THE ORGANIZATION OF ANCIENT ECONOMIES

In this book, Kenneth Hirth provides a comparative view of the organization of ancient and premodern society and economy. Hirth establishes that humans adapted to their environments, not as individuals but in the social groups where they lived and worked out the details of their livelihoods. He explores the variation in economic organization used by simple and complex societies to procure, produce, and distribute resources required by both individual households and the social and political institutions that they supported. Drawing on a wealth of archaeological, historic, and ethnographic information, he develops and applies an analytical framework for studying ancient societies that range from the hunting and gathering groups of native North America to the large state societies of both the New and Old Worlds. Hirth demonstrates that despite differences in transportation and communication technologies, the economic organizations of ancient and modern societies are not as different as we sometimes think.

KENNETH HIRTH is Professor of Anthropology at Pennsylvania State University. An economic anthropologist who has conducted archaeological research in Mexico, Honduras, Peru, and Turkey that has spanned 12,000 years of human development, he has authored, edited, and coauthored nineteen books on different aspects of Mesoamerican society and economy. Hirth is currently a Senior Fellow at Dumbarton Oaks Library and Research Collections in Washington, DC. He has received the National Geographic Society's Career Achievement Award in Archaeology (2000) and the Excellence in Lithic Studies Award from the Society of American Archaeology (1998).

THE ORGANIZATION OF ANCIENT ECONOMIES

A GLOBAL PERSPECTIVE

KENNETH HIRTH

Pennsylvania State University

CAMBRIDGE
UNIVERSITY PRESS

CAMBRIDGE
UNIVERSITY PRESS

University Printing House, Cambridge CB2 8BS, United Kingdom

One Liberty Plaza, 20th Floor, New York, NY 10006, USA

477 Williamstown Road, Port Melbourne, VIC 3207, Australia

314–321, 3rd Floor, Plot 3, Splendor Forum, Jasola District Centre, New Delhi – 110025, India

79 Anson Road, #06-04/06, Singapore 079906

Cambridge University Press is part of the University of Cambridge.

It furthers the University's mission by disseminating knowledge in the pursuit of education, learning, and research at the highest international levels of excellence.

www.cambridge.org
Information on this title: www.cambridge.org/9781108494700
DOI: 10.1017/9781108859707

First published 2020

Printed in the United Kingdom by TJ International Ltd, Padstow Cornwall

A catalogue record for this publication is available from the British Library.

Library of Congress Cataloging-in-Publication Data
NAMES: Hirth, Kenneth, author.
TITLE: The organization of ancient economies : a global perspective / Kenneth Hirth.
DESCRIPTION: 1 Edition. | New York : Cambridge University Press, 2020. |
Includes bibliographical references and index.
IDENTIFIERS: LCCN 2020013540 (print) | LCCN 2020013541 (ebook) |
ISBN 9781108494700 (hardback) | ISBN 9781108796880 (paperback) |
ISBN 9781108859707 (epub)
SUBJECTS: LCSH: Economic history.
CLASSIFICATION: LCC HC21 .H487 2020 (print) | LCC HC21 (ebook) | DDC 330.9–DC23
LC record available at https://lccn.loc.gov/2020013540
LC ebook record available at https://lccn.loc.gov/2020013541

ISBN 978-1-108-49470-0 Hardback

CONTENTS

FIGURES

MAPS

TABLES

PREFACE

A book can be written for many different reasons. It can chronicle the life and times of notable individuals, tell a spellbinding tale, or follow a personal quest of the author. This book fits in the latter of these three categories. I was fortunate to be raised on my family's 1850s homestead farm in southern Wisconsin. Nothing was ever thrown away in my German–American family. The farm was overflowing with wooden tools (mallets, flails, pitchforks, pulleys), farm implements (sickles, ropes, draw knives, adzes), crocks and caskets, harnesses and the equipment to go with our two working horses, and an endless supply of 19th- and early 20th-century items squirreled away in corners of the barn, outbuildings, and the attic and cellar of our stone house. The abundance of old items sparked my curiosity in what they were and how they were used. Fortunately, my grandfather and grandmother still had one foot planted in the late 19th century and could explain how all the old technology was used to plant, harvest, butcher, preserve, and manage a farm household before the advent of hybrid seed, store-bought food, and electrical appliances. With the vantage of hindsight I realized that they also imparted an understanding of how a self-sufficient family farm needed to operate in order to survive. This was my introduction to history and the beginning of an academic career as an archaeologist and anthropologist that sought to understand how ancient societies were organized to get work done.

This book was written with two audiences in mind. The first is that group of general readers who are interested in how ancient societies developed and produced the food and other resources needed to support themselves, build civilizations, and engage in long-distance trade using simple preindustrial technologies. Although not written for the classroom, these topics can be of interest to eclectic students and lifelong learners interested in the broad sweep of economic history. We have all have grown up with a basic understanding of 20th- and/or 21st-century capitalistic society. But does that understanding overlay neatly onto the past? This volume explores how ancient and premodern societies were similar or different from the modern one in which we live.

The second audience is comprised of my archaeological colleagues who are interested in the economy and comparative analysis but have to put the majority of their efforts into developing an up-to-date mastery of the culture areas where they conduct their research. Developing a detailed understanding of a single past society is a full-time job for scholars pursuing serious research. This book uses a comparative approach to summarize alternative forms of economic organization found in both large- and small-scale societies. All ancient and premodern societies were economically plastic with different forms of organization coexisting and operating simultaneously in different contexts and levels of society. The comparative approach reminds us to beware of monolithic models that propose an ideal form of economic organization without taking into consideration the heterogeneity inherent in both the domestic and institutional economies. The examples provided are intended to help researchers think broadly about the economy of the societies that they study.

All authors have their biases. My family heritage together with professional training in business administration, anthropology, and archaeology have shaped the presentation and rationale of this book in several ways. My upbringing along with later experience in sales and marketing had taught me the importance of organization in shaping the cost and operation of economic enterprises. Anthropology and archaeology have provided insight into the structure of small-scale societies and illustrated how simpler forms of organization continued unchanged over long spans of time enabling households to adapt to changing cultural and environmental conditions. The anthropologist in me believes in the inherent value of the cross-cultural approach for understanding the diversity of ways that human societies developed over time. In this sense it runs contrary to historical particularism that views all societies as intrinsically unique and unable to be compared with one another in structural terms.

The format of the volume follows anthropological conventions. In-text citations are used for bibliographic references, and endnotes provide supplementary information not included in the text. One of the distracting aspects of a cross-cultural and comparative approach is keeping track of the many different societies where parallel and divergent cultural practices are found. There is no easy solution to this, and I do not assume that readers have a global knowledge of all the place names, provinces, and ethnic groups that existed in the ancient and premodern past. As a partial remedy to this issue, four maps are located at the end of this Preface that provide general locations for the more than 250 archaeological sites, regions, and ethnic groups mentioned throughout this volume. Finally, I feel that the examples used in the comparative discussions are one of the most valuable aspects of this volume. They naturally reflect my research interests, which are centered on state- and chiefdom-level societies more than on foraging or pastoral groups. Nevertheless, research suggests that there are similarities in organization across both small- and large-scale societies that fit within the analytical framework for studying the economy proposed here.

Albert Einstein believed that time was an illusion. Calculating time in a uniform way is a problem that archaeologists are intimately familiar with despite the many ways we have for counting it. Time can be calculated in tree ring growth, radiocarbon years, geological eras, and atomic clocks using uranium isotope decay, potassium–argon ratios, paleo-magnetic measurements, and thermo-luminescence differences. Once calculated, time can be expressed in different calendar series including BP (before present), BC/AD (Julian calendar), BCE/CE (modified Julian calendar), and calibrated or uncalibrated radiocarbon years. Preference for one calendar scale over another depends on the age of the material studied and the regional or academic traditions of the investigators that use them. I have chosen to express time in Julian calendar dates (BC/AD) because they are well established in the archaeological and historic literature in both the New and Old Worlds. Rather than tracking time with chronological charts for each area discussed, dates and time spans are identified within the discussion by the century or millennium BC or AD. When a specific archaeological period or phase is used (e.g., Ur III or third dynasty), the time span is provided in parentheses (e.g., 2112–2004 BC) to contextualize the discussion.

Finally and most importantly I want to thank my family and colleagues for the advice and assistance they have provided over more than a decade of reading and research that led to this volume. First in line is my wife Susan, who fueled this research with gifts of books during holidays and other family celebrations, which dealt with merchants, trade commodities, and general economic history. Her encouragement and interest in my work have endured despite being subjected to reading drafts on all manner of tedious economic topics ranging from lithic technology, craft production, and market development to the present volume. A shout also goes out to all of my archaeological colleagues in Mesoamerica with whom I have conducted research and exchanged ideas over the years, including Ann Cyphers, Jorge Angulo, Raul Arana, Frances Berdan, David Carballo, Susan Evans, Norberto Gonzalez, David Grove, George Hasemann, Gloria Lara, William Sanders, and David Webster. Economic anthropology provides the theoretical foundation of this volume, and I thank Timothy Earle, Thomas Hakannson, Paul Durrenberger, Donald Kurtz, and Della McMillan for our many stimulating discussions about the economic organization of ethnographic societies. Finally, I want to thank Mark Munn and Gonzalo Rubio for their comments on Classical Mediterranean society, and my son Colin Hirth for many insightful and invigorating discussions on medieval Icelandic and European society and economy. I thank them for their contributions and recognize any errors in describing the ancient economy are my own creation.

1 Europe, the Mediterranean, and the Middle East

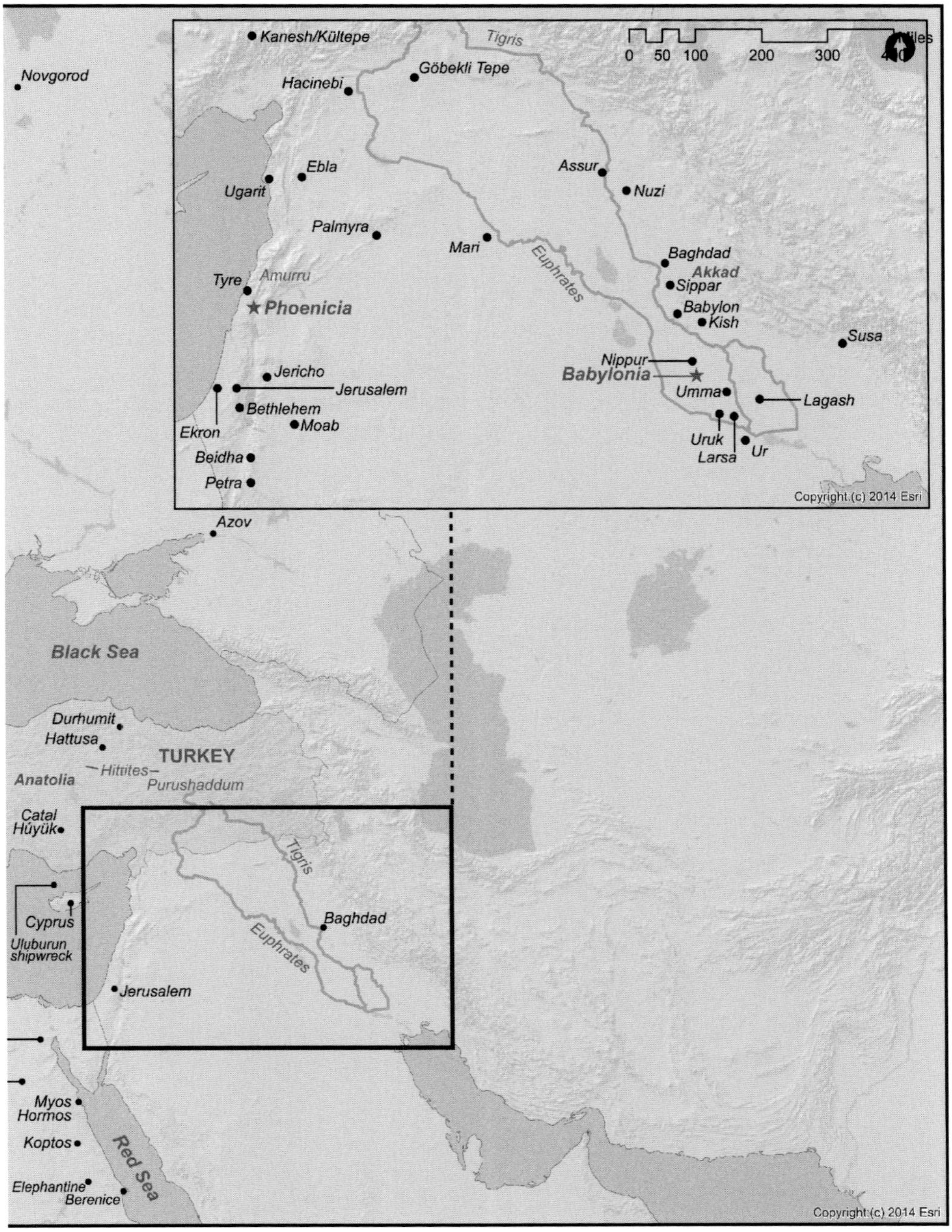

Kanesh/Kültepe
Tigris
0 50 100 200 300 400 Miles
Göbekli Tepe
Hacinebi
Ebla
Ugarit
Assur
Nuzi
Palmyra
Mari
Euphrates
Baghdad
Akkad
Sippar
Tyre
Amurru
Phoenicia
Babylon
Kish
Susa
Nippur
Babylonia
Jericho
Jerusalem
Umma
Lagash
Bethlehem
Moab
Ekron
Uruk
Larsa
Ur
Beidha
Petra
Copyright (c) 2014 Esri
Novgorod
Azov
Black Sea
Durhumit
Hattusa
TURKEY
Hittites
Anatolia
Purushaddum
Catal Hüyük
Tigris
Cyprus
Uluburun shipwreck
Baghdad
Euphrates
Jerusalem
Myos Hormos
Koptos
Red Sea
Elephantine
Berenice
Copyright (c) 2014 Esri

1 (*cont.*)

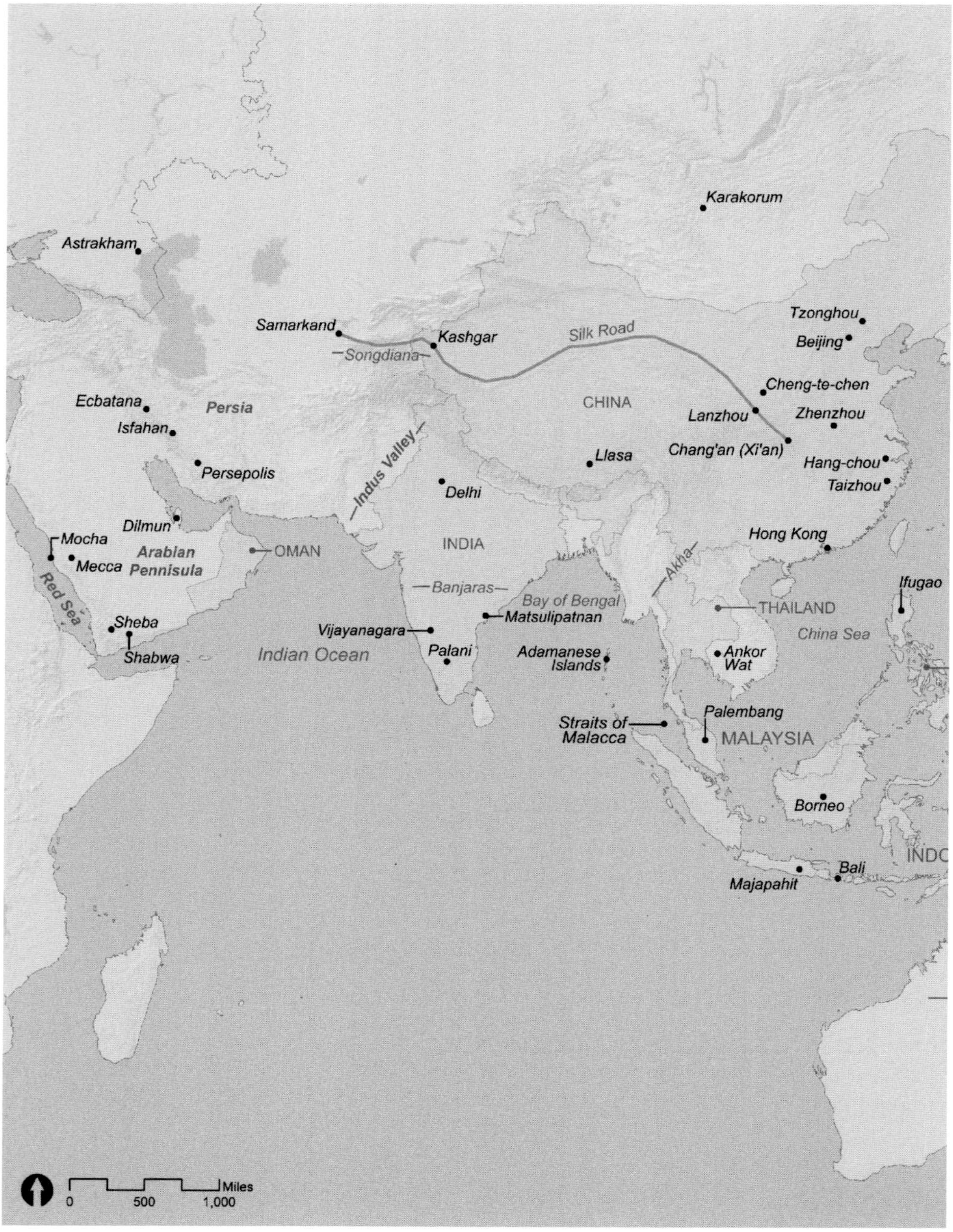

2 India, Asia, and the Pacific

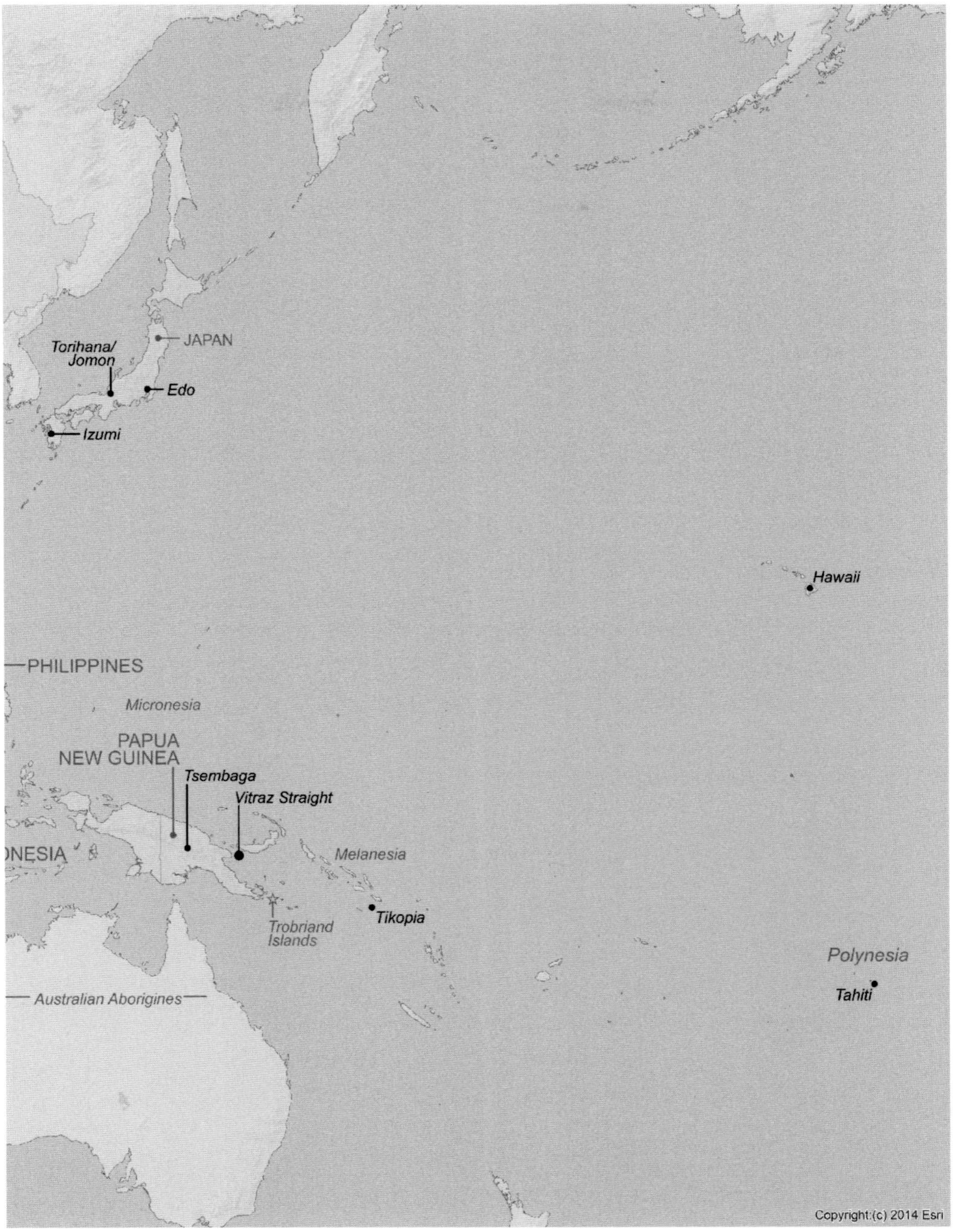

JAPAN
Torihana/
Jomon
Edo
Izumi
Hawaii
PHILIPPINES
Micronesia
PAPUA
NEW GUINEA
Tsembaga
Vitraz Straight
NESIA
Melanesia
Trobriand
Islands
Tikopia
Polynesia
Australian Aborigines
Tahiti
Copyright:(c) 2014 Esri

2 (*cont.*)

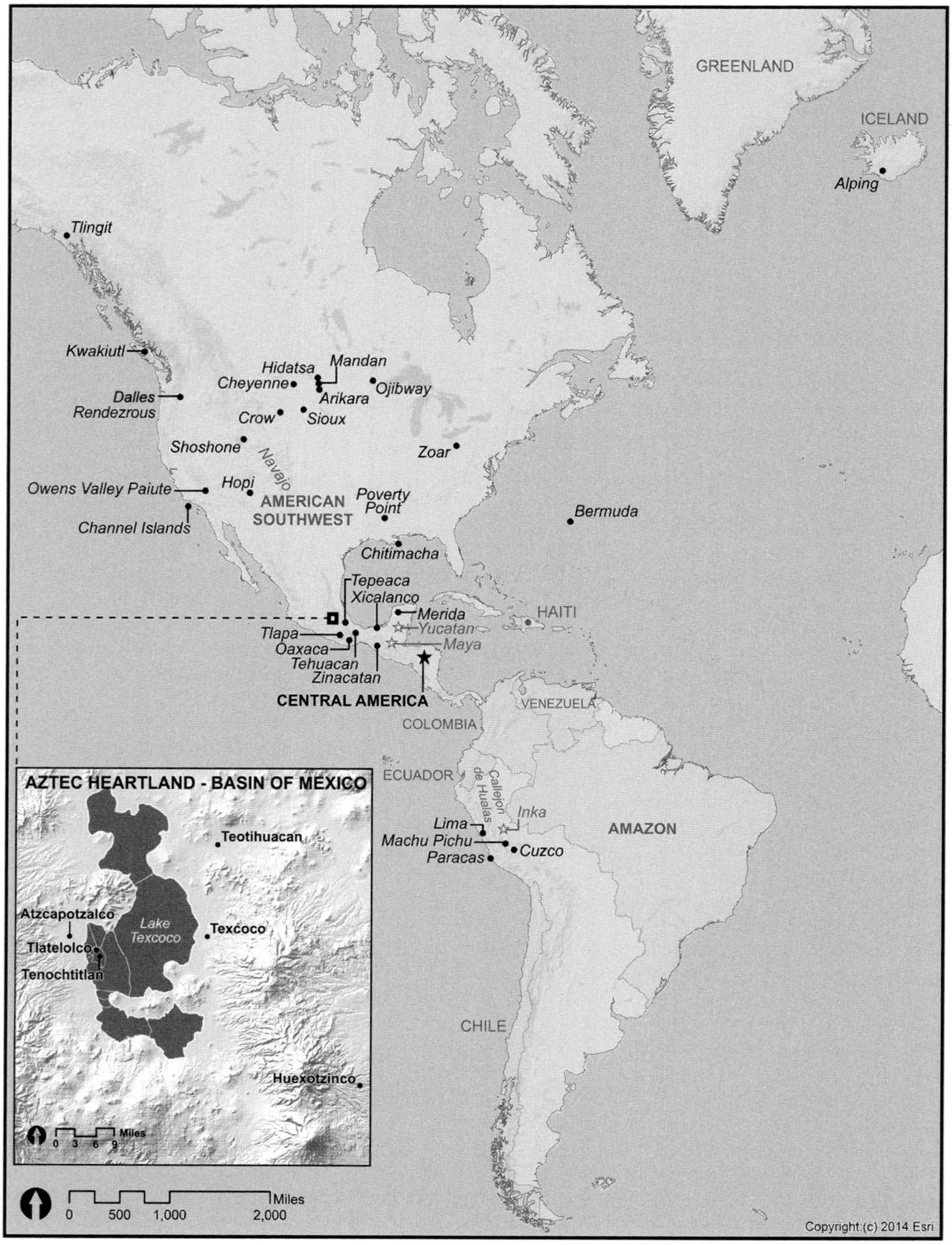

3 The Americas

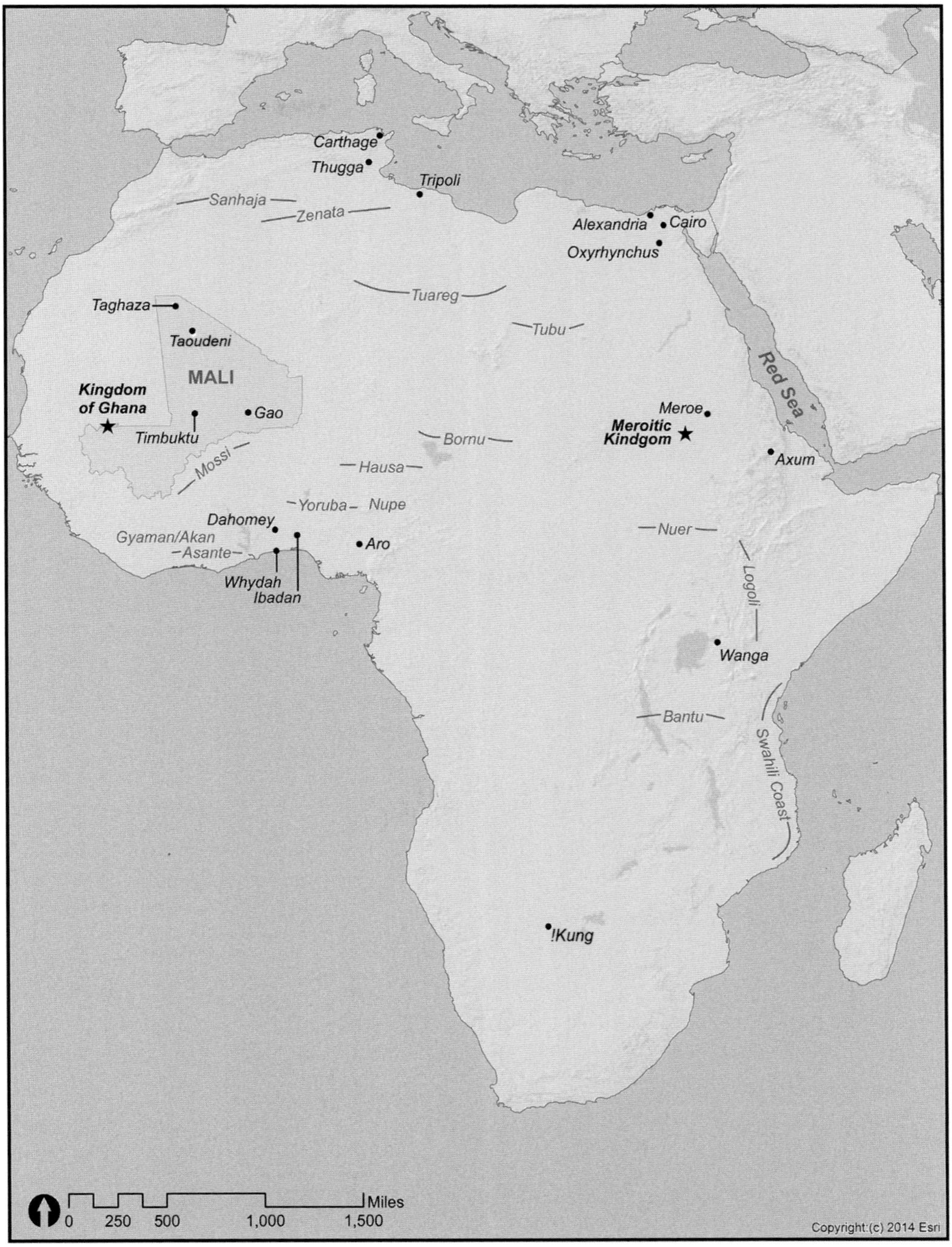
Carthage
Thugga
Tripoli
Sanhaja
Zenata
Alexandria
Cairo
Oxyrhynchus
Tuareg
Tubu
Taghaza
Taoudeni
MALI
Kingdom
of Ghana
Gao
Timbuktu
Mossi
Red Sea
Meroe
Meroitic
Kindgom
Bornu
Axum
Hausa
Yoruba
Nupe
Dahomey
Gyaman/Akan
Asante
Aro
Nuer
Whydah
Ibadan
Logoli
Wanga
Bantu
Swahili Coast
!Kung
Miles
0
250
500
1,000
1,500
Copyright:(c) 2014 Esri

4 Africa

ONE

THE STRUCTURE OF ANCIENT ECONOMY

> Ancient economic history is still in its infancy, both because few economists have learned much about the ancient world and because ancient historians have typically not incorporated economics into their analysis.
>
> (Temin 2006:133)

The economy is the foundation of society today, just as it was in the ancient past. It is the source of material support for all of society's households as well as its social, political, and religious institutions. While our modern economy is often described as a result of the industrial revolution, this is not really the case. Today's economy is actually the collective byproduct of more than 10,000 years of economic development. It is a composite of *formal* and *informal* forms of production and distribution that have evolved over time. Ancient, premodern, and modern economies all developed in the same way, by adding new types of production and distribution to existing forms of work to meet specific needs.

This book is about the organization of ancient and premodern economies. It starts from the premise that just like today, the scale, complexity, and organization of the economy was a primary factor in determining the direction and development of ancient societies. The preceding epigraph suggests that the study of ancient economy is still in its infancy. If this is true, then the pages that follow will only attempt a few cautious steps to advance what can be said about how economies operated in the past. The lack of progress in the field is primarily one of omission rather than commission. Researchers have often examined how aspects of the economy reinforce social and political relations rather than focusing specifically on the economy as its own specific domain of investigation.[1] While Temin chooses to criticize the lack of discourse between economists and economic historians as the reason for this, the blame is not theirs alone. Anthropologists and archaeologists likewise have not focused enough on the premodern economy despite having the tools to do so. At least three obstacles have stood in the way of the concerted study of past economic systems.

The first obstacle is empirical and methodological, and reflects the difficulty of reconstructing ancient economic activity from a single disciplinary perspective. Historians make excellent use of textual records for the periods for which there are documents. Unfortunately, that eliminates all preliterate societies from the discussion, and the records available from historic periods rarely include detailed information about the life of commoners within society. Archaeologists can reach back into the prehistoric past and examine economic behavior using material remains from production, distribution, and consumption activities. The limitation for archaeologists is that they rarely have large enough samples of material remains to reconstruct economic systems, or the inclination to view them in a holistic and systematic way. To write an economic history of even one society is an enormous and complex task. It requires the use of multiple data sets that include textual sources, art historical depictions, archaeological remains, and comparison with ethnographic cases to develop a synergistic understanding of past economic patterns.

The second problem is one of competing research paradigms. The strong evolutionary focus in anthropology of the 1960s and 1970s affected the way that social researchers viewed the economy. The holistic approach of anthropology together with the influential work of Karl Polanyi argued that the economy could not be examined as a separate sphere of activity because it was deeply embedded in other aspects of society. The result was that the economy came to be viewed largely as subordinate to larger social and political processes. At the same time, the strong evolutionary current within archaeology focused on identifying cause and effect relationships to explain major cultural changes such as population growth, warfare, agricultural intensification, and state development. Obscured in the process was a concern for basic economic structures that were the mainstay of traditional Marxist analysis. While social anthropology constructed detailed analytical frameworks[2] for studying kinship, jural relations, political organization, marriage, religion, forms of exchange, and production technologies, archaeologists struggled to develop the means to apply them to the past. The result was a lack of attention to identifying organization and change in the economic structures that define the economy.

The third and final obstacle to studying the ancient economy is the most challenging. The view adopted here is that the study of the ancient economy is most productive if it is undertaken from a comparative perspective.[3] Solutions to similar economic problems at different points in time can take similar forms. Nevertheless, the amount of time needed to develop an in-depth understanding of an ancient society can lead investigators to see them as unique and overlook the structural dimensions of the economy that they share with other societies unless they have a direct historical connection. Comparative economic research needs to look beyond the particularism that defines regions, cultures, and individual societies. This is a daunting proposition given the enormous variation that existed in the past and the limited or incomplete information available to researchers to explore it. Nowhere is this more evident than in the economy, which can be organized in similar and different ways in societies at different levels of organizational complexity.

This study examines the ancient economy from a comparative perspective. It does not attempt to develop a single synthetic view of what ancient and premodern economies were, how they were organized, or how they developed. That would be impractical given the enormous variation in the scale, structure, and integration of past economies. In fact, it does the opposite. It attempts to identify a broad range of different organizational structures found in, and shared by, societies at different levels of complexity at different points in time. The emphasis is on modes of organization and how they operated. Humans are problem solvers and it should be no surprise to find similar forms of economic organization in different societies to meet similar needs and get work done. Identifying this variation provides the foundation for a comparative analysis of past economic structures, and supplies the basis for exploring the evolutionary forces behind their development.

WHAT IS THE ECONOMY?

Definitions have value because they both clarify a domain of meaning and identify the specific variables or attributes that concepts encompass.[4] Nowhere is this more true than when investigators attempt to define the economy. Karl Polanyi (1957) argued that there were two ways to define the economy: a formal or neoclassical way and a substantive way. The neoclassical approach views the economy as a domain of human behavior concerned with material provisioning that can be studied separately from the rest of society. Material provisioning is based on rational choice theory where individuals make conscious choices about how to meet their needs or desires (Samuelson 1967:5). Lionel Robbins defines economics from this perspective as "the science which studies human behavior as a relationship between ends and scarce means which have alternative uses" (Robbins 1935:16).

The substantive view of the economy is different. It holds that processes of material provisioning cannot be understood apart from the broader social structures in which they are found (Dalton 1961; Polanyi 1944). For those favoring the substantive view, the economy is embedded in the social systems where provisioning takes place. As a result, behaviors such as maximization, utility, and rational choice can*not* be understood in the universal terms used by neoclassical economics because they are culture-specific. The literature on these differences is vast and defines what have been called the Formalist–Substantive and the Modernist–Primitivist debates in anthropology and archaeology (Dalton 1961; Kaplan 1968; Plattner 1989b: Polanyi 1957; Polanyi et al. 1957; Schneider 1974). The important question is, What view of the economy provides the *best* approach to studying and understanding the ancient economy?

The economy is defined here as a *socially mediated form of material provisioning and interaction involving the production and allocation of resources among alternative ends*. Several things are implied by defining the economy in this way. First, it focuses on the behaviors and interactions associated with the material provisioning of everyday life. Interaction at this level involves the interplay of individuals with the resources in their natural environment and the groups who use or control them. Second, the economy is a socially mediated realm of behavior. This recognizes that the values and behaviors that shape provisioning decisions are learned and acquired in the societies in which individuals live. It also recognizes that material provisioning was often embedded in other social, religious, and political activities. Third, the production and allocation of resources refers to the decision-making processes that individuals and groups go through with regard to the production, distribution, and consumption of resources. It is here that altruistic or self-motivated choice confronts the cultural norms that shape them. Judging the rationality or irrationality of those choices depends on the cultural and ethnocentric vantage point from which individuals observe them.

The perspective adopted here contains elements of both formalist and substantive views of the economy. The formal view of the economy derives from Adam Smith (1827), who argued that economic provisioning was the result of rational decision making by individuals who allocate their time and resources to different ends. It is based on the empirical fact that humans are problem solvers who make choices that determine their physical and social well-being. They have to eat to survive, select mates to reproduce, and raise offspring that represent the next generation. To this end people are decision makers who mediate these and other issues through their own calculations and/or the advice and counsel of others. People are rational within the cultural universes where they operate, but they are not the emotionless, fully informed, rational *Homo economicus* at the core of neoclassical economics. Instead, they are bounded by their beliefs, rationality, and cultural experiences, which bias their selection choices in different ways (Sandstrom 2008; Thaler 2015).

The substantive perspective is valuable because it emphasizes the variation in how each society defines the scope of its economic interaction. Societies set the parameters of the economic base. They establish the specifics of economic interaction (value, exchange equivalencies, the expectations of reciprocity), define the norms of material and social well-being, and set standards of expected economic involvement in preserving social and community values (Dalton 1961; Gudeman 2001). Nevertheless, while society defines the ideology of economic interaction, people operate creatively within it. They make individual decisions set within the culturally mediated range of acceptable and nonacceptable options open to them.

This dimension of individual economic action blends the formal and substantive views of the economy together. Every ancient household was responsible for its own livelihood. Households understood the economic risk of resource shortfall and worked both individually and collectively to ensure that they had sufficient resources to survive. The result was that households formed collective action groups that worked at improving their economic well-being through their individual effort and participation in broader, community-based social interaction. The strategies that households adopted were a multifaceted mix of intensified and diversified production activities that, together with mutual aid networks at the community level, helped meet their everyday material and social needs (Netting 1981, 1993; Sahlins 1972).

The formalist and substantive perspectives are alternative but compatible theoretical positions about how the economy was structured. The debate between these two views is no longer foremost in the minds of anthropologists and economic historians. Nevertheless, the legacy of the substantivist perspective continues to frame how researchers view the organization of, and sources of change in ancient economies. Polanyi argued that the economy did not grow organically through individual decision making or maximization strategies, but was created and operated through society's social, political, and religious institutions. The reason was that he saw barter and other forms of commercial negotiation as dangerous and disruptive forces if they were left unchecked to operate freely within society. Researchers who argue for strongly centralized economies and elite-centered explanations for culture change carry with them Polanyi's top-down view of cultural organization and change (Carrasco 1978; Finley 1985; Murra 1980).

On the other hand, researchers who focus on individual decision making see economic development from a different perspective. They often favor a bottom-up view of economic development with considerable latitude for technological innovation and organizational change emanating from households on all levels of society (e.g., Reina 1963). A number of scholars have argued that Polanyi's denial of individual decision making has impeded our understanding of everything from household level economic structure to the development of markets, merchants, and commerce in ancient societies (Blanton and Fargher 2010; Feinman 2013a; Hirth 2016; Silver 1995). Individual incentive and the rational economic choices that people make are compatible with a recognition of the embedded nature of the economy. After all, it was Adam Smith who said that "economic actors tend to make strenuous efforts to re-entangle economic relations in a nexus of social relations for the stability and predictability of the markets" (cited in Oka and Kusimba 2008:365).

COMPARING ANCIENT, MODERN, AND PREMODERN ECONOMIES

The 21st century has a rapidly changing and growing world economy. Technological advances in computers and telecommunications have led to significant restructuring in manufacturing, distribution, and consumerism at the global level. The International Monetary Fund, the World Bank, the European Common Market, and Wall Street are some of the large-scale trade and financial institutions that help make the global economy work. The result is that the modern economy is often perceived as being very different from economies of the ancient past. But is it? From the perspective of economic anthropology, the similarities between modern and premodern economies are closer than one might think.

Take our financial institutions, for example. A drive down any major street in America will reveal more banks than grocery stores. The scale of our financial institutions would lead us to think that the implementation of economic change in the modern world occurs at a scale much larger than it did several hundred years ago when Thomas Jefferson argued strenuously against the need for a strong central bank. But if we adopted the top-down view of economic development, it would contradict recent Chinese experience. The current business revolution in China occurred largely through informal lending relationships and mobilizing capital along kinship lines that have dominated ancient and premodern societies for thousands of years. While formal banks and banking institutions exist, they have not provided the capital to fund the many recent small business ventures in both China (Ayyagaria et al. 2011; Dong et al. 2012; Turvey and Kong 2010) and India (Kumar 2009; Ravi 2003).

Another example is the replacement of general purpose money with formal currencies, which are argued to represent an important evolutionary advance in the development of commercial economies (Dalton 1965; Polanyi 1957; Schneider 1974; Weatherford 1997). Be that as it may, special purpose monies are still with us and even growing in importance. Community currencies such as Ithaca HOURS and other local exchange trading systems (LETS)[5] have developed in a number of places as ways to procure and trade services against one another instead of buying them with dollars (Jacob et al. 2004). Bitcoin and the Facebook Libra are more recent examples of nonregulated virtual currencies, which operate in the restricted world of cyber exchange (Segendorf 2014). Add to this the way that Internet business has facilitated the emergence of independent contracting in the form of Uber, Lyft, and Airbnb as replacements to formal taxicab companies and hotels makes for an increasingly decentralized and informal business environment.[6]

Many of the same structures found in ancient and premodern societies continue to operate today. Livelihoods continue to be organized around work in domestic settings. Social and religious institutions continue to be funded and operate through voluntary contributions and tithes as they have for centuries. Political institutions still rely on taxation, tolls, fines, and tariffs to fund their administrations. Societies in the ancient world built and supported urban centers and engaged in long-distance trade. Commerce and the production of goods for sale was carried out at all levels of cultural complexity, from tribal societies to states. Marketplaces developed and operated alongside private enterprise in virtually all large state societies, although not in the same way that capitalistic markets operate today.

Ancient and modern societies are similar to one another in two ways that make comparisons between them possible. First, they are both economically plastic. *Economic plasticity* refers to the principle that as economic systems grow in size, new forms of economic organization appear alongside preexisting ones without replacing them (Hirth and Pillsbury 2013). New forms of economic organization usually appear as solutions to special problems or circumstances. They normally are not initiated as rapid, broad-scale changes in the organization of work. They occur, instead, as small, new ways of doing things in the existing economy. New introductions can become important over time as they demonstrate their efficiency and supplant existing forms of production, resource mobilization, or product distribution. Economic innovation is largely an egalitarian process. New technology and forms of work will be added to the economy in proportion to their ability to increase productivity, reduce effort, and agree with existing ideological norms.[7] But that does *not* mean that older forms of economic organization will disappear.

Second, both ancient and modern societies are heterogenous. *Economic heterogeneity* is a function of the natural conservativeness of economic systems. It refers to the diversity of organizational structures created over time as new forms of economic organization are added to economic systems (i.e., plasticity) without discarding existing forms. Preexisting economic arrangements may continue to be practiced even in the face of new, more productive or efficient ones depending on a variety of circumstances. The perpetuation of older technologies and economic practices can be the result of their being appropriate solutions for small-scale economic activities. Domestic economies are

1.1 20th-century *dhoukani* threshing sled with close-up of its stone chert blades. (Photographs by Nicholas Kardulias. Photography on top modified by author with permission of Nicholas Kardulias)

generally conservative because of limited labor and/or capital resources. Older practices and technologies will continue in use as long as they get the job done (Langlands 2017). This explains why rural farmers in Cyprus, Greece, and Turkey still used animal- and human-drawn sledges (*dhoukani*) edged with sharp chert flakes and blades (Figure 1.1) to thresh grain well into the middle of the 20th century (Anderson et al. 2004:figure 5; Kardulias and Yerkes 1996; Pearlman 1984). The result is a heterogenous economy where old technologies and traditional practices such as mobilizing resources through gifts or along kinship lines continue to be important even in today's modern capitalistic world.

RECONSTRUCTING ANCIENT AND PREMODERN ECONOMIES

How can a comparative understanding of past economies be developed given the diversity, plasticity, and heterogeneity of their economic practices? The place to begin is to recognize that no single discipline can do it alone. Temin is correct in the epigraph that few economists have displayed an interest in past economic systems, but this should not be a surprise. The field of contemporary economics is concerned with explaining the operation of capitalistic markets, not ancient or premarket economies.[8] Economists rarely examine historic trends in the economy unless they have the measurable data to do so. The recent study by Thomas Piketty (2014; Piketty and Zucman 2013) on the distribution of income and wealth is important in this regard as it examines trends over a 300-year time period, brief from our perspective, but valuable in what it demonstrates in terms of the nature of capital accumulation and long-term historic analysis.

Economic historians have been called on to provide the field with longer term analyses (North 1978; North and Thomas 1973). The requirements of good scholarship for the economic historian follows that of all historians: reliance on good textual records. When records exist, economic history can provide detailed insights into past economic behavior. But historians face two significant shortcomings. The most obvious is that many societies either lacked writing or existed before writing was introduced.[9] Second, when textual documents are preserved, they usually record a specific or narrow dimension of economic life such as palace economy (Heltzer 1982; Lipinski 1979; McGeough 2007), merchant activity (e.g., Casson 1989; Gotein 1967, 1973), estate operation (Rathbone 1991), or political activity such as conquest levies or taxation (Berdan and Anawalt 1992; Lee-fang Chien 2004). The result is often an in-depth discussion of one particular facet of society, rather than a holistic and integrated view of the entire economy. Aspects of the domestic economy, for example, can be particularly difficult to reconstruct.

Archaeology provides another entrée into the study of the ancient past. Archaeologists reconstruct history from durable material remains (e.g., Harris 1993). The advantage of archaeological research is twofold. It can examine all levels of the society from commoners to kings, and it is not time-bound or restricted to periods of written history. Careful analyses of material remains make it possible to reconstruct an array of economic topics ranging from agriculture (Barker and Gilbertson 2003; Harrison and Turner 1978) and craft production (Costin 1991; Hirth 2006b) to trade (Lobell 2009), type of storage (Christakis 1999; LeVine 1992; Rickman 1971), and the presence of complex economic institutions such as a marketplace (Camp 1986; Hirth 1998; Stark and Ossa 2010). The strength of archaeology is that the materials recovered from domestic contexts reflect consumption at the family and household level, information frequently missing from other sources. The disadvantage of archaeology is the issue of *equifinality*, namely that distributions of material remains could have been produced by several alternative social processes. Nevertheless, careful modeling and problem-oriented research make it possible for archaeologists to reconstruct different forms of both production and distribution (Costin 2001a; Earle and Smith 2011; Hirth 1998, 2008, 2010; Hirth and Cyphers 2020).

Finally, there is the voluminous work of countless economic anthropologists and ethnographers who have compiled detailed accounts of indigenous premodern and semi-modern economies in different cultures around the world. These studies provide actual descriptions of economic behavior that can be used as testable models for past economic systems. They encompass a wide range of economic diversity from foraging and tribal groups (Evans-Pritchard 1940; Strathern 2007; Wiessner 1982) to chiefdom societies (Codere 1966; Malinowski 1922) and states (Halperin 2013; Netting 1981). They touch on a wide array of topics from the domestic economy (Wilk 1989b) and agriculture (Chibnik 1994; Netting 1989, 1993; Stone 1986) to merchants (Harding 1967), markets (Beals 1975), and market systems (Smith 1976a, 1976b). Many of these scholars follow the ethnographic tradition of providing a holistic description of society. In addition to materialist discussions many ethnographers probe the ritual (Monaghan 1995) and emic meaning of economic activity (Drucker and Heizer 1967; Gudeman 2001). The utility of ethnographic studies is that they provide models for how different economic activities (e.g., foraging, pastoralism, agriculture) were perceived and structured in societies of different size and complexity that lived in different types of environments. While they are not perfect analogues for ancient societies that have long since disappeared, they provide useful points of comparison with which to examine them.

A COMPARATIVE FRAMEWORK: DOMESTIC AND INSTITUTIONAL ORGANIZATION

A goal of this study is to develop a comparative perspective of the economic structures found in ancient and premodern (traditional) economies. It seeks to develop an organizational framework that is applicable for cross-cultural analysis in which different economic practices and activities can be analyzed and compared. The discussion draws heavily on economic anthropology to frame this understanding. Anthropology contains detailed ethnographic descriptions of different forms of production, communal labor, feasting, elite sponsorship, self-sufficient householding, usufruct property, traditional systems of land tenure, and an array of gift exchanges like those mentioned in many ancient and historic accounts. No assumption is made that any of these forms of organization are perfect analogies for past societies. But it does assume that there are commonalities and continuities in human behavior and ways of doing things that can be identified and profitably compared across a broad range of time.

While cross-cultural comparisons are an anathema for many historians, they provide a landscape of possibilities against which the key organizational features of the domestic and institutional economy can be examined. Moreover, it is the economic plasticity and heterogeneity of human societies that makes cross-cultural comparisons of economic systems possible.

The principle of economic plasticity recognizes that older (simpler) and newer (more complex) forms of economic organization are compatible with one another to the extent that they can carry out the same type of work at different levels of production efficiency. Older forms of economic organization can be retained or shifted to those sectors of the economy where the opportunity costs of change are high. The result is that even industrial societies can retain preindustrial forms of work. Identifying this principle provides a framework for studying how, where, and under what conditions older, less efficient forms of economic organization can survive and even thrive.

All economic activities within ancient and premodern societies can be grouped for purposes of comparative analysis into one of three broad organizational sectors: (1) the domestic economy of individual families and households, (2) the informal institutions that households use to support each other, and (3) the formal institutions that embrace society as a whole. How these three dimensions of society differed from one another in terms of form, scale, complexity, and integration is essential for understanding economic plasticity and heterogeneity. This study presents examples that illustrate the diversity of economic structures found in premodern societies while at the same time evaluating their fit into the threefold analytical framework. Rather than a specific region or set of regions, examples are selected from a diverse array of different societies. This was intentional since the goal of this volume is to explore the applicability of the analytical framework used to examine economic organization. The only stipulation was that the economies of the different case studies used were well documented through historic and/or archaeological research.

Two caveats are important to this discussion. The first is that the focus of the discussion is on forms of organization and their utility for describing past societies. The economic models proposed are empirical constructs that can be reworked when new data become available. They are first iteration models of economic organization, and, while not complete, they serve as useful points of departure for exploring the economic structures on which ancient societies depended. To the extent possible, these models assist in our understanding how economic systems developed over time. But they are organizational rather than developmental models. Nevertheless, they provide insight into how economies *may* have changed by adding new forms of organization to existing ones without replacement. Recognizing different forms of organization provides the building blocks for identifying how complex economic organizations were shaped. The goal is to advance the discussion of comparative economic analysis, achieve a more meaningful understanding of past economic structures, and broaden our understanding of the forces of change shaping past economic systems.

The second caveat is that the comparative perspective adopted here uses a synthetic rather than a single theoretical perspective to evaluate the empirical information drawn from different disciplines. Theory is indispensable in scientific inquiry because it helps make sense of disparate fact (Flannery and Marcus 2012:xiii). But the important question is, What brand of theory should investigators adopt? Behavioral economic research has demonstrated that individuals in nonmarket societies make rational economic choices within the scope of their own experience (Sandstrom 2008; Thaler 2015). Adam Smith would have approved of that. However, it is also clear that the economic choices that people make are socially conditioned. The substantivists argued that more than fifty years ago. Furthermore, agency theory (Eisenhardt 1989) is pertinent to any discussion where wealthy elites instituted new administration practices, where religious specialists modified belief or ritual practices, or where enterprising merchants engaged in new commercial ventures or organized long-distance trade missions. And what about Marxist perspectives? Anytime the forms of production are discussed, the Marxist framework is useful for conceptualizing the structure of economic activities. In more general terms, a "modes of organization" approach can be used to model a wide range of economic activities, from forms of distribution and sharing to resource control within the institutional economy. Additionally, world systems theory is useful for examining long-distance interactions.

Is the use of a collective theoretical approach just weak theory? Perhaps for some. I, however, view theoretical eclecticism as a strength and adopt it here since it enables researchers to incorporate the strongest aspects of different theoretical approaches into their interpretations of disparate facts. It facilitates a more middle-range economic analysis that connects different types of economic interactions and organizations to the theoretical perspectives that best explain them. While the dogmatic adherence to single theoretical approaches demonstrates strong philosophical convictions on the part of the researcher, the one-hammer approach does not fulfill all the needs of a carpenter. Neither does it describe all aspects of how an economy works unless one is satisfied with focusing on a narrow range of data or adopts a single analytical perspective. While that may be done for the sake of parsimony, it is not a good application of the comparative method.

THE FRAMEWORK OF DISCUSSION

Archaeologists often discuss the economy in terms of production, distribution, and consumption activities. This functional approach is useful because it fits the type of data available for discussion and allows investigators to focus on particular domains of economic activity in considerable detail. The analytical framework used here is different. Instead of activities, it focuses on the three levels of economic organization mentioned above: the domestic economy and the informal and formal institutions that regulate broader social and economic interactions. The relationship between domestic and institutional realms of economic activity is represented in Figure 1.2. It illustrates that while formal institutions are designed to embrace all households in society, informal institutions operate on an interhousehold basis and form networks that vary in size and permanence based on the initiatives of the households involved.

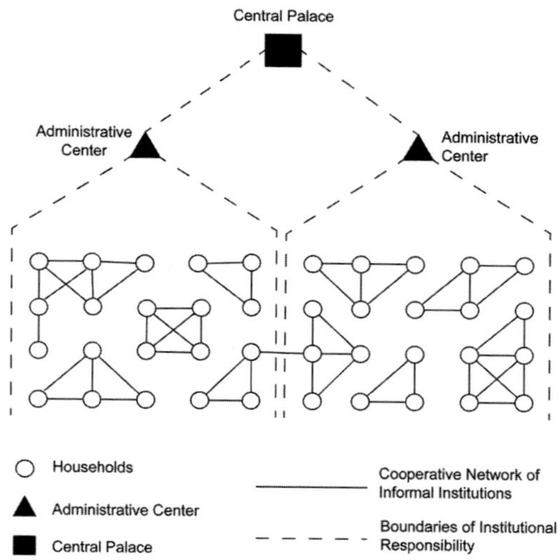

1.2 The organizational relationship between the domestic economy and formal and informal institutions. (modified from Hirth 2016: Figure 2.1)

The *domestic economy* is the foundation of all human societies both past and present. It is organized to support individual families and includes all of the ways that households access or produce the resources needed to meet their biological and social needs. While not particularly glamorous in terms of the types of activities that households engaged in, the domestic economy was the most durable and largest economic component of ancient societies. It was organized to obtain the food, clothing, housing, knowledge, and technology necessary for life and reproduction (Johnson and Earle 1987:11). Today as in the past, the domestic economy supports the greatest number of people, accounts for the greatest volume of goods produced and consumed, and is the foundation on which all other economic activity is based. As a framework of analysis, it applies equally well to commoner and high-status households in both sedentary and mobile societies.

The important and dynamic nature of the domestic economy is discussed in Chapter 2. It explores some of the organizational principles of the domestic economy and the variety of ways that households dealt with subsistence risk. Households were small but flexible adaptive units that were linked by networks of interhousehold interaction. Their overarching goal was feeding, raising, and socializing the next generation, and they operated as entrepreneurs taking advantage of subsistence opportunities when they presented themselves. This included becoming involved in local and extra-regional trade networks to exchange the goods they produced for those that they could not. The chapter examines two household examples to illustrate these points: the way 16th-century households in Central Mexico diversified their economic activities to meet subsistence needs, and how the domestic production of hand-crafted cotton textiles fueled the trans-Asian global economy and textile trade during the 13th through 18th centuries (Abu-Lughod 1989).

While the domestic economy is easily equated with the operation of the household, Chapters 3 and 4 deal with the issue of defining what constitutes the *institutional economy*. Institutions represent the regularized and agreed-on structures of socioeconomic interaction within society.[10] They carry with them norms and values[11] of how interaction should be defined and conducted within society. Institutions from the perspective used here consist of *both* the rules that govern socioeconomic interaction *and* the forms of organization created to carry them out.[12] Institutions in this sense range along a continuum from informal and spontaneous to formal and inviolate. Chapter 3 explores the nature of *informal institutions* within society. Informal economic institutions include all of the structures, principles, and customs that households employed on a voluntary and ad hoc basis to mobilize labor, access resources, minimize risk, and provide other forms of interhousehold support needed for their maintenance and social reproduction. Examples of these practices are drawn from past and premodern societies in Africa, North America, ancient Israel, and medieval Iceland.

Formal institutions are the focus of Chapter 4. Formal institutions are special-purpose organizational structures that operate at the level of the whole society. They developed alongside informal institutions and increased in scale, complexity, and permanency as societies grew in size. From a historic and archaeological perspective, they represent many of the stand-alone organizations identified as temples, libraries, marketplaces, and the varied installations associated with political governance, including palaces, courts, and assembly halls. Four important forces for social integration are examined along with the role that leaders and their households have in shaping institutional development: the need for mutual protection, the formation of land holding and resource pooling associations, the intensification of resource production, and the need to mediate relationships with neighboring groups. It also explores how the household served as a template for some of the earliest forms of institutional organization.

Formal institutions in early state-level societies required resources to sponsor celebrations, construct special-purpose facilities, and support administrative personnel that oversaw their activities. These resources were obtained in a combination of ways that included producing them directly within institutional contexts or mobilizing resources from the population that the institutions served. Chapter 5 explores the first of these options and how resources needed for institutional support were produced by the institutions that used them. Examples of direct production systems are discussed for Sumeria, China, the Aztec, and Inka, along with decentralized production and peripatetic consumption across the Middle East and medieval Europe.

Benjamin Franklin is credited with the saying that "in this world, nothing can be said to be certain, except death and taxes." Taxation is another way to obtain resources for institutional support by mobilizing resources from the households of its constituents. Chapter 6 explores this second dimension of institutional financing. Resource mobilization and taxation are complex topics, and the discussion begins by examining the difference between compulsory institutional donations and the voluntary *euergetism* characteristic of the Greco-Roman world. Two forms of taxation are discussed: tolls and duties levied on imported goods and taxing agricultural production; the difference between land tax, rents, and leases in agrarian states is also clarified. Finally, the role of conquest taxation is examined along with systems of tax collection including tax farming.

Merchants were economic agents that shaped the ancient economy in important ways. They traveled long distances, sought out products for sale, and faced the dangers of the road. Whether they worked as independent operators, agents for institutions, or members of family firms and diaspora communities, they made commercial decisions to buy and sell goods on the basis of incomplete information. Chapter 7 examines who merchants were and how they operated to move goods over space under conditions of high transportation costs. Merchants self-organized to conduct business and overcame what has been called the *merchant's dilemma.* The forms of organization discussed include commenda partnerships, family firms, merchant guilds, temple collaborations, and the phenomenon of merchant diaspora. The examples discussed include the Banjaras pastoral merchants of India, the Old Assyrian merchants of the Middle Bronze age, and the Aztec *pochteca* of pre-Hispanic Mexico.

Craft production was an important component in the economies of both state and pre-state societies. Chapter 8 explores the nature of noninstitutional craft production carried out in domestic and commercial settings. It examines the origins of craft production, the associated risks involved, and the strategies that artisans employed to mediate the obstacles to full-time specialization referred to as the *craftsperson's dilemma.* The discussion examines differences in production scale found within ancient societies together with how guilds and the putting-out system shaped manufacturing strategies and harnessed labor for commercial production in late medieval and early modern Europe.

The marketplace was a prominent economic institution in societies with high population densities for mobilizing and assembling resources in a central locale for consumer access. Chapter 9 examines the role of the marketplace, market exchange, and the variety of conditions under which markets could develop in ancient societies. The variation in the scale and structure of marketplaces is examined using the examples of native North American rendezvous; the retail markets of Greece, Rome, and Aztec Mexico; and wholesale entrepots in Greece and medieval France. The chapter concludes with an evaluation of the marketplace as a formal institution where both commercial and noncommercial interests intersected.

The volume concludes with observations about the ancient economy and how the comparative approach contributes to its study. The value of the domestic and institutional framework is its ability to separate, compare, and contrast economic activities in different settings. General observations are presented on the evolution of institutional economy along with the need for more research on identifying and understanding the forms of economic organization as a basis for understanding how economic systems changed over time.

A final word is warranted regarding terminology. Both in this chapter and throughout the volume, I use the phrase "ancient and premodern societies" to bracket the breadth of societies that I describe and compare in economic terms. Although the societies discussed were separated by thousands of years of development and differed greatly in scale, they all were organized to operate in a preindustrial economic landscape. Most of the food consumed was produced locally, transportation and communication were slow and costly, and formal financial institutions as we know them today did not exist or play a major role in economic development. They were traditional societies in the sense that labor and organization rather than technology and capital investment were determining factors affecting the scale of production. Similarly, they are preindustrial in the sense that they did not make extensive use of energy from fossil fuels. While entrepreneurial behavior and profit motivations could be found in these societies, production regimes did not respond, or responded slowly, to anything resembling the type of market competition and contemporary price-setting mechanisms found in modern industrial societies. Within this shared economic landscape, similarities in forms of economic organization can be found in both ancient and premodern societies.

TWO

THE DOMESTIC ECONOMY

> The subsistence economy is the family economy. It is organized at the household level to meet basic needs including food, clothing, housing, and procurement technology. The simplest form of the subsistence economy is the "domestic mode of production." Each household is ideally self-sufficient, producing all that it needs.
>
> (Johnson and Earle 1987:11–12)

The domestic economy refers to the full array of provisioning activities carried out by the co-resident household or family unit for its social and biological maintenance. Without question, households are the most important economic and social units in human society. Households are where a society's members are born, nurtured, and often educated. They are interactive social units whose primary concern is the day-to-day well-being of their members. Households reproduce themselves both biologically and socially. In addition to basic staples, households provide their members with the social, psychological, and economic resources needed to live their lives. They vary tremendously in size, composition, and rank, but despite this variation, households have always been the primary social settings in which families reinforced their shared cultural values through a combination of work, play, and domestic ritual.

The domestic economy represents the largest sector of every ancient and premodern society. Households, however they were composed, produced and consumed the majority of all the food and fiber resources in society. Survival and reproduction were their business, and the productivity of their economic pursuits determined the success, survival, and well-being of their members. Households provided the vehicle through which resources were pooled, stored, and distributed both to their members and to other sectors of the economy. They contained most of the labor available for work, military service, and religious activity. The domestic economy was always the backbone of ancient society, and the development of political complexity is largely a history of how labor and resources in the domestic sector were mobilized by emerging elites and the institutions that they supported (Johnson and Earle 1987). Given these factors, it is amazing that the importance and organization of the domestic economy is often overlooked in discussions of past economies.

This chapter explores three topics. It begins by examining what the household represents and why it can be difficult to define in absolute terms. This is followed by a general discussion of the domestic economy and why it is the basic organizational unit of society. As the quotation at the beginning of this chapter states, households have to meet the family's subsistence requirements, and the constraints and strategies to do this are discussed. Households often diversify their production strategies to reduce risk and to expand net return. An example from 16th-century Central Mexico is presented to illustrate how individual households utilized different economic activities to broaden and diversify their subsistence base. A second example of household textile production is presented for the Indian subcontinent to illustrate how household production could be expanded to the point that it underwrote the development of the trans-Asian global economy. Finally, the role of the household as an organizational template is discussed, and the house model of society is presented as an example of how the household served as a conceptual framework for early institutional development.

THE CONCEPT OF HOUSEHOLD

While the household's importance is easy to understand, it has not always been considered an important analytical unit within anthropology. This is because the compositional elements of the household are difficult to define and distinguish from those of the family (Yanagisako 1979). Bender (1967) observed that the family and the household have been treated as separate analytical units. The family was defined in terms of kinship relationships regardless of where individuals resided or whether they cooperated in mutually beneficial economic activities. In contrast, the household was viewed as a task-oriented residential unit that could contain both kinsmen and nonkinsmen who were expected to cooperate in a range of social, economic, and ideological activities.

The view adopted here is that most ancient households were co-resident groups that shared householding tasks and decision making (Blanton 1994:5; Netting et al. 1984:xxvi). Households are useful units of analysis that are readily identifiable in archaeological contexts from the dwellings that members occupied, and the activities carried out at them. They are dynamic action groups, and no attempt is made here to define family separately from the household. Individuals who resided together tended to coordinate their activities with one another whether they were directly related by kinship or not (Douglass 2002).

The household as an analytical unit can be found in all human societies irrespective of size or cultural complexity. In mobile societies they represent the nuclear food-sharing unit in both foraging and pastoral groups. In sedentary societies household composition ranges from simple, two-generational nuclear residential groupings to larger complex households composed of multiple generations that can incorporate a range of married offspring, wards, and other attached individuals.

Archaeology is the primary way that households in the distant past are studied. Historic documentation of households is rare and, where it occurs, often is confined to wealthy, high-ranking, and literate families. Domestic structures, architectural constructions, and associated artifacts can be used to reconstruct household size and activities. The degree of transhumance in society directly affects the type of these remains, with sedentary groups producing more robust archaeological records than mobile ones. The reality of the situation is that the domestic remains that archaeologists encounter often reflect time-series accumulations of household debris. When households reside in the same place for long periods, the physical remains recovered may span several generations (Binford 1981, 1982; Kent 1987). The result is that the physical remains associated with a single dwelling can represent the accumulation of multiple rather than single households (Hirth 1993; M. Smith 1992:12).

Comparative analysis has identified tremendous variation in how households were organized and perceived by the individuals who occupied them. Social scientists have defined household composition using different criteria including co-residency, food sharing, resource pooling, post-marital residence, kinship, and the product of work groups (Wilk and Netting 1984). But problems always arise in identifying household boundaries. How, for example, is the household defined in diaspora settings where a family member has emigrated to a new setting but regularly sends resources back to his natal household, as Bronze Age merchants in Kanesh did to their families living in Ashur? (See Chapter 7.)

The variation in household composition can frustrate social scientists who want to develop precise definitions of what they represent, but it underscores their fundamental strength as highly dynamic adaptive units. Small size allows households to respond quickly to problems or new economic opportunities. Ethnographic research has documented that households are flexible and innovative social units that can intensify production on their own initiative when economic conditions require them to do so (Netting 1990, 1993; Stone

1986; Sundström 1974). They can change their composition quickly by adding or hiving off members and changing their work regimes. The rapidity with which these changes can occur makes them difficult to study in the historic perspective[1] (M. Smith 1992).

HOUSEHOLDS AND THE DOMESTIC ECONOMY: SEVEN DYNAMIC FEATURES

The best way to understand the structure of the domestic economy is to examine what households actually do. Households did not become an important focus of study in anthropology until the 1980s (Arcury 1984; Bossen 1981; Netting et al. 1984; Wilk 1989b, 1991). This was because early ethnographers felt that larger kin groups such as lineages, clans, and phratries were the basis for social organization in early societies (cf. Engels 1978; Morgan 1877; J. Smith et al. 1984). Households were viewed as secondary social units. Rather than seeing the diversity in household structure as a key to their adaptive success, variation in form was equated with a breakdown of earlier forms of kinship organization.[2] To understand how the domestic economy operates requires recognizing their seven core economic features and strategies.

First and foremost, all households are the basic units of demographic reproduction within society (Wilk and Netting 1984; Wilk and Rathje 1982). Survival and reproduction are their only business. Households utilize the resources around them to ensure their success, and they thoughtfully deploy household labor to produce or procure the resources needed. Their primary goal is to enhance their economic well-being, and it is within this framework that work is planned, organized, and implemented in premodern societies. Increased economic well-being enhances their survivability and results in larger and healthier households with more labor to reinvest in production activities (Wood 1998). Labor availability is a key constraint on resource production needed for household growth, which is expanded through natural reproduction, recruitment, and the formation of reciprocal labor networks between households (Chapter 3).

Second, households are not passive in their subsistence pursuits. The delayed interest in households until the 1980s resulted in a lack of information on how they operated and adapted to outside opportunities (Wilk 1989a, 1991). This created the false impression that households were passive or, at best, had a limited capacity to address all their resource needs. Nothing could be further from the truth. Instead, households actively search for ways to meet their resource needs because failure to do so threatens their survival. They were highly motivated because there were few social safety nets in ancient and premodern societies.

While the ideal situation would be for all households to meet their resource needs, there are always cases of free riders in societies who consume more resources than they produce. Sahlins (1972) identified this problem and felt that some households intentionally produced below their recognized subsistence needs. Reaching subsistence goals is more difficult than estimating them. Annual fluctuations in rainfall or temperature can lead to decreased availability of resources. The common response by households is to set production goals at levels to meet their needs during years of below-normal yields (Halstead and O'Shea 1989). The result in normal and good years is the production of a food surplus that is available for normal consumption, intracommunity sharing, and intergroup feasting (Allan 1965:38; Halstead 1989). The problem for households is they generally lack the ability to plan for and manage extreme resource shortfalls. When these occur, households can be in serious trouble if higher-level social institutions cannot supply aid (see Chapter 3) (O'Shea 1989).

Third, household self-sufficiency is the primary goal of the domestic economy (Gudeman 2001:43). Commoner households in antiquity regularly consumed the food that they produced and did not rely on other households or the market for the *majority* of the food they needed to survive. For most households, anything else would have been a high-risk economic strategy. That said, it would be incorrect to assume that ancient households existed as isolated, autonomous units and consumed only the goods that they produced themselves. Self-sufficiency does not mean premodern households limited their production goals to auto-consumption only. This view of household self-sufficiency is derived from the Marxian contrast of production for use in traditional society with production for exchange in capitalist economies (Sahlins 1972:83–85).

Self-sufficiency as a household objective also involved production for exchange. Trade was an important component of the domestic economy even if it involved the movement of small quantities of goods. Archaeological research has established that completely self-sufficient households were rare. Instead, past households regularly interacted with neighbors both inside and outside their communities to obtain goods and to enhance their overall economic well-being. There are two reasons for this. First, households in antiquity lacked the time and labor to produce all the resources and items that they desired. Strict adherence to the principle of self-sufficiency would have deprived households of many different items. Second, as will be explored more fully below, complete self-sufficiency would have lowered their overall survivability. Research has shown that household survival is enhanced by the development of multiple resource strategies and cross-cutting exchange networks with other households. Interhousehold exchange networks provided a network through which households could mobilize resources during times of shortage (O'Shea 1989).

The fourth characteristic of the domestic economy is the ability of households to intensify production and increase their ability to produce or acquire food. Resource shortfalls were always a concern for households, especially in large, sedentary societies.[3] One way to offset this problem was to intensify the use or production of the most productive resources (Hayden 1990; B. Smith 2001). The best example of this is the cultivation of high-yield grains in agricultural societies (Aldrete and Mattingly 1999; Bar-Yosef and Meadow 1995; Flannery 1973) and the practice of animal pastoralism (Zeder 1988).

The view that premodern households lacked the ability to intensify production has been shaped by three factors. The first was the development of neo-evolutionary theory that advocated the role of centralized political authority as the engine behind culture change (Carneiro 1970, 1974; Wittfogel 1957). From this perspective households were too small to intensify their production systems and required institutional assistance to do so. The second contributing factor was the assumption that households could not produce a surplus, consumed all the resources they produced, and the only way a surplus could be extracted was through forms of taxation (Harris 1959). That households consumed a large percentage of what they produce is congruent with their overall production strategy. But that does not imply that they could not intensify production. Although production levels could vary, many households regularly produced surpluses above their biological or subsistence requirements to meet social and ritual obligations, to satisfy special needs, and to protect themselves from subsistence risk (Allan 1965; Hayden 2001b; O'Shea 1989). Third, small household size was also seen as restricting the ability to intensify production. It is true that households have a limited labor supply, but that does not mean they could not intensify production with the available labor. Ethnographic research has demonstrated that households have intensified agricultural production by building terrace and irrigation systems in different places around the world.[4] Agricultural intensification is only one facet of diversified subsistence strategies employed by small households.[5] Sustainable intensification is the essence of the smallholder adaptation and would be expected in the past under conditions of limited or restricted access to agricultural land (Netting 1990, 1993; Stone 1986).

Research by Alexander Chayanov (1966) established that agricultural households faced internal stresses that were part of the normal household life cycle that encouraged the intensification of production. He showed that newly formed households with young children were under more resource stress than older households with adolescents or unmarried adults. The reason was that young children consumed more resources than they contributed to the household resource pool. Adults, therefore, had to work harder than if they were just producing for themselves (Durrenberger 1984), resulting in a small degree of intensification. An alternative response to reduce stress was to reside in larger, multigenerational households that had a higher ratio of working adults to young dependents. Large families can lower the consumer-to-producer ratio, but that does not mean that members would work less. In fact, the efficiency of work in large households could increase since they can effectively handle the multiple simultaneous (inelastic) labor demands that occur within the annual work cycle (Wilk 1991:182–183). For example, the ability to share child care releases women to expand their scope of work by engaging in subsistence production, trade, craft activity, and/or alternative forms of service labor (Clark 1989).

A great deal of variation in household size can be found in every society. Nevertheless, large households always had an advantage over small households in the amount of labor they could mobilize for production or invest in agricultural improvements such as terrace building, fencing, or manuring (Bernbeck 1995; Hajnal 1982). Household members often seek to optimize the returns to their labor the best that they can (Mayer 2002). The higher marginal productivity of large households helped buffer them against food shortages, and their labor advantage explains why many households in agricultural societies were organized as multigenerational domestic units (Hajnal 1982).

A fifth feature of households is that they systematically sought to minimize subsistence risk by adopting a resource diversification strategy.[6] Diversification involved exploiting multiple resource groups and broadening the scope of food resources consumed or exploited to ensure household survivability[7] (O'Shea 1989). A diversified production strategy helped to offset cyclical and seasonal resource shortfalls throughout the year (Arnold 1988; Davies 1996; Halstead and O'Shea 1989; Messer 1989). While diversification strategies potentially involve more work than specialized production (Winterhalder 1981), they provided households with predictable food stocks. According to O'Shea (1989), the need to minimize risk was the most important variable in determining the structure of domestic production systems. The reason is that it provided a safer and more predictable strategy for households than the more productive but riskier strategy of production specialization (Cashdan 1990; Winterhalder et al. 1999).

Scott (1976) has argued that households consciously opt for a safety-first subsistence strategy. But that does not mean that they do not take risks in order to increase production returns. Agricultural households will gamble on riskier, higher-production activities when they know that their subsistence needs are met, that their members are secure, and that success in a risky activity could measurably increase their economic well-being (Popkin 1979:21). Risk minimization and maximization strategies are not incompatible activities but involve conscious decision making to balance risk versus potential benefits. Gallant (1991:38–42) makes the case that rural agricultural households in ancient Greece used a variety of agricultural strategies including intercropping, crop diversification, and small field dispersal as ways to maximize agricultural yields while minimizing risk.

A sixth characteristic of the domestic economy was the use of interhousehold exchange as another strategy to minimize subsistence risk. That does not mean that the quantity of goods exchanged had to be large to be important. The establishment and maintenance of alternative networks of resource access can be vital for household survival. Polly Wiessner has shown that !Kung San foragers spent a significant amount of time manufacturing small gifts to exchange with individuals in different bands to establish mutual support networks that stretched across different resource areas (Lee 1993; Scott 2003; Wiessner 1977, 1982, 2002). As societies grew in size, production for exchange increased in importance as rural households produced food, fiber, or craft goods consumed by centralized elite institutions, urban settlements, or growing interregional commercial networks (D'Altroy and Earle 1985; Earle 1994; Fall et al. 2002; Finley 1985).

Interhousehold food-sharing networks were important for family survival in premodern societies even when it involved the exchange of similar commodities that were available in abundant supply (Bliege Bird and Smith 2005; Bliege Bird et al. 2002; Gregory 1981). The value of food-sharing networks was that they were maintained and could be activated when they were needed. Sen's theory of exchange entitlement looks at how the construction of exchange and social network relationships helped to buffer families and households against resource shortfalls in difficult times. He feels that many famines are just as much a result of faulty systems of food distribution as they are shortfalls in resource production (Sen 1981). Households that develop better ways to access food resources through trade, production, labor access, and charitable networks have a better chance of surviving famine and other forms of social stress.

But interhousehold exchanges involved more than just food; they also involved the exchange of finished goods. Archaeological research has proposed that ad hoc, special purpose crafting appeared early in human societies to fulfill both ritual and personal needs (White 1993, 2007). Examples of early specialized craft production date to as early as the Upper Paleolithic period (40,000–9000 BC), which included the production of both ceramic figurines[8] and chert blades for ritual and utilitarian purposes.[9] Items of personal adornment traded over distances of 100–800 kilometers included beads and pendants manufactured from ivory, amber, soapstone, and marine shell (R. White 2003: figure 9; 2007). Obsidian for sharp cutting tools likewise moved over 200–600 kilometers by land and 600–1000 kilometers over water (Grebennikov et al. 2010; Izuho and Hirose 2010; Kuzmin 2010:149; Tsutsumi 2010). Of course, these are the materials that have been preserved. One can only imagine the quantity of perishable materials including food and hides that also moved through interhousehold exchanges.

Interhousehold exchange networks became more important for resource provisioning as societies became less mobile and individual households had less direct access to different resource zones with increased sedentism. The items often produced for exchange among agriculturalists include cooking pots, baskets, special apparel, cloth or hides, items of personal adornment, wooden implements, and cutting tools, as well as figurines and other items used in social, ritual, and mortuary activities (Clark and Blake 1994; Harding 1967; Helms 1993; Hughes 1973, 1977). In sedentary societies, craft production became an important component of the domestic economy for some households (Hirth 2009b).

The production of goods for exchange increased in importance within the domestic economy when craft goods began to move in reciprocal exchanges for food.[10] That was the point when craft production was incorporated into household subsistence strategies. It enabled households to utilize labor available during slack periods of the annual work cycle and to produce items without disrupting other subsistence activities (Hagstrum 1999, 2001). The practice of small-scale intermittent craft production is common in societies where seasonal agriculture is the primary subsistence activity.[11] It allows households to micro-manage their labor, moving easily from one activity to another on a daily or even hourly basis[12] (Hagstrum 2001:49). Craft production is an additional diversification strategy that enables households to expand their subsistence base through exchange if other households chose to participate.

A seventh and final feature of the domestic economy is that households are social organisms that need to reproduce socially as well as biologically. Household social reproduction involves engaging in intracommunity activities that often require material accumulations or expenditures to achieve the social statuses desired for household members and their offspring (Blanton 1994:19). Children change their status as they grow and mature into adulthood. These changes frequently are marked by feasts and celebrations that require special durable goods that often have to be obtained outside the immediate household. Material expenditures accompany the socialization and education of offspring.

The most economically demanding change in social status of household members occurs at marriage. First and foremost, a spouse must be obtained from outside the family, which often involved considerable planning, economic accumulation, and the expenditure of effort to mediate the transition. Economic transactions associated with obtaining a spouse included bridewealth, brideprice, dowry, arranged marriage, marriage payments, groomprice, and bride service (S. Anderson 2007; Dalton 1966; Goody and Tambiah 1973; Kaplan 1985; F. Pryor 1977). A fundamental economic feature of these different spousal arrangements was whether the goods or services required were provided by the family of the bride (dowry, groomprice) or the groom (brideprice, bride service). These payments varied from society to society, but they all entailed the movement of economic goods or services before, during, and/or after the marriage ceremony.

On the whole marriage was an expensive undertaking. Assembling the array of staple and durable goods for a new household took a long period of time. Finding a hardworking and compatible spouse for raising offspring was essential for the success of the household. In the premodern era this often involved long and careful negotiations between family groups through preexisting social connections. These interactions often involved establishing interhousehold gift relations as an important preamble to these negotiations.[13]

The combination of these seven factors led to the creation of mixed household economies that went beyond production of subsistence goods. The diversity of intersecting and divergent goals found in each household shaped the domestic economy in different ways. Households allocated labor to different tasks as their goals and opportunities permitted. The result was that households engaged in a mix of production strategies to produce goods for their internal consumption and for exchange. It is this combination of different production activities for both use and exchange that defines a mixed household economy. It can combine different food production strategies such as agriculture, pastoralism, foraging, and hunting (Bates 2001), with different forms of nonfood production including crafting, commercial trade, wage or service labor, and cash cropping as means to meet household needs. Rather than specializing in a single pursuit, households commonly diversified their economic activities by engaging in a mix of both subsistence and commercial activities (Castanzo 2009; Netting 1990, 1993; Sundström 1974). This could result in a remarkable diversity of microeconomic activities within households as they followed their strategic self-interest. The practice of diversifying household production strategies was common in early state societies where commercial opportunities allowed agricultural households to use their intermittently available labor surpluses in creative ways.

HOUSEHOLD SUBSISTENCE DIVERSIFICATION IN 16TH-CENTURY CENTRAL MEXICO

The Aztecs of Central Mexico were conquered by the Spanish and Hernán Cortes in AD 1521. With conquest, the indigenous society underwent significant population reductions caused by the introduction of new, infectious diseases from Europe (Cook and Simpson 1948). Nevertheless, except for increasingly high labor demands imposed by the Spanish, the economic activities of most indigenous households continued much as they had prior to conquest. Many Central Mexican households practiced a mixed household economy, engaging in a wide array of production and service activities. They demonstrate how indigenous households used the marketplace to diversify their subsistence activities and improve their economic well-being by providing services or becoming involved in production for commercial exchange.

The term "Aztec" is used in a generic sense to refer to the general way of life found across Central Mexico during the 15th and early 16th centuries AD. The society was agrarian. Commoners were farmers, elites were supported by their agricultural estates, and even merchants and artisans had small agricultural plots that provided food to support their households. Land was not held privately; elites had hereditary and prebendal estates and controlled the assignment of state and communal lands.[14] Commoners accessed land through communal land-holding bodies known as *calpultin*, or directly from elites by entering into special service relationships with them. All households had access to land, including those located in urban centers, even if they were small house plots.[15] Farming, therefore, was the foundational subsistence base that all households engaged in. Each commoner household farmed the land assigned to them, and corvée labor was used to work the estate lands of the elite. Slave labor was not employed in agriculture except in restricted and unusual circumstances[16] (Hirth 2016).

The centerpiece of the Aztec economy, as in other groups across Mesoamerica, was the presence of marketplaces in many large- and medium-sized communities (Chapter 9). Marketplaces were important for the domestic economy for two reasons. First, the marketplace was organized for household provisioning. Marketplaces were spaced closely to one another and were held on a rotating schedule, so most households had access to a market within a single day's walk from home. Surplus goods were sold there, and households could purchase anything they needed either through barter or by using one of the native currencies, particularly cacao beans or woven cotton textiles (Berdan 1975, 2014; Rojas 1995; M. Smith 2012).

Second, the marketplace was open to all members of society and provided commercial opportunities for any household with goods for sale. Most crafting was carried out in individual homes, and finished goods were brought for sale in the marketplace. There were no restrictions on the number of craftspersons who could produce goods in society, and most crafting was carried out by intermittent and part-time craft producers rather than full-time artisans. Fresh vegetables were available in the marketplaces of the Aztec capital throughout the entire year, which suggests that some farmers raised crops for commercial sale.[17]

Women vendors prepared food in their homes which they brought to sell in the marketplace. This often was a part-time activity because most markets, including those in large cities, met on a rotating 5-day schedule. The marketplace provided every household with the opportunity to diversify their internal production regimens, make use of intermittent labor surpluses, and offer goods for sale even in small quantities. Women were active in the marketplace as vendors even during the agricultural cycle when men worked in the fields. The few existing Aztec period land registers suggest that some households were land poor in relation to others (Williams and Harvey 1997; Williams and Hicks 2011), and the importance of market commerce for the household subsistence was inversely proportional to the amount of land available for household cultivation.

But the question of interest here is, How diversified were households in the production of secondary food products, craft goods, or the practice of service activities to augment the agricultural activities that every household engaged in? A document entitled the *Matricula de Huexotzinco* compiled in AD 1560 contains a rich array of information that addresses this issue.[18] The document is a census of twenty-two indigenous rural communities in the Huexotzinco province of Puebla-Tlaxcala, Mexico (Brito Guaddarrama 2011; Prem 1974; Warren 1971). The *Matricula* was prepared by pre-Columbian scribes as a pictorial document (Figure 2.1), listing each commoner household, whether they rented or had direct access to communal land, and whether they engaged in any supplemental craft or service activity in addition to farming (Brumfiel 1987). This document was compiled 39 years after the conquest but reflects the types of economic activities that indigenous households practiced both before and after the conquest. Large-scale population declines impacted the labor and taxation demands placed on native populations, but the Spanish did not attempt to change the indigenous market system or how native households supported themselves. Forty-six crafts, service professions, and wage labor activities were identified in these communities (Table 2.1). They reflect the range of activities that pre-Columbian households used to support themselves along with basic farming. Table 2.2 summarizes how these activities were distributed among the twenty-two communities.

Several aspects of this census are particularly noteworthy. First, fully one-quarter (26.7%) of the agricultural households in the census also engaged in a supplemental income-generating activity as a craftsperson, collecting wild resources for sale, providing a service, or working for wage labor. The number of households involved in nonfarming activities was closer to 29–30% since one of the native scribes did not record any information on supplemental forms of work in one large community.[19] Most communities have 20–36% of households engaged in part-time, supplemental income activities, with one community of specialized merchants having as many of 94.2% of households engaged in income-generating activities in addition to farming (Table 2.2) (Hirth et al. 2017). The penetration of colonial society into the rural economy

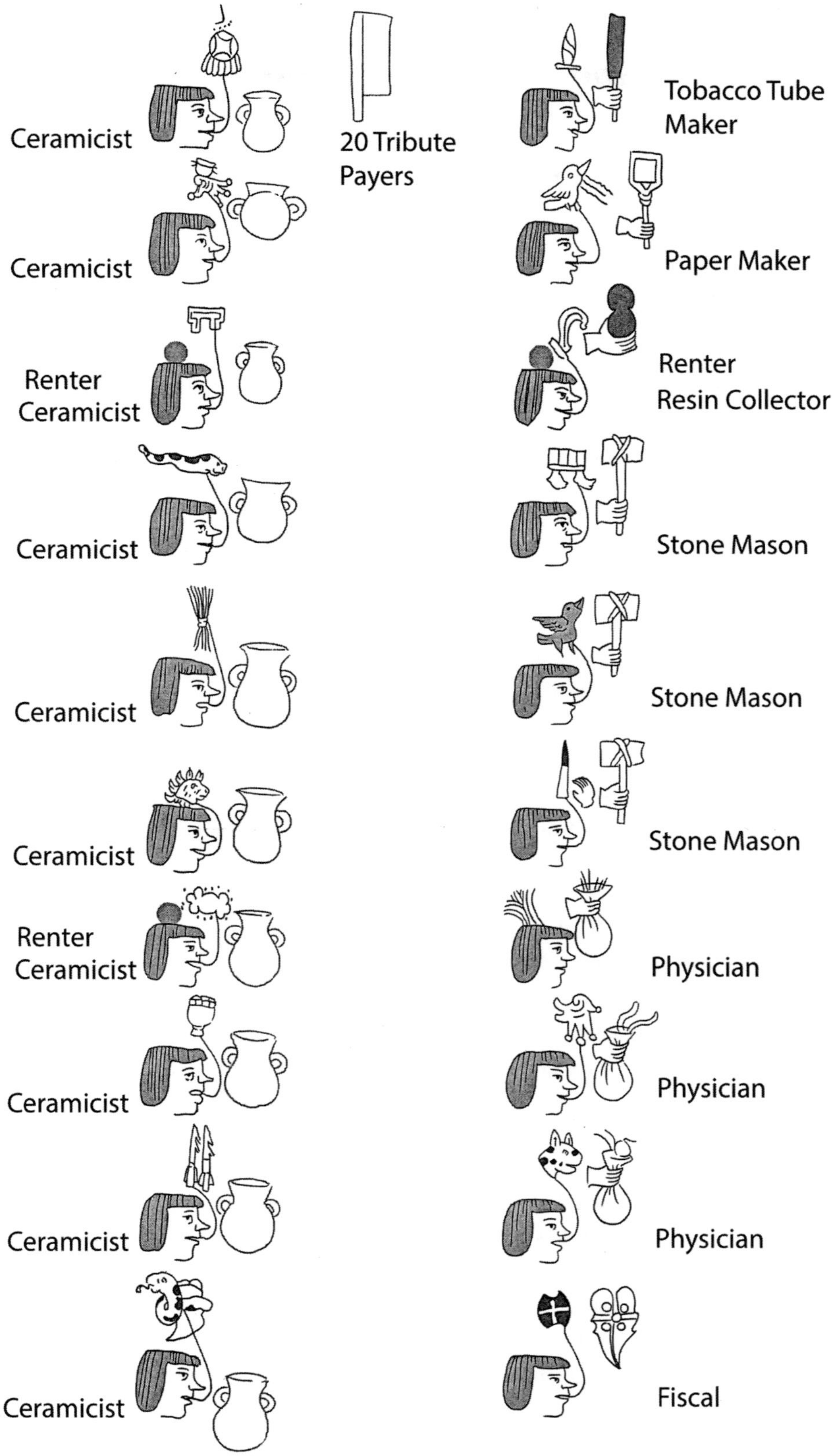

2.1 Domestic activities of households in addition to farming in AD 1560 in the community of Santa María Acxotlan, Mexico. (Illustration redrawn from page 628v of the Matrícula de Huexotzinco by Karin Dennison and author)

TABLE 2.1 *Households involved in nonfarming income activities in Huexotzinco*

Craft artisans	Commercial specialists
Basketmakers	Cochineal raisers
Ceramicists	Merchants
Cobbler	Retailers
Copperworkers	
Dyers	**Wild resource foragers**
Featherworkers	Fishermen
Flowerworkers (dry)	Herb collectors
Flowerworkers (fresh)	Hunters
Limeworkers	Quail hunters
Obsidian craftsmen	Resin collectors
Paper makers	Wild honey collectors
Petate makers	
Rope makers	**Professions**
Sandal makers	Butchers
Silk thread spinners	Doctors
Stoneworkers	Land purchasing agent
Thread spinners	Painters
Tobacco tube makers	Scribes
Unidentified craftsmen	Tailors
Woodworkers	Tortilla makers
	Unidentified profession
Administrative service providers	
Boundary watchers	**Laborers**
Catechists	Bell ringers
Fiscal administrators	Cart drivers
Guardians	Plow workers
Preachers	Porters

is evident in some of the wage labor and administrative services listed.[20] This indicates that indigenous households were quick to adapt to new opportunities in addition to continuing to hunt, fish, and collect wild resources that could be sold in the marketplace (Table 2.1). A few cases are also listed of households combining two crafting and service activities with farming, but census takers normally did not record more than one nonfarming activity in each household.

All of the communities in the Huexotzinco region were small rural towns, and despite their size, households actively produced goods and services for sale that were either sold in regional marketplaces or contracted individually within communities. The Huexotzinco information documents that households practiced a diversified subsistence economy in this rural setting. What is important is that the 29–30% estimate of households involved in secondary subsistence activities still significantly underrepresents the number of households practicing a mixed subsistence economy. The reason is that two commercial activities of

TABLE 2.2 *Summary of household economic activities in Huexotzinco*

Communities	No. of tribute households	Nonfarming income activities	Households engaged in nonfarming income activities	% of households engaged in nonfarming activities
San Agustín Atzompan	215	11	53	24.6
San Antonio Tlatenco	80	6	8	10
San Bartolomé Tocuillan	220	9	78	35.5
San Esteban Tepetzinco	158	12	54	34.2
San Felipe Teotlaltzinco	349	11	124	35.5
San Francisco Tianquiztenco	163	8	45	27.6
San Gregorio Aztatoava	713	13	203	28.5
San Juan Huexotzinco	295	20	88	29.8
San Lorenzo Chiauhtzinco	207	11	48	23.2
San Luis Coyotzinco	669	17	106	15.8
San Martín Tianquizmanalco	54	5	10	18.5
San Nicolás Cecalacohuacan	236	16	68	28.8
San Pablo Ocotepeque	192	11	45	23.4
San Pedro Atlixco	75	6	12	16
San Sebastián Tlayacaque	83	11	14	16.9
San Simón Tlanicontlan	171	12	44	25.7
Santa Cruz Atenco[a]	652	1[b]	1[b]	0.2[b]
Santa María Acapetlavacan	668	21	147	22
Santa María Acxotlan[c]	347	9	327	94.2
Santa María Asunción Almoyahuacan	278	13	98	35.3
Santa María Tetzmollocan	1018	15	289	28.4
Santiago Xaltepetlapan	374	16	65	17.4
Total	**7,217**	**N/A**	**1,927**	**26.7**

[a] Nonfarming activities were not recorded in this community.

[b] Scribe did not record nonfarming activities.

[c] Includes the merchants from this community who moved to the town of San Salvador.

2.2 An Aztec woman weaving on a backstrap loom. (from Hirth 2016:Figure 2-5)

women were not taken into account by census takers that were important contributors to household incomes: the preparation of food items offered for sale in the marketplace and the production of textiles.

The failure to mention textile production is understandable because it was common knowledge that *every woman* produced textiles in Aztec society. Young girls were taught to spin and weave at a young age and produced cotton or maguey fiber textiles for internal household use, to meet tribute obligations, and for household income through sale in the marketplace. Women produced textiles on backstrap looms in their homes during spare moments throughout the year (Figure 2.2). Cotton textiles referred to as *quachtli* were one of the two native currencies used in Aztec marketplaces for making purchases. This meant that women were the real money makers in Aztec society. Textile production was a highly profitable additional production activity that *every married household had the potential to engage in*. Many women spun thread and wove cotton textiles for sale or use as currency in the marketplace (Berdan 1987). The degree to which women produced for the marketplace is unclear since it depended on the time available in their very busy days. One thing is certain, however. It was the most immediately lucrative diversification opportunity that households could engage in. But this is not a situation unique to pre-Columbian households in Mesoamerica.

TEXTILE PRODUCTION AND THE DIVERSIFIED HOUSEHOLD ECONOMY

Textile production was a common way for households to diversity their production strategies in many societies in the ancient and premodern past. Plant and animal fibers were important resources that were processed into a range of useful products including cordage, net bags, fishing nets, and woven textiles. The earliest evidence for twisted cordage and possibly netted garments dates to the Upper Paleolithic period,[21] and the use of woven textiles for clothing has been recovered from the onset of the Neolithic period 8,000–9,000 years ago.[22] The manufacture of spun thread and woven textiles was a major technological innovation in human prehistory (Good 2001) because of their wide array of uses for apparel, household furnishings, currency, and even for making sails for maritime vessels.

Textile production in Mesoamerica was carried out in households at all levels of society as well as in supervised locations where communities had to produce cloth to meet tribute demands. It originated as a domestic activity that was most often carried out by women, for two reasons. First, Becker (2014) feels spinning emerged as a common female activity because it could be done intermittently throughout the day in between food preparation and child care (Barber 1994; Berdan 1987). Second, both weaving and spinning were low-energy tasks that could be carried out just as well by women and children as by men. The result was a division of labor with a higher concentration of women in these tasks, while men engaged in subsistence activities requiring greater energy expenditure.[23]

Textile production was a labor-intensive activity no matter what type of fiber was used. Both plant and animal product fibers had to be cleaned, carded, spun, woven, dyed, and calendered to produce the desired products. It was the labor invested that gave textiles value. The creation of cloth with fine weaves, mixed fibers, or attractive printed, woven, or embroidered designs took time. Textiles were a durable, high-value good that could be traded for food or other commodities the household needed. Their production provided commoner households with a means of diversifying subsistence strategies by producing a value-added item that was lightweight and relatively easy to transport in bulk using premodern forms of transportation. For elite households the production of high-value textiles provided an avenue to increase their durable wealth.

Domestic textile manufacture provided the opportunity for households to become integrated into broader commercial networks. Whether they did so or not depended on three factors: having the incentive to do so, having access to sufficient raw materials, and having the ability to connect to a source of demand for the textiles that households produced. As discussed above, the incentive to diversify production strategies in commoner households was part of the normal risk-reduction strategies that were just as strong in tribal and foraging societies[24] as they were for households in agricultural ones (Krech 2000; Morrison and Junker 2002; Murphy and Stewart 1956). The raw materials employed could be a by-product of raising animals for other purposes (e.g., sheep, goats) or produced specifically for textiles (cotton, flax, maguey) or other things.

The more challenging problem for households was connecting to a source of demand for the textiles produced. Fortunately, textiles were recognized for their value and were widely traded throughout the ancient world, so there was natural demand that households could connect with. Textiles were among the most highly valued wealth goods in New World state societies (Berdan 1987; Berdan and Anawalt 1992; Costin 1998, 2011; Hendon 2006; Murra 1962). The importance of domestic textile production is well documented for medieval Europe (Dyer 2005), West Africa (Kriger 2011), Southeast Asia (Clarence-Smith 2011:129), and India, the latter of which will be discussed separately below. In Japan, textile production was a strong component of the domestic economy. A survey of agricultural households in a rural village in the Izumi district in AD 1843 revealed a mixed domestic economic strategy that combined agriculture with cotton textile production. Some 74–94% of households with fewer than 2 hectares of land engaged in some form of nonagricultural work, which included heavy involvement in both cotton spinning and weaving (Tanimoto 2011:table 18.3).

China is famous for its production of silk textiles, but cotton production was more important for both domestic use and commercial exchange.[25] The production of cotton textiles for sale was a major domestic activity throughout the Ming dynasty (AD 1368–1644) (Zurndorfer 2011:55). The 17th-century poet Dong Hongdu praised the importance of women's weaving for the maintenance of the Chinese household with these words:

> Hungry, she still weaves. Numbed with cold, she still weaves shuttle after shuttle after shuttle. The days are short, the weather chill. Each length hard to finish. The rich take their rent, the clerk the land tax, knocking repeatedly with urgent insistence. Her husband wants to urge her on. But has no heart to do so. He says nothing, but stands beside the loom.
>
> (Zurndorfer 2011:57)

By the 18th century, women's income from weaving was vital to household maintenance since it was close to what a man earned by farming[26] (Pomeranz 2005:243). Rural households did not have to look for a market to sell their textiles. Homespun cloth was bought by wealthy families, who sold it to merchants, who then resold it in local and international markets (Zurndorfer 2011:57–59).

INDIAN HOUSEHOLDS, TEXTILES, AND THE WORLD ECONOMY

The industrial revolution and the rise of 19th-century European capitalism was closely tied to the manufacture and distribution of cotton textiles. Eric Hobsbawm summed it up concisely when he stated, "Whoever says industrial revolution says cotton" (Hobsbawm and Wrigley 1999:34). The forgotten point is that England's industrial revolution in cotton manufacturing would never have occurred without the preexisting, premodern global trade in Indian textiles. English cotton manufacturing grew by replacing a range of well-crafted handmade textiles with cheaper industrial ones, which eventually destroyed the native Indian textile industry (Beckert 2014; Bernstein 2008:299; Riello 2013).

When Portuguese traders reached India at the start of the 16th century AD, they encountered an immense trade network of Indian merchants[27] that extended from the east coast of Africa through Indonesia and into the China Sea (Chakravarti 2000:35; Das Gupta 2001d; Jain 2005). Trade networks extended inland from the coasts as far as Iran and into Russia (Dale 1994). The antiquity of this trade network stretched back to as early as AD 1 when Indian cotton textiles are known to have reached ports in the Red Sea, Egypt, and China (Riello 2013:15, 35). By AD 1000, Indian cotton textiles were at the center of a trans-Asian global network (Riello 2013:5). Merchant ships from India carried expensive and inexpensive textiles west to Saudi Arabia[28] and East Africa (Goitein 1963, 1973; Ramaswamy 2006:71), as well as to the East, reaching Southeast Asia, Malaysia, China, Japan, and the Philippines during the 11th century (Das Gupta 2001b; Kayoko 2011; Parthasarathi 2011:17; Pires and Cortesão 1944:45; Sinopoli 1988).

Small-scale domestic textile producers enabled India to become the greatest producer and exporter of cloth in the premodern world. Indian households during the 18th century AD produced more than one million cotton textiles for export each year, representing perhaps as much as 25% of the world's textiles[29] (Bayly 1986; Pomeranz and Topic 2006:234). The majority of these textiles were manufactured within the context of households as a facet of their domestic economy. According to an East India Company official, spinning was done by women (Hossain 1988:39). Likewise, Parthasarathi (2011:30) notes that a great deal of cotton thread was spun in domestic households in areas of seasonal agriculture. In these areas, "spinning provided a valuable source of income for peasant families in the slow months. In addition, spinning provided a form of insurance for peasant families in lean years. When agricultural work was unavailable, all hands turned to spinning for survival" (Parthasarathi 2011:30).

Weaving was normally done by men working in the patios of their homes, which developed into a full-time profession over time (Parthasarathi 2011: illustration 1.3). Weaving, like other work in India, was frequently organized by caste through the Jajmani system where different groups of people and the work they engaged in were defined in terms of relative degrees of spiritual purity or pollution (Appadurai 1974; Fuller 1989; Lewis and Barnouw 1956). These weaving communities served as their own regulatory groups, mediating intracaste disputes, establishing quality standards, and even organizing into larger lobbying groups to protect their interests both economically and politically (Mines 1984; Sinopoli 1988). While a few master weavers existed, tax records from the late 17th century AD reveal that single-loom households were the most common, with some households having two looms, possibly reflecting the existence of multigenerational households with two male weavers.[30]

Indian cotton textile production is historically significant because it was a global market that was organized on the backs of a multitude of small-scale domestic spinners and weavers. Peasant households farmed the cotton, spun the yarn, wove the cloth, and sold the finished cloth to merchants.[31] Domestic weavers interfaced with merchants on a number of different levels across India. Merchants supplied households with raw cotton and spun yarn if it was not available locally, provided households with credit when necessary, and guided the style and quality of the weaving (Das Gupta 2001c; Sinopoli 1988). Indian households engaged in these activities on a part- or full-time basis, depending on how these activities interfaced with other subsistence pursuits. Subsistence production in many households was organized as a mixed economy strategy, with some activities supplying the food they consumed and textile production providing the income needed to pay taxes and purchase alternative goods. Perhaps as many as a million households or more supplied the labor, resources, and the finished textiles that moved over thousands of miles and defined the trans–Indian Ocean global textile economy.

THE ROLE OF THE HOUSEHOLD IN INSTITUTIONAL DEVELOPMENT

The foregoing discussion has focused on the economic functionality of the domestic economy. In this regard the household was the basic unit of support for commoner and elite households alike. But the household also served as the structural template for other organizational entities in society, including the development of formal institutions. The household is the setting where children learn the social norms and behaviors expected in society. It is where interpersonal relationships are defined, first within the household and then outside it. The dwelling where individuals are raised is the physical arena where the principles of socialization are defined and cultural categories achieve sensory existence (Blanton 1994:9; Bourdieu 1977). In short, families are where children learn pertinent social categories and norms of behavioral interaction, while their residential dwellings provide the physical context where meanings are given material reference and expression. They both work together to teach and ingrain each generation with the models and meanings of interaction they need in life.

The idea that the household provides the model for the political community can be traced back to Aristotle and his treatise *Politics* (Jowett 1943) where he discusses the origin of the polis. Aristotle felt that the household was a natural association that served to meet the family's needs. The union of several households formed a village, and the union of several villages formed the larger political entity of the polis, or city-state. While not a family per se, it had analogous features and functioned to regulate the conflict that arose out of obtaining the necessities of life (Nichols 1992:17). For Aristotle, shared identity was a critical element in defining households, villages, and political groups as integrated groups and communities (Yack 2002:23).

More practical discussions of the household as a structural template for the organization of formal institutions in society was proposed independently by Max Weber (1978) and Claude Levi-Strauss (1982). While many early researchers focused on kinship[32] as the basis for sociocultural organization (Firth 1939; Fortes 1949; Kroeber 1917; Leach 1961; Morgan 1871; Radcliffe-Brown 1941), proponents of the *house model* of society have viewed the household as a more appropriate model for understanding the organization of emergent complex societies and the institutions that shaped them. The household incorporates elements of kinship together with other variables important in the formation of integrated social groups. These other variables included a concern for marriage, location, subsistence, production, religion, gender, rank, wealth, inheritance, and the incorporation of nonkinsmen into unified groups (Gillespie 2000a). As such, households served as a flexible organizational model for early institutions that sought to unify societies with many competing groups and interests.

Claude Lévi-Strauss (1969) developed an early interest in kinship, but he came to the conclusion that it did not explain the organization of all societies equally well. He proposed the house society as a transitory form of organization between kin-based societies and the more complex institutions and class-based social orders of ancient states (Carsten and Hugh-Jones 1995b:10; Lévi-Strauss 1982, 1987, 1991). House societies were organized along the lines of large expansive and integrative households. His examples of house societies were the noble houses of continental Europe, which he compared to the large houses found among the Kwakiutl of the American Northwest Coast (e.g., Boas 1897; Drucker 1965). Lévi-Strauss defined the house in these societies as "a corporate body holding an estate made up of both material and immaterial wealth, which perpetuates itself through the transmission of its name, its goods, and its titles down a real or imaginary line, considered legitimate as long as this continuity can express itself in the language of kinship or of affinity and, most often, of both" (Lévi-Strauss 1982:174).

The origin of more complex forms of organization was viewed as originating in the simpler or more elemental structures of society. Levi-Strauss argued that the house as a model of organization existed "on all levels of social life, from the family to the state" (1982:184). The house for Lévi-Strauss had both a spiritual and material heritage that conveyed and included tradition, dignity, origins, kinship, names and symbols, position, power, wealth, and history.

Researchers have found the house society model useful for examining the structure of complex societies where bilateral kinship systems dominate over unilineal ones (Gillespie 2000b). The house has been used as a conceptual model for integrating society because it provides a mechanism for bringing together rulers, kinsmen, nonkinsmen, and dependents, including slaves, into a single society whether small or large (Waterson 1995:53). In this regard, large kinship units such as the clan were often described as houses in southwest Asia (Gillespie 2000a:6). Among the Tikopia, the patrilineal clan is called the *paito*, which refers to a house or building in which people live (Firth 1939:346). Anthropologists have found the house society model useful for discussing organization structure in a number of areas around the world (Fox 1987; Hugh-Jones 1995; Sandstrom 2000; Waterson 1995). Similarly, archaeologists and historians have applied the concept to a range of ancient societies including those in the Near East (Chesson 2003), the Maya (Gillespie 2000c), Indonesia (Errigton 1989), and Polynesia (Kirch 2010; Kirch and Green 2001:201–205).

Max Weber developed a separate house model for the organization of state-level societies in European society. Weber saw medieval societies as patrimonial states organized around the ruler's family household (Weber 1978:1013–1014). He labeled this system of rule *patrimonialism* where the state's administrative apparatus was developed from the organization of medieval manorial households (Weber 1978:372). Weber's patrimonialism has been reworked into the patrimonial household model by David Schloen (2001), which has been applied to a number of ancient societies including Egypt, Rome, Byzantium, China, and across the ancient Near East, including many Islamic states (Fleming 2002; Lehner 2000; Schloen 2001; Weber 1978).

THE HOUSE MODEL PARADOX

There is a paradox regarding the house society model that has to be addressed to understand how it can serve as an organizational template for formal institutions in ancient societies. Households are viewed largely as nurturing bodies where one-sided generosity and generalized reciprocity are the norms in raising children to adulthood. This contradicts the situation found in early complex societies that are characterized by hierarchical relations, social inequality, and restricted access to resources. If the household is a nurturing body, where do individuals learn these nonegalitarian values and behaviors? The answer is simply "in the household," because it is here that individuals first encounter two general principles that carry over into broader institutional life: an understanding of social inequality and the principle of resource control and ownership.

Households may be nurturing, but household members are not all equal. There are fundamental differences within households on how work is distributed based on age and gender. Children learn these differences at the elbow of their parents and observe elder household members doing different and less arduous tasks than younger individuals. Moreover, elders are often credited with knowing more and in charge of ritual activities, or are engaged in tasks that require less physical force or endurance. The unequal distribution of work within households provides the basis for the differential allocation of labor and rationalizing the separation of task responsibilities at the broader level of society.

The inequality of resource control is also learned in the household in several ways. Children are the economic dependents of their parents; they are consumers beyond their ability to support themselves (Durrenberger 1984; Fortes 1958; Goody 1958). From the perspective of food distribution, therefore, households are composed of food givers and food takers, with the latter being dependent on the former for all their resource needs. This is so ubiquitous that it often passes unnoticed in discussions of household interaction. But it is important because it establishes a pattern of differential control over resources. This principle carries over to public situations where food is given and received, as occurred in labor mobilization feasts between households (Chapter 3). Public feasting is another setting where social inequality is defined through the relationship of food giver and food receiver (Hayden 2001a; Dietler 2001; Dietler and Hayden 2001b; Drucker and Heizer 1967). Furthermore, while all members of the household may contribute to the production of subsistence resources, not everyone is involved in the decision making regarding their allocation.

Household interaction established patterns of both individual authority and collective responsibility. While 21st-century western society emphasizes the importance of self-expression and maximization strategies as the model for economic behavior, this was not the way households operated in the past. In traditional societies, households operated more as corporate units under the household head, who directed the collective actions of household members. The household head was an authority figure even if this status was expressed in subtle ways. According to Max Weber, the broader domains of authority found in society could be traced back to the responsibilities that men and women had within the household. Ancient Babylonian, Greek, and Roman law allowed the patrimonial household head to sell wives and children into slavery if need be, and to adopt individuals as full members of the household (Gallant 1991:121–128; Hudson 1998:152; Weber 2003a:48). The respect of leadership, the control over resources, and the roles of food givers and food takers established a framework of unequal social and economic relationships that can be manifest in both egalitarian and nonegalitarian societies.

Life within agricultural households established a second important principle concerning property rights, ownership, and resource control. The concept of ownership or resource control, as it is used here, refers to the rights over the use and disposal of a particular material good. While ownership may be defined as codified law in complex societies (Hoebel 1967:58), small-scale societies commonly assign ownership, that is, the right to the use or disposal of an object, in terms of how it was created or produced (Gregory 1981). For

Marx (1975:67) the fundamental claim of ownership was the labor invested in the creation of an object, whether it was a field, a house, or a tool.

Marx's "labor investment" principle seems to hold for both movable and landed property (Earle 2000). The general rule for movable property is that the individual who manufactured a tool or weapon was its recognized owner because they created them[33] (Bishop 1998). Native Americans in North America could claim individual ownership over specific fishing and hunting spots as well as trade routes because of the time and labor invested in discovering them (Herskovits 1965:333). Ownership in this sense did not necessarily involve exclusive use but represents a sort of stewardship and sharing like that found in intrahousehold interactions. Among the Tlingit an individual who discovered and owned a particular fishing spot would never deny a request by another household to use it (Drucker 1939:59). Nevertheless, instances are known where Native American societies did lay claim to specific stands of natural resources for their exclusive use by individual households[34] (Krech 2000; Vennum 1988). Among the Owens Valley Paiute, the linkage between labor invested and the individual ownership of piñon nut trees is explicit by the fact that they irrigated them to ensure a bountiful harvest of piñon nuts (Steward 1938).

The principle of labor investment is especially important for ownership claims to land by agricultural groups. The labor that a household invests in clearing and cultivating a plot of land establishes their exclusive claim to the harvest even if crops were produced on open or common-pool land.[35] The Asante express this principle with the proverb, "The hoe is the one to lay claim to the land" (Herskovits 1965:367). In Melanesia and Polynesia planting fruit and nut trees prolonged usufruct control over land even while it was in fallow because the labor invested in the trees established a household's right to harvest their fruit (Barton 1969:43; Conklin 1957, 1969; Hiroa 1932). Among the ancient Maya the practice of planting cacao orchards enabled elite households to claim ownership over the land and the tree's fruit as individual property. It is here that usufruct rights to land or other group resources was converted into the right of ownership through the labor invested in producing goods.[36]

The same principle applied to the establishment of broader systems of land tenure. Labor investment expressed in the use and possession of land, as well as the construction of landesque capital in the form of terraces, mounds, and other commemorations, forms the claims that larger groups and communities make to the territory that they occupy (Dillehay 1990; Håkansson and Widgren 2014). Among agricultural groups, ownership or control over land is secured through a combination of original possession, improvement, inheritance, and conquest (Earle 2000; Flannery and Marcus 2012:74). The mixing of a person's labor with natural resources creates a landscape with attached property rights that establishes the household's claim for their exclusive use (Earle 2000:41; Gilman 1998:220; Hunt 1997).

Finally, the principle of ownership is expressed most fully with regard to the dwelling that the household occupies. The construction of a house in a specific locale established a claim of occupancy and ownership. This is the case even among pastoral groups like the Bantu people of south and east Africa where the construction of a *kraal* hut with a fence as a grazing outpost is recognized as personal property, even if it is 50–100 miles from the permanent village (Herskovits 1965:344; Schapera and Goodwin 1937:156). But residential structures take on a deeper meaning among sedentary groups because the daily activities, life events, and rituals that are carried out there have cultural meaning for household members. The dwelling can symbolize the trans-generational group to which household members belong. The burial of ancestors under the floors of houses (Kirch 2000; McAnany 2014) or in cemeteries within or adjacent to the house yard (e.g., McKee 2006) provides household members with a means of remembering their heritage as well as calculating the future. The dwelling can reflect the social position and the wealth of its occupants and, as a trans-generational entity, provide for the transfer and inheritance of property between household members (Goody 1976; Yanagisako 1979:163).

The house society model, therefore, provides a framework for conceptualizing and structuring early institutions in emerging complex societies. Households loomed large in the minds of the people who grew up in them, and it is logical that they were used as a model for larger forms of integration. The household can incorporate a range of kinsmen, affines, and unrelated clients, servants, and slaves under one roof. As a form of institutional organization, the household projected strong personal ties between the ruler, his family, and nonfamily dependents. Administratively, the household of the ruler could include servants, chief officials, and the heads of prominent families who made up the royal court. According to David Schloen, "In a patrimonial regime, the entire social order is viewed as an extension of the ruler's household – and ultimately the god's household" (Schloen 2001:51). It included all the lands and all the individuals in the ruler's domain.

SUMMARY

The domestic economy has always been the foundation of society. The household is the basic unit of biological and social reproduction at all levels of society, and nothing about that has changed. The primary occupation of the household was to provide its members, whether commoner or elite, with the material base to live their lives. The economies of all ancient societies were built on this fact, which is why the domestic economy was examined first.

Households worldwide have demonstrated the ability to adapt quickly to new opportunities and crises. Failure to do so often meant that they did not survive, since ancient societies rarely provided broad-based public assistance for household support.

To be self-sufficient meant that households had to be entrepreneurial. They could intensify production when they had the opportunity to do so while at the same time trying to minimize subsistence risk. Households were not islands unto themselves. They established interhousehold support networks to obtain the resources that they could not produce in exchange for the goods that they did. Economic diversification was an important risk-reduction strategy, and households incorporated alternative forms of work into their domestic labor budgets to take advantage of different income opportunities. Textile production provided one attractive opportunity for households in premodern India to produce cloth for local and interregional trade. The case of Huexotzinco, Mexico, during the 16th century AD demonstrates that households used many different means to diversity their subsistence base. Analyses of land-holding sizes in ancient Greece suggests that peasant households had to do much the same thing, since as many as 30% did not have sufficient land to support their households (Gallant 1991:84).

The household was the setting where social roles and values were learned and fundamental ideas about social hierarchy, status inequality, and resource control were acquired. The social relations established between kinsmen and nonkinsmen *within* ancient households provided a cognitive template for modeling and expressing social relationships in other settings *outside* the household. This has made the household a useful framework for modeling the organization of many ancient societies. While the house society model is an ideal type, researchers have found it useful for describing the organization of a wide range of small (Carsten and Hugh-Jones 1995a; Hugh-Jones 1995; Lévi-Strauss 1982), intermediate (Errigton 1989; Kirch and Green 2001), and large-scale societies (Lehner 2000; Schloen 2001; Weber 1978) around the world. The chapter that follows explores the role of informal institutions established and used by households to further their own prosperity, to overcome the limitations of size, and to safeguard against resource shortfalls.

THREE

THE COMMUNITY OF HOUSEHOLDS

Informal Institutions

Alone we can do so little; together we can do so much.

(Helen Keller)

Many hands make light work.

(John Heywood)

Institutions are forms of organization and modes of operation created to accomplish specific ends (Acheson 1994). *Informal economic institutions* are the special practices, norms of behavior, and economic arrangements that households initiate and employ to assist one another in meeting their social and biological needs. They are forms of mutual assistance that operate on a voluntary or quasi-voluntary basis between households. Informal economic institutions are structured through the social linkages that households and their members form with one another. The support available through these arrangements can be highly variable, depending on whether interactions are convened on a regular schedule or operate on an ad hoc basis as needs arise and means permit. Likewise, the leadership that coordinates these interactions is also informal. Informal institutions provide the mutual support networks that households need to produce and access the resources they require both for their normal maintenance and to provide assistance when unanticipated events placed them in peril (Hirth 2016:22).

In all ancient and premodern societies, the first line of economic support for households came from social networks composed of kinsmen, friends, and social partnerships. Households built their social networks through interactions with consanguineal, affinal, and fictive kinsmen as well as formal reciprocal trade partners.[1] These were the networks that linked households and through which people, labor, and resources could be requested and mobilized. Anthropology has documented tremendous diversity in the structure and organization of informal institutions. This was a product of the incentive and creativity of households to self-organize under a variety of different social and environmental conditions. The voluntary nature of informal institutions meant that they did not always operate smoothly. Nevertheless, they were the primary means that enabled households to prosper in times of abundance and survive in times of scarcity.[2] Informal institutions are as old as the households that shaped them and were a dynamic feature of ancient economic landscapes.

The discussion that follows examines four areas of support that informal institutions provided to households to meet their social and biological needs. The first of these deals with labor shortages, which were a constant problem for small households that needed to mobilize labor for both subsistence and communal ends. The need for labor was particularly acute in agricultural societies at key points in the planting and harvesting cycles (Erasmus 1956; Moore 1975). The solution was the formation of informal labor groups or reciprocal labor pools that mobilized voluntary labor from multiple collaborating households. The discussion begins by examining two scenarios of labor mobilization from ancient Israel. The first examines how communal labor was used to rebuild the wall surrounding the city of Jerusalem in 445 BC. The second example discusses small-scale labor mobilization through the practice of bride service.

A second group of examples discusses how households used informal institutions to shape their social networks. Household social networks were indispensable for accessing resources, providing protection, finding spouses, moving to take advantage of better economic opportunities, and fleeing famine, plague, or other disasters. Three case studies of social network formation are presented. The first examines social network formation among the !Kung foragers, who used gift exchange to forge linkages that allowed individuals to shift bands and move to more productive resource areas when needed. This is followed by a discussion of how child fosterage was used to build interhousehold alliances for safety in medieval Iceland. Finally, everyone likes a party and the practice of feasting is examined as a general mechanism to build interhousehold solidarity. The case of native American Northwest Coast societies is examined to discuss the general practice of household-level feasting.

Households also had to look beyond the limits of their communities if they wanted to access resources that were not locally available. This third dimension of economic interaction examines how voluntary, interhousehold relations were used to form a bridge between unrelated, even enemy groups through which crucial resources could flow. The North American calumet ceremony is used to illustrate one example of how these trade relationships were established.

The discussion of informal institutions closes on a depressing note. Even under the best of circumstances, bad weather, unanticipated deaths, disease, or war can put households at risk. Informal institutions often provided the only safety net for households when this occurred. The final case examines how Iron Age Jewish households attempted to deal with social and natural calamities when they faced poverty or death.

RECIPROCAL HOUSEHOLD LABOR EXCHANGES

Labor was in short supply in most ancient and premodern households, and a division of labor was employed to use it more efficiently.[3] In most societies the basic unit of labor cooperation was the household. Alexander Chayanov (1966) demonstrated that large, multigenerational households had an advantage over smaller households since they had more labor to deploy in production tasks (Durrenberger 1984). Nevertheless, there were some tasks that required more labor than a single household could supply. It was at this point that households collaborated and engaged in voluntary labor exchanges to mobilize the workforce needed to get work done. Cooperative labor groups have been found in every society (Haviland 1990:191), and it was probably one of the earliest forms of interhousehold collaboration found in prehistoric societies.

The need for cooperative labor is most acute in agricultural settings when getting work done at key points in the agricultural cycle is critical for household survival. When work is time sensitive, households will collaborate in reciprocal labor exchanges. In tropical environments weeding and land clearing may be the main production constraints, while in other areas the critical factors may be timing the harvest and processing food resources before they spoil (Conklin 1969; Langlands 2017). Households often collaborate when the work can be done faster by a group than by an individual, and where tasks can be done more efficiently by working together (Erasmus 1956:454). A case in point is the way that peasant households in medieval Europe collectively shared oxen used for plowing agricultural fields (Homans 1960:76).

But need is not the only reason why households engaged in reciprocal labor. They also provided motivation and encouraged work. Ian Hogbin found that collective labor groups were used for jobs in New Guinea even when there were no significant benefits in using them.[4] People engaged in reciprocal labor groups because they felt as if they got more work done by working together. Hogbin (2013) concluded that social approbation offset a tendency to procrastinate in carrying out subsistence tasks. While this may be true, there are two other reasons why collective labor may be employed. The first is when it is more enjoyable than working alone, and the second is when labor exchanges reinforce other social networks that households rely on. One clear benefit from the use of collective labor is the joint investment created when groups work together in the construction of landesque capital (Brookfield 1984; Håkansson and Widgren 2014; Widgren 2007) to increase productivity through the construction of terraces, irrigation systems, and wetland agricultural fields (Denevan 2001; Donkin 1979; Håkansson and Widgren 2007).

Charles Erasmus identified two important forms of household labor collaboration in societies around the world: reciprocal exchange labor and festive labor. *Reciprocal exchange labor* operates on the principle of tit-for-tat. That is, one day's labor is expected in return for each day given (Erasmus 1956:445). The groups involved in reciprocal labor exchange are usually small, fewer than ten individuals in size. These groups are relatively stable and engage in redundant activities such as moving from field to field during planting or harvesting times. There is a level of egalitarianism built into these groups that require little oversight because all members understand the tasks that need to be done (Moore 1975:274). Reciprocal exchange labor has been widely documented in many premodern societies. It remains a durable form of interhousehold labor exchange even in the face of wage labor because of its low cost and the interdependence that it fosters between small farmers.

Festive labor is another form of collaborative labor with a different set of obligations.[5] Festive labor is a sponsored labor group, and as the name implies, it operates more as a labor party. A host calls for the labor party and provides worker-guests with good food and appropriate beverages. In Africa, brewing beer is a basic requirement for this type of work (Stone et al. 1990). What is important is that there is no obligation that the host reciprocate with return labor. The reward or "wage" that workers receive is the food, beverage, and occasional music provided at the end of the work day. These groups typically are large in comparison to reciprocal labor exchanges, containing 10–100 individuals depending on where they are held (Mahir 1983; Stone et al. 1990:12).

Festive labor requires mobilizing a good amount of food and drink to host the labor group and provides an opportunity for conspicuous giving. Not only is there frequently a disparity in status and wealth between host and worker, but these work parties also operate to raise the prestige of the individual sponsoring it. In Africa, beer-driven work parties serve as commensal politics (Arthur 2003; Dietler 2001) as well as providing the opportunity of an individual to mobilize labor to intensify production or to invest in the formation of landesque capital. Festive labor is a pre-wage method of mobilizing labor. Today, wage labor has largely eradicated festive labor because it is more cost-effective and dependable than this form of work (Moore 1975:287).

While collective labor is often associated with agricultural work, it is not its only application. Collective labor has also been employed for tasks such as repairing buildings or clearing fields of pests, as well as community activities including building roads or defensive features, and working in temple fields (Moore 1975:277; Widgren 2007). A number of communities in the Near East (e.g., Jericho, Beida, Tell Meghzaliyah) probably used collective labor to build defensive walls and ramparts during the Pre-Pottery Neolithic period (8500–6000 BC) since they were constructed without clear indications of having centralized political leadership. The section that follows examines a later case from the 5th century BC when voluntary household labor was mobilized to reconstruct the defensive wall around the largely abandoned city of Jerusalem.

Rebuilding the Wall of Jerusalem (445 BC)

In 586 BC the city of Jerusalem was conquered and destroyed by Nebuchadnezzar II, who dispersed or enslaved its resident population. In 539 BC Jerusalem fell under the control of the Achaemenid or Persian empire when Cyrus the Great defeated Nabonis, king of the Neo-Babylonian empire in the battle of Opis (Haerinck 1997). Jerusalem remained under Persian control when Artaxerxes I became the new king. Artaxerxes I ruled for 41 years (465–424 BC), and the account of the rebuilding the wall of Jerusalem began in the twentieth year of Artaxerxes's reign (Nehemiah 1–6).[6] Nehemiah was an ethnic Hebrew who had risen to the important position of the king's cup bearer and was distressed over the condition of Jerusalem because its walls and gates lay in ruin.[7] Artaxerxes, seeing that Nehemiah appeared sad, asked him what was wrong. Nehemiah responded by saying, "May the king live forever! Why should my face not be sad, when the city, the place of my fathers' tombs, lies waste, and its gates are burned with fire?... If it pleases the king ... I ask that you send me to Judah, to the city of my fathers' tombs, that I may rebuild it" (Nehemiah 2:3–5).

Artaxerxes granted Nehemiah's request[8] because his concern for his ancestor's tombs was honorable and implied religious and family concerns rather than political ones. To accomplish his goal Nehemiah made the following request:

> If it pleases the king, let letters be given to me for the governors of the region beyond the River, that they must permit me to pass through till I come to Judah, and a letter to Asaph the keeper of the king's forest, that he must give me timber to make beams for the gates of the citadel ... for the city wall, and for the house that I will occupy.
>
> (Nehemiah 2:7–8)

The king granted the request, and in addition to allocating resources,[9] Artaxerxes supplied Nehemiah with a military contingent to ensure his safely (Nehemiah 2:9). When he arrived at Jerusalem, he assessed the work that needed to be done, and it is at this point that the account gets interesting. Although Nehemiah had the permission to rebuild the wall of Jerusalem, it was not an imperial mandate. Instead, he snuck out at night to assess the work to be done because he anticipated opposition from local administrators. Resistance was not slow in coming. After seeing the extent of the destruction, he addressed the Jewish population:

> "You see the trouble we are in, how Jerusalem lies in ruins waste, and its gates burned. Come and let us build the wall of Jerusalem, that we may no longer suffer disgrace." And they said, "Let us rise up and build." So they strengthened their hands for the good work.
>
> (Nehemiah 2:17–18)

Here is the crux of the building project. Nehemiah did not command the local population to rebuild the city walls. Instead, he entreats them as good Jews to return Jerusalem to its place of honor before its conquest in 586 BC. Cyrus, the previous king of Persia, had ordered the rebuilding of Jerusalem's central temple (Ezra 1:1–2), which was completed around 516–515 BC (Blenkinsopp 1988:75). Nevertheless, the rest of the city remained largely depopulated and in ruins.

What is important is that participation in the project was voluntary. Nehemiah did not have the participation of the whole province of Judah to rebuild the wall (Blenkinsopp 1988:226). He rallied support for the project by appealing to Jewish groups living in and around the city. Not all responded even though the construction of city defensives benefited the entire community (Moore 1975:277; Widgren 2007). While community labor projects may be mandatory, this one was not. Nehemiah provided supervision, encouragement, and some support, but the decision to contribute labor to the project (or not) was made by the groups of participating households that undertook it.

The work was organized using a form of unsupervised, segmented construction.[10] Since the task was to rebuild the old wall, there was no need for a new design; construction followed the wall's preexisting foundation. What Nehemiah did was divide the construction project into forty-one unequal parts, with one segment assigned to each participating group. This allowed them to work at their own pace and with the labor at their disposal. The participants involved were a cross-section of society and included priests, Levites, artisans, gatekeepers, merchants, commoners from nearby towns, and the private households of wealthy families already residing in the city (Nehemiah 3:1–32).

There was no need for direct supervision of the construction because each group only had to connect their work to the segment of the wall located on either side. How work was constructed within each party was up to them. In one case, workers from the town of Tekoa, located 12 miles south of Jerusalem (Blenkinsopp 1988:234), worked unsupervised because "their nobles did not put their necks to the work of their Lord" (Nehemiah 3:5). While Nehemiah obtained the timber needed for the construction of the gates, the rest of the project was self-financed by each respective group. They supplied their own food and almost certainly recycled stone from the rubble of the previous wall. Food shortages are mentioned during the project because each group had to feed their own workers.

Opposition to the construction was immediate once it got underway. In the words of Flavius Josephus, when several groups in the region heard that the walls of Jerusalem were being rebuilt,

> They tried to interfere with the builders. They killed many of them and hired foreigners to assassinate Nehemiah himself. But Nehemiah surrounded himself with bodyguards and was not deterred. Not that he feared death, but he knew that if he were killed, the walls of the city would never rise. He also gave orders that the builders should have arms when they worked, and . . . [t]rumpeters were stationed at intervals of 500 feet to signal if the enemy approached, so the builders would be ready for them.
>
> (Maier 1994:193)

The wall of Jerusalem was completed in a relatively short time. Nehemiah says it was completed in 52 days on the twenty-fifth of the month of Elul (Nehemiah 6:15). This contradicts Josephus, who said that it took 2 years and 4 months to complete (Maier 1994:193). It is possible that both commentaries hold grains of truth. The perimeter of the wall could have been closed in 52 days to protect the builders.[11] Bringing the wall to its final height would have taken longer, for which 28 months is not an unreasonable estimate.[12]

Forms of segmented construction projects were common across both the ancient and premodern world. It was the way that the Athenians reconstructed their city wall after the Persian defeat at Plataea in 479 BC. According to Thucydides, everyone, including men, women, children, resident aliens (*metics*), and slaves, took part with the work being completed in record time. Eighty-six years later the same system was used to reconstruct the long wall protecting the road leading to the port of Piraeus after the defeat of the Spartan fleet at Cnidus (Blenkinsopp 1988:232–233).

The section that follows explores the topic of labor mobilization at the level of an individual household. With marriage, new households are formed and existing households obtain or lose labor. The example examines the mobilization of labor associated with bride service, where a young male works for the household of his bride-to-be in exchange for the right to marry a daughter. The example is coupled with what appears to a post-marital labor contract, suggesting that households contracted labor for specific purposes perhaps as early as the Bronze Age.

OBTAINING A SPOUSE: HOUSEHOLD REPRODUCTION

After food, nothing is more important for the biological reproduction of households than obtaining spouses for young adults to marry. The process in premodern societies was often involved. Norms of post-marital residence varied. Newlyweds could reside with or near the family of the groom (patrilocal), with or near the family of the bride (matrilocal), or in a separate location by themselves (neolocal). But all forms of marriage involved the loss of at least one young adult from the natal household. This loss, irrespective of gender, was significant because it removed productive labor from households where labor already was in short supply. The result was that marriage was often accompanied by some compensatory transfer of wealth or labor in the form of bride service, bridewealth, or dowry.

Bride service represents a labor transfer that is a precondition to marriage. It is a period of labor service, often expressed in numbers of years, where a young prospective groom works for the household of the bride-to-be. This type of compensation is frequently associated with small-scale societies with limited internal social differentiation and economic stratification (Collier 1993). *Bridewealth*, also known as brideprice, involves the transfer of goods and/or services from the kin group of the groom to the kin group of the bride (Bossen 1988). In broad terms the material goods are compensation for the loss of the bride's labor in her household. This type of marriage compensation is common in societies where female labor is important to household well-being. Finally, *dowry* is the reverse of bridewealth. It is the transfer of goods from the bride's kin group to the kin group of the groom as their contribution to the new household (Goody and Tambiah 1973).

Two questions are of interest here. First, how common was the accumulation and transfer of wealth and labor at or before marriage in ancient societies? Second, if it occurred, what impact did this practice have on household economic strategies? Regarding the first question, Goody and Tambiah (1973) have summarized the presence of these three marriage transfers in premodern societies represented in Murdock's (1967) ethnographic atlas. The results show that 61% of the 860 preindustrial and premodern societies in that sample have one of the three forms of marriage compensation.[13] This level rises to 67% when marriage gift exchange is included (Goody and Tambiah 1973:22). Bridewealth occurs in almost one-half (47%) of these societies, followed by brideservice at 11% and dowry at 3%; all these practices vary by region.[14]

Several lines of research suggest that these practices have considerable antiquity. Bridewealth can be traced back to 3000 BC in Near Eastern[15] and Egyptian societies, and to perhaps as early as 2000 BC for Germanic tribes in western Europe (Anderson 2007; Hughes 1985; Quale 1988; Stol 2012, 2016:112–145). It was required under Islamic law in the Arab world and it also occurred in China (Bianquis 1996; Rapoport 2000; Quale 1988). Dowry was common in both Greece and Rome, and Quale (1988) believes that there was a shift from bridewealth to dowry across Mesopotamia with the increase in urbanization perhaps as early as the 18th century BC. Similar shifts are argued for Egypt during the 6th century BC and during the 1st century AD across the Levant. Dowry is frequently mentioned in Neo-Assyrian and Neo-Babylonian texts during the first millennium BC (Stol 2012:155–159; 2016:139). The shift from bridewealth to dowry is believed to have been the result of increased social stratification, a decline in polygyny, and a change in the nature of female labor within the household (Anderson 2007:155–157).

Wealth transfers with marriage had three economic advantages for past households. First, they established the need to accumulate marriage wealth, which required that households intensify production and produce a surplus that could be converted into the goods, property, or currency for these transfers.[16] Second, the accumulation of goods required long-term planning at the household level. While intended for use in marriage arrangements, these goods provided a fund of durable wealth that could be reconverted into food during times of subsistence stress, illness, or famine (O'Shea 1989). Third and finally, the movement of wealth at marriage broadened the participation of family members to ensure that marriages succeeded and new households stayed together.

Bride Service in a 19th-Century BC Israelite Community

Bride service did not involve the transfer of wealth as a precondition for the marriage. Instead, bride compensation took the form of a labor transfer where the groom joined the wife's household for a period and added his labor to the productivity of her family. While not as well documented in antiquity as bridewealth or dowry, a case of bride service is recorded in the Hebrew Bible in Genesis chapters 28–31. The story of Jacob describes how he obtained two wives and established a new household in a society that practiced a mixed economy of horticulture, pastoralism, and foraging[17] (Stol 2016:122).

The story begins with Jacob's mother Rebekah telling him to "go to Paddanaram to the house of Bethu'el your mother's father; and take as a wife from there one of the daughters of Laban your mother's brother" (Genesis 28:2). Laban was Jacob's maternal uncle and had two daughters, Leah and Rachel. What Rebekah is suggesting is a maternal cross-cousin marriage, which was common in both foraging and small-scale agricultural societies (Haviland 1990:235). So, Jacob journeyed to Laban's household and lived with him for a month before the following conversation ensued between Laban and Jacob:

> "Because you are my kinsman, should you therefore serve me for nothing? Tell me, what shall your wages be?" Now Laban had two daughters; the name of the older was Leah, and the name of the younger was Rachel . . . Jacob loved Rachel; and he said, "I will serve you seven years for your younger daughter Rachel." So Jacob served seven years for Rachel.
>
> (Genesis 29:15–20)

The bargain for bride service was struck. The Hebrew word for bride service is *maskôreth* and a better English translation would be marriage reward (Strong 1995:88). Jacob served 7 years in Laban's household, and on the wedding night, after a substantial amount of wine was consumed, Laban pulled a fast one. He substituted his older daughter Leah for Rachel, which Jacob did not discover until the following morning after sleeping with her.[18] He is angry and they had the following discussion:

> Jacob said to Laban, "What is this you have done to me? Did I not serve with you for Rachel? Why have you deceived me?" Laban said, "It is not so done in your country, to give the younger before the first-born. Complete the week of this one, and we will give you the other also in return for serving me another seven years."
>
> (Genesis 29:25–27)

A compromise was reached, and Jacob agreed to another 7 years of service for Rachel. He was now in a polygamous marriage, and after the 14 years of service were completed, Jacob decided to take his family and return to his homeland. But Laban wanted Jacob to remain in his household, so he made the following proposition:

> Laban said to him . . . "the Lord has blessed me because of you; name your wages, and I will give it. . . ." Jacob said, "You shall not give me anything; if you will do this for me, I will again feed your flock and keep it: let me pass through all your flock today, removing from it every speckled and spotted sheep, and every black lamb, the spotted and speckled . . . goats; and such shall be my wages. So my honesty will answer for me later, when you come to look into my wages. . . . Every one that is not speckled and spotted among the goats and black among the lambs, if found with me, shall be counted stolen." Laban said, "Good! Let it be as you have said."
>
> (Genesis 30:27–34)

Here a labor contract was struck. The English translation for wages clouds the meaning of what is being proposed. The Hebrew word used for wages that

Laban asked about is *sâkâr*, which is best translated as compensation or the payment resulting from a contract (Strong 1995:142). Jacob agrees, using the same word to confirm their agreement. What is important in this service contract is that there was no guaranteed return. Instead, Jacob was proposing something very much like working on commission or working on a share's basis. Since speckled and black sheep and goats are rare, Jacob proposed that those be his herd and he keep only the speckled or black offspring that they produced. Any white animals would be considered "as stolen," but not really. What is meant is that any white sheep or unspeckled goats produced would still be considered Laban's property.

But true to his character Laban pulls another shady trick. He culls all the speckled sheep and goats from his herd and sends them away with his sons so that Jacob had only white sheep and unspeckled goats to breed. To Jacob's credit he uses selective breeding and a home remedy (Demsky 2012:211–212) to increase the size of his flock of speckled sheep and goats (Genesis 30:43). Jacob grew rich at Laban's expense, leading to jealousy and a separation of the two households. Jacob's explanation to Laban and his wives for leaving is instructive as the Hebrew words reveal some of the distinction between bride service and contracted labor:

> [Y]ou know that I have served your father with all my strength.... If he said, "The spotted shall be your wages [*sâkâr*]," then all the flock bore spotted; and if he said, "The striped shall be your wages [*sâkâr*]," then all the flock bore striped.
>
> (Genesis 31:6–8)

> These twenty years I have been with you [Laban].... That which was torn by wild beasts I did not bring to you; I bore the loss of it myself; of my hand you required it, whether stolen by day or stolen by night.... I served you fourteen years for your two daughters, and six years for your flock, and you changed my wages [*maskôreth*] ten times.
>
> (Genesis 31:38–42)

Fourteen years was not unusually long to spend in bride service for two wives. After Jacob's 14 years of bride service, however, the relationships changed. Jacob became more of an independent contractor within Laban's household, working for shares based on reproduction within the herd under his supervision. The fact that Laban continually renegotiated the terms of their labor agreement during the six contract years suggests considerable flexibility in their construction from year to year. The words for wages fluctuate between *maskôreth* for reward for bride service and *sâkâr* specifying that the increase to flocks was the proper payment from their labor contract.

Jacob's statement that he bore the loss of Laban's animals himself implies that contracts at this time were based on a percentage of net return on the increase of the herd with animals killed by carnivores exempted from shepherd contracts under Hebrew law.[19] This is exactly what is found in herdsman contracts in southern Mesopotamia during the 6th and 7th centuries BC. Here herdsman operated as entrepreneurs, managing flocks of sheep for the Eanna temple at Uruk using share-breeding contracts. These contracts required herdsmen to produce a two-thirds increase on every 100 ewes in their charge as well as 1.5 mina of wool for every ram and ewe in their flock. Contracts allowed for a 10% loss in the herd due to death. Any additional increase in the number of animals or the secondary products that could be produced from them (i.e., milk, cheese, butter) represented the herdsman's profit (Kozuh 2014). As in the case of Jacob, share-contracts combined with good herd management was the key to profit and success.

FORGING SOCIAL NETWORKS

Social networks were critical to household survival, and households conscientiously worked at building and maintaining them over time through a range of activities including gift giving, feasting, visitation, and other informal means. Social networks provided the interhousehold connections through which households accessed resources, organized informal work groups, obtained spouses, and arranged marriages. The breadth of one's social network was important because it defined the individuals who might provide help or support in times of stress and resource shortfall. The first example of how households shaped their social networks is *hxaro* gift exchange among the !Kung bushmen.

Social Networks and Hxaro Gift Exchange among Bushmen Foragers

The !Kung bushmen (Ju/'hoansi) were mobile foragers who occupied the Kalahari desert in northwest Botswana and northeast Namibia, Africa (Lee 1993; Lee and DeVore 1976; Marshall 1976, 1999; Wilmsen 1989). Bushmen hunted and gathered across a high-risk environment that received only 6–10 inches of rainfall annually. An important staple of the !Kung diet throughout the year was the collection of edible nuts from the Mongongo tree.[20] During the wet months (November–March) groups ranged widely across the landscape, but during the seven dry months (April–October) foraging was confined to the area around water holes. Hunting was risky, and as a result, the collection of nuts accounted for fully 50% of the !Kung diet (Lee 1968:33).

The Ju/'hoansi lived in small nuclear family units within bands whose normal group size ranged from ten to twenty-five individuals. They represent what anthropologists call egalitarian societies.[21] The use of groves of mongongo nut trees around permanent water sources created territories (*n!ore*) that were occupied recurrently by related kinsmen (Lee 1993). Because marriage was exogamous (outside the band), children inherited rights to two different *n!ore*, one from their mother and one from their father. Establishing rights to multiple *n!ore* was important because the environment was risky and the resources they contained were unpredictable. The two primary ways that families minimized risk was to diversify the range of foods they consumed and to broaden mobility options that allowed them to move to other *n!ore* where resources were more plentiful during seasons of unanticipated shortfall. Mobility options were maintained through the construction of gift and sharing networks involving *hxaro* exchange.

Hxaro exchange was a form of informal gift exchange between formal trade partners (Wiessner 1977, 1982, 2002). Multiple trade partners were established over an individual's life, creating a network of contacts that could be mobilized in times of need. Partners could be consanguineal kinsmen, affinal kinsmen, or unrelated individuals both inside and outside the local band. *Hxaro* was structured as a form of delayed, reciprocal gift exchange involving a range of durable goods. The purpose of the exchanges was to form a long-term, semi-formal network of mutual assistance partners. This network provided individuals with vital information about environmental conditions and resource availability in different areas.

A *hxaro* relationship was established between two individuals. The most common relationships were between a parent and child, spouses, siblings, the spouses of siblings, and with friends or distant relatives. Detailed study of 955 *hxaro* partnerships held by 73 individuals (59 adults and 14 children) revealed that adults averaged 16 partners apiece.[22] The number of *hxaro* partners increased over the early life span of an individual and included individuals of both sexes. Partnerships were strategically placed over space at distances as much as 200 kilometers from the base camp of any individual. According to Wiessner (2002:421), 18% of *hxaro* partners were in the same camp, 24% with individuals in camps 1–15 kilometers away, 25% with individuals in camps 16–50 kilometers away, and 33% in camps 51–200 kilometers away.

The gifts offered in *hxaro* exchanges consisted of material goods only. Food was distributed along kinship lines and to *hxaro* partners, but it was never included in *hxaro* exchanges per se. The most common items moving through these exchanges were ostrich eggshells, dogs, jewelry, digging sticks, ostrich eggshell bead necklaces, pots, arrows, clothing, blankets, and other items made by hand[23] (Lee 1993:104). Gifts were exchanged during visiting trips. The first item given was a return gift from a previous exchange. The second was an opening gift of the next exchange. A delay of months or even years could transpire before a return gift was presented for the second exchange. Of course, when it was given it was countered with the first gift of a third exchange. In the words of one !Kung man, "If you give me something and I give you something back, we are even, we are finished. In *hxaro* you are never finished. One or the other is always waiting to see what comes back" (Lee 1993:106). It was the ongoing indebtedness and the expectation of reciprocal return (Mauss 1990) that kept the relationship active and open. The result of this structure was that exchanges went on forever throughout the lives of linked participants.

The key question is, What was the function of *hxaro* exchange? While it resulted in the movement of goods, it was not intended as a resource procurement network. Instead, its purpose was to establish a network of social contacts that provided access to groups with different resource pools. This was critical in areas where resources were scarce or could fluctuate from year to year. *Hxaro* enabled people to adjust band size and incorporate themselves into groups in different areas when resources were insufficient to support them. It also provided an outlet for individuals to move when conflict emerged within bands.

Hxaro exchange networks helped groups minimize subsistence risk by increasing their mobility options. Wiessner (1982:65) feels that these networks allowed the Ju/'hoansi to pool risk by developing social obligations of hospitality and sharing. These networks enabled families to move and integrate themselves into the groups of their *hxaro* partners. The maintenance of these networks spread subsistence risk over as many individuals and as great a distance as possible. Individuals made an average of 1.5 *hxaro* visits per year with a mean length of visits lasting 2.2 months. This meant that even during periods without resource stress, approximately 25% of the year was spent in camps that accessed other resource pools.

Archaeological research suggests that *hxaro* exchange networks had significant time depth within the Kalahari region and were a fundamental feature of bushman regional adaptation (Scott 2003:5; Wiessner 1982). Similar forms of exchange have been suggested for interaction across mid-continental North America during the Late to Middle Archaic period (6000–1000 BC) (Jefferies 1995). In ancient Greece a system of guest friendship (*xenia*) and reciprocal support (*proxenia*) between rich men was the framework through which grain and other resources could be mobilized in times of hardship (Gallant 1991:167–168; Herman 1981). *Hxaro* was an adaptation to a high-risk environment where families relied on mobility to access resources in areas of sharp regional variation in resource availability.

SOCIAL NETWORKS AND INFORMAL INSTITUTIONS FOR ACQUIRING CHILDREN

When Thomas Carlyle called economics the dismal science, he was referring to the practice of slavery, but he might as well have been describing the study of premodern demography. Children were indispensable for the survival of the household, but infant and childhood mortality in antiquity was depressingly high.[24] This sentiment was captured by Marcus Aurelius during the 2nd century AD in his *Meditations* where he said, "As often as a father kisseth his child, he should say secretly with himself . . . tomorrow perchance shall he die."[25]

Households that did not raise children to adulthood were doomed to fail. The maturation of children provided households with the hope of future support for aging parents. In the same vein, households with too many children put an economic strain on household resources especially where dowry or bridewealth was practiced. There were two ways to achieve a balance of young adults in households: adoption and fosterage. Adopted children generally became full members of the household, while foster children might not.[26] This is an oversimplification of these practices, but they are a useful starting point for discussing how child acquisition practices varied from society to society.

Adoption was widespread across the eastern Mediterranean throughout antiquity. It was common in the ancient Near East (Malul 1990; Stone et al. 1991) and was a regular part of family life in both the Greek and Roman worlds (Huebner 2013). The reasons for adoption varied from continuing the family name and providing homes for orphans to obtaining social and ritual progeny and supplying heirs for inheritance and the consolidation of an estate (Goody 1969). The focus of adoption was often on perpetuating the biological household (Silk 1990). Joan Silk (1987b:39) has argued that adoption in Oceania and the North American Arctic often involved the natural parents maintaining a close interest in the welfare of their adopted children. A strong motivation for adoption in these societies was to adjust family sizes and to increase their overall economic well-being (Silk 1980, 1987a).

The practice of fosterage was widespread in ancient and preindustrial societies. It was found across Europe (Bremmer 1976), the Middle East (Parkes 2004), Africa (Notermans 2004; Scelza and Silk 2014; Silk 1987b), Oceania (Brady 1976; Donner 1999), and Central and South America (Halbmayer 2004). In the Muslim world suckling a foster child created a strong bond referred to as "milk kin," and this type of fosterage is represented in the Homeric epics and writings of ancient Greece (Parkes 2004:592–595). Scelza and Silk (2014:449) observed that the practice of fosterage often conferred a range of social benefits for the foster parents who took in a child. In Micronesia, children of large, higher-ranking families were fostered by lower-ranking households to solidify social ties (Betzig 1988). The implication is that fosterage was a flexible arrangement that could also be used by households to strengthen interhousehold relationships and dependencies.

Fosterage in Medieval Iceland

In medieval Iceland the role of fosterage was used as a strategy to build and strengthen interhousehold social and safety networks from the 10th to 13th centuries AD. Iceland was colonized between AD 870 and 930 by voyaging Vikings from Scandinavia (Gelsinger 1981; Miller 1990:13). The society was unique in three ways. First, it was a decentralized, largely egalitarian society run by local chieftains known as *goði*.[27] While medieval Iceland had a highly developed set of legal codes known as the *grágás* (Dennis et al. 2006), there was no public law enforcement. The result was that violence, interhousehold feuding, and blood revenge was a way of life (Byock 1993; Miller 1990). Second, the society was largely rural, and because the climate was harsh the economy focused on sheep raising and limited agriculture (Gelsinger 1981; Ingimundarson 1995). Iceland could be productive, but by the 11th century population growth began to stress the limits of the island's resources (Byock 2001:55). When twenty-seven trading ships from Norway were forced to winter in Iceland in AD 1118, this extra population created famine in several areas of the island (Jónsson 1953; Miller 1990:16). Third, medieval Iceland was a literate society whose legal codes and rich oral tradition were recorded in the sagas (Olasson 1932) and provide valuable information on lifeways back to the 10th century AD (Byock 2001; Durrenberger and Pálsson 1999; Miller 1990).

The combination of these three conditions provides a picture of a precarious social and natural environment. Life was hard, and resources were often in short supply, but that is not the reason why fostering children was common in this society. Instead, fosterage was used along with marriage, oath and blood brotherhood,[28] and patron–client alliances as a means of building and reinforcing support networks that provided protection for households. Social and kinship networks were indispensable for household survival because of the perpetual violence and blood feuds within society (Miller 2014). Bravado and force of arms was one avenue to raising one's status in medieval Norse society. Physical conflict was common and, with it, death and reprisal. Individuals had to choose sides in these disputes, which was complicated, as any household could contain individuals with multiple different family allegiances.[29] The best assurance of survival was to have a large network of supporters that included strong and sometimes violent men, as well as good arbitrators to resolve disputes peacefully in the Alþing law court.[30]

Fosterage was used to expand and cement linkages between households. One fairly common practice was for a low-status household to foster a child from a large or higher-status household that could provide support and protection for the foster family (Miller 1990:172). The request for fosterage often was initiated by a foster father to the biological father to create a linkage and a level of social indebtedness of the latter to the former. Fosterage did not occur free of charge. It normally involved providing protection and support for the fostering family or an outlay of funds called a *fóstrlaun* to raise the child. The link between foster father and foster child was a close one, and the law codes gave the foster parent specific rights including the right to kill on behalf of his charge (Hansen 2008:77). Foster children were expected to be treated as well as or better than natural-born children within their foster families. Not surprisingly, biological parents monitored the welfare of their children.[31]

Fosterage was instrumental in building relationships between families. In Njal's saga, Njal was an aspiring man of influence and legal knowledge who married his son to the daughter of a wealthy chieftain (*goði*) named Asgrim Ellida-Grimsson to cement a political alliance and to build his social network. To strengthen this linkage, Njal also became the foster parent of Höskuldr Hvitaness, Asgrim's precocious son, under the pretense of providing legal training (Magnusson and Pálsson 1960, 16:37; Miller 1990:124). In the Laxdæla saga a man named Þordr in desperate need of protection petitioned a strong man named Höskuldr to be allowed to foster his son and make him the heir to his estate (*arfsal*) if Höskuldr would grant him physical protection (Magnusson and Pálsson 1969, 16:37; Miller 1990:172, 348, fn49). Fosterage in this society was about building social capital.

It also was used as a means of gaining status by demeaning another. An Icelandic proverb in Laxdæla saga says that "he who fosters another's child is always the lesser man" (Miller 1990:172; Magnusson and Pálsson 1969, 27:75). In Sturlu saga, Sturlu buys flour from a man named Þorvarthr that he feels is wormy and of poor quality. Sturlu gives Þorvarthr a choice: either to take in his son Halldorr as a foster child or to be summoned to the law court at the Alþing for shady dealings. Sturlu's bullying works, and Þorvarthr takes Halldorr in fosterage[32] (Byock 1993:233; McGrew and Thomas 1970–1974). In a similar scenario, Njal agrees to foster the son of another man that his sons had killed to avoid the risk of their condemnation as outlaws at the Alþing (Magnusson and Pálsson 1960, 94:236; Pálsson 2001).

Fosterage, therefore, was never done purely for altruistic reasons to help orphans or to even out differences in family size. It was used to build social networks between households. As Jesse Byock has observed, a "way to gain protection either before or during a feud was the creation of ties between families. Fosterage, a bond of fictitious kinship was especially common" (Byock 1993:247). The combination of bilateral kinship and a dispersed settlement spread the kinsmen who might support you over considerable distances. For that reason, it was important to build a support clientage with other families close to home in case a feud broke out. Icelanders continually were embroiled in feuds and routinely faced the dilemma of having to "uphold pre-existing kinship, fosterage, or political obligations to individuals on opposing sides in a dispute" (Byock 2001:214). In this case the economic value of fosterage was that it provided protection for households in an insecure economic and social landscape.

FEASTING BETWEEN HOUSEHOLDS

Communal eating is one of the fundamental ways that social solidarity is built and maintained in human societies. Whether it is an ordinary meal within the household or a special meal between friends or strangers, sharing food is an act that fosters trust and mutual well-being. Because of this, feasts and feasting played a central role in building social networks between households. A feast is defined here as the communal consumption of food and drink among individuals for a special purpose or to commemorate an important occasion. It could involve special types of food (Hayden 1990, 2001b:28) or be intended for specific guests. The fact that a feast is designated for a specific purpose or to convey special information makes feasting a ritualized event[33] (Dietler 2001:67).

Feasts constitute a domain of social action that, in the words of Michael Dietler (2001:69), "bind people together in various intersecting groups ... from the local household cluster to the regional political community." The feasts that specifically linked households were those involving mobilizing work groups (the festive labor groups described above), marriage, coming of age ceremonies, reinforcing gender roles, soliciting favors, and maintaining inter-household cooperation and support networks (Dietler 2001; Dietler and Hayden 2001; Hayden 2001a, 2014). Among the Akha of northern Thailand, feasts were indispensable for creating and maintaining life-crisis support networks (Clarke 2001:144).

While not of specific concern here, feasts were common as part of community-wide celebrations sponsored by formal institutions within and between societies. Several scholars see feasts as indispensable for building alliances and political relationships as well as displaying differences in the wealth of the groups or individuals who sponsored them (Friedman and Rowlands 1978a; Junker 2001; Perodie 2001). These types of feasts include mortuary feasts of leaders, establishing alliances between polities, mobilizing surplus from the community, and competitive displays to validate claims of individuals to leadership offices (Codere 1966; Dalton 1977; Hayden 2001a; Wiessner 2011). Whether they occurred as formal celebrations or within households, feasts were viewed as wasteful by colonial administrators and missionaries (Hayden and Villeneuve 2011). A general disgust for feasting is described by Diego Durán,[34] a Dominican friar and missionary to New Spain in the early 16th century. He describes how people from indigenous communities in Central Mexico disguised their feasts and religious rites with the following words:

> I can only imagine how many times the following has happened to our priests. Three or four months have gone by since a holy day, and how the Indians come to ask for [a priest's] services.... And if our priests question the natives regarding this great delay ... [t]hree thousand excuses and lies are offered, but when one looks into the native calendar, one finds that the feast of the idol ... falls on that day.
>
> (Durán 1971:409)

And regarding the celebrations, "The most elaborate rites were found in celebration of the feasts. And everything was associated with heathenism and idolatry, even bathing in the river" (Durán 1971:55). Durán probably did not have anything against bathing; he just did not understand the positive benefits that interhousehold feasting had for the individuals involved. Marshall Sahlins (1972) was the first to identify the free rider problem where some households relied on others to produce a portion of the resources they required for subsistence. This is a dangerous situation in societies where it occurred. The practice of feasting forced households to produce above their anticipated households needs (e.g., Harris 1959) to meet both household and society's feasting requirements throughout the year. The larger the demand for household-level feasting, the more important storage and intensified food production to create a surplus became at the household level (Hayden 1990; Malinowski 1967b). Creating a social requirement for food consumption created a work obligation that could not be questioned solely based on household subsistence needs (O'Shea 1989).

Native American Feasting on the Northwest Coast

Nowhere has feasting been more prominently discussed than among the native American societies of the Northwest Pacific Coast (Boas 1897; Codere 1966; Drucker and Heizer 1967; Piddocke 1965). These societies occupied the rich coastal waterways where salmon and other species spawned annually, providing access to a wide array of marine resources. Social organization revolved around the clan or local kin group that possessed lands and fishing places of economic importance. Individuals within each clan were ranked from high to low status within the general categories of chiefs and commoners (Drucker 1965).

A prominent feature of Northwest Coast society was the elaborate potlatch feasts conducted to validate the claims to status positions within clans by eligible claimants. The potlatch has been used as an example of redistribution as formulated by Karl Polanyi (1957). What is often overlooked is that the elaborate competitive potlatches discussed by Codere (1966) were brought about by high post-contact death rates after the introduction of European diseases. Anthropologists have made the mistake of calling every celebration where food was served a potlatch. Native informants of the southern Kwakiutl say that, before contact, "feasts were frequent but potlaches were few and far between" (Drucker and Heizer 1967:35). While both were used to validate changes in status within society, feasts and potlatches were different events in the minds of Northwest Coast groups that sponsored them.

The difference between feasts and potlatches was one of scale, frequency, and formality. Prior to European contact, everyone gave feasts while only the highest-ranking chiefs sponsored a potlatch (Drucker and Heizer 1967:36). A feast among the Tlingit was called a *wuš-kana-wuti-at*, which literally meant "we gather together." They were small informal gatherings hosted by the house group for nearest relatives and individuals with whom they were in frequent contact. According to Tlingit informants, "a man gives a feast because he 'feels-good-inside'" (Oberg 1973:97). Food at feasts was supplied by the household, prepared by its women, and served by young men and slaves, which was different from how it was prepared and served at a potlatch.[35] Among the Tlingit, feasts were given whenever the household head had plenty and was in a benevolent mood. Occasions for feasts included births, naming a child, puberty rights, declarations of marriage eligibility, celebrations of successful fishing or hunting expeditions, before and after a successful trading venture, and after a son had returned from days of shamanistic training (Drucker 1965; Oberg 1973).

Feasts increased in formality as one moved from small household feasts to more inclusive group celebrations. Larger feasts were held to commemorate burial ceremonies, marriages, return of brideprice ceremonies, house building events, and dance society events where children learned the importance of their social roles. In comparison to household feasts, potlatches were infrequent, large-scale affairs that lasted multiple days with formal rules of seating, gift display, gift giving, dancing, and formal speeches establishing claims of heredity[36] (Barnett 1938; Codere 1966; Drucker and Heizer 1967). Feasting operated at all levels of society and was especially important in building informal social networks between households.

TRADE AND EXTERNAL RESOURCE PROCUREMENT IN PREHISTORIC NORTH AMERICA

In prehistoric North America, not all resources could be obtained locally and households often had to look beyond their own communities to obtain them. As a result, a range of formal and informal visiting trade institutions was used to mediate this problem (Heider 1969). Social networks were established between households that provided the bridge between different groups through which resources flowed. The archaeological evidence for these interactions is found in the broad array of resources that moved as gifts and trade goods over long distances. Native groups in North America display a long tradition of both regional and interregional trade (Baugh and Erickson 1994) that can be traced back to the Archaic and Paleoindian periods (Jackson and Ericson 1994; Lafferty 1994; Walthall et al. 1982). Native North American societies ranged from mobile foraging bands and semi-sedentary tribes (Steward 1938, 1972) to complex chiefdoms practicing agriculture (Milner 1998; Pauketat 1994; Snow 1996). All these societies employed trade as a component of their overall provisioning strategies, which operated through informal interactions at the household level.

There were two levels of exchange in native American societies: local exchange and intertribal trade over long distances. Exchange within societies circulated food and other staples through a range of gifts, local redistributions, feasts, and reciprocal exchanges. Intertribal trade involved the movement of goods between different societies and ethnic groups. Intertribal exchanges were negotiated, competitive, and involved immediate reciprocal exchange of goods (Driver and Massey 1957:373–375; Wood 1980:98). Exchanges were initiated and transacted on an individual basis; men interacted with men, and women with women inside a structured environment. The goods exchanged in intertribal exchanges consisted of a wide range of subsistence goods. Before European contact, groups that produced horticultural products such as corn or beans would exchange them with foraging groups for items such as dried meat, buffalo robes, clothing, and other goods (Wood 1980:100). Foraging groups occupying different environmental zones exchanged goods such as fish for buffalo robes (Steward 1938). After contact, European trade goods were in high demand and French and American fur traders entered into these exchanges.[37]

The North American Calumet

The movement of resources over long distances and between groups was fraught with danger because it involved interactions between groups that, outside of specific trade interactions, often were enemies of one another. Intertribal trade in North America was carried out through the calumet ceremony both as interactions between individual groups and within the context of annual trade meetings or rendezvous known from the western fur trade (Blakeslee 1975, 1977). In both cases trade was embedded within the broader social and ritual dimensions of the calumet ceremony. Much of the information on the calumet ceremony and rendezvous trade meetings (see Chapter 9) is based on European eyewitness accounts. While Turnbaugh (1979) argues that rendezvous trade fairs (Chapter 9) were the result of European contact, archaeological evidence suggests that both calumet trade and larger rendezvous events had their own trajectory of development within North American prehistory (Brown 1989; Meyer and Thistle 1995; Rodning 2014). Blakeslee proposes that the calumet trade system was a response to drier

3.1 George Caitlin portrait of Eh-toh'k-pah-she-pee-shah, Black Moccasin, aged chief holding his calumet. (Reprinted with permission from Smithsonian American Art Museum, Gift of Mrs. Joseph Harrison, Jr.)

climatic conditions that started around AD 1200 that produced fluctuating resource levels and a greater need for trade across western North America.

The calumet ceremony was an informal institution that established a temporary peaceful relationship between two potentially hostile groups. The term "calumet" comes from the medieval French word *chalemel* (and later *chalumeau*) that means reed, cane, stem, tube, or pipe (Brown 1989:312). The modern American term associated with the calumet ceremony is the peace pipe[38] (Figure 3.1). The pipe was the symbol of the ceremony, and trade was essentially carried on "under the pipe" (Fletcher and Murie 1904; Jablow 1950:47). Tobacco was an important element in the symbolic minds of North American groups that touched many dimensions of religious life (e.g., Paper 1988; von Gernet 1995). The bowl of the pipe was carved from red pipestone, normally catlinite or argillite, a densely grained but soft metamorphic stone (Fishel et al. 2014; Gundersen 1993). The pipestone used to manufacture calumets was highly prized and the raw material to make them was traded over long distances.[39]

While the calumet ceremony was especially prominent among Plains groups of western North America, it extended east into the Mississippi Valley and across the American Southeast. The importance of the ceremony was immediately evident to Jacques Marquette, the first Frenchman to encounter it. He described its importance in AD 1673 in the following way:

> There remains no more, except to speak of the Calumet. There is nothing more mysterious or more respected among them. Less honor is paid to the Crowns and scepters of Kings than the Savages bestow upon this. It seems to be the God of peace and of war, the Arbiter of life and of death. It has but to be carried upon one's person, and displayed, to enable one to walk safely through the midst of Enemies – who, in the hottest of the Fight, lay down Their arms when it is shown. For that reason, the Illinois gave me one, to serve as a safeguard among all the Nations through whom I had to pass during my voyage.
>
> (from Jacques Marquette's journal, in Thwaites 1896–1901:59:129, 131)

The calumet ritual established a temporary truce and relationship between otherwise hostile enemies that enabled groups to engage in the intertribal exchange of goods. The calumet ceremony established a fictive kinship relationship between two male individuals who could serve as representatives of different clans, bands, or ethnic groups (Blakeslee 1981:759). This was expressed as a ritualistic father–son adoption that enabled members of warring groups to trade with one another through their fictive kinsmen. This relationship provided a bridge for conducting important intertribal trade in a climate of intertribal conflict. According to Bruner (1961:201), groups along the middle Missouri including the Mandan, the Hidatsa, and the Arikara "were adopted by fictitious fathers, and in turn had adopted sons in tribes with whom they dealt." Intertribal trade, therefore, was conducted not between enemies but between fictitious relatives or family members of fictitious relatives (Blakeslee 1975:145–150).

3.2 Ceremonial presentation of a calumet to initiate interaction between Chitimacha Indians and Europeans in Louisiana (AD 1758). (Redrawn from Brown 1989: Figure 4 and Le Page du Pratz 1758:1:facing 105 by Shae Rider and author.)

Figure 3.2 illustrates a presentation of a calumet from a group of Chitimacha natives in Louisiana to a group of Europeans in AD 1758. The leader of the procession is the presumptive leader of the Chitimacha group who initiated the contact after which extended social and ritual interaction took place. Some of the more common events of the calumet ceremony are summarized in Table 3.1. Central to establishing the linkage between groups was the ceremonial adoption of one member of the group by the other. These were recognized and enduring relationships that were reactivated in future exchanges.

The calumet ritual, therefore, served as the umbrella under which groups with different foraging, hunting, and horticultural practices could engage in the exchange of foodstuffs, skins, and craft goods. According to Blakeslee (1975:180), the movement of subsistence goods through this trade was enormous; sometimes the returns from an entire buffalo hunt would change hands during a calumet ceremony. Of course, participation in exchange was wholly

TABLE 3.1 *Most common events associated with the calumet ceremony*

Order of appearance	Activities
1	Sending a messenger by the visiting group to announce their arrival and initiate contact by presenting the calumet
2	A mock attack by the visitors reciprocated by the hosts
3	Agreed-on pricing and equivalences of items to be exchanged by leaders of both groups in an established relationship
4	For establishing a new trade partner relationship, carrying the son to be adopted or father doing the adopting into the village and the ceremonial lodge, depending on who is visiting
5	Initiation of the formal calumet ceremony: the adopted son is presented with a new set of clothes by the adopting father, the calumet is danced, and gifts are exchanged
6	Feasting between the two groups during the calumet ceremony and sometimes before
7	Informal trade and exchange between the members of the two groups. These exchanges occur during dances or through gambling, and involved immediate reciprocal exchange of goods
8	Presentation of gifts at the departure of the visiting group

Source: Information is from Blakeslee (1975:176–177; 1977:82).

voluntary once the linkage between groups was made, although few households passed up the opportunity to exchange the goods they that had for those that they needed (O'Shea 1989:62).

Establishing value and trade equivalents was especially important. Because participating groups were always potential enemies, the establishment of fixed equivalencies helped to avoid disputes that could occur as a result of hard bargaining. To offset these difficulties, some trade was conducted under the guise of reciprocal gift giving via the leaders of the groups linked by the calumet ceremony. Charles McKenzie, an early fur trader, describes how trade with the Crow occurred in a Hidatsa village in AD 1805. The Hidatsa

> made the [Crow] . . . smoke the pipe of friendship, and, at the same time, laid before them a present consisting of two hundred guns, with one hundred rounds of ammunition for each, a hundred bushels of Indian corn, a certain quantity of mercantile articles, such as kettles, axes, clothes, etc. The [Crow] in return brought two hundred and fifty horses, large parcels of [buffalo] robes, leather leggins, shirts, etc., etc. This exchange of trading civilities took place dancing; when the dancing was over, the presents were distributed among the individuals in proportion to the value of the articles respectively furnished.
>
> (Jablow 1950:46–47)

This negotiation represents an early form of collective bargaining with each household contributing horses, robes, guns, or other items to be exchanged as a group and then taking away the items obtained in the exchange in proportion to what individuals contributed. While this formal group exchange was going on, women from each group bartered individually with one another for corn, dried meat, buffalo robes, and provisions (Jablow 1950:48).

The calumet ceremony provided the ritual framework through which group and individual trade took place between members of different ethnic groups. In many other societies around the world a good deal of exchange occurred through established trade partners (Heider 1969). The calumet ceremony and the situational alliances that it created was the framework through which individually motivated exchange could take place. In this regard the calumet ritual served the same function as Kula ring gift exchange did in the Trobriand Islands. Kula gifting provided the incentive and the conditions for groups from different islands to peacefully engage in the individual barter of basic resources referred to as *gimwali* (Malinowski 1922). Trade was important for household provisioning in prehistoric North American (O'Shea 1989), and it was embedded in the calumet ceremony to ensure that household-to-household exchange could be conducted if individuals chose to do so.

HOUSEHOLDS AND NETWORKS OF EMERGENCY SUPPORT

Mahatma Gandhi once said, "There are people in the world so hungry, that God cannot appear to them except in the form of bread." His point was a simple one: famine and food shortage are the greatest threats to household survival. As discussed in the previous chapter, all societies recognize this problem and devise means to safeguard against predictable resource shortfalls (Halstead and O'Shea 1989; O'Shea 1989; Sen 1981). Nevertheless, resource shortfalls occur that place households in peril. When this occurred, households had to rely on their informal interhousehold support networks to provide resources for them to survive. Rare were the instances in antiquity where households could count on support from higher-order institutions for their survival.[40] For the most part they had to depend on their own ingenuity.

One important line of defense for agricultural households during famine was to revert to collecting wild plant resources, often called famine foods, which foraging groups would have exploited in the same region. Theft can be a problem during famine once stored food is depleted. Fields where a few crops could be grown can be stripped clean by starving individuals, further endangering the households to whom they belonged. The Aztec made allowances for desperate households. While theft was punishable by death, they allowed hungry individuals to take up to twenty ears of corn from the first row of a maize field along a public road (Alba 1949:22). The idea was to help the individual without stripping the field of the family who owned it. Likewise, gleaning a field after it was harvested was allowed and not considered theft.

The two primary networks for household assistance were its consanguineal and affinal kinsmen and the informal, mutual assistance networks built up over time by gift giving, labor exchanges, and feasting. Besides supplying access to food, these networks provided opportunities for individuals to move to households that were in better economic shape. Of course, these two networks were not mutually exclusive and overlapped to the extent that they could provide emergency support. While the *hxaro* networks discussed above extended over several hundred kilometers, most agricultural household networks were more limited in their spatial extent. This was a problem because resource shortfalls created by climatic conditions were usually regional in nature and affected many households in the same way. Nevertheless, these networks were the first line of assistance for households facing desperate situations.

When all else failed, people could resort to begging. The widespread acceptance of begging as a means to support oneself led to the emergence of a whole collection of wandering monks across Europe during the 4th and 5th centuries AD who begged for their subsistence as a dimension of their ascetic, religious lifestyle (Caner 2002). In the most desperate situations families might resort to selling their children into slavery to save them from starvation. This is what happened among the Aztecs during the great famine of AD 1452–1455 in the Valley of Mexico when parents sold children to merchants for as little as a basket of maize (Durán 1994:240). Some societies had more elaborate means than others for supporting households in times of stress. The section that follows explores the informal institutions that operated in traditional Jewish society to provide a safety net for failing households.

Desperate Housewives: Jewish Widows in Ancient Israel

As a rule, early state societies in the Near East made few social provisions to help poor and destitute families in times of need. This was left to the customs, informal institutions, and mutual assistance networks operating at the household and community level. One instance where the cultural guidelines for interhousehold assistance were well developed was in Old Testament Hebrew society. Jewish theology emphasized the need for faithful Jews to show concern for the sick and destitute. There are many exhortations to help the poor and to provide them with loans throughout both the Old and New Testament scriptures.[41] The following quote from the book of Isaiah illustrates the general expectations for how individuals should help the poor: "Is it not to share your bread with the hungry, and bring the homeless poor into your house; when you see the naked, to cover him, and not to hide yourself from your own flesh? Then shall your light break forth like the dawn, and . . . your righteousness shall go before you" (Isaiah 58:7–8).

Other expectations included giving gifts to the poor on holidays, allowing them to eat the sacrifices offered in the pilgrimage feasts, and to have access to the 10% tithe brought into the town every 3 years (Deuteronomy 16:11, 14; Haran 2007). Jewish tradition had the Sabbatical and Jubilee years, designed to help families in economic difficulty recover and climb out of debt every seventh year.[42] These were the years of release (Deuteronomy 15:1–11) when debts were canceled, vineyards and olive orchards were left unpicked so they could be harvested by the poor, and bondsmen tied to wealthy households had the option to be released with a financial stipend for their years of service (Deuteronomy 15:12–14; Lieber et al. 2007).

As helpful as these practices were, Jewish customs went further and provided multiple options for households that had fallen on hard times to reestablish themselves and their families. The Old Testament book of Ruth, written between the 5th and 3rd centuries BC (Schipper 2016:22; Weinfeld et al. 2007), provides a glimpse of how a widow could deal with hard times. The account describes how informal mechanisms were intended to support destitute individuals in Jewish society (Schipper 2016:38–51).

The story begins with a famine in Judah where Elimelech and his wife Naomi lived. Their response to the famine was to take their two sons, Mahlon and Chilion, and move to the land of Moab on the eastern side of the Dead Sea where they took up residence. They resided there for 10 years during which time Elimelech died and their two sons married local Moabite women named Orpah and Ruth. Eventually, both sons also died, leaving a household of three childless widows. Naomi decides to return to her hometown in Judah because the famine was over. As she sets out on her journey, she bids farewell to her two daughters-in-law with the following instructions:

> "Go, return each of you to her mother's house. The Lord grant that you may find a home, each of you in the house of her husband!" And they said to her, "No, we will return with you to your people." But Naomi said, "Turn back, my daughters, why will you go with me? Have I yet sons in my womb that they may become your husbands?. . . even if I should have a husband this night and should bear sons, would you therefore wait till they were grown?"
>
> (Ruth 1:8–13)

Naomi tells her daughters-in-law to go home because she was not in a position to provide them with husbands through the custom of the *levirate*. The levirate was the practice where the brother of the deceased man was obligated to marry his brother's widow. The purpose of the levirate was twofold. First, it reincorporated the widow into her husband's family and provided her with support instead of leaving her destitute. Second, the first son born was considered to be the son of her first husband, which continued his paternal line with an heir to his estate (Davies 1981; Leggett 1974). Jewish widows could find themselves in difficult straits because inheritance was patrilineal, and wives were not recognized as their husband's heirs; therefore, wives could not continue to cultivate their husbands' patrilineal land (Weisberg 2009:5, 8).

Naomi and her daughters-in-law were in a bind. There was no one to marry Naomi or her daughters-in-law. Their best option was to return to their own patrilineal households where they might remarry. Orpah takes that option, while Ruth decides stay with her mother-in-law. They set off together for Judah and return to Naomi's home town of Bethlehem at the beginning of the barley harvest. Facing the problem of obtaining food, Ruth has a suggestion:

> Now Naomi had a kinsman of her husband's, a man of wealth . . . whose name was Boaz. And Ruth the Moabitess said to Naomi, "Let me go to the field and glean among the ears of grain after him in whose sight I shall find favor.". . . So she set forth and went and gleaned in the field after the reapers . . . to the part of the field belonging to Boaz.
>
> (Ruth 2:1–3)

Ruth understood two things about Jewish culture. First, Ruth is going to search out the *pe'ah* to glean, and second, she is going to put herself in position for an alternative form of levirate marriage with Boaz, Naomi's kinsman. One of the interesting stipulations of Jewish law was that the corners of things, or the *pe'ah*, should be left uncut.[43] This command applied equally to agricultural fields, orchards, and vineyards. The *pe'ah* were left unharvested so that the poor would have resources to glean and support themselves. Jewish law is clear on this where it says:

> When you reap the harvest of your land, you shall not reap your field to its very border, neither shall you gather the gleanings after your harvest. And you shall not strip your vineyard bare, neither shall you gather the fallen grapes of your vineyard; you shall leave them for the poor.
>
> (Leviticus 19:9–10)

All the poor of a Jewish community would have waited eagerly for the harvest to begin because they would be allowed in the fields to glean their corners and borders. How much grain was left uncut in fields was up to each land owner so that if even one stalk of wheat or barley was left, the law was fulfilled. Jewish rabbis recommended that one-sixtieth of the harvest (1.67%) should be left in the field, but the actual amount left was for the owner to decide. The poor could glean the *pe'ah* three times during the day: in the morning, at midday, and in the afternoon.[44] Gleaning had to be done by hand rather than with a spade or a sickle so that the poor would not assault one another in their haste to collect food (Berenbaum and Skolnik 2007:632).

It was also a time that could be dangerous for young women, and for this reason Boaz tells Ruth, "Listen my daughter, do not go to glean in another field or leave this one, but keep close to my maidens.... Have I not charged the young men not to molest you?" (Ruth 2:8–9). Apparently, young women gleaners were subject to derision and worse.

Boaz took a fancy to Ruth because of her dedication to Naomi (Ruth 2:10–11) and because she was a hard worker (Ruth 2:7). After instructing her to eat with his harvesting crew, he tells his workers, "Let her glean even among the sheaves, and do not reproach her. And also pull out some of the bundles for her, and leave it for her to glean, and do not rebuke her" (Ruth 2:15–16).

These commands reflect another set of informal gleaning customs called *leket* and *shikh ah* afforded the poor by Jewish law. *Leket* in a barley or wheat field refers to the stalks of grain that fall to the ground in the process of bundling the stalks into sheaves. The idea here was that if a stalk or two fell to the ground during the bundling, then God must have intended them to be left for the poor and they were not retrieved. The same concept applied to harvesting in a vineyard. Here the grapes that fell to the ground were known as *peret*. Likewise, small clusters of only a few grapes, *olelot*, were also believed to be intended for the poor.

The term *shikh ah* is *leket* at a slightly higher level of magnitude. Rather than a single stalk of grain, a bundled sheave of grain could be forgotten or broken in the field as it was taken to the threshing floor. These sheaves were not to be collected but were to be left for the poor. The same concept applied to trees in an orchard as well as the vineyard. Late-ripening olives might not fall from the tree when the boughs were beaten and were supposed to be left for the gleaners to collect. These practices are clear in the biblical instructions laid out in Deuteronomy:

> When you reap your harvest in your field, and have forgotten a sheaf in the field, you shall not go back to get it; it shall be for the sojourner, the fatherless, and the widow; that the Lord your God may bless you in all the work of your hands. When you beat your olive trees, you shall not go over the boughs again; it shall be for the sojourner, the fatherless, and the widow. When you gather the grapes of your vineyard you shall not glean it afterward; it shall be for the sojourners, the fatherless, and the widow.
>
> (Deuteronomy 24:19–21)

It appears that Boaz was thinking about these two practices when he tells his workers to allow Ruth to find stray stalks (*leket*) and to pull out some bundles (sheaves) and leave them for her (*shikh ah*) (Berenbaum and Skolnik 2007:632). Gleaning was hard work and even at the end of the day Ruth had been able to collect only about an *ephah* of barley, which was enough for 5 days of bread.[45]

Gleaning helped the poor, but it was only a partial contribution to household survival. Ruth gleaned through both the barley and wheat harvests, roughly from the spring equinox to late May. By the end of the wheat harvest access to food through gleaning had ended, and except for begging there were no further prospects on the horizon (Eskenazi and Frymer-Kensky 2011:47). The only real hope for Ruth and Naomi was for Ruth to remarry and bring Naomi into her new household with her. This was a challenge because Ruth was recognized as a Moabite the moment she entered Bethlehem (Ruth 2:6). Recognition as a foreigner was as much a statement about not owning local land as it was about growing up in a different place. Naomi understood this, but with honorable intentions and in hope of arranging a marriage with Boaz, she tells Ruth to bathe, anoint herself with perfume, and declare herself available for Boaz after the grain was threshed. Boaz eats, drinks a little wine, and, feeling happy with the harvest, goes to sleep next to the pile of threshed grain. Ruth arrives, uncovers his feet, and lies down at them. At midnight he awakes, startled to find a woman at his feet:

> "Who are you?" And she answered, "I am Ruth, your maidservant; spread your skirt over your maidservant, for you are next of kin." And he said, "May you be blessed by the Lord, my daughter, you have made this last kindness greater than the first, in that you have not gone after young men, whether poor or rich. And now, my daughter, do not fear, I will do for you all that you ask, for my fellow townsmen know that you are a woman of worth. And now it is true that I am a near kinsman, yet there is a kinsman nearer than I. Remain this night, and in the morning, if he will do the part of the next of kin for you, well; let him do it; but if he is not willing . . . then, as the Lord lives, I will do the part of the next of kin for you."
>
> (Ruth 3:9–13)

This was not a case of Ruth sleeping her way into a marriage. Naomi and Ruth were using the avenues available to them to establish a marriage through the practice of *go'el* (Eskenazi and Frymer-Kensky 2011:44, 59–60). Ruth asks Boaz to spread his skirt over her. The custom of placing a corner of his garment over a maiden was a way of asking for a marriage (Pfeiffer and Harrison 1990:271). Ruth in effect is asking Boaz to be her *go'el*, and he was flattered and delighted. It is possible that he may already have been thinking about it. In any case, he tells her to stay on the threshing floor, probably to avoid the danger of a late-night return home (Leggett 1974:202). The next morning, so that it won't look like she had spent the night with him, he sends her away with six measures of barley (Ruth 3:15). It is possible that food was bought or could be gifted at the threshing floor as another opportunity for an individual to express *hesed* and kindness to the poor.[46]

Go'el refers to the practice of blood and property redemption. The *go'el* is a "redeeming kinsman" who helps a near or distant kinsmen in time of need (Eskenazi and Frymer-Kensky 2011:lv). If, for example, a poor family was forced to sell their property, another kinsman (the *go'el*) could redeem it and buy it back for them[47] (Leggett 1974:83–84). The practice also extended to redeeming a person from slavery or debt (Leggett 1974:98–106). Here Ruth is proposing that Boaz function in that capacity for her, for Naomi, and to perpetuate the name of her husband Mahlon as practiced in the levirate. Boaz knew he was not her closest kinsman and could not be her *go'el* unless the other kinsman refused.[48] Boaz pursued the issue and approaches the other claimant stating that Naomi is selling Elimelech's land and he could buy it; if he did, he also had the obligation to take Ruth as his wife to perpetuate Mahlon's name. The nearest kinsman could not do so because of financial difficulties, and Boaz, as next in line as *go'el*, makes the claim. They marry and produce a son.

The story of Ruth and Naomi is one of tragedy, difficult times, and redemption. It illustrates the rich array of customs and informal institutions that households in Jewish society had available to them to mediate household failure. Was this typical of other ancient societies? It is hard to say, but it is easy to imagine that not all similar stories had a happy ending. There is not a lot of literature from ancient societies that describes informal institutions intended to help the poor and destitute. It is likely, however, that as societies moved away from kinship-based forms of organization, the number of these mutual support networks may have been reduced to those that could be built and maintained by the initiative of individual households.

SUMMARY

This discussion has examined some of the informal institutions that households used to support themselves. A variety of examples was presented to illustrate how households coped with the problems of reproducing themselves both biologically and socially. The onus of survival resided with household members, so they creatively networked with one another for this end. How this interaction was structured varied from society to society. But these forms of interaction were *informal* institutions because how they operated and who was involved was a voluntary prerogative of each household.

Households needed food, safety, spouses, and children to reproduce both biologically and socially. Only fundamental economic needs have been considered here to illustrate how households created the conditions for their success. Adding a sexually receptive mate to an economically stable household was the first step in producing children. Since young adults represent productive labor, marriage usually entailed at least one household losing a worker.

Several ways this loss was mediated was through bridewealth and bride service (Dalton 1966). Whether children could be produced and successfully survive to adulthood was another matter, and forms of adoption and fosterage were identified that were used to even out the demographic irregularities of high infant mortality throughout antiquity.

Resources, eligible mates, labor support, and emergency assistance were all accessible through networks of interhousehold support. Labor was always in short supply in agricultural households during key planting and harvesting seasons. Households solved this bottleneck and increased their subsistence productivity through voluntary, reciprocal labor exchanges; the construction of the wall of Jerusalem provided an example of how cooperative labor was carried out in antiquity for a nonagricultural pursuit.

Building interhousehold support networks was key for mobilizing material resources, and two examples were provided for how households in different times and places did this. *Hxaro* gift exchange was used as an example of how foraging groups could build a social network that allowed families to offset resource shortfalls by relocating to areas where food was available. Environmental diversity creates differential distributions of natural resources that groups often could exploit only through exchange. The calumet ceremony provided an example of how that was accomplished even between declared enemies. While the example used was from the trans-egalitarian societies of native North America, it serves to illustrate how trade also served as a way to access resources in more complex chiefdoms and states.

Households could not survive without their social networks. These were the networks that provided access to both labor and spouses. Two examples of how households forged these networks were provided. Feasts were important for commemorating life-cycle events and establishing linkages between households. The example of feasting in native American Northwest Coast societies illustrates this point. Social networks also were used to build alliances for physical protection as well as economic support. The case of child fosterage in medieval Iceland is an example of this practice.

Even under the best of circumstances households failed due to illness or famine. In most ancient societies there were no social support networks available to households beyond those that they created or activated on their own. Our understanding of these forms of support is limited because, like most household behavior, they either escape detection in the archaeological record or went unnoticed in recorded history. The example from the book of Ruth illustrates the informal social mechanisms that were available to 5th- to 3rd-century BC Jewish households.

The informal institutions fostering interhousehold support were a staple of ancient and premodern societies. What is important to recognize is that they continued to operate in much the same way over thousands of years under conditions of significant sociocultural change. Informal forms of cooperative and voluntary labor certainly existed in early agricultural societies and they continue to operate every time there is a communal barn building for an Amish household. Their frequency and application could change, but households always recognized the importance of mutual support networks and sought to maintain them. Significant new forms of economic organization appeared in ancient societies to integrate households from different communities, regions, or ethnic groups into stable political entities. The nature of these developments is explored in the chapter that follows.

FOUR

FROM HOUSEHOLDS TO PALACES

Leaders, Chiefs, and Their Households

When the best leader's work is done the people say, "We did it ourselves."
(Lao Tzu)

Households were both the primary units of adaptation and a model for organizing some of the earliest formal institutions in ancient society. Whether in the form of the house of the gods, or the palace and residence of the ruler, households provided a template for expressing and organizing a range of social relationships between groups of unrelated people. The house was a useful model for early formal institutions because households are both inclusive and corporate. They are inclusive in the sense that both kinsmen and nonkinsmen can be members of the same household. They are corporate in the way that all members are part of a mutually supportive and internally integrated body. The house and household provided a model for collective and hereditary interaction that could also be used to organize groups in nondomestic settings. Within this context, the house society model is useful for examining the structure of early formal institutions.

This chapter explores some of the factors that played a role in the development of formal institutions within early complex societies. Two fundamental assumptions guide this discussion. The first is that large, internally heterogenous social groups occur as a result of the benefits they afford their members. If they didn't afford benefits, groups would fission instead of remaining integrated as they grew in size. From an evolutionary perspective many early complex societies represent collective action groups (Blanton and Fargher 2008; Blanton et al. 1996; Carballo 2013a; Olson 1965), where pro-social behavior affords greater chances of success within a competitive environment (Boyd and Richerson 2009; Boyd et al. 2003; Henrich 2004). The second assumption is that the growth of large social groups is not automatic. Face-to-face interactions within and between households lead to disputes that can result in fission and out-migration (Feinman 2013b:38; Kopytoff 1987). Forms of social control, ways to mediate disputes, and incentives for integration also need to be developed or it is unlikely that large social groups could ever have developed (Service 1978).

The discussion begins by identifying what formal institutions are and how they relate to group size. This is followed by an examination of four forces of integration that helped shape cooperative action groups and the institutions that developed from them. The forces that fostered integration include the factors behind resource pooling, conflict and the need for mutual protection, intensification of resource production, and regulating interaction with neighboring groups. The question of leadership is also explored, because leaders represent the human capital involved in resolving problems in societies when they occur. Finally, the role of leaders and their households is considered in relation to the development of palaces. The two Bronze Age societies of Old Kingdom Egypt and Canaanite Ugarit are examined to evaluate whether they conform to the house society model of early institutional development.

FORMAL INSTITUTIONS AND GROUP SIZE

Just as informal institutions structure interaction between households, *formal institutions* create the social cohesion and organizational structures that integrate whole societies. Formal institutions are special arrangements, modes of operation, and organizational structures created by groups to accomplish specific ends (Acheson 1994). Institutions consist of both the rules of operation and forms of organization that bind individuals together to achieve social objectives.[1] In this sense institutions are task-oriented organizations. This view combines the behavior of individuals with the structural properties of the organizations in which they operate (Ostrom 1992:19–20, 2015). Not only does the structure of groups shape the behavior of their members, but it is the organization of institutions and their architectural manifestations that are most apparent in the archaeological and historic records. While it may be difficult to envision the rules and norms of institutional operation, it is possible to detect traces of feasting celebrations, ritual enactments, the monuments of rulers, and the architecture associated with lineage or clan buildings, ritual areas, and centers of political authority.

Descent groups were important organizational structures, and many institutions started out within lineages and clans. The men's huts and ritual buildings of early foraging and agricultural groups are a case in point (Flannery and Marcus 2012). Nevertheless, the task-focused orientation of institutions provided the framework for scales of interaction that cross-cut and transcended the boundaries between descent groups. For example, the practice of feasting *within* a descent group can develop into an institution for reciprocal interaction *between* groups as occurred with moka celebrations in New Guinea and the potlatch among native Americans (Drucker and Heizer 1967; Strathern 2007). Similarly, reciprocal gift giving between households can develop into broader networks of ritualized gift exchange such as that associated with the calumet ceremony and the Kula ring (Blakeslee 1981; Brown 1989; Malinowski 1922, 1967a). Institutions are designed to fulfill specific purposes or needs in society. These needs may be permanent and ongoing or periodic, spontaneous, and cyclical depending on the situation.

Formal institutions existed and operated at different scales throughout antiquity. Examples of organizations found at the smaller end of the spectrum include warrior fraternities, dance associations, healing societies, craft guilds, land holding associations, secret societies, and men's hut organizations. In state societies formal institutions are the "bricks and mortar" organizations that fulfill primary social, political, religious, educational, and economic roles. These institutions are represented in ancient states by an array of military organizations, temples and religious superstructures, oracles, palaces, theaters, sports arenas, marketplaces, judicial courts, and specific offices of political administration or economic regulation (Hirth 2016).

The scope of activities and the procedures employed by institutions are unique and particular to each society. Because they are designed to meet specific needs, formal institutions often require resources to fulfill their respective missions and to operate effectively. These resources may range from food and attached service personnel to large-scale cooperative labor needed to build facilities or activity spaces. How these resources were generated, whether through forms of production, exchange, or taxation, is the essence of what constitutes the political economy (Engels 1973; Godelier 1978c; Hirth 1996; Robotham 2012; Terray 1972). Rather than political economy, these forms of resource mobilization are best referred to as the institutional economy. The reason is that not all institutions are political, and labeling them as such downplays those that are primarily social or religious in nature, but still require resources to operate. How the institutional economy was organized and supplied with economic resources is discussed in Chapters 5 and 6.

Finally, formal institutions provide the integration and social solidarity that allows societies to grow in size, to diversity internally, and to increase in hierarchical complexity[2] (Feinman 2013b:table 2.1). Elinor Ostrom (1992) aptly points out that institutions are crafted entities. Both the rules of operation and their organizational infrastructures were shaped by their users to achieve specific objectives. This could involve the creation of new ideological principles as well as new ways of producing or mobilizing the resources necessary for institutional support.[3]

Aristotle was perhaps the first to allude to the role that institutions played in ordering interaction between individuals in the growth of society. For Aristotle, Greek society was embodied in the *polis*, which was composed of associations (*koinēnia*) instituted with the intent of attaining a common good (*agathón*).[4] In this sense Aristotle shares common ground with advocates of collective action theory (Blanton and Fargher 2008; Carballo 2013b; Ostrom 2007; Saitta 2007). Integrative theories of social change have advocated that formal institutions developed to counter the centrifugal forces of society that work against social integration (Cohen 1978:5; Dahrendorf 1959; Service 1978). Not only did they provide ways of bridging households and kin-related forms of organization, but they also helped to mediate and resolve intrasociety conflicts, allowing societies to grow and their participants to enjoy the benefits that larger size affords.[5]

Empirical research has shown that the size of society is directly proportional to the development of its integrative institutions. Individuals living within small societies or the same community can be organized through face-to-face interactions. Interpersonal relationships can fulfill some of these integrative functions at the regional level within small groups as discussed in Chapter 3 for the !Kung bushmen. But there is a ceiling at which this becomes ineffective. The larger a community or group grows, the greater the possibility of more disputes. The relationship between social complexity and group size is referred to as the *size–complexity rule*. Research has shown that group size is directly correlated at all levels of social complexity with the number and type of integrative institutions that a society contains (Carneiro 1967; Ember 1963; Feinman and Neitzel 1984; Johnson 1982; Kosse 1990; Lekson 1985). As Gary Feinman points out,

> both total population and maximal community size corresponds closely with organizational complexity (hierarchical organization) . . . groups over 400–500 generally have suprahousehold integrative institutions of some kind, while population numbering 2,000–3,000 are almost always organized hierarchically.
>
> (Feinman 2013b:39)

The size of a group's social network, whether in the thousands or hundreds of thousands, is closely related to the hierarchical complexity of its formal political and religious institutions (Feinman 1995, 1998). If group size is a benefit to survival, then institutions will be developed to hold societies together. If size confers a competitive advantage to groups with regard to either resource exploitation or competing with their neighbors, then they will likely expand at the expense of smaller groups (Boyd et al. 2003; Carneiro 1978; Sahlins 1961; Stanish 2013).

KINSHIP AND DESCENT GROUP ORGANIZATION

Systems of kinship reckoning are a universal feature of human societies. Virtually all of the 565 societies in Murdock's ethnographic atlas calculate kinship relatedness through some form of descent system.[6] Kinship relationships are the basis for defining descent groups and kindreds. A descent group according to Haviland (1990:269) is a "kinship group in which being a lineal descendant of a particular real or mythical ancestor is a criterion of membership." Descent groups assign individuals to kin groups with clear boundaries based on specific rules of relatedness (patrilineal, matrilineal, ambilineal, double descent). A kindred is a group of related kinsmen calculated from the perspective of one living individual through both parents (Haviland 1990:284). Both systems define kin groups with different degrees of inclusiveness. The principle of unilineal descent serves to define a lineage as a corporate descent group composed of consanguineal kin related by birth. As lineages grow in size, they have a tendency to split off from one another. This fission, together with the recognition of common ancestry between lineages, gives rise to the formation of clans. Clans are composed of multiple lineages and are large enough that direct kinship to all individuals cannot be traced and clan members assume descent from a common ancestor.

Kinship networks help to define groups and group boundaries. They have formal rules of membership, help to determine which individuals can marry, and provide a group structure through which households can claim resources and seek mutual support and protection from outsiders. Descent groups are reinforced by religious traditions and rituals. In addition to the assistance that they supply in meeting material needs, descent groups provide strong emic identities at both the group and individual level.[7] They define who people are and where they came from, both basic questions in the existential dilemma that all groups and individuals attempt to explain.

Kinship networks are the frameworks in which social interaction occurs and institutions develop. They define characteristic modes of expected behavior between related individuals. They provide settings in which leaders may emerge and institutions develop that promote group solidarity within descent groups and cooperation or competition between them. Descent groups may be largely egalitarian in structure or sharply ranked on the basis of ancestral myth and heredity. However they are composed, they provide a preexisting social landscape within which individuals operated and institutions were created and modified within the context of changing environmental and social conditions. The following discussion considers some of the forces that help to create and shape institutions within society designed to bridge individual descent groups.

FORCES OF INSTITUTIONAL DEVELOPMENT

Social integration carries with it costs of operation in terms of time, energy, and the resources necessary to maintain peaceful interaction. The fact that societies grew in size and complexity throughout the Holocene attests to the fact that the value of integration and cooperation overrode the associated costs. Experimental research in evolutionary game theory has shown that humans exhibit pro-social behavior and cooperate with one another when there are clear benefits to do so (Axelrod 2006; Henrich et al. 2001, 2010; Myerson 2013; Richerson et al. 2003). The conclusion from these studies is that humans are rational decision makers that can balance self-interest with more altruistic, group-oriented behavior if it produces benefits to participating households. In short, humans act as rational agents who are able to evaluate the benefits of cooperative action within institutional settings.[8]

Four stimuli for institutional integration are discussed below. They are by no means the only examples that could be chosen but they do supply a framework for understanding how formal institutions provided social cohesion within society. The benefits that emerging institutions could provide included establishing exclusionary claims to land and other resource pools, providing mutual protection, enhancing or enabling forms of production, and regularizing relationships with neighboring groups. These institutions developed first within kin groups and were modified into more inclusive non–kin-based organizations as societies grew in size and complexity.

RESOURCE-HOLDING ASSOCIATIONS

Resource access was critical for group survival. Where resources are abundant and usage demands are low, there is no risk to household survivability and open access may predominate. However, under conditions where competition for resources is strong, groups may attempt to control access through forms of territoriality or land tenure systems.[9] Dyson-Hudson and Smith (1978) have demonstrated that territoriality and willingness to defend a resource domain is a function of the abundance and predictability of resources. Where resources are unpredictable or widely scattered, there will be little incentive to develop resource-control mechanisms because of the high costs of monitoring and defending access to resources. However, where resources are densely concentrated, highly predictable systems of resource control may develop among foraging groups. Food production increased the predictability and concentration of resources, so it is little surprise that resource-holding associations were ubiquitous among agricultural groups around the world (Herskovits 1965:355).

The initial push for increased social solidarity usually occurred within the context of local groups. Increased sedentism associated with the exploitation of high-density and predictable resources brought households in more continuous interaction than was found in the periodic aggregations of mobile foraging groups. The pull of these resources, the desire for positive social interaction, and the threat of competition with other groups could serve to minimize group fissioning and reduce households moving away from established inter-household support networks (Johnson and Earle 1987:316). Kin groups provided a framework for mutual assistance groups. The solidarity within and between kin groups at the local level was enhanced by ceremonial and ritual activities (see below) that broadened and created collective household interaction.

One incentive behind the development of formal institutions was the need to establish proprietary claim to necessary resources. Timothy Earle (2000:40–41) has argued that the "emergence of social groups can in part be explained by a need to defend and allocate land." He sees the emergence of corporate groups (i.e., lineages, clans) as closely linked to systems of land and resource control (Earle 1991; Johnson and Earle 1987). The rationale for household resource ownership, discussed in Chapter 2, is expressed as a function of the labor and energy invested in production. This same rationale is used at the group level to validate corporate land-holding claims.

Corporate land-holding claims were established in one of four ways: by demonstrating original possession, by establishing ancestral inheritance, by modifying the landscape, and by conquest (Earle 2000:41). All four of approaches changed the landscape in some way. Groups often based land claims on original possession that they validated by constructing burial mounds, boundary markers, or other features that established deep time associations with the land (Dillehay 1990). The construction of burial mounds was often contextualized within a rich mythology that linked ancestors to the landscape using both household and group rituals (McAnany 2014). In the Bronze Age, chiefdoms of southern England (2500–800 BC) constructed long earthen barrows (burial mounds), causeway camps, rectangular enclosures referred to as cursus monuments, and special ritual sites with calendric and/or astronomical importance such as Stonehenge (Bradley 1984, 1991; Earle 1991:80–95; Renfrew 1973).

Landscape improvements involved with the intensification of production such as terracing or irrigation provided another claim to landscapes. The forceful seizure of territory was another. Claims made through warfare could be solidified in chiefdom and state-level societies by establishing new territorial boundaries and erecting public monuments commemorating conquest and territorial expansion. Examples of this type of land acquisition can even be found among tribal societies. Among Tsembaga and other warring tribes in north central New Guinea, planting a rumbin tree by a successful tribe in an abandoned area after a cessation of hostilities is a regional declaration of territorial expropriation and the establishment of new group boundaries (Rappaport 1967).

Differential access to resources and control of property has been argued to be a major factor in the development of regional chiefdom societies (Earle 1991, 1997; Fried 1967; Johnson and Earle 1987). Ownership of land in these societies normally was vested in large corporate kin groups such as clans with the allocation of land in the hands of chiefs and clan leaders. It is through the management and access to land that chiefs could gain power over the production, accumulation, and distribution of food important to systems of staple finance (D'Altroy and Earle 1985; Earle 1994). This general relationship is summed up in the Asante proverb, "The farm [meaning the farm produce] is mine, the soil is the chief's" (Herskovitz 1965:367). It was the acquisition of land for individual use along with rights to use communal labor that was the foundation for the development of inequality in many agricultural societies.

Polynesia provides good examples of how land and resource rights were held and allocated among chiefdom societies. The structure of Hawaiian chiefdoms in the late 18th and 19th centuries AD is well understood and illustrates how resources were allocated within a system of hierarchically ranked ruling lineages (Earle 1977, 1978, 1980, 1991, 2002b; Johnson and Earle 1987:229–245; Kirch 1989,1997; Kirch and Sahlins 1994). Each community had its territorial land (*ahupua'a*) to which community members had hereditary access,[10] which permitted generalized self-sufficiency. Land was allocated to households by the chief of each *ahupua'a* who, at the time of European contact, was appointed as manager (*konohiki*) of the community by the paramount chief. In earlier times land assignments may have been made by ranked kinsmen of the community as occurred in other Polynesian chiefdoms, but this was not the case at the time of European contact. Instead, the *konohiki* was an appointed high-ranking member of the royal lineage. The paramount chief claimed control over all of the land and the polity was held together by a constant state of conflict between chiefs.

Corporate land-holding associations continued to operate in state-level societies at the village and community levels long after corporate kinship groups had weakened or largely disappeared. Among the Aztecs the corporate land-holding unit was the *calpulli*, organized around the principle of hereditary co-residence rather than kinship. The *calpulli* was an internally stratified corporate group that served as the basic unit of organization in both rural and urban settings. Each *calpulli* had its own temple and was the organizational framework for both corvée labor assignments and military service. Individuals were born into a *calpulli* and their birthright gave them usufruct rights to land held in common for its members. The *calpulli* leader, known as the *calpullec*, kept a book of land assignments that were made when a new household was established. It served as a collective action group for its members whether they were actual kinsmen or not (Berdan 1982, 2014; Carrasco 1971; Dycherhoff and Prem 1976; Hirth 2016; Rojas Rabiela 1979; M. Smith 2012).

INSTITUTIONS FOR MUTUAL PROTECTION

Another important stimulus for integration was the need for protection and defense. Here size matters because there is more protection in a large group than when households stand alone. Conflict theorists feel that external pressures are essential motivators for cultural development. Intergroup conflict is argued to be a human universal and an important factor in cultural evolution (Carneiro 1970, 1978; Gat 2006; Keeley 1997; Webster 1975). Early evidence for human violence can be traced to the site of Jebel Sahaba in the Nile Valley where the excavation of a 15,000-year-old cemetery revealed evidence of fighting and hostility between groups (Wendorf 1968). Paul Roscoe (2013:59) feels that "polities as political communities are and were almost everywhere defensive organizations, aimed at securing the collective benefits of mutual protection against enemy attack." In short, people recognize the danger of hostile attack to their families. The need for defense both serves as an incentive for mutual cooperation and provides an opportunity for emerging leaders to create durable and centralized structures of internal control.

When considering the effect of warfare on human groups, it is important to recognize that it has both defensive and offensive incentives for group cooperation. Defensive action motivated by the threat of attack is a powerful unifying force. It can galvanize lineages and whole communities to integrate for the common good. The need for defense can stimulate the construction of defensive features around towns or defendable nonresidential locales in both small- (Milner 1999; Parkinson and Duffy 2007; Spence 1993) and large-scale societies (Jones 2010; Kern 1999). Offensive warfare in small-scale societies is often situational and motivated to revenge a homicide or theft and/or to enrich the participants (Roscoe 2013). While members of a community will cooperate for purposes of joint defense, they may not be interested in participating in an attack emanating from family or kinship disputes.

The importance of protection as an integrating stimulus was directly proportional to the size and duration of the threat that groups and individuals faced. If the threat was strong and ongoing, the response by groups would be stronger and more significant in shaping an organized response than if the threat was weak and intermittent. Three responses that groups commonly made were the construction of defenses, the emergence war leaders, and the appearance of warrior sodalities. The construction of defensive works around a community differed with the nature of the threat. The threat of ongoing attacks would lead to the construction of more permanent defenses or individuals stationed as lookouts for raiders than when attacks were situational or seasonal.[11] While archaeologists utilize defenses as an indicator of regional hostility, not all societies constructed them even in hostile environments. Sparta, the most militaristic city-state in ancient Greece, did not have fortifications. Plutarch says that when a stranger visited Sparta he asked King Agesilaus why the city had no walls, at which point the king pointed to his men and said, "These are the walls of Sparta."[12]

Warfare appears to have played a role in the origin of early leadership in ancient Mesopotamia. What the exact form of leadership and protection was during the Ubaid period and earlier time periods is far from clear, but it appears to have resided in the collective consensus of kin-based assemblies. Jacobsen (1943, 2008) originally speculated that the authority structure of early Mesopotamian communities resided in the assembly of elders, probably representing the collective male lineage heads.[13] He felt that this assembly was responsible for selecting the leader based on a reading of a tablet from Akkad that states, "in the common of Enlil, a field belonging to Esabad, the temple of Gula, Kish assembled and Iphurkish, a man of Kish . . . they raised to kingship" (Jacobsen 1943:165). Likewise, he feels this form of rule is implied in the Epic of Gilgamesh when Gilgamesh, lord of Uruk, approached the elders of Uruk to entreat them to not submit to Kish but to fight them. In the epic dating to the late third millennium BC, Gilgamesh addresses two assemblies, an assembly of elders (*abba uru*) and the assembly of townsmen (*guruš*), before resistance can proceed (Jacobsen 1943:165, fn 44). Whether formal assemblies operated in this manner is highly questionable. Daniel Fleming (2004:190, 232–234), drawing on cuneiform texts from the city of Mari, suggests that Jacobsen's references to assemblies probably refer to broad groups of individuals and the collective decision making in towns and tribal groups instead of formally constituted administrative groups.

Nevertheless, group protection was an excellent arena for individuals to exert their leadership abilities and to solidify a position of leadership in society. The ethnographic and ethnohistoric record documents that war leaders were common in tribal and chiefdom societies as a special-purpose and temporary position of influence (Flannery and Marcus 2012; Godelier 1986; Hoebel 1960). Wright et al. (1974:125) have suggested that the role of warfare was important in the emergence of leadership in early Mesopotamia. In an increasingly bellicose environment, the need for defense possibly led to the war leader becoming a permanent office within early Mesopotamia. Petr Charvát (1982:51) speculates that it was the accumulation of wealth through raids and warfare that allowed war chiefs to develop a specific clientage of followers and to purchase private lands that served as estates to increase their wealth and influence. Defense and protection appear to have been important in the emergence of leadership in ancient Mesopotamia as well as in Egypt where pre-dynastic nomarch rulers are shown in their guise of military leader (Trigger 2003:84, 245).

A third way that protection can be organized through cooperative group action was by the formation of defense-oriented action groups. This solution transferred the primary responsibility of defense and internal protection to a specific subgroup within society. Anthropologists refer to special-purpose groups as associations. They arise out of common interest or community need and occur in a wide range of societies from tribal bands to large states. Associations are especially important in small-scale societies because they provide action groups that cross-cut groups organized by kinship.[14] They can span a whole array of different activities, but those concerning defense are the ones of interest here. Understanding how defense associations were organized in traditional societies is often difficult because of the pacification that occurred under colonial rule. The example of Cheyenne warrior associations discussed below illustrates how authority and institutional responsibilities could be divided in society where the task of group protection was relegated to a special-purpose group.

Cheyenne Warrior Associations

The Cheyenne were one of the bison-hunting tribal groups that occupied the Great Plains of the western United States. At contact in the 19th century AD the Cheyenne numbered approximately 3,500 people organized into ten major bands (Moore et al. 2001:879). The Cheyenne lived in an environment of continual raids between neighboring groups intended to steal women, children, horses, and to obtain status by killing or counting coup against enemies.[15] There were six warrior associations or clubs among the Cheyenne that cross-cut the ten main bands.[16] Each warrior association had their individual ritual insignia, songs, dances, and initiations. Dorsey (1904) estimates that two of the largest of these associations (Fox, Elk) each had about 150 members. Each warrior club had four officers or leaders who served as the main war chiefs within the tribe. Warrior associations were a defense mechanism, not an offensive weapon. Any Cheyenne warrior could lead a raid as long as he could engage the support of a few followers[17] (Hoebel 1960:34–35).

The warrior associations did more than just protect Cheyenne from their neighbors. They also were responsible for maintaining order and protecting bands while they were on the move. They played an important supervisory role when bands came together for large communal buffalo hunts. Warrior associations were responsible for maintaining the peace and stopping disputes that arose between individuals of different bands who did not know each other well or that resulted from trading, gambling, theft, or illicit sexual relations. As a body they served as a court of appeal with the ability to summon individuals accused of wrongdoing and to resolve disputes that emerged from it.[18] They operated as a general-purpose law-and-order group.

The warrior associations and their leaders were not the sole authority in Cheyenne society. Each band also had four peace chiefs who were independent of the warrior associations. These leaders were the primary voices of collective representation within the band, and the warrior associations were under their authority. Peace chiefs were selected by consensus from the elders of their bands and formed the Council of Forty-four, which was the sacred body that presided over all ten bands. They were "protectors of the people" and were addressed as "father" out of respect for the secular and religious duties that they performed (Grinnell 1972; Hoebel 1960:38). Whereas the warrior associations served as a combination defense and police force, the peace chefs acted as conciliatory mediators to unify the bands and to rehabilitate individuals with consistent bad behavior.[19]

The Cheyenne did not have single leader or a unified form of governance. Instead, the warrior associations provided protection, order, and leadership in both raids and major bison hunts. The peace chiefs held authority over them but not enforcement rights; rather, they worked for unity and consensus within the bands. This dual organization is distinct from, but reminiscent of, the dual organization that is believed to have developed in early Mesopotamia, where war leaders dealt with secular matters of protection while religious leaders oversaw the ritual events associated with the temple (Trigger 2003:84; Wright et al. 1974:125).

Offensive warfare was also a unifying force within groups. Leaders attracted and rallied bands of warriors to raid other groups especially when there was the promise of plunder to enrich the participants. The Roman historian Tacitus identified an early version of this in AD 98 when he described the comitatus bond between a German lord and his supporting warriors (Peterson 1914). The warriors were clients of the leader who rewarded their faithful service in battle with training, material rewards, and prestige. Likewise, the power of Viking leaders stemmed from the acquisition and distribution of wealth from raids or trading ventures to their supporting warriors and retinue (Earle 2002c; Winroth 2012:42). The collection of a personal retinue of warriors was a characteristic of many complex chiefdoms across Africa (Dike and Ekejiuba 1990; Evans-Pritchard 1971; Roberts 1987).

Military orders consisting of warrior fraternities continued to be important with the emergence of state societies. In medieval Europe examples include the Knights Templar, the Knights Hospitallers, the Teutonic Knights, and the Order of Santiago, to name a few. Among the Aztecs, associations of warrior knights were the engine behind military conquests and the expansion of the empire. Aztec warfare was intimately tied to their religious cosmology since human sacrifices were necessary to nourish their gods and forestall the end of their world.[20] Warriors who took enough captives for sacrifice on the battlefield were eligible for admittance into one of the prestigious knight societies (Berdan 1982, 2014; Berdan et al. 1996; Hassig 1988; Hirth 2016; M. Smith 2012). These military orders were the backbone of the Aztec army, and their households were given wealth and supported by the state. For commoners, entry into a knight society was the primary means of upward social mobility (Hassig 1988; Hirth 1989).

LANDESQUE CAPITAL, RESOURCE CONTROL, AND THE INTENSIFICATION OF PRODUCTION

The management of public or common-pool resources such as land and water have long been recognized as important factors in cultural development. The question here is, How did the management of these resources or the development of more intensive forms of production contribute to the formation of formal institutions within society? The development of terracing, irrigation systems, intensive grazing, or the construction of other forms of landesque capital certainly increased the usufruct and ownership claims that groups made on their environments (Håkansson and Widgren 2014). They could also foster the need for increased control over their operation and the coordination of planting and harvesting cycles (Donkin 1979; Lansing 1987; Scarborough 2003).

Researchers have a long-standing interest in how the construction and control of irrigation systems and other forms of hydraulic agricultural production have contributed to the development of complex social institutions (Steward 1955; Wittfogel 1957). Water is a necessary resource for human life in both agricultural and pastoral production strategies. Scarborough (2003) argues that water management and the human-developed landscape that resulted from it was a powerful force that shaped economic, social, and political institutions in the societies that practiced it. Managing water flow requires hydraulic engineering. Irrigation systems involved the construction of canals, dams, and reservoirs; their maintenance once they are in operation; and monitoring and distributing water to the users.

The construction of hydraulic systems required the expenditure of human labor. Peter Blau (1970) has observed that the larger the work group, the greater its organizational complexity and internal differentiation. Charles Spencer (1993) proposed that the construction of the large earthen Purron dam[21] with a storage capacity of 1,430,000 cubic meters of water led to the emergence of centralized leadership in a small chiefdom in the Tehuacan Valley, Mexico around 600 BC. He argues that the construction of the dam required the coordination of labor from multiple villages, which bound the participants and individual farmers to the irrigation system and the leaders who managed it.

Not all hydraulic systems required the collaboration of large labor groups. Small drained fields and agricultural terraces could be constructed by individual households. Furthermore, some irrigation systems could be constructed and regulated collectively by labor associations without centralized top-down organization (Ostrom 1992). Nevertheless, Hunt (1988) feels that demands for water within irrigation systems created competition between users that led to centralized authority structures (Flannery 1972; Scarborough 2003:92). The way to mediate these conflicts was through coordinated organizational use. Stephen Lansing's (1987, 2009) work on Balinese irrigation systems illustrated that the systemic use of water resources could be coordinated through a range of social and religious structures. Coordinating use is a motivating factor for institutional development that can take many different forms.

The need to manage common pool resources can be an incentive for the development of institutional leadership if societies want to avoid overexploitation and the tragedy of the commons (Chibnik 2011:142; Hardin 1968). This is especially the case when common pool resources are indispensable for human life or when there is threat of their being converted into individual wealth. According to James Acheson, "In virtually all societies, there are controls on access to resources and various kinds of rules and arrangements to limit exploitive activities. Individuals are not allowed to seek their short-time goals at the expense of society" (Acheson 1989:375–376).

One such critical resource is drinking water. Under normal conditions humans require 2–3 liters of water per day to meet their needs (Scarborough 2003:1; White et al. 1972:table D). In this regard, Lisa Lucero (2006) has argued that the control of drinking water was important in the emergence of social complexity among the ancient Maya, who lived in a karst environment with 4–6 months of seasonal drought and no permanent rivers or lakes. Lucero argues that the control of rainwater collected in natural sinkholes and constructed reservoirs allowed the emerging elite to exchange access to potable water for labor from client farmers (Chabot-Hanowell and Lucero 2013:223). Individualized control of other critical resources such as forest resources or salt can have the same effect in different circumstances (Carballo 2013c:252; Flad 2011). Likewise, indirect leadership could emerge through the ritualization of planting and fertility cycles as Malinowski (1935) discussed in his examination of how agricultural production was embedded in garden magic (Stanish 2013).

REGULARIZING RELATIONSHIPS WITH NEIGHBORING GROUPS

It is generally believed that human groups throughout prehistory have always been aware of their neighbors. Anthropologists working across the globe in the late 19th and early 20th centuries never encountered a society that did not interact with neighboring groups through peaceful or hostile means. Colin Renfrew (1986; Renfrew and Cherry 1986) has argued that intergroup interaction was an important stimulus in the emergence of early complex society. His basic contention is that the internal structures of social integration, ritual communication, and political organization were stimulated by interaction between autonomous and independent sociopolitical groups in close proximity to one another. Competition over resources, warfare, and the exchange of material goods were all forces that helped to solidify hierarchies of internal social control.

George Dalton (1977) felt that hostility was the inevitable result of having neighbors. In state-level societies conflict resolution and avoidance was carried out by their leaders. But in stateless societies the situation was more complex because of the absence of absolute authority and the monopoly of force that defined society-wide control. In stateless societies hostility in the form of raiding, feuding, and conflict at various scales of intensity was a constant threat among neighboring groups. The threat of warfare was dire in stateless societies because leadership was weak and there was a limited ability to control the actions of all members of society once hostility erupted. The result could be an endless chain of raids, feuding, and revenge killings as individual families defended their honor or reciprocated violently to avenge the wrongs committed by their neighbors. The danger of hostility in pre-state societies is reflected in the written sagas of medieval Iceland where families were caught in continual feuds and revenge killings with limited ability to end the cycle of violence (Miller 2014).

There were two solutions to this problem. One was to embrace warfare openly and attack neighbors with both regularity and vigor. Robert Carneiro (1992) argued that chiefdoms developed as a result of warfare and the integrating forces that it produced. The second solution was for societies to wage peace instead of war. This was achieved through the establishment of intergroup alliances and interdependencies using a variety of means to quickly reestablish peaceful relations or to avoid conflict altogether. Dalton (1984) identified four mechanisms that were used to regularize relationships with neighboring groups: intergroup marriage, ceremonial exchanges, trade, and regularized forms of conflict mediation. The economy and the exchange of valuables played a role in all four of these mechanisms. Lineage groups were the interaction spheres through which alliances were established and maintained in stateless societies (Dalton 1981:23). Once alliances were established, they also served as emergent support networks through which food or refuge could be obtained in times of need (Dalton 1977:202).

The practice of intergroup marriage replicates the pattern of obtaining a spouse found in every household but involved the movement of individuals from one group to another. In stateless societies members of the same lineage shared a set of common beliefs and ideally did not fight with one another. Marriage between lineages in different groups extended this bond through the reciprocal transfer of women as spouses. Intergroup marriage also could involve the transfer of bridewealth and the establishment of lifelong reciprocal transactions between affinal relations. A second common alliance mechanism was the use of ceremonial exchanges accompanied by feasting.[22] Here alliance networks were maintained through the perpetual exchange of prestige goods and the social interactions that accompanied them.

A third stimulus for maintaining alliances between neighboring groups was the need to continue intergroup exchange of utilitarian goods. This could occur simultaneously with ceremonial exchange as it did within the Kula ring (Malinowski 1922, 1967a) or through reciprocal exchanges between trade partners (Harding 1967; Heider 1969; Rappaport 1968) such as that discussed in the previous chapter for calumet trade. Besides providing needed resources, these exchanges maintained contacts through which other social interactions occurred. Fourth and finally, despite alliance initiatives, hostilities often would break out between families or lineages in neighboring groups. Conflict mediation mechanisms provided a way of reestablishing peaceful relations. These often involved some form of death-compensation payment, exchange of valuables to the aggrieved parties, and/or feasting that recognized the cessation of conflict.[23]

The important point is that between-group interaction was a powerful force for institutional development. It stimulated the emergence of full-time leaders as political intermediaries and/or the development of alternative means of regulating group interaction. In stateless societies alliance relationships were forged through an amalgamation of social, political, and economic activities. But with the development of permanent centralized leadership, institution building took on a new dimension.

INSTITUTIONAL LEADERS AND LEADERSHIP

Leaders are found in all situations that required coordinated group activity. Institutional leaders have decision-making authority that extends across households and over nonkinsmen. Whether they act alone or as a collective body, leaders are individuals who provide decision-making benefits for followers as well as themselves (Kantner 2010; Vaughn et al. 2010). In egalitarian societies leaders were often defined situationally on the basis of needs such as directing communal hunts, supervising ritual events, or leading group raids. The need for leaders could be cyclical or could occur on an ad hoc basis. There often were strong leveling forces in small- and middle-range societies to limit leadership authority and to keep it from becoming permanent (Kantner

2010:259–260). A challenge for the study of institutional development, therefore, is understanding how emergent leaders overcame these leveling forces and extended their authority across household and kinship boundaries.

One trend that can be observed in both ancient and ethnographically studied complex societies is that leadership became increasingly prominent as societies grew in size. Institutionalized leadership refers to the appearance of permanent rather than situational leaders. Just as social forces and conditions shaped the need for organizational action, leaders shaped the structure of the institutions that developed to meet social needs. They operated as both agents of change and guardians of tradition. As societies grew in size, leaders became increasingly important and essential for organizing group activities, keeping order, preventing fission, and mediating disputes[24] (Feinman 2013b:38).

What are the attributes required for leadership? That is a difficult question to answer because it largely depends on the unique conditions of society, the circumstances they face, and the personality and leadership style that followers would support. In their book *Leading Minds,* Gardner and Laskin define a leader in the following way: "a leader is an individual (or, rarely a set of individuals) who significantly affects the thoughts, feelings, or behaviors of a significant number of individuals . . . leaders fashion stories – principally stories of identity. It is important that a leader be a good storyteller but equally crucial that the leader embody that story in his or her life" (Gardner and Laskin 2011: xiii). While their study is based on studying prominent individuals in the modern era, they feel that leaders in different types of societies share many of the same traits (Gardner 1993; Gardner and Laskin 2011:xiv).

Obviously, the prerequisites for leadership were different in ancient and premodern societies than they are in the modern world, but there is a good degree of commonality in leadership traits seen in historic sources (e.g., Scott-Kilvert 1960; Strauss 2012) and the recent ethnohistoric and ethnographic literature (e.g., Flannery 1999). John Kantner (2010) identifies many of the same leadership traits as Gardner and Laskin in his study of leadership in stateless societies. The first of these is charisma, the ability to inspire devotion and enthusiasm in one's followers. The second is diplomacy, the ability to seek advice from others and develop a consensus of agreement with possible dissenters. The third characteristic of good leaders is their ability to solve problems whether through intelligence or strength of will. Fourth, leaders need to be able to manipulate situations and get enough individuals to cooperate to solve the problem at hand. Nehemiah, discussed in the previous chapter, displayed all four of these characteristics as he mobilized voluntary labor to reconstruct the wall of Jerusalem. Finally, leaders need to have intelligence and be good storytellers. Ideology is as important to the organization of economic and political systems as it is to religious beliefs (Demarest 1992:8–9; DeMarrais et al. 1996; Friedman and Rowlands 1978b; Godelier 1978a; Miller and Tilley

1984). It is in the telling of myths and legends that new ideological principles of organization and rationales for resource allocation can be formed through the reinterpretation of old traditions. In this sense the ability to reinterpret historical tradition is foundational.

The value of the leader to a group is their ability is to dispel uncertainty. Three sources of uncertainty are especially important for leaders to address. The first is resource supply. Food shortages were always a concern, and one avenue to leadership was the demonstrated ability to produce resources in abundance. This is the reason that feasting was a prominent feature of premodern societies. Feasts allowed aspiring leaders to demonstrate their generosity, wealth, and ability to provide (Dietler and Hayden 2001; Vaugh 2010) while at the same time reinforcing the inequality of food giver and food receiver found in every household (Chapter 2). The ability to provide was the basis for the euergetism of leaders in the Greco-Roman world, which is discussed in Chapter 6. A second area of uncertainty was that of physical protection, discussed earlier as an important force for institutional development (Carneiro 1992). Third and finally, there was the need for spiritual safety and the uncertainty associated with unseen forces. It is here that shamans, priests, and other ritual specialists emerged as leaders to deal with the causes of unexplainable events such as disease, plague, famine, and death (Eerkens et al. 2010:10; Hirth 1996).

Researchers interested in the evolution of leadership have proposed a range of hierarchical, heterarchical, scalar, and social agency models for its development (Drennan 1991; Ehrenreich et al. 1995; Flannery 1972; Johnson 1982, 1983; Marcus and Flannery 1996; Roscoe 1993; Saitta 1999). Two models of leadership development that have received considerable attention are the network and corporate strategies. While often referred to as the dual-processual theory (Blanton et al. 1996), these two models are actually two ends of a spectrum of leadership strategies. *Network strategies* develop around personal prestige, wealth, and power of individual leaders.[25] Network leaders employ patrimonial rhetoric and prestige goods to build their followings. Patrimonial rhetoric emphasizes membership in kinship groups as a starting point for building their followings. Likewise, aspiring leaders may control the production of prestige goods or their procurement through interregional exchange to develop a clientage of individuals and leaders within groups. Network leaders stimulate a demand for these goods within political and religious contexts and attract a following by being their primary suppliers (Brumfiel and Earle 1987b; Earle 2002c; Friedman 1982; Friedman and Rowlands 1978a; Hayden 2001b; Kusimba and Kusimba 2010:225–227).

Leaders following a *corporate strategy* emphasize leadership offices and collective action within groups rather than competing for a personal clientage. Collective action strategies emphasize communal activities and rituals including public construction, food production, and religious celebrations to build group solidarity (Carballo 2013a). Leaders in corporate-based systems are often financed through systems of staple finance, using food and other durable staple goods, rather than wealth items or prestige goods which are prominent features of network strategies (D'Altroy and Earle 1985; Earle and D'Altroy 1982). Corporate strategies on the whole deemphasize building personal wealth in favor of managing the creation and the distribution of corporate wealth (Feinman 2001; Kusimba and Kusimba 2010). Corporate strategies produce a range of less centralized forms of leadership. Johnson (1982) refers to these as sequential leader hierarchies; the warrior associations among the Cheyenne discussed above are one such example.

The key element in the development of institutionalized leadership is concentrating power in a single person or office of leadership. Arnold (2010:122) argues that the key for this was the development of "inherited leadership and leaderships with sustained and renewable control over nonkin labor." The control over staple goods, prestige goods, and/or knowledge is viewed by Arnold (1995) as a precondition for the inheritance of leadership roles rather than determining them through collective means. The emergence of institutionalized leadership brings with it the development of leader households as a prominent and highly visible feature in the sociopolitical landscape of ancient societies. We now turn to a discussion of these households.

THE PALACE AS A VISIBLE INSTITUTION

Leaders grew up and lived in households just as their followers did. However, differential access to resources associated with the development of permanent and hereditary leadership led to sharp differences in levels of household wealth. Because leaders had more responsibilities, their households did as well. As a result, leaders' households tended to grow in size and complexity to meet their expanded responsibilities and because they controlled more resources to meet them. Cross-culturally and historically, households of leaders have always been large as a result of the work they performed, the special privileges they were granted, and the followers that they attracted (Blanton 1994; Evans and Pillsbury 2008; Mack 1951; Netting 1982; Webster and Inomata 2004). The size of a leader's household is represented by larger domestic spaces. Increased wealth and social position can be reflected in the type, scale, and decoration of a leader's residence, which may include special features or facilities for the activities they engage in (Price 1978). Finally, the involvement of leaders in sponsoring feasts and entertaining dignitaries may produce a different material cultural assemblage related to these activities (M. Smith 1987).

Leaders have always led from their households in both small-scale societies and complex states. As a result, the leader's household emerged as an early, prominent institution and the locus of social and political interaction within society. The result was twofold. First, government and its associated social and political activities often were organized as an extension of the leader's household. The result was the creation of a house model of political organization like that discussed in Chapter 2. Second, it is from the leader's household that the institution of the palace developed. Palaces as royal residences are the physical embodiment of the house society. They contained both the residence of leaders and the nonresidential spaces and facilities needed for the secular and ritualistic activities that they engaged in. The transformation of the leaders' households into administrative centers was an early hallmark of complex society. Ritual architecture in the form of religious sanctuaries and temple buildings representing the house of god was another (Schloen 2001).

Leaders' households were transformed into palaces when residential areas were expanded to include nonresidential or extra-household functions and activities. This transformation coincided with the centralization of decision making within society. But in operational terms, what is a palace? Winter provides a definition that is both concise and applicable to a broad range of leader households.

> "By folk definition, the palace is where the ruler resides. In the successive kingdoms of ancient Mesopotamia, however – Sumerian, Akkadian, Babylonian, Assyrian – the palace was the seat of many activities: administrative, bureaucratic, industrial, and ceremonial as well as residential. In brief, it was an 'institution,' not just a 'residence'; part of the state apparatus, not merely a container of state apartments"
>
> (Winter 1993:27).

Working from a New World perspective Webster and Inomata define the palace in very similar terms: "Palaces are the residences of individuals of wealth or high social rank, along with their families and retinues, and they include facilities appropriate to the ritual, political, recreational, and economic functions of elite households and individuals as foci of social power" (Webster and Inomata 2004:149). Both of these authors are discussing the role of the palace in state-level societies where the ruler's residence was the center of political governance and social power. While Winter was specifically discussing palaces in Near Eastern societies, the same was true elsewhere in the Mediterranean (Carile 2012; Hägg and Marinatos 1987; McNally 1975; Schoep 2010; Spawforth 2008) and across the ancient Old and New World.[26] But palaces were not confined to state societies. They also were common in many chiefdom societies.[27] They were multifaceted centers of governance that, rather than being a single residential building, often were organized as a complex of structures where the leader, his family, and entourage resided. As architectural entities palaces could be distinguished from other residential buildings in society by their size, internal layout, type of construction materials, unique architectural features, and/or the degree of internal or external decoration.

TABLE 4.1 *Common functional areas found within palace complexes in chiefdom- and state-level societies*

Class	Area
Residential/domestic areas	
	Leader residence
	Residence of wives
	Residence of royal family
	Residence of attendants
	Residence of officials
	Food preparation facilities
	Food storage facilities
	Guards
Civic areas	
	Public plazas and assembly areas
	Marketplace
Administrative areas	
	Council chamber or equivalent
	Reception areas for functionaries and ambassadors
	Adjudication areas
	Installation areas
Ritual/ceremonial areas	
	Temples
	Ancestor worship and chiefly burial areas
	Oracle shrines and divination areas
Specialized or unique areas	
	Craft areas
	Educational facilities
	Stables, armories, treasury, and other nonfood storage

James Sheehy (1996) has identified more than twenty different activity areas commonly associated with palace structures in chiefdom and state-level societies around the world. These can be grouped into five general classes of distinct residential and nonresidential activities, summarized in Table 4.1. The five classes of activities include the ruler's residence, civic areas, administrative areas, ritual/ceremonial areas, and specialized areas unique to the society under examination. As a general rule, the larger the society, the greater the degree of internal differentiation found within the central palace.

The core of the palace is the ruler's residence. Rulers of states, just like leaders of chiefdoms, often had multiple wives and special activity areas within their residence. The number of apartments that a palace contained depended on the number of wives, servants, attendants, and members of the ruling family that the residence had to house. In some cases, the royal residence included apartments for resident court officials who were not kinsmen. Sheehy's study showed that palaces often had special kitchen areas needed to fulfill entertainment obligations, although in some cases food was prepared outside the palace and brought in. Storage facilities were common to feed the royal family, to supply resources for sponsoring public events, and as a show of wealth under conditions of staple finance (D'Altroy and Earle 1985; Earle and D'Altroy 1982). In about half of the situations, a bodyguard either resided in the household or was stationed nearby (Table 4.1).

The palace was the arena of administrative and civic activity that required assembly areas. Within these spaces, joint celebrations and feasts were held and where the ruler publicly addressed his followers. It is also where public rituals could be performed and where processions and pageants could be held. In short, public assembly areas were where the pomp and circumstance of centralized rule could be witnessed or experienced by all or a select group of society's members. Depending on the level of sacredness or seclusion, it was also where followers might catch their only glimpse of the ruler. A second type of civic area was the public marketplace. If a society had markets, their location could vary. But where caring for the people was an important ideological component of rulership, permanent or periodic marketplaces could be found adjacent to the ruler's palace.[28]

A common feature of palaces was the presence of reception areas where individuals could meet with the ruler. It was where chiefs and functionaries from the leader's domain could assemble and where the leader could meet with leaders, ambassadors, and representatives from neighboring polities. Council chambers were where leaders met with their advisors or assembled a council of war. One of the prerogatives of centralized leadership often included the right to use force to enforce laws or other prescribed cultural practices. As a result, palaces often included a location for the adjudication of jural affairs and disputes within society. They also were where oaths were taken by officials when they were installed in office.

Palaces frequently had ritual areas for the private use by rulers or for ceremonies related to their leadership roles. In chiefdom societies this could include oracle shrines and divination areas for foretelling the future or casting spells. Rulers who were thought to be divine or semi-divine were intimately involved in ceremonial activities and could have temples within or close to palace structures. Likewise, an emphasis on the sacredness of the leader could produce greater degrees of seclusion within the palace, buffering the leader from followers. The palace might also contain a burial place for the ruler as well as family members. This could be a continuation of ancestor worship practiced at the level of individual households and used to maintain the inheritance of rulership within one lineage.

Finally, the palace could house a number of society-specific types of activities. As discussed above, the control and distribution of wealth goods was an important feature in the development of network leadership strategies

(Blanton et al. 1996). One way to do this was to control their production, which could locate craft workshops in or adjacent to the ruler's residence. An alternative approach was to control the procurement of wealth goods through trade. Under these circumstances storage areas for both trade goods and goods mobilized through taxation could be expected if the palace also functioned as a general treasury. Furthermore, where military defense was an issue the palace could serve as a central armory. A miscellany of other less common but important features could be found that included stables, gardens, orchards, and entertainment areas.

The appearance of permanent, centralized leadership was an important step in the development of complex society. One result was the emergence of leader households as early multipurpose institutions. They formed the core of early complex societies, and as they grew in size the house of the leader eventually was transformed into the ruler's palace. The discussion that follows examines the two Bronze Age societies of Old Kingdom Egypt and Levantine Ugarit and how the ruler's household or palace was the central administrative feature for organizing society.

Old Kingdom Egypt (2686–2181 BC)

Herodotus said that Egypt was the gift of the Nile and the land of the pharaoh. The state and its associated institutions began to develop in the late fourth millennium BC. Multiple small chiefdoms developed along the Nile that increasingly fought with one another. Instead of developing forms of peaceful coexistence, increasing hostilities led to the conquest of one group by another and the eventual unification of Egypt through military conquest.

The Palermo stone was inscribed in the fifth Dynasty of the Old Kingdom (2498–2345 BC) and depicts the names of the early rulers of Egypt. Egypt was always seen by its inhabitants as representing two kingdoms: Lower Egypt representing the area of the northern delta, and Upper Egypt, which represents the valley of the Nile from the delta south and upriver.[29] The Palermo stone depicts several early rulers wearing the red crown of Lower Egypt followed by subsequent rulers wearing a crown with the emblems of both Lower and Upper Egypt. Wearing the double crown indicated that Egypt was ruled as a unified entity. The later Egyptian scribe of Manetho said that the first pharaohs of Egypt originated in the Thinite nome of Upper Egypt.[30] Inscriptions and hieroglyphic texts place the conquest unifying Egypt at around 3100 BC, which marks the beginning of the Early Dynastic period (3100–2686 BC) (Trigger 1983:44–52).

With the unification of Egypt, the great traditions of Egypt can be said to begin. Herodotus identified Menes (who may also be the individual known as Narmer) as the conqueror who unified Upper and Lower Egypt and

4.1 The Narmer Palette. (Redrawn from Flannery and Marcus 2012:Figure 59 by Shae Rider and author)

founded Egypt's first dynasty (Figure 4.1). Whatever his name, the unification brought with it centralized governance. He established the capital at Memphis where Upper and Lower Egypt met. It was here that the pharaoh built the main temple of Ptah and established his royal residence. Memphis remained the symbolic center of the Egyptian state throughout its development. It was shortly thereafter that a pharaoh named Aha established a cemetery on the Saqqara plateau behind Memphis that contained the tombs of important officials who were part of the pharaoh's Early Dynastic administration. During this period the pharaoh's divine nature was established as the earthly manifestation of the solar creator god. The religious ideology maintained that only the pharaoh could make offerings through his priests to the gods and ancestors throughout Egypt (Trigger 2003:79). With the construction of mortuary pyramids as a component of the pharaoh's royal household, the early Egyptian state reached its fullest expression and the Old Kingdom (2686–2181 BC) had begun.[31]

Max Weber (1978:1013) proposed that ancient Egypt was organized as a patrimonial state with all economic and political activities directed from the pharaoh's household (Janssen 1978:234). Lehner (2000) concurs with Weber but argues that the state had a more segmental organization with households nested within households. The household worked well as a generalized organizational principle for the Early Dynastic state. Even the word for "pharaoh" is derived from the Egyptian term for "great house" (Lehner 2000:333; Moreno Garcia 2012:1). The Egyptian household included core kinsmen (parents, siblings, children, etc.) as well as nonkinsmen acting as servants, household administrators, concubines, attached acquaintances, and serfs. They also included deceased family members.

The Egyptian household had two levels of inclusiveness. At the core were blood kinsmen who were defined in relation to the household head much like a kindred. More on the periphery, but still integral to the household, was the collection of clients and servants attached to the household head through patronage and dependency relationships. Coffin texts express the household of the deceased as "all his kindred together with the household" or "all my people" (Moreno Garcia 2012). The implication is that kinsmen and dependents formed one household. Middle-range households could have eighteen to twenty individuals,[32] while high-ranking households could have many more. The highest-ranking households in Egypt could have several hundred people including dozens of servants and 60–150 serfs. Individuals actively sought the patronage of influential people, and when they obtained it, they were considered members of the elite household. An individual in service to a patron might be referred to as "son" even when no kinship relationships existed. Moreover, the extensive use of patronage relationships made it possible to be a patron to one person and a client to someone higher in the social hierarchy (Moreno Garcia 2007:135–136; Warden 2013:20–21).

The flexible structure of Egyptian households was well suited to accommodate the administrative responsibilities and activities of a ruler of a small state. Butzer (1976:83) estimates the population size of the entire Old Kingdom at 1.6 million people. While this was a lot of people, Egypt was easy to govern with a relatively simple administrative hierarchy. The Nile flood provided subsistence without the need for a large-scale investment in agricultural infrastructure. Because of its unique situation, Egypt could be ruled with relatively little cost. It was protected to the east and west by stretches of desert, and there was little fear of invasion from its more powerful neighbors in Mesopotamia. Likewise, because the majority of its population was dispersed throughout small towns and villages, there were no centers of population where revolt could foment. Finally, the narrow Nile Valley and the delta were the only inhabitable areas in Egypt so that there were no refuge areas where dissidents could organize a rebellion. There was no need for Old Kingdom Egypt to maintain a large standing army, and no military titles are evident among the important officials within the state hierarchy (Janssen 1978:225).

The pharaoh's palace residence was the administrative center of the early Egyptian state, and the officials involved in its operation were client members of his household. Most of what is known about the internal organization of the Old Kingdom is derived from the titles and textual inscriptions found in the tombs of officials buried in the pharaoh's mortuary complex. There were other, lower-level officials who lived and carried out their duties in the provinces, but the ones buried with the pharaoh were members of his extended household. In many cases more is known about the individuals who held important titles than the actual duties they carried out. What makes things complex is that individuals accumulated titles over the course of their lifetimes as they worked their way up the administrative hierarchy so it is difficult to know if they had concurrent responsibilities in different branches of the government or just changed their duties over time.

While all authority flowed from the pharaoh, several key political officials can be identified in the pharaoh's household who were instrumental in the operation of the state. The four most important of these were the vizier and the overseers of works, the granary, and the treasury.[33] The administrative hierarchy grew in size and complexity from two main officials (vizier, chief of works) during the Third and Fourth Dynasties (2686–2498 BC) to about ten or more during the Fifth and Sixth Dynasties (2498–2181 BC) as a result of the growing workload. What is important in terms of pharaonic household structure is that during the Fourth Dynasty all the viziers, chiefs of works, and high priests claimed to be close relatives of the pharaoh (Warburton 2001). After that time nonrelatives entered the administration, but even they often carried the honorific title of king's son (Strudwick 1985).

The vizier was the highest-ranking official in the Old Kingdom directly under the pharaoh. He supervised all of the departments involving resource production and collection, and only the most trusted individuals held this office. His presence was pervasive and the vizier appears to have had authority over fiscal administration and judicial affairs (Kemp 1983:84). The overseer of works was responsible for the pharaoh's architectural projects. These included the construction and repair of temples and the planning and completion of his mortuary complex. Since labor and materials were required in construction he probably also oversaw mining activities and organized the corvée workforce. He may also have supervised craftsmen who worked in the palace on different types of materials (Strudwick 1985).

The number of administrators expanded in the Fifth Dynasty. Two important administrators, the overseer of the granaries and the overseer of the treasury, appeared at this time. The Old Kingdom operated largely on the basis of staple finance and the production of grain. Collecting, storing, and managing grain, therefore, were of primary importance to the operation of the state. As a result, there were administrative divisions of this office both in the royal residence and in the provinces. This office possibly had the responsibility of providing bread and beer to individuals involved in corvée labor (Warden 2013). The overseer of the treasury was a parallel office to that of the granaries and dealt with a separate range of high-value items that included oil, wine, and linen, and raw materials such as metal, precious woods, and ivory. He probably was in charge of all taxes as well as equipping official trade expeditions to Nubia and other foreign countries. The treasury also inventoried and supplied furnishings for the pharaoh's residence and lavish offerings for his tomb (Strudwick 1985; Warburton 2001).

These high-ranking administrators lived in the royal palace and conducted their activities as members of the pharaoh's household. Other important administrators in the palace during the Fifth Dynasty include the overseers of great mansions and the king's documents. The overseer of great mansions was a judicial title; this individual oversaw the six courts located in the royal residence. The position of overseer of the king's documents refers to the scribal administration involved in sealing granaries, inventorying the treasury, and keeping general accounting records. Lesser officials and stewards worked under these administrators to carry out the work of the state both in the palace and throughout Upper and Lower Egypt. How one advanced in the hierarchy had everything to do with an individual's personal standing with the pharaoh. This is evident from an elaborate tomb of a man named Ty who had the position and title of hairdresser. One can only imagine the exchanges and discussions that occurred as the pharaoh was coiffured in the royal palace (Strudwick 1985:343).

Compared with other ancient states, the budgetary requirements of Old Kingdom Egypt were minimal. The administrative hierarchy was small and most of the resources needed to support the state were produced on institutional estates. Tax-in-kind was collected from individuals granted private estates for their personal support and administrative duties, but this income was small in relation to the institutional estates. Institutional estates took two forms: those that produced grain and other income used by temple and state administrators during the Old Kingdom, and the royal domains of pharaohs and other top administrators that became entailed estates held in trust to fund the mortuary rituals carried out for individuals after death. The labor for these estates was supplied by tenants who were provided land for their own support as well as being provisioned with food when they provided corvée labor (Kemp 1983; Quirke et al. 2001; Warden 2013).

Old Kingdom Egypt extended from the Mediterranean Sea to the site of Elephantine in Upper Egypt, a distance of approximately 1,000 kilometers along the Nile. Although this distance was great, the Nile facilitated both transportation and communication, making it possible to rule the kingdom from the capital of Memphis. The pharaoh was the undisputed ruler of the land, and the state administration of the Old Kingdom was directed from his household. While Egypt was ethnically homogenous, this was not the case to the east in the Levant and across Mesopotamia. There ethnic diversity, multiple urban centers, and a tradition of interpolity conflict created a very different political environment. The question addressed next is whether the ruler's household also served as the model of political organization in the Levant. The Bronze Age state of Ugarit is examined for this purpose.

Bronze Age Ugarit

Ugarit was a small city-state along the northern coast of Syria that flourished during the Middle and Late Bronze Age (1900–1180 BC). It corresponds to what has been called Canaanite culture, which played an important role in the development of Jewish and Levantine history. Ugarit was the most important Canaanite kingdom in the Late Bronze Age. The city of Ugarit corresponds to the archaeological site of Tell Ras Shamra where the recovery of important textual materials and archaeological excavations have provided detailed information about the city from 1500 to 1180 BC. While the city accumulated considerable wealth because of its involvement in maritime trade, the kingdom was small, covering only 2,000–2,200 square kilometers. In military terms Ugarit was never very strong. It could muster an army of 4,000–5,000 soldiers, and the city was conquered, destroyed, and abandoned by attacks from the Sea People around 1180 BC (Vita 1999; Yon 2006).

David Schloen (2001) has examined the available textual, linguistic, and archaeological information and feels that the political organization of Ugarit along with other ancient Near Eastern states conforms to what he calls the *patrimonial household model*[34] fashioned after Weber's (1978) concept of patrimonialism. In the ancient Near East social governance was intimately tied to the ruler's household. Political organization was structured as a patrimonial regime where "the entire social order is viewed as an extension of the ruler's household – and ultimately the god's household. The social order consists of a hierarchy of subhouseholds linked by personal ties at each level between individual 'masters' and 'slaves' or 'fathers' and 'sons'" (Schloen 2001:51).

In Ugarit and elsewhere in the Near East, the ruler held control over all of the land and personnel in his domain. The result was that everyone in the ruler's domain was linked conceptually to the royal household through a nested hierarchy of household relationships. Small households were viewed as incorporated into larger, higher-ranking households (Gelb 1979:7). There was no effective difference between individuals in rural areas or the capital of Ugarit; all were obliged to serve and support the ruler and the state (Schloen 2001:65).

The foundation of Late Bronze Age Ugarit was the large joint family household. Schloen (2001) feels that the household in Ugaritic society was patriarchal, patrilineal, and patrilocal. The typical family was a self-sufficient agricultural unit that included around ten individuals. The preference for large joint families stemmed from their success in minimizing risk by pooling resources such as land, animals, and labor. Impartible patrilineal inheritance combined with brideprice[35] concentrated resources in patriarchal households (Gray 1960). Archaeological data on house size together with the Levitical laws against sexual intercourse with kinsmen and affines reinforce the model of the large extended household as the normal form of residence (Bernbeck 1995; Noth 1965:135; Schloen 2001:148–149).

The joint patrilineal household was called the *bet ab* in Hebrew, which translates as "house of the father." The composition of the household could include the senior living male and his wife, sons, unmarried daughters, his married sons' wives and children, as well as slaves, landless clients, and livestock. Schloen correlates the *bet ab* with the joint family household, and while he is undoubtedly correct in doing so, the term also has the capacity to represent larger, multigenerational groups of up to 50–100 persons (Gottwald 1999:285–292). At this scale the term is able to encompass something more akin to a lineage or kindred like the "house of Jacob" rather than just a single extended household. In any event each *bet ab* had its own hereditary and inalienable land allocation known as the *nah la* (inheritance) (Schloen 2001:150). In Israel these households were members of a larger clan or patronymic land-holding association known as the *mispaha*[36] (Gottwald 1999:257–267).

While all households had permanent usufruct claims to land, Schloen (2001:120) argues that this did not represent private property in the sense that it developed in Iron Age societies. Instead, the gods were the ultimate owners of the land who gave proprietorship to the patrimonial ruler to allocate to subjects in return for service and a share of the crop. For Schloen the land allocation system was akin to that of the ruler allocating land to sharecroppers. Other scholars disagree with this view and feel that there were two separate sectors of land allocation throughout the kingdom: one where land was held by the free inhabitants of rural villages and another involving land under direct control of the ruler's palace (Diakonoff 1982; Heltzer 1976, 1979, 1982:424).

The gods were always recognized as the proprietors of the land, and the rulers of Ugarit probably did not obtain this right as proxy until after the formation of the Bronze Age state. Land rights during the preceding Neolithic period would have been vested in the hands of local villages and clan groups rather than a single ruler.[37] With the emergence of centralized leadership, a ruler's claim for eminent domain over all or some land could be made. Nevertheless, in Bronze Age Ugarit, land was granted and rations of food were issued to individuals who provided service to the ruler's household, which indicates that the ruler had superordinate control over at least a portion of the land.

The kingdom of Ugarit, like that of its neighbors, was organized as a hierarchy of households nested within larger and more influential ones with the royal household at the top. The importance of the household as the cognitive template within the kingdom is reflected in kinship terminology used to characterize generalized organizational relationships. Terms such as house, father, son, brother, master, and servant were used extensively in textual documents to characterize the social order of relationships between nonkinsmen. Schloen (2001:255) argues that these terms were not simply metaphors for describing social and political relationships, but were employed because there were no alternative concepts for characterizing the social hierarchy available for use in Bronze Age societies. Kinship continued as an important organizational structure in the development of early state societies, but household relationships and terminology provided a natural framework for integrating nonkinsmen into a large corporate body.

The terms "father" and "son" are used in royal correspondence throughout Canaan and the middle Euphrates to describe hierarchical political relationships and subservience. The terms "father" and "master" were used to address individuals of exalted position, while "son" and "servant" expressed positions of subordination. Similarly, individuals at the same relative social positions often referred to each other as brothers. These terms were used in politically calculated ways to flatter and appease their peers, to grant their wishes, or to acquire a favor.[38] The master–servant and father–son forms of address are common in royal correspondence, and both can be traced back to intrahousehold relationships applied to social and political relationships within and between early states.

The household terminology used to describe social and political relationships within the kingdom of Ugarit makes it difficult to determine who actually resided within the royal palace. The king, his wives, the queen mother, and his immediate family certainly would have resided at Ugarit. The regent or vizier referred to as the *sakinu* was the king's primary deputy and representative when he traveled outside the kingdom. There are individuals who held the title of *mar sarri*, or son of the King, who are not directly related to him. Other important head functionaries included the chief of the palace, chief of works, chief of the field, chief accountant, and the chief of the war chariots. Less important palace personnel included scribes, gatekeepers, and eunuchs, as well as a range of ancillary service personnel for domestic tasks and entertainment.[39] What is confusing about the palace administration is that the texts do not distinguish between individuals resident in the city and those residing in rural areas. All individuals who provided service were referred to as royal dependents (*bns mlk*) because they received economic support for the services they provided (Heltzer 1982, 1999; Vita 1999).

Nevertheless, *all* of the people of the kingdom were referred to as the sons and daughters of Ugarit. Likewise, at the regional level, political superiors in large cities were masters and fathers, while their subordinates in towns and villages were servants and sons. In the nearby kingdom of Ebla, the term of "house" is used to refer to a whole village or a large estate in close proximity to one. This is evident in a text that provides a royal land grant to an individual named Ingar:

> Thus [says] the king to Ingar: Listen. For ten years the king will set aside and give to you a "house" in Baytan which is 2,000 [measures of land]. Moreover, I will not take [it] [or: receive (revenue from it)] for ten years. It is set aside [for you] and it will be your residence outside the city [of Ebla]. From time to time you will reside outside the city [of Ẹbla].
>
> (Schloen 2001:270)

The grant of 2,000 measures of land is large and probably represents an area of about 720 hectares.[40] This grant established a house or dependency for Ingar in the village of Baytan. In another royal text, the king of Ebla gave land grants (expressed as houses) to the three sons of his chief vizier, a man named Ibrium. Included in these grants are the names of individuals who were incorporated as subordinates into their service. One of these individuals was the same Ingar named in the quotation above.[41] These royal grants illustrate how household terminology was used to express the social and political relationships within Bronze Age societies. The village of Baytan was given as a house to Ingar, which in turn was granted to Ir-Damu (son of Ibrium), who was already a member of his father's house, who served as vizier and member of the royal household to the ruler of Ebla. The hierarchy of households expressed in this royal land grant depict a five-tier relationship of ruler–vizier (Ibrium)– Ir-Damu–Ingar–sons of Baytan.

Like Old Kingdom Egypt, the ruler's household served as an organizational model for structuring social and political relationships within Bronze Age Ugarit.[42] One reason this was possible is because Ugarit was small, encompassing an area of only about 2,000 square kilometers. Its population could be administered effectively through patron–client relationships following a household model. The result was that interpersonal relations were more important in the organization than are often ascribed to early states. Individuals were members of a royal household, and there was no sharp political or economic distinction between public and private, or rural and urban parts of the kingdom. The state was personal rather than impersonal, with little to no conceptual difference between personal economic obligations and those owed to the ruler's household (Lehner 2000:280–281). Scale and complexity were important factors mediating the operation of household forms of governance, and they continued to operate effectively in many areas of the world until systems grew beyond their capacity to effectively integrate their constituent populations.

SUMMARY

The foregoing discussion has explored the relationship between the development of complex society and the formal institutions that supported it. The discussion focused on three general issues: the forces for social integration within society, the effect these forces have on forms of leadership, and how the emergence of permanent leaders transformed their households into one of the early formal institutions in complex societies. The conditions under which these events occurred varied from society to society and from situation to situation. No pretense is made to suggest that this process can be understood outside the specific cultural and environmental circumstances in which individual complex societies developed. Nevertheless, there are some general features associated with the emergence of formal institutions that span the transition from small chiefdoms to early states. Any hope of understanding these developments requires the use of a multidisciplinary approach that combines archaeological and textual research with the structural models and analogies that can be drawn from chiefdom and state-level societies described in the ethnographic, ethnohistoric, and historic records.

If there is one constant in the emergence of complex society, it is that size matters. There is a consistent positive correlation between the size of society and the development of institutions and forms of integration that kept it together. This is often referred to as the size–complexity rule. I see this as a chicken and egg relationship. As the population of a group or society increased, so too did the internal pressures that could tear it apart. Groups fissioned when internal pressures could not be resolved. Population growth incentivized the development of integrative institutions, but leaders also created the conditions for collaborative social interaction that enabled societies to grow in size without fissioning.

Four integrating forces were presented that provided conditions or incentives to develop cooperation, collection action, and leaders within groups. All societies recognized relatedness within groups through different forms of kinship. Kinship, therefore, provided an organizational framework through which social hierarchy and heterarchy (Crumley 1995) could be expressed and within which leaders could address problems through individual initiatives. Two of the forces for interaction – the development of resource-holding groups and the intensification of production – dealt with internal pressures and benefits of collective and cooperative group interaction. The other two – the need for mutual protection and regulating interaction with neighboring groups – addressed external pressures that groups faced within their cultural environments. While these are only a few of the situations that could be cited, they all provided stimuli for the development of social institutions to solve these problems. In some situations, they resulted in centralized leadership, while in others they did not.

Leaders are found in all societies where coordinated group activities take place. Whether leaders are temporary and situational or permanent and multifunctional, they represent the human capital to resolve problems within society. Archaeologists have identified and dichotomized two general strategies that past leaders used in shaping group action. These are a network strategy where individuals built a personal clientage through patrimonial rhetoric, personal charisma, and the use of prestige goods, and a corporate strategy where leaders emphasized unity and engaged in cooperation-based activities that emphasized the collective benefits of mutual participation. Whatever the leadership strategy selected – and most societies employed both – the result could be the emergence of permanent leaders who organized and/or sponsored group activities from their households. A resulting by-product was the development of the ruler's residence as a palace within developing complex societies.

The palace is the ruler's residence writ large. As an institution and center of political governance and authority, palaces can be found in complex societies from small chiefdoms to territorial states. This was as much a function of efficiency and expediency of leadership as it was a strategy for appropriating control over social resources. All members of a leader's household would have been involved in leadership-related activities. Max Weber (1978) and Lévi-Strauss (1982) both observed how the household served as a model for sociopolitical organization in both ancient and ethnographic societies around the world. The reason for this was that households readily incorporated both kinsmen and nonkinsmen into integrated workgroups under a household head. It was a preexisting rationale that could be used to integrate, coordinate, and express relationships between individuals (nonkinsmen) from different lineages and clans. Until that could be done, it would have been a challenging task to coordinate activities across and between different kinship groups.

Two examples were presented to illustrate the existence of the household model of political organization in early Bronze Age states: Old Kingdom Egypt and the Canaanite kingdom of Ugarit. Evidence for the household model is found in the way that political relationships were structured as personal relationships and expressed in household and familial terminology. Hierarchy was expressed as a system of households nested within superordinate households, with the ruler's household at the apex (Moreno Garcia 2012:4; Schloen 2001:208; Warden 2013:21). This nesting was accomplished by incorporating the head of a subordinate household as a conceptual member or dependent of a higher-ranked household.

No assertion is made here that the household model is either a universal feature of ancient societies or a rigid analytical type that should be applied to all societies. But it is *one way* of expressing and conceptualizing bureaucratic relationships within a functional framework organized around the leader's household. After all, kinship and its associated forms of organization did not disappear with the advent of complex society. It continued to be a way of expressing interpersonal relationships between both the governing and the governed. The next two chapters explore some of the types of formal institutions found in ancient society in greater detail. They examine some of the variation in how formal institutions covered the cost of their activities in different societies across the ancient and premodern world.

FIVE

FINANCING FORMAL INSTITUTIONS

Systems of Direct Production

[Moctezuma] housed separately, those who were his feather workers, who pertained to him. He gave them a house of their own. And they made the array which was Moctezuma's own . . . wherefore [the craftsmen] were called . . . feather workers of the palace, artisans of the ruler.

(Sahagún 1959:91)

The institutional economy is composed of a combination of both formal and informal organizations that provide structure and produce benefits for the groups they serve. While informal institutions are voluntary associations between collaborating households, formal institutions are more explicitly constituted organizations in terms of the way they are structured and the functions they provide within society. As discussed in the previous chapter, formal institutions often emerge to solve specific problems and to integrate societies as they grow in size and complexity. Formal institutions vary in both size and purpose. Whether they are designed as society-wide institutions (temples, palaces, courts, marketplaces) or as special-purpose organizations (trade guilds, warrior associations, charitable foundations), they provide cohesion for groups within society. Whatever their purpose, most formal institutions require resources in the form of labor, food, or goods to support personnel, provide needed infrastructure, and carry out the activities for which they were formed.

This chapter examines the economic organization of formal institutions. It explores one dimension of this organization: how institutions internally produced the resources they needed for their normal operation. Three characteristics are central to this discussion. First, the examples were selected to illustrate different forms of institutional organization. No pretense is made to suggest that they represent the earliest, the most common, or the only ways that institutions produced the resources that they used. Second, the cases discussed focus on only one dimension of institutional finance: the creation of resources used through systems of direct production. The above epigraph describes one such form of institutional production among the Aztecs of Central Mexico. Third, as societies grew, so too did the number of ways that institutions financed their activities. In many societies, society-wide institutions were supported through multiple, different forms of resource creation because of the quantity and type of resources required in different situations.[1]

The discussion begins by examining the structure of institutional resource creation. It explores how different social and environmental conditions can result in different forms of institutional finance, mechanisms of resource creation, and costs associated with production and mobilization of resources. The focus then shifts to a comparative examination of different ways that formal institutions can be funded using systems of direct production. Examples are presented from several different state societies: the temple estates of ancient Sumer, the prebendal estates of the pre-Columbian Aztecs, the production monopolies of ancient China, institutional production and distribution within the Zoar community and the Inka state, and manorial production and peripatetic institutional consumption in medieval Europe and the Middle East. These examples were selected because they represent well-documented instances of how large-scale, society-wide religious and political institutions were funded. As a small collection they illustrate the diversity of ways that formal institutions solved their resource needs using direct production in different cultural settings.

THE COST OF INSTITUTIONAL COMPLEXITY

Karl Polanyi (1957) was keenly interested in the role of institutions in shaping economic behavior. He took the position that all past economic activity was embedded in, and shaped by, the social and political institutions of ancient societies. Proponents of new institutional economics (NIE) have revisited this relationship from a different perspective (North 1981, 1995). Faced with a world of imperfect knowledge, NIE argues that humans created institutions as both rules of conduct and forms of organization to reduce risk and regularize economic behavior. In this sense NIE addresses two dimensions of institutional development not usually addressed by traditional economics. The first is that ideology and the rationales of operation are just as important as necessity in shaping the structure of institutions (Williamson 2000:figure 1). The rules defining the structure of property rights are an example of how ideology and law govern resource access and control (e.g., Kehoe 1997, 2007). Its second contribution is its focus on identifying the transaction costs associated with economic activity in terms of the time, effort, and material expense that institutions incur to accomplish their intended purposes (Acheson 1994:11; Coase 1937, 2008; Klein 1998:466–469; Williamson 2008).

All organizations incurred costs of operation, and three dimensions of institutional organization are important in evaluating how they were met. The first of these involves the types of resources needed and created to meet institutional costs. This topic has been addressed for ancient societies in terms of the system of resource finance that institutions employed (e.g., D'Altroy and Earle 1985; Earle 1994). The second issue is how resources were produced. This question has historically fueled a great deal of discussion concerning the structure of the political economy and how the flow of wealth was controlled in society (e.g., Brumfiel and Earle 1987a; Earle 2002a; Marx 1975; Murra 1980; Wittfogel 1957; Wolf 1982). Third and finally, the costs of moving, managing, processing, and/or converting resources into the forms required for institutional consumption need to be identified. Each of these factors is examined briefly below to identify how they affect the mobilization and use of resources in institutional contexts.

Forms of Institutional Finance

One way that community and group activities were funded was by collecting resources from the participants. This was the common practice for intra- and intercommunity feasting as well as for moka and potlatch celebrations. Whether produced or collected for the event, resources were assembled with a specific end use in mind. Early states often financed institutions in much the same way; consumable staples and food were produced and stored for specific usages. Researchers have referred to this manner of institutional funding as *staple finance* (D'Altroy and Earle 1985; Earle 1994; Earle and D'Altroy 1982). It involved the collection and storage of staple goods such as grain, wine, oil, or livestock in special facilities for use when needed as food, drink, adornments, costumes, and/or gifts.

The evidence for staple finance systems is represented in the archaeological and historic records in two ways. One is the presence of large storage facilities located in areas close to where individuals supervised their use. Examples in the ancient world are found in Egypt (Baines and Malek 2000:97–98; Bleiberg 2001; Kemp 1991:192–196), Mesopotamia (Hunt 1987; Nissen 1986, 1995:799; Zeder 1991), China (Bray 1984; Lee-fang Chien 2004; Will et al. 1991), Japan (Berry 1982), Rome (Rickman 1971, 1980a; Vitelli 1980), Mycenean Crete, the Indus valley (Wheeler 1968:figure 9, plate V), Mongol imperial storage at

Karakorum (Weatherford 2004), and in state societies in the New World among the Inka (Huaycochea Nuñez de la Torre 1994; LeVine 1992; Pozorski and Pozorski 1991) and the Aztecs (Hernandez Xolocotzi 1949; Hirth 2012a, 2012b; Kobayashi1993b; Rovira Morgado 2014).

Systems of staple finance used by institutions replicate the way that households fund their participation in informal institutions by collecting and storing consumable resources needed for different events. The difference, of course, is in the scale and location of staple storage facilities. For that reason, centralized storage is often associated with the palace or house of the leader. It is this association that led Karl Polanyi to advocate redistribution as an important form of economic organization. Large storage facilities are associated with palace complexes in Mycenaean Crete, but this was a function of provisioning the institution of rulership and the palace rather than the way that society was organized as a whole (Christakis 1999, 2011; Halstead 1988; Nakassis et al. 2011). The centralized storage and display of food surpluses was important in chiefdom societies where social relations and rank were reinforced through feasting and the control over scarce resources.[2] This is evident among Trobriand Islanders where community chiefs had the largest storage cribs for yams and were the only ones in the village whose contents were not hidden from view for the express reason of proclaiming their wealth (Malinowski 1922; Ward 1985:98; Wesson 1999). Staple finance was always important for supporting activities in the central palace. It just changed in frequency in relation to relative importance of wealth finance.

A second way that staple finance systems are expressed is in the written records of early states when staples were used to pay for services, support labor drafts, or sustain the households of state administrators. A great many of the early texts from Bronze Age societies deal with issuing rations of food or beer to state workers in Mesopotamia[3] (Beale 1978; Postgate 2004; Renger 1979; Schloen 2001; Steinkeller 2007; Van de Mieroop 1999:154) and Egypt (Strudwick 1985; Trigger 2003:330–331; Warden 2013:32–34). Grain, salt, and cattle were staples of survival and served as a form of commodity money in early exchanges. Karl Polanyi recognized the importance of staple finance and felt that staples were used as submonetary accounting units in early states (Dalton 1968:186–187, 321–324). Mobilizing staple resources within institutional contexts to compensate corvée workers for their labor was a continuation of the type of economic compensation associated with interhousehold work parties and labor feasts.

Staple finance systems were common in small agrarian states where goods were used locally and did not have to be transported over large distances (Dodgshon 1998; Earle 1994; Stein 1994). As societies grow in size, however, staple finance encounters problems. Food and other staples are bulky and can be costly to transport over long distances. These costs can limit the growth of both large chiefdoms and early states.[4] One solution to this problem was to shift from staple to wealth finance systems as a means of funding formal institutional activities.

Wealth finance refers to the use of high-value commodities or prestige goods to fund formal institutions and elite-sponsored activities (Earle 1987b; 1994). These goods are high-value products, sometimes referred to as special-purpose money (Dalton 1965), that were used as a means of payment in lieu of staple goods. Systems of wealth finance have several advantages over staple finance. The first is that these goods functioned as a form of currency within society. Second, they are normally nonperishable goods (e.g., jewelry, textiles, spices), which have a longer use life than food and allow for the accumulation of durable wealth. Third, where wealth goods were manufactured items, the state could control or sponsor craftspersons to produce them.[5] Fourth and finally, these goods were both compact and lightweight compared with staple goods. The result was that they could be transported over greater distances at lower costs than was possible with bulk commodities (D'Altroy and Earle 1985:188).

The development of wealth finance systems is generally associated with large, territorially extensive states. Wealth goods can be centrally collected, assigned, and transported to points of administrative use within a regionally dispersed or extensive territorial domain with greater ease than staple goods. The key for wealth finance systems was the ability to convert wealth goods into staple goods at their point of use. Food staples were required to support the households of administrative personnel and the feasts associated with public celebrations and ceremonies. This presupposes two important conditions for operation: first that there is sufficient local production to make those conversions possible, and second that there is sufficient demand for wealth goods to move comfortably between spheres of exchange for high- and low-value goods (e.g., Bohannan 1955). It is for this reason that systems of wealth finance in early states are often associated with the development of market systems, with the Andes being the possible exception to the rule (see below).

While the distinction between staple and wealth finance is important, both are usually combined to generate the resources needed to support the institutional economy. For example, staple goods can be consumed in feasts or used to feed corvée laborers or to support client craftsmen who produce items used as gifts or in trade. In this way staple goods can be used to support local activities, while wealth goods can be used to finance state functions and mobilize resources over long distances (D'Altroy and Earle 1985; Earle 1994).

Mechanisms of Resource Creation

How were resources obtained for formal institutions? This question is critical for understanding the development of institutional economies. Households in mid-range societies normally were expected to make contributions to public rituals, community defense, or labor projects as required. In many instances, emerging leaders set the example and contributed more time and resources to community ventures than other households. For others, leaders organized and managed the production and assembly of resources using labor drawn largely from outside their household. In both situations, leaders functioned as managers of the community's assembled wealth. As a result, leaders had the ability to benefit individually from community activities especially if the accumulated wealth flowed into and through their households (Hirth 1996).

As a rule, the institutional economy of early complex societies was supported by a mixture of resource creation strategies. For purposes of discussion they can be classified into resource production, service, and mobilization strategies. Of these three, production and mobilization strategies were the most important. Resources raised through the services that leaders or institutions provided were often small and viewed as direct compensation for the services rendered. Examples include collection of fines for jural services and fees for divination, healing, casting spells, issuing writs, or conferring rights and immunities (Hirth 1996; Netting 1972; Rosenwein 1999). Production and mobilization strategies have a greater capacity to create resources, but they each face their respective obstacles of operation.

The assembly of staple goods for institutional use can be accomplished either by mobilizing donations from participating households or by creating the resources needed through forms of direct production. The direct production of agricultural goods for institutional support involved designating a plot of land for that purpose and mobilizing corvée labor to cultivate it. Resource ownership at the level of individual households was a function of the labor invested in its creation (Chapter 2). The same principle held for institutional production. The collaborative labor invested in agricultural activities on designated institutional lands made all participants collective stakeholders in the resulting harvest. The fruits of the labor were community resources or, in terms of institutional economy, resources designated for specific institutional use.

The same would be true of raising livestock in a communal herd or using collective labor for building community defenses, ritual structures, terraces, fencing, or irrigation systems on community or institutional lands. While these forms of direct production may be easy to initiate, they required careful planning to ensure that all needed resources were produced. Nevertheless, even with planning, the ability of direct production to meet institutional needs can be limited by the constraints of staple finance and the scale of production required to meet institutional needs.

Systems of direct production can also be used to finance the production of wealth goods. As mentioned above, leaders can support craftsmen to create wealth goods used for purposes of social reproduction (e.g., marriage, funerals) or trade. Wealth goods produced through patron–client relations could be used to build alliances with other leaders or to foster their own political ambitions (Brumfiel and Earle 1987b; Clark and Parry 1990). In precolonial Africa, local chiefs established patron–client relationships with foreign ironworkers to control the accumulation of metal spears important in bridewealth, hunting, and warfare (Guyer 1986). Once established, formal institutions often produced wealth goods as a means to support their own activities. A range of craft activities in Mesopotamia was carried out in temple and palace complexes. The Uruk palace was directly involved in the production of textiles and the manufacture of a range of products (and sculptures) in bronze, ivory, glassware, and other precious materials (Kemp 1972:673; Moorey 1994; Postgate 2004; Potts 1993; Renger 1979; Stein and Blackman 1993; Van de Mieroop 1987). In addition to local consumption, many of these goods were used in long-distance trade to obtain resources that were not locally available. Forms of direct production could include mining natural resources (e.g., salt, copper, jade, turquoise); harvesting and processing natural products such as dyes, spices, aromatic woods; hunting animals for their pelts, feathers, and ivory; or collecting resources like coral, marine shell, wax, and resin.

Resources can also be assembled the old-fashioned way by mobilizing them from individual households. When the quantity of resources required exceeded the limits of voluntary donations, resource mobilization could be mandatory or even coerced. This occurred as societies increased in size and the need for institutional resources expanded. The term most often used to refer to nonvoluntary forms of resource mobilization is taxation. Taxation has a long history of development in the ancient world and differed in form and severity depending on whether it was imposed on local or conquered populations. The most common forms of taxation include those on production and property, commercial tolls and tariffs, and individual head taxes. While the reasons for taxation varied, they were often imposed or increased during times of war when the need and cost of military defense increased (Brewer 1988; Finer 1975; Levi 1989:105–108).

Taxation has been called a mark of civilization by some (Samson 2002) and a curse of oppression by others (Fisher 1996). Whatever one's predisposition to being taxed, it differed from production strategies of institutional support in one very different and significant way. Taxation removed resources from the domestic budget of households *after* inputs and costs of production were expended. In this respect, taxation is a *net tax* on household production. This makes it distinct from direct production strategies that used corvée labor to produce resources on land set aside for institutional use. In direct production, labor is an *input* in the production process. While corvée labor was drawn from commoner households and reduced the amount of work they could perform for themselves by a small amount, it removed nothing from the harvest that the households relied on for their survival. It was less intrusive on the domestic economy than forms of taxation. Scholars who lump "labor tax" with taxation in finished goods miss this fundamental and important point. While labor service removed some labor from the household, it did not necessarily reduce the household domestic product since labor was often rotational and there was enough flexibility in the timing of subsistence tasks that labor service could be scheduled to not interfere with household agricultural production (Hagstrum 1999, 2001).

Costs of Institutional Resource Management

The costs of producing resources for institutional use varied depending on the form of production and the effort required to manage the physical, human, and social capital involved in production activities (Coleman 1998; Ostrom 1992:13). Even after resources are created, additional costs may be incurred preparing them for use. Management costs differ for staple and wealth goods. On the whole, however, management costs fall into three general categories: costs of storage, costs of transportation, and costs involved in resource conversion and/or use.

Costs of storage are highest under conditions of staple finance. Food is perishable and costlier to store than imperishable goods. Besides being bulky, food resources require the construction of storage facilities appropriate for preservation. Likewise, both perishable and imperishable resources required supervisory oversight to protect against spoilage, unauthorized use, and theft. While centralized storage may reduce the cost of supervision, it can increase the cost of moving and accessing institutional resources.[6]

All movement incurs costs of friction. These are especially high for bulk goods, and for this reason a good deal of long-distance trade involved lightweight, high-value goods. Renger (1999) reasoned that the cost of overland transportation in the ancient Near East made it prohibitive to move grain beyond 50–100 kilometers. He cites as an example the fact that barley did not move 70 kilometers in northern Assyria to alleviate a famine in AD 350 (Renger 1999:157). One way to reduce transportation costs in staple finance systems was through decentralized storage and warehousing grain and other resources on the institutional lands where they were produced or initially processed (e.g., at the threshing floor or olive press), and incurring transportation costs only at the moment of use. Storage at the household level prior to taxation is decentralized storage by definition. Of course, transportation costs became irrelevant when they were shifted to conquered groups as part of their tax obligation as occurred in early state empires (e.g., Sluyter 1993). Reliance on staple finance in areas with high transportation costs can pose special problems for managing institutions. One solution to this problem is to move the primary institutional consumers to where resources were stored instead of moving the resources to the consumers. This type of system is associated with the operation of peripatetic courts, discussed below (Kobishchanow 1987).

Finally, there are the costs of converting goods into the forms needed for final use. This can involve cooking, brewing, or other forms of resource processing. The presence of marketplaces provides institutions with a low-cost means of converting resources into alternative products (Chapter 9). An example of how the cost of resource conversion and transportation can be shifted to the commercial sector without using the marketplace is illustrated in medieval India. Here grain had to be mobilized from rural areas to supply the military and to provision large cities. The solution was to institute a head tax on farmers payable in coinage, thereby shifting the cost of resource conversion onto individual households. Farmers converted their grain to coin by selling it to Banjaras tribal pastoralists at their fields, who in turn transported it on their livestock across India to major points of consumption as part of their normal annual transhumance (Chapter 7). The Banjaras absorbed the transportation costs, while the government collected taxes in ready-to-spend coin (Habib 1982:83; Levi 1994). In this sense demanding payment of taxes in coinage reduced the institutional cost of converting grain to cash or other goods.

The question explored next is how systems of direct production were organized in different settings to produce resources for the institutional economy. The discussion begins by examining the organization of one of antiquity's earliest formal institutions, the Sumerian temple estate.

SUMERIAN TEMPLE ESTATES

Early state institutions appeared during the fourth millennium BC in the Tigris and Euphrates basin of southern Mesopotamia. Social complexity during the Uruk period (3900–2900 BC) is evident in the development of irrigation agriculture, intensive wool production, the development of a weaving industry, and long-distance trade to obtain metals and other goods (Algaze 2008; McCorriston 1997). An urban civilization emerged at this time that developed into Sumerian society during the third millennium BC. Writing appeared during the Uruk period as an instrument of institutional management, and the appearance of southern Mesopotamian–style texts in distant areas has been argued to represent an Uruk expansion to obtain resources not available in the alluvial lowlands of southern Mesopotamia (Algaze 1993; Stein 1999b). While the exact structure of economic and political relations during the Uruk period remain unclear, it was a period of dynamic interaction during which the main institutions of Sumerian civilization were forged and spread.

The ritual house or temple was the first formal institution in the Middle East. One of the earliest examples of special-purpose ritual buildings is found at the site of Göbekli Tepe in southeastern Turkey dating to Pre-Pottery Neolithic A and B periods (9000–7000 BC). Here round and rectangular structures were constructed using large T-shaped stone pillars weighing up to seven tons. A number of these pillars contained the engraved images of animals with ritualistic symbolism. Archaeologist Klaus Schmidt (2001, 2006, 2010) suggests these structures were early temples used by a dispersed population practicing a mixed economy that incorporated hunting and wild plant collecting with food production. Banning (2011) feels that the structures at Göbekli Tepe were ritualized domestic houses. Flannery and Marcus (2012:128–137) identify the ceremonial structures at Göbekli Tepe, Nevali Çori, and Cayönü as ritual clan houses. While not direct forerunners to the Sumerian temples of southern Mesopotamia, the elaborate stone architecture found at Göbekli Tepe indicates that the idea of temple households (Chapter 4), with or without permanent residents, was already well established in the Near East by the eighth millennium BC.

The fluorescence of civilization in Sumer occurred during the third millennium BC. The earliest institution in southern Mesopotamia was the temple, whose development can be traced both in the archaeological record and in textual sources. One of the earliest examples of a formal temple in southern Mesopotamia occurs at the site of Eridu where a small shrine was transformed into a platform temple during the fifth millennium BC (Stone 2013:157). While much remains to be learned about the organization and operation of Sumerian temples, their antiquity makes them an important place to begin the discussion of institutional economy in ancient state societies.

The temple was viewed both figuratively and literally as the deity's household (Hudson 1999a:119). The Sumerian word *é* or *e2* refers to a dwelling, house, room, family, clan, or household. It was used in textual sources to refer to two types of households: the familial household and the large public household of a temple or palace[7] (Gelb 1979). The deity resided in its temple house, and the temple's presence in the community gave residents the visible assurance that their god was with them (Robertson 1995). Deities had to be cared for and the priests who performed these duties were members of the temple household. Typical duties included offering sacrifices, conducting ceremonies, and overseeing rituals, as well as washing or clothing the god. Deities also required nourishment, so, like any familial household, temple households had lands on which their attendants could produce the requisite resources.

A series of small independent city-states developed in southern Mesopotamia by the beginning of the third millennium BC. Each of these city-states had patron deities that represented the community, the state, and the identity of its members. The territory of the city-state was the property of its patron deity, which was described as the fields of the god. Since the temple represented all the people in the community, there was a moral and spiritual obligation to sustain its deity (Postgate 1979). Whether a city had one or multiple temples, the community obligation remained the same: to serve the households of the gods and to provide the corvée labor needed to farm the temple, crown, and noble estates.

Early Assyriologists believed that the temple was more than the center of community and religious life; they believed that it was the political and economic center of a temple-state (Rubio 2007:12–18; Schneider 1920). The temple-state hypothesis held that all agricultural land was owned and controlled by the temple as the nucleus of a theocratic state. According to its proponents the basis of the temple's power was twofold (Deimel 1931; Falkenstein 1974; Renger 1979:250). The first was that the temple developed and controlled the irrigation systems on which agriculture in southern Mesopotamia depended. Second, since all of the land was the property of the gods, it was through service to the temple that households received access to farm land to cultivate.

The temple–state hypothesis no longer accurately reflects the role of the temple in Sumerian society (Foster 1981). Yes, the temple was a central institution, but subsequent research has shown that the temple neither owned all the land nor employed all of the population in its cultivation. Analysis of textual sources reveal that there was more land in Sumerian city-states than the temple directly controlled (Diakonoff 1991:38). Moreover, records of land sales on stone stelae indicate that some land was privately owned (Gelb 1969; Gelb et al. 1991; Liverani 2013:text 6.2). If the temple was not the center of a monolithic state economy, how should it be viewed within the context of the institutional economy?

The most parsimonious view is that temple households were organized for their own support like familial households. They were corporate organizations, and the architectural layout of Early Dynastic temples suggests that they were internally diversified institutions that had "spaces dedicated to the gods ... courtyards for communal gatherings, and areas for the accumulation of surplus (storehouses) and economic and administrative activities (archives and workshops)" (Liverani 2013:98). The temple's institutional economy was multifaceted and evolved over time in the face of economic opportunities and constraints. While agriculture was a primary source of income, temples also maintained large animal herds, produced textiles in temple workshops, granted loans with interest, and received gifts and pledges from individual donors. Considerable variation certainly existed in the way that temple households were organized from one city-state to another, and this is recognized explicitly in the characterization presented below.

As corporate entities, temples provided complete support to individuals who were full-time members of their households and partial support to those who worked on a periodic or part-time basis in specific tasks. Support for service was provided as rations of barley, oil, and wool. The dividing line between full- and part-time association with the temple is difficult to establish except where individuals appear in the textual sources as receiving food rations for an entire year (Gelb 1965). Nevertheless, the ration lists provide an inventory of the array of activities and specialists that temple estates supported. Textual sources identify six general categories of supervisory personnel,[8] nine specialized craftsmen and tradesmen,[9] eight general categories of service personnel,[10] and eight classes of supervisors who oversaw agricultural activities in addition to general farm labor.[11] The temple also supported women, children, and destitute members of society (Gelb 1972), many of whom were involved in processing wool and flax used in the weaving industry.[12] The importance of woolen textiles together with the need for animals in temple sacrifices and for food meant that temples kept herds of tens to hundreds of thousands of animals (Kozuh 2014). Temples also provided food rations for the shepherds, accountants, and herd supervisors that kept track of these herds.[13]

Temples controlled large quantities of land and operated as large corporate estates. Temple holdings were large, but they were not concentrated in a single locale; instead, the estate often consisted of large fields scattered across the landscape. Widell (2013) calculated the average size of domain fields for the kingdom of Lagash at 32–49 hectares (79–121 acres), 55% of which ranged from 36 to 45 hectares (89–111 acres).[14] These fields were long and narrow and would have been prepared for planting using coordinated teams of plowmen, who received food rations for their service. The identity of the workers who cultivated estate land is unclear. Temple administrators who supervised agricultural activities, stored the surpluses produced, and maintained temple infrastructure were supported by the resources of the temple household. But the system evolved over time. While seasonal corvée laborers were provided with food rations during the Early Dynastic period (ca. 2600 BC), permanent staff members eventually were provisioned with shares of the harvest or plots of land with farmers to cultivate them (Liverani 2013:105).

How temples originally acquired their land is a separate question. The view taken here is that temple lands were corporate estates that expanded their control over land in concert with the incorporation of rural communities into an expanding regional economy. The dynamic factor was the expansion of regional irrigation networks beginning in the fourth millennium BC. New estate lands were probably unused areas that were brought into cultivation with the expansion of local irrigation systems. This could have been done without dislocating preexisting fourth millennium communities, or with minimum disruption by offering existing rural communities access to new and more productive irrigation lands than they previously cultivated. In this fashion temples could have accumulated domain lands without dismantling older systems of community land tenure as suggested by Diakonoff (1975). As discussed in Chapter 4, community and kin-based systems of land holding were ubiquitous in pre-state societies around the world, and certainly would have existed from the Neolithic period across the Near East everywhere settled villages were found.

A second important source of institutional revenue was the production of textiles. According to Joy McCorriston (1997), woolen textiles fueled the political economy of ancient urban Mesopotamia. Linen and wool textiles were high-value goods because of the time and energy used to produce them. Their light weight made them natural trade items that groups used to obtain resources like timber, stone, and metal (Crawford 1973:233; Sallaberger 2014). The production of linen cloth stretched back into the Neolithic period (ca. 9000–6000 BC) (Schick 1988), but wool became the fiber of choice in textile production during the fourth millennium BC because of its lower labor requirements.[15] It was during the middle of the third millennium BC that texts from southern Mesopotamia began to refer to flocks of sheep linked to an emerging textile industry that funded the operation of temple households[16] (Breniquet 2014; Foster 2014).

The wool textile industry increased in importance into the Ur III period (2119–2004 BC), and textiles were used as a form of currency throughout the third millennium. Raw wool served as a unit of account, a standard of value, a reserve of value, and means of payment for land sales (Breniquet 2014:74; Charvát 2014:88). It is likely that finished textiles served the same purpose. Temples served as a failsafe collection center for poor women and orphans without other means of support where many were employed in textile manufacture in centralized workshops (Gelb 1972: Liverani 2013:106; Wright 2013). By the Ur III period, temples, palaces, and the households of wealthy elite were all involved in textile production.

By the end of the third millennium the scale of institutional textile production was massive. Large-scale production has been documented in at least seven cities, including Alsharraki, Lagash, Nippur, Puzrish-Dagan (Drehen), Umma, Ur, and Uruk. These weaving workshops could be quite large with the largest weaving mill at Guabba in the territory of Lagash employing 4,272 women and 1,800 children (Potts 1997:94). Together they controlled more than a million sheep for their wool (Algaze 2008:82), and textile workers received rations for their labor. Hartmut Waetzoldt, in a careful study of cuneiform texts, identified 15,000 textile workers in Lagash and 13,200 weavers in Ur (Waetzoldt 1972: 99, 106). Since 32–45% of the textile workers in Lagash were weavers, the implication is that the total number of textile workers in Ur was 20,000–22,000 individuals. Algaze (2008:85) estimates that 50,000–60,000 workers were involved in textile production in southern

Mesopotamia during Ur III, which represented an approximate ten-fold increase over a several-century period.

The foregoing discussion provides a partial description of what is known about the institutional economy of Sumerian temples. But what about the palace and the broader administration of secular affairs? Unfortunately, both the archaeology and the textual information do not provide much information about that until the late third millennium with the conquest of Sumer by Sargon the Great. It is during the Sargonic dynasty (2350–2193 BC) that the palace became a more visible institution in southern Mesopotamia, taking direct political and economic control of temple estates. Prior to that time, it is difficult to identify the palace and the political administrators as separate from the temple. Temple structures have been identified archaeologically from their architectural floor plans back into the fourth millennium BC (Heinz 2013). Separate palace structures have not been located (but see Bretschneider 2007), so it is likely that the head of the temple was also the chief administrator of the Sumerian state (Van De Mierop 2013:283). Marlies Heinz summarizes this problem in the following way: "To seek out which is a palace or a temple among the public buildings in the Sumerian world . . . seems unlikely to lead to definitive answers. The problem of the lack of clarity could be due to the fact that we are looking for a functional exclusivity that never existed" (Heinz 2013:198).

Nevertheless, warfare between city-states was a constant feature of the early Sumerian landscape, making military leadership the most likely pathway to permanent secular authority. From this perspective conflict between groups supplied the need for military leaders on a temporary basis that became permanent as episodes of conflict became more frequent (Charvát 1982; Van de Mieroop 2013). The accuracy of this interpretation for the pre-state period in Mesopotamian history remains to be seen. Unfortunately, the early cuneiform texts do not provide much information about secular administration and its relation to military activity. While there are texts that inventory military equipment such as bows and arrows, it is often unclear whether the institution acquiring them is the temple or a separate institution like the palace (Rubio 2006). These requests range from hundreds to the thousands of units, implying that a large and significant military force was provisioned.[17] All that is certain about these cuneiform texts is that they were recorded by scribes from a central urban institution.

The Sumerian temple was an internally complex and diversified corporate institution that supported itself and its members through a combination of agricultural, pastoral, and commercial craft activities. The temple economy was organized as a direct production system that combined both staple and wealth finance (Gavin 1987). The control of large blocks of land for grain cultivation supplied the food rations that supported the personnel working in the fields, the temple, and temple workshops. Where it could be shipped in bulk, grain was used to acquire resources that it lacked.[18] The temple owned large herds of animals used for meat, as beasts of burden, and for the secondary products they provided. Oxen were used for plowing and sheep provided wool. Woolen textiles were wealth goods that were produced in centralized workshops (*ergastula*) managed by institutional personnel similar to the way textile workshops were apparently run in Mycenean palaces (Nakassis et al. 2011:figure 4). The workers in Sumerian workshops included both poor dependent women and slaves (Gelb 1972) as well as craftsmen who supplied the temple with the tools it needed to operate, all of whom were supported with food rations. Finally, commercial relations were managed through merchants who operated as agents on their behalf. Analysis of Ur III administrative texts from Umma reveals that merchants regularly made purchases for institutions using raw wool valued in silver shekels (Sallaberger 2014).

Characterizing the institutional economy in Sumer during the third millennium BC is a challenging task. Not only did institutional economies change over time, but they varied in structure from urban center to urban center. One specific change that can be observed over time is the shift from subsistence rations to the use of prebends for the support of administrative personnel. Prebends are an assigned income derived from an institution in return for services rendered. They are a substitute for direct rations and appear to have developed as an alternative form of support for personnel within temple contexts.[19] What is important about prebends is that they tended to become hereditary and were passed down to family members rendering the same service unless they were sold to outsiders (Bongenaar 1997:140–141). Within the context of prebendal assignments, institutional land may have passed into the hands of individuals as private property.

Some of the earliest evidence for the use of prebends comes from cuneiform texts recovered from Fara during the Early Dynastic period (ca. 2600 BC). Here fields of different sizes were assigned to support tradesmen, scribes, fisherman, and other professionals. The size of these fields ranged from 1 to 3.6 hectares depending on the service duties involved. These fields were apparently sown and cultivated by temple personnel because allotments of seed grain for these fields were also recorded in the texts (Nissen et al. 1993:58–59). The section that follows explores another example of prebendal assignments that existed in pre-Columbian Central Mexico at the time of the Spanish conquest. Although much later in date, it provides a comprehensive description of how this system worked within the Aztec empire.

AZTEC PREBENDS AND PREBENDAL ESTATES

The term "Aztec" is a colloquial designation for the groups of Nahua people residing in Central Mexico that Hernando Cortés encountered in AD 1519.

The capital of the Aztec state was the city of Tenochtitlan in the Basin of Mexico where Mexico City is located today. The Aztec empire grew through conquest to cover an area of 160,000 square kilometers stretching from the Atlantic to the Pacific coasts between AD 1428 and 1519 (Berdan et al. 1996). It was composed of multiple small polities known as *altepemeh* (sing. *altepetl*), which together generated a huge tax revenue that flowed into the Aztec capital from conquered provinces (Berdan and Anawalt 1992; Hirth 2016:table 2.2). The result was a significant increase in the level of wealth within the Basin of Mexico, which was used to sponsor religious festivals and political activities and to support the warrior knights fundamental to military expansion. Tribute wealth was distributed by state institutions through gifts and grants of various sorts.

The competitive advantage that the Aztecs had over adjacent areas of Mesoamerica was the high population density in the Basin of Mexico, which was supported by a highly productive form of wetland agriculture known as *chinampas*.[20] The result was that the basin supported a contact period population of one million or more (Sanders et al. 1979). There were no beasts of burden in Mesoamerican or navigable rivers in the highlands, which resulted in high transportation costs for moving goods. Agriculture was intensified in the Aztec heartland, while high-value wealth goods were manufactured in the tributary provinces and transported to the capital on the backs of human porters (Blanton and Feinman 1984; Drennan 1994). The result was an institutional economy that combined staple and wealth finance.

Staple production within the Basin of Mexico was focused on the cultivation of four basic storable foods: maize, beans, amaranth, and chia. The turkey and the dog provided most of the animal protein in the diet.[21] Most of the goods used in wealth finance (e.g., plain and decorated cotton textiles, jade, gold, copper axes, exotic featherwork) were manufactured from nonlocal materials. Raw materials (feathers, raw cotton, precious stones, metals) were imported and made into an array of exotic goods and regalia by both independent and attached craftspersons. Agricultural production was intensified under the supervision of the Aztec state,[22] but the way that institutional support was organized remained relatively unchanged even as the Aztec empire grew in size.[23]

Land and labor were the basis for systems of staple finance that individuals accessed through the social system depending on their social standing and their rights to prebendal land assignments. All land fell within the territorial domain of a city-state (*altepetl*) which had a primary patron deity and was ruled by one or more elite lords (Hodge 1984). The traditional land-holding units within these domains were *calpultin* (singular *calpulli*). These were internally stratified land-holding groups organized around a shared identity based on ethnicity, kinship, hereditary membership, and/or a common profession. Commoners had hereditary, usufruct rights to *calpulli* land that was assigned to households for their support.[24] Land for the support of religious and administrative institutions as well as elite families was cultivated using corvée labor by members of the *calpulli*. The fields cultivated for the elite could be centralized and worked rotationally or attached to individual commoner fields (López Corral and Hirth 2012; Martínez 1984).

The formal institutions of the Aztecs resembled those of other ancient complex societies. At the center of the state was the palace of the ruler and the temple of its patron deity, Huitzilopochtli. The relationship between the palace and the temple was intertwined as the ruler's primary responsibility was maintenance of the gods. Other components of the institutional economy included the military, the judiciary, formal schools, marketplaces, noble families who filled administrative roles within the state, and the priests and temples of the many lesser deities. The personnel and the costs of operating these institutions were all supported through staple finance in essentially the same way, by the allocation of land as a prebendal assignment for a specific purpose. As a general principle, lands were attached to the institution rather than the individual. While prebendal land was under the control of the individual fulfilling a specific duty, it retained its institutional affiliation and was reassigned to the next officeholder as needed. In principle, institutional land circulated among users in much the same way as land did within the *calpulli* without it becoming permanently alienated from its social context in the way that private property did.

Nahuatl was the language of the Aztecs, and its vocabulary provides a great deal of insight into the different types of institutional land. Seventeen types of land are known from documentary sources, which can be grouped into six different usage categories (Table 5.1). All of these land categories were subdivisions of community or institutional lands within the *altepetl*. Temple lands (*teopantlalli*, *teotlalli*) were assigned to support religious institutions; many of these were small temples in individual *calpultin* and land allotments were made from their respective land holdings. Military lands (*milchimalli, yaotlalli*) provided food for the army during military campaigns as well as provisioning garrisons established throughout the empire. Noble family lands (*huehuetlalli, pillalli*) were those controlled by the elite as individual patrimonial estates. These land assignments tended to be hereditary as long as families retained their elite status. As such, elite estates tended to resemble prebendal estates whose size waxed and waned (or disappeared) with their family's political fortunes and status. Included in this category is woman's land or dowry land (*cihuatlalli*) that elite women brought into their marriage (Terraciano 2001). There is some evidence that the hereditary entrenchment of noble families allowed some transfer of land through purchase (Offner 1983), although it is likely that most of the purchased land (*tlacohualli*) was a post-conquest phenomenon (Table 5.1).

TABLE 5.1 *Types of land in preconquest Central Mexico*

Land category	**Nahuatl term**[a]	Type of land
Community land	*altepetlalli*	Land of the *altepetl*
	calpullalli	Land of the *calpulli*
Administrative land	*mexicatlalli*	Land of the Mexica (conquest)
	tecpantlalli	Land of the *tecpan*
	tequitlalli	Tribute land, tribute field
	teuctlalli	Land of the lord, ruler
	tlatocatlalli	Ruler's office lands, ruler's palace land
Temple land	*teopantlalli*	temple land
	teotlalli	Sacred lands, land of the temple and the gods
Military land	*cacalomilli*	Land for military supplies
	milchimalli	Land for military supplies
	yaotlalli	War land
Noble family lands	*cihuatlalli*	Woman's land, possible dowry
	huehuetlalli	Inherited land, ancestral land, patrimonial land
	pillalli	Private land of noble families
	tecpillalli	Ancient land of the nobles
Other	*tlalcohualli*	Purchased land

[a] *Tlalli* is the word for land with the functional assignment attached as a prefix to form a composite word.

Administrative lands were assigned to support specific activities. Land within each *calpulli* was assigned to support their elite leaders, their administrative center known as the *tecpan*,[25] and its associated activities. Prebendal lands were attached to specific offices. Foremost among these were lands to support the paramount rulers (*teuctlalli*) and the operation of the palace (*tlatocatlalli*) (Table 5.1). Other functionaries also were supported with prebendal land. Judges, for instance, had lands set aside to finance their administrative duties even though as members of the elite they had a hereditary estate to support their families. Knight societies were especially important in Aztec society for military operations. Commoners inducted into one of these military orders were awarded land for their support and were eligible for additional low-level administrative positions within society (Hassig 1988:29). It appears that prebendal assignments also were made to ambassadors and tribute collectors to carry out their duties (Hirth 2016).

The key ingredient in prebendal assignments was how the land was cultivated.[26] In Mesoamerica this land was worked with corvée labor drawn from commoner households. Labor service was based on the concept of *tequitl*, that is, the duty and service that everyone in society had to serve the gods (Carrasco 1978:29). The *tequitl* of the nobles was to rule justly and attend to religious matters. Commoner males were expected to supply labor to farm fields, transport goods, engage in public construction projects, and produce the other goods that society needed. Female labor likewise was mobilized through *tequitl* obligations to provide a range of tasks including cooking, cleaning, child care, spinning, and weaving textiles.

Corvée labor was mobilized from communities on a rotating basis to minimize its effect on individual households.[27] This was possible because the participating population was large and corvée rotations were short or scheduled in a way that allowed households to cultivate their own fields around service obligations. Colonial documents provide insight into how a large institutional field (*tlatocatlalli*) was cultivated to support the ruler's palace of Texcoco. The field was 110–121 hectares in size and was cultivated using rotational labor drawn from households in several different communities. The work was a collaborative effort with the labor commitment divided equally based on community size to cultivate, harvest, store, and transport the food produced to the palace where it was used. The available data suggest that corvée labor probably averaged only about 10% of a household's annual work budget.[28]

Military conquest was a major source of wealth goods for the institutional economy. Looting was not a common facet of Aztec conquest. Instead, conquered provinces were required to pay specified levies of tribute goods four times per year as their tax obligation (Berdan and Anawalt 1992). Thirty-eight provinces in the Aztec empire paid regular tribute in goods produced using corvée labor often from locally available materials (Berdan 1992b). Regions required to supply goods they did not produce exchanged what they had with merchants for what they needed (Hirth 2016). Although the range of tribute items was diverse, the most important items collected were finished textiles (Hirth 2016:table 2.2). Berdan (1992a) estimates that 128,000–255,360 finished textiles entered the Aztec capital each year, fully one-half of which were highly negotiable plain cotton *quachtli* that was used as a form of currency in the marketplace. The next most abundant and valued materials were green, blue, red, and yellow feathers used by craftspersons and in the state-sponsored palace workshop known as the *totocalli* to make special regalia given to visiting dignitaries and used in special celebrations throughout the year. While important, the level of state-sponsored craft production as a basis for institutional support was minimal in comparison to the multiple textile workshops associated with institutions in Mesopotamia.

Corvée labor was also mobilized for public work projects that included building or repairing temples, administrative buildings, streets, and canals. Particularly important for the Aztec capital was the construction of dykes to regulate water levels and prevent flooding within the central lakes region.[29] The Aztecs undertook large-scale hydraulic works to regulate lake levels and manage agricultural production in the wetland *chinampas* fields. Similarly, when weapons or craft goods were needed for military or administrative use, artisans were mobilized to supply them in lieu of other forms of service.

The expansion of the Aztec empire was dependent on its citizenry supplying military service. State expansion was linked to religious doctrine. The Aztecs believed that they lived in an unstable world that was stabilized by providing sacrificial victims to their patron deity Huitzilopochtli, who was nourished and strengthened on human blood and hearts. It was through conflict that large numbers of sacrificial victims were procured. Individuals who procured a sacrificial victim in battle were rewarded with gifts of wealth goods that included embroidered textiles obtained from the tribute network. As warriors were successful in obtaining sacrificial victims, they increased their status, eventually becoming eligible for entrance into a knight society. Warfare expanded the empire, but it had a high overhead cost that was covered by the wealth goods the tribute network provided.

Political and religious institutions funded an array of public feasts carried out each month for different Aztec gods (Durán 1971) and the inauguration of political functionaries (Broda 1978). These celebrations required large quantities of food, dance entertainments, and gifts for all who attended them. Particularly spectacular were the sacrificial events when both allies, enemies, and leaders of the groups that the Aztecs planned to conquer were invited to witness the sacrifice and unfortunate demise of warriors who chose to oppose them. All attendees were showered with gifts during these celebrations, which were intended to intimidate their enemies into submission. They were an expensive but effective form of political propaganda.

The marketplace was another institution that played an important role in the institutional economy. While staple and wealth goods provided a variety of complementary resources for funding institutional activities, having the right quantities of food and gifts defied even the most careful institutional planning. It was here that the marketplace was indispensable for converting staples to wealth goods and vice versa. The prebendal and hereditary estates of noble families produced more food than they could realistically consume. What they did was sell their surplus to retail merchants who resold it in the marketplace. Likewise, goods entering through the tribute system represented stored wealth that could be converted to food, cacao, and manufactured wealth goods as circumstances required. The marketplace reduced the costs of converting resources needed for institution support as well as providing opportunities for households to produce goods for sale to augment their domestic productivity (Chapter 9).

PRODUCTION MONOPOLIES AND THE CHINESE INSTITUTIONAL ECONOMY

Control of scarce or vital resources has always been an avenue to power and wealth. As discussed in the previous chapter, the production and control of wealth goods could be an important source of political power and alliance building in prestige goods economies (Blanton et al. 1996; Brumfiel and Earle 1987a; Junker 1993; Trubitt 2003). It could be argued that the control of basic necessities and utilitarian items could have a greater potential impact on the lives of the larger population than wealth goods even if it was difficult to achieve except in special circumstances (e.g., Clark 1987; Flad 2011; Junker 1993). The control of salt was one of those special circumstances.

Salt is a necessary resource that the human body needs for proper metabolic maintenance. It aids in digestion, helps to regulate blood pressure, maintains hydration levels, invigorates the nervous system, aids in proper musculatory functions, protects the stomach lining, and helps to prevent stroke or heat prostration. Salt was the world's first food preservative for both meat and vegetables. In meat preservation, salt draws out moisture and creates an inhospitable environment for bacterial growth. Likewise, it slows decomposition and serves as a pickling agent for vegetables.[30] Wars were fought and political policies shaped around the control of salt sources (Kurlansky 2002). It functioned as a form of commodity money in some societies (Godelier 1978b) and served as the basis for extensive interregional trade in others (Andrews 1983; Bovill 1970). Trade in salt provided profit for merchants. Combine this with the leverage that the control of salt has over the people who need it on a daily basis and you have an effective strategy that could be used to fund aspects of the institutional economy.

Ancient China stands as one of the best examples of how control over the production and distribution of a basic resource like salt could be used to support state institutions. The sale of salt was a cash mobilization strategy used to support the political bureaucracy. Archaeological evidence indicates that salt was produced and traded across central China as early as the fourth millennium BC (Flad and Chen 2013:146). The early support base of imperial China was corvée labor and a tax on land. Nevertheless, in 119 BC the emperor Han Wudi instituted a new policy. Propelled by the need for money to fund military campaigns, Wudi instituted the first state-wide salt monopoly. The salt monopoly was designed to support the central political bureaucracy and involved the following organizational features:

> In the system of monopoly prohibitions (*quejin*), also referred to as monopoly sales (*quemai*), the Han state restricted entry into the market, took ownership of all salt, and assumed command over production, which had been in the hands of small local producers. The government

> provided equipment and funds to workers, often landless peasants it had drafted into salt production. It specified the size of evaporation pans to facilitate reckoning how much was manufactured each day ... the product was not the producer's to dispose of freely; all salt had to be submitted to the state, which punished private production. After collecting salt, the state undertook to transport it to points of distribution. It implemented empire-wide sales to consumers in which the price greatly exceeded the costs of production and distribution.
>
> (Chien 2004:6)

The high universal demand for salt, the localized nature of its production, and the high revenue stream it could provide made it a perfect target for a state-controlled monopoly. This was a vertical monopoly in the sense that the state controlled all related forms of production and distribution. The rationale for control over salt production can be traced back to the Guanzi treatise, a 7th-century AD philosophical and political text written by Guan Zhong. The logic for a salt monopoly was that any increase in the head tax for adults and children would have resulted in opposition, while the cost of salt purchases by consumers provided revenue without resulting in a separate tax payment (Chien 2004:5). The salt monopoly was organized as a separate bureaucratic administration or directorate within the state to manage production and to collect revenues. While the organization of the salt monopoly changed over time, it remained an important source of institutional revenue for more than 2,000 years until the beginning of the 20th century AD (Kwan 2001). The broader citizenry was required to purchase salt, which resulted in the extraction of revenue that has been referred to as a "salt tax" (*gabelle*) (Kwan 2001) even though it does not conform to the normal definition of what constitutes a tax (Chapter 6). This type of forced transaction is more correctly referred to as a compulsory purchase order (CPO).[31]

Salt was produced using four distinct processing technologies. Sea salt was produced along the coast using evaporation techniques. It produced the greatest quantity of both product and profit. Pond salt was processed using evaporation from a large salt lake owned by the state at Xiezhou. Earth salt was extracted from alkaline soil by boiling brine. It produced both the lowest quantity and least desirable form of salt. The fourth type of salt production was well salt (*jingyan*). This form of salt production is one of the most fascinating, not because of the quantity of salt produced but because of the technology involved. Wells were dug and salt brine was hauled out by buckets and the brine boiled to remove the salt. In the 11th century AD production shifted to something more akin to modern well drilling employing bamboo piping and reaching depths of up to 1,000 meters below the surface. While the natural gas encountered in deep drilling was originally thought to represent devil spirits, it was eventually captured and employed to fuel the stoves to boil the brine perhaps as early as the 4th century AD (Chiang 1983; Flad 2011:38–39). Income records from AD 997 provide a breakdown of relative contributions of these four types of salt to the overall production enterprise and revenue stream: sea salt (69%), pond salt (21%), well salt (7%), and earth salt (3%) (Chien 2004:43).

The organization of the salt monopoly evolved over time, but it always involved tight bureaucratic control over production. The country was divided into 15 administrative directorates[32] that represented autonomous production and marketing districts. Salt produced within each directorate had to be sold there and could not move between them under severe penalty.[33] Production levels in each directorate were geared to regional population levels. Each saltern had a production manager who hired peasants to produce salt, set production quotas, supplied the equipment, and stored the finished product in special warehouses. Households were paid for their work and supplied with fuel and other supplies needed for production; some households also may have received a rice stipend along with wages. Each directorate was also responsible for the fiscal accountability of expenditures and collecting revenues.

The scale of these operations was immense. Finished salt was collected, stored, and then moved to centralized warehouses for later collection by secondary agents or merchants, who sold it to retailers for distribution to consumers (Chiang 1983). According to the Songshi Salt Treatise, disruptions in salt production in the Huainandong directorate in AD 1165 required that 20% of the salt produced at the towns of Tzonghou and Taizhou be moved to the neighboring administrative district of Jingxibei and stored at the town of Zhenzhou. The Huainandong directorate was on the coast and had eight different production towns that processed sea salt. The salt had to be moved over 900 kilometers by a combination of overland and canal transportation to reach Zhenzhou. While 20% of the salt from two towns does not sound like much in the whole scheme of things, the enormity of the move can be appreciated by the fact that 280 new warehouses had to be built in Zhenzhou to accommodate the moved salt stocks. Similarly, when the government organized the transportation of salt, it did so in large convoys of boats and carts using corvée labor. Again, the scale of movement was immense. Waterborne convoys employed anywhere from ten to thirty boats. During the Song dynasty (AD 960–1279), 170 convoys were employed to move salt each year on a regular basis that involved between 1,700 and 5,100 individual boats (Chien 2004:50, 229–230, maps 3, 5, 8).

As in all things managed by government, the salt monopoly did not always run smoothly. The system was fraught with problems. Corruption was the norm, the flow of salt fluctuated between gluts and scarcity, smuggling was common, and salt was spoiled or contaminated in storage or transport.[34] Government bureaucrats were corrupt and made money from the system through clandestine sales and by manipulating units of measurement to their benefit. Managers often were irresponsible and did not care if salt was damaged or spoiled once it was out of their control. The general rule was that the further salt moved, the more unusable it became as people stole it and mixed contaminants in with shipments to replace the bulk illegally removed.[35] Consumers recognized this problem, which meant that smuggled salt was preferred, not only because it was cheaper but also because it was cleaner. Problems in supply were common within regions because bureaucrats ran their directories as franchised monopolies and protected them from encroachment. Finally, salt prices were often too high for the poor to purchase it, resulting in the accumulation of unused surpluses while the most needy segments of the population often went without this necessary resource (Chien 2004:51–54, 229).

The organization of the salt monopoly changed over time in an attempt to remedy the problems that beset it. Beginning in AD 706 private merchants were given the right to move salt in an attempt to make distribution more efficient. Of course, this was another institutional income opportunity, and merchants had to pay a surcharge for the ability to resell salt. The involvement of private merchants was tightly regulated, restricting where they could obtain and sell salt. The advantage of using merchants was threefold. First, it was more efficient since government directed transportation organized using corvée labor ruined a large quantity of salt during transport. Second, government transportation often expropriated the carts, animals, and boats of villagers to move salt, which was a burden on the peasant population. Third, and most important, merchant transportation was cheaper. Merchants supplied their own carts or boats at no expense and were willing to operate in areas of low demand. Since merchants also transported fodder and grain for the army, it was a complementary means of distribution that the government could employ when it was to their advantage to do so. Nevertheless, the role of merchants in salt transportation was far from consistent. In the late 10th century AD, the Song court rescinded and reinstated the use of merchants to transport pond salt five different times. Eventually, merchants came to dominate the distribution and sale of salt up into the 20th century (Chiang 1983; Chien 2004:7–9, 49–59; Ho 1954; Kwan 2001).

The important question is, How important was the salt monopoly in generating institutional income? In a word: very. From the 9th century AD onward salt revenues produced more income than agrarian taxes! But salt was not the only production monopoly that the state derived revenue from during the Song dynasty. As early as the 10th century AD the government became involved in iron production both to obtain raw material for the manufacture of weapons and to extract revenue from smelters. Because large iron pans were used in salt boiling, the two forms of production were combined into a single Salt and Iron Bureau. The wine monopoly was the second most productive money maker for the state, only exceeded by salt sales. Since the production of wine was more difficult to control, the state resorted to franchising wineries for fixed-rate production and charged fees for retail sales. Tea was the third major monopoly of the state (Rossabi 1970:142–143). The production and distribution of tea was organized in much the same way as salt, and from the 12th century AD onward tea and salt were combined in the same directorate. Spice and alum production were other commodities that the state used to extract revenue through monopolistic production (Chien 2004:36–37; Wagner 2001).

The importance of these direct production systems is evident in their fiscal contribution to the institutional economy. Documentation of total fiscal expenditures from AD 1168 indicates that monopolized industries were the state's primary source of institutional income. Of the year's total expenditures, the controlled substances of salt (38%), wine (25.5%), and tea and spices (5.5%) contributed fully 69% of the state's total annual revenue. Salt constituted anywhere from one-third to one-half of the state's total budget revenue depending on the century. Salt was an important revenue source throughout China's long history and still constituted 11.9% of state revenues in AD 1753 and 15.4% as late as AD 1908 (Chien 2004:34–36; Wang 1971).

It is estimated that 60,000–100,000 commoner households were employed in salt production under this managed production system during Song dynasty (AD 960–1279). This benefited the producer households by supplying them with a steady income and exempting them from ancillary corvée labor. But labor relations did not always go smoothly. Throughout the 13th century more than 100 uprisings occurred that were instigated either by salt-producing households because of poor work conditions or by the salt-starved peasantry. The purchase of salt was a requirement rather than an option and the state mandated purchases of salt. Wealthy households were required to buy twice as much salt as poor households.[36] Most notable was the creation of special purchase obligations where consumers were required to purchase salt whether they needed it or not. Some of these special-purchase levies included fisherman salt, shop owner salt (both of these for preserving food), land-selling salt, winning-a-case and losing-a-case salt for litigants, scholarship salt, corvée and completing-the-corvée salt, long-life salt, and afterlife salt (Chein 2004:43, 57, 81). The unique nature of Chinese institutional economy is that rather than extracting increasingly larger quantities of resources directly from household subsistence budgets, the state required that households buy important inputs for household maintenance such as salt and tea from institutionally controlled monopolies.

REDISTRIBUTION, ZOARITES, AND THE INKA STATE

Karl Polanyi (1944, 1957) identified redistribution as an important form of economic redistribution, which John Murra (1956, 1980) argued was the foundation of the Andean institutional economy. Redistribution is important because of the implied importance that it has for household provisioning (Polanyi 1944, 1957; Service 1962, 1975). Redistribution is no longer recognized as a major form of economic organization and organizing force in the evolution of leadership and social complexity as Polanyi and Service originally proposed (Christakis 2011; Earle 1977, 2011; Nakassis et al. 2011; Silver 1995). Yet the collective production, assembly, and redistribution of material goods did occur in ancient and premodern societies. It is evident in the organization of the traditional potlatch in North America, in New Guinea moka feasting, and generalized forms of patron sponsorship at different levels of society (Chapters 3 and 4). The following discussion examines the relationship between collective production and redistribution in two past societies. It begins by examining how collective production and redistribution operated in the 19th-century community of Zoar, Ohio. This is followed by an examination of Inka institutional economy in AD 1532,[37] which Murra (1980) argued was organized around the principle of redistribution. It is generally argued that the structure and integration of the Inka state employed the same principles of within-group reciprocity and forms of redistribution that were found at the level of small, individual communities. To understand Inka institutional economy, therefore, requires contextualizing it in relation to Andean community organization.

A few words need to be said about redistribution as a preamble to this discussion. There has been constructive discontent with Polanyi's original proposition that redistribution was a fundamental mode of organization for ancient economy (Earle 1977, 2011; Nakassis et al. 2011; Silver 1995). Polanyi was wrong about redistribution as a unitary mode of economic organization in the same way that Marxists were wrong about fixed stages of economic evolution based on forms of production. But that does not change the fact that redistribution is a documented form of economic organization that can work under specific circumstances. Examples include production for feasts and the assembly and distribution of specific prestige goods mobilized through the social hierarchy. The key, however, is understanding what those circumstances were and how redistribution interfaced with other forms of economic activity including prestation, reciprocal exchange, barter, and even market activity.

Redistribution and the Community of Zoar

Redistribution works best as a form of economic distribution in small-scale settings,[38] where a narrow range of goods is collected and redistributed, and where it was used as a provisioning strategy for *specific* purposes. One such case was the German separatists of Württemberg who emigrated to the United States and founded the religious community of Zoar in Tuscarawas

County, Ohio, in AD 1817 (Fernandez 2003). The Zoarites established a communal society to pay off the debt for the 5,500 acres of land purchased to support themselves. Their community operated as a perfect redistributive society until collective ownership of resources was abandoned through formal vote on March 10, 1898, as a result of pressures from the outside world and failure to adapt to new economic circumstances at the beginning of the 20th century (Ohio State Historical Society 1952:27, 63–68). The communal nature of the society was documented by Emilius Randall (1904), who visited and interviewed members of the community in 1898 and 1899. The principles of redistribution were laid out in the community's articles of association: "The members of the Society agree with each other that their property of every description should be held and used as a common fund for their general benefit and they appointed certain agents to manage their concerns and provide for their support" (Randall 1904:24).

The Zoar community agreed to a universal partnership of profits for all its members[39] "whether from property or industry," and it continued to operate that way well after the community's debt was paid off in 1830. The community operated communally and collectively. It collectively farmed its land; maintained herds of sheep and cattle; operated a range of enterprises, including a dairy, a brewery, a bakery, and a mill; and established a variety of shops to provide the community with the goods it needed (Figure 5.1). Any surplus produced was sold for profit to the outside world.[40] Bread, sweetbread, meat, cheese, butter, milk, beer, cider, and other food staples necessary for daily life were distributed equally to community members based on household size. So too were goods such as shoes and cloth for manufacturing clothes. The items the community could not produce (e.g., tea, coffee, rice, sugar, spices) were purchased from the outside and redistributed to households from a central magazine. Work was carried out collectively. The work horn blew each morning at 6:00 AM, and people who did not have regularly assigned jobs would assemble at Number One House to be allocated their work for the day (Ohio State Historical Society 1952:50). Children from 3 to 14 years of age were kept in a central nursery that allowed women to work full-time outside the household. The success of the system is evident in that the community maintained a central park, constructed a hotel for tourists, loved music, and maintained their own public band. In terms of the essentials, community members ate well, enjoying up to five meals per day (Ohio State Historical Society 1952:49).

The community of Zoar operated as an efficient redistributive society for more than 80 years because it was small and did not exceed about 300 people at any point in time. Redistribution, however, does not work well as a *general* organizational principle for large-scale societies because of the colossal managerial costs involved in mobilizing, storing, and redirecting all of the different

5.1 Men and women of the Zoar community collectively harvesting one of their communal grain fields in AD 1888. (Photograph courtesy of the Ohio History Connection (AL00003) (Photograph dated AD 1888).

resources and services needed by *all members of society*. The enormity of this task is compounded when the scale of the society is considered alongside the different internal economic subsystems operating in and across regions at the household and institutional levels. The only effective way this could be accomplished is if strong administrative control was maintained over specific resource domains that were efficiently and equitably distributed to the households and institutions that needed them. As already seen in the case of the Chinese salt monopoly, bureaucratic efficiency was inversely proportional to its size, often leading to graft and resistance (e.g., smuggling, theft) when the system did not work equitably for all those it was intended to serve. The combination of these circumstances makes the examination of the model of Andean redistribution particularly interesting for developing a comparative understanding of both household and institutional economy.

The Inka Economic System

At the outset it is important to understand the unique set of environmental conditions that structured resource distributions throughout the Andes and how they influenced pre-Columbian economic interaction. The Andes are characterized by exaggerated vertical relief of up to 5,000 meters within a compressed horizontal landscape averaging about 400 kilometers. This brings sharply differing resource zones with different rainfall levels into close proximity of one another as one moves from west to east across the Andes mountains (Figure 5.2). The Pacific coast is rich in marine life that includes fish, shellfish, sea mammals, and fishing birds. The shore along the coast is a desert[41] except in the coastal valleys, which were transformed into productive agricultural land using irrigation. In the middle valley, or *yungas* zone (300–2,300 meters), people produced a range of products including maize, cotton, coca, chili peppers, and a range of tropical fruits. Higher up the valley are the *quechua* (3,100–3,500 meters) and *suni* zones (3,500–4,000 meters) where maize and vegetable agriculture give way to the cultivation of the native grains of quinoa and cañihua, and a variety of different tubers including the potato, ulluco, and oca. The *puna* above 4,000 meters is a tundra grassland and home to the Andean camelids: llama, alpaca, guanaco, and vicuña. Further to the east, the Andes drop down into the tropical lowlands again crossing the *quechua* and *yungas* zones before reaching the Amazonian rain forest (D'Altroy 2002:27–32). The microvariability created by relief makes it possible to be within a single day's travel or less from another major resource zone.

Households residing in these different zones wanted resources produced in each of the others. Meat and wool were produced from llama and alpaca herds pastured in the *puna*, while fish and cotton were available on the coast. Likewise, maize, coca, and peppers were grown in the mid-valley zones on

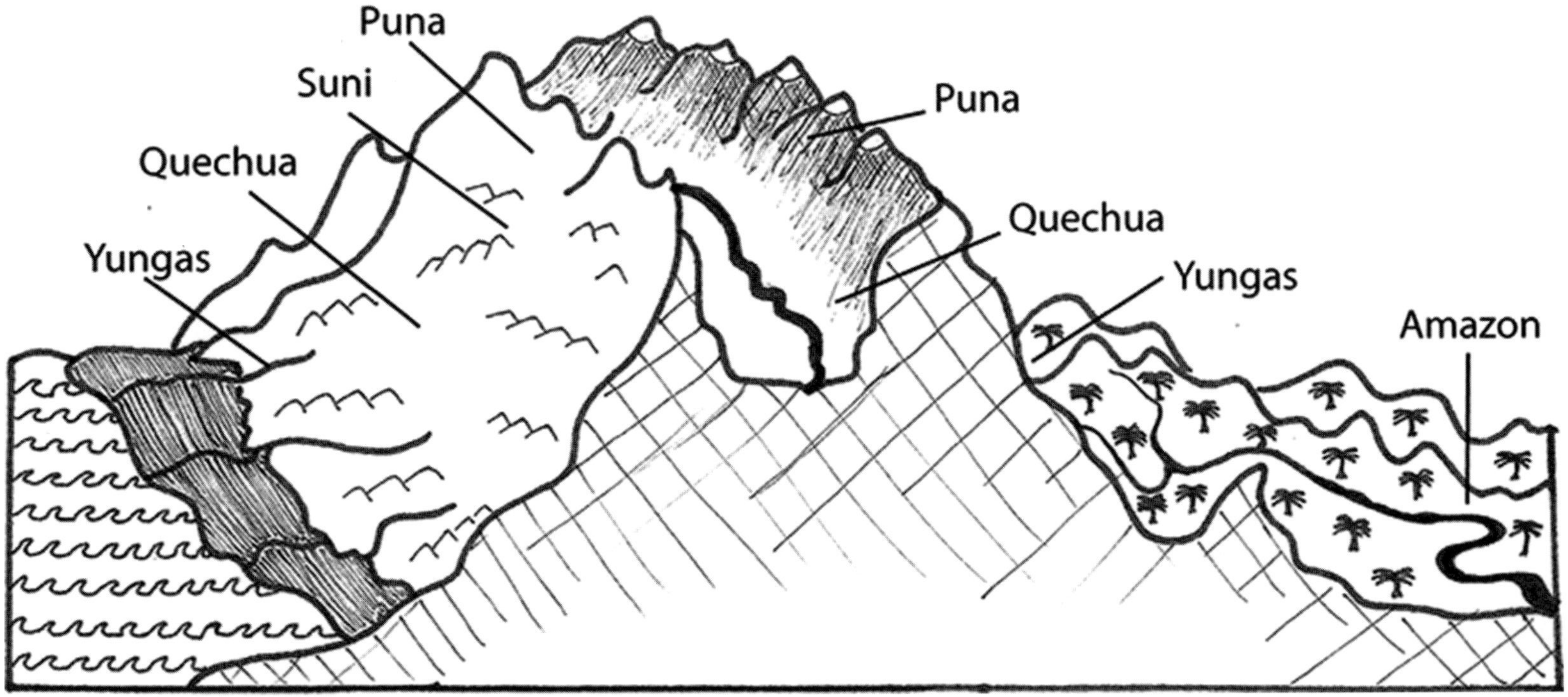

5.2 A cross-section of major environmental resource zones in the Andes. (Redrawn from D'Altroy 2002:Figure 2.1 by Shae Rider and author)

both sides of the Andes compared with the grains and tubers cultivated in the low and high mountain valleys. The fundamental goal of Andean households was self-sufficiency, or at least the ability to access all the staple goods used in everyday life. There were two ways that households accessed this diverse array of resources. One way was to move goods through formal and informal interregional exchange networks that might include some form of market system. The development of marketplaces was not the Andean way (Earle 2001:313). The other was through regional redistribution where households accessed resources from different environmental zones through centrally coordinated systems of production and distribution at the community and regional levels.

Murra proposed that the Andean economy was based on two fundamental principles. The first was that of the *ayllu*, and the communities to which they belonged sought to obtain direct access to resources in each of the different ecological zones across the Andes. The *ayllu* were local corporate and hereditary descent groups that held land and resources for use by its members (D'Altroy 2002:326). The strategy employed was one of zonal complementarity where community leaders sought to establish colonies in different areas to produce resources that could be accessed by the community as a whole. Second, Murra proposed that resources from these different zones were collected and transported between colony segments by communal llama caravans that moved from the highlands to the coast and back again, acquiring and redistributing resources and craft goods as they went. The strategic placement of satellite colonies in different resource zones created an archipelago of group segments distributed over space that maintained membership in their parent *ayllu* communities and the rights to the resources communally produced.[42] In theory, the resources mobilized from each of these different ecological zones were redistributed to all the participating households. Murra's model was a highly centralized and top-down form of institutional organization that both accounted for the relocation of ethnic groups within the Andes and provided a model for the movement of resources between different ecological zones in the absence of marketplaces.

This model of zonal complementarity has rightly or wrongly dominated the thinking about Andean economic organization for more than half a century (Goldstein 2013; La Lone 1982; Murra 1956, 1985a, 1985b; Van Buren 1996; Wachtel 1981). While it accounts for aspects of how groups accessed land from communities in different environmental zones through the reciprocal exchange of labor groups, it does not serve as a general model for a large-scale redistributive economy for two reasons. First, the model proposes that zonal complementarity was designed to produce, move, and redistribute large quantities of food and other staple goods to households from the Pacific coast to the Amazonian lowlands and back again. Archaeological research has demonstrated that this did not happen. Food and staple resources generally did not move long distances. Instead, households primarily relied on local resources, and goods generally remained within their immediate regions (Costin 2001b; Earle 2001:table 12.1; Hastorf 2001a). Second, even if the system was organized as Murra proposed, it would not have distributed resources evenly to all participating households as the classic model of redistribution predicts. Why? Because the archipelago colonies were small and did not have the production capacity to fulfill the consumption needs of the entire ethnic group of which they were a part.

It is true that small colonies were established in the territories of adjacent polities through reciprocal agreements between their respective leaders. But this relationship is more reminiscent of a share-cropping arrangement with local elites. A lord in one area would send subjects to reside and work on lands of an adjacent lord located in a different resource zone. The host lord would receive a share of the resources produced from their labor as did the lord who sent them and to whom they owned their primary allegiance (Ramírez 1985; Topic 2013). Under these conditions a lord could mobilize small quantities of resources from different resource zones (Van Buren 1996). But these resources were not necessarily redistributed to the broader community for individual household consumption. In her study of colonial documents, Rostworowski de Diez (1977:265) argued that state redistribution *never* provided subsistence resources for the commoner population. Instead, Inka households were self-sufficient units, and where they could not produce all the resources they required, they procured them through a range of household gift and exchange relationships (Mayer 2002; Stanish and Coben 2013).

Nevertheless, research by John Murra has been instrumental in identifying the basic structure of direct production systems in the Andean world that have been enhanced by subsequent archaeological and ethnohistoric research (Bauer 1996; D'Altroy 2001:42, 2002; D'Altroy and Hastorf 2001; Earle 2001; Goldstein 2013; Mujica 1985; Stanish 1992; Topic 2013). He established that in local settings, land was owned and cultivated "*ayllu* by *ayllu*" with people residing in communities made up of several *ayllu* (Murra 1980:29). Households were granted usufruct rights to *ayllu* land that they cultivated for their individual support. Land was assigned based on need and function.[43] *Ayllu* land also was assigned to support the *curaca*, or community leader, as well as religious shrines for local deities. The local *curaca* drew on corvée labor to cultivate their fields and tend their herds in exchange for the service that elites provided as leaders of the community (Hastorf and D'Altroy 2011:11).

The important point within the Andean system is that these fields were worked corporately by all members of the community using the *mita*, the corvée work obligation. According to Cobo (1979:212), everyone, including leaders, participated in cultivating institutional fields. Work was divided into equal parts depending on the number of households in the community. Each *mita* task, or section of work,

> was called a *suyu*, and, after the division, each man put into his section his children and wives and all the people of his house to help him. In this way, the man who had the most workers finished his part, or *suyu*, first and among them he was considered a rich man; and the poor man was he who had no one to help him finish his work, so he spent a longer time working. This same system was followed by each of the lords and *curacas* in his district, the most important man starting the work and soon leaving it, and the nobles following him according to their rank and social standing.
>
> (Cobo 1979:212)

The assertion that elite were involved in working the fields is likely an exaggeration, with their involvement in the work being more symbolic than real. But the important point is that collective action was the operative principle in producing the food and other staple resources that institutions and community leaders required. Planning was important in staple finance systems, and this carried over to the allocation of land within the *ayllu*. Even the needs of individual families were collectively assessed in terms of their respective subsistence needs. In the words of Father Bernabé Cobo:

> Every year the caciques distributed . . . lands among their subjects, not in equal parts, but proportionate to the number of children and relatives that each man had; as the family grew or decreased, its share was enlarged or restricted. No one was granted more than just enough to support himself, be he noble or plebeian, even though a great deal of land was left over to lie fallow and uncultivated.
>
> (Cobo 1979:213)

The Inka state grew through conquest and replicated this system writ large across its empire. With conquest, the Inka reorganized local economic systems in two ways. First, after conquest all land, pasture, and herds were claimed as crown property. Land is said to have been subsequently reapportioned with one-third of the land claimed by the Inka state, one-third allocated to the Temple of the Sun and other religious deities, and one-third left for the common people (Murra 1980:33). This model of reapportionment probably was more conceptual than actual, but it likely paralleled the division and assignment of lands at the local level.[44] While there certainly were important changes in production after Inka conquest (Rowe 1982), it is unlikely that there were many changes in traditional land assignments to local *ayllu* who were allowed to remain on the land.[45]

Second, the Inka implemented large-scale population relocations to reorganize the empire. These relocations, referred to as the *mitmaq*, mimicked the traditional practice of colonizing new environmental zones with kinsmen and community members, but on a larger scale. The Inka used the model of zonal complementarity and removed groups from their home regions as a device in shaping the political organization of the empire. One reason conquered groups were moved was to divide their support base and to minimize the chance of future rebellion. Another was to relocate groups with special skills to areas where they could be employed to meet the needs of the empire. These skills could include the construction or expansion of irrigation systems in coastal valleys, the cultivation of specific crops, or mining and processing natural resources such as copper, gold, and silver.

The Inka empire extended more than 4,200 kilometers from southern Ecuador to northern Chile, and the cost of transportation precluded the large-scale flow of staple goods into the capital of Cuzco from tributary provinces. Instead, the empire was organized into multiple localized systems of staple finance that were integrated with one another using gifts of wealth goods to reinforce the state's administrative operation (D'Altroy and Earle 1985; Earle 1994; Earle and D'Altroy 1982). Food and other resources were produced for institutional use and stored in special storage facilities known as *qollqa* around Inka administrative centers (Earle and D'Altroy 1982; LeVine 1992; Morris and Thompson 1985). The food produced on institutional lands was used in large public feasts and religious celebrations, as well as to feed the army and to supply food and drink for corvée labor and general administrative activities. How resources were assigned to these different functions is unclear, although state and religious institutions operated independently to the extent that crops from state land were stored in *qollqa* separately from those of church lands (Murra 1980:124). While production and storage were decentralized and organized at the regional level, detailed records were kept by accountants (*khipo kamayoq*) on where resources were stored around the empire on the *khipu*, a counting device using knotted string (Figure 5.3). Careful record keeping along with a detailed annual census enabled the Inka state to manage affairs within their far-flung empire (Julien 1988; Urton 2009).

The centralized management of resources at the level of the empire led Murra (1956, 1980) to argue that the Inka economy was based on redistribution. In his words, "Having monopolized for state use corvée services of the peasantry ... the crown had at its disposal vast storehouses only a fraction of which went for strictly court use. The bulk of these resources were distributed where it was thought that it would do the most good. In this sense the Inca state functioned like a market" (Murra 1980:121).

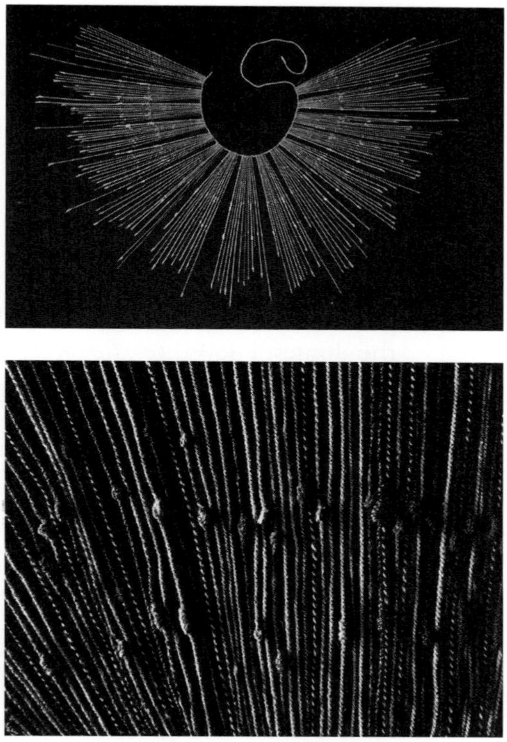

5.3 An Inka *khipu* with a close-up showing the different types of knots tied in different colored and textured strings. (Photograph taken by Joanne Pillsbury)

The Andean economy at both the local and regional levels operated under the principle of balanced reciprocity called *yanantin* (Platt 1986) or *waje waje* (Fonseca Martel 1974; Hastorf 2001b:315–316), and this is what generated the large-scale movement and distribution of food, staple resources, and wealth goods to the communities of individuals who served the state. But this is not redistribution at the level of subsistence support for households that Murra implies. Like the allocation of food for work parties around the world (Chapter 3), the distribution of food and gifts by the local *curaca*, or state administrators, was an acknowledgment of the value of the labor that individuals provided. The Inka state reciprocated for contributed labor service by providing elaborate feasts that included the distribution of wealth goods during important religious celebrations.

Wealth finance was used to balance and repay services important to the state. Sally Moore (1958) was one of the first to identify the importance of wealth goods in the Inka economy when she discussed how wealth goods produced by state-supported craftspersons were distributed down the institutional hierarchy as reciprocal payments, gifts, and indicators of social status and administrative offices that individuals held (Owen 2001:267). The most important wealth goods involved in reciprocal service payments were textiles, precious metal goods, and *Spondylus* shell objects (Costin 1993; Earle 1994; Murra1962; Owen 2001). Of these, textiles were the most widely produced and circulated form of wealth. Textiles were manufactured of cotton, camelid wool,[46] and maguey fiber[47] in two types of cloth: *awasqa* coarse weave produced for domestic purposes and *kumpi* fine cloth (Murra 1962:711). The military were great consumers of *awasqa* textiles; soldiers received two suits of clothing annually (Murra 1962:717).

Textiles as gifts factored into every major service and life event ceremony in Andean society. Fine *kumpi* textiles were used as religious sacrifices, to clothe the gods, and as a backdrop against which god effigies were viewed. Some of the images of Sun and Thunder gods were even made of carefully folded combinations of textiles. They were indispensable in mortuary offerings; a single mummy burial in the Paracas culture of coastal Peru could require up to 300 square yards of fine cloth. The initiation rites of royal youth consumed large quantities of textiles worn by the participants as well as those given away as gifts to attendees. All individuals who served the state, including administrators, messengers, and even the sons of provincial *curacas* held as hostages in Cuzco, received fine textiles as reciprocal compensation. Exchanges of cloth were integral to diplomatic and military negotiations. The Inka even gave cloth as gifts to groups after conquest to establish a conceptual indebtedness to their overlords that could only be reciprocated by sending subsequent textiles and other products to the Inka warehouses. At the domestic level, textiles were given as gifts in all major life events (birth, puberty, death) and were a fundamental ingredient in marriage bridewealth (Murra 1962).

State storehouses are described as filled to their ceilings with bundles of textiles of all different types and qualities. While some of the finest *kumpi* textiles were woven by specially chosen women (see below), most of the *awasqa* cloth was manufactured in domestic contexts as part of the annual service requirement placed on commoner households. Cieza de León (1998) claimed that each household had to produce one blanket each year and each person one shirt as their annual obligation (Murra 1962:716). Interestingly, households were only required to supply the labor; the raw material, whether cotton or wool, was supplied by the local *curaca* from community or state herds. According to Cabello Valboa, everyone from humble peasants to high-ranking elites considered themselves well rewarded if they received a gift of garments from the local or Inka state rulers (Murra 1962:720).

The Inka applied the principle of direct production across their empire by producing food and other staple goods and storing them in areas where they were needed. The same was true for wealth goods such as textiles that used domestic labor in their production. Likewise, bronze and other metal wealth goods were produced in regionally specialized state workshops (D'Altroy et al. 2000; Earle 1994) and in Inka administrative centers where copper and tin ore were imported (Earle 2001:311; Owen 2001).

While corvée labor was the traditional way that goods were produced for institutional consumption, there is evidence that the Inka state was developing greater control over the labor used in institutional production. The Inka established royal agricultural estates and created a class of permanently dependent client laborers to work them. These were the *yanakuna*, full-time and lifelong workers who farmed, provided service, and tended to the herds of Inka estates. Many of these estates were located in and around Cuzco and were developed to support the kindred of the ruler both during and after his death as a mortuary complex to underwrite related political and ceremonial activities (D'Altroy 2002:278). The *yanakuna* are described as perpetual servants with low status because they were removed from their *ayllu* kinsmen.

Given that fine *kumpi* textiles were important wealth goods, it is not surprising that the Inka likewise created a class of hereditary full-time weavers. These were the *aqllakuna*, or chosen women (Figure 5.4), who were young girls taken from their families when they were about 10 years of age and trained to weave fine textiles and brew maize beer (*chicha*) in Inka administrative centers across the empire[48] (Cobo 1990:172–174). In both these cases the Inka appear to have been in the process of creating a more tightly integrated institutional economy that did not rely entirely on the traditional mobilization of labor through community corvée (D'Altroy 2002; Murra 1980).

5.4 The *aqllakuna* chosen women of the Inka. (Redrawn from Guaman Poma de Ayala 1980 and D'Altroy 2002:Figure 8.3 by Shae Rider and author)

While the Inka state mobilized a vast quantity of peasant labor to produce institutional revenue, it did not assume the responsibility of provisioning peasants with subsistence goods as the model of redistribution implies. There were areas in the northern and southern Andes where zonal complementarity did not exist. In these areas, goods moved within and between regions through systems of barter exchange and caravan trade (Murra 1985a:4; Nielsen 2013; Salomon 1977, 1987). La Lone (1982) argues that small marketplaces existed in several areas both at the capital of Cuzco and in the northern portion of the Inka empire to help distribute goods. Others have suggested that small markets may have been intentionally suppressed by the Inka after conquest to institute a more top-down control over the institutional economy (Hirth and Pillsbury 2013; Mayer 2013; Stanish and Coben 2013). Yet the archaeological evidence for marketplaces and market exchange in the Andes remains weak. A comparison of household assemblages between the Aztec and the Inka reveals a much higher degree of commercialization among the former as would be expected with the operation of marketplaces (Earle and Smith 2011). Inka household assemblages, in contrast, reveal greater self-sufficiency and noncommercial involvement along the lines that Murra's nonmarket model originally suggested. In summary, the Inka institutional economy is an excellent example of how the direct production of staple goods together with the production and circulation of wealth goods provided the basis for a state economy when it was combined with careful planning and organization.

PERIPATETIC CONSUMPTION AND THE GAFOL

Direct production on agricultural estates provided leaders, rulers, and other functionaries with food and staple goods in many societies. As with all cases of staple finance, the movement and storage of bulky staple goods involved some form of cost. The cost of funding institutions using staple finance rose as the scope of activities carried out was increased. There were two solutions to this problem when the costs of transporting staple goods became prohibitive. One solution was to convert staple goods to coin or some other wealth good that could be shipped over space to the point of consumption. This is the essence of wealth finance systems, and they function smoothly as long as wealth can be reconverted into food and other staple goods when and where they were needed. This worked well where markets and merchants were involved in moving goods across the landscape independent of the institutions that consumed them. Where transportation costs were too high and staple goods could not be mobilized in sufficient quantity to meet institutional needs, an alternative solution could develop: the institution and its associated consumers may relocate to where staple goods were assembled and consume them there.

The movement of institutional consumers to where resources were produced is referred to here as *peripatetic consumption*. It produces the phenomenon of the peripatetic court, where a ruler's household and court circulated constantly and consumed resources from estates scattered throughout his domain. This was a common feature of European feudal society where rulers and their retinues circulated throughout their domains residing with their hosts for periods of time and consuming resources in the locations where they were produced and stored (Bernhardt 2002; Bloch 1961). In discussing the nature of itinerant courts in the 10th to 11th centuries AD in medieval Germany, Geary states that

> Germanic kings were not only sacred, they were peripatetic. Like other early medieval monarchs, they had no fixed capital or permanent abode. Their court traveled to the far-flung lands over which they reigned but which they could rule only by regular visitations. Such travels had an additional, practical purpose: at any given time the royal entourage might number between three hundred and one thousand people, and given the weak level of monitarization of the German economy as well as the realities of foodstuff preservation and transportation, the most effective means of feeding such an entourage from royal income was to travel to the sources of revenues and consume them on the spot. These payments comprised the *servitium regis*, which ... made up the contributions ... to the monarchy.
>
> (Geary 1996:111)

The German court (Bernhardt 2002) was highly mobile in comparison to the earlier Carolingian state that also moved through the kingdom, but did so through more finite territories as a result of a better developed institutional structure (Airlie 2000:2; McKitterick 2011). Kobishchanow (1987) refers to peripatetic consumption with the Anglo-Saxon term *gafol*, which he believes was a feature of many societies around world where staple finance was coupled with high transportation costs and a weak central government. Feudal kings who ruled large domains would circulate throughout their kingdoms with their household entourage in tow. Instead of mobilizing surpluses to a central location, lords would "collect" surpluses from their vassals by moving to where they were produced and consuming the surpluses on the spot through a form of imposed hospitality.[49] The result was a form of "movable feast" as rulers traveled through their domains consuming what their subjects produced[50] (Vale 2002). According to Homans (1960:229), "If the lord held many manors, he probably would not reside at any one of them for more than a week or two during the year."

A good example of how this type of adaptation operated is provided by Bishop Thomas Arundel, who traveled from manor to manor throughout the bishopric of Ely, England, between AD 1375 and 1388 (Stone 2005). Medieval bishops were as much civil servants as they were men of the cloth, and they moved throughout their bishoprics regulating both secular and ecclesiastical matters. The bishopric of Ely had nearly sixty manors scattered across an area of 10,000–11,000 square kilometers.[51] Bishop Arundel moved peripatetically throughout the year by horse and barge,[52] checking on maintenance activities at each of his manors. His movements were most frequent between the eight major palace residences located in the western half of the bishopric and his house in London, although he would have stayed at other locales when he visited manors in the east. In addition to his own peripatetic movements, the bishop also received and entertained his peripatetic superiors. For example, it is known that in July of AD 1383 he received and entertained Richard II, Queen Anne, the duchess of Brittany, and other members of the royal court (Stone 2005:22).

Peripatetic consumption was an adaptation to situations where political leaders were supported through staple finance in areas of high transportation costs. But it also served other functions. It provided rulers with some political control and a way to monitor supporters and judge their loyalty. It allowed rulers to be seen by their subjects along with the holy relics they often traveled with, and which provided supernatural validation of their right to reign (J. Smith 2010:80). Political authority and dependency relationships were personal rather than bureaucratic in feudal society (Bloch 1961:145–151), and rulers reinforced allegiances by circulating through their kingdoms evaluating the loyalty of their subjects. It was advantageous in this regard for the ruler and his court to be somewhat nomadic. In addition to maintaining a level of cohesiveness in what otherwise might be a loosely organized domain, rulers could resolve disputes that arose between lords in adjacent territories, dispense justice, and conduct any religious functions required of them.

According to Kobishchanow (1987), peripatetic consumption represented an early form of feudal rent and was the prototype for other forms of taxation used to support royal courts. He proposed that it was important in many early state societies outside feudal Europe, including the ancient Hittite kingdom, the Meroitic kingdom in Sudan, 11th-century Iceland, the Angkor and Majapahit kingdoms of southeast Asia, Tahitian and Hawaiian societies of the South Pacific, as well as the African societies of Axum, the Hausa, and the Bantu groups in the lower Congo. He views it as an early form of resource mobilization that eventually was replaced by more direct forms of taxation. He feels that with a more secure fiscal base peripatetic consumption was transformed into alternative forms of royal touring whereby rulers circulated throughout their domains to conduct ritual activities, initiate feasts, commence spring planting, or just evaluate loyalties and reassert their authority. In this sense the *gafol* and other forms of peripatetic consumption can be seen as evolving over time, taking on new functions beyond simple resource mobilization.

A somewhat different example of peripatetic consumption can be found in the Achaemenid empire of ancient Persia (ca. 559–331 BC).[53] It was customary for Persian kings to move in formal processions between their various palaces at different times of the year. They wintered in Susa, summered in Ecbatana, resided in Persepolis in the autumn, and spent the rest of the year in Babylon. The Greek historian Aelian compared the institution of court migration to the yearly migration of fish and birds (Wilson 1997). When the king moved, all the members of his family, court, household staff, bodyguards, state administrators, and courtiers moved with him along with images of the gods and their attendant priests. This was a procession of several thousand people.[54] When the king and his court were on the move, the royal tent was the center of the kingdom (Briant 2002:184–189).

The peripatetic court of Persian kings combined political, economic, and ideological functions as it moved through the realm. The king was received along his route with great pomp and circumstance. Careful preparations were made weeks in advance of his prescribed movement, which included cleaning the roads, preparing food to feed his entourage, and assembling an array of extravagant gifts. City rulers and local officials would meet the king outside their city walls to illustrate their submission to his authority, and failure to perform any of the prescribed preparations was seen as an act of rebellion. The arrival of the king was also a time of massive gift giving. He was presented with a wide array of exotic animals, gold and silver cups, crowns with gems, rich textiles, furniture with elaborate inlays, and all the other rich bounty of the province. In turn the king performed sacrifices to local deities to underscore that the gods of the city also received him (Briant 2002).

The common people also presented gifts to the king during his tour. The practice is described by Aelian (I.31) when Artaxerxes II's royal procession passed peasant fields and villages on his way to Persepolis:

> A custom most carefully maintained by the Persians, when the king drives to Persepolis, is that each and every one of them, according to his means, brings an offering. Since they are engaged in farming and toil on the land, living by what they produce, they bring no pretentious or unduly expensive gifts, but rather oxen, sheep, or corn, or in other cases wine. As the king passes and drives on his way these objects are laid out by each man, and are termed gifts; the king treats them as such. Men who are even poorer than these farmers bring him milk and dates and cheese, with ripe fruit and other first fruits of local produce.
>
> (Wilson 1997:55)

The people would line the roads to see the king pass by in his glory, and it was considered shameful to disregard the practice of giving even small gifts to the king. Hosting the king's annual visitations provisioned his court and financed his treasury, while at the same time reinforcing his right of dominion over the kingdom. What the exact balance was between the costs and benefits of his peripatetic movement cannot be measured with any precision. But coming in person to receive the best the land had to offer left no doubt who held dominion over his subjects.

SUMMARY

The structure of institutional economies can be examined from at least three different perspectives. The most fundamental is what type of goods were needed and used for institutional support. Here the issue revolves around whether institutions used staple consumables such as food, wealth goods like textiles or metals, or some combination of both to finance their activities and support associated personnel. A second equally important question is, How were these goods obtained and what were the mechanisms used to create them? The two most common forms of resource creation employed in ancient economies were direct production systems and voluntary and involuntary resource mobilization and taxation. This chapter has focused on the first of these, where institutions undertook the task of directly producing the resources that they required for operation. The final aspect of institutional economy that is important to consider is the overall cost and efficiency of its operation. These involve costs of producing, collecting, processing, storing, transporting, and otherwise managing institutional resources. A great deal of change in institutional economies is related to the ways of increasing net returns either by increasing gross revenue or reducing costs of operation, or both.

All of the examples discussed here were state-level societies with differing degrees of centralized bureaucratic control. They all relied on systems of staple finance, combining them with wealth finance when they could. The temple and palace institutions in southern Mesopotamia were based on highly productive irrigation agriculture (Adams 1965, 1981; Adams and Nissen 1972; Gasche and Tanret 1998). The development of institutional herds of sheep allowed them to produce high-value textiles that were used in trade to obtain other staple and wealth goods, including the metals vital for military equipment in Bronze Age societies. The Inka organized their empire around the regional production of staple goods to provide food and drink at feasts in return for community corvée labor. Textiles and precious metals were important wealth goods, but these moved primarily as reciprocal gifts and distributions to supporters along the same lines as staple goods.

The Aztec institutional economy was based on a combination of staple and wealth finance. Primary institutions in the Basin of Mexico were supported by the production of maize, beans, and other products on lands set aside for specific purposes. Wealth goods were important, and these came into the economy through the tribute flowing from conquered provinces throughout the empire. A vibrant market economy provided the mechanism whereby wealth goods could be converted into both food and other valuable items. In this case wealth goods flowed into the capital of the empire through taxation, while the local population focused on food production.

The Chinese case is interesting because of the range of staples that it chose to control. Instead of controlling food production, it concentrated on the essentials of salt, tea, iron, and spice, products that were important as consumables at all levels of society. By controlling the production and distribution of these commodities, the state established a monopoly and set the price for essential goods that evolved from voluntary consumption to mandatory purchase.

Wealth goods were important to individuals in all of these societies as units of value and durable storage; when needed, they could be converted to other goods through exchange. In institutional contexts, they seemed to have somewhat different functions. In Sumer they were used for trade to obtain metal and other goods not locally available. Among the Inka and the Aztec, they were used as gifts to retainers and supporters. Among the Chinese, wealth goods were the objects of elite consumption. But in the example of the

Chinese salt monopoly the society already operated as a cash economy so that the proceeds from salt could be used to purchase military equipment; pay soldiers, bureaucrats, and other retainers; buy land; or simply purchase the luxuries important for elite courtly life.

A common denominator of these examples was the use of community corvée labor to greater or lesser degrees within these direct production systems. In Sumer this is evident in both the food ration lists allocated to workers and the large quantities of beveled, rimmed "ration bowls" recovered in archaeological excavations throughout southern Mesopotamia during the third millennium BC. Among the Aztecs the rationale for corvée labor was expressed in the concept of *tequitl*, or the duty that everyone in society had to serve the gods and those individuals that the gods placed in authority. Among the Inka it was the *mita* corvée work obligation that everyone in society had to fulfill, with men providing agricultural labor while women wove textiles. What is especially notable about the Inka case is that even royal persons were involved in initiating work projects in the fields alongside commoner retainers. The Chinese case is somewhat different because the workers involved in the salt monopoly received direct support. Nevertheless, the general population was still responsible for corvée work for different tasks, including general construction activities and in the transportation of salt and other commodities when merchants were not involved in their distribution.

Determining the efficiency or costs of institutional management is difficult without detailed data, which are hard to obtain and difficult to discuss especially within a synchronic perspective necessary for describing the structure of economic organizations. Nevertheless, a few observations are possible. First, the direct production of food and other staple goods such as salt is expensive. In terms of equipment and technology, direct production involved the construction and maintenance of irrigation systems and plow animals in Sumer, salt production equipment in China, the construction of terraces and irrigation systems in the Andes, and agricultural *chinampas* in the Basin of Mexico. Similarly, corvée labor was not free labor; it also had costs. It involved organizational costs as well as the customary practice among the Sumerians, Aztecs, and Inka of feeding corvée workers. Available labor among the Aztec and Inka was kept track of in pictographic codices or *khipu* records at the community level. Given the economic importance of writing in the Near East the same was almost certainly true in Sumer.

It is notable, therefore, that organizational changes can be detected in institutional economies that appear to be related to reducing costs or otherwise increasing the level of net revenue. Changes in the management of institution lands in Mesopotamia from the third to the second millennium BC included shifts from the use of corvée labor to prebendal land allocations for service positions to equivalent payment as rents on land to institutional personnel.

While institutional support among the Aztecs was largely in the form of prebendal and hereditary land assignments worked by corvée labor, there was an emerging tendency toward private control of land and the use of dependent (*mayeque*) labor, rather than free commoner (*macehualtin*) labor in cultivation. Among the Inka corvée labor was the norm, but a lower class of perpetual servitude was emerging for both agriculture and general service workers with *yanakuna* and *aqllakuna* personnel. The weaving industry in Sumer witnessed similar developments with destitute women, children, indentured servants, and slaves being given to temples for this purpose. All these changes involved greater control over labor that would have translated into more efficient forms of institutional production.

The Chinese production monopolies had a long history of management, mismanagement, and reorganization either to increase revenue by increasing efficiency of operation or to reduce the level of fraud and corruption within the organization. While the Chinese preferred to transport and distribute salt within the organizational structure of the monopoly, they often found themselves having to contract merchants to distribute salt either when it was unprofitable to do so or in an effort to reduce fraud and waste. The Chinese also reflect one of the most blatant cases of revenue exploitation by establishing mandatory purchases of salt for different purposes. The examples of winning-a-case salt, land-selling salt, corvée and completing-the-corvée salt, long-life salt, and afterlife salt are clear instances of the state mandating and forcing individuals to purchase salt simply to increase its flow of institutional revenue.

Storage is a key ingredient in direct production systems involving the production of staple goods like food. Food spoils, animal herds must be fed, and the products from both need to be protected from the natural elements. Storage is one of those dimensions of economic behavior that is visible in the archaeological record at both the household and institutional levels. It is interesting that only with the Inka are storage facilities prominent and visible. Storage facilities were built at provincial centers and along roads throughout the empire for a vast array of goods ranging from food to textiles to military equipment. Storage facilities are not prominent in either Aztec or Sumerian administrative areas. There was some storage in Aztec palaces for wealth goods and food for everyday use, as well as a central storage facility for grain within the Aztec capital (Kobayashi 1993a). But in many cases the storage of food was decentralized with granaries located on the same estate fields where food was grown, and corvée labor was used to transport it to the point of consumption when needed (Hirth 2012b). In Sumer large storage facilities for grain are also absent and it is possible that storage facilities were located at or near the threshing floors and fields where grain was processed.

Finally, two examples were discussed that identified the problems of managed production systems of staple finance: the 19th-century AD community of

Zoar, Ohio, and the practice of peripatetic courts. Zoar supported itself by combining direct production with the redistribution of goods to all community members. It was successful because of its small size and shared religious ideology but ceased to operate once its founding members passed away. The topic of peripatetic consumption was presented as a special case of staple finance where itinerant royal courts moved to where resources were produced and stored, instead of the reverse. It is argued that this type of consumption was a product of high transportation costs and a solution to how staple finance systems could be organized. As such, they provide an interesting contrast to the staple goods economy of the Inka empire. Peripatetic courts were common across medieval Europe and the Near East. Royal itinerancy in these situations, however, was not simply the result of moving retainers to where resources could be consumed. They also played an important role of consolidating authority in weakly integrated systems of governance. In the chapter that follows, the other major form of resource creation is examined: the mobilization of resources for institutional support through voluntary donation and involuntary taxation.

SIX

TAXATION, RENT, AND PATRONAGE

Mobilization of Institutional Resources

There is no art which one government sooner learns of another than that of draining money from the pocket of people.

(Adam Smith)

Institutional finance in the modern world is dominated by a variety of different types of taxation at both the private and corporate levels. The fiscal systems of ancient economies were different. The word "fiscal" comes from the Persian term *fisc*, which was the basket used to collect money and resources from Persian provinces (Hudson 2000:11). That is a good way to envision how ancient economies funded institutional activities, as a mixed basket of different production and resource transfer/mobilization strategies. Resources that went into the basket were available for use, and when the basket was empty expenditures were postponed. Taxation was a very flexible strategy to fund institutional needs and took many different forms across the ancient world.

What Adam Smith is lamenting in the epigraph[1] are the two well-known institutional practices from late 18th-century England: the heavy burden of taxation on the population for institutional use, and the new ways that governments adopted to raise revenue by emulating the taxation practices of their neighbors. The preceding chapter discussed some of the direct production strategies used to support institutional activities. This chapter examines some of the mobilization strategies employed by societies to extract resources from households for institutional use. It focuses specifically on economic transfers, which are one-way transactions involving the conveyance of goods or services from one individual donor or group-donor to another (F. Pryor 1977:3). Transfers are unbalanced in the sense that there is no tangible or immediate counterflow of goods or services in return for the resources offered. It is in this regard that voluntary tithes and mandatory taxes can be considered together as analogous forms of institutional support.

It is important to clarify two aspects about transfers at the outset. First, the motivations behind transfers can vary greatly from donor to donor as can the intangible benefits that they believe are received in return for making them. Transfers may be completely voluntary or coerced depending on the circumstances involved. It is in the shift from voluntary to mandatory contributions that donations were transformed into taxes. Second, the scope of donors involved in making transfers can range from individual households to large corporate groups such as guilds or estates that represent institutional organizations in their own right. The feature that all donors have in common is that the resources involved are mobilized from their respective income or revenue streams. They are *net donations* after all production costs have been incurred. For domestic households, transfers, as either voluntary donations or mandatory taxes, are direct withdrawals from their subsistence budgets.

The chapter examines a selection of different resource mobilization strategies that range from voluntary patronage to taxation and rent collection. It begins by discussing what constitutes taxation in the formal sense of the term. This is followed by an examination of forms of elite patronage in the Greco-Roman world and their importance in funding dimensions of the institutional economy. Important here is the relationship between compulsory and voluntary (euergetistic) patronage. The scope of ancient taxation is too broad to examine *all* of the direct and indirect ways that people were taxed and resources were mobilized. Instead, the discussion is selective and addresses only three of the most common forms of taxation: tolls and tariffs, land and production taxes, and the taxation of conquered provinces. This is followed by an examination of forms of revenue collection with attention to tax farming and the conditions under which it developed. The chapter concludes with a discussion of another important way that resources were mobilized through rents and leases. Although often classified as a form of taxation, rents and leases are empirically distinct because they provide the right to access a set of resources in return for payments made.

WHAT CONSTITUTES TAX? THE LANDSCAPE OF TRANSFERS

In the ancient Near East, as well as in early Christian ecclesiastical circles, a sharp distinction was often made between a tithe and an offering. Both were transfers in the sense that money or resources were given to a religious institution often without an immediate or tangible material return. While similar in form, the circumstances surrounding these two types of transfers were very different. In ancient Israel and across Mesopotamia, the tithe was the expected 10% increase from fields or flocks that was owed to God and the associated religious institutions[2] (Pirngruber 2017:67–68; Stol 2016:153). In Israel, compliance was viewed as compulsory in religious terms:

> You shall tithe all the yield of your seed, which comes forth from the field year by year. And before the Lord your God, in the place which he will choose, to make his name dwell there, you shall ... tithe of your grain, of your wine, and of your oil, and the firstlings of your herd and flock; that you may learn to fear the Lord your God.
>
> (Deuteronomy 14:22–23)

Failure to tithe brought divine rather than secular sanctions, while compliance brought blessings:

> Will man rob God? Yet you are robbing me.... In your tithes and offerings. You are cursed with a curse, for you are robbing me; the whole nation of you. Bring the full tithes into the storehouse, that there may be food in my house; and thereby put me to the test, says the Lord of hosts, if I will not open the windows of heaven for you and pour down for you an overflowing blessing.
>
> (Malachi 3:8–10)

The offering was different from the tithe because it was a completely voluntary gift above and beyond the expected tithe. Failure to provide it did not carry spiritual or secular sanctions, only incentives, as the preceding quote implies. It was given out of respect, gratitude, adoration, or as a pledge.

These two examples capture the extremes of resource transfers from the compulsory but unmonitored payments (the tithe) to the completely voluntary donations (the offering). Scholars who follow the rational choice model find it difficult to explain voluntary donations of resources unless they can be balanced with some tangible economic, emotional, or psychological return. Ideological compliance like that described does not make pure economic sense because it is an unbalanced transaction. It does make sense, however, if it provides personal or existential fulfilment or builds visible social capital within society for the individuals who practice it. Even strong adherents to the rational choice model, such as Douglas North (1985:394), recognize that ideology beliefs and values structure rational economic behavior. The concern here is not whether voluntary donations were made for personal altruistic, spiritual, or social reasons. Instead, we simply recognize that they existed even when the motivation behind them is hard to discern.

Taxation, in contrast, is a nonvoluntary and enforced transfer. According to international taxation guidelines, a tax is defined as "a compulsory levy made by public authorities for which nothing is received directly in return" (James

1998). While some individuals may pay their taxes willingly, the implication of it being a compulsory payment is that coercive force will be used to collect from those who choose not to pay. Likewise, the idea of "no direct return" refers to the delayed or nebulous benefits received from paying taxes. Yes, taxes may pay for services or contribute to roads and schools, but revenue essentially goes into a black box, and it is never clear exactly how it is used. Taxes are paid in the hope that they will be used wisely. This is quite a different economic relationship compared with payments made in a grocery store or a car dealership.

The key to effective fiscal policy, according to Margaret Levi (1989), is the development of quasi-compliance among taxpayers. The working assumption is that taxpayers will normally want to avoid paying taxes because avoidance enhances the economic well-being of themselves and their households. Enforced compliance by institutions levying taxes carries with it both monitoring and enforcement costs. The most effective and efficient system of taxation, therefore, is one that induces individuals to pay on a semi-voluntary basis. To achieve this end, institutions must demonstrate that the taxation system is reasonably fair and that there is a high probability that punishment will result from nonpayment. Compliance will be enhanced, of course, if taxpayers believe that there are benefits from paying their taxes. Nevertheless, there will always be some who attempt to avoid paying. The key for an efficient system of taxation, therefore, is to attain quasi-compliance among the majority of taxpayers so that enforcement can be directed toward the few who are noncompliant (Levi 1989:52–55).

Adam Smith (1827:347–348) identified the four components of a sound system of taxation. The first of these is that the system is equitable and fair to the taxpayers in terms of their ability to pay. Second, there must be certainty to the system so that the taxpayers can plan their tax payments and produce to meet them. Third, the payment of taxes has to be convenient without incurring large additional costs to meet payment obligations. Fourth and finally, the system must be efficient and easy to administer so that taxpayers will not attempt to avoid their fiscal obligations.

Achieving equity in a tax system depends on three interrelated factors. The first is that the fiscal needs of the kingdom have to be predictable so that individuals can calculate their tax expenditures. One of the forces that consistently created unanticipated tax burdens within societies was the cost of war. The second factor was determining the composition of the revenue base that institutions could draw on. What were the activities that could be taxed (e.g., agriculture, trade, mining, services) and what was the scale of the taxable revenue base? Finally, what were the management skills and fiscal priorities that shaped the system of taxation? It is here that there is considerable potential for administrative mismanagement, which can create distrust and opposition to paying taxes.

Levi (1989) models the structure of taxation systems under what she calls the *theory of predatory rule*. She asserts that revenue is the primary factor limiting or enhancing a leader's ability to rule. The greater their revenue, the more leaders can extend the range of governance and the number of institutions that support it. In this regard they are revenue maximizers and employ taxation as a means to that end. Whether institutions extract as much revenue as they desire depends on the constraints placed on them, the nature of their objectives, and their ability to effectively manage institutional costs and maintain a level of quasi-compliance among taxpayers. The costs involved in managing a tax system are complex and include the cost of predicting revenue yields, organizing the collection agency, monitoring tax compliance, and punishing noncompliance. These costs dictate whether collection procedures are structured through bureaucratic means or through tax farming (Coşgel and Miceli 2009; also see below).

But perhaps the most important factor in the structure of taxation systems is how institutional decision makers value the immediate or long-term effects of tax policy. Levi (1989) labels this as the tax discount rate, which refers to the time frame for taxation. The more a ruler values the future value of taxation in relation to the present, the lower the overall discount rate. The discount rate employed directly affects the benefits and long-term stability of tax policies. In other words,

> Rulers with high discount rates care little for the future. They will be less concerned with promoting the conditions of economic growth and increased revenue over time than with extracting available revenue even at the risk of discouraging output. Rulers with low discount rates do have an interest in securing future revenues, they will extract revenue up to the point at which further extractions would put future output at risk.
> (Levi 1989:32–33)

It is here that the balance in tax policy that Adam Smith advocated can be achieved or lost depending on the disposition of institutional leaders.

Any attempt to generalize about the system of taxation for a society is fraught with difficulty. Not only is it usually composed of multiple different forms of taxation, but they often change and expand over time as institutions seek new sources of revenue. Attempts to classify societies by their primary fiscal regime (Bonney and Ormrod 1999) are not useful because they fail to recognize the variation in the forms of taxation used[3] and how they may be combined with forms of direct production within institutional economies.

The variation in taxation found in ancient societies is a testimony to the fiscal creativity of institutional leaders.[4] Taxation can be calculated as a fixed or flat tax against adult members or individual households as it was with poll taxes. It may be calculated on finished goods or raw materials moving through trade; custom fees and import duties are examples of this type of tax. Perhaps the oldest and the most common form of tax was levied on the production of food used in staple finance systems (Chapter 5). How this tax was calculated also varied from society to society. It could be calculated on agricultural and herding output as a tithe as it was across the ancient Near East. The problem was that output was difficult to monitor unless processing was done in a central locale such as a threshing floor, oil press, or shearing pen. For this reason, it was often easier to calculate the tax using production inputs such as the amount of land cultivated or quantity of trees owned. Production taxes were also levied on craft producers frequently calculated against their level of output (Monson and Scheidel 2015:16–18).

Taxes could also be calculated against the estimated value of fixed assets rather than the size of a herd or the quantity of land that an individual owned. Solon of Athens is credited with creating one of the earliest general property taxes around 594 BC when he divided the citizenry into four social groups based on wealth[5] calculated in terms of the value of the land, houses, slaves, furniture, and money that a household possessed (Finley 1985:48–49; Samson 2002:23). A similar wealth census was conducted every 5 years in Rome against which a fixed percentage of tax was assessed.[6] Wealth from conquest was also important whether it was collected as plunder or a regular assessment of resources.[7] Finally, economic transactions were taxed in a dizzying array of ways every time wealth or resources moved between individuals. Examples include taxes on inheritance, sale of property, manumission of slaves, sale of offices, marriages, gifts, establishing licenses, executing contracts, and eventually through sales taxes.[8] An early form of inheritance tax of 10% can be found in Egypt during the 7th century BC, which required that detailed land registers be kept to track the transfer of property from generation to generation. As in all things related to taxation, people found ways around inheritance tax using phony sales of property from parents to children to avoid payment (Monson and Scheidel 2015; Samson 2002).

It was not unusual for different kinds of taxes to coexist with one another. The same was true for the different practices of collecting tax. As a rule, tax was collected to minimize expense or to conform with other organizational practices in society. Calculating taxes on production outputs or trade, for example, could be more variable and riskier for fiscal purposes than taxes calculated on inputs. The discussion that follows illustrates only a few of the many diverse forms of economic transfers. Rather than beginning with forms of taxation, I focus first on examples of voluntary transfers common throughout the ancient Mediterranean and referred to as forms of euergetism.

LITURGIES AND COMPULSORY PATRONAGE IN THE GRECO-ROMAN WORLD

One of the expectations of ancient societies was that leaders would act in the interest of all its members. This often involved bearing the financial costs that leadership activities entailed. This certainly was the case in ancient Greece where Aristotle considered general taxation of its citizens a form of state tyranny (Beck 2013:292). Nevertheless, citizen farmers among the peasantry generally were required to pay a small tax on the grain harvest (Bresson 2016:104). In the Greco-Rome world it was expected that people would contribute to society in proportion to their ability to do so. That meant a heavier expectation fell on wealthy members of society.[9] The Greeks felt that a just division of wealth and power in society should be linked to their demonstration of individual moral excellence. As a result, elites needed to validate their elevated social position by demonstrating they possessed a high level of virtue (Zuiderhoec 2009:13).

The result was that the *wealthy were expected to serve as society's social patrons and shoulder the primary burden and expense of the institutional economy*. The patronage duties that wealthy families performed were referred to as the *leitourgia*, from which we derive the word "liturgies." The sponsorship of liturgies was both compulsory and honorific within Greek society. They could be undertaken voluntarily in the euergetistic spirit (see below) or compelled through social and legal pressure. In this sense, compulsory liturgies and voluntary sponsorship of civic activities lay on opposite ends of the spectrum of elite patronage. Nevertheless, however the liturgies were fulfilled, wealthy patrons received public acclaim for funding institutional activities. The way that euergetism was proclaimed was through dedicatory inscriptions that commemorated the donor and the nature of the gift. It is through these commemorating inscriptions that archaeologists have identified the nature of public service and gifting activity.

The financial cost of compulsory liturgies could be a heavy burden for wealthy families. In *Oeconomicus*, Xenophon satirizes the obligation of sponsoring liturgies in Athens in a conversation of his character Sokrates with the immensely rich Kritoboulous where he says,

> You must keep horses, pay for choruses and gymnastic competitions, and *prostateiai* [patronages]; and if war breaks out, I know they will require you to undertake trierarchies and pay *eisphora* taxes that will nearly crush you. Whenever you seem to fall short of what is expected of you, the Athenians will certainly punish you as though they had caught you robbing them.
>
> (Beck 2013:344)

An important sphere of liturgical activity was for religious festivals. According to Finley (1985:151), there were ninety-seven liturgical appointments each year in Athens that required sponsorship of religious rites and festivals. This number rose to 118 every fourth year with the commemoration of the Panathenaic Games. Liturgical sponsorships provided funds for civic banquets, torch races, gymnastic competitions, musical choruses for civic festivals, funding comedy and dramatic performances, leading processions, and even heading delegations outside the city-state (Davies 1967; Gabrielsen 1994:7). On average the cost of many liturgies ranged from 100 to 1,000 drachmas per year (Beck 2013:293). In return for sponsorship, the wealthy received public recognition that they used to foster individual political ambitions. When their political ambitions went awry, they would use the quantity of past sponsorships to avoid punishment. Lysias (XXI.1–4) records the speech of a young man who was brought before a court and accused of taking bribes. As a main feature of his defense, he lists the large amount of money spent on public services during an 8-year period as evidence of his innocence and the unlikeliness that he would defraud the state:

> [G]entlemen of the jury ... in the archonship of Theopompus: appointed to produce tragic drama, I spent thirty minae [3,000 drachmas] and two months later, at the Thargelia, two thousand drachmae, when I won a victory with a male chorus; and in the archonship of Glaucippus ... eight hundred drachmae on pyrrhice dancers.... I won a victory with a male chorus ... and spent on it ... five thousand drachmae; then ... three hundred on a cyclic chorus at the Little Panathenaea. In the meantime, for seven years I equipped warships, at a cost of six talents [36,000 drachmas]. Although I have borne all these expenses, and have faced daily peril in your service abroad, I have nevertheless made contributions – one of thirty minae [3,000 drachmas] and another of four thousand drachmae – to special levies. As soon as I returned to these shores ... I was producing games for the Promethea ... after spending twelve minae [1,200 drachmas]. [L]ater, I was appointed to produce a chorus of children, and spent more than fifteen minae [1,500 drachmas]. In the archonship of Eucleides I produced comic drama ... spending ... sixteen minae [1,600 drachmas]; and at the Little Panathenaea I produced a chorus of beardless pyrrhic dancers, and spent seven minae [700 drachmas].
>
> (Lamb 1930:477–479)

While we do not know if this young man escaped his accusers, his donations and list of sponsorships are impressive and showed his civic spirit. Yes, he might have exaggerated the level of his public expenditures, but they were still enormous. The young man spent nearly 10 talents of silver[10] for public services that included sponsoring tragic and comedic dramas, adult and children's choruses, dancers, and athletic games, as well as sponsoring and commanding a warship in the Athenian navy. The time frame for these expenditures was the end of the 5th century, between 410 and 420 BC. These were years when

Athens was at war, and Finley (1985:151) characterizes the level of expenditure of this young man at more than twenty times of what the cost would have been for hoplites to equipment and provision themselves for military service during this same period.

While festive liturgies varied in cost, the most expensive liturgy that an individual could undertake in Athens involved the sponsorship and command of a warship in the Athenian navy. The young man in the foregoing quotation indicates that he sponsored a warship for 7 years. All wealthy families were required to pay the *eisphora*, which was a war tax levied against the total value of their estate. Because estate worth was a self-assessment declared by the owner, it should be considered a semi-voluntary contribution rather than a formal tax evaluation and levy. The military might of Athens resided in its navy where the trireme was the fighting ship of the day (Casson 1991:81–92; Morrison et al. 2000). The trireme was an oared warship propelled by three decks of oarsmen and equipped with a battering ram on its prow. It was sleek, fast, and turned quickly, making it a lethal warship. They were specialized vessels that lacked storage capacity, required a crew of around 200 persons to operate, had no other serviceable function, and were too costly to operate outside war.

Funding the navy and the cost of its operation involved undertaking a military liturgy called a *trierarchy* that was assigned to only the wealthiest of Athenian families. The institution of the trierarchy is believed to have originated in the early 5th century BC. Themistocles is said to have orchestrated the purchase of twenty triremes from Corinth that were then outfitted and commanded by wealthy Athenians who paid the crews who rowed and operated them. Several aspects of the trierarchy are particularly noteworthy. First, the ships were state owned and built rather than privately owned. Second, the men who commanded them were not professional seamen even if they privately owned a ship for personal use or to engage in commerce. Third, the primary criteria for becoming a *trierarchos*[11] was having the wealth to shoulder the cost of the office. The *trierarchos* could be a farmer, although a wise one would want to have a seasoned crew and pilot to captain the ship in a naval engagement.

Trierarchs were required to cover three primary costs. The first was to equip and supply trireme hulls with whatever equipment was necessary for their operation. This could be expensive if the previous trierarch had stripped them of sails, oars, cable, and other equipment at the end of his service. Second, triremes were manned by free citizens and seamen instead of galley slaves; this involved paying the salaries for a crew of around 200 men. Third and finally, triremes had a very limited storage capacity. They could not carry many provisions, which meant that trierarchs had to make logistical arrangements and provision their crew with food and other supplies while they were on maneuvers. Who covered the cost of a ship that was lost or damaged in combat is less clear, although it is likely that they were shared by the trierarch and the state.

The total cost of a trierarchy is hard to calculate, although Gabrielson (1994:216) estimates its average cost at 6,000–7,000 drachmas per year, which is slightly higher than the 7-year average of 5,142 drachmas spent by Lysias' young defendant quoted above.[12] While civic and religious liturgies were often held in successive years by wealthy individuals, this was not the case for individuals serving as a trierarch. The reason was simple; a trierarchy could cost anywhere from three to seven times more than even the most expensive religious and civic liturgies. In recognition of this, individuals were not required to serve as trierarchs in successive years. Instead, they were given a 2-year exemption from repeat service to recuperate their private and family wealth. Nevertheless, the burden was considerable especially during wartime when Athens attempted to maintain a navy of around 300 triremes at any given point in time.[13] To meet this need, a registry of wealthy families was established to spread the service burden of naval sponsorship between eligible individuals (Gabrielsen 1994:70).

Despite the importance of the navy for the defense of Athens, there was plenty of shirking among those expected to bear its cost. One strategy that rich citizens used to their hide wealth was to put it in merchandise, loans, and commercial ventures instead of investing it in land where wealth was most visible (Christ 1990). The best evidence that there was resistance to serve in a trierarchy was the practice of *antidosis*, which was a formal legal procedure that individuals could employ to shift the responsibilities of fulfilling a trierarchy. An *antidosis* allowed an individual to transfer a trierarchy to another eligible candidate either through a voluntary agreement or by a formal challenge. The way it worked was that the individual selected for a trierarchy (person A) could either find a replacement or identify another eligible candidate (person B) who was financially more able to undertake it. If person B refused to accept the trierarchy, then person A could challenge his refusal by proposing a direct exchange of total assets with him. If the challenged person refused to exchange property, then the affair could be brought before a jury, which would assign the disputed liturgy or trierarchy to the individual that they deemed to be wealthier. As Christ points out, "On a strictly practical level, the *antidosis* procedure was a bureaucratic convenience that enabled the city to keep its liturgical ranks full with minimal commitment of public resources. Only if private negotiations failed was the state called upon to intervene through its courts" (Christ 1990:161–162).

The Romans followed a similar pattern of elite patronage where "town finance was essentially 'liturgical,' with much or most cash revenue coming from a narrow tax-base of well-to-do office-holders" (Duncan-Jones 1990:160). Holding civic office carried with it the expectation of covering the costs of operation from personal finances, which were considerable. These obligations were the *munera* that came with the office. Town inhabitants could be called on to fulfill *munera civilia* or *munera personalia* from their own finances, which included maintaining buildings or heating public baths. *Munera patrimonni* involved service at a higher and more expensive level that included mobilizing work parties, providing billets for soldiers, covering transportation costs, supplying regional recruits for the army, sponsoring gladiatorial events, or holding the office of a priesthood (Coleman 2003:62; Duncan-Jones 1990).

The financial burden of civic office was considerable, and individuals understandably tried to evade excessive service obligations. Nevertheless, the "law ruled that if a town did not have enough men with the wealth needed to hold office, then existing office-holders must go on repeating their tenures of office" (Duncan-Jones 1990:161). Like the liturgies of Greece, formal rules came into play to mediate financial burdens placed on the wealthy as a result of holding public office. "Holding a magistracy gave five years' respite from holding the same post, but only three years' immunity from holding some other office. Going on an embassy for the town gave only two years' worth of immunity" (Duncan-Jones 1990:161).

How immunities from service were handled varied over time and space with the availability of officeholders. In some places, professionals in the middle-income strata including doctors, teachers, and rhetoricians could be given exemptions from *munera* service in limited numbers. Providing services to the community as part of one's profession could also win immunity from service. Army veterans had automatic immunity for 5 years after discharge unless they agreed voluntarily to serve as a town councilor. The immunity for veterans was made indefinite during the early 3rd century AD.[14] Merchants who shipped grain to Rome for *annona* food distributions also obtained indefinite exemption from local *munera* service. Similarly, merchants who shipped oil and oil retailers received exemptions for a period of 5 years between service.

The expectation was that people would fulfill their civic obligations to the extent that they were physically or financially able. This included the poor. Roman construction projects were undertaken using convicts condemned to forced labor as *ad opus publicum*. When this did not supply sufficient labor, citizens were conscripted. The shortage of wealthy individuals to fulfill civic services led Trajan to grant the town of Aquileia permission to make foreigners eligible for *munera* duties. The expectation of civic patronage was pervasive throughout both Greek and Roman society. The reward was public recognition and honor to the individuals who fulfilled them. The honor was amplified the more that individuals voluntarily donated their time and resources to euergetistic activities.

EUERGETISM AND VOLUNTARY PATRONAGE IN THE GRECO-ROMAN WORLD

Philanthropy, munificence, lavish generosity – these are all words used to describe the practice of euergetism. The term is derived from the Greek word *euergetēē*, which means doing good deeds.[15] It refers to the practice of patronage by wealthy elites across the Greco-Roman world who *voluntarily* used their wealth to finance secular and religious institutional activities. The level of civic generosity displayed was high in the eastern Mediterranean world and was unmatched by elites in other ancient societies.[16] Donations and gifts were made publicly in the spirit of benefiting the whole community. The practice of euergetism has been discussed in a variety of contexts (Hands 1968; Veyne 1976, 1990; Zuiderhoec 2009:11–12). Here the focus is on voluntary euergetism, namely public generosity that was unattached to compulsory donations like those associated with public office.

Most scholars agree that euergetism was an expected feature of Greek society. Aristotle identified generosity as the third virtue and moral responsibility of every individual. The Greek *polis* was defined as a community of citizens, and the munificence and public generosity of wealthy citizens represented a celebration of this civic ideal.[17] Scholars often link euergetism to earlier forms of gift-giving and reciprocity (e.g., Mauss 1990), sometimes referring to it as a form of wealth redistribution (Barnard 2011:10; Isin and Lefebvre 2005:13). They are correct in the former and incorrect in the later. While public gifting can be linked to earlier practices of leader patronage, it was not a form of redistribution. Redistribution (Chapter 5) involves the collection and distribution of resources to contributing members (Polanyi 1957; Sahlins 1972), which was not the process involved with euergetistic donations. The *euergetes* who made donations did so from the private property of their individual households. It was a transfer of personal wealth within the context of the moral economy (Gudeman 2001) back to the community in which the individual lived.

Euergetism increased in frequency in Greece during the Hellenistic age (323–31 BC) as democracy gave way to imperialistic rule. It was a way to validate the emerging inequality in both wealth and power through the outward celebration of collectivist ideals (Barnard 2011), a process that continued into the Roman period (Zuiderhoec 2009). Its early origins most likely lie in religious gift-giving, where the goodwill of the deity was thanked with the presentation of a votive offering.[18] Dedicatory inscriptions often commemorate the sponsorship of voluntary building projects. A study of euergetistic dedications at the sanctuary of Demeter at Eleusis found that during the 4th century BC most commemorations celebrated agricultural productivity or religious celebrations. During the 3rd century BC the tenor of the dedication inscriptions shifted to commemorating the civic honors of notable individuals (Barnard 2011:38).

While the Greeks can be credited with a high level of public euergetism, most public building projects drew on public funds. The reason for investment in building projects may lie in high level of public recognition associated with them. For example, in the 5th century BC, Pericles used public revenue to fund the construction of the Parthenon and other buildings in Athens, drawing complaints from his political opponents in the process. When he responded to those complaints by stating that he would pay for the temple construction himself and "dedicate all the public buildings in my name" (Scott-Kilvert 1960:181), it created such an uproar among his critics that they agreed that the use of public funds was a better option. While letting Pericles cover these construction costs would have made good economic sense, public acquiescence to using public funds was because his opponents[19] feared the public acclaim he would have garnered from sponsoring them (Beck 2013:298–299). Munificence was designed to bring an individual public honor and increase their influence and social standing within the community.

Another 5th-century notable and rival of Pericles named Cimon engaged in his own campaign of public gifting, particularly to members of his own *deme*.[20] According to Plutarch, Cimon was a rich man who used his wealth honorably toward his fellow citizens in the following way:

> He had all the fences on his fields taken down, so that not only poor Athenians, but even strangers could help themselves freely to whatever fruit was in season. He also provided dinner at his house every day, a simple meal but enough for large numbers. Any poor man who wished could come to him for this.... He always went about attended by a number of young men ... each of whom was ready, if Cimon met some elderly and poorly dressed citizen, to change clothes with him, and this custom made a deep impression. The same attendants carried with them plenty of ready money, and would go up to the better class of the poor in the marketplace and quietly slip some change into their hands.
>
> (Scott-Kilvert 1960:151)

There are few dedications to munificence in the form of feeding the poor. Nevertheless, we know that Polykritos lent money to the city to buy grain during a food crisis in 275 BC, for which he was greatly honored (Colpaert 2014:195).

While voluntary euergetism may have originated with the Greeks, it continued to be practiced within Roman society. Public inscriptions provide a wealth of information about the donations that private individuals made to fund public activities, but they do not distinguish between voluntary donations under discussion here and the donations required to fulfill the liturgies of public office. Despite vagueness in the inscriptions, there is enough evidence to indicate that voluntary donations were a regular feature of public life throughout the Roman empire. The Roman mob was an expectant lot and politicians did their best to curry their favor.

Voluntary donations varied from community to community. The three most common forms of euergetism involved funding building projects, public festivals, and public distributions of money. Cicero said Rome was built for nothing because forced public labor[21] was used in construction projects (Duncan-Jones 1990:174). This is true, but he was also acknowledging that private sponsorship of building projects was the most common form of euergetistic activity. In an analysis of 529 dedicatory inscriptions from Roman Asia Minor, Zuiderhoec (2009:table 5.1) identified 58% related to public building projects, 17% for public distributions of money, 13% linked to festivals and games, and the remaining 12% associated with a miscellanea of different activities. These are approximate estimates since many distributions of money were made during festivals (Zuiderhoec 2009:98).

Public construction was the favored activity, or at least the one with the most durable evidence. It may have been favored because the buildings carried the sponsor's name in an inscription. According to Kalinowski (1996), private donations accounted for the construction of most of the public buildings in the city of Ephesus in Rome's eastern empire. Cicero expressed his opinion about the importance of public construction with the statement: "the expenditure of money is better justified when it is made for walls, docks, harbours, aqueducts and all works which are of service to the community. There is to be sure, more of present satisfaction in what is handed out, like cash down: nevertheless public improvements win us greater gratitude with posterity" (Miller 1913:233).

While most building sponsorships were made by local residents, some important donations were made by nonresidents. Kalinowski (1996:28–30) documents huge contributions by Pliny the Younger to construction projects in two Italian towns while he was a senator and resident in Rome. These two towns were Comum, which was his birthplace, and Tiernum Tiberinum, where he was adopted as a community patron after inheriting a local estate from his uncle. Pliny spent 5 million sesterces in these two towns. His donations in Comum paid for one-third of the cost for a school, a library, the construction of a public bath, and the establishment of a foundation for its upkeep. His donations also founded an alimentary institution to feed children as well as a civic association to fund an annual public banquet. At Tiernum Tiberinum he funded the construction of a temple and commissioned the statues that adorned it (Kalinowski 1996:29).

Ward-Perkins (1984:3) feels that most of the public buildings constructed in Italy before AD 300 employed money from private donations. A comparative analysis of two communities (Thugga and Thamugadi) in northern Africa illustrates the variability in civic sponsorship that was associated with architectural construction (Duncan-Jones 1990:181–183). While most of the buildings in Thugga were constructed by private patrons, the majority of those in Thamugadi were paid for using public funds. Together the sample of 115 buildings from these two communities reveals that 58% of all public buildings were financed by private funds, while the remaining 42% of buildings were from public funds. While this sample is small, it underscores the importance of private donations in civic building projects.

Arjan Zuiderhoec (2009) has provided a detailed profile of euergetistic patrons in eastern Asia minor under the Roman empire. He notes a significant increase in public euergetism in the second and early 3rd centuries AD, which he credits to an increase in economic inequality that the wealthy attempted to mediate by increased displays of public munificence. His conclusion, based on a sample of 514 benefactions, was threefold. First, the total quantity of donations represented only a small percentage of total elite income. Second, most of the donations made were relatively small.[22] Third and finally, more than 50% of the money spent on donations came from only 5–6% of the donors represented in these inscriptions. While most big donors in the Roman world were male, prominent women could also play a role. A woman priestess named Eumachia funded and dedicated the construction of a large civic building that was probably used by the fuller's guild on the east side of the forum at Pompeii.

A final comment needs to be made regarding euergetism and support for the poor, especially given the *lex frumentum* and the practice of distributing food to the poor in Rome and other Italian cities (Rickman 1980a; Woolf 1990). While this would seem like a natural arena for munificence as it was for Cimon in 5th-century BC Athens, charity to the poor was not a driving factor for Romans. As Finley (1985:40) points out, the debt policy toward the poor was harsh, hereditary, and unyielding. Finley feels that the *alimenta* food programs implemented by Trajan (AD 98–117) were to encourage demographic growth rather than out of concern for the poor. Peter Brown (2002) has pointed out that rich *euergetes* were always praised for loving their home cities rather than helping the poor. Where did public charity and concern for the poor originate in the Mediterranean world? Brown characterizes its appearance in the following way:

> Love of the poor ... did not grow naturally out of the ideals of public beneficence.... It could only come to the fore as a meaningful public virtue when the ancient "civic" sense of the community was weakened. In the period of late antiquity ... Christian and Jewish charity ... was a new departure. It was frequently presented as a challenge to the classical, pagan image of "civic" community.
>
> (Brown 2002:5–6)

Charity for the poor originated in the 1st century AD within the Judeo-Christian world.[23] It did not fit well into the overall pattern of Greco-Roman euergetism.

TOLLS AND TARIFFS

Trade between regions can be traced back to the dawn of human civilization (Chapters 2 and 7). Trade was always risky because of the possibility of theft from robbers and pirates. Nevertheless, as the movement of goods grew in scale and frequency, local leaders realized that it was more profitable to charge a recurrent tax for safe movement through their territories than it was to rob the occasional passerby. This had two advantages. First, it provided access to nonlocal, often exotic goods that could be obtained through a tax-in-kind. Second, by regularizing interaction with merchants, they could also place orders for particular types of merchandise that could serve as payment for safe passage through their territories. The result was that tolls and tariffs became a profitable source of institutional revenue in every area of the ancient world where long-distance trade occurred.

A distinction is drawn here between tolls and tariffs even if they are hard to distinguish from each other. Tolls refer to a fee charged for the privilege of moving through a territory, on a road, or along a transportation route. Tariffs are duties or surcharges imposed on goods imported into or exported from a specific area. There is a considerable degree of inconsistency in the way that scholars interpret this information[24] and whether goods were taxed simply as a result of moving between regions or when goods actually changed hands or left specific jurisdictions. While these distinctions are important for understanding the structure of economic activity, tolls and tariffs are considered together as means of taxing goods moving through commercial channels. How lucrative tolls and tariffs were for the groups collecting them depended on a great many variables, including the scale of trade, how revenue was collected, the purpose for which tolls and tariffs were collected, and what alternative sources of taxable income were available for institutional use. On the whole, however, transient fees needed to be relatively modest and provide value for the services provided. If they were too expensive, they would impede the movement of goods or merchants would seek alternative routes.

Transient tolls were charged by societies at all levels of complexity ranging from tribes and chiefdoms to states and empires. In pre-colonial Africa indigenous merchants and merchant caravans regularly paid tolls for safe passage across the territories of different ethnic groups. Sedentary groups such as the Logoli often positioned their settlements at key junctions along rivers and trade routes specifically to collect tolls from passing merchants.[25] No caravans were allowed to pass through the territory of the Mossi if they did not pay a transient tax; wise caravan leaders paid the tax and established relationships with the chiefs to ensure their protection (Stevenson 1968:127, 140; Sundström 1974:9). West African merchants such as the Maraka balanced safety against cost and traveled with their own warrior escorts, avoiding areas with high tolls and tariffs (Roberts 1987:68).

Tolls along transportation routes were especially prevalent in north Africa where gold, salt, and slaves moved through the trans-Sahara trade. Salt was needed as a dietary supplement throughout Africa and was traded for gold and slaves that moved into the Mediterranean. The key production locales for salt were Taghaza and Taoudeni, located in inhospitable areas of the western Sahara; trade routes passed through the territories of hostile pastoral tribes such as the Tuareg, Sanhaja, and Zenata, among others[26] (Bovill 1970:47–50). Salt moved by donkey from Saharan production areas southward into more settled regions. Here merchants had to pay a duty of 1 gold dinar for every donkey-load of salt entering the kingdom of Ghana and 2 for leaving. A 10% in-kind duty on salt entering and leaving domains was common. Tolls also were paid to the Tuareg for salt leaving Taoudenni as well as in multiple locations throughout the Niger region.

The community of Timbuktu was a key location in the trans-Saharan salt trade, and its founding is claimed to have been the result of Djenné merchants who wanted to obtain salt without paying tolls to Mali fiscal authorities. The tolls and tariffs paid on salt were high and ranged from one-third (one salt bar out of three) to 75–90% of total volume shipped between Timbuktu and areas 800 kilometers further south (Sundström 1974:133–136). Relationships along trans-Saharan trade routes were fragile, resulting in the construction of desert forts along trade routes and the need for military escorts accompanying caravans. The payment of tolls and guarantees of safe passage from one tribe did not protect caravans from others. Constant conflicts in the early 19th century AD between the Tubu and the Tuareg led to continual attacks on caravans along the Tripoli–Bornu route (Bovill 1970:245, figure 9).

Tolls along trade routes also were common throughout the Near East. Interpolity relations were important in regulating trade between state-sponsored merchants. A treaty ratified between Ebla and Assur in the 24th century BC stipulated that merchants could operate tariff and toll free if they paid their normal taxes to their respective administrators (Aubet 2013:136). By the Old Babylonian period (2000–1600 BC), conditions had changed.[27] Documents from the city of Mari indicate a toll was levied on traders moving along the Euphrates by boat or caravan (Renger 2003:29). From then on, tolls, tariffs, or market taxes were a common source of institutional income. Throughout the Neo-Assyrian period (911–612 BC) tolls were regularly levied on goods moving into and out of their empire (Jursa and Moreno Garcia 2015:130). One of the first references to trade between Assyria and the kingdom of Saba (Sheba) refers to the failure to pay tolls. A caravan of 100 people and 200 camels from Saba carrying myrrh, wool, iron, alabaster, and blue and purple dyed cloth apparently skirted the customs station and was apprehended for nonpayment of tolls (Robin 2005:17).

Tolls and tariffs in the Greco-Roman world commonly were collected in harbors where ships docked to load and unload goods. In the Greek port of Piraeus and others across the Mediterranean, customs officials normally levied a 2% duty on the value of the cargo that ships loaded or unloaded at the port. This was not a protective tariff but, together with fees collected for use of harbor facilities, was a way of covering the cost of the port facilities (Casson 1991:99). Athens attempted to charge a 5% tariff on all imports and exports throughout its empire as well as a 10% toll on ships passing through the Bosporus. But these levies were hard to enforce and were not enduring forms of taxation compared with the 2% harbor tariff (Ober 2015:509).

In ancient Rome indirect levies in the form of tolls, tariffs, and duties were referred to as the *portoria*. They ranged from 2% to 5% within the empire,[28] and individuals traveling with merchandise could expect to pay tolls several times in the course of their travels. Tan (2015) identifies tolls as one of the three major forms of tax during the Roman republic.[29] Zuiderhoec (2009) feels that tariffs on goods entering communities was an important income stream even at low rates of only 2–4%.[30] The importance of local tariffs is evident at the city of Palmyra where a public inscription referred to as the *portoria palmyrenorum* lists tariffs due on goods sold in its local marketplace. While Palmyra was an important center of long-distance trade (Young 2001), the majority of the goods enumerated in the tariff lists are staple goods such as dried produce, purple-dyed fleece, goat skins, olive oil, animal fat, and salt fish.[31] The public proclamation of tariff rates was intended to reduce debates between merchants and administrators collecting these surcharges. Interestingly, no charge was exacted on produce brought into the city from the region around Palmyra compared with goods brought in from outside its territory. Most of the tariffs on staples were on *exports*, highlighting the importance of keeping food and staple goods in the city for consumption (Matthews 1984).

High-value imports entering from outside the Roman empire had a higher *portoria*. A great deal of the trade with India took place via Egypt. According to information recorded in the *Periplus Maris Erythraei*, in the 1st century AD[32] ships left Egypt via the ports of Myos Hormos and Berenicé on the Red Sea. The round-trip voyage from these ports to India normally took a year, when they returned laden with precious stones, pearls, ivory, silk, cotton textiles, frankincense, myrrh, nard, pepper, cassia, cinnamon, and other high-value goods (Casson 1989). Ships would unload at the two ports and goods would be carried overland by caravan to Koptos (Qift) on the Nile where they would be stored in a warehouse until a *portoria* was paid that covered the cost of policing the eastern roads from the Red Sea ports. Once the tax was paid, goods were loaded on boats and shipped down the Nile to Alexandria where they were stored in a public warehouse, inventoried, and a second *portoria* of 25% was levied against all goods. This was the general tariff for goods entering the empire by overland routes from the east (Casson 1989; Young 2001).

The structure of tolls and tariffs changed with the politics and the conditions surrounding interregional trade. Tolls were often suspended throughout the Mediterranean during festivals to promote the flow of goods to places where they were needed. Ögödei, son of Genghis Khan, abolished local tolls and garrisoned troops along the Silk Road in the AD 1230s to foster the flow of trade between east and west (Weatherford 2004:136). While Ögödei died in AD 1241, the cost-saving efforts that he instilled could still be felt in the early 14th century when the Venetian merchant Francesco Balducci Pegolotti (1936) estimated that the total round trip cost of tolls and duties for a trip to China was only about 6% of the total value of the merchandise.[33] In some areas, however, tolls more closely resembled extortion. For example, ships sailing through the straits of Malacca on their way from India to China could either stop and pay a toll at the port of Palemban or be attacked by pirates (Hirth and Rockhill 1911:60). What is clear is that tolls and tariffs were an important component of fiscal policy in most complex societies where goods moved over long distances. While tariffs were employed as a form of protectionism in emerging industrial countries as they were in the United States at the beginning of the Civil War (Bernstein 2008:324), in the ancient world tolls, tariffs, and custom duties were primary vehicles for generating institutional revenue.

AGRARIAN LAND TAXATION: TAXING FARMERS

Most early complex societies were based on agriculture,[34] so it is important to examine the relationship between political institutions and the agrarian base. After all, commoner farmers made up the overwhelming majority of the population in preindustrial agricultural societies and provided the labor to support the institutional economy. Two general questions need to be answered in this regard. The first is, How was the broad commoner base organized to produce tax revenue for higher -order institutions? The second question is, How did the structure of this revenue system develop and change over time? Peasant farmers were heavily taxed in a number of ancient societies, but the important question is, Was this was a ubiquitous feature of all early agrarian states, or did it develop gradually as institutions grew in size and the need for revenue increased?

The unfortunate truth is that there is very little systematic discussion of how agrarian populations were taxed in early states. Most of the information on taxation comes from later states that had writing. Nevertheless, there are clues.

As discussed in Chapter 5, the institutional economy of many early state societies was organized in whole, or in part, by forms of direct production using corvée labor that received food rations for their time and effort. This contrasts with forms of direct taxation of agrarian producers that mobilized resources from commoner households. Although a large percentage of institutional costs in the Greco-Roman world was financed by elite patronage, citizen farmers in Athens also were required to pay a small agrarian tax on the grain they produced. According to Aristotle, this tax was one-tenth of the harvest (a *dekatē*) at the time of Peisistratos (ca. 550–527 BC). The grain tax was reduced to one-twentieth of the harvest (an *eikostē*) under the sons of Peisistratos between 527 and 510 BC. Farmers were freed from this agrarian tax entirely during the 5th century BC and good years of the 4th century BC when income from mines, tribute from allies, and other sources provided the state income. During these years, citizen farmers paid tax only when the state was in dire need of resources (Bresson 2016:104). Not only was the agrarian tax a small percentage of the total harvest, but it decreased over time, at least for a while. The early Greek tax on citizen farmers was not an oppressive levy that ruthlessly exploited commoner households.

Agrarian taxes were more consistently collected in the external possessions of Athens. In the early 4th century the law of 375/4 BC levied a tax of one-twelfth (a *dōdekatē*) on the grain produced on the islands of Imbros, Lemnos, and Skyros. Likewise, in the 3rd century the leaders of Samos levied a one-twentieth, or 5%, tax on its possessions in Anaia. As Bresson points out, the other known tax rates never exceeded more than a one-twelfth (8.33%) assessment. The wealth tax rate of the *eisphora* that was applied to citizens was never this high, nor would it have been tolerated. Lending rates of more than 8.33% were considered usurious; land rent in Athens never exceeded 8%. In Sparta helots paid a tax of 50% of their harvests, but they were not free citizens and were taxed accordingly at a high rate (Bresson 2016:104–106).

One area of the Hellenistic world that had high agricultural tax rates was Ptolemaic Egypt where Bresson (2016:104) cites a 50% tax rate on grain and a one-sixth production tax on vineyards and orchards. Closer inspection of the information, however, indicates that this 50% rate was not a tax, but the combined rent and tax paid by individuals leasing land from state estates for their own use (Manning 2003:123). A good deal of the arable land in Egypt was held privately, with personal claims based on long-term use (Manning 2003:89). Manning (2003:60) says a flat tax was charged on domain lands using a fixed measure of grain, calculated in artabas, for a given area under cultivation calculated according to aroura.[35] The tax rates ranged from one-half to 2 artabas of grain per aroura, which probably reflected differences in land quality and yield. When these figures are converted to metric equivalents, they represent a tax of one-twenty-fifth of the harvest for the half-artaba tax rate, one-twelfth of the harvest for the 1-artaba rate, and one-sixth of the harvest for the 2-artaba tax rate. While not low, the highest one-sixth rate is fully three times less than the 50% rental rate extracted from those leasing state domain lands.

Like Egypt, the great kingdoms of the Indian subcontinent were agrarian states and land taxation was the mainstay of institutional support as early as the Vedic period around 1000 BC. Comprehensive taxation was based on the principle that the king received one-sixth (16.7%) of all the produce of the land in exchange for maintaining peace and justice. Tax rates given in Hindu texts range from one-sixth to one-twelfth of the harvest yield, with the former being the most frequently mentioned over the length of Indian history. Whatever the rate of taxation used, the guiding principle was that taxation should never take so much as to threaten the livelihood of peasant households. Taxation in India was based on the principle that taxes had to be fair, predictable, and low enough so as to avoid creating hardships among the people being taxed. These views are expressed in different ways in the Panchatantra, an ancient Indian collection of animal fables attributed to the scholar Vishnu Sharma. These texts reveal that taxation should operate just as "the gardener plucks fruits and flowers but does not harm the trees and the bees sucks honey without damaging the flower, so also the king should collect taxes but should not cause any suffering to his subjects" (Prasad 1987:27).

Although different levels of taxation were used over time by governments across the Indian subcontinent,[36] the one-sixth levy was established as the most common rate for land taxation by the 4th century BC. This is made clear in the Mahābhārata epic where it states, "With the sixth part upon a fair calculation, after the yield of the soil, as his tribute, with fines and forfeitures, levied upon offenders, with the imposts according to the scriptures, upon traders in return for the protection granted to them, a king should fill his treasury" (Prasad 1987:56).

How this tax levy was assessed as a percentage of the total crop is suggested by an account in the Jākata tales believed to date to the 4th century BC. Prasad summarizes the account dealing with the collection of the tax on a rice field in the following way:

> an official of the king . . . once the crop in the fields was ripe for being cut, came to see it in person. Then under his supervision, the crop was measured by making it into heaps and in this process marks (*lakkham*) appear to have been used. Then the king's share (*rāja-bhāga*) was first set apart and later the balance could be stored in the granary of the owner of the field of rice and not before.
>
> (Prasad 1987:57)

The percentage division of the harvest as described was a simple and straightforward procedure for collecting an agricultural tax. As a result, states where agricultural production was the basis of their institutional economy often developed comprehensive land surveys and censuses to monitor production yields. Examples of where this occurred include ancient Egypt, Japan, India, Byzantium, and Persia. The practice of land surveying appeared early in Egypt as a function of relocating property boundaries after the annual flooding of the Nile. Later land surveys were initiated primarily in response to the need to estimate revenue to cover growing institutional costs.

How burdensome, therefore, was the land tax on households in ancient agrarian states? Any level of taxation can be seen as burdensome from the point of view of the taxpayer. The perspective of rulers in subcontinental India, however, was to tax fairly and not kill the taxpayer. Their solution was the adoption of a one-sixth tax rate, or 16.67%, on production on agrarian production. Whether they applied this fairness principle on a consistent basis is another question. Determining if a given tax rate was light or burdensome would vary from region to region,[37] but this at least was a baseline for evaluating institutional intrusiveness into the domestic economy. While taxation probably stripped agrarian households of most of their disposable surplus, no ruler wanted to see the tax base reduced through revolt, migration, or the starvation of taxpayers (Kiser and Levi 2015).

In general, agrarian tax rates throughout antiquity appear to have been relatively low compared with modern tax rates. They rarely exceeded 16.67%, the one-sixth tax rate on production output, and often are well below it. Solon the Athenian law maker saw the one-sixth rate to sharecroppers renting land as too high and brought about reforms that made in-kind taxes on agriculture rare in Attica. Agricultural taxes in the Roman world[38] ranged from 10% to 12% (Hopkins 1980:116), which is below the one-sixth tax rate on private land in Ptolemaic Egypt. During the 10th to 12th century AD, the yearly land tax in Byzantium was 10–12% of the yearly crop yield (Haldon 2015:361) and compared favorably with the one-eighth to one-tenth tax rate on grain harvests in the Ottoman empire (Coşgel 2015:408). Within the Neo-Assyrian empire (911–612 BC), the king levied a 10% tax on the produce of the land (Sharlach 2004:167). In early imperial China agricultural tax rates were even lower. During the Qin (221–206 BC) through Han (206 BC–AD 220) dynasties, the tax rate on grain was one-fifteenth of the harvest, or 6.67% of the total annual yield. In 178 BC Chao Cuo wrote that a 10% tax would represent a colossal burden on peasants, which was about what they paid when their additional poll or hearth tax was added in (Lewis 2015:291).

Of course, these low tax rates were high-level rules-of-thumb, and one has to wonder about the extent of abuse and exploitation that took place at lower bureaucratic levels at the hands of corrupt administrators and tax collectors. The recourse for appeal by individuals who felt they were abused was to go to the higher authorities, just as tenant farmers did who worked on royal estates in Roman Egypt (Kehoe 2007). Roman law makers recognized that the agrarian peasantry was vulnerable to excessive exploitation through taxation and other demands. A concern for taxation fairness can be found in the legislative reforms invoked by rulers who were concerned about the welfare of their agrarian majority. Solon's reforms of 594/593 BC were a partial response to the dire straits of peasant farmers who had gotten themselves into debt by renting land at one-sixth of the harvest rate from wealthy landowners. Farmers pledged themselves as collateral for loans, and when they were unable to pay, they were sold into slavery. Solon canceled those debts, thereby protecting rural farmers from exploitation by the wealthy (Scott-Kilvert 1960:57–58; Starr 1977:181–184).

The law codes of Mesopotamia mention abuses to farmers and common laborers, and often canceled the debts used to enslave them or strip them of their property. One of the earliest of these debt relief initiatives was the Reforms of Urukagina in 24th century BC, which returned farms taken from their original owners (Liverani 2013:113–114). The most frequent basis for land transfer in Old Babylonian times was through forfeiture of debt. Clean-slate proclamations of debt were needed since the tax collector could also function as a money lender.[39] The edict of Ammisaduqa in 1646 BC was a big one; it canceled debts and bond service established since the last clean-slate proclamation made by the king 16 years earlier in 1662 BC. Likewise, the earlier 18th-century law code of Hammurabi blocked the practice of farmers pledging their land as collateral for loans to prevent privatization of their ancestral crop land (Hudson 1999b:467; 2000:15; Van de Mieroop 1999:206).

The same fairness principles were the basis for the Jubilee Year celebration every 50 years in ancient Israel. In principle, slaves and bondsmen would be freed at this time, debts would be canceled, and rural properties that were sold could be redeemed by their original owners. "And you shall hallow the fiftieth year, and proclaim liberty throughout the land to all its inhabitants; it shall be a jubilee for you, when each of you shall return to his property and each of you shall return to his family. A jubilee shall that fiftieth year be to you" (Leviticus 25:10–11).

The model of the good ruler in all ancient societies was one who was just and fair and who protected his people. That was not always the case, but there is evidence to show that exploitation of the agrarian farmer was just as often the result of incurring debt from borrowing to pay taxes, buy seed, or meet other needs as it was the result of excessive land taxation. Of course, systems of land taxation evolved and changed over time. One of the most rapid ways this occurred was through the annexation or incorporation of territory into a larger empire through conquest and the introduction of new demands that this could create.

EMPIRES, TRIBUTE, AND TAXATION

Empire building involved the subjugation and annexation of new territory. Subjugated areas were always required to provide goods and resources as tribute to new overlords both at the moment of conquest and afterward for as long as they remained a tax-paying province within an empire. How these resources were extracted could vary widely. Tribute could be extracted as compulsory and voluntary gifts, the removal of population as slaves, the confiscation and reassignment of lands, the introduction of foreign colonists, the expropriation of craft industries, or the levying of a whole array of taxes on land, property, and commerce. Revenue could also be extracted by creating new classes of fines, fees, and licenses. If existing elites remained in place after conquest, they were forced either to pay tribute levies out of their existing fiscal regimes or to pass the burden of creating more wealth onto the general population. All things being equal, local elites preferred the latter even though it could increase economic stress within their province.

Revenue was collected from tributary provinces in three different ways. The most common was to use existing forms of revenue collection since both the rationale and means of collection were already in place. While this could create considerable variability in how revenue was mobilized across the empire, it left most of the cost of its collection in the hands of regional administrators. The Aztec tribute empire (Berdan et al. 1996) and the Persian empire under king Cyrus (550–530 BC) and Cambyses (530–522 BC) are examples of this type of organization.[40] Alternatively, existing revenue-producing institutions could be left in place but modified to accommodate new economic practices of the conquerors. Ptolemaic Egypt (305–30 BC) fits this model; it maintained the same tax and administrative structure of the preceding Egyptian pharaonic state but added several new Greek institutions to it, including banking, tax farming, and auctions of property (Manning 2003:137). Third and finally, a new single tax standard or method of tax calculation could be implemented across all provinces in the kingdom. This normally occurred in more mature empires to increase revenues or to make their collection more efficient. Darius was the first king to standardize taxation on land within the twenty provinces of the Persian empire by setting a value on land along with an assessment in proportion to its valuation (Briant 2002:70). According to Herodotus, to establish the value of this land tax, "The land was precisely measured in parasangs and classified according to crops cultivated or even according to the size of the harvest" (cited in Hudson 2000:11). The general approach to fixing tribute levies at the provincial level under Darius is described in the following way: "After fixing the amount of taxes which his subjects were to pay, he sent for the leading men of the provinces, and asked them if the taxes were not perhaps heavy; and when the men said that the taxes were moderate, he ordered that each should pay only half as much" (Briant 2002:393).

An important consideration of early state tribute empires was the relationship between their overall size and the structure of their system of institutional finance. As discussed in the previous chapter, institutional economies can be characterized as systems of staple finance, wealth finance using an array of high-value items, or, in its final form, as a monetized economy. Of course, these are not mutually exclusive categories and the actual organization of revenue collection can involve all three of these systems. An example of composite revenue collection was when the land tax or a poll tax on the individual was calculated in coin but collected as in-kind resources such as grain.

Of these three fiscal systems, staple finance was the most difficult to manage within large territorial states and empires. Systems of staple finance throughout antiquity always mobilized grain, livestock, and or other types of consumables. Some of the problems in organizing and managing these systems included (1) supervising and/or monitoring the production of staple goods, (2) organizing their collection at harvest, (3) storing them in appropriate facilities, (4) planning production levels against consumption needs, (5) developing an inventory tracking system to monitor resource levels against consumption, (6) transporting staple goods to their point of use, and (7) converting staples into alternative goods when they were required. All of these activities have transaction costs associated with them in terms of the time and personnel involved in carrying them out (Hopkins 1980:123; Levi 1989; North 1978, 1981).

How these activities were organized had a strong bearing on their total cost and who incurred them. For example, the stipulation that an in-kind tax on grain be paid at a central storage facility transferred the costs of transportation to the taxpayer. Furthermore, the requirement that the tax on grain be paid only in coin similarly placed the cost of converting the grain to cash onto the taxpayer. These changes could have secondary effects within society beyond reducing the costs of revenue collection for the central state. Keith Hopkins (1980) has argued that the collection of tax in coin had a strong positive effect on the Roman economy by increasing the level of trade across the Mediterranean between 200 BC and AD 200. Farmers had to sell their crops to raise the money to pay their tax in the same way that artisans had to sell their goods. Hopkins feels that the shortage of currency in mid- to late 3rd century AD forced a return to in-kind tax payments, which reduced the general level of economic activity across the Mediterranean. The same was the case in Japan when the Tokugawa shogunate switched from collecting taxes in coin to collecting them in rice during the late 16th century AD in what is referred to as the *kokudaka* system (Osamu 1975; Yamamura 1988).

One of the earliest systems of provincial taxation for which there is documentary information is the bala system, which operated in southern Mesopotamia during the Ur III period (2112–2004 BC). Staple finance was the primary way that institutions were supported during this period.[41] The bala was the system used to mobilize resources from nineteen provinces in the central core of the Ur III state and distribute them to temple and administrative institutions in the primary centers of Ur, Nippur, and Uruk (Steinkeller 1987). In keeping with the complexities of organizing a system of staple finance, the region the bala administered was relatively small, covering an area 400 kilometers long and 100 kilometers wide along the Tigris and Euphrates Rivers. It was a complex accounting system that shifted goods produced in the provinces to cities and other areas where they were needed.

The bala was the central administrative mechanism that matched institutional needs with the production and allocation of tribute goods. Tonia Sharlach (2004) provides a detailed discussion of the bala system, which she sees as an organized system of revenue allocation. "Bala" means rotation, and each province was allocated a period during which its designated tribute would be turned in throughout the year. The resources mobilized through the tribute network were diverse and included grain, flour, reeds, timber, and manufactured goods, as well as labor for specific service activities for both men and women.[42] Livestock were particularly prominent in the bala system because of the need for sacrificial animals in temple rites and ceremonies. The site of Puzriš-Dagan, located 10 kilometers southeast of Nippur, was a central administrative and accounting center for cattle, small livestock, animal products, and the goods manufactured from them, including shoes.

Sharlach (2004:35) believes that institutional needs were determined on a yearly basis and forwarded to bala administrators for tabulation and assignment. Resources were collected within each province during its bala period and then allocated for institutional use within the three major cities, other provinces, or within the same province where they originated. How tribute was mobilized within each province is less clear, but revenue appears to have come from both royal and temple domains as well as private holdings. Tribute quotas had to be met on time, but it was also possible for a governor of a province to "pay forward" into the bala, contributing more than was requested during the year and receive a credit against future revenue levies. The system was flexible enough to allow institutions to charge expenses to their accounts as needed. The textual evidence from the city of Umma indicates that "When courtiers or even members of the royal family traveled through Umma, expenses for their upkeep could be charged to the bala account" (Sharlach 2004:46).

In this sense the bala and all of its associated administrative apparatus served as record of taxation and a system for the assembly, transportation, and allocation of goods to where they were used. Because the taxation system was in staple goods, institutional accounting had to plan and keep track of where and when specific goods were needed. This was achieved by careful recording of each of the different resource categories involved.

The Aztec empire (AD 1428–1521) provides a view of how a tribute network was organized using a combination of both wealth and staple goods. The Aztec empire was a discontinuous patchwork of conquered and tax-paying provinces and client states (M. Smith 2012:table 7.1), which extended over 160,000–165,000 square kilometers and contained 6 million to 10 million people.[43] Two things make this case interesting for purposes of comparative study. First, Mesoamerica lacked beasts of burden, which meant that all staple and wealth tribute mobilized from the provinces of the empire was moved into the Aztec capital on the backs of human porters. Second, it is the only area of the ancient world where a complete itemized list exists for all the yearly tribute entering the Aztec capital from tax-paying provinces (Berdan and Anawalt 1992; Berdan et al. 1996; Reyes García 1997). This provides a unique opportunity to see how wealth and staple goods were used together to mobilize revenue from tax-paying provinces under difficult transportation conditions.

The central palace of the Aztec king contained a room where records were kept that recorded the type and quantity of goods that provinces paid quarterly throughout the year. Figure 6.1 illustrates a leaf from one of the tribute ledgers recorded in pictographic style. The toponym glyphs down the left side and across the bottom of the document list the names of the tribute-paying towns in the province, while the rest of the images record the types and quantities of goods paid as tribute. This figure illustrates several characteristics of the Aztec tribute system. Every province had its own individual list of goods that they were required to pay. Each list was itemized to the specific amounts required, and none of the provinces turned in the identical type or quantity of goods. Tax levies were a mixture of both staple and wealth goods. The exact goods required depended on the location of the province within the empire, its distance to the Aztec capital, and what goods were available through trade with nearby areas, or could be produced by the tax-paying population.

Table 6.1 provides a list of the annual tribute from the Aztec empire and reveals the diversity of goods demanded. Food was included in the levies as granaries of maize, beans, amaranth, or chia;[44] other consumables included chili, honey, maguey syrup, salt, prepared war rations, and cacao. The majority of the tribute items listed in Table 6.1 were wealth goods or the raw materials to make them. Cotton textiles were at the top of the list and included both richly decorated cloaks as well as plain white *quachtli*, which, along with cacao beans, served as a form of currency among the Aztecs (Chapter 9). The feathers of tropical birds were especially prized and were used to make elaborate apparel worn by the elite (Berdan 2006). A range of other items also was collected from the provinces that produced them. Examples of these goods

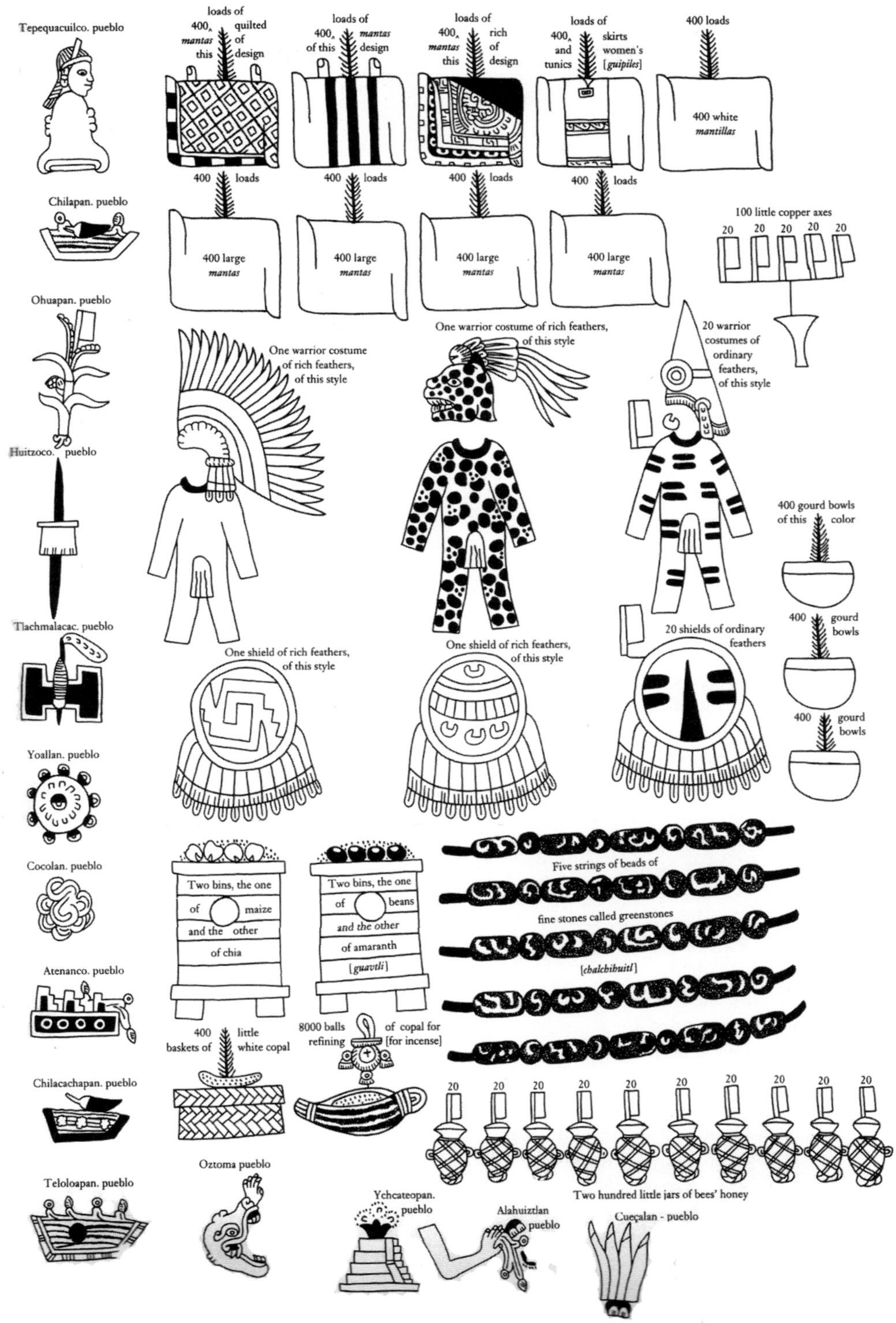

6.1 The Province of Tepequacuilco tribute leaf from the Codex Mendoza. (Reprinted with permission from Berdan and Anawalt 1992, volume 4:Folio 37r)

TABLE 6.1 *Annual tribute paid to Tenochtitlan listed in the Codex Mendoza*

Tribute items	Quantity
Manta cloths	
Plain white	68,000
Decorated and quilted	52,000
Richly decorated	8,000
Total manta cloths	128,000
Clothing	
Men's loincloths	7,200
Women's shirts and tunics	12,000
Warrior's costumes and shields	665
Food	
Bins of foodstuffs	88
Loads of chili	1,600
Jars of honey and syrup	3,800
Loaves of salt	4,000
Baskets of *pinolli* (war rations)	160
Cacao: loads and baskets	840
Miscellaneous items	
Loads of raw cotton	4,400
Loads of lime	16,800
Bags of cochineal	65
Beams and planks	14,400
Carrying frames	800
Loads of firewood	4800
Reed mats and seats	16,000
Sheets of paper	32,000
Canes	48,000
Smoking canes	32,000
Gourd bowls	17,600
Pottery bowls	2,400
Rubber balls	16,000
Copal: balls and baskets	67,200
Pans of yellow ochre	40
Exotic goods	
Seashells	1,600
Live eagles	2 or more
Live enemy warriors	Unspecified
Deerskins	3,200
Jaguar skins	40
Liquidambar: jars and cakes	16,100
Lip plugs	82
Amber ornamental items	2
Turquoise ornamental items	15
Jade ornamental items	22
Copper bells	80
Copper axes	560
Gold: bowls, bars, and disks	130
Gold ornamental items	5
Feathers and skins	
Quetzal feathers	2,480

Blue and red cotinga feathers	17,600
Green and yellow feathers	9,600
Green and yellow bunches	4
Feather ornamental items	3
Bags of feather down	20
Bird skins	160

include lime for soaking maize, paper for recording accounts and sacrificial offerings, natural rubber, copal incense, and cochineal and yellow ochre for use as dyes.

All these goods were transported by porters to the Aztec capital where they were stored in the palace and other imperial storehouses (Hirth 2016; Kobayashi 1993a). The emphasis on lightweight, high-value goods was a result of the high cost of transporting them (Hassig 1985). Unlike the bala system where production was matched to institutional needs, the Aztec tribute system was more generalized. Regionally specialized consumables were included in the tribute lists, as were local raw materials,[45] but there does not seem to have been a one-for-one attempt to match institutional needs with tribute levies. Instead, the focus was on mobilizing generalized wealth from the provinces, which could be converted into alternative goods in the capital's central marketplace to meet specific institutional needs[46] (Chapter 9).

The goods paid as tribute from provinces were produced in the typical fashion using corvée labor (Chapter 5). Cotton textiles were produced by growing cotton and having women spin the thread, weave the cloth, and dye or embroider it as required. When cotton[47] or another requested resource was not available in the region, residents obtained it from neighboring groups or from merchants engaging in commerce between regions (Berdan 1987; Hassig 1985). The principle of generalized equivalencies operated within the tax system. Tribute records from the provinces of Tlapa,[48] Cihuatlan, and Tepequacuilco in the modern state of Guerrero reveal that the tribute turned in to the Aztec tribute supervisors did not exactly match one-for-one with what was turned in at the Aztec capital (Gutiérrez 2013; Litvak King 1971). It was higher. This indicates two things about the Aztec tribute system: first, that tax was computed in terms of the relative value of alternative goods, and, second, that tribute supervisors assisted in procuring the items required to meet tribute demands using the goods turned in at the provincial level.[49]

The Aztec and Ur III states both imposed taxes on their conquered provinces. Both empires were of short duration and developed economies that lacked coinage but used wealth good currencies as units of value and units of account.[50] The result was that tax levies were paid in both staple and wealth goods. The bala was a carefully organized collection and accounting system where provincial resource levies were matched to institutional resource needs. The Aztecs also collected food and utilitarian goods from their empire, but most of the tribute from outlying provinces consisted of wealth goods. The cost of tax collection and transportation was absorbed at the provincial level. Where the Aztec system differed sharply from the bala was in their reliance on commercial agents and a system of marketplaces that absorbed the cost of converting resources from the tribute network into alternative goods as they were needed.

METHODS OF TAX COLLECTION

Just as there was a great deal of variation in the types of activities that governments taxed, so too there was variation in how taxes were collected. As discussed above, the structure of the revenue system in terms of goods or currency strongly affected the costs of estimating, collecting, inventorying, transporting, and using the resources required. All things being equal, systems of institutional taxation tended to evolve toward maximizing net revenue while minimizing transaction costs or passing them on to the taxpayer. One way to reduce taxation costs was by changing how they were collected. The two alternative ways of collecting taxes involved using institutional administrators or private contractors. Determining which to employ depended on the specific circumstances of the tax being collected.

In both the bala and Aztec tribute networks, government officials were directly involved in supervising the collection and inventorying the tax collected. Likewise, civic officials were involved in assigning and monitoring the civic liturgies in the Greco-Roman world. Voluntary elite patronage was largely self-organized by the donors because of the social recognition it afforded them. The way that tolls, tariffs, rents, leases, and agricultural taxes were collected was a completely different affair. Here there was considerable latitude as to whether governmental officials or private contractors were used. The difference between using administrators versus private contractors to collect agricultural taxes illustrates their relative advantages in specific circumstances.

The ideal fiscal system would be one where individuals voluntarily brought their tithes, offerings, and taxes to institutional storehouses without inducement. This did not happen because all forms of taxation resulted in net reductions in the subsistence incomes of peasant households. For that reason, institutions had to monitor or estimate the projected revenue stream against actual returns. One of the oldest and most direct ways of collecting agricultural taxes was as a percentage of the harvest. Examples of this method from the Mediterranean world, China, and the Indian subcontinent were identified above. Since peasant farmers lived by the sweat of their brows, institutional administrators could safely assume that they would maximize production on their individual holdings because failure to do so threatened the survival of their families. The key to honest evaluation and collection of the agricultural tax was to closely monitor harvest yields.

One way that the grain harvest was monitored in the Old World was to collect agricultural taxes at the state or community threshing floor where the tax could be calculated and collected as a percentage of the total harvest yield (Bresson 2016:294). Van de Mieroop (1999:149–150) feels that rents from tenants and sharecropping also were traditionally taken by the landowners at the threshing floor because it was the most direct way to calculate agreed-on shares. Steinkeller (2007) believes that granaries were located adjacent to threshing floors on royal domain estates during the Ur III period (2112–2004 BC) where grain was stored until it was needed. Rural villages may also have had communal threshing floors since one is implied in the Boaz–Ruth narrative from the southern Levant described in Chapter 3. Grain was taken to the threshing floor where Boaz and his attendants slept to guard the harvest, which would not have been necessary if the grain was threshed in his own compound. Manning (2003:59) says that grain taxes in Ptolemaic Egypt were paid at state granaries throughout the year, although it is unclear whether these were located at threshing facilities or not.

Collecting taxes at centralized processing facilities appears to have been practiced in the southern Levant shortly after the kingdom of Israel was conquered by the Assyrian empire during the late 8th century BC. Archaeological explorations at the city of Ekron identified more than a hundred olive oil presses within the city, suggesting that it was a central processing center for this important commodity (Gitin 1997; Welch 2015). One interpretation for the concentration of oil presses at Ekron was that it facilitated the collection of oil as tax during the period when it was a tribute-paying province in the Neo-Assyrian empire (Schloen 2001:145–146). If this interpretation is correct, then the tax on oil would have been taken at the press in the same way that tax in grain could be collected on the threshing floor.

In the past, some governments contracted with private entrepreneurs rather than using institutional employees to collect taxes. The reasons for this varied from passing the collection costs to private contractors and reducing risk, to expediting collection and obtaining a fixed sum useful for planning fiscal expenditures. Coşgel and Miceli (2009) identify three types of private contracts that were used by governments to collect taxes in the past: (1) *share contracts* where the government and the private collector shared the revenue collected; (2) *fixed rent contracts*, also called tax farming, where the collector paid the government a premium for the right to collect the tax; and (3) *fixed wage contracts* where subcontractors were hired to collect all the tax as representatives of the government. Both share contracts and fixed wage contracts incurred the risk of fraudulent reporting by contractors if administrative oversight was not provided to keep them honest. Unlike the other two, tax farming did not require secondary supervision except to monitor whether contractors were collecting taxes in a fair manner as the law prescribed.

Of the three, tax farming was the most widely used form of private contracting to collect taxes in the ancient world.[51] Pomeranz and Topik (2006:33) estimate that by AD 1500 every state bordering on the Indian Ocean used tax farming to collect some portion of its taxes. The structure of tax farming was similar across many of these areas. Governments offered the right to collect a type of tax in a certain region at auction to a group of tax collectors. Prospective tax collectors then bid for the right to collect the tax for a specified period of time.[52] The high bidder won the contract and either paid the price up-front or in increments over the length of the contract. The goal of the tax farmer was to profit on the margin between the bid price paid for the tax contract and the actual amount of money that could be collected in taxes. This did not always happen but was the risk that the tax farmer took when submitting bids.

There were advantages and disadvantages to using tax farmers. The advantages were threefold. First, while institutions lost some income by selling their tax base at a discounted rate, they benefited from receiving a fixed amount of revenue either up-front or on a prearranged schedule that was useful for planning fiscal expenditures. Second, governments saved money by passing costs of estimating and collecting the tax on to private contractors. Third, the state reduced the risk of shortfall due to drought, revolt, or other disruptions that might temporarily or permanently reduce its revenue stream. Nevertheless, where tax returns were predictable and where deviation in payment can be detected easily, states collected taxes using their own bureaucracy (Levi 1989). The disadvantage of using tax farmers is that collectors often had no organic connection with, or concern for, the population being taxed. Taxpayers were subjected to contractors who wanted to maximize their returns and often had the liberty to use force to extract what they could. In short, they could squeeze the peasantry dry if need be, which could lead to discontent, resistance, and revolt (Fleet 2003).

Tax farming was a speculative business, so why did contractors engage in it? The reasons varied. From an organizational perspective, tax farmers served as an informal bank whose advance payments were much like loans against future earnings to the governments that used them. Risk could be mediated to some degree by knowledge of local conditions. The *publicani* were tax farmers who collected taxes for Rome and often were provincials themselves who understood local conditions much better than the central government (Levi 1989:82). Collusion also helped to reduce risk. In Rome the same group of wealthy individuals who served as tax farmers also ran the government. The result was that the rules guarding against abuses or excessive profits from tax farming were never tightly enforced (Kiser and Kane 2007). Tax farming also was especially well suited for newly conquered areas, where population levels or customary forms of taxation were unknown. Here tax farming provided a quick source of revenue for the state.

One of the biggest attractions of tax farming was the opportunities that it provided for alternative commercial endeavors. Wealthy merchants were often active tax farmers. Besides providing a profit-making opportunity, it allowed merchants to monitor trade and obtain commercial advantages in other ways. Genoese merchants were tax farmers within the Ottoman empire for key commodity taxes on wine as well as collecting custom duties during the 14th and 15th centuries AD. It benefited the merchants to increase the level of trade into and out of Ottoman ports if they were the ones who collected the duty charged as a percentage of imports and exports rather than as a fixed rate (Fleet 2006:134–140).

Tax farming also provided merchants with an entrée into other government-related forms of work with less risky forms of income. Muhammed Sayyid Ardestani was a prominent Persian merchant in the 17th-century AD trans-Indian Ocean horse trade.[53] In the course of these dealings, he parlayed his connections with the Indian sultanate of Golconda into controlling one of the province's diamond mines and becoming the governor and tax farmer over commercial trade in the port city of Masulipatnam on the east coast of India. Ardestani also used his connections to become a primary factor in the lucrative Indian textile trade (see Chapter 2) and in the 1640s served as a general in one of Golconda's military campaigns (Pomeranz and Topik 2006:33–35). Depending on the circumstances, tax farming could provide opportunities for other profitable ventures.

Perhaps one of the best-documented cases of tax farming is associated with the Athenian grain tax law of 374/3 BC. Rather than a law, this was a case of tax farming intended to collect and transport the one-twelfth (8.33%) in-kind grain tax called the *dodekate* from islands of Lemnos, Imbros, and Skyros to Athens. This case of tax farming is well known because it was inscribed and erected on a stone monument in the Agora, the central marketplace of Athens

6.2 The monument for the Athenian grain tax-farming law of 374/3 BC (Stele I 7557). (Image courtesy of the American School of Classical Studies at Athens: Agora Excavations.)

(Figure 6.2). The monument was erected to declare the public auction of the tax, the purpose of which was to bring grain to the city in the wake of its war with Sparta (Stroud 1998). Recent research has reevaluated the nature of this monument and concluded that the *dodekate* collected probably was a form of rent rather than a tax (Moreno 2003:99; Osborne 2000). How the grain was collected in the islands is uncertain, but the stipulations of the contract are clear on how the bid was to be made, how the grain was to be delivered (without contamination, not as flour), and what assistance would be provided by the city in terms of overseers and storage in a building called the Aiakeion. In this case the contractor served the public good by supplying the city with grain while at the same time making a profit.

RENTS AND LEASES

Rents and leases are another source of institutional or private revenue when land or other resources are available for lease to another party. They are not technically a tax because the use of land or some other income-generating asset is received in exchange for the payment made. They are important to consider here because they are another way that resources were mobilized for institutional or private use without being directly involved in production. Nevertheless, the dividing line between tax and rent is difficult to draw, with the right to receive payment in exchange for use based on the right to maintain exclusionary control over the resource in question. Renting private property to another individual is a well-known example of this process. Domain lands held by an institution (e.g., temple land, palace estate) is another. Public land is a third category when the state claims exclusive control over its usage and principles of common pool usufruct no longer apply or apply in restricted form. Exclusive control over public resources was always an important source of public and private revenue, which included things as diverse as land, subsurface minerals, water, forests, and fisheries.

Public land (*ager publicus*) was important for institutional income in ancient Rome. According to Hopkins (1980:104), renting public land was just as important as taxation for raising revenue. Under Trajan, the *ager publicus* rented in northern Italy represented nearly one-quarter (22%) of all the lands cultivated by private individuals.[54] Uncultivated public land left in pasture also had value and was rented out for a grazing fee referred to as *scriptura* (Hollander 2013). Rents could also be collected from the use of forests and fisheries (Tan 2015:212). Towns had their own public lands that were rented to tenants and which provided an important civic revenue stream. Depending on the area, public land could represent anywhere from 3% to 20% of a town's holdings, which could be leased to individuals for perpetual use. One common practice was to establish a foundation or fiscal trust that rented land for a specific purpose such as *alimenta* programs for feeding children or funding festival activity. The land for these foundations could originate from private donations, allocations of civic land, or land from imperial assignments (Duncan-Jones 1990:121–123; Woolf 1990).

Income from domain land was also important. In Rome this included income from imperial estates. Conquest often resulted in large blocks of land becoming the personal property of the emperor and members of the imperial family. In 30 BC emperor Cesar Augustus conquered Egypt and took over the estates of his Ptolemaic predecessors, transforming them into imperial estates under his direct control and that of subsequent emperors.[55] Imperial and private estates were established in north Africa where land was rented to tenants as sharecroppers, who agreed to pay one-third of their crop as rent as well as working on the lands of their landlords (Kehoe 2007; Rickman 1980a:111–112). This rental agreement was called the Lex Manciana. It was designed to extend grain cultivation into unused lands and was an important strategy that made north Africa along with Egypt an important producer of grain for feeding Rome (Rickman 1971, 1980a). The quantity of resources controlled by imperial estates was enormous and enabled emperors to fund a tremendous amount of public activity. The funerary inscription of the emperor Augustus summarizes the personal expenditures that he made in the public interest, which include more than twenty large-scale building projects and illustrate the type of patronage activities that emperors regularly engaged in (Coleman 2003:appendix). Elsewhere in the eastern Mediterranean temples in Egypt also rented out their domain lands as a source of institutional income (Duncan-Jones 1990:123; Manning 2003).

It is in southern Mesopotamia at the beginning of the second millennium BC that evidence for the rental of domain lands replaced direct production systems as an important source of institutional income (Chapter 5). According to Renger (1979), the rental of domain fields[56] became common during the Old Babylonian period (2000–1600 BC) as a strategy to reduce institutional costs. In Mari, the "palace relieved itself from as many activities as it could . . . large parts of the available fields were given to individuals who either had to pay a rent or who were obliged to render services to the palace" (Renger 1979:253). Hudson (1999a:129) believes that temples were history's first landlords earning rent and revenue from their domain holdings long before private land holdings existed.[57] Foster (1981:240) feels that domain land designated for the maintenance of the city ruler was already being leased out to individuals as early as the 24th century BC.

A process that may have accelerated the shift from direct production to the rental of domain lands was the involvement of merchants in sharecropping and agricultural production on a large scale. From the second millennium BC onward small agricultural plots of about 6.5 hectares in size became increasingly prevalent as rental fields. While these plots were big enough for the maintenance of a family of five to seven persons, they could not provide significant institutional revenue unless the number of lease holders was great. At this same time, however, land also began to be rented to entrepreneurs in large allotments ranging from 200 or 300 to 3,000 hectares in size (Renger 2003:20). This type of arrangement continued into the Neo-Babylonian period (626–539 BC) when a case can be found at Larsa where two men leased 7,410 hectares of land at a discounted rate. As part of their rental contract, they were given 540,000 liters of barley as seed, 300 kilograms of iron for plowshares, 400 farm laborers, 400 oxen, and 100 large cows. In return for this lease, they were obliged to pay the temple a yearly stipend of 4.5 million liters of barley and 1.8 million liters of dates (Van de Mieroop 1999:210).

This certainly was a good arrangement for the two entrepreneurs since they are able to use the tools, labor, and seed of the temple in their venture. Nevertheless, they were speculating and taking a risk by underwriting a fixed level of return. The appearance of this early form of agro-business[58] may have been prompted by a general shortage of agricultural labor under the control of temple administrators. Texts from the Ebabbara temple in the city of Sippar during the Neo-Babylonian period indicate that only one-third of its total domain land was cultivated by its 120 temple farmers. The remainder was rented out to sharecroppers, with the temple supplying the tools and livestock to cultivate the land (Dandamayev 1999:366–367).

These early rental agreements involved payment in-kind since coinage did not serve as a medium of exchange in this area until after the 5th century BC.[59] The way agreements would have been structured was either in the form of fixed return contracts, as was the case of the two entrepreneurs from Larsa, or as a percentage of the crop at harvest.

Political leaders always retained the rights to control specific resources within their domains. Because of their importance in long-distance trade, African chiefs often claimed exclusionary ownership of valuable hides or feathers collected by hunters within their territories. Elephant hunters were required to hand over one tusk to the chief in whose domain the hunting occurred, with chiefs holding monopolies over the interregional trade in ivory (Stevenson 1968:79, 82; Sundström 1974:61; Terray 1974:325). The same was true in the west African gold trade. In the Kingdom of Gyaman,[60] gold prospecting was a free activity. Anyone could mine gold within the territory of their village and only had to pay a fee to the local chief if they mined for gold in a neighboring village. Nevertheless, while everyone could keep the gold dust they encountered, all gold nuggets recovered were considered the property of the chief and had to be turned over to him[61] (Terray 1974).

It was natural, therefore, that minerals and mining rights were leased out as another important source of institutional economy. In ancient Athens, land was held as private property, but subsurface resources were owned by the state (Ober 2015). The Laurion area in southern Attica had deposits that provided the silver for Athenian coinage.[62] During the 4th century the state leased the rights to private individuals to mine silver for periods ranging from 3 to 10 years (Davis 2014:266–267). Each lessee was responsible for operating the mine; who smelted the ore and whether this was done by the lessee or in beneficiation workshops (*ergasteria*) run by other specialists remains unclear. Refined ore was made into coins in Athens's state mint. Along the way the state charged a one-twenty-fourth (4.17%) tax on silver production along with a "processing fee" for minting coins.

The total revenue from these fees must have been substantial for Herodotus (7.144.1) to make the following claim: "[W]hen the Athenians had a great amount of money coming to their public funds from the mines at Laurion, and proposed to distribute 10 drachmas a man to each of them; then Themistokles persuaded the Athenians to stop this distribution and to have 200 ships built from this money for the war . . . against the Aiginetans" (from Davis 2014:268). Davis (2014:273) calculates that the 4.17% lease together with a 3–5% minting fee would have been enough to supply 50 talents of silver for the war fund.[63] While this may not have been sufficient to pay for the purchase of 200 triremes, it still would have been a significant contribution to the state's institutional coffers.

The Persians also considered subterranean resources such as metal and gemstone to be the property of the state. The foundation charters of Susa hint at the exclusive control of resources including gold, lapis lazuli, turquoise, and carnelian. The region of Lydia in western Turkey was rich in silver, which was controlled by the royal family. The mines were leased to private individuals as they were in Attica. In Lydia the lease-holders were required to turn over a portion of the bullion recovered to the royal treasury where it was minted into coins (Briant 2002:400–401). Leasing the rights to resource access, like the rent of domain land, was an important source of institutional revenue.

SUMMARY

This chapter has examined only a few of the many ways that ancient societies mobilized resources for institutional use. The forms of resource mobilization were diverse and complex. In the Greco-Roman world, elite patronage was important in funding aspects of the institutional economy. Voluntary patronage and forms of euergetism were important components of the institutional economy in both Greece and Rome but are often overlooked as important forces in other institutional economies. Taxation was the central focus of the discussion, which was defined as a resource transfer from the unit of production, whether it was a household, an estate, or a commercial enterprise. The important feature of taxation levies is that they were net transfers of goods, or their monetary equivalent, from production units after production inputs were made. From a Marxist perspective this makes the taxation of goods different from the mobilization of corvée labor, which like tools and resources, are inputs in the mode of production.

Taxation is a complex topic and only a few forms of tax were discussed: tolls, tariffs, agricultural taxes, and taxes at the level of empire. Other forms of taxation were left out of the discussion, including property taxes, inheritance tax, war levies, manumission taxes, sales taxes on goods and people, licensing fees, and poll taxes, to name a few. The reason for omitting them was simply a matter of space. Also unaddressed were the forms of valuation used to make tax assessments. If there is one thing that is true about ancient societies, it is Adam Smith's quotation at the beginning of this chapter: ancient societies were extremely creative when it came to developing new ways to tax people once it became an established feature of the fiscal environment. How and when that occurred are aspects of fiscal history that have yet to be written (Hudson 2000).

A particularly thorny issue that needs to be addressed in greater depth is the historic relationship between taxation and rent. They are distinct in principle but are hard to distinguish from one another in the textual sources. That is why the issue of rent was included in this discussion of transfers and taxation. The distinction between tax and rent is based on whether something is received in exchange for the payment made. With taxation nothing immediately tangible is obtained, while with rent the use of land or some other form of property is received. The distinction is easy to overlook when domain lands from temple or palace estates begin to be rented to individuals. The fee paid to the institution is rent, although, because it is going to a state or temple institution, it can easily be misinterpreted as a tax. Likewise, the distinction between a farmer bound to state lands and one who works the land on a share hold or as a tenant is difficult to distinguish without a clear understanding of the land tenure system and what was obtained for the payment made (Kehoe 2007).

A primary feature of ancient fiscal systems is that forms of taxation were function- or target-specific. Specific sources of public revenue were earmarked for different categories of civic activity. Institutions did not run up large public debt. Instead, they operated with cash on hand or tailored their activities to the planned or anticipated revenues they expected to generate. Temple and palace institutions mostly operated with a fiscal logic of not incurring large-scale debt. What appears to be a recurrent problem in Bronze Age societies in the Old World was not that the agrarian base was overtaxed, but that private debt owed by farmers to wealthy elites overpowered the ability of rulers to collect taxes. The evidence for this is found in the reforms of benevolent rulers that canceled debt and returned indentured or enslaved individuals to their families. While agriculture was always important, early public institutions do not appear to have supported a high, broad-based agricultural tax on its citizenry (Hudson 2000:7). Tax on land, at least initially, appears to have been relatively small and limited in terms of what it took from its agrarian citizens. It was not until states expanded and conquered other groups that broad-based systems of general taxation and higher tax rates appeared.

Taxes were collected and resources mobilized in premodern societies using both institutional officials and private contractors. Tax farming was widely practiced in specific situations across the ancient world. These tax farmers could be members of the society in which taxes were collected, but this was not always the case. In fact, foreign merchants sometimes were well positioned and often the most eager to take on this responsibility when they had no direct moral connection to the community they sought to exploit. The next chapter examines the broader role of merchants in the ancient societies, some of the constraints they operated under, and how they were organized to produce and distribute the finished goods that circulated throughout the ancient world.

SEVEN

THE ROLE OF MERCHANTS AND TRADE IN ANCIENT SOCIETY

There are very honest people who do not think that they have had a bargain unless they have cheated a merchant.

(Anatole France)

People have been involved in the exchange of food, craft goods, personal adornments, and exotic goods for thousands of years. Whether these exchanges were structured as gifts or trade, they served to bring people together in settings where social interaction took place. Economic exchanges served the dual purposes of reinforcing social relationships between individuals and the societies that they represented, at the same time that they provided an opportunity to obtain resources and goods that were not locally available. Exchange met both the social and provisioning needs of society. Two conditions helped to promote exchange as a means of resource provisioning: the unequal distribution of resources across the landscape and the cyclical fluctuations in the availability of food and fiber resources that individuals depended on for everyday life. Exchange relationships increased in importance in these situations and often became formalized in regularized trading partner relationships, periodic trade rendezvous, and centralized market exchanges as societies grew in size and internal complexity.

Within these contexts, trade interactions increased in frequency, and professional merchants made their appearance. A *merchant* in general terms is an individual who participates and assists in resource provisioning within society as an aspect of their livelihood. The merchant is an agent dedicated to the procurement, movement, and exchange of goods. The more vital resource movement is in meeting provisioning needs, the more important the role of merchant traders becomes within society. From a developmental perspective, merchants appeared when informal trading relationships and trade partner arrangements were insufficient for moving the quantity of goods needed or desired across the landscape. Likewise, an economic system can be said to increase in its level of commercialization as the number of goods moving through exchange rises in frequency and more people become dependent on exchange for the resources they consume.

This chapter explores the role of merchants, the conditions that gave rise to their appearance, and some of the ways that merchant trade was organized and carried out in the ancient and premodern past. Merchants were important for the development of maritime societies such as Venice and Phoenicia. While a merchant could operate as an individual, they commonly self-organized and operated through a series of informal and voluntary institutions that helped them transact business and exchange goods both inside and outside their local, ethnic, and religious communities.

WHO IS A MERCHANT?

Webster's New World Dictionary (1968) defines a merchant as an individual whose livelihood or business is buying and selling goods for profit – in short, a person involved in professional trade. While this definition was based on 20th-century views of the economy, it is simple, to the point, and applicable to a discussion of merchant behavior in the ancient world. Moreover, it highlights three important aspects of merchant behavior: the role of agency in establishing trade relationships, the desire for profit or personal gain as an impetus for trade, and the function that merchants provide as trade intermediaries.

The first of these features is the role of merchants as *exchange agents*. Agency theory emphasizes the role of individual actors in structuring contractual relationships and interactions of various kinds between individuals. Agency theory developed out of information economics to understand agent opportunism, organizational behavior, and principal–agent relationships such as employer–employee, lawyer–client, and buyer–supplier interactions (Eisenstadt 1989). As such, it is a perfect framework for characterizing how merchants establish, negotiate, and manage commercial dealings with the individuals with whom they do business. After all, the goods and commodities that merchants traffic in do not appear on their own. Commodities must be found, assembled, and transported to locations where they can be distributed and/or sold to their respective consumers. Merchants, whether working for themselves or as agents for institutions, have to make the decisions about what to buy, where to sell it, and how to navigate the associated business risks of doing so largely as individuals.[1]

While merchants fit the model of commercial agents, they did not conduct business in a vacuum. Instead, they pooled their knowledge and shared the risk of travel with others who also were involved in trade. In some societies, this resulted in the formation of formal groups, such as merchant guilds, that allowed groups of like-minded merchants to pool capital resources, share investment risk, and draw on the business contacts and relationships established by other guild members to do business in local and distant areas. Furthermore, most novice merchants did not learn the trade on their own. Rather, it most often was a generational profession. Like the young Marco Polo, novices usually learned their profession from veteran merchants and established their own commercial contacts building on the business relationships of their older colleagues. Commercial success was based to a large degree on an individual's experience and the ability to evaluate future gains or losses. But the uncertainties of ancient trade meant that merchants also had to be lucky if they were to survive the risks and dangers of the road.

The second aspect of merchants' behavior is that their primary motivation is to *make a profit* from their dealings. The idea that profit motivation is the raison d'être for trade is controversial since there are many social reasons why individuals or groups may engage in exchange beyond economic ones (e.g., Dalton 1977). Profit is the marginal increase in value that occurs from an economic transaction. In this regard, Gudeman (2001) equates profit with the creation of value through exchange.[2] Among the Aztecs, for example, profit was glossed simply as an increase, in the same way that a harvest is an increase reaped from an agricultural field. In an environment of resource shortages or shortfalls, profit or an increase in material goods acquired through trade can be represented as an increase in either the quantity or variety of goods obtained. The former dominated in settings where goods could be readily bought, sold, and converted into standardized durable currencies. The latter reflects a world where transportation costs were high and the variety of goods and resources essential for everyday life were limited and could be obtained only through trade. Profit from the perspective of any merchant was the increase that contributed to the merchant's livelihood and provided the resources to live on.

Profit, therefore, represents a gain in either the quantity or quality of the economic base. In antiquity, these gains can be measured at the household and institutional levels by increases in the movement and consumption of both local and nonlocal resources. Whether through production or exchange, gains in value at the household level are the result of economic activities that improve overall economic well-being (Gudeman 2001:102). Agency and entrepreneurial activity, therefore, were fundamental for improving economic well-being at the household level (Sewell 1992). They also supply the incentive and motivation behind the emergence of the professional merchant.

The third and most obvious feature of merchants is that they are *trade intermediaries*. They provide the linkages to procure and move goods over space (e.g., Milton 1999). Merchants are exchange specialists who supply the intermediate connection and facilitate the movement of goods from their place of origin to the point of final consumption. Two factors were fundamental to their operational success. The first was knowledge about where resources could be found and how to obtain them. It is no surprise that merchants recorded this information in closely guarded operational travel manuals. One such travel manual is the *Periplus Maris Erythraei*, which provides information for ancient Roman maritime trade conducted during the 1st century AD between the Red Sea, the Gulf of Aden, and throughout the Indian Ocean.[3] Another is the 14th-century AD account of Francisco Balducci Pegolotti, who wrote a handbook on caravan trade operations along the Silk Road between Azov in southern Russia and Hang-chou, the capital of Song, China.[4] The second factor was the knowledge of the social connections through which resources could be obtained. In the premodern past those connections were established between relatives, co-religionists, and cross-culturally through established relationships and communities of practice. This knowledge represented the trade secrets by which merchant groups operated. It would be shared internally by members of merchant communities and carefully guarded from nonmembers as it directly impacted competition and the overall success of their trade operations.

A merchant's success depended on being able to obtain reliable stocks of high-quality goods at a reasonable price. In premodern societies the networks through which merchants obtained and sold goods were determined by the durable social relationships established between interacting parties as much as they were their economic interests. Even within market contexts, favored client relationships developed that structured both the purchase and sale of goods (Chapter 9). Mintz (1964) refers to these social relationships as *pratik*, and they are the social setting in which goods were contracted for purchase or sale, credit was granted, prices were negotiated, and bulk discounts were arranged. In the imperfect world of ancient merchants, these social networks served to secure and stabilize sources of supply and loci of demand (Mintz 1964:262).

Merchants are often characterized as simply buyers and sellers of goods. Their role was far more dynamic than that. As will be discussed below, to obtain goods for sale required that merchants became involved in the discovery, processing, or manufacture of the goods they trafficked in at both the wholesale and retail levels. English merchants created the *putting-out* system during the 15th century to produce the textiles they sold (Dyer 2005). Similarly, African merchants who sold kola nuts and palm oil were eventually forced into production when demand rose and stocks became scarce (Dike and Ekejiuba 1990:215, 235). At the retail level, rural shopkeepers in colonial North America sold on credit and regularly took produce in return as payment (Cuddy 2008). The result was that shopkeepers often had to process the produce into alternative goods before it could be resold and profit realized.[5]

Finally, the scholarly view of merchants often suffers from the 100% problem. This is the view that an individual qualifies as a professional merchant only if they dedicated 100% of their time to commerce. Many did, but it is important to realize that the range of individuals who functioned as merchants in the ancient past was much broader than that. It included many individuals who engaged in trade only part of the year, either because of seasonal transportation issues or because they combined their merchant activities with other subsistence activities (Chapter 2). The question of who qualifies as a merchant or trader runs the gambit from individuals who might engage in a trade venture only once a year to those involved in commerce on an everyday basis. Similarly, merchants operated with different commercial portfolios. Some merchants specialized in a single commodity like grain in ancient Rome (Rickman 1980a, 1980b), or a particular provisioning activity like supplying raw cotton or spun yarn for textile manufacturing in India and Japan (Tanimoto 2011:376). But most merchants involved in long-distance commerce adopted a more diversified approach to trade,[6] either because of the widely varying cycles of demand for goods (e.g., Polanyi 1966) or because merchants followed a more opportunistic strategy of trading in a wide spectrum of commodities from which they could make a profit (Gotein 1973).

FACTORS THAT SHAPED THE MERCHANT'S WORLD

The factors that shaped individual trading strategies depended on the natural and cultural conditions of the trade environment in which merchants operated. The natural environment shaped adaptation and the opportunity for exchange. Equally important was the cultural environment that shaped the opportunity costs of trade. Three factors had a strong effect on the structure of intergroup exchange relationships: the distribution of environmental resources, the transportation technology available for moving resources, and how differential adaptation to environmental conditions provided opportunities for economic interaction between groups.

Environmental Conditions and the Distribution of Natural Resources

Cultural geographers have long recognized that the environment played a strong role in human adaptation, population location, and economic interaction.[7] The type and distribution of resources affects a group's livelihood and whether they adopt a sedentary or mobile lifestyle (Bates 2001; Steward 1938, 1972). Likewise, the overall productivity of the landscape affects the size and organization of communities, the longevity of a community's occupation, and the capacity to develop urban centers. The landscape also has a direct effect on the direction and ease of movement. Transportation geographers are interested in how the natural and cultural environments shape human interaction. The three factors considered to be particularly important in shaping interaction between human communities are distance, size of the community, and the differential cost of movement within different types of terrain[8] (Haggett 1965; Taafe and Gauthier 1973). All three of these conditions were important factors that influenced the behavior of merchants and the structure of the trade networks. Additional factors that affected merchant activity were safety, the risk of shipwreck or robbery, the return from the time invested, and the desire to avoid tolls and duties whenever possible.

There are two constants in human interaction. The first is that the resources that people want are differentially distributed across the natural landscape. The second is that trade consistently has been the way that groups have resolved problems regarding the spatial and seasonal availability of resources[9] (O'Shea 1989). It is here that the environment provides incentives and obstacles to procurement and trade. In heterogenous environments, groups will favor location near, or at the interface of, different environmental zones to broaden their access to resources. Rapid changes in relief like that found in the Andes (Chapter 5) or the Himalayas bring different natural resource zones in close proximity to one another. Differences in resource availability foster the development of procurement systems and the flow of resources across different ecozones (e.g., highland–lowland, coastal–inland). When these zones are close to one another, procurement can be solved at the household or community level. In highland Mexico, this occurred via interhousehold exchange, leading to the formation of markets (Sanders 1956; see also Chapter 9), while in the Andes, the movement of resources between different zones was managed through intracommunity procurement networks, with some community segments located in different elevations (Murra 1972, 1985a; see also Chapter 5). Where resources were widely spaced and difficult to obtain, some households specialized in trade and thus merchant behavior was born.

This is not to suggest that staple resources were the only or even the primary stimulus for trade. This certainly was not the case. Items of adornment made from exotic materials were exchanged, gifted, and transported over long distances as early as the Upper Paleolithic era (40,000–9000 BC). The desire for luxuries as well as the need for necessities can stimulate the appearance of merchants. Trade is evident in the early history of southern Mesopotamia, which, although rich in grain production, lacked basic resources such as timber, building stone, and mineral resources important for the development of urban communities. Hudson (1996:298) feels that the need for imported raw materials made merchants instrumental to the newly emerging temple and palace institutions in southern Mesopotamia during the third millennium BC (e.g., Aubet 2013; Ratnagar 2004; Renger 2003). This certainly was the case throughout the Bronze Age (3100–1200 BC) when long-distance exchange and the operation of merchants was indispensable for obtaining copper and tin for the manufacture of bronze weaponry (Algaze 2007, 2008; Monroe 2009, 2010)

An important ethnographic case study of tribal merchants was carried out in the 1960s among groups of the Vitiaz Strait along the northeastern coast of New Guinea. Here the need for resources promoted the development of merchant households that used trade as a strategy to provision themselves with necessary resources (Harding 1967). The Vitiaz Strait is 320 kilometers long and 50–65 kilometers wide and was composed of many distinct ethnic groups. Six island groups operated as maritime merchants within this area, linking upward of 150,000 persons in an intertribal exchange system that extended from the coast of New Guinea to its interior upland range.[10] Unlike the more ritualized Kula ring that operated throughout the Trobriand Islands off the east coast of Papua New Guinea (Malinowski 1922, 1967a), this exchange system was based primarily on the exchange of food and other useful durable goods. Approximately three dozen items manufactured in different villages within the Vitiaz Strait were obtained by merchants who then resold them to other groups as they made their rounds.

The motivation for Vitiaz merchants to engage in trade was a scarcity of food on their home islands. The islanders fished, but they lacked sufficient land to cultivate taro, sago, or bananas, or to raise pigs. Trade was their solution, and they exchanged fish, shellfish, and the manufactured goods they obtained through trade to provision themselves with sufficient food for daily and festive consumption. Most trade was conducted during the nonagricultural season, especially at or after harvest time when food was abundant and could be exchanged for other products. Merchant canoes were 10–14 meters in length, with a single masted sail and a crew of five to six men made up of household members and friends. Trade occurred between trading partners or trade friends. These linkages defined the trade roads through which products moved between suppliers, merchants, and consumers. Where there were no linkages between trade partners, there was no exchange (Harding 1967:19, 92). In this sense trade was carried out as interactions between households and modeled along kinship relationships within society.[11]

Approximately three dozen items were involved in Vitiaz commercial dealings. These included fish, taro, pigs, dogs, pottery, wooden bowls, hand drums, obsidian, stone adzes, paints, bark cloth, net bags, pandanus products, tobacco, and bows and arrows. Many of the items exchanged had important social functions. Wooden bowls were important for brideprice along with valuables that included boar tusks, dog teeth, cowrie shells, tambu shells, and other ornaments. Exchanges could occur anywhere, from the platforms of the trading canoes and the houses of trade friends to mini-markets[12] held in coastal villages during festivals when highlanders came to trade products with their coastal trading partners.

The Vitiaz merchants are instructive for several reasons. First, they illustrate that resource scarcity can be a motivating force behind the development of merchant activity as individual households sought to meet their provisioning needs. In addition to food, Vitiaz islanders traded for the capital equipment essential for their way of life, including timber for their canoes and fiber for fishnets. Second, merchant trade was not for subsistence alone; it also was profit-oriented and involved the accumulation of socially valued commodities. Wealth was defined in terms of durable goods, especially those that involved large amounts of labor to manufacture and that were used in meeting social obligations (Harding 1967:72). Pigs were especially important in the ceremonial cycle of all Vitiaz communities, and since they could not raise them,[13] merchants employed a wide array of trade transactions to pry loose a quantity of pigs from the communities that bred them (Harding 1967:141–142). Third and finally, this example illustrates how geographic differentiation stimulated both the need for trade and the production of specialized products in different environmental zones as a response. A 4-hour canoe trip, like a 24-hour walk from the coast to the highlands, allowed individuals to traverse all the environmental resource zones in the region. The differentiation of craft production within these zones fostered organic solidarity within the trade sphere (Durkheim 1984; Harding 1967:239–242). The advantage for the Vitiaz merchants and what made the trading system operate was the fact that they could employ maritime transportation to move goods over space.[14]

Transportation Costs and Their Effect on Trade

Fernand Braudel (1995:355, 357) pointed out in his discussion of 16th-century AD Mediterranean society that distance was the first enemy of premodern civilization. The same was true for ancient societies. It goes without saying that the type of transportation available directly affected both the scope and profitability of merchant ventures. Transportation was the highest transaction cost that ancient merchants had to contend with in their commercial dealings. The more goods they could transport, the greater was their potential profit per unit of time. Cost of transportation, however, was calculated in terms of weight of goods involved. Where transportation costs were high, as they were throughout much of the ancient world, trade focused on high-value goods with low bulk weight. Conversely, where transportation was less expensive, lower-value and bulkier goods could be profitable items of exchange. Even better was when the two could be combined, as occurred when bulk goods moved as ballast in ships along with lightweight products of high value. Nevertheless, innovations that lowered transportation costs always had the ability to reshape the structure and volume of ancient trade.[15]

An often-cited example of how improvements in transportation fostered trade was the development of the *fluyt* by Dutch shipbuilders whose efficient and low cost of operation helped to promote Dutch commercial success during the 16th and 17th centuries AD (Bruijn 1993; Landers 2003:78; Unger 1973; Van Zanden et al. 2009). Menard (1991) questions the accuracy of the belief that early trade was dominated by the movement of high-value, low-bulk items. After all, grain, wine, and olive oil figured prominently in maritime trade within the Mediterranean, and they were bulk goods (Casson 1991:171). Nevertheless, it is easy to understand how merchants would use forms of transportation and transportation routes that increased the safety and/or speed of travel, or lowered the overall costs of movement (e.g., Fletcher 1958; Geels 2002).

Compared with the modern world, all forms of transportation were slow and costly. But some were slower and costlier than others. Comparative studies on the relative efficiencies of different forms of transportation exist for different areas of the ancient and premodern worlds (Adams 2012: Braudel 1986:349–372; Duncan-Jones 1990:7–29; Hassig 1985; Landers 2003:73–97; Ratnagar 2004:212–245; Renger 1999:157). A considerable amount of information on the costs of transportation by different means is contained in Diocletian's Edict on Maximum Prices of AD 301 (Kent 1920; Meijer and van Nijf 1992:133–135). Diocletian's edict was a response to inflation and sought to limit price fluctuations rather than to set fixed prices (Morley 2007:97). The edict was composed in Asia Minor, and using general costs of the time, arrived at the conclusion that a 1-kilometer-long journey by oxcart cost the same as traveling 57 kilometers by sea (Hopkins 1978:43). Scheidel (2014:9) calculates that the relative price ratio of transporting a given unit of cargo over the same distance was cheapest by sea, five to ten times more expensive if transported by river depending whether it was up- or downstream, and fifty-two times more costly than moving goods by cart.[16] These differences made it cheaper to transport grain across the Mediterranean to Rome by ship and up the Tiber river by boat and barge than it was to move it 120–160 kilometers by wagon from the region around Rome (Rickman 1980a:14).

But other forms of transportation were used in the ancient world that the Edict on Prices does not address. Cargos also moved by donkey, mule, camel, and, of course, human porters. While an oxcart could move a heavy load, beasts of burden were efficient when used in teams or in small strings of animals. Furthermore, they do not require the prepared roads that cartage requires; simple paths are sufficient for load-carrying animals, and they are perfectly suited for traversing undeveloped areas and irregular mountainous terrain (Lattimore 1995; Rizvi 2012). Comparison of the relative efficiencies of these different forms of transportation is difficult. Nevertheless, Hassig (1985:216–217) places the efficiency of a wagon in 16th-century AD colonial Mexico at twice that of a load carried by a team of mules. Canoes like the small vessels used by Vitiaz Island merchants were twelve times as efficient as using mules. Commerce in areas such as Africa, Mesoamerica, and across the Himalayas, however, was conducted profitably using human porters. While human porters are limited in what they can carry, historic and ethnographic evidence indicates that they could carry heavy loads approaching and even surpassing that of mules (Hirth 2016:table 8.1; Malville 1999). For all animal and human transport, carrying large cargoes was a function of the number of individuals involved in trade caravans.

Improvements in transportation technology developed very slowly, so merchants took advantage of every opportunity to reduce shipping costs or shorten travel. The domestication of the camel revolutionized communication across desert areas and opened the sub-Saharan trade into west Africa (Bovill 1970; Gilbert and Reynolds 2006:64–75), but these types of innovations were few and far between. Instead, merchants focused on ways to speed up loading and unloading cargoes within ports, made more efficient use of the shipping available to them, and looked to reduce risk or otherwise lower costs. The emperor Claudius built the port at Ostia in AD 42 to speed up the transshipment of grain shipments to Rome. Before Ostia was built, all grain shipped from Egypt and north Africa had to be unloaded at Puteoli in the Bay of Naples and transported by riverboat along the coast and up the Tiber river to Rome (Casson 1991:199). An important innovation in stowage aboard maritime vessels was the use of wooden barrels instead of clay amphora to ship oil, wine, and other liquids in late antiquity.

All forms of long-distance trade were risky (Braudel 1973:312–314), but none more so than maritime voyages. As a result, all efforts to reduce the possibility of shipwrecks were welcomed. One of the most spectacular of these was the construction of the Diolkos paved road or trackway by the tyrant Periander across the Isthmus of Corinth in Greece during the early 6th century BC (Lewis 2001). The Diolkos was a paved limestone road 6–7 kilometers in length whose primary purpose was to transport commercial goods over the narrow isthmus between the Aegean and Ionian Seas (MacDonald 1986). Thucydides states that ships were portaged along this road or trackway, although Pettegrew (2011) questions whether this included merchant ships. The advantage that the Diolkos provided was that it allowed merchants to avoid the treacherous storms that ships could encounter when circumnavigating the Peloponnesian peninsula.

Although the cost of the Diolkos would have been very high, its construction benefited the economy of Corinth and the merchants who frequented its emporium (market) in a number of ways. Strabo referred to the Diolkos as a portage and said that sailors preferred to buy and sell at Corinth's emporia instead of sailing all the way around the Peloponnesian peninsula (Pettegrew 2011:370). One source of income, and undoubtedly the reason for constructing the Diolkos, was the collection of transit duties on goods transported overland along the tramway. The natural harbor of Schoinos was located on the eastern side of the portage, although no port facilities have been located to date on the west. One possibility is that cargos were sold at the emporium in Corinth and the cost of portage across the Diolkos was added to their value as they were shipped to Corinth or transferred to vessels for transshipment elsewhere. While Pettegrew questions the commercial basis for the Diolkos, it remains the best single explanation for its construction. After all, its role as a transportation feature was underscored in AD 67 when the Roman Emperor Nero attempted to construct a large canal across the isthmus to allow ships and not just cargo to pass between the Ionian and Aegean Seas.

Location, Adaptation, and the Carrying Trade

Some locations and the adaptations that groups make to their environments provide better opportunities for engaging in trade than others. Coastal locations are one such example. Exploitation of marine resources requires watercraft for deep water or coastal fishing. The use of watercraft, in turn, provides the ability to move across the seascape and interact with other groups they encounter. The example of the Vitiaz merchants presented above illustrates the opportunities that a coastal location provides for individual households to engage in trade. Coastal households apparently engaged in trade alongside fishing–foraging activities in the Mediterranean on a fairly broad scale during the fourth millennium BC, if not earlier. Obsidian used for cutting tools during this period occurs in natural deposits on a number of islands in this area, the most important of which are Sardinia, Lipari, and Pantelleria islands near Sicily; Palmarola off the west coast of Italy; and the island of Melos in the Aegean Sea (Dixon et al. 1968; Renfrew et al. 1966). The obsidian source on Melos was exploited more than 12,000 years ago during the Upper Paleolithic period (Carter 2016; Renfrew and Aspinall 1990). Maritime groups visited, collected, and mined obsidian and other useful resources from these islands, which they exchanged with other coastal groups over a circuit of several hundred kilometers.[17] From coastal villages, obsidian was traded inland passing through down-line trade partners in much the same way as was observed in northeastern New Guinea (Harding 1967:figure 1). In this sense, involvement in the *carrying trade* was an important corollary activity undertaken alongside mobile fishing–foraging activities.

Coastal locations were an opportunity for exchange throughout Mediterranean history. The Phoenicians and Venetians are examples of small city-states that rose to prominence based on the development of merchant trade (Fox 1977). The wealth mobilized and accumulated through trade could also result in port cities being provisioned through exchange rather than through agricultural production in their hinterlands. Throughout history, many of the great cities of the Mediterranean were located along the coasts or had ready access to it via rivers. As a result, their leaders often took more interest in overseas trade than did the rulers of inland agrarian societies with large peasant populations that could be taxed in staple goods (Pearson 1991:69–70).

Another preadaptation to trade can be found with mobile pastoralists. The need to move animals to grazing lands across the landscape created the opportunity to simultaneously transport goods and engage in trade. Pastoral groups regularly developed symbiotic relationships with agricultural communities to exchange food, hides, and other animal products from their herds for grain, tools, and manufactured craft goods (Barth 1956; Bates 2001:109; Evans-Pritchard 1940). Excavation of an early site in Israel's southern Negev recovered evidence for small-scale craft activity by pastoral nomads between 3000 and 2700 BC who manufactured millstones, beads, and smelted copper to produce items that they exchanged with nearby agricultural communities (Rosen 2003). The relationships between pastoral nomads and settled communities was a dynamic relationship that went beyond ecological symbiosis. Pastoral nomads often took up the business of transporting goods over long distances as well as protecting (or robbing) the merchants who passed through their territories. Camel pastoralists of the northern Sahara and the Arabian Peninsula were notable in this regard (Bovill 1970).

An interesting example of cattle pastoralists that also were itinerant merchants were the Banjaras tribesmen, located in central and southern India.[18] In Indian literary texts the term *banjara* is used to denote any type of itinerant peddler (Chakravarti 2005:25). The Banjaras were organized into four large tribes, spoke their own language, and traveled across India throughout the year buying and transporting goods as they moved their cattle from pasturage to pasturage. They moved goods in carts pulled by bullocks as well as in bags and packs strapped to the backs of their animals. Banjaras tribes were subdivided into clans that were organized internally into family units called *tandas*, with the elders of five *tandas* forming a *panchayat*. Families on average had about 100 oxen (Habib 1993). Altogether a Banjara clan could command up to 100,000–180,000 bullocks all moving across the landscape, picking up and transporting goods while they grazed (Levi 1994).

Grain was the principle, although not the only, commodity that the Banjaras trafficked in. Habib (1993) estimates that the oxen of the four Banjaras tribes conveyed 1,140,000 metric tons of grain over an average distance of about 1,200 kilometers throughout the year.[19] The first reference to Banjaras activity dates to AD 1357 when peasants were forced "to sell grain to the *kāravānīs* (caravan people) who took it to Delhi for sale" (Habib 1982:83). Peasants were required to pay their taxes in cash under the Mughals during the 16th century AD (Habib 1999:85), and this was one way that cash could be raised. They were also a major source of rural credit when rural farmers needed it (Habib 1993:375). While Banjaras were the principal suppliers of grain, they also trafficked in a wide range of other commodities that included salt, sugar, raw cotton, butter, and textiles, as well as a wide range of household consumables in demand in rural areas.[20] Finally, they also were major suppliers to the military. In medieval India a soldier had to buy his own food from merchants in temporary bazaars that followed the armies. The Banjaras supplied the armies with large quantities of rations and were even allowed to pass unharmed amid rival armies on the verge of conflict.

The Banjaras moved large quantities of goods on a continental scale across India. They were the principal suppliers of grain to urban areas, which they bought in the countryside and transported to cities. Their organization into family units allowed them to move in small groups across the landscape interfacing and supplying the small village communities on which they grazed their cattle. They moved large quantities of resources, but they did it slowly at a pace of about 10–12 kilometers per day. While they were one of the major means of transporting goods across India, it is hard to think of them as specialized merchants. They were cattle pastoralists who provided important merchant and transportation services at a very low cost because they integrated it into their normal seasonal transhumance (Habib 1999:373). Although the Banjaras were organized as a large tribal society, Irfan Habib (1993:379) has characterized their overall method of operation as analogous to a large joint-stock company.

THE PERCEPTION OF MERCHANTS

Merchants without question performed important economic functions for society. The fact that they often are perceived as doing so for self-gain rather than as benefactors for the communities in which they lived resulted in merchants being held in low esteem. In traditional Chinese and Japanese societies, merchants occupied the lowest social strata. In China the Confucian view held that merchant wealth should not be used as a basis for political power.[21] Instead, the Confucian view advocated that rulers should come from the educated literati; as a result, merchants sought to get their children educated and into that class (Gungwu 1993:400). The same was true in Greek and Roman societies where farming was considered the noble profession and involvement in trade was less so. Aristotle considered production of goods for use as morally superior to production for exchange (Meijer and van Nijf 1992:11). Among the ancient Greeks, merchants (*emporoi*) normally were foreigners and noncitizens (*metics*), whether they were involved in maritime or local trade (Reed 2003:7–8, 55).

The Romans likewise held commerce in low regard. A law was passed in the 3rd century BC that prohibited senators from engaging in trade; the law was still in force in the 3rd century AD even though there were plenty of ways around it (Meijer and van Nijf 1992:15). The general attitude of the Roman elite toward commerce can be summarized in this quote by Cicero in his treatise *On Duties* (I.150–2):

> Another disreputable class includes those who buy whole lots from wholesalers to retail immediately. They would not make a profit unless they indulged in misrepresentation, and nothing is more criminal than fraud.... Commerce should be considered vulgar if it is a rather small affair. If it is extensive and well-financed, importing many products from all over the world and distributing them to many customers honestly, one should not criticize it severely. In fact, it even seems to deserve the highest respect if a merchant ... retires from the quayside to his farmhouse and estates. Of all pursuits by which men gain their livelihood none is better than agriculture.
>
> (Meijer and van Nijf 1992:16–17)

The general European view of merchants throughout the Middle Ages was no kinder, having added a Christian suspicion of commerce and merchants to the previous Roman attitudes.[22] The merchant was important in medieval society, and most money lending as well as a great deal of trade was in the hands of Jewish merchants who were outsiders to the Christian community (Pounds 1994:352). As outsiders, merchants were strangers, and as strangers they were the object of suspicion. Georg Simmel (1967), in his seminal work on the stranger, summarizes the status of the merchant through time in the following way:

> Throughout the history of economics the stranger everywhere appears as the trader, or the trader as stranger. As long as economy is essentially self-sufficient, or products are exchanged within a spatially narrow group, it needs no middleman: a trader is only required for products that originate outside the group. Insofar as members (of the community) do not leave the circle in order to buy these necessities ... the trader must be a stranger, since nobody else has the chance to make a living.
>
> (Simmel 1996:38)

For Simmel, the merchant was an outsider who lived on the margins of society and did not fully belong to it. As such, they were viewed as the source for foreign, intrusive, and even dangerous views.

The widespread and common dislike of merchants stemmed from their practice of buying goods when prices were low and selling them when prices were high.[23] Nowhere was this more evident than during famines when merchants sold food at rates that demand could bear. Even if they lacked food to sell, they were viewed as hoarders working against the common good of society. To illustrate how widespread the general dislike of merchants was, consider the agreement between the two most unlikely bedfellows, Karl Marx quoting Martin Luther on the nature of merchants:

> Now there is among merchants much complaint . . . because they must trade under great danger and run the risk of being kidnapped, beaten, blackmailed, and robbed. If they would suffer these things for the sake of justice, the merchants would be saintly people.. . . But since such great wrong and unchristian thievery and robbery are committed all over the world by merchants . . . is it any wonder that God should procure that such great wealth, gained by wrong, should again be lost or stolen, and they themselves be hit over the head or made prisoner?
>
> (Marx 1967:331)

Of course, not all ancient and premodern cultures had this disdainful view of merchants. In Islamic teachings trade and commercial activities are a divine calling and necessary part of life. The Prophet Mohammed was a merchant himself, as was his wife Khadija. The ascendancy of the Umayyad caliphate during the 6th and 7th centuries AD emphasized the importance of trade as well as conquest in the spread of Islam. Mohammed praised the role of the merchant when he said, "He who brings supplies to our market is like a warrior in the war for God" (Ali and Al-Owaihan 2008:8). Besides holding merchants in high esteem, Islam is governed by Sharia law, which includes rules about fair trade, the virtue of honesty, and equal treatment of coreligionists in trade irrespective of their ethnic origin. As a result, it provided a valuable framework for both conducting business and spreading Islam across Africa and Southeast Asia (Bernstein 2008:108; Chaudhuri 1985:34–62; Gilbert and Reynolds 2006:35; Labib 1969). As a rule, merchants often had higher status in smaller kingdoms,[24] which relied more on trade for income than did rulers with large peasant populations that could be taxed (Pearson 1991:69).

The truth about ancient merchants is that they were overwhelmingly honest, at least among themselves. They followed Benjamin Franklin's maxim, that honesty is the best policy, because it was more profitable to do so. Trade between merchants operated on trust and fair practice. A good reputation for honesty took years to establish and, once achieved, ensured continued interaction as well as attracting new opportunities for trade through referrals from established trade partners (Greif 2000:272). Granovetter (1985) argues that durable social relationships rather than institutional arrangements or generalized morality were the basis for trust and enduring economic relationships. This especially was the case for intercultural trade in premodern societies that operated without careful monitoring institutions.[25]

A good example of this is found in the trust and credit interactions operating between Fulani pastoralists, Hausa commercial agents, and Yoruba meat processors in west African cattle markets. In the Nigerian market of Ibadan, 75,000 cattle were sold each year by Fulani pastoralists to Hausa agents, who extended unsecured credit to Yoruba butchers who paid for the animals after meat processing was completed. The entire system operated on the reputation of agents and the trust engendered between interacting parties. The value of the credit exceeded 100,000 pounds sterling when the study was made in the mid-20th century. Credit was extended based on personal agreements, without signed contracts or the involvement of formal financial institutions such as banks or money changers (Cohen 1965). This practice was widespread and operated similarly for long-distance exchange relationships in the kola nut trade (Cohen 1966).

THE MERCHANT'S DILEMMA

The discrimination that merchants faced as disreputable hucksters throughout society was compounded by other problems they encountered in their home communities. I refer to these problems as the *merchant's dilemma* and they were twofold. Their first problem was that as prominent members of society merchants were expected to invest some of their wealth in the social institutions and economic base of the communities where they lived. The expectation within peasant communities is that wealthy members would serve as benefactors supporting local institutions and building social capital within the community (Evers 1994b; Geertz 1963:125; Mauro 1993:274; Schiel 1994:16). Failure to do so fosters resentment within the community, like that observed in the community-sponsored cargo systems of Latin America.[26] The expectation that wealthy individuals take on the burden of financing festivals and institutions for the benefit of the community creates enormous social pressures on merchants and their families since any finances invested in the community takes away from the economic capital needed for commercial endeavors (Evers and Schrader 1994; Lloyd 1953:42).

Second, merchants serve as an external conduit for marketing products produced in local communities as well as obtaining goods produced outside them. When they buy products such as grain from their fellow villagers, they do so at the lower discount rate dictated by their *use value* established by the moral economy operating inside the community. This produces a profit when merchants sell that grain or other goods outside the village using the *exchange value* established by the market. In some cases, this ability may be recognized, and when it is, it was frowned on (Wilk 1989b:147). However, they face a dilemma when they are asked to obtain and sell goods within the community. When they do so, they are expected to sell goods to community members using prices established by the internal moral economy instead of the external market price used to obtain them (Evers 1994a:85). Furthermore, merchants are recognized as individuals with capital resources and can be asked for loans by friends, neighbors, and family members who may feel little obligation to repay them (Evers 1994b).

Several strategies were employed by merchants in the ancient world to mediate the merchant's dilemma. None was a perfect solution if they wanted to remain full members of their respective communities and retain *all* their economic capital for their personal commercial use. The first approach was to physically leave home and concentrate on trading outside the community for a period of time. A spouse and/or other family members would remain in the community to provide a permanent home base that enabled merchants to maintain their affiliation without being permanently engaged in community affairs. There were two ways of doing this. One was to become an itinerant peddler involved in interregional exchange and who returned to the natal community for periodic, short visits. They also could leave for long periods of time and return home permanently only after they retired from active trading and reengaged in normal community life. Both strategies allowed merchants to keep their community affiliations while insulating them from being pressured into undertaking significant community sponsorships. Pursuing commercial life outside a merchant's natal community produced many of the ethnic trade diasporas that were fundamental to accessing products and lowering the transaction costs of long-distance exchange in the ancient and premodern world (Bonacich 1973; Curtin 1984; Evers 1994a). A discussion of trade diasporas is presented below (see also Baghdiantz McCabe et al. 2005).

A second solution was for merchants to insulate themselves within the communities where they lived. One way was to depersonalize economic relationships, which can be difficult to do in small communities. They could also semi-isolate themselves from the rest of the community through ethnic barriers or distinctive religious practices. This is what the long-distance merchants of the Aztecs did who lived as commoners, maintained marital endogamy, and did not display their wealth in public lest they raised the ire and jealousy of the political elite who might take it from them (Hirth 2016; M. Smith 2012:120–123).

A third way was to accumulate social capital that allowed merchants to shelter their financial assets or use them in a manner that could be combined with trade outside the community. Undertaking a religious pilgrimage was one way to do this. The yearly *hadj* to the holy city of Mecca in the Arabian Peninsula by Muslims was an opportunity for commerce. It was the way that the taste for coffee and the coffee trade was spread through the Muslim world: pilgrims purchased coffee as they passed through the port of Mocha on their way home (Bernstein 2008:243; Das Gupta 2001a, 2001c:183). Likewise, pilgrims traveling to Jerusalem or the Vatican in Rome regularly bought and sold goods along the way to defray costs.

Merchants faced a range of personal and occupational challenges as they moved resources over short and long distances. That they did so is a credit to both their entrepreneurial spirit and the commercial incentives that trade provided. Merchants also were practical opportunists who affiliated themselves with existing political and religious institutions when it was in their benefit to do so. An alternative way that merchants protected capital assets was to donate them to temple institutions and religious orders and then borrow them back at little or no interest. The result was that in some societies religious institutions played an important role in supporting the merchants involved in interregional trade (Liu 1988:107–114) (see below).

MERCHANTS, INSTITUTIONAL AFFILIATION, AND THE LUXURY TRADE

What were the avenues leading toward "merchanthood" in the ancient economy? While the information is far from clear, we know that trade was a regular part of the economy from very early times, providing access to resources that were not locally available. The fisher–foragers who traded obsidian across the Mediterranean during the fourth millennium BC illustrate this. Nevertheless, recorded history does not talk much about small-scale merchant groups or the trade they engaged in. Some of the earliest mention of merchants in written records comes from Bronze Age cuneiform texts from the Near East. Moses Finley (1985) and others (Jones 1974; Polanyi 1957, 1981) championed the view that the ancient economy was composed of largely self-sufficient agricultural communities with relatively little interregional trade.[27] They argued that the high cost of transportation limited trade to high-value luxury goods that were consumed by a small number of political and religious elites. Similarly, because the volume of trade was restricted, the status and role that merchants had in society was correspondingly low. Merchants were perceived primarily as agents of institutions and the elite to obtain luxury goods through interregional trade (Hopkins 1983).

Some of the earliest information on merchants in Mesopotamia comes from the Ur III period of the late third millennium (2112–2004 BC). Textual information suggests that merchants had dual functions: they were involved in managing economic activities of the state while at the same time engaging in trade for their own households. Much of the commercial activities for themselves involved making purchases and making loans. Garfinkle (2008:69) proposes that merchants were organized as local associations along the lines of extended families that were most active within the boundaries of their own kingdoms but could travel widely when they engaged in business for the state. Merchants also served as facilitators of exchange who transferred and converted surpluses into different types of goods (Garfinkle 2004:25). At the institutional level, merchants obtained raw materials for the operation of temple and palace workshops. Toward the end of the Ur III period merchants became increasingly involved in tax farming to collect institutional revenues (Garfinkel 2010:188). Based on documents from Lagash, merchants apparently were involved in making collections of staple goods for the bala distribution system in Mesopotamia (Sharlach 2004; see also Chapter 6).

The range of economic activities that merchants engaged in privately is revealed in an Ur III archive of an urban entrepreneur named Ur-Nusku who resided in the Mesopotamian city of Nippur in the 21st century BC. The documents reveal that Ur-Nusku engaged in three different types of economic activities: (1) procuring goods for the temple's weaving workshop, (2) serving as a broker for a group of reed cutters that involved extending them credit and delivering their harvest to its final destination, and (3) procuring large quantities of copper and importing it into Mesopotamia. While the household of Ur-Nusku was not under institutional control, some of his biggest clients were the temple estates of the Nippur city-state. What the archive of Ur-Nusku indicates is that Ur III merchants actively represented their institutional clients at the same time that they engaged in numerous private commercial ventures on their own behalf (Garfinkel 2010:195–196).

Bronze Age Trade and the Uluburun Shipwreck

An important feature of the Bronze Age was the development of copper–tin metallurgy and the long-distance trade associated with it. The trade in copper and other metals can be traced back to the fourth millennium BC with Uruk culture, centuries before written accounts mention merchant activities (Algaze 1993:113–116; 2008; Özbal et al. 1999; Stein 1999a, 2001). It is likely that this trade was conducted by merchants, with some individuals working as contract representatives of Uruk institutions as well as on their own behalf. Cuneiform tables from the Early Dynastic period (2900–2350 BC) record that foreign merchants from Dilmun on the Persian Gulf brought copper to Lagash for trade (Ratnagar 2004:25). The archive of Ea-nāṣir, a 19th-century BC copper merchant from the city of Ur, provides information on how this trade probably was organized. The Dilmun copper trade was in the hands of private merchants who worked in association with one another to procure copper for themselves and the palace. Ea-nāṣir relied on Dilmun merchants to deliver copper in exchange for textiles, reed baskets, and silver assembled by Ea-nāṣir and his fellow commercial associates (Garfinkle 2010).

A valuable glimpse as to how this trade was organized comes from the Late Bronze Age Uluburun shipwreck dating to the 14th century BC. The ship sunk off the southern coast of Turkey, and its well-preserved cargo illustrates a number of important aspects about how maritime trade was conducted (Bass 1986; Pulak 1998). The dimensions of the ship have been reconstructed from the displacement of the cargo and preserved wooden remains: the ship was 15 meters long, 5 meters wide, and had a cargo capacity of about 20 tons. Most of the goods on board were Syro-Canaanite and Cypriot in origin, and it is believed that it sunk while on course to somewhere in the Aegean Sea (Pulak 2008). The estimated value of the ship's cargo was very high when calculated in the exchange rates of that time. Monroe (2009) calculates the total cargo value at 12,000 Ugarit silver shekels, which at modern prices would represent an investment of approximately $57,000.[28] The cargo consisted of a mixture of high-value goods including copper, tin, resin, gold, and glass, and low-value goods including ceramics and perishable foodstuffs.[29] The copper ingots weighed a total of 10,069 kilograms, while the tin weighed 1,000 kilograms, which together was sufficient to produce 11 tons of bronze artifacts (Monroe 2010:table 1).

While the high value of the cargo makes it a good candidate for state-sponsored gift exchange (Pulak 2008), Monroe concludes that the cargo was well within the range of what a wealthy merchant – or, more likely, a consortium of merchants – could have managed financially. Several lines of evidence support this interpretation. First, the presence of four different types of copper ingots and three types of tin ingots[30] suggests that the ship did not procure them from a single port or political trade partner, but obtained its cargo through a series of stops and commercial exchanges throughout its voyage. Despite the richness of the cargo, this suggests that the Uluburun practiced a form of cabotage or tramping to multiple ports to obtain cargo. Second, nine weight sets and two pan sets were recovered on the shipwreck, suggesting that four different merchants were on board who carried weight sets of different shapes and types. Third, while Pulak (2008:302) proposes that two passengers onboard were Mycenaean elites based on the personal items recovered, this is contradicted by the absence of elaborate sealstones, which would be expected if political emissaries or elite individuals were on board. Instead, only steatite sealstones were recovered, like those found in simple burials that were appropriate for merchant use. However this expedition was organized, the loss of the vessel and its cargo would have been a significant economic setback for its owners.

MERCHANT PARTNERSHIPS: THE COMMENDA

How maritime voyages were financed and organized varied depending on their overall goals and the individuals involved. In ancient Athens maritime trade was largely in the hands of small businessmen who worked with partners to arrange shipments and conduct trade. Grain was an important import for Athens, and good descriptions are available about how partnerships were formed to import shipments to the city (Casson 1991:102–103; Finkelstein 1935; Reed 2003). Trade normally was conducted with borrowed money and involved the collaboration between three to four individuals: a merchant shipper, shipowner, investor, and wholesaler. Each of these individuals had a different task or contributed different expertise to the venture. The investor provided funding; the shipowner provided transportation; the merchant bought, sold, and traveled with the cargo; and the wholesaler sold the cargo once it reached the home port.

The merchant shipper was a central figure in the enterprise. He normally worked on credit and arranged a loan with a wealthy investor for the price of the cargo and freight charges. The merchant would charter or contract space on a vessel with a shipowner for a specific voyage destination. The loan for the voyage would be secured by a pledge against the sale of the future cargo. In those rare circumstances where the merchant was also a shipowner, then the loan would be secured by a pledge against the ship. Otherwise, the merchant would travel with the vessel throughout the length of the voyage arranging purchases and selling cargo as necessary. If the vessel was lost in a shipwreck, attacked by pirates, or seized by enemies, the investor lost his investment and the merchant and ship's captain risked losing their lives. Because risk was high, interest on the loans ran 22.5–30% for a 4- to 5-month period depending on the length of the voyage.[31] At the end of the voyage the ship would arrive at the port – Piraeus if the final destination was Athens (Chapter 9) – where the cargo would be unloaded and the wholesaler would auction all or portions of the cargo to local retailers, millers, or other consumers. Once the cargo was sold, the merchant could pay off the loan along with customs and port fees and settle any outstanding charges for freight (Casson 1991:102–103).

A three-way arrangement between a merchant, shipowner, and investor was the most common collaboration and is normally referred to as a commenda partnership[32] (J. Pryor 1977). It was a contract where the individuals invested different abilities and talents in a commercial venture. One invested capital, one invested knowledge and labor, one invested the means of transportation, and so forth (Bayly 1983:419). It was a practical way to finance commerce in an undercapitalized economic environment and to avoid contracting wage labor. The commenda was an arrangement used by investors to spread risk across multiple small commercial ventures. While it is often cited as a medieval institution (Harris 2009; Weber 2003b), its roots are earlier. Frederic Pryor (1977:5–6) credits the first instance of this form of business organization to ancient Babylon and cites the Athenian maritime partnerships and Roman sea loan agreements as early examples of this type of arrangement.

The commenda as a form of business organization was found across Eurasia and around the world. The term for the Persian, Muslim, Armenian, and Jewish merchants (*ortoy*) operating along the Silk Road actually means partnership in the Turkic-Arabic lexicons of the 11th and 14th centuries AD (Allsen 1989). This arrangement was common in Europe (Braudel 1986:206–207; Weber 2003b:71–74), India (Dale 1994; Goitein 1963), Russia (Martin 1985), China (Rossabi 1993; Yoshinobu 1970:30–31), and the Muslim world (Goitein 1967; Greif 1989), and extended into Africa (Amselle 1971). While a number of researchers have tried to trace the spread of this institution across the ancient world,[33] it probably originated independently in different times and places as a logical way of sharing commercial costs. One thing, however, is clear: commenda contracts were based on the personal relationships, abilities, reputation for honesty, and a high level of trust between the participants.

Avner Greif (1989:876) feels that commenda contracts were largely used for short-term relationships and specific targeted enterprises because gains could be calculated easily after each venture along with any amount of cheating by its participants. While this may have been generally true, it does not describe the activities of the Armenian merchant Hovhannes, son of David, who kept a careful account book of his commenda transactions over an 11-year duration from AD 1682 to 1693. Hovhannes traveled more than 1,000 miles from Isfahan, Iran, to India and Tibet where he spent several years in Lhasa with other Armenian merchants trafficking in a wide range of commodities that included silver, gold, precious stones, cotton and wool cloth, musk, tea, and indigo. He worked with capital acquired from commenda investors, but he also used his own capital as well as money he borrowed in his own name.[34] He constantly worked between money, goods, bills of exchange, and money loaned at interest to calculate profit and returns of trade ventures. He appears to have been a faithfully honest merchant and entrepreneur who kept scrupulous accounts of his commercial transactions. His account book illustrates the freedom, complexity, and ingenuity that ancient merchants employed to conduct business (Braudel 1986:122–124; Khachikian 1967).

FAMILY FIRMS, MERCHANT HOUSES, AND MERCHANT GUILDS

The commenda, of course, was not the only way that commerce was organized. Merchants guarded, pooled, and assembled their capital in a variety of organizations. The most fundamental and no doubt the earliest business organization was the family firm. There is evidence for large private family firms (*bītum*) in later third-millennium BC Akkad. The household was the model of early firms. The phrase, "my house is your house" was used when business partners needed to smooth out disputes, and kinship terms were used in a metaphorical sense to refer to business relationships (Silver 1985:39). Burton Benedict (1968) has argued that family firms have always been, and continue to be, important in the initial growth of young, under-commercialized economies as would have existed in many areas of the ancient and premodern world. Family firms were well equipped to take risks in a developing and unstable economy. They could make investments in training that large firms could not, raise capital through its social network, and provide long-term financial security to members willing to take risks because they could see the benefits that would accrue to them. Their small size provided flexibility, which was an advantage in small-scale commercial systems.

Family firms grew not only through biological means; adoption and the purchase of slaves were used to add members when additional labor was needed. Keeping business in the family protected trade secrets. It was within the family that women often assumed important roles as business persons (Silver 1995). The size of the family firm depended on incorporating kinsmen, in-laws, slaves, servants, and adopted sons and daughters into the enterprise. The household model of the firm continued in use over time and was the foundation of some of the great merchant houses of Europe, India, the Orient, and across the Muslim world (Chapman 2006; Miyamoyo 1997; Parks 2005; Um 2011). In Europe, the great banking house of the Medicis was a family firm that could not loan money at interest because of usury laws; they made money using bills of trade and exchange that essentially did the same thing (Parks 2005:40).

Larger associations of merchants found across the ancient and premodern world[35] were often referred to as guilds following the medieval European convention. Moore and Lewis (1999:85) trace merchant associations back to the Phoenicians where all merchants (*mkrm*) traded as members of their guild association rather than as individuals. Whatever the term used to describe these associations,[36] merchants, whether elites or commoners, shared a number of commercial concerns that were better addressed as a group rather than individually. Safety during travel abroad was one of them; security could be improved when they traveled in groups or could negotiate assurances of safe passage or fair treatment from the leaders of the areas they visited. For the most part, their effectiveness and ability to obtain these types of considerations depended on having the backing of their representative political governments, as was the case with Venice.[37] Merchant associations from multiple towns could also band together, as was the case for the German Hanse, which functioned as a confederation of guilds (Epstein 1991:134; Mauro 1993).

One of the concerns of merchants was fair trade. They were always directly involved in the operation of the local marketplace, and to the degree possible in fair dealings abroad (Braudel 1986:314–315). The behavior of medieval merchants in Europe was governed in general terms by the *lex mercantoria*, a body of customary law that varied from region to region. To avoid exploitation from local rulers, merchants in Europe lobbied for legal jurisdiction over economic disputes as early as the 9th century AD. In Italy this was confirmed in community charters where merchants claimed the right to establish guild courts to mediate commercial disputes. This was especially important in fairs and marketplaces where merchants needed to have contracts upheld and be able to travel securely without having their goods confiscated to pay the debts of others (Pounds 1994:427–428). It was over a concern for fair merchant practices that led the Reverend Johannes Nider (1966) to write *De Contractibus Mercatorum* in AD 1468, which is the earliest known printed discussion of business ethics in the western world. His work was intended as a moral guide to business practices that was guided by Christian doctrine.

Merchant associations also had more than just economic functions. In the Hanseatic league, merchant associations also had religious, choral, and recreational purposes in addition to their professional ones. They shared a house or a meeting hall where they held their meetings, which usually was the most important structure in the community. When merchant associations traded in a single commodity, they often became involved in production to ensure they had a sufficient supply of goods to trade. This was common in China where specialization in a single product (e.g., opium) frequently made membership in a specific merchant association dependent on regional or ethnic origin (Golas 1977:563). In terms of their general functions, Mauro (1993:278) argues that merchants in both the east and the west were organized in much the same way.

MERCHANT ORGANIZERS: THE PUTTING-OUT SYSTEM

Merchants got involved in production when they had to as a means to ensure they had product to sell. An example of this was described in Chapter 2 in the discussion of the weaving industry across the Indian subcontinent. Merchants also were directly involved in the organization of rural textile production systems in preindustrial Europe. This system has been referred to as the *putting-out system*, or the *Verlagssystem*.[38] This system is important for its historic role prior to the industrial revolution. Merchants organized female rural labor to produce woolen textiles in their homes. It was a short step from that to moving workers to a centralized location at a factory and adding machinery, which initiated the industrial revolution.

The putting-out system is well known for rural England. The issue for urban-based woolen merchants was to obtain good quality woven cloth for export. Their solution was to organize rural women, all of whom knew how to spin wool into thread and weave cloth, into a dispersed rural cottage industry to make textiles that merchants would collect and export. The merchant would supply the raw wool to women, who would spin the thread and manufacture the woolens to the specification of the merchant. On completion, the merchant would pay a stipulated amount of cash for the finished goods. This system centered production in the home, provided additional income for households, and allowed the work to be carried out by women and children during down times in the work cycle. Dyer (2005:230) has characterized this form of production as proto-industrial. One reason given for the widespread development of the putting-out system in England is that craft guilds there were weaker than they were in countries on the European continent (A. Smith 1991:114). Nevertheless, it was applied as a form of production across Europe for a variety of products including the manufacture of nails, silk textiles, lace, paper, metal goods, and printed books (Braudel 1986:300, 317–318, 321).

The role of merchants as an organizing force in production was not confined to Europe. It appeared in many other areas of the premodern world. In India, merchants gave cash advances to rural craftsmen to produce finished cotton textiles without supplying them with raw material (Ramaswamy 2006:144). The desire for cotton textiles allowed merchants from China and Thailand to introduce a form of putting-out system throughout Southeast Asia[39] to manufacture woven goods for local consumption (Clarence-Smith 2011). The structure of the putting-out system is discussed more fully in Chapter 8.

MERCHANT DIASPORAS

In 587–586 BC, Nebuchadnezzar destroyed the city of Jerusalem and carried its population off as slaves to Babylon. This was not the first or even the last time Jewish populations would be forcefully deported from Israel. Previous conquests by the Assyrians had forcefully removed Jewish populations from the northern kingdom of Israel, with Sennacherib deporting more than 200,000 people from the kingdom around 705 BC (Unger 1966:181). Conquest was one way that people could be relocated from their native homeland. But it was not the most common. While many factors were involved in the dispersal of ethnic populations around the globe, economic motivations including trade were particularly important.[40] Here the discussion focuses on the trade diaspora, which was both the Internet of ancient commerce and the highway along which goods moved and commercial relationships were structured.

Philip Curtin (1984) first identified the importance of the trade diaspora as one of the most widespread human institutions and a primary mechanism for long-distance trade in the ancient and premodern world. Curtin (1984:3) defined trade diasporas as "communities of merchants living among aliens in associated networks." Trade diasporas typically share three important characteristics in common with one another. First, the trade diaspora was made up of merchants, or at least groups of individuals whose primary objective was to enhance their economic well-being through trade. In this way the Viking colonies in Iceland and Greenland that were settled in the late 9th and 10th centuries AD in search of walrus ivory, furs, and hides (Brown 2015:56–61) qualify as diaspora settlements, as do the early Greek colonies dispersed throughout the Mediterranean (Garland 2014). A second feature is that the diaspora group often represents a minority group in the land that they occupy. They frequently represent what Bonacich (1973) refers to as middleman minorities based on the economic role they play in the societies where they are found. And third, diaspora groups were not isolated. Rather, they were part of a system of interconnected communities that formed a network-based economy[41] that operated through personal and established economic relationships (Wai-keung 2005).

Trade diasporas were a ubiquitous part of the ancient world wherever long-distance trade was practiced. The reason for this was that the ancient world was an ethnic world in which cross-cultural economic interaction took place only where established social relations bridged the cultural divide. The Portuguese had trouble buying spices and other goods on their arrival in India at the dawn of the 16th century AD because they had no established local connections to work through.[42] Time was a critical variable in a system where maritime transportation was slow and costly. Having reliable agents to procure goods for merchants in advance of their arrival and being able to leave goods with trusted colleagues instead of having to sell themselves expedited commerce.[43] The key to amassing profit was to keep on the move. Trade diasporas represented communities of individuals with similar religious, ethnic, and ethical backgrounds. They were the best solution to the merchant's dilemma of having to leave his hometown to preserve working capital while not becoming isolated from his cultural background. Members of a diaspora community shared a common origin and cultural background that enabled them to generate capital, mobilize labor, assemble and store goods, keep information secret, and respond to new opportunities in distant markets on behalf of others when prices were low or new opportunities arose.[44] Shared social ties provided the network through which information flowed (Greif 1989). As autonomous groups in the societies where they resided, diaspora communities maintained internal order, protected themselves, and disciplined members who deviated from established moral or economic practices (Cohen 1971).

Trade diasporas have been found in one form or another everywhere where long-distance trade occurred on a large scale. They were a driving force behind the dispersal of minorities throughout the ancient[45] and premodern[46] worlds. They are, however, difficult to study with a synchronic approach without taking into consideration population movement, marriage patterns, and descent (Cohen 1971:268–269). From an archaeological perspective, trade diasporas can be difficult to distinguish from other types of colonies unless researchers specifically look for economic linkages. Even where enclaves were settled for political motives, trade often followed the flag or was the reason for conquest or political expansion (Webb 1975; Wells 1992).

Gil Stein (1999b, 2001) proposed that the presence of Uruk features at Hacinebi, Turkey, during the fourth millennium BC was an early trade diaspora. This is based on four criteria. The first is his identification of ethnic markers that he believes reflects the actual presence of Uruk foreigners at Hacinebi instead of trade interaction between the two regions. Second, there was no evidence of fortifications, warfare, or forceful domination of the Hacinebi community during the Uruk presence. Third, the Uruk population represented a very small minority of the site's inhabitants, who lived in their own encapsulated and autonomous neighborhood within the community. Finally, the Uruk population did not dominate the larger community of Hacinebi either politically or economically. Instead, they appear to have lived side by side in a peaceful fashion for a period approaching 400 years without disruption. If Stein is correct, then it suggests that trade diasporas were a dynamic factor in the economic relations among peer polities during the formation of early states (Renfrew and Cherry 1986).

One of the primary keys for the success of a trade diaspora was the maintenance of trust and shared cultural values between its members. Greif (1989) feels that a diaspora community is best thought of as a coalition of interdependent individuals. He notes that members of the medieval Jewish diaspora operating across the Muslim world and into India always preferred to incorporate new emigrants into long-distance trade rather than incorporating local individuals into their businesses. Non-Jews were excluded from the network because they felt it was costlier to keep nonmembers honest than fellow Jews. Religious and ethnic origins provided the boundaries for the coalition, which made it difficult for outsiders to break into the trade network that they controlled (Cohen 1971). The result was that large commercial centers were transformed into heterogenous, multicultural urban centers with merchants from different ethnic groups residing in small enclaves within the city. Port cities and commercial centers like Novgorod (Russia), Timbuktu (Mali), Astrakhan (Russia), and Hong Kong are examples of communities with multicultural populations (Dale 1994; Martin 1986; Miner 1953).

Maintaining the ethnic homogeneity and distinctiveness of the diaspora community was more difficult than one might think, especially when communities were widely scattered over space. This was less difficult when individuals moved from community to community throughout the diaspora or only stayed away from their home communities for short periods of time. However, when individuals remained in diaspora for long periods of time, they would often seek local wives, begin to adopt local customs, and assimilate into the local culture, losing some of their ethnic distinctiveness. Indian merchants normally traveled without their wives. Since they could be gone for periods of 10–20 years when traveling and trading in Central Asia, they made accommodations with their family life.[47] It was common for their wives to have children with other men in their absence, who were recognized as full members of the merchant's family (Levi 2002:142).

A well-known diaspora in ancient Mesoamerica was a network of small Zapotec groups located in communities spaced over 400 kilometers between the Basin of Mexico and the Valley of Oaxaca. Small enclaves of Zapotecs have been identified in the large urban center of Teotihuacan and contemporaneous communities between AD 200 and 600 that formed a trade network through which ceramics, mica, and other trade goods moved (Spence 2005). One commercial specialty of several Zapotec communities was mining, processing, and trading quick lime used for stucco floors, plastering walls, and sealing exterior roofs. The problem of maintaining a strong ethnic identity within these multigenerational communities was solved by the recruitment of young Zapotec women from the Valley of Oaxaca and relocating them to diaspora enclaves in Central Mexico. Isotopic analysis of human burials indicates that the emigrating women actually traveled between diaspora enclaves while they were breast-feeding infants. Christine White and colleagues (White et al. 2004) suggest that the movement of women and infants between Zapotec enclaves created a diaspora citizenship for new emigres and inducted infants into the broader ethnic network through the practice of sojourning (White et al. 2004).

Trade, Diaspora, and the Old Assyrian Merchants of the Middle Bronze Age

The Middle Bronze Age (2000–1600 BC) began with the collapse of the Ur III dynasty of Sumer in southern Mesopotamia and the emergence of multiple city-states that competed for political influence with one another. Several of the most important city-states during this period were Babylon in the middle Euphrates, Mari in the northern Euphrates, Assur on the northern Tigris, and Ebla in northwestern Syria. Considerable evidence exists during the Middle Bronze Age for extensive trade of both bulk commodities and luxury goods over long distances. Trade routes extended from the Persian Gulf and Iran to the Black Sea and into the Aegean world (Larsen 1987, 2008a:13; Potts 2010:126–127, 131). The Assyrian city of Assur was particularly important during this period in the development of commercial trade with central

Anatolia in modern-day Turkey. Assur depended on commercial trade for a major portion of its income, producing, importing, and exporting goods through its extensive network of merchants.[48] The following discussion describes how merchant commerce operated between the home city and its diaspora colonies.

Fundamental to the successful operation of this trade was the establishment of diaspora merchant enclaves in the Anatolia communities. Much of what is known about the Old Assyrian trade comes from a large body of more than 23,000 preserved clay tablets excavated from an Assyrian merchant enclave located in the ancient Anatolian community of Kanesh[49] (modern Kültepe, Turkey). The city of Assur negotiated trade agreements with the rulers of distant areas establishing the rights of Assyrian merchants to trade while at the same time theoretically prohibiting their competitors from doing the same (Larsen 2008b:71–72; 2015). These treaties granted permission to establish a *kārum*, or diaspora community of Assyrian merchants, through which trade was monitored and taxed by both their foreign hosts and the city of Assur. The *kārum* was a corporate administrative unit of merchants under the control of the economic office of the *bīt ālim* at Assur. The *kārum* had a secretary, central storerooms, a building, and rotating administrative officials who monitored transactions, collected fees, and settled disputes as they arose between merchants. Within this setting, Assyrian merchants conducted their business as private entrepreneurs who borrowed money, worked with their own capital, and conducted trade for investors. They worked for profit and understood the price-setting mechanism of supply and demand (Meijer 2000:334; SVeenhof 2003a:78; 2003b:78).

The city of Assur was controlled by a merchant oligarchy that together with the king negotiated the placement of its *kārum* merchants in strategic locations to access key resources fundamental to commercial success.[50] They founded *kārum* (pl. *kāru*) enclaves in the kingdom of Nuzi, Kurdistan, to get access to tin. Another *kārum* was established in the Akkadian city of Sippar to get access to textiles and grain from southern Mesopotamia. The trade enclave at Durhumid obtained copper from the Black Sea that in turn was traded to other diaspora colonies in Anatolia. The *kāru* of Kanesh, Hattuŝa (modern Boğazköy), and others in Anatolia were oriented primarily toward the sale of tin and textiles to acquire gold and silver (Moore and Lewis 1999:60). Goods imported into Assur would pass through the *bīt ālim* economic office at Assur, which oversaw trade for the city and acted as a clearing house for accounts. The *bīt ālim* appears to have inventoried textiles manufactured for export and goods coming into the city for resale, collected export taxes, and sold merchandise to *kārum* merchants in other enclaves (Veenhof 2003b:75). Trade enclaves were the economic extensions of Assur. In addition to their goods being taxed by the city, they could be called on for special levies of silver as occurred when the city wall of Assur needed repair (Aubet 2013:281; Larsen 2015, 1976:163).

The main items of trade in Anatolia were tin and textiles exchanged for silver and gold. Documents from *kārum* Kanesh suggest that business was generally handled in three steps. First, silver would be turned over to a transporter at Kanesh with a contract stipulating the amount and the individual to whom a shipment would be delivered in Assur. Then a merchant in Assur would notify his agent in Kanesh that a shipment of goods would be sent with a specified carrier. Third and finally, after receipt of the goods, the agent in Kanesh would send a letter notifying[51] the merchant in Assur that the goods were received, how they were handled, and how much taxes and duties were paid, along with any other expenses (Aubet 2013:300). Goods were transported by donkeys over 1,000 kilometers, a trip that usually took about 50 days. It was the responsibility of the local ruler to provide for safety in route, and a toll was charged on the quantity of tin and textiles transported.[52] Veenhof (1972:69–80) calculated that over a 60-year period a total of 14,500 textiles and 13.5 tons of tin were sent from Assur to Kanesh. When this is projected over the life of *kārum* Kanesh, the volume of trade is upward of 100,000 textiles and 80 tons of tin moving from Assur into Anatolia through the Kanesh merchants (Van de Mieroop 1999:190).

Caravans arrived at the *kārum* in Kanesh, at which point the local palace would be notified of their arrival. Goods would then be carried up to the palace where they would be inspected and a tax levied on the value of their contents. By agreement with Assur, local rulers received an in-kind tax of 20% on linen and 30% on tin. The palace also had the right to buy an additional 10% of the merchandise at an agreed-on price if they chose to purchase any (Larsen 2008b:72). After that, the cargo was returned to the *kārum* center where merchandise would be sold in smaller lots, most often on the basis of credit, to merchants to sell in other towns in Anatolia. Some thirty-five to forty towns in Anatolia had resident Assyrian merchants in them (Larsen 2008b:71). Large Anatolian towns like Kanesh and Purushaddum had their own *kārum*, while smaller communities had a reduced trading station known as a *wabartum* (Barjamovic 2011; Dercksen 1996:155–156). Kanesh was a central node in the Anatolian trade network and helped to initiate trade agreements with other communities together with the *bīt ālim* and its envoy from Assur (Veenhof 2003b:86–88).

Tin was in high demand throughout Anatolia and a main item in the Assyrian trade because all of it had to be imported to manufacture bronze. Textiles were also significant. Assur imported and resold Akkadian textiles manufactured in southern Mesopotamia. Especially important, however, were the textiles manufactured in Assur from wool obtained through trade. Women were important in textile production, and the city assembly of Assur protected this manufacturing sector with penalties. A letter sent by two colleagues in Assur to a Kanesh merchant named Pushuken makes this clear. It identifies a fine levied against merchants who bought and sold Anatolian textiles instead of importing textiles manufactured at Assur. The letter states:

> Here (in Assur) it has come to a lawsuit concerning *saptinnu-* and *pirikannu*-textiles, woollen products, and many people have been fined. You too have been obliged to pay 10 pounds of silver; you must pay one pound each year.... Please do not get involved in (the trade in) *saptinnu-* and *pirikannu*-textiles, don't buy them.... The ruling of the City is severe.
>
> (Veenhof 2003b:89–90)

The merchants in residence at *kārum* Kanesh were part of a broad Assyrian trade diaspora (Curtin 1984:67–70; Kuhrt 1998:26). The Assyrian *kārum* was located in the lower city, which existed as a separate ethnic enclave within Kanesh. The names of customers listed on clay tablet documents reveal that Kanesh was a multicultural place where Hittite, Luwian, and Hurrian were spoken in addition to the Semitic languages spoken in Assyria and Ebla (Larsen 2008b:71). It is clear from the documents that merchants from Assur often lived there for long periods of their adult lives. First-generation merchants kept their wives and families in Assur, but second- and third-generation merchants more frequently married Anatolian women, which produced tensions with their in-laws back in Assur.[53] While husbands understood that they had to support their families back home, the relationship was not always smooth. In the following letter written by a wife to her wealthy merchant husband residing in Kanesh, she entreats him to stop pursuing profit for profit's sake and return to his family in Assur that needs him:

> Here we ask the women who interpret oracles, the women who interpret omens from entrails, and the ancestral spirits and the god Ashur sends you a serious warning: "You love money! You hate life!" Can't you satisfy Ashur here in the city? Please when you have heard the letter then come, see Ashur's eye and save your life! As to the proceeds from my textiles, why don't you send that to me?
>
> (Larsen 1982:214)

Assur and the Assyrian merchants in its diaspora enclaves lived by trade. They operated as family firms with members in enclaves like Kanesh who communicated with family members in Assur. Merchants also entered into partnerships referred to as *naruqqum* where rich merchants in Assur would invest large sums of money in the commercial transactions of traders in Kanesh (Aubet 2013:284). In a sense these rich merchants functioned as investment bankers. The goal of trade was to make a profit, and merchants understood the pull of supply and demand. The following is a letter sent by a merchant named Puzur-Ashur, residing in Kanesh, to his wife Waqqurtum, who lived in Assur. In it Puzur-Ashur requests that Waqqurtum make or purchase specific kinds of cloth that were popular at that moment in the Anatolian market:

> [Concerning] the fine cloth that you sent me: you must make cloth like that and send it to me via Ashur-idi, then I will send you [as payment] half pound of silver [per piece]. Have one side of the cloth combed, but not shaved smooth: it should be close-textured. Compared to the textiles you sent me earlier, you must work in 1 pound of wool more per piece of cloth, but they must still be fine! The other side [of the cloth] must be just lightly combed; if it still looks hairy, it will have to be closeshaved, like *kutānu*-cloth.[54] As for the *abarnê*-cloth ... which you sent me, you must not send me that sort of thing again. If you do want to do so, then make it the way I used to wear it. But if you don't want to make fine textiles as I have heard it they can be bought in quantity over there [i.e., where you are]; buy [them] and send them to me. One finished [piece of] cloth, when you make it, should be nine ells long and eight ells wide [4.5 × 4 m].
> (Kuhrt 1998:27)

Veenhof (1972:350–351) was the first to note the entrepreneurial nature of Assyrian commerce. He was also the first to observe that the purpose of buying and selling was not simply to meet basic domestic needs; instead, its goal was "to make money (silver)" (Aubet 2013:296; Veenhof 1972:363). Merchants made profits by exploiting the highly varied exchange rates for copper, silver, and textiles found in different areas of Anatolia (Dercksen 1996:157–159). Profit margins were as high as 100% on tin and more on textiles, even after taxes were deducted (Dercksen 1996:181; Moore and Lewis 1999:65).

MERCHANT SPECULATORS AND THE FUTURES MARKET IN ANCIENT ROME

The desire for profit often led to speculation, and speculation led to the development of an early form of a futures market in ancient Rome. A futures contract is an agreement between a buyer and a seller to purchase a commodity at a future date at an established price. Futures contracts entail risk because the future value of the commodity may be higher or lower than the price paid at the moment of sale. In ancient Rome a futures market developed where merchants bought agriculture products from elite estates. It was a risky venture, but it allowed estate owners to sell their harvest before harvest time at a discounted rate to merchants who hoped to capitalize and profit on the margin between what they paid and what they hoped to collect from anticipated sales.

According to Neville Morley (1996), the landowners had three options for selling the crops produced on their estates. The first was that they could transport goods to the city themselves and sell them through family connections or in their own family shops (*tabernae*) (Chapter 9). The second alternative was to transport products to the city and sell them to merchant wholesalers or retailers. In both cases selling one's own produce was exempt from the prevailing view among Roman elite that involvement in trade was a demeaning activity (Morley 1996:160). The third option involved selling estate produce "at the gate" of the estate to a merchant (*marcellarius*, *negotiator*) either at harvest time or as a futures contract through an auction. The futures contract for the estate harvest was paid at the completion of the auction either by the merchant who purchased it or by the auctioneer (*argentarri*) who extended credit to the merchant.

The futures contract is described by Cato in *De agricultura* as selling "olives on the tree, grapes on the vine, wine in jars and increase of the flock" (Morley 1996:161). The futures contract for sale of something like grapes on the vine before harvest was referred to as *emptio rei speratae*, that is, the sale of something that may or may not come into existence. Wine bought as a future product before the grape harvest was a bit more involved because it had to be processed and held for a longer period of time. In this case the futures transaction was finalized only after the wine was tasted to ensure that it had not spoiled and turned to vinegar. But by any stretch of the imagination, futures contracts were risky. Nowhere is this better expressed than in the words of Pliny the Elder, who sold his grape harvest as a futures contract on the vine: "I had sold my grape harvest to the *negotiatores*, who were eager to buy, when the price quoted at the time was tempting and prospects seemed good. Their hopes were frustrated" (Morley 1996:162).

TEMPLES AS COMMERCIAL INSTITUTIONS

Temples always had important economic roles in early societies and were important property owners in the Near East at least as early as the fourth millennium BC (Falkenstein 1974). They owned large flocks of sheep, and the wool they produced was woven into textiles by female labor working in temple workshops (Gelb 1972, 1979; Kozuh 2014; Liverani 2013). In Egypt, pious foundations created to support deceased pharaohs formed their own distinct economic entities (Kemp 1991:85, 89). In both these cases, temples produced large quantities of goods beyond their internal consumption needs. Merchants, whether members of the temple and the palace institutions that they served or independent commercial operators, were instrumental in transporting, marketing, and converting institutional resources into alternative, high-value products that were not available locally or could be stored indefinitely and converted into other resources at a later date. Merchants always maintained a symbiotic relationship with the important social, political, and religious institutions that produced resources for their own use and consumption. But that is not the relationship of interest here.

The focus here is on how temples fit into fostering commercial relationships within society. The discussion looks beyond how merchants may have worked for the temple as a specific economic institution. Instead, it considers the role that religious institutions played in supporting merchants, reinforcing contract agreements, serving early lending and banking functions, and fostering interregional trade in a variety of different ways. It was within this context that some religious institutions spread across the ancient world coincident with the increase in interregional, long-distance trade. Ethnicity and religion were closely linked in the ancient world, and they were important characteristics in defining the membership and solidarity of many trade diasporas. Shared religious practices built communities of trust in which merchant-to-merchant interaction and relationships were forged.

Throughout antiquity, religion was a powerful force in the lives of people. The gods played an important economic role as protectors of honest business practices within society.[55] The gods might be personified as merchants or serve as patron deities for specific crafts, but where they were particularly important was in reinforcing honesty in interpersonal business agreements. Divine oversight and potential retribution was the primary assurance that commercial contracts were fulfilled in the absence of a strong secular framework for protecting commerce (Rauh 1993:340–341). Oaths before god were how individuals pledged to fulfill their obligations. In the ancient Near East, oaths were used to seal contracts, dissolve partnerships, confirm the honesty of testimony,[56] and stipulate inheritance divisions (Postgate 2004:280). In Babylon, merchants settled accounts in the temple of the sun-god Shamash, and if they broke their oaths, they forfeited protection of the gods (Silver 1995:11, 17).

Declaration of commercial oaths before god was a cross-cultural practice. This normally involved three steps: invocation of the gods, declaration of a promise to be fulfilled, and guaranteeing the outcome with a curse that accompanied failure to complete the specified agreement. Altars were often found in marketplaces before which oaths could be declared. It is for this reason that the Ara Maxima of Hercules in the forum Boarium of Rome was the most celebrated market altar in the ancient world (Rauh 1993:147). Oaths often were accompanied by the sacrifice of animals[57] to reinforce their meaning before god (Sundström 1974:21).

Not surprisingly, temples were also sites of commerce.[58] In Greek mythology the island of Delos was sacred to Apollo, was the location of his temple, and became an entrepot in the eastern Mediterranean for merchants involved in both the grain and slave trade (Hudson 1999a:142–144). Similarly, in 5th-century BC Egypt, the Phoenician trading enclave from Tyre was located adjacent to the temple of Aphrodite in the town of Memphis (Silver 1995:18). One of the attractions of temples as early sites of commerce was that they also served many of the functions of early banks. In the late third millennium BC, Near East temples supplied loans to merchants who engaged in trade for copper and other goods obtained through maritime commerce to Dilmun via the Persian Gulf (Ratnagar 2004:25–27). Greek temples also provided loans and were often the safest places to store wealth (Andreau 1999:124). It was this banking function that led Polanyi (1981:141) to suggest that the temple and the palace were the original providers of harvest credit for farmers in the ancient world.

Temples also provided a partial solution to two aspects of the merchant's dilemma. The first problem was how to avoid drains of working capital from wealthy individuals who were expected to sponsor activities in the community where they resided. If a merchant lived up to expected social obligations and hosted feasts or sponsored the construction of a building, a high proportion of that capital would be lost to future economic ventures. A more attractive alternative was to make a gift of that capital as an endowment to a temple and then borrow it back at an interest rate well below that of standard commercial loans. The net effect of this practice was the merchant still had control of a large percentage of his capital for economic ventures while at the same time being perceived within the community as a respected patron. Temple endowments and donations of both land and money were common across south India as early the 9th century AD and were used for a range of functions in addition to supporting trade.[59] In terms of financial endowments, temples could serve as a form of bank trust for working capital.

A second challenge that merchants faced was how to establish themselves in a new community when they entered it as an ethnic outsider. Again, examples from south India are instructive. Tamil merchants referred to as Nattukottai Chettiars established themselves as outsiders in key market towns using temple affiliations. They built and endowed temples to local deities, which helped to establish them as trusted and contributing members of the community. An example of this process is illustrated by a Chettiar salt merchant by the name of Kumarappan who arrived in the south Indian town of Palani in AD 1600 to explore salt trading possibilities. Kumarappan stayed in the house of a temple priest and opened a shop next door. He sold his salt at just over cost and gave the proceeds to the temple, thereby establishing a relationship with the temple deity. After 4 years he brought five additional salt merchants to the community who replicated the same pattern.

Religious gifting provided a mechanism for outside groups like this Tamil caste of merchants to establish themselves in the local Hindu economy and eventually form resource groups within the community. Kumarappan eventually became a ritual master within the temple and a chief administrator of temple business with the responsibility of investing funds endowed for the deity. Can you guess where he invested those funds? In a range of business ventures including his own! Kumarappan took charge of collecting contributions to the temple and, in exchange for this service, also received a share of the endowment that he managed. In this context there was no separation of worship and economics. Gifts to the temple had specific economic functions, and as an elite merchant Kumarappan could reinvest in mercantile enterprises for the temple, which included loans to himself for commercial ventures (Dobbin 1996:133–135; Rudner 1987:365–369, 374–377). As Rudner (1987:377) states, "The Nak [Nattukottai] caste and other castes of itinerant traders engaged in worship as a way of trade, and they engaged in trade by worshiping the deities of their customers."

Merchants endowed temples as investments to further their interests. It should come as no surprise to find temples built along the same routes that merchants traveled. This is exactly the process, according to Xinru Liu (1988), that accounts for the spread of Buddhism from India into China over the first 6 centuries AD. Buddhist merchants established monasteries along trade routes leading into China, which over time were transformed from congregations of monks to special cloisters associated with names of specific commercial sponsors. Some monasteries were associated with specific guild groups and provided safe lodging for merchants while they were on the road. Four different financial practices found in China may have originated in Buddhist monasteries or at least were closely associated with them. These include the pawn shop, the mutual financing association, the auction, and the sale of lottery tickets. While Buddhist monks did not drink, archaeological investigations in India indicate that some monasteries made liquor, not for consumption, but for purposes of trade (Liu 1988:107–114, 122).

MERCHANTS ON THE ROAD: THE AZTEC *POCHTECA*

The best-known case of merchants in the New World are the long-distance Aztec merchants known as the *pochteca*. While there were other pre-Hispanic merchant groups in the northern Andes (Salomon 1977, 1987, 1988) and caravan traders in the southern Andes (Dillehay and Núñez 1988; Nielsen 2001, 2013), the Aztec *pochteca* remain the best known because they were documented by Spanish friars interested in Aztec culture and history in the early 16th century AD (Durán 1867–1880, 1994; Sahagún 1959, 1961; Zorita 1994). The *pochteca* are interesting for two reasons. First, all trade was carried out by transporting goods using tumplines (Figure 7.1) on the backs of human porters.

7.1 Aztec *pochteca* merchants carrying merchandise with a tumpline. (from Hirth 2016:Figure 4.1)

As such, they provide a valuable point of comparison with Old World merchants in Africa where human porters were used (Dike and Ekejiuba 1990; Forde 1956; Northrup 1978) and in areas where goods could be transported on donkeys, camels, in wagons, and on ships. Second, the *pochteca* normally did not organize long-distance trade using diaspora communities. One trade outpost is documented among the Aztecs at Tochtepec, but it was an adaptation to special circumstances and did not have permanent residents. Instead, the *pochteca* operated through the widespread network of marketplaces where business transactions were negotiated through a range of individual buyer–seller relationships (Chapter 9). In this sense long-distance trade was organized differently from how it was in the Old World.

Wealth within the Aztec state came from two primary sources. The first was from the agricultural estates where food was produced by rotating corvée labor from the commoner population; these estates supported both local elite families and the majority of local institutions (Harvey 1984, 1991; Hicks 1976, 1984). The second was from taxes that flowed into the Aztec capital from conquered provinces, which covered the costs of the state and rewards to soldiers (Berdan and Anawalt 1992; Berdan et al. 1996). Merchant wealth was not an avenue to elite status. The *pochteca* were members of the commoner (*macehualtin*) class. While commerce was a way to amass a substantial private fortune, merchants had to hide their wealth lest they incur the jealousy and wrath of less wealthy elite. Merchants were required to pay a tax in the goods they trafficked in, most often expressed in quantities of cacao beans (Martínez 1984). But they operated primarily for themselves and on occasion as commercial agents for the state. Nevertheless, the wealth they imported and accumulated was vital for the growth of Aztec craft industries, and the *pochteca* provided important service to the state as economic advisors, as market supervisors, and as spies, ambassadors, and guides to the army as they moved through foreign territory.

The *pochteca* were organized as stratified corporate groups called *calpultin* (sing. *calpulli*) that resided together usually as a separate barrio or neighborhood[60] (Calnek 1976; van Zantwijk 1970, 1985). *Calpultin* were organized around a common group identity based on profession, hereditary land holdings, or ethnicity. Because of the lucrativeness of their trade, *pochteca* were largely endogamous; that is, they married members of other merchant families within their *calpulli*. All *calpultin* had their own temple, and the *pochteca* worked together as a group in organizing and carrying out trade expeditions. Status within the *pochteca* was based on wealth and experience, and those who could acquire both became leaders within their community. The primary way this was achieved was by using their wealth to sponsor sacrifices in public ceremonies that served to raise their individual stature within the *pochteca* community through their society-wide contributions.

For the *pochteca*, success in commerce involved direct trade in the marketplace. They did not use agents or formal intermediaries that we know of, but instead they traded their goods directly with local people in the different markets that they visited both within and outside the Aztec empire. This involved trading with commoners, elites, and other foreign merchants. High transportation costs using human porters made high-value, lightweight commodities the focus of this trade. Merchants traveled from market to market hundreds of kilometers from their home communities seeking out and buying exotic goods in areas where they occurred naturally and where the prices were low. Because they bought in the marketplace, the *pochteca* took a range of both utilitarian and high-value goods[61] with them that could be sold to the commoners, craftsmen, and retailer venders located there. The Mesoamerican marketplace is discussed more fully in Chapter 9, but the items the *pochteca* sought to obtain included both finished goods (embroidered textiles, necklaces, gold jewelry) and raw materials (e.g., feathers, jade and greenstone, marine shells, liquidambar, and exotic pelts and skins).[62] They also trafficked in slaves, who may have been used to transport goods on return trips of expeditions (Hirth 2016:297, fn 2).

A number of scholars (Carrasco 1978l; Chapman 1957) following the work of Karl Polanyi have proposed that the *pochteca* were an official arm of the state's administered economy. We now know that this was not the case, and that merchants operated as independent operators in a commercialized economy. But the *pochteca* did operate as agents of wealthy individuals, including the Aztec king, taking goods on consignment to trade for a commission. The best documented case of this was their serving as commercial agents for the Aztec king of Ahuitzotl. Not all areas were open to Aztec merchants; the province of Xicalanco on the Gulf Coast of Mexico was one of these. Nevertheless, a specific treaty with the ruler of Anauac Xicalanco[63] allowed the *pochteca* to enter under his protection where they presented gifts on Ahuitzotl's behalf to him and the other rulers with whom the treaty had been arranged. The following quote describes how this occurred:

> when the merchants reached Anauac Xicalanco [and] the rulers who governed the cities of Anauac, thereupon they ... [the merchants] ... gave to each of them all the items of trade – the precious capes, precious skirts, precious shifts, the property of Auitzotzin ... And then the rulers of Anauac Xicalanco, Cimatlan, [and] Coatzaqualco reciprocated with the large green stones, ... and fine bottle-green jadeite, and turquoise mosaic shields; ... and large red sea shells, ... feathers of the red spoonbill, the toupial, and the blue honeycreeper; ... and the skins of wild animals.
>
> (Sahagún 1959:18–19)[64]

This was inter-elite trade under the guise of reciprocal gift giving, and was common among elites where reciprocal gifting signaled a closer social relationship between the interacting parties than did impersonal haggling over equivalent value. In this instance, the *pochteca* were serving as personal agents of the king. Once gifting ceremonies were concluded, merchants traded on their own behalf. The elite in Xicalanco were different from the Aztec elite in that they also were involved as merchants in long-distance trade (Scholes and Roys 1968:58–60). A similar form of reciprocal gift giving is recorded in the Old World in the El Amarna letters where diplomacy and trade were linked (Liverani 2008a, 2008b; Moran 1992).

Taking oaths and establishing contracts was not a dimension of Mesoamerican commerce because trade normally took place between strangers and established trade partners in the marketplaces. The goods traded were carried with the merchant, so exchanges were immediate and did not have to be left with agents for later sale. The *pochteca* also acted as agents for other wealthy individuals parallel to what they did for their king. As far as can be determined, however, most of the goods consigned for trade were for other members of the merchant community. Fair trade return for the merchandise consigned was judged somewhat subjectively because of the opportunistic nature of the goods available in the marketplaces where merchants traveled. The sources tell us that consigned goods were not entrusted to a particular merchant but were assembled and put on display in the house of the merchant leading the trade expedition. This allowed the whole community to see the type of goods consigned as well as to judge whether the goods accrued by the end of the expedition were reasonable in relation to the amount invested in the venture. Instead of returning home at the end of an expedition, merchants took all the merchandise directly to the house of another well-respected and honest merchant where it was left presumably for public display, evaluation, and distribution to the consignors involved[65] (Hirth 2016:260–263).

Ritual was important for merchants at the beginning of an expedition where they faced the dual uncertainties of danger from the gods and robbery on the road. All wealth was seen as divine property, which made trade risky since acquiring it for yourself meant expropriating it from the gods. Second, there was the physical danger of being attacked on the road, especially in those areas where the *pochteca* were forbidden to enter but did anyway by disguising themselves as merchants from different areas.[66] The Mesoamerican pantheon was replete with capricious deities, so merchants made small sacrifices at their altars as they traveled throughout the land. They also decorated and revered their walking staves as the embodiment of their god Yacatecuhtli, who "went before them" on their travels (Hirth 2016:224–227). The Aztec *pochteca* were independent entrepreneurs who were motivated by profit and the desire to accumulate wealth, like merchants elsewhere. Nevertheless, the conditions under which they operated were different from merchants in the Old World and, as a result, so too were the ways that they conducted business.

SUMMARY

Ancient merchants were individuals whose livelihood depended on buying and selling goods for profit. They were self-actualizing entrepreneurs who sought opportunities for trade, served as trade intermediaries in moving goods over space, and in the process were indispensable in converting resources into alternative commodities. The motivation behind their activities was profit, the proceeds from which were important for supporting their individual households. No attempt was made to define what a merchant was in terms of any specific set of activities because the road to becoming a merchant could take many paths. Likewise, I have avoided talking about merchants as full-time professionals, as many Assyrian merchants or Aztec *pochteca* certainly were. The reason for this is that merchants often combined their commercial activities with other subsistence pursuits. Merchants could buy goods for wholesale or retail resale at the same time that they produced what they sold, engaged in agriculture, moved their herds to pasture, loaned money, collected taxes, or transported goods for others. Nevertheless, where merchant behavior was most strongly expressed in antiquity is where the majority (50% or more) of their time was spent in commercial activities.

Karl Polanyi (1957, 1981; Polanyi et al. 1957) did not feel merchants operated as independent entrepreneurs. Instead, he felt that because the economy was based on agriculture, most merchants mentioned in the early cuneiform texts were agents of large institutions where they received their support. The origin of merchants for Polanyi was as agents of the temple conducting administered trade (Chaudhuri 1991:426). For him the commercial middle class with its enterprising merchants was a late 19th-century AD development associated with the emergence of western capitalism (Silver 1995:167–172).

The reality of the situation is that the origin of merchants was not an either/or situation. They operated on their own to improve their individual economic well-being, and they willingly served as agents for institutions when they were needed. The orientation of merchants in both these cases was the same: to convert available resources into alternative goods to meet consumption needs. Bronze Age merchants of the ancient Near East worked as agents of institutions trading textiles produced in temple workshops for copper and tin to manufacture bronze as well as other wealth goods consumed by the social elite (Garfinkle 2010). But merchants always operated for their own economic well-being, and for this reason merchants can be found even in small-scale, tribal societies. The example of the Vitiaz Island merchants underscores this point. Exchange was important as a provisioning strategy throughout human history. The early movement and exchange of obsidian in the central and eastern Mediterranean demonstrates that exchange was an important component linking fisher–forager groups to coastal and inland settlements as early as 12,000 years ago.

As merchants acquired wealth, commerce became a full-time pursuit and merchants faced a socioeconomic dilemma: How to retain the resources and economic capital that they needed for their commercial enterprises, while still maintaining their social standing in the communities where they lived? Wealthy members of society were expected to invest their time and resources in the economic base of their community. The solution to this problem for merchants was far from ideal. One response was to preserve their capital by leaving home and focusing their attention on trade outside the community. This suspended community obligations with merchants being reintegrated into the community at a later date if some family members remained behind. This was a common solution when merchants were part of a broader trade diaspora and could change their location by becoming actively involved in long-distance trade. The community of Kanesh represents a trade diaspora where young Assyrian merchants from Assur learned the ropes of long-distance trade.

A second solution to the merchant's dilemma was to insulate themselves from requests to spend their capital in noneconomic activities. The *pochteca* were insulated from the larger society by their *calpulli* membership and commoner status. When they spent their money on socially prescribed functions, it was to raise their status within the community of merchants as they became wealthy toward the end of their careers.[67] An alternative practice across the greater Indian subcontinent was to invest working capital in temple endowments within the communities where they lived and traveled. Becoming temple patrons had two positive results. It gave merchants social status within the community while at the same time allowing them to stipulate how temple endowments would be used. By remaining active patrons in the temple, they could borrow back their capital at reasonable interest rates for use in trade. This had the dual benefit of building their individual social capital while maintaining some control over their economic capital.

A trade diaspora was the solution in antiquity to the problems of poor communication, slow and dangerous transportation, and the need to establish local contacts through which intercultural exchange could take place (Curtin 1984). There are multiple examples of strong, durable, trade diasporas that were the conduits for the continued movement of resources over hundreds of years. Some well-documented examples of trade diasporas include the Arab penetration into Africa and Southeast Asia (Abu-Lughod 1989:306–310; Curtin 1984; Tibbetts 1957) and the early Sogdian diaspora into Central Asia that established some of the first long-standing contacts along the Silk Road into China (de la Vaissiere 2005; Hansen 2012). These enclaves are evident in both the archaeological and historic record because they represent Bonacich's middleman minorities, which engaged in commerce while reinforcing their membership with strong ethnic and religious affiliation.

What is interesting is that diaspora networks were not a vibrant part of long-distance trade among the Aztec *pochteca* or other groups in Mesoamerica. They occurred occasionally in Mesoamerica (e.g., Spence 2005), but are a dim reflection compared with what can be observed in the Old World. One might expect that they would be necessary in an environment where the cost of transportation was very high. This was not the case in Mesoamerica because marketplaces provided an environment for exchange that served many of the same functions and reduced the need for permanently settled communities to negotiate interaction. The topic of marketplaces is examined in greater detail in Chapter 9.

The examples described here certainly do not capture all the variation in merchant activity found across the ancient world. The commercial relationships established between Assur and Kanesh certainly were not the same for every other kingdom during the Middle Bronze Age. Long-distance trade was slow and dangerous. But here is the paradox. For those brave and hearty individuals who chose to undertake long-distance trade throughout antiquity and into the premodern era, the potential for economic return was greater than it is today. Why? Because modern communication and transportation networks have leveled the playing field. The great discrepancies in prices for what goods were worth in the ancient world no longer exist. Variation in currency types and valuation rates drove European traders in Africa to the point of exhaustion (Polanyi 1966). But these differences eased with the appearance of modern currencies. Even where gold and silver were used to calculate value, there were still cultural preferences for one over the other that allowed ancient merchants to capitalize on differences in their relative worth, as occurred in the trade between China and India. In the chapter that follows, another dimension of the ancient and premodern economy is examined: the economic structures involved in the manufacture of craft goods and other commodities.

EIGHT

THE NATURE AND ORIGIN OF INDEPENDENT CRAFT PRODUCTION

Against the rising tide of automation and increasingly digital complexity, we are becoming further divorced from the very thing that defines us: we are makers, crafters of things.

(Alexander Langlands)

Craft production is an important topic in any discussion of the ancient economy. It has been proposed as a fundamental element in the emergence of civilization and the political and economic complexity that accompanied it. The role of craft production has been incorporated into debates about the appearance of social differentiation, wealth inequality, the division of labor, and the development and expansion of trade in early complex societies (Childe 1936; Marx 1967). Much of this discourse has been set within the conceptual framework of social evolutionary theory (Patterson 2005). Evolutionary treatments of craft production are valuable, but they often fail to provide detailed reconstructions of the scale or organization of specific craft activities.[1] This chapter seeks to expand on this discussion and contribute to a more complete understanding of the structure of ancient craft production.

Craft production was carried out in both institutional and noninstitutional contexts in ancient societies. The recognition that wealth goods were manufactured in institutional contexts is one of the reasons why craft production has been central to many discussions of the development of complex society (Clark and Parry 1990). The role of how institutions derived income and controlled the production of key commodities[2] was presented in Chapter 5. Here the focus is on noninstitutional forms of crafting where individuals worked as independent artisans for their own support in a range of domestic and commercial settings. In the aggregate, most independent production was carried out by many small-scale producers. How these crafting systems differed in scale, complexity, and integration from society to society depended on specific historic conditions, the demand for the goods produced, the forms of organization used to produce them, and the transportation systems used to distribute them.

It is important to recognize our modern bias at the outset of this discussion.[3] The industrial and digital revolutions have divorced us from processes of manufacture, which was the very essence of what defined the makers and crafters of things. Crafting was more than just a livelihood for the artisans producing goods for sale. It was a system of knowledge, a demonstration of artisan skill, and the creation of meaning through the transformation of raw materials into finished products. Crafting shaped the identity of the artisan as much as it did the products they produced (Hendon 2007; Hruby and Flad 2007). Aelfred the Great, King of Wessex (AD 871–899), referred to crafting in his many writings, which he described as a way to display an individual's power, talent, learning, excellence, merit, and virtue. The rise of consumerism coincident with the industrial revolution has been identified as the impetus behind the Arts and Crafts movement in late 19th-century AD England (Langlands 2017:17–33), which promoted the value of hand-crafted goods against the flood of mass-produced industrial commodities.

The discussion that follows examines several aspects of ancient craft production while remaining mindful of our modern bias. It begins by clarifying what noninstitutional craft production is and what commodities were produced by the artisans who practiced it. Theories for the origin of craft production are examined along with their ability to explain the development of ancient complex economies. The discussion then considers what I refer to as the *craftsperson's dilemma* and the risks that independent artisans faced in practicing their craft. This is followed by an exploration of production scale and the variation in organizational complexity associated with craft production in the ancient world. The scale, efficiency, and quality of craft production was enhanced through the coordination of production activities between groups of individual crafting households. Two examples of these broader manufacturing networks are explored: the development of craft guilds and the organization of the putting-out system. Finally, craft production did not exist in a vacuum. The scale that craft production could attain depended to a large degree on the forms of distribution through which finished goods were exchanged. This relationship is explored using a simple example of informal craft production in a modern college town.

THE NATURE OF NONINSTITUTIONAL CRAFT PRODUCTION

The primary goal of independent craft production was to meet the subsistence needs of its artisans by producing goods that other households could use. In institutional production artisans were attached to and supported either permanently or temporarily by the institutions that employed them (Clark 1995; Clark and Parry 1990; Costin 2001a). In noninstitutional crafting, artisans were independent and derived all or most of their livelihood from the work they performed under difficult conditions. Artisans involved in independent craft production incurred greater risk than those attached to institutions, and they employed a range of strategies to mediate it. It is in the increase of independent craft production that greater economic complexity and diversification can be found.

Independent crafting involved the manufacture of goods for use beyond the boundaries of the production units that created them. Two things are important about production orientation and output. First, artisans are specialists who engage in production for exchange rather than production for their own use. Archaeologists recognize that all ancient households produced food, tools, clothing, adornments, and other items for household consumption. These forms of ad hoc production were important but are not included in the discussion of specialized craft production presented here no matter how skilled the makers were. Specialized craft production represents the creation of items intended for consumption by groups, households, and individuals elsewhere in society. It is the increased reliance on the goods that these artisans produced that raised the level of economic integration within society. It also reflects the emerging division of labor within society as individuals focused their productive work on more specialized tasks.

A second feature of independent production is that it involved the manufacture of a broad range of utilitarian products for exchange that included food and durable goods in both finished and partially processed form. Archaeologists often focus on craft goods because they produce durable remains that can be identified in archaeological contexts. But food was a staple that also was gifted and exchanged between households as part of normal social interaction, which could involve special production effort. These could include a range of secondary food products (e.g., wine, oil, sugar, dried fruits) and specialty items including spices that were objects of trade throughout antiquity (Fall et al. 2002; Hayden 1990, 2014; Miller 1969; Morrison 2002; Zeder 1998). Specialized production of craft goods increased in importance once the process of population nucleation and urban growth was underway and the residents of urban communities manufactured fewer of the items that they consumed through their systems of ad hoc production.

The distinction between *production for use* and *production for exchange* is a useful conceptual dichotomy that can be traced back to the work of Karl Marx

(1967:I:chapter 7). For Marx, the growth of economic complexity revolved around the creation of commodities that could be exchanged for other specialized goods. The oversight in this reasoning was that Marx linked the creation of commodities and their exchange value to trade in the marketplace. He failed to recognize that exchange in the marketplace was not the only means by which goods were distributed. Ethnographic studies illustrate that artisans produced craft goods for a variety of reasons that included the distribution of finished products as gifts, as tribute, for exchange, and for sale in commercial settings. Furthermore, household members often produced a small range of items that were given away as gifts to maintain social relationships important for their subsistence survival. The production of items used in *hxaro* exchange by !Kung foragers to broaden their economic options (Chapter 3) underscores this point.[4] Nevertheless, the important issues in identifying specialized production are (1) whether the items created represent a significant factor in the work budgets of the production units, and (2) how they contributed to changing economic interdependencies within society. In general terms the importance of independent specialized production in society should be evident in the level of reliance that consumer households had on commodities that they did not produce.

PERSPECTIVES ON THE ORIGIN AND IMPORTANCE OF CRAFT PRODUCTION

Gordon Childe was the first archaeologist to propose a general theory for the origin of craft production based on the development of bronze metallurgy in Mesopotamia in the fourth millennium BC. Childe knew that cuneiform texts referenced the production of bronze objects, so he proposed that the origin of full-time craft specialization was the result of elite sponsorship in institutional contexts (Childe 1936, 1958:162–173). He reasoned that only institutions had the resources to obtain the raw materials, develop the technology, and support craftsmen needed to create bronze artifacts (Wailes 1996). Childe (1950) linked the expansion of craft production more broadly with the growth of urban places as centers of both production and consumption. For Childe, craft production was a hallmark feature of the early urban revolution.

Childe was correct in correlating bronze metallurgy with the rise of early states in Mesopotamia since the production of bronze weaponry was instrumental for their armies. Where he was misled was in assuming that metallurgy originated in institutional contexts (e.g., Gibson 1996). Subsequent research suggests that institutions were not responsible for the development of bronze metallurgy, but rather reorganized production in new ways to meet their specific needs. Gil Stein (1996) has argued that independent craft specialists already were producing bronze in noninstitutional contexts as early as the mid-sixth millennium BC. Regarding the production of bronze metallurgy in institutional contexts, he concludes that

> there is no good evidence for either prestige goods or attached craft specialization until the emergence of state societies in the Uruk period [3900–3100 BC]. Even in the Uruk period, both attached and independent craft specialization appear to have co-existed in a dual economy where the "great institutions" (palace, temples) only attempt to monopolize control over the production of prestige goods, while independent specialists continued to mass-produce utilitarian goods in all sectors of society.
>
> (Stein 1996:27)

The same was also true for the large-scale production of textiles in institutional contexts (Chapter 5), which was preceded by a long tradition of weaving at the household level.[5]

Another model for the development of craft production is linked to the appearance of prestige goods economies[6] in ranked and pre-state societies (Friedman 1982; Friedman and Rowlands 1978a). In this model, elites sponsored and controlled the production of wealth goods through patron–client relationships with individual artisans (Brumfiel and Earle 1987a; Clark 1995; Costin 2001a; D'Altroy and Earle 1985; Earle 1987a:295; Hayden 1995; Schortman and Urban 2004). The goal of craft sponsorship was to increase elite access and control over wealth goods that they could use to augment their power through lavish displays, feasting, and gift giving. The goods produced were used to build political alliances that cross-cut traditional kinship boundaries and provided the foundation for creating a nested hierarchy of political leaders who exercised power at the local and regional levels (Brumfiel and Earle 1987a:3; Earle 1987a; Frankenstein and Rowlands 1978).

This elite control model conforms to examples found in the ethnographic record. While artisans can be permanently attached to elite households, ethnographic research reveals that elite sponsorship of crafting was more commonly an intermittent practice unless the demand for specialized goods was high and continuous. Under conditions of intermittent production, elites may supply raw materials and consign production requests to artisans on an as-needs basis (Clark and Parry 1990; Malinowski 1922). With consigned production, elites employed existing artisans to produce the goods that they needed. Whether consigned production was carried out under elite supervision or without oversight in the households of the artisans varied from situation to situation (e.g., Hirth 2009d). The important point is that in most cases, crafting in domestic and noninstitutional settings was a precondition for patron–client production to occur.

If there is one fundamental truism in all economic systems, it is that trade does not occur in the absence of goods or resources to exchange. In this sense,

Marx was correct in seeing production as the starting point for analyzing economic interaction even though he recognized that there was interplay and feedback between production, distribution, demand, and consumption (Marx 1973:83–100; Patterson 2005:319). While elites could mobilize artisan labor for specific purposes, the production of most craft goods, including textiles, ceramics, lithics, basketry, leather, and wooden goods, was carried out in noninstitutional contexts because they were items used in everyday life. The demand for finished goods increased as communities grew in size and urban centers appeared, just as Childe (1950) predicted. Henri Pirenne (1974) associated the revival of European economy and trade in the 11th century AD with the resurgence of merchant activity in medieval towns and cities. The manufacture of goods for trade, including spices, dyes, incense, and textiles made of cotton, silk, wool, and linen, drew heavily on forms of domestic production throughout antiquity (Abu-Lughod 1989; Dercksen 1996; Riello and Parthasarathi 2011; Schneider 1977; Veenhof 2003b).

It is important to recognize that the majority of all ancient crafting took place in noninstitutional contexts. There are three reasons for this. First, the greatest aggregate demand was for utilitarian goods consumed by all levels of the population regardless of social standing. Second, any attempt to monopolize control over the production of a broad spectrum of utilitarian goods was impractical because of the transportation costs that would have been involved in distributing them to a widespread population. Third, and most important, even low levels of crafting were a profitable enterprise for individuals and artisan households to engage in because it helped lower their overall subsistence risk (Chapter 2). The reason for this resides in what can be called the *marginal advantage of crafting* found within agricultural societies. The normal work cycle for agricultural households often consists of periods of intense labor activity followed by periods of labor inactivity (Conklin 1957; Hagstrum 1999, 2001; Mattingly and Salmon 2002; Netting 1981, 1993). Crafting provided a way to employ idle labor in a secondary subsistence pursuit if tools and resources were available to do so. Even small-scale crafting provided households with a marginal advantage over noncrafting households in terms of the returns obtained in exchange for the goods produced.[7] The marginal advantage of crafting for households helps explain why it occurred early in prehistory in domestic settings, while at the same time restricting the scale of production because of limitations in available labor, the forms of distribution, and the problems inherent in the *craftsperson's dilemma*, described below.

Of course, there are other aspects of crafting that make it a compelling topic for historic and archaeological research. Scholars have recognized the importance of craft production in establishing meaningful social identities for the artisans who practiced it (Costin 2013; Costin and Wright 1998; Halperin and Foias 2010; Schaffer 2011). Researchers have looked at the meaning and value of the objects that craftspersons produce. Mary Helms (1988, 1993) argues that individuals with skill, the knowledge of crafting, and access to exotic goods moving through long-distance networks have the intrinsic abilities to become political leaders. Furthermore, all durable goods represent forms of resource storage (O'Shea 1989), and many of the craft goods produced played important roles in societies as bridewealth, insignia of office, and symbols of ethnic or group affiliation (Costin 2016). Artisans who practiced their crafts did not invent them on their own. They learned the knowledge important for craft work from their parents or within other communities of practice (Hughes et al. 2013; Minar and Crown 2001; Wenger 1998). Finally, craft production has been studied from the perspective of *techné*, a holistic view of the knowledge necessary to carry out a task (Costin 2016; Roochnik 2010).

RISKY BUSINESS, SPECIALIZATION, AND THE CRAFTSPERSON'S DILEMMA

We live in a world where the food and goods consumed are produced at an industrial scale by highly specialized forms of production. It is natural, therefore, to be interested in the origin and development of specialized production and the forms of organization associated with it. While the scale of production and the degree of specialization may interest us because of our modern evolutionary bias, they were not factors that entered into the economic calculus of ancient artisans. To comprehend the origins and development of ancient craft production requires that we understand the problems that crafters faced and identify the solutions that they devised to solve them.

Most ancient artisans were small-scale producers who operated out of their households or workshops with limited labor. As household enterprises they had the same goal as noncrafting households: developing an effective subsistence strategy in order to survive. Small crafting households had to solve the same challenges and problems that faced larger production enterprises. They needed skills and technology, access to necessary raw materials, and the ability to trade or sell the goods they produced for the food and other goods that they required. All three of these dimensions involved a level of cost and risk. Whether craft producers were located in rural or urban settings affected both cost and risk in different ways.

Archaeologists tend to associate craft specialists with the special knowledge and skill needed to perform their craft. There is no doubt that most craft specialists had a high level of skill that they applied to the production of the goods they made. But Alexander Langlands (2017) has demonstrated that a great deal of skill and knowledge could be found in *every* agricultural or pastoral household. If fact, it can be argued that every technological skill that craftspersons employed was developed in households for normal subsistence tasks *before* they were applied to production of goods for use outside the household. The processes used to work leather, wood, fiber, stone, clay, plant, and animal products were well known at the household and community levels even if they have been forgotten in the modern world. Even the practice of metallurgy and copper working that Childe (1936, 1958) argued required specialized knowledge can be linked to simple pyrotechnology used in cooking and the production of both pottery and lime. Hagstrum (1999, 2001) views the origin of early craft producers in terms of the *complementary* and *intersecting technologies* that households use for different forms of work. An example would be the application of pyrotechnology used in cooking to baking objects formed of clay that leads to the development of pottery and ceramic crafting.

The procurement of resources involved in craft production represents a specific challenge. Artisans normally used or adapted locally available resources to the tasks at hand. Stone, clay, and other mineral resources could be mined and used where they occurred or transported to areas where they were more easily processed. Organic renewables like wood or fiber resources that had specific uses were not just collected in the wild but were fostered within the landscapes where they grew or were side-products of other production activities including agriculture.[8] Acquiring resources for craft production was more difficult in urban areas and could have required developing special sources of acquisition or symbiotic relationships with other craftspersons through which they could be obtained (e.g., Hirth 2008). Examples of inter-craftsperson relationships could include cobblers using finished leather from tanners to manufacture shoes or the symbiotic relationship between weavers and fullers as proposed for some Roman cities (Goodman 2016; Wilson 2000).

The biggest problem that artisans faced if craft production was to become a significant component of their individual livelihoods was finding a predictable and steady market for the goods they produced. It is finding the reliable market that represents the essence of the *craftsperson's dilemma* and governs the scale that craft production could attain. When a reliable market cannot be found, craft production is a risky business. In the words of Max Weber (2003a:163), "An irregular market is fatal to the entrepreneur." The market must be large and constant for regular, full-time crafting to be successful. Morley (2007:92) contends that most farmers were not market-oriented because farming was risky enough without adding the uncertainties of the marketplace. The craftsperson's dilemma is the subsistence risk that artisans face because of the variable or fluctuating demand for the goods they produced. Craftspersons cannot escape this problem and have to deal with its unpredictability head-on. The two dimensions of market risk that crafters have to contend with are the location of demand and its constancy or periodicity over time.

The location or concentration of demand can be characterized in both spatial and contextual terms. It can be viewed as *aggregate demand*, which can be different for each type of product produced. Demand can also be distributed unequally across society. It can be concentrated in a particular sector of society or spread out widely across a broad consumer base. How demand was distributed shaped the structure of production decisions, especially when the goods produced were those consumed by households at all levels of the income spectrum. *Per capita demand* is another way of assessing and quantifying demand. There can be a large aggregate demand for certain consumables even if consumption is limited within each family. This was often the case for goods consumed by low-income families. Nevertheless, it is incorrect to assume that low per capita demand resulted in limited consumption of items such as luxury goods. De Light (1993:107) points out that not all Roman peasant households were poor, and even luxury goods were consumed in rural areas in small amounts. Luxury goods such as imported spices were purchased for their medicinal value to combat illness and declining health. When per capita demand is low, the best market for goods is in urban centers where the concentration of population is high.

A greater problem for craft producers is the *periodicity* and *elasticity of demand*, which can vary cyclically throughout the year (Douglas and Ischerwood 1979; Gormsen 1978:251). Periodicity of demand varies by product as well as by household. According to Stuart Plattner, "The need for goods varies with time: The demand cycle for food is short, either daily or weekly; that for clothing is usually seasonal; and that for durables such as tools is annual or longer" (Plattner 1989c:186). Each of these different types of goods required different crafting and marketing strategies. Periodic markets provided one solution for the distribution of goods where demand was seasonal or could be accumulated and delayed throughout the year.

The elasticity of demand is a function of household or consumer income. Purchases occur when households have the need and ability to make them. The result is that the purchase of some durable goods may be determined in relation to cyclical social needs such as births, marriages, deaths, and festival needs. This was a major factor in ancient societies where the bulk of the consuming public were farmers, or where the disposable income of the elites was derived from agrarian pursuits or seasonal commerce. The amplified purchasing power of peasant households after agricultural harvests has been documented ethnographically in many rural agrarian societies around the world. In these settings, "[t]he demand of rural households for manufactured goods is income-elastic, both seasonally and in the long run. The hungry pre-harvest season is usually a time of minimal purchases, limited to necessary goods. The post-harvest season is the time of expanded demand for goods" (Plattner 1989c:187).

In agricultural societies demand increases at harvest time. This pattern has been documented in Africa, Latin America, China, and Medieval Europe (Braudel 1986:177–180; Landers 2003:43; Shiba 1977:411; Wrigley 1969:66–68). Craftspersons and artisans had no choice but to adjust to the punctuated nature of these demand cycles. Furthermore, poor families often defer their purchases until the need is most pressing, creating a different cycle of demand than households that are better able to anticipate their needs and take advantage of bargains or normal price cycles for the goods they consume (Moore and Roux 2006). In these cases, absolute need is more important than absolute price (Sen 1981).

OVERCOMING CRAFT RISK

One must wonder, given the high level of risk and the cyclical nature of demand, how craft production ever developed outside patron–client relationships. The answer is that most early forms of independent craft production adopted the same survival strategy as households. They diversified their economic base. Early crafting did not develop as an independent pursuit. Instead, it developed as a subsidiary component in a broader, diversified household economy. Broadening the household subsistence base had two important benefits for the domestic economy. First, it provided greater stability and predictability to household subsistence streams (Annis 1987:50; Clark 1989:106; Messer 1989:162). Diversification reduced risk by following the old adage of not putting all your eggs in one basket. It allowed households to combine more productive, but riskier craft endeavors with more predictable subsistence activities.[9] Second, it provided a context in which crafting could take place without the risks associated with periodic and elastic demand for the goods that crafters had to deal with. The most stable and risk-averse domestic subsistence strategy in both the short and long term was a diverse one that included a mix of agriculture, pastoralism, crafting, wage labor, and/or mercantile activities since diversification reduced the chances of bad outcomes from a single economic choice (Chibnik 2011:70–73; Netting 1981, 1990, 1993; Scott 1976:24).

Forms of diversified craft production are found ethnographically in non-industrial settings the world over[10] (e.g., Beals 1975:20–21; Geertz 1963:67–70; Stolmaker 1996). Combining crafting with subsistence agriculture or pastoralism ensured that households had food to support themselves during periods when craft goods could not be sold. Craft production also was a way to use small-scale labor surpluses in creative ways. As mentioned above, societies that practice seasonal agriculture have labor regimens characterized by periods of heavy labor demands during planting and harvest times, interspersed with periods of low labor demand during winter or dry months (e.g., Netting

1981). It is during periods of low labor demand that craft activities could be profitably carried out.[11] Furthermore, households frequently micromanage their labor on a daily or hourly basis, moving from agriculture to craft activity during the heat of the day, during intervals of rain, or in the evenings (Hagstrum (1999, 2001). Crafting is a type of work that can be carried out intermittently on a work schedule set by the practitioners rather than seasonal or climatic conditions. Finally, crafting allows households to make full use of *all* available labor by providing productive work opportunities for women, children, the aged, and the infirm who are unable to participate in other, more strenuous forms of work (Hirth 2009a).

Wang Fu, the Han dynasty political commentator, was well aware of the tendency of rural households to diversify their economic activities. He credited the failure of rural agricultural policies in China during the 2nd century AD to the "plague" of rural crafting and service activities.[12] In his words, "The people engaged in lesser occupations are ten times as many as the farmers; the people engaged in worthless occupations are ten times as many as the people engaged in lesser occupations" (Liu 1988:49). For Wang Fu, the lesser occupations represented individuals engaged in handicrafts and commerce, while the worthless occupations were those involving service and entertainment. Likewise, Pan Gu, the 1st-century AD Chinese poet, cited the relative profitability of crafting and trade with the proverb, "Among the means of obtaining wealth when you are poor, agriculture is not as good as handicrafts; handicrafts is not as good as trade; just as doing embroidery is not as good as leaning on the market gate" (Liu 1988:49).

What then can be said about the origin of full-time craft production in ancient societies? While some households may have shifted to craft production when agricultural land was in short supply (Arnold 1985), this was not the basis for the origin of crafting in the ancient world. The origin of most craft production resides in intermittent crafting combined with one or more primary subsistence pursuits. Intermittent, part-time craft production appeared early in the Neolithic societies in both the Old and New Worlds long before there was a shortage of good agricultural or pastoral lands. The profitability of intermittent crafting as part of a diversified household subsistence strategy, and the importance of durable goods in gift-giving economies (Dalton 1977; Lee 1993), were dual incentives for the early implementation of crafting on a part-time basis within domestic settings (Hirth 2009a). What needs to be explained are the factors that enabled individuals involved in intermittent or part-time production to dedicate increasing amounts of time to crafting at the expense of other subsistence pursuits.

One of the primary obstacles that impeded the emergence of full-time crafting was the craft risk imposed by the seasonal and periodic fluctuations in demand. As discussed above, this made independent crafting a risky business that could be practiced securely only within a diversified economic strategy that included some form of food production (Rosen 2003). There appear to have been two routes from intermittent crafting to full-time craft production: crafting in urban communities and the practice of multicrafting. Multicrafting will be described first because it is found in pre-state societies and in nonurban contexts in both the New and Old Worlds and was likely an early route to full-time craft production in many ancient societies.

Multicrafting refers to the practice of artisans engaging in multiple crafts within the same household or workshop setting instead of specializing in a single craft activity (Costin 2001a; Feinman 1999; Hirth 2006a, 2009c; Shimada 2007a; M. G. Smith 1955:159; Widmer 2009). The goal of production is to increase the diversity of items produced that have different demand curves to enhance the predictability and continuity of sales. Regarding crafting in ancient Greece, "In small towns the same man makes couches, doors, ploughs, and tables, and often he even builds houses, and still he is thankful if only he can find enough work to support himself" (Finley 1985:135).

The crafts practiced can be independent of one another, or interrelated if they used the same technology, knowledge, or production facilities (e.g., kilns, ovens, processing materials, tools). An example of the former would be the combination of producing cutting implements out of obsidian alongside the production of wealth goods (beads, earspools, pendants) out of the same material using lapidary techniques (Hirth 2006b). A corollary of interrelated production streams in the Old World would be producing utilitarian goods out of iron and wealth goods in bronze, silver, or gold using similar metallurgical processes.

Another related form of multicrafting has been referred to as *contingent craft production* where a set of finished goods or tools is needed and manufactured in the process of producing a particular type of good. Examples would be manufacturing ceramic boiling or evaporation pans used in the process of manufacturing salt, making cutting tools for woodworking, or processing dyes as a step in textile manufacture (e.g., Anderson and Hirth 2009; Brumfiel and Nichols 2009; De León 2009; Dike and Ekejiuba 1990:113–114). In all these cases, dyes, cutting tools, and salt pans were tools or consumables produced to meet the needs of the artisans who used them in specific production processes. They have the practical value of minimizing any purchases that would have to be made for tools or goods used in the production process, while at the same time diversifying manufacturing activities within the production unit, which could lead to developing secondary craft products. In any case, the issue of craft consumption, that is, the production of tools and items used and consumed in production, is always a question that needs to be addressed separately in archaeological investigations since it represents the diversification of manufacturing activities within production units.

Multicrafting and diversified household economic strategies have been found in a wide range of societies at different levels of cultural complexity in both stateless and premodern state societies. It was widely practiced across pre-colonial Africa to produce goods for interregional trade (Sundström 1974; Vansina 1973, 1978). Both multicrafting and contingent crafting were found among the Nupe where iron workers produced bellows and charcoal, and made their own tools along with finished products. Other Nupe households engaged in four related textile professions as tailors, hat makers, embroiderers, and cushion makers. Virtually all agricultural households engaged in mat making (Nadel 1942: 257–288). Among the Hausa, "the great uncertainties attached to farming also led most men to practice some other subsidiary occupation, as a form of insurance" (Smith 1955:157).[13] All rural crafting in Africa was practiced alongside agriculture, with full-time crafters found only in urban areas.[14] The importance of mediating risk through diversification was reflected by full-time leather workers hiring labor (*kodago*) to farm the agriculture plots that they used as partial support for their families (Smith 1955:160).

Intermittent craft production combined with agriculture was the dominant pattern in all state and pre-state societies in the New World. It was the pattern in the highly commercialized Aztec society, among the Maya, as well as in the more centralized institutionalized economies of Andean states including the Inka. Multicrafting was prominent where craft production comprised an increasing percentage of artisan time (Feinman 1999; Feinman and Nicholas 2007; Goldstein and Shimada 2007; Hirth 2006a, 2016; Inomata 2007; Isbell 2007; Otero and Cremonte 2014; Shimada 2007b). There are also indications that multicrafting was a successful adaptation to economic conditions in other areas, including the American Southwest (Mills 1995, 2007), Africa (Smith 1955:159), the Indus Valley (Kenoyer and Miller 2007), and the Shang state in China (Li 2007).

The second route from intermittent crafting to full-time craft production was for craftspersons to relocate to urban centers, which was common in the ancient Old World. There were obvious advantages to urban locations for craftspersons. The first was the larger aggregate demand of its nucleated population. Second, urban centers often contained the residences of wealthier individuals and institutions that had their own periodic demand for goods. The effect of both conditions was a larger and potentially more continual demand for the products that crafters produced. Xenophon, commenting on the relationship between multicrafting and the tendency to find full-time specialists in urban centers in 5th-century BC Greece, states that "it is impossible for a man of many trades to do all of them well. In large cities, however, because many make demands on each trade, one alone is enough to support a man" (Finley 1985:135).

The concentration of artisans in urban centers provided the opportunity for crafters to develop more efficient forms of craft organization that could include periodic labor sharing and the establishment of vertical production linkages. The formation of guilds also helped to protect craftsperson's interests by restricting the proliferation of new artisans, who could provide unwanted competition for their products. This was the clear response of the artisans in ancient Carthage. When Greek goods began to flood the market after 400 BC, Punic merchants and craftspersons formed protectionist guild associations rather than becoming more competitive with the quality or price of imported goods (Moore and Lewis 1999:204).

THE ORGANIZATION AND SCALE OF NONINSTITUTIONAL CRAFT PRODUCTION

How then was craft production organized in noninstitutional contexts across the ancient world? While archaeologists often begin their discussion from the perspective of the technology employed, the focus here is on the three interrelated issues of context, scale, and the organizational structures associated with specialized craft production. Robert Carneiro (1974) pointed out that organization had a greater effect on the scale of production in the ancient world than did a change in the technology used.[15] These three aspects of production, therefore, are a useful starting point for reconstructing the different modes and past structures of production since change in organization can lead to enhancements in the efficiency of production, increased output, or the scale of the crafting activity practiced.

Craft production can be organized in many different ways. Variation in organization can be the product of the type of labor used (slave, family, indentured, reciprocal, wage, apprentice), the gender of the artisans and whether they were mobile or sedentary[16] or full- or part-time, the technology used, whether production was conducted independently or organized within a larger network of guilds by merchants, and whether artisans sold their products directly to consumers or through intermediaries. Rather than attempting to describe each of these different forms of crafting, four polythetic categories are described into which these different organizational variants can be fit. While they lack specificity, they are flexible categories that capture the variation in the scale and context associated with noninstitutional craft production. Moreover, they draw on the work of previous researchers who have investigated independent craft production, ranging from ceramics and lithics to textile manufacture (Costin 2011, 2013; Costin and Hagstrum 1995; Peacock 1982; Santley et al. 1989; Sinopoli 2003; Spence 1981; Torrence 1986; van der Leeuw 1976).

The four crafting categories discussed are specialized domestic production, workshop industries, nucleated workshop industries, and manufactories.

These are ideal types, which are useful for discussing relative production scale but are not mutually exclusive of one another for any given craft. Instead, they lie along a continuum of size and organization with the lines between them blurring when they shared organizational characteristics. *Specialized domestic production* and the *workshop industries*, for example, are both independent and small-scale production units. Nucleated workshop industries and manufactories, in contrast, are larger manufacturing entities. The *nucleated workshop industry* represents a form of cooperative production where multiple artisans locate their workshops in the same locale to make the same commodity. The *manufactory* is a form of organization more akin to a segmented assembly line. It involves the linkage of work by artisans conducting different specialized tasks in the production of a single product.[17] When taken together, these four types of production provide a template for characterizing the organization of many forms of ancient and premodern craft production.

Specialized Domestic Production

As the name suggests, this form of craft production takes place within or adjacent to the domicile where artisans and their families reside. It represents the small-scale production of goods intended for consumption and sale outside the household. This is what distinguishes it from ad hoc production carried out in all domestic settings where tools, ceramics, ornaments, and other goods were produced by households for their own consumption. It was the basic and most widespread form of independent crafting found cross-culturally in both simple and complex societies. It represents the context in which the first craft specialists would have originated and operated, facing all the risks and uncertainties of the craftsperson's dilemma. The labor for production most often was drawn from household or family members in the same or adjacent residences. In many circumstances craft production was a secondary rather than a primary subsistence activity of the household and was practiced intermittently throughout the year alongside other primary subsistence practices such as farming or herding.

The proto-industrial term for specialized domestic production is the rural cottage industry where goods were produced in low quantities within domestic contexts (Houston and Snell 1984). In the Roman world the household was the foundation for craft production in most urban settings (Flohr and Wilson 2016:10). Another example of this type of production unit was the itinerant artisan who traveled and took their craft with them producing goods where they were needed. Itinerant production was often the result of low or sporadic demand for the product where the best solution was for the artisan to travel to where the good could be sold. Examples of itinerant crafting include metal workers in Bronze Age Europe (Childe 1936; Wailes 1996:5), iron smiths in premodern Africa (Northrup 1978:103; Sundström 1974:188), and the greater array of traveling nomads who produced goods for sale alongside those that they transported in the carrying trade[18] (Rao 1987; Rosen 2003).

Historic accounts often ignore forms of domestic production, and the archaeological signatures of specialized domestic production can be difficult to identify depending on the frequency of crafting and the type and quantity of production refuse created in the process. A special work area may be separated from the household if the production process or the waste produced was hazardous to other household members, especially children.[19] More often than not, however, production activities were carried out in normal living spaces and open-air patios alongside other domestic activities. The result may be no clear separation of crafting and domestic activities, with the waste produced from crafting activities mixed with other domestic refuse. Small-scale domestic craft production was the predominant way that craft goods were created in all small-scale and complex societies across the New World (i.e., Aztec, Inka, Maya) and in Africa. It never dropped out of the historic record and was a common form of craft production in premodern India, China, and across Europe. It was a viable form of production at all levels of cultural complexity and continues today with many of the home-based service and production businesses that operate through the Internet.

The Workshop Industry

The workshop industry is another type of small-scale production unit. Two features set it apart from specialized domestic production. The first is that the production workshop always exists as a separate work area or atelier. It may have a domestic residence attached to the atelier or work area, but for the most part there is a clear separation of crafting activity from domestic life. The separation of domestic and craft activity is an important feature for this type of production, and Brun (2016:81) considers this type of arrangement essential for identifying artisans in ancient Rome. While Brun's view of crafting is culturally specific, the presence of dedicated work areas generally suggests greater, often full-time involvement in craft production. Second, the workshop industry may employ multiple different forms of labor in crafting activities that can range from kinsmen to indentured, apprenticed, and slave labor.[20] The presence of special production facilities can also indicate the involvement of multiple artisans in the production process. The existence of a dedicated work area normally is interpreted as a signature of more continual specialized production.[21] A lead craftsperson would normally supervise the work from beginning to end irrespective of how production activities were organized within the workshop. In general, work groups remain relatively small, with 10 individuals or fewer involved in production (Starr 1977:86).

8.1 Dedication monument by the cobbler Dionysios showing his workshop, first half of the 4th century BC. (Bottom: Photograph of the dedication monument courtesy of Mark Munn.)

One expression of this form of production is the shop economy. Shops in the ancient world were associated with a wide array of retail, wholesale, service, and production activities. Examples of shop economies are well known from medieval Europe where goods were modified and sold to consumers from the workshops where they were made. In the shops of medieval Europe, a master artisan along with a small staff of apprentice workers produced most of the craft goods circulating in society. It is likely that shops grew out of domestic workplaces as additional labor was added to meet need and demand (Braudel 1986:62; Cox 2000). The single proprietor shop was common in China for the manufacture of utilitarian goods (shoes, paper lanterns, straw products, fans, furniture, wooden ladles) and where little capital investment was required (Shiba 1977). In addition to operating independently, commercial partnerships occasionally were established within shops when it was advantageous to share production facilities as occurred in the medieval Arab world where Muslim and Jewish silversmiths and glass workers operated shops together (Goitein 1967:85).

Individual shops and workshop industries were the backbone of craft production in Greek and Roman urban centers. Figure 8.1 illustrates a small cobbler's workshop where four men and one boy work at making sandals. In Athens the potter's quarter was located on the west side of the city along the Panathenaic Way. Small workshops in Athens have been recorded for sculptors, shoemakers, and bronze workers, the latter of which are documented by curse tablets left by unhappy customers condemning the artisan for work not completed to their satisfaction.[22] Many workshops were located in and around the Agora and Socrates apparently met his young students at the house of Simon the cobbler, which was probably at or near his workshop. A cobbler's

8.2 The house of Simon the cobbler in the Agora of Athens. (Image courtesy of the American School of Classical Studies at Athens: Agora Excavations)

shop found in Athens near the Tholos (Figure 8.2) could be Simon's workshop; even if it is not, it provides a model for their scale and organization that can be compared with Figure 8.1 (Camp 1986:145).

Small craft workshops in Roman cities were often located in *tabernae*, the small rectilinear shops that line many of the main avenues (Figure 8.3). The Roman author Varro specifically connects *tabernae* with commercial activity, which has been confirmed by archaeological investigation.

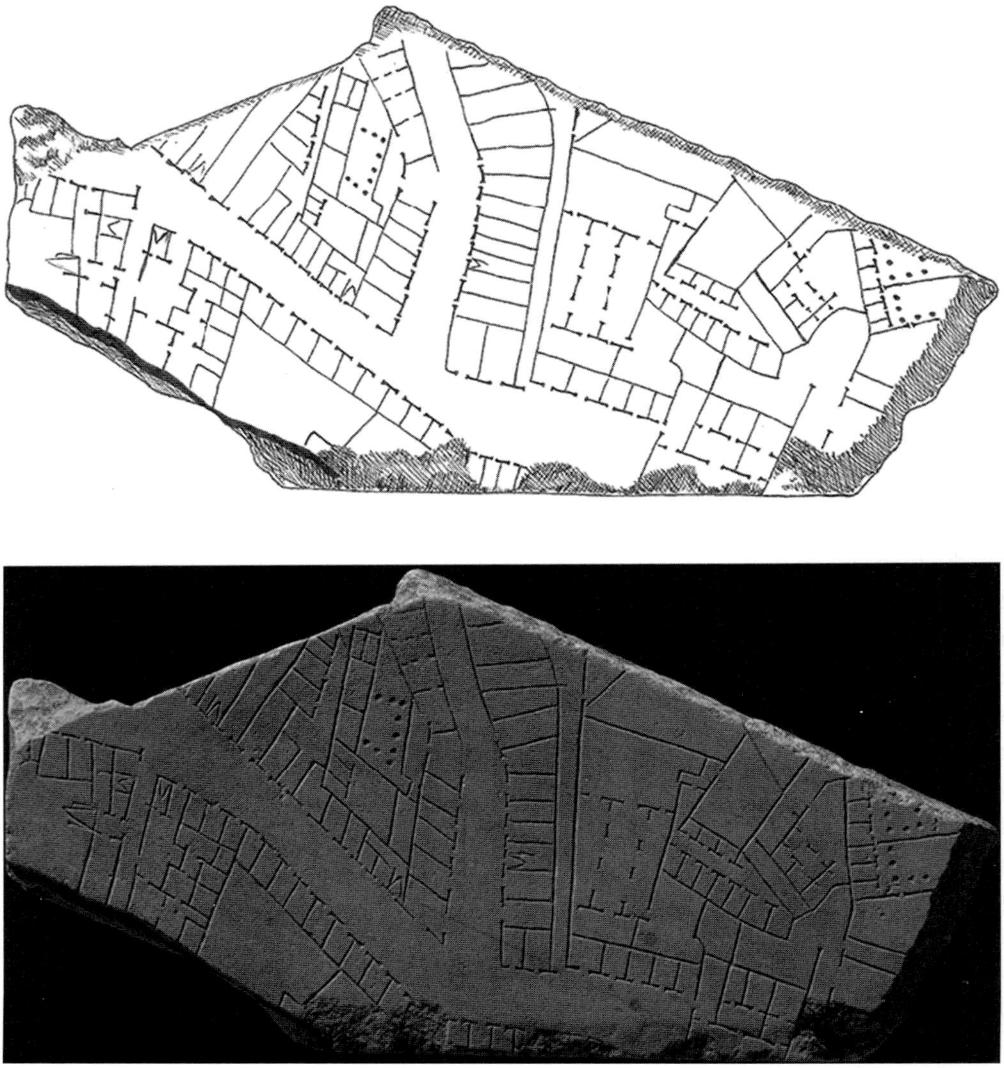

8.3 *Tabernae* represented on the Marble map of ancient Rome and a line drawing of the plan. by Shae Rider and author. Bottom: Photograph of Marble plan (Photograph © Roma, Superintendent of cultural heritage).

Tabernae had wide doorways appropriate for viewing goods and a grooved threshold for the placement of vertical wooden shutters to close the shop at night. Like those in Athens, shops in Rome and Pompeii were used for a variety of manufacturing, retail, wholesale, and service functions.[23] Craft production including ceramic and glass making have been identified in *tabernae* from the permanent installations (kilns, ovens) required to carry out the work (Putzeys and Lavan 2008). A *taberna* identified in Herculaneum had tools, a furnace, lead ingots, and production debris associated with smelting metal as well as fabricating and repairing lead pipes. Literary sources mention making leather goods, dyeing purple cloth, and making shoes in Roman *tabernae*. According to Holleran (2012:125), "the sheer number of these units in Roman towns and cities . . . underlines the small scale and fragmented nature of ancient urban production."

The size of individual workshops, the number of workers that they contained, whether they used slaves, and how production was organized varied widely by craft from establishment to establishment. Most workshops were small, and Peacock (1982:9) uses twelve workers as the dividing line, or a working average, between individual workshops and the aggregated workshop industries found in rural ceramic production. Although this number is arbitrary, it underscores that most workshops in the ancient Mediterranean world were small by modern production standards. Slaves often supplied the workforce for Roman workshops, although artisans also operated as independent contractors in the practice of their craft.

Nucleated Workshop Industries

This form of production refers to a clustering or concentration of multiple individual workshops that engaged in the same or a related craft activity in a specific location or region. Archaeologists often characterize this type of production as community or coordinated group-level craft production (e.g., Santley et al. 1989; Sinopoli 1988; Stein 1996) even when there is no direct indication of intracommunity collaboration in production activities. An example of the latter would include the ad hoc clustering of manufacturing specialties observed in some urban centers even when there was no intentional collaboration in production activities between production units (Goodman 2016; Ruffing 2016:125). Peacock (1982) linked the appearance of nucleated industries with the exploitation of key natural resources in rural areas and was particularly interested in the large nucleated workshops that produced *terra sigillata* red-slipped ceramic wares in Italy, Gaul (France), and areas of the eastern Mediterranean (Poblome 1999:289–291, 2004). *Terra sigillata* was a major, mass-produced ceramic that was widely consumed throughout the Roman world from the 1st century BC to the early 3rd century AD. It is used here to explore the nature of how nucleated

8.4 Photograph of a *terra sigillata* red-ware modiolus cup manufactured in the production center of Arezzo, Italy, between AD 5 and 40. Image courtesy of the Metropolitan Museum of Art (Item 17.194.896).

workshop industries could have been organized in the ancient world. Despite the large-scale production of this ware, there were no qualitative differences in the size or organization of the individual workshops found in these aggregated industries.

While *terra sigillata* ceramics were a major long-distance trade item in the Roman world, several of the major production centers are not located in areas where bulk goods like ceramics could be easily obtained for long-distance transportation. The major *terra sigillata* production center of Arezzo, Italy, is located in the mountainous region of Umbria, 250 kilometers north of Rome. Figure 8.4 illustrates a small modiolus, or drinking cup, manufactured in Arezzo in the early 1st century AD. The river Arno that runs through the region is not navigable, which meant that all ceramics were transported over difficult terrain for at least 150 kilometers before reaching the nearest seaport. Similar conditions existed for *sigillata* production centers in Gaul at La Graufesenque and Lezoux, France. What this indicates is that production was organized independent of transportation considerations even though they were significant in the overall scheme of interregional trade. *Sigillata* vessels simply were produced in large quantities where they could be made. While merchant middlemen would have preferred more accessible locales, they went to where the products were fabricated and available rather than attempting to move production to more accessible port areas like Pisa or Puteoli (Peacock 1982:119).

Jeroen Poblome and colleagues have proposed that the manufacture of *terra sigillata* ceramics was organized using *locatio-conductio* contracts between landowners who controlled key resources (clay, fuel), the artisans who produced them, and the merchants who mobilized the finished goods for sale across the Mediterranean. In ancient Rome *locatio–conductio* agreements were the legal basis for a wide range of economic activities ranging from leasing farmland, dwellings, *tabernae*, and storage facilities to hiring labor and contracting services for a range of different activities. In this type of contract, an owner or landlord (*locator*) rented an establishment, often with equipment, to a tenant (*conductor*) for a specific task and period of time. The use of *locatio–conductio* agreements to produce ceramics is known from the recovery of three papyri that describe these contracts for pottery production from 3rd-century AD Roman Egypt.[24] In each contract, the potter agreed to make a specific number of wine amphorae vessels for the landlord over a period of time so that they were ready for storing wine at the end of the grape harvest.

The stipulations of these agreements contain details that provide insight into how *locatio–conductio* agreements generally operated for ceramic production. As part of the contract, the landlord provided the working establishment for the potter, along with the clay used for the vessels, fuel for the kiln, pitch for coating the inside of the vessels, and water from a cistern. In addition to the resources needed to produce the amphorae, the building rented was fully equipped with production equipment: a potter's wheel, a kiln, and storerooms for drying and finished pots. The level and method of payment for the potter's work was also stipulated in coin once the finished vessels were completed, along with an in-kind monthly supplement to support the potter while production was underway (Poblome and Brulet 2005:31).

The potter was required to supply any additional personnel needed for manufacturing the pottery, including assistants, porters, and stokers for the kiln. Independent craftsmen used *locatio–conductio* contracts in the same way as landlords to obtain the additional labor they needed including contracting slaves from their owners. The modiolus cup illustrated in Figure 8.4 reflects this practice as it was manufactured in the workshop of a P. Cornelus by a slave named Rodo. The contract placed the responsibility of production on the potter, who could have shared production facilities with other potters operating under similar contracts within areas of nucleated industries. Evidence for interworkshop collaboration between artisans involved in the production of *terra sigillata* ceramic wares can be found in the distribution of pottery stamps and other production debris recovered from workshops and kiln refuse. *Locatio–conductio* contracts were generally of short duration lasting no more than 1–2 years, which gave both the landlords and the craftspersons the ability to strike different bargains when it was in their interest to do so.

Marketing the vessels was *not* the responsibility of the potter in large-scale nucleated industries. All the potter apparently had to do at the completion of the contract was turn in the finished vessels to the landlord. The landlord or contracting agent would have worked with merchants (*institores*, *negotiatores*) to find and move finished vessels to final markets (Murphy and Poblome 2016:196; Poblome and Brulet 2005:32). The greatest profit was probably made by the wealthy landlords through their relationship with merchant middlemen. But the structure of production released the potter from risk and the craftsperson's dilemma of having to find a market for the large quantity of finished goods. Poblome (2004:499) suggests that *locatio–conductio* agreements may have been used to mobilize free labor in the production of other goods including textiles. What is important to note is that the production unit for each contract was the individual workshop, and as a result there were few economies of scale to be achieved on the production side by grouping more artisans together into larger and larger enterprises (Poblome 2004:500). What aggregated production industries do, of course, is to make a large quantity of finished goods available in a central locale that can be mobilized commercially.

Poblome and Brulet (2005:27–28) suggest that the production of *terra sigillata* was organized as complex manufactories based on the number of artisans involved and the overall scale of manufacture associated with it across the eastern and western Mediterranean. The scale of production was large, but that by itself does not imply a sharp division of production tasks like Marx and others (e.g., Peacock 1982; Santley et al. 1989:110) associate with the operation of manufactories (see below). Instead, the aggregated production industries of *terra sigillata* ceramics more closely resemble a holonic enterprise organized by landlords acting as mediator agents to convert the resources that they had in their possession (clay, water, fuel) into salable commodities.

A *holonic business enterprise* is a self-regulated network of production and service units, each with their own competence, that arrange themselves in a system to meet a specific production objective (McHugh et al. 1995). The term "holon" comes from the Greek work *holos* meaning "whole" with the suffix -*on* meaning "part," that is, part of the whole (Koestler 1967). These networks represent partnership collaborations between semi-autonomous units that would have been difficult for any contributing unit to organize on its own. The holonic enterprise is a self-organizing production system where interactions between its members are collaborative and symbiotic rather than exploitive and competitive. The production of *terra sigillata* ceramics corresponds to this type of intra-enterprise organization where many small producers in adjacent workshops were following their individual interests toward the same end, the production and sale of fine tableware (Ulieru et al. 2002). Landlords owned workshop facilities and contracted master potters who, in turn, contracted other workers to assist them. Once the work was completed, ceramics from multiple workshops were purchased by merchants for distribution and sale.

The network relationships were mutually beneficial, and while the landlords owned the natural resources, they were worthless without potters to convert them into vessels and merchants to mobilize them for sale beyond the production area. These interdependencies resulted in clusters of landlords, artisans, merchants, and laborers that formed a flexible production enterprise with the capacity to reorganize itself on a yearly basis as opposed to a fixed and permanent business firm. The use and flexibility of *locatio–conductio* contracts allowed these networks to change over time as well as allowing the individual production units (e.g., potters, workers, workshops) to collaborate with one another and form parts of different holonic groups (Chacón et al. 2008). The scale of production in nucleated workshop industries was large, but the work carried out was redundant rather than integrated on a large scale.

The Manufactory

The manufactory was the most complex form of craft organization found in the ancient and premodern world. It was a large-scale organization that differed in two ways from the nucleated workshop industry. First, production was integrated and under the supervisory control of one or more individuals who directed production and were responsible for the goods produced. Second and more important, production within the manufactory took advantage of task specialization and the manufacturing efficiency that accompanied it. Craft production was broken down into logical steps of preparation, shaping, assembly, and finishing, with artisans performing specific tasks linked together into a single production process. Ruffing (2016) associated the manufactory with what he called vertical specialization as opposed to horizontal specialization,[25] where artisans with different skills were used in the production of a single item. This type of reciprocal dependence is represented in mortuary inscriptions in the Roman world with regard to producing bread, where sifters of flour are distinguished from formers and bakers of bread (Ruffing 2016:124). This distinction might seem trivial until one considers the importance of the *lex frumentum* and the scale of production needed to provide bread to feed the poor in ancient Roman (Rickman 1980a, 1980b).

Marx (1967:I:338) identified this type of production in his discussion of the way work and different materials were used and integrated in a carriage factory. Poblone and Brulet (2005:28) made the claim that, except for the scale of manufacture and the level or capital investment, there was "no clear distinction between a well-organized workshop and a manufactory." Identifying the division of labor within archaeological contexts is always difficult, but that does not mean it did not exist or cannot be addressed in archaeological analyses (e.g., Hirth 2006b). There always was some division in tasks within workshops as artisans were trained and more skilled individuals carried out certain tasks. But it was the use of the division of labor as an organizational principle to increase production efficiency that defines the presence of a true manufactory. Workshops were not as internally complex, although the spatial extent of some nucleated workshop industries such as the production of *terra sigillata* was extensive, surpassing the scale of individual manufactories. What made manufactories distinct was their internal organizational structure.

Peacock (1982:5) associated early manufactories in the eastern Mediterranean with the *ergasteria* directed by master craftsmen in the Greek world (van Leur 1967:18). Unfortunately, there is no specific association of this term with a specific level of organization. The term *ergasterion* is used for both a single-room shop where the artisan lived and a large factory establishment where large numbers of slaves worked to produce a particular item (Marzano 2012). Nevertheless, a passage from Xenophon's *Cyropaedia* (Miller 1914) for an *ergasterion* involved in shoe production identifies the presence of task specialization within a large functioning workshop: "One man makes shoes for men, another for women, and there are even places where one man earns a living by only stitching shoes, another by cutting them out, another by sewing the uppers together, while there is another that performs none of these operations, but only assembles the parts" (Camp 1986:146–147).

Perhaps the best example of an early manufactory from ancient Greece was the shield factory of Polemarchus located in the Athenian port of Piraeus during the late 5th century BC. Polemarchus was a wealthy *metic* (noncitizen) who is reported to have employed 120 slaves in his shield-making enterprise. Demosthenes's father likewise had a knife and ivory-bed factory where fifty-two to fifty-three slaves were employed. These examples appear to be on the large end of the range of *ergasteria* found in ancient Greece (Burford 1972:43).

Possibly the largest manufactories to operate in the ancient world date to the late Ming (AD 1368–1644) and Qing (AD 1644–1911) periods in China and again pertain to ceramic production.[26] Pottery manufactories in the town of Ching-te-chen engaged in the large-scale production of porcelain vessels distributed across China that ranged from elaborate tableware used in the royal palace to the simple plain wares used in commoner households. This was a factory town with a population of 250,000–400,00 people, 80% of whom were directly involved in porcelain manufacture (Frank 1983:371). The firms in Ching-te-chen ranged in size from large manufactories to small family workshops. Of the 2,000 or so workshops, about 110 are estimated by Wright (1980) to have been large firms. The largest of the manufactories were the imperial potteries, which made special-order porcelain for the royal household. Sheehy (1992:76, 97–102), using information provided by Wright (1980), estimates that the largest firms produced anywhere from 2 million to 2.5 million vessels per year.

The level of craft production found in the largest porcelain factories is described in a letter dated September 1 of AD 1712 by Pere d'Entrecolles, a Christian missionary who visited Ching-te-chen and recorded the production operations that he witnessed there:

> In the less frequented districts of Ching-te-chen are vast sheds surrounded by walls, where one sees [ar]ranged, stage upon stage, a great number of jars of earth. Within these walls live and work an infinite number of workpeople, who each have their allotted task, and a piece of porcelain, before it is ready to go into the oven, passes through the hands of twenty persons, and that without any confusion. Doubtless they have proved that the work is done much more quickly in this way.
>
> (d'Entrecolles 1906:89–90)

What d'Entrecolles described is a high level of task specialization that took vessels quickly from their shaping through firing in what was the closest thing to an assembly line form of production as can be found in the preindustrial world. Several segments of this production process are illustrated in Figures 8.5 and 8.6. He goes on to describe some of the specialists that he observed at work, listing fourteen to sixteen specialists involved in the production of a simple cup.[27] What he was describing is a commercial enterprise that achieved an industrial scale of production because of the large demand for high-quality ceramic vessels both inside China and as an item of foreign trade.

The four types of specialized craft production described here are ideal types that lie along a continuum, from specialized household crafting to truly industrial-scale manufacturing with internal task specialization organized along an assembly line. Not all types of crafting fit neatly into one of these four types of production, so it will always be necessary for investigators to redefine categories to accurately characterize the specific forms of craft activity in which they are interested. An example of a difficult form of production to characterize is the *ho-ku* partnerships of Late Imperial China that were used to manufacture luxury goods, and which seems to be a hybrid of the nucleated workshop industry and the manufactory. The demand for luxury goods in China spiked at the lunar new year when people regularly bought more gifts. Makers of luxury goods frequently faced seasonal capital shortages as they purchased expensive raw materials and hired artisans to meet demand. Credit often got so tight by the end of the year that large workshops had to suspend production.

The *ho-ku* partnership sought to solve this problem through collaboration between other shop owners. Workshop owners would temporarily come together and pool their working capital, materials, tools, workshops, and labor to meet the end-of-the-year demand for luxury goods. The types of crafting

8.5 Ceramic production at Ching-te-chen, China (1816). (Courtesy of the Division of Rare and Manuscript Collections, Cornell University Library.)

where this occurred included carving wood, inlaying furniture, making lacquer ware, and working precious and nonprecious metals. Shiba (1977:411) reports 36 craftsmen working in two *ho-ku* shops where 20–25 separate manufacturing processes were carried out under the supervision of 12 master artisans. This coalescence of artisans in temporary forms of production most likely occurred where they had skills that could be quickly transferred to working different mediums. Its primary advantage probably was that it helped individual workshops offset the problems of capital shortfall in the wake of cyclical changes in the demand for goods.

The creation of the *ho-ku* partnership again illustrates the accuracy of Carneiro's (1974) ethos that changes in the organization of production could more quickly and effectively change the scale of craft production than the introduction of a new technology. The foregoing discussion has focused on the scale and organization of individual production units. A new level of organizational control was achieved when production units were integrated into larger coordinated systems of manufacturing. The economies of scale achieved through the creation of a network of coordinated production could result in the creation of larger surpluses of higher quality goods then when

8.6 Preparing a kiln for ceramic firing at Ching-te-chen, China (1816). (Courtesy of the Division of Rare and Manuscript Collections, Cornell University Library.)

artisans produced for the market independently of one another. The discussion that follows examines two coordinated production systems: the craft guild and the putting-out system.

THE CRAFT GUILD

A guild was a corporate group of artisans or merchants that operated to benefit and safeguard their collective commercial interests. Craft guilds were an association in the anthropological sense in that they were organized around a common interest, namely the practice of a particular craft or trade. They were corporate in that they were formal organizations often operating as co-fraternities with specific membership requirements and internal organizational structures. Craft associations could be organized along ethnic, caste, or ritual-istic lines (Goitein 1967:82–83; Lloyd 1953). The type of guild discussed here, however, is what Weber (2003a:137) called the free association guild, made up of members who were linked by common profession rather than kinship criteria. The craft guilds of medieval Europe are well-known examples of this type of organization. While craftspersons were organized collectively on the basis of a common profession, artisans continued to work independently of one another in their individual shops and workshops.

The origin of craft guilds in medieval Europe was a function of both economic and historical processes. Crafting as an economic process was built into the domestic economy. In addition to being important to the subsistence livelihoods of households who practiced it, skilled artisans (smiths, tanners, saddlers, carpenters, weavers, harness makers, etc.) were indispensable for the operation of rural manorial estates. Craft guilds developed historically within the independent towns across Europe. Rural artisans could achieve a level of independence by moving to towns and practicing their crafts under the jurisdiction of town lords independent of manorial control. Towns became the seats of craft groups who produced for the local and broader regional market. The prerogatives of artisans to town lords included forms of town service and some form of tax or rent payment. As guilds developed and became stronger over time, they sought to free themselves from these obligations, often converting them to a fixed payment for the group as a whole (Weber 2003a:149). While it can be argued whether the Roman *collegia* did or did not operate as guilds (Epstein 1991:11–13; Finley 1985:138), it was not until the 12th century AD that guilds began to flourish in many urban centers across Europe.[28] As might be expected, guilds grew rapidly in cities located along important trade routes. By the middle of the 13th century, guilds were well established, with as many as 101 separate guilds operating in the city of Paris in AD 1260 (Braudel 1986:315).

Craft guilds were first and foremost protectionist organizations. They were designed to protect the livelihood of their members and the integrity of their craft. They regulated work and working conditions, and attempted to build a monopoly against outside competition. They were rigorous in protecting their monopoly over certain goods and services, and even employed an early version of trademarks to protect the recognition of product origin. Members participated and socialized in group activities, often involving religious celebrations. This fostered social solidarity between members and enabled the guild to act as a charitable organization or mutual aid society when individual members fell on hard times, needed help for funerals, or required assistance in the performance of their craft. They also passed regulations that helped to ensure a level playing field for artisans within the guild. One such regulation had to do with *forestalling*, which made it forbidden for a guild member to supply himself with raw material that would enable him to work ahead of fellow guild members. This helped to control the pace of production and reduce the opportunity to prepare, stockpile, and sell more products ahead of other members of the guild (Cox 2000:30; Weber 2003a:140–141). Likewise, master artisans were prohibited from hiring workers away from other guild members, which became a problem during the 14th century AD after the Black Death (Dyer 2002:315).

Maintaining a high standard of quality also was important and became more so as competition to guilds arose from other sectors of the economy during the 16th century AD. One area that was particularly important to the guild was the regulation of artisan training through the master–journeymen–apprentice system. Masters took apprentices into their homes to train them, who, after reaching journeyman status, would work for the master for an established period of time at an agreed-on wage. Formal contracts would be written when apprentices were not immediate family members, and tensions could arise when journeymen attempted to leave early (Epstein 1991:102–126; Wood 2002:141–142). Although the practice of informal apprenticeship was probably common throughout the ancient world, formal training for apprentices can be traced back to the 1st century AD in Roman Egypt (Freu 2016). Here formal contracts known as *didaskalikai* were drawn up between apprentice and master that specified the economic opportunities and advancement of the well-trained journeyman. Dedicatory texts indicate that skilled workers (*technitai*) benefited directly from their master's expertise and good name. One of these benefits was the transfer of a master craftsman's social network and customers (*patrocinium*) to good pupils (Freu 2016:188–189).

Quality was expressed in the workmanship and skill of the artisan that was acquired in the process of apprenticeship. Quality was a product of careful work, and the philosophy of medieval guild craftsmanship was that "the raw material must take the longest possible course in the individual shop, that the individual workman must keep the object worked upon in hand as long as possible" (Weber 2003a:139). This placed guild craftsmen in an interesting and awkward position in relation to more efficient forms of production that emerged both before and during the industrial revolution. Guilds viewed specialization in production on a product-by-product basis and not by production task. On the whole, guilds strongly opposed the types of task specialization that emerged in later forms of factory production.

As an organization, medieval guilds were stalwart in the defense of their domain against competition from other groups or communities. Dealing with competing interests was an ongoing problem for guilds and eventually led to their demise. Guilds sought to monopolize rights to provide specific goods and services, even though goods could be produced outside towns. Monasteries that were free from tax and other secular obligations were able to set up diversified commercial establishments that enabled them to compete effectively with certain guilds and accumulate considerable wealth (Weber 2003a:150). Guilds also had to fight the problem of infringements on their rights by other guilds. Most guilds were formed by splitting off a specialization from a previous broader sphere of work (Epstein 1991:53), but it also worked the other way. Guilds protected the rights of their members, but they seemed to have no compunction against encroaching on the protected rights and exclusive domains of other guilds. As a result, a bill presented in AD 1571 to the mayor and aldermen of the city of London by the wardens of fourteen guild companies could make the statement that "in the name of all the handicraftsmen in the city . . . the great number of encroachers of handicrafts [have] brought [guild members] to such ruin and decay that they are not able to maintain their families" (Rappaport 2002:111).[29]

Two sources of competition eventually led to the decline and ultimate demise of guilds as powerful economic organizations in European towns. The first and most significant of these was the organization and movement of production to rural areas. The reason was that rural labor was cheaper and the price of goods produced was lower than that of those manufactured in town centers (Wrigley 1978:301). This new form of production known alternatively as *Verlagssystem*, or the putting-out system, was organized by merchants interested in mobilizing goods for export production. This system is discussed below and had the effect of interjecting cheaper goods into the market that guild members had difficulty competing with (Braudel 1986:316; Friedrichs 1978). A second area of competition emerged with the appearance of wholesalers and retailers who bought in bulk and/or sold diversified arrays of products.[30] Serious cracks in guild solidarity began to appear in England when some guild members branched out into retailing by buying and reselling goods in their specialties instead of making them (Davis 1966:62–63). The advent of retailing doomed the guilds in urban contexts when goods were sold at lower prices than guild artisans could produce them. Even as craft guilds declined in size and influence, it is interesting that the earlier system of apprenticeship continued as the means of training salesmen in the new retail trades (Cox 2000:225).

VERLAGSSYSTEM, INDUSTRIAL HOUSEWORK, AND THE PUTTING-OUT SYSTEM REVISITED

Several different terms have been used to describe the form of production referred to here as the putting-out system.[31] It refers to a system of subcontracted production organized by an agent using independent labor. In the ancient and premodern past, these systems used rural laborers who were contracted to produce goods in their homes or other production facilities. The coordinating agent would usually supply the raw materials to be worked, specify the type of finished product required, and reimburse workers for their labor on a piecework basis when finished goods were collected. Historically, most of the labor employed in this form of production was drawn from rural farming households where the pace of agricultural activities allowed those who were periodically idle to be put to work in other activities (Laslett 1971:17). Although instances of full-time production are known, most individuals who were engaged in putting-out contracts worked in their homes on a discontinuous, part-time basis as time permitted throughout the year.

The success of this system was that it was mutually beneficial for both producers and agent organizers. It enabled merchants to use their capital to build an extensive production network to mobilize finished goods that could be sold in both regional and international markets. It was advantageous for producers to the extent that it allowed households to deploy otherwise idle laborers in an activity that brought a measurable return and improved their overall economic well-being. The putting-out system was successful because it was compatible with the general strategies of domestic economies and the creative ways that households sought to sustain themselves (Chapter 2). While not strictly a rural phenomenon, it was readily adopted in areas where agricultural activities provided only a marginal livelihood for households, while at the same time fostering an increased separation of production and trading activities (Clarkson 1971:103; Landes 1969:118–119).

The putting-out system was well known for Europe and was incorporated into many of the early discussions by Adam Smith, Karl Max, and Max Weber. Franklin Mendels (1972) proposed it as a proto-industrial stage of production that presaged the movement of labor from rural households into wage-based factory settings. Like Marx (1967:3:335–336), Mendels saw the involvement of merchants in the production process as initiating the transition to industrial capitalism. While this fits the historic development of the English textile industry, the putting-out system should not be viewed as a specific stage in the development of industrialization. Instead, it is an enduring form of capitalist production that reappeared in different areas of the ancient, premodern, and modern worlds. It is closely associated with textile production in Europe where spinning and weaving were dependent on female labor before industrialization. But the putting-out form of production also was associated with textile production in India, China, Japan, Thailand, North Africa, Malaysia, Indonesia, and across the Ottoman empire (Abé and Saito 1988; Beckert 2014:19–20; Clarence-Smith 2011:129–139; Geertz 1963:63; Ramaswamy 2006:142–144; Riello 2013:63–66).

Moreover, the putting-out system was not confined to textile production and was applied to the manufacture of a wide range of products. In Europe, it was used to produce everything from knitted goods, leather gloves, shoes, lace, nails, chain, metal goods, books, rosaries, and ceramics to complex items such as firearms (Braudel 1986:317, 321; Clarkson 1971:101–102; Hounshell 1984:17; Littlefield and Reynolds 1990:362). In China, the putting-out system was used by merchant entrepreneurs to produce both finished goods and smaller components for later assembly. An agent known as a *chan*, *chuang*, or *hang* would organize and finance the production of craft goods in households, either as finished goods or as components for products assembled elsewhere. Examples of the production of components included the manufacture of latticework, beds, and the ribs of bamboo umbrellas. The manufacture of finished goods included the production of straw hats, straw mats, embroidered silk cloth, and cotton cloth. Straw hat production involved several organizational layers. A merchant would contract straw from a large estate owner, who would then factor it out to twenty or so agents, who in turn arranged the production of straw hats in thirty to fifty households. This allowed a single wealthy merchant with his agents to harness the labor to produce hats in 600–1,000 rural households (Shiba 1977:412). Ancient and premodern merchants understood the supply chains for the goods that they sold. In very real terms they coordinated and organized cottage craft production at a proto-industrial level.

The putting-out system appears early in Germany and spread across Europe during the 13th century AD. In Germany, putting-out production was referred to as *Verlagssystem* or *Verlaswessen* where a merchant (*Verleger*) distributed raw materials and work orders to artisans for production. Braudel (1986:316) identified the operation of the *Verlagssystem* in Paris in AD 1275 where the Provost of Merchants forbade spinsters from pawning the mercers of silk they were given to weave into finished goods for money to support themselves. What is often overlooked is that the putting-out system developed alongside and in response to the operation of craft guilds. Craft guilds fostered the division of work, resulting in the separation of spinning, weaving, finishing, and dyeing activities in textile manufacture. Furthermore, guilds often were forced to work with merchanges, on whom they were dependent for the importation of raw material or to sell their goods. By the 16th century AD merchants in Germany regularly contracted with guilds for the products they produced and largely absorbed the majority of their manufacturing capacity (Kieser 1994:612–613).

Urban textile guilds, however, could not keep up with the demand for finished goods at a reasonable price. Competition between cities made textile sales price-sensitive. The city of Ulm in southern Germany competed with Lombard in northern Italy for the production of fustian and cotton textiles sold in Flanders and other important mercantile centers from the 14th century AD onward (Riello 2013:73–74). In both centers, production moved from the cities to rural areas were labor was cheaper. Beckert (2014:27) reports that in comparison to the 2,000 workers producing cotton textiles in the city of Ulm, there were 18,000 weavers in the countryside working under the *Verlagssystem*. The same transpired in Italy where urban centers also could not keep up with the high cost of labor. Rural cotton weaving moved to rural areas around Lombard, and by AD 1585 the weaver's guild in Milan attempted to claim commercial jurisdiction over seventeen small towns, boroughs, and villages around the city (Mazzaoui 2011:82–83). Guilds fought the expansion of putting-out systems, sometimes even resorting to force (Wrigley 1978:301).

Nevertheless, they continued to expand during the 17th and 18th centuries AD because it was a durable, flexible, and cost-efficient form of production that produced large quantities of goods and quickly adapted to changing circumstances in the market when they occurred. By AD 1800 it is estimated that 42% of the entire German workforce was involved to some degree in the *Verlagssystem* (Henning 1974; Kieser 1994:613).

Lest we think that the putting-out system is an antiquated thing of the past, it is alive and well in the modern world. Geertz (1963) recorded a vibrant putting-out system in Indonesia that produced a wide variety of different goods that included finished clothing, construction brick, woven baskets, and bean curd. More importantly, it remains an important feature of the modern manufacturing landscape where domestic households and small-scale firms produce goods for the international market. It is the system used in Yucatan, Mexico, where several thousand weavers, mostly women, work for piece-rate wages in their homes to produce leisure hammocks for the international tourist market (Littlefield and Reynolds 1990). The home embroidery industry in Mexico is another case involving production for the tourist industry (Waterbury 1989). The world-famous Harris Tweed cloth likewise is a highly successful example of the putting-out cottage industry where textiles have been woven in homes of the inhabitants of the Outer Hebrides islands of Scotland since at least the early 19th century AD.

But perhaps the best example of how the putting-out production has been adapted to large-scale production is the Italian knitwear industry. This fast-changing fashion industry employs 16,000 people in the modern province of Modena, Italy. Here fashion companies design the knitwear; provide patterns, color specifications, and access to materials; and subcontract with individuals who work separately[32] or in small firms and collectives to manufacture finished garments for sale nationally and internationally (Lazerson 1993a, 1993b).

The putting-out system was, and remains, an important form of large-scale craft production. While it could not adopt new, more efficient forms of mechanized technology as fast as factories during the industrial revolution (Mokyr 1990:77), its continued existence today reveals that it is a flexible form of organization that fits certain sectors of the modern economy better than large-scale manufacturing. The independent development of putting-out production in different parts of the premodern world attests to its adaptability and persistence in production sectors that remain labor-intensive, require little capital investment, and use a technology and workforce that can be decentralized (Littlefield and Reynolds 1990:369–370). If it was only a stage of proto-industrialization, it would not be found in the world today.

One of the greatest economic changes in the 21st century is how the Internet has fostered the proliferation of cottage industries and small-scale domestic businesses. The Internet provides access to the global marketplace in ways that drastically reduce the type of craft risk associated with the limited transportation and communication networks of the ancient world. Still, there are lessons to be learned about the scale and productive capacity of intermittent, part-time craft production and the challenges that it can face. This is clear from the example below that examines the organization of periodic pie making in an informal institutional setting.

PERIODIC PIE MAKING AT HARMONY METHODIST CHURCH

The Harmony Methodist Church[33] is a small congregation with a big heart in central Pennsylvania. It supports a free afternoon daycare for low income families, a Montessori school, and a variety of other community services as part of its commitment to social ministry. The problem is that they are a small congregation of fewer than 200 members and their weekly offerings are not enough to fund the scope of social services that they want to support. Their solution is to raise money by making food and producing craft goods that they sell at Christmas, Easter, and at sporting events throughout the year.[34] Many of these goods are produced in voluntary work or fellowship groups at the church or in members' homes.[35] One of their tastiest fund-raising activities is making and selling ready-to-cook apple pies.

There is nothing more symbolically American than a home-cooked apple pie. What the apple pie makers at Harmony Methodist Church do is produce apple pies that can be immediately baked or frozen for later use in festive events throughout the year. The pie-making group makes pies to sell twice a year during the fall and the spring. The production date is distributed by word of mouth, but it is well known among pie aficionados within the community. Individuals who want to purchase pies for themselves or for their groups inform the pie coordinator of the number desired, and a time is set for pick-up at the church on the day they were made. The church makes only one type of pie, which simplifies the production process and enables them to mass-produce pies in a short period of time.

The church normally sells 950–1,000 pies each year, with the fall being the time when about 60% of the pies are sold because of their demand for Thanksgiving and Christmas holidays. In the fall of 2009, I participated in the pie-making event. A total of 563 apple pies were assembled and sold to eager consumers in the fall sale. Forty-four people were involved in the event over 2 days.[36] What is particularly noteworthy is that all apples were peeled and sliced, and pies were assembled and sold to consumers, in a space of 4 hours in a single afternoon! All the production technology used was essentially preindustrial in nature with rapid distribution made possible using modern transportation.[37]

Why are apple pies of interest here? Because of the scale of production that a simple mode of production *makes possible*. In 1 year, there are approximately

260 working days in a five-day work week. Thus if 950–1,000 pies can be made in two half-days (one full day) of work, then 247,000–260,000 apple pies could be made by the Harmony Methodist Church each year if they chose to work on a full-time basis. Harmony Methodist Church is located in a town of 42,000 people, which represents an average production capacity of 23–25 pies per family each year if they worked full-time. The available statistics suggest that is 15–17 times greater than the national average of pies purchased from supermarkets and consumed in US households.[38] The point is simply to show that the scale of production, even using simple nonindustrial technology, can significantly exceed the local demand for pies if taken to its logical extreme.

A similar problem existed during the industrial revolution where the productive capacity of factories often outstripped the market demand for the products they produced. The result was high levels of intra-industry competition and a corresponding high incidence of firm bankruptcies (McKendrick 1982; McKendrick et al. 1982). The efficiency of production assisted by machines far exceeded the ability of distribution systems to get the goods produced to the consumers who might want them. The result was that firms could choke on the quantity of unsold goods produced, underscoring the fact that the industrial revolution was constrained to a large degree by the nature of the transportation and distribution systems available at that time.

SUMMARY

Craft production was an important dimension of the ancient economy. The reliance of households on goods produced by specialized crafters provides a useful measure of the degree of commercialization within society. Emile Durkheim (1984) felt the same and proposed that the economic interdependence in society could be expressed in terms of its mechanical and organic solidarity.[39] The use of social evolutionary theory, beginning with Gordon Childe, together with our modern industrial bias has overemphasized the scale of production and the presence of full-time specialists as important benchmarks for the development of craft production. Likewise, these two characteristics have been incorrectly used for measuring the level of economic integration within ancient societies. They are not well suited for these purposes.

Market integration is best viewed in terms of the flow of goods and services between different sectors of society, as Durkheim originally proposed. Crafting reflects this process and developed as the demand for acquiring (rather than producing) consumer goods increased across society. The role of the independent craftsperson, their level of specialization, and the scale of craft production are important, but they should not be used by themselves as proxy measures for characterizing economic development since they reflect different underlying conditions within society. The scale of crafting followed demand

and the commercial circulation of goods, while the level of craft specialization was a response to the level of risk that artisans faced in pursuit of their craft. Small-scale production units continued to predominate over time as long as they could meet the need for goods in their respective societies. Conversely, larger-scale production units were held in check or allowed to develop to the extent that forms of distribution enabled higher levels of output to reach the range of intended consumers.

This chapter has focused on the independent craftspersons who produced goods for their own support in noninstitutional contexts. Identifying the scale of production is important for understanding how craft goods were produced and circulated in the ancient past. Four types of production were discussed that describe the variation found in the modes of craft organization: specialized domestic production, workshop industries, nucleated workshop industries, and manufactories. What is clear is that most craft goods throughout antiquity were produced in relatively small-scale domestic and commercial venues. The shops and craft workshops of even highly commercialized systems such as those of ancient Greece, Rome, Persia, and China were organized largely as extended family affairs, adding slaves, wage labor, or indentured apprentices as needed.

Large-scale manufactories and *ho-ku* enterprises such as those found in ancient China were rare. Even the large conglomerate production centers that archaeologists have identified as nucleated workshop industries had a greater degree of internal, small-scale organization than previously thought. The production of Roman *tierra sigillata* ceramics was used as an example. While these were large-scale production centers, the production units appear to have been organized through *locatio–conductio* agreements into holonic networks of largely self-regulated craft producers. These production conglomerates were located in areas of natural resources (clay, fuel for firing) at some distance from urban markets and other intended zones of consumption, which made them dependent on merchants to mobilize and distribute the wares produced.

The origin of craft specialization lies in the forms of ad hoc production and systems of craft knowledge that every household employed in utilizing the resources of their environment to meet their individual subsistence needs (e.g., Langlands 2017). Specialized craft production did not begin with patron–client production or the forms of institutional production found in chiefdoms or early states (Brumfiel and Earle 1987b; Childe 1936; Clark 1987). Instead, the more likely scenario is that patrons mobilized existing artisans in society to produce goods of special significance and for the specific usages that they were interested in. Institutions took preexisting systems of crafting knowledge and provided new domains of application and a framework of support for them to flourish.

All artisans had to deal with craft risk and the conditions of the craftsperson's dilemma. The problem of craft risk was twofold. From the perspective of the artisan it was the problem of fluctuating demand for the goods they produced. This is the essence of the craftsperson's dilemma and an obstacle to relying on crafting for a large proportion of their yearly income. From the perspective of society, the problem was one of assuring access to the quantity and availability of goods that the market demanded. Solving the first of these problems was the solution to the second. It was most often achieved through the development of redundant small-scale and part-time crafting units situated close to the markets or areas where goods were needed. The risk to artisans was reduced by situating intermittent crafting within a diversified domestic subsistence strategy. Crafting could be conducted as an important secondary pursuit in conjuncture with agriculture or pastoral subsistence activities by taking advantage of periodically or seasonally available labor (Hagstrum 1999, 2001). This provided households that incorporated craft production into their subsistence pursuits with what can be called the *marginal advantage of crafting*. It increased the diversity of household subsistence pursuits and reduced overall subsistence risk, which, in turn, increased their overall reproductive success (O'Shea 1989).

The road to full-time crafting was hazardous and required solving the aspect of artisan risk in the craftsperson's dilemma. One pathway to a fuller involvement in crafting was through multicrafting. Multicrafting continued the successful practice of diversification by adding new forms of crafting to the work regime and broadening the scope of goods produced that tapped into different demand cycles. Diversification could range from preparing cooked food or brewed beverages to sell in marketplaces alongside durable utilitarian goods like ceramics or basketry to producing higher-value luxury goods with different short- and long-term cycles of demand. An alternative approach was to practice crafting in areas where the demand for goods was larger or more continuous. Urban centers were one such location. Not only was aggregate demand greater in large communities, but the location of formal institutions and wealthier elites in urban centers provided the opportunity for production consignments to independent artisans, thereby providing more reliable long-term support (Clark and Parry 1990).

Craft guilds and the putting-out system were larger-scale solutions to the problems of craft risk and the craftsperson's dilemma. From the perspective of the market, craft guilds served to regulate the quality and consistency of the goods produced. This was good for both the consumers and the merchants who purchased goods for resale outside the region. For the artisan, however, they served as protectionist organizations that restricted the entry of new producers into the market who would reduce the share of consumer demand that any individual craftsperson could hope to reach. The putting-out system, or *verlagssystem*, was an adaptation to the long-established system of rural household diversification. It allowed merchants to systematically tap into seasonal workflows and labor availability in rural agricultural settings to produce and mobilize goods for export. Franklin Mendels saw the putting-out system as a form of proto-industrialization where the "existence of seasonal [labor] shortages does not preclude the existence of seasonal surpluses which can be trapped at no opportunity cost for (pre-factory) industrialization" (Mendels 1972:254).

For Mendels, the putting-out system allowed labor to shift into the industrial sector without incurring the opportunity costs of regional food scarcities for the households supplying labor. It successfully exploited the diversification tendencies that rural households employed for their own security to produce manufactured goods. While the putting-out system did not result in a great increase in the material standard of living found in rural households, its benefits to households is reflected by the increase in rural population that occurred coincident with their engagement in crafting activities (Mendels 1972:252). Rural households largely ate the improvements in their standard of living, resulting in larger and healthier populations.

Small-scale production units involved in intermittent and part-time craft production were adaptations to both the risky environment for artisans and the structure of the distribution networks through which craftspersons distributed their goods. The production of apple pies at Harmony Methodist Church illustrates that even informal forms of production using preindustrial technologies have the capacity to outstrip the accessible demand for goods if taken to full-time production. Specialized craft production was a risky business if distribution systems were not adequate for artisans to sell their products. The following chapter discusses the development of the marketplace and market systems, which were one of the solutions to broadening and enhancing distribution on multiple levels.

NINE

ON MARKETS AND MARKETPLACES

In one and the same place you will find all kinds of things for sale together at Athens: figs – Policeman! Grapes, turnips, pears, apples – Witnesses! Roses, medlars, porridge, honey-comb, peas – Lawsuits! Milk curds, myrtle-berries – Allotment machines! Bulbs, lamps – Water clocks, laws, indictments!

(Euboulos on things for sale in the Agora marketplace in Athens)

The city has many open squares in which markets are continuously held and the general business of buying and selling proceeds. One square in particular is twice as big as that of Salamanca and completely surrounded by arcades where there are daily more than sixty thousand folk buying and selling.

(Hernan Cortés's description of the Aztec market of Tenochtitlan, Mexico)

The marketplace was the heart and soul of the ancient commercial economy. As a primary location for economic interaction, it was one of the great institutions and developments of the ancient world. Markets in different forms were part of the economic landscape in both large- and small-scale societies. They were a hallmark of complex societies with high population densities and were one of the ways that cities with large urban populations were provisioned. In fact, it is difficult to find a state-level society in the ancient world that did not develop markets as a means of mobilizing and distributing resources to the groups and individuals who needed or wanted them.[1] The marketplace was a conspicuous provisioning engine behind the operation and development of economic complexity in many ancient societies. From an economic perspective, the appearance of markets was an evolutionary development equivalent to, and as revolutionary as, the origin of the state. It is this facet of the ancient economy that is examined here.

The marketplace was a formal institution on two levels within society. Its primary function was economic. It mobilized resources from where they were produced and assembled them in locations where they could be acquired by the individuals or groups who wanted or desired them. Markets could develop spontaneously and informally, but they operated more smoothly and efficiently when they were convened with some administrative oversight. The marketplace facilitated exchange by allowing kinsmen, foreigners, and nonkinsmen to engage in reciprocal exchanges. Because this involved both economic and social risk, the marketplace could not operate without the development of a special ideology and place-specific mode of behavior that allowed individuals of different ethnic backgrounds and social statuses to interact as economic equals. Marketplaces by definition were specially created liminal places where negotiation could take place without social repercussions to the individuals involved (Blanton 2013:28–29; Hutson 2000; Weber 1978:637). While the incentive for market interaction was economic, the special places and circumstances under which they were convened normally were socially constructed through a sponsoring individual, a deity, during a festival, or by a political official.

The second dimension of the marketplace was its role as a social institution. People did not go to the marketplace just to buy and sell. They also went to see friends, to gossip, and to socialize. People sometimes went to the marketplace when they did not have to or sold small amounts of items that did not make economic sense in terms of the time invested.[2] In the premodern world, the marketplace was where news and information were most effectively disseminated. As the first epigraph of this chapter illustrates, the Agora of Athens was where a great deal of political intrigue took place.[3] It was where people heard the news of the day. Theophrastos made this clear when he wonders, "in what stoa, in what shop, in what part of the agora do they (the newsmakers) not spend the day?" (Wycherley 1978:92). The marketplace also was a place of social display, where rulers could be associated with the creation of wealth and bounty (Sen 1998:14–15). Finally, the marketplace often was where courts were convened, and legal disputes were resolved.[4] Among the Aztecs, criminals were executed in the marketplace as a public declaration to obey the law.

The term "market" has been used in so many ways that it is necessary to explain how related concepts are employed here. The discussion then examines several types of marketplaces found in societies of different size and complexity to illustrate that "the market" needs to be approached as a multiscalar phenomenon rather than assuming that it represents a single form of behavior. The examples discussed range from the spontaneous and periodic marketplaces found in small-scale societies in Africa, India, Iceland, and North

America to the types of markets found in the urban state-level societies of ancient Athens, Rome, and Aztec Tenochtitlan. This is followed by a brief examination of market systems and how marketplaces fit into the broader landscape of mobilizing goods at the regional level. The question of market origins is explored beginning with the influential work of Karl Polanyi. The discussion illustrates that there were multiple factors that contributed to the formation of marketplaces that varied with local conditions. The chapter concludes with a discussion of the marketplace as a primary institution in society where multiple economic activities intersect.

MARKETS, MARKET EXCHANGE, MARKET ECONOMY, AND THE MARKETPLACE

We live in a world where the terms "market" and "marketplace" are tossed around in so many contexts that the terms lose relevance for discussing the ancient economy without clarification. Financial markets, labor markets, perfectly competitive markets, Internet marketing, real estate markets, black markets, currency markets, and global markets are all terms and phrases bandied about to characterize different commercial settings and relationships within the modern 21st-century economic landscape. They are not all relevant to discussing premodern economic systems. Financial and currency markets related to acquiring credit are modern concepts. Nowhere in antiquity are speculators found borrowing money on a large scale[5] to buy land or to make a killing in investments, as this was the first step in losing one's property (Hudson 1999c:489). Labor markets in the sense they are used today refer to the ability to hire people under the conditions of modern wage labor. It does not apply to a market for slave labor, and while wage labor was known in the ancient Mediterranean world, it was a limited and often seasonal dimension of work relations. Black markets always existed and were linked to smuggling and tax evasion, but the data on this topic are difficult to come by. There was no such thing as a global price-setting market for different classes of goods. Information was scarce, transportation was slow and expensive, and the merchants who engaged in long-distance trade exploited the discrepancies in the value of goods over space to make a profit (Chapter 7).

The term "market" has been used across the field in three general ways for discussing economic interaction in the ancient and the premodern world. The first and most common is as a place where goods were bought and sold. The second use is in reference to a general demand stream for specific products such as a grain market or the market for Indian textiles. The third usage of the term is to describe situations where a product is offered for sale and its value or price is determined by some level of interaction between buyer and seller (Berdan 1989:102). This last usage of the term is fine as long as researchers are careful with their assumptions about how the prices of goods sold determined or influenced production schedules. For this reason, it is important to clarify what is meant by the terms "market exchange," "marketplace," "market system," and "market economy" because they bear directly on the discussion of market function.

Market exchange as it is used throughout this volume follows the definition of Frederick Pryor (1977:104) as a balanced transaction involving the exchange of goods or services between two or more interacting parties where the forces of supply and demand are active and visible. They are commercial exchanges where price is determined through negotiation, whether through the barter of goods or the use of formal currency (Plattner 1989c). The exchange of goods is usually immediate rather than involving delay. What is specifically important about market exchange is that it implies nothing about the location of the exchange or the commercial complexity of the economic system in which it occurred. It can occur in centralized locations such as a shop or marketplace just as easily as it can in decentralized contexts between trading partners (Heider 1969) or in the chance encounters of customers and street peddlers (Plattner 1975a, 1975b).

Similarly, market exchanges occurred in societies at all levels of cultural complexity, from foraging groups to states.[6] They were not restricted to societies with a market economy since the principle of balance and equivalency is well understood in situations where exchanges take place. An examination of how gifts are exchanged in both bridewealth systems and intergroup feasting (e.g., moka, potlatch) around the world reveals that they were often carefully scrutinized and even hotly negotiated to achieve an agreed-on notion of balance. Market exchange as defined here was a simple negotiated way to obtain products and services. It also covers situations where prices may be set by tradition or administrative oversight to protect buyers from unfair price inflation. It was not necessarily the disruptive force that scholars such as Polanyi and his followers often ascribe to it (Polanyi 1944, 1957; Polanyi et al. 1957).

Marketplaces are centralized locales where many market exchanges take place on a periodic or regular basis (Plattner 1989c). Marketplaces make exchange more efficient by bringing buyers and sellers together as economic equals in a centralized location. In so doing, they reduce the costs of resource procurement by providing access to a wide array of goods that allows buyers and sellers to engage in multiple face-to-face transactions on a repeated basis in a single locale (North 1995; Silver 1995:153). The marketplace does not presume preexisting social relationships between interacting parties, although these may exist. What it does require, however, is that individuals be able to negotiate as economic equals, without regard to social status. As mentioned above, this requires establishing a certain market logic or liminality that suspends existing social identities so that transactions between individuals or groups can be smoothly negotiated and accepted or rejected without the fear of social reprisal.

Marketplaces developed as separate institutions because of the special rules or conditions required for them to operate efficiently and without conflict. They usually were convened on predictable schedules so individuals could plan provisioning decisions. Marketplaces often had their own internal supervision to oversee the honesty of transactions and to resolve disputes when they occurred. For this reason, it has been argued that marketplaces required elite oversight (Dyer 2005:20; Hicks 1987; Polanyi 1957) despite known cases where political supervision of marketplaces was weak or absent (Benet 1957; Blanton 2013). When supervision was absent, other informal means were used to establish a social framework for peaceful negotiation (Khuri 1968; Mintz 1964).

Elites often were interested in sponsoring marketplaces, not because they derived a great deal of material benefit from them but because of the prestige that they could confer. The cost of market sponsorship was low when compared with feasts, redistributive events, and other social activities that elites were called on to underwrite. Moreover, because marketplaces were anchored in space, the prestige associated with them was durable for communities where they were held. Prestige of place can increase over time with the number and type of events sponsored. This was the case in New Guinea where the ceremonial fields where feasts were held increased in prestige over time with the size and number of moka events that a clan and their big men were able to sponsor (Strathern 2007). This also was the case for marketplaces. The sponsorship of markets was one way that big men in Papua, New Guinea gained prestige from their size, the variety of goods sold, and distances over which individuals traveled to attend.[7] The relationship between place, prestige, and leadership grew together with the size and frequency of the markets convened.

Marketplaces may occur alone or as part of larger, regionally organized *market systems*. These are networks of marketplaces convened on regular schedules that facilitated the movement of merchants between them and made access to products more efficient for consumers. Market systems are usually associated with mature economic landscapes, higher population densities, and state-level societies (Garraty 2010:10). How these systems were organized and articulated could take many forms depending on regional geography, transportation constraints, and how regional populations were distributed (Garraty and Stark 2010; W. Skinner 1964; C. Smith 1974, 1976c, 1983). Particularly important was the development of hierarchical relationships between marketplaces in terms of the type of goods sold and the frequency with which they were convened (Santley and Alexander 1992).

A *market economy* is an economic system where the production and distribution of products is strongly determined by the connectivity between supply, demand, competition, and price. In these systems the price and availability of goods and services directly influences the production decisions of individuals who make them. Market economies are often referred to as having price-setting markets, whether they are regulated or not. A major characteristic of these economies is that supply and demand is the pervasive feature regulating the price of all commodities ranging from land and labor to goods and services.

These characteristics make it difficult to apply the concept of market economy to most ancient societies for two reasons. First, a market economy was not simply an economy with marketplaces. Many ancient societies had complex market systems but lacked correspondingly active markets for land, labor, or capital. Different rules and conditions governed these commodities, which often could be accessed only through social rather than economic relationships. Second, fast and efficient forms of communication need to be present for supply and demand to directly affect the production and distribution of goods. This was not the case in most premodern societies. Instead, transportation was slow, communication was imperfect, and long-distance trade was often dependent on wind and weather cycles that could result in long delays between when orders for goods were placed and when they arrived at their final destination (Morley 2007:95). The result was that production units remained small, were focused on quality over quantity, and were relatively resistant to innovation (Homans 1974; Silver 1981).

Marketplaces, market exchange, and market systems were all found in ancient and premodern societies and are relevant for any discussion of economic interaction. The concept of a market economy is not. Prices did vary somewhat with supply and demand, and some producers attempted to respond to them as would be expected in any commercial setting. But as a rule, production responses to changes in demand were slow. The average farmer was not market oriented since agriculture was risky enough without being subject to the vagaries and vicissitudes of the marketplace. A change in the price of grain in Rome had little effect on production decisions in its hinterland (Morley 2007:92–95). The main responses to agricultural opportunities came from prosperous estate owners who approached farming as an economic investment.[8] Nevertheless, individuals actively engaged in market exchanges inside and outside marketplaces to meet their individual wants and needs. The variation found in marketplaces across the ancient world underscores the diversity of ways in which these needs were met.

THE FORM AND FUNCTION OF THE MARKETPLACE

Research on marketplaces has focused primarily on four separate questions: what types of goods were sold, the periodicity with which they were held, where they were located, and how they operated. But the important and underlying factors that dictated the form and function of the marketplace

TABLE 9.1 *Differences in the structure, location, periodicity, and operation between domestic- and sector-oriented marketplaces*

Market functions	Domestic-oriented markets	Special sector markets (merchants, elites)
Types of goods sold		
	Retail sales	Wholesale sales
	Staples	High-value goods
	Generalized goods	Specialized goods
Market location		
	Rural and urban	Urban
	Border locations	Ports and harbors
Periodicity: varies with reliance on marketplaces		
	Regular scheduling in areas of high population density	Regular periodic scheduling with regard to seasonal and transport constraints
Operation		
	Commodity barter	Use of formal currencies and equivalents
	Supervised and unsupervised	Supervised and regulated

pertained to who or what sectors of the economy the marketplace was intended to serve. If market institutions were structured to service the society as a whole, then marketplaces would be regularly scheduled, evenly distributed, and would deal in a wide range of both staple and specialty goods. If markets are oriented to supply special sectors within the society, such as merchants or political institutions, then marketplaces would tend to operate as wholesale exchanges, have a narrow array of high-value or specialty goods, or mobilize resources for export. Scheduling would be more variable and could correspond to harvest or production cycles when large quantities of goods became available.

Table 9.1 lists the different ways that market functions and activities have been dichotomized in terms of the four most commonly asked questions about the organization of ancient marketplaces. The listing overgeneralizes and simplifies how marketplaces operated, but it illustrates the difficulty of developing a classification of market types. One of the primary cross-cultural functions of marketplaces was to provide provisioning functions for the domestic economy. Marketplaces could mobilize high-value goods used by elites and for institutional consumption, but the raison d'être for the development of most marketplaces was to provision households with food and staple goods. Markets were not needed for the exchange of wealth goods since they usually were restricted to a small sector of society and could be conducted through other forms of exchange, including house trade[9] or through institutional arrangements (Chapter 5). The public marketplace was for the public. As discussed in Chapter 2, households are the primary units of production and reproduction in society. As such, they are responsible for provisioning themselves with the resources necessary for their survival. The marketplace was an organic solution to their provisioning problems by allowing households to use exchange to obtain the resources that they could not produce.

It is not possible to provide examples for all the forms of marketplaces summarized in Table 9.1. Six types of marketplaces are presented below that illustrate the type of variation found. They range from the spontaneous marketplaces found in cross-cultural interactions within small-scale societies to the highly regularized retail and specialty markets of Rome, Greece, and Aztec Mexico. They reflect the range of market diversity and the use of markets to solve provisioning problems in societies of different size, and they highlight the organizational features that appear in different cultural settings.

UNPLANNED SPONTANEOUS MARKETPLACES

Since Malinowski (1922) described the practice of *gimwali* barter as a form of market exchange, anthropologists have debated the role of marketplaces in societies of different size and complexity. *Gimwali* was a form of barter carried out between crafting villages in the interior of the Trobriand Islands[10] as well as on the beaches between residents and visitors who went out to Kula (Malinowski 1967b:218–220). Hoyt (1926:121–123) reports similar behaviors for groups in the Andaman Islands. These informal assemblies in places where individuals engaged in market exchanges are referred to here as spontaneous marketplaces. They were unplanned and ad hoc marketplaces that occurred when people came together on an impromptu basis. While it is easy to assign them to small-scale societies, they actually can occur in societies of different scales wherever the opportunity to conduct ad hoc market exchange arises.

Spontaneous marketplaces occurred along caravan routes where merchants traveled with their goods. Owen Lattimore (1995:157) reports that it was common for caravans traveling the old silk route in central Asia during the early 20th century AD to trade flour with local groups as a part of normal interactions as they traveled. Caravans of traders moving through nonhostile areas of west Africa were characterized as slow-moving markets selling a range of goods in route. Roberts (1987:63) argues that sales along the way were just as important for these caravan merchants as those in their final destinations. The same was true of llama caravans in the southern Andes of South America that carried salt from the highlands to areas on the coast and traded it for other goods in nightly stopovers along the route (Nielsen 2001, 2013).

Perhaps one of the most intriguing cases of mobile and spontaneous marketplaces is that provided by the Banjaras. As discussed in Chapter 7, they were an ethnic group of tribal merchants who held a monopoly on trade of bulk items such as grain, raw cotton, and salt across India at least as early as the 15th century AD. The Banjaras were cattle pastoralists who moved goods in carts and on the backs of bullocks from rural to urban areas as they grazed their herds across the Indian subcontinent (Habib 1999:69). By the late 16th century, the Banjaras were the primary suppliers of the Mughal imperial army as well as the opposing forces. In medieval India, it was traditional for soldiers to buy the food they consumed from dealers (*banyas*) in temporary bazaars that followed armies when they were on the move. The Banjaras became the primary suppliers of these military marketplaces (Levi 1994:38–42). They provided food and other supplies to opposing forces, were considered neutral, and were allowed to cross enemy lines to provide provisions where needed. They were a hardy, self-reliant group that carried thousands of tons of bulk commodities on the backs of their oxen and were able to set up spontaneous marketplaces wherever and whenever it was convenient or necessary to do so (Varady 1979).

Another type of spontaneous marketplace was the beach market that appeared when merchants arrived to trade imported items for local goods directly on the beach or cove where they landed their ships. These types of marketplaces were known from Roman Africa. An anonymous Christian preacher from the 5th or 6th century AD describes the Mediterranean beach-side marketplaces of northern Africa when he says, "O how lovely the beach looks when its filled with merchandise and it bustles with businessmen! Bundles of different clothing are pulled from the ships, countless people delight at the sailors' cheerful singing, and the rich man dances in the sand" (McCormick 2001:84).

The 1st-century AD Greco-Roman manuscript known as the *Periplus Maris Erythraei* records numerous places to obtain goods down the coast of eastern Africa but contains few references to marketplaces (Casson 1989). The goods in demand were luxury items such as gold, ivory, cassia, and medicinal products, and it is likely that some of these were obtained through direct trading in beach markets. Jeffrey Fleisher (2010:151) feels that much early trade along the Swahili coast of eastern Africa was conducted through beach marketplaces until the 11th and 12th centuries AD when visiting merchants began to be sponsored by local merchants who moved trade from the beach to the confines of their private stone houses. This type of house trade probably was structured in the same way that it still is in some areas of Africa (Cohen 1965; Hill 1966, 1969) where the resident merchant serves as the visitor's agent, exchanging the goods that are brought for those that he has stockpiled or procured from other members of the community. Another form of spontaneous marketplace is recorded for medieval Iceland, where "the usual practice was for markets to spring up ad hoc whenever and wherever a trading ship might land. This tended to be at the most frequented natural harbors, but the existence of a market depended on the presence of a recently arrived ship" (Miller 1990:80).

There were no permanent marketplaces in medieval Iceland, although some exchanges occurred at Alþing meetings and at fairs held in conjunction with feast days. The Icelandic law codes are clear that local chiefdoms set the price of goods that arrived in Iceland. This included both the goods brought in the ships that they owned as well as ships owned by foreign Norwegian merchants (Gelsinger 1981:38). In the saga of Hen-Thorir, a foreign merchant by the name of Orn ignored the local chieftain and tried to set his own prices, which were promptly boycotted because of the chief's opposition (Pálsson 1975:97). Most of these spontaneous markets probably occurred during the summer and early fall, after which return sailing to Norway could be difficult because of bad weather.[11] Local chieftains exerted control over these marketplaces and probably had the first choice of the goods offered for sale within them.

Spontaneous marketplaces occurred without scheduling when the opportunity arose. They occurred in areas of low population density and were most common in connection with some form of interregional or long-distance trade. While they frequently occur in areas of underdeveloped economic infrastructure, they are not confined to simple or small-scale societies.

PERIODIC MARKETPLACES IN SMALL-SCALE SOCIETIES: THE NORTH AMERICAN RENDEZVOUS

While Karl Polanyi (1957:255) associated marketplaces with the development of complex economic systems, they also have been documented in a number of small-scale and tribal societies around the world. They can occur in stateless societies as periodic fairs associated with festivals, feasts, or other culturally prescribed events that helped set the condition for peaceful interactions between individuals and groups with different ethnic or cultural identities. What makes these marketplaces distinct from those discussed in the previous paragraphs is that they were regularly scheduled rather than occurring spontaneously. Scheduling allows for planned attendance, the assessment of needs for those who decide to go, and the preparation of goods to be exchanged. It also enables household attendees to use their time efficiently in production and provisioning pursuits. These marketplaces operated as points of direct resource procurement and may or may not be integrated into larger spheres of resource mobilization or distribution.

Paul Bohannan and George Dalton in the classic study *Markets in Africa* (1962b) discuss the variation in marketplaces and market exchange in different societies across the continent. They were attempting to evaluate the distribution of what they referred to as the "market principle" in African societies. What they demonstrated was that variation in marketplaces depended to a large degree on whether it was focused on exchange of goods for local consumption or for external trade. Furthermore, they found that scheduled, periodic marketplaces were not the primary vehicle of resource provisioning for some of the societies studied. Instead, the livelihood of many of the premodern African societies depended on nonmarket production and distribution activities. Market participants primarily were target marketers who obtained small quantities of necessary items from the marketplace and satisfied the bulk of their subsistence needs in other ways (Bohannan and Dalton 1962a:7).

A major periodic market among the Kapauku people of Papua, New Guinea, was held in conjunction with the *juwo* pig feast. This was the most important and complex ceremony in Kapauku culture, and it was sponsored by wealthy individuals to enhance their prestige by selling the meat from slaughtered pigs in specially built feast huts. A market was convened coincident with the *juwo* feast where individuals sold a wide array of goods in exchange for shell money (cowries), which could be used to buy pig meat at the feast. Up to several thousand individuals from both local groups and neighboring tribes attended this marketplace, which provided a forum for the interregional exchange of goods. The *tapa* money-collecting ceremony was another important occasion for convening a marketplace. The purpose of the ceremony was to publicly collect shell money and cancel debts owed to the sponsor of the feast.[12]

Periodic trade fairs known as rendezvous took place between indigenous hunting, gathering, and agricultural groups in prehistoric North America. Although the antiquity of these periodic trade meetings is unknown, Jackson (1991) argues that they may have extended back as much as 3,000 years ago to the Late Archaic period (1500–1000 BC). Whatever their age, the cultural context that made these trade meetings possible was the calumet ceremony, discussed in Chapter 3. The calumet ceremony provided a ritual framework and established a temporary truce between otherwise hostile enemies that permitted the intertribal exchange of goods. The conceptual basis for this truce was the establishment of fictive kinship relationships between males of different groups through which trade took place (Blakeslee 1981:759). The intertribal linkages created by the calumet ceremony served as the basis for establishing annual trade meetings at predetermined locations during different times of the year, most often at the intersection of natural communication corridors and trade routes. Joseph Jablow (1950) makes the point that meetings with sedentary horticultural groups like the Hidatsa and the Arikara always took place at their villages, while the location of meetings between mobile groups varied from year to year.

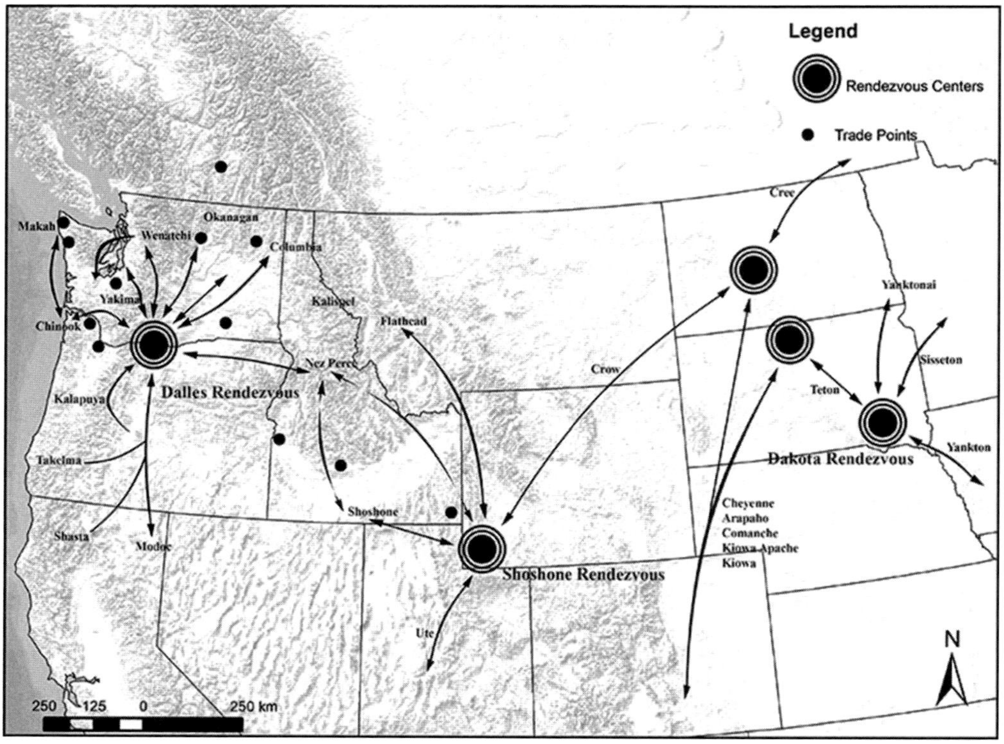

9.1 Five different periodic rendezvous or trade fairs held in the area of what is currently the western United States before European contact. (Illustration modified from Wood (1980:Fig 1) by Dylan Davis. Service Layer Credits: ESRI, USGS, NOAA.)

Figure 9.1 identifies the locations of five of the most important 19th-century AD rendezvous trade fairs in the western United States. They were the Mandan/Hidatsa, Arikara, and Dakota trade centers along the upper Missouri and James Rivers; the Shoshone rendezvous in southwest Wyoming; and the Dalles rendezvous along the Columbia River on the Washington/Oregon border. Twelve other secondary trade locations are also known, nine in the area around the Dalles rendezvous and three others between Dalles and the Shoshone rendezvous (Wood 1980:figure 1). Multiple different groups descended on these centers at the same time and engaged in trade on a peaceful basis through their calumet intermediaries even if they otherwise were hostile and mortal enemies. This does not mean that tense situations and confrontations did not occur, but when they did, they were mediated by their calumet intermediaries. This especially was the case when the Cheyenne and Sioux met to conduct trade through the Arikara, who functioned effectively as trade intermediaries for both groups (Jablow 1950:57).

In a similar pattern, groups of Cree would assemble each spring in the northwest along Saskatchewan River to harvest and trade birch bark, which was important for the maintenance of their canoes (Meyer and

Thistle 1995). These types of large yearly aggregations were common among mobile foraging groups (Conkey 1980; Hayden 1993:164) and provided the opportunity for a range of social interactions that included recruiting spouses, gambling, and learning songs, dances, and folktales (Wood 1980:106).

Social interaction notwithstanding, the primary purpose for these trade meetings both before and after European contact was the acquisition of subsistence products that they either did not produce or did not have in enough supply. The Mandan, Hidatsa, and Arikara were horticulturalists, and nomadic hunting and foraging groups came to centers along the Missouri River to exchange buffalo hides, horses, and other goods for maize, beans, and eventually guns (Ewers 1968). An account by two Frenchmen (La Vérendrye 1927) in AD 1739 reported that a number of allied nomadic tribes visited the Mandan in June and stayed for a month (Ewers 1968:4). Groups known to have visited the Mandan and Hidatsa included the Crow, Cree, Assiniboine, Cheyenne, Arapaho, Comanche, and Kiowa-Apache. The Crow also traveled to the Shoshone rendezvous (Figure 9.1) where the Ute, Flathead, and Nez Perce interacted (Ewers 1968:14). After contact, these trade centers were magnets for European traders and trappers, and quickly were incorporated as trade and procurement nodes in the Rocky Mountain fur trade.[13]

Groups planned for these trade interactions throughout the year. They intensified production and stockpiled goods that they could use in exchange for food and other products that they could not produce. Interaction along the Columbia River revolved around the Dalles rendezvous held every fall, where large quantities of dried fish were stockpiled and traded. Lewis and Clark reported more than 50 tons of dried fish near the Dalles meeting area and Griswold (1970:21) estimates that up to 500 tons of dried fish were traded there each year (Wood 1980:102). Trade within these centers occurred as both individual barter and collective group exchanges.[14] In the latter, items would be pooled and exchanged in large quantities by the leaders of different groups, with the goods obtained redistributed to individuals in proportion to their contributions (Blakeslee (1975:145–150; Jablow 1950). One such pooled exchange in June 1805 records the Hidatsas trading 200 guns to the Crow for 250 horses (Ewers 1968:27).

PLACE AND MARKETPLACES: PILGRIMS AND BORDER MARKETS

Natural and cultural environments shaped where people lived and how they moved over space. The natural environment affects where crops grow, where animals live, and where mineral resources can be found. Terrain configurations, ocean currents, wind patterns, and river networks shaped the transportation landscape and the cost of moving goods over space in very definite ways (Landers 2003:73–103; Meijer and van Nijf 1992; Scheidel 2012b; www.orbis.stanford.edu). Political and cultural conditions did so as well but were more susceptible to change over time than were natural conditions. Since marketplaces are institutions designed to facilitate access to resources, it is no surprise that they would be located along natural communication corridors and in areas that minimized transportation costs.

Mackinder's dictum states that no human settlement is more difficult to supplant than an established market (Bird 1958:464; Bromley et al. 1975:531). The truth of this statement resides in the fact that markets tend to be located in optimal physical locations for purposes of transportation and tend to persist in those locations because of the services they provide for communities in those areas. Geography affects market location and helps to create natural ports of exchange. Market emporia are more likely to be found where the forms or costs of transportation change or at break-bulk locations where conditions required repackaging goods for continued transshipment. Maritime harbors and river crossings are examples of where this occurs (Blackmann 1982a, 1982b; De Graauw 2013; Harding 1967:16). Geography also creates natural bottlenecks to movement that funnel transportation traffic, shape linkages between communities, and create hierarchical relationships between networks of sites (Hirth 1978; Lloyd and Dicken 1977; Rodrigue et al. 2016; C. Smith 1976c; Taaffe and Gauthier 1973). The availability of key resources such as water shaped trade routes and the location of communities and marketplaces across arid regions. Likewise, ecological diversity created border markets at the interface of different environmental zones and the human groups that occupied them (Boenisch Burrough 1978:49). A common expression of this is the location of border markets where pastoral groups can exchange their products for grain and craft goods produced by sedentary agriculturalists[15] (Bates 2001:109–110; Bradburn 1981).

Cultural factors such as ethnicity and political policies also shaped the commercial landscape. Border markets were common at the interface between different cultural groups because they served as neutral places where they could exchange products and safely interact[16] (Benet 1957:189–191; Boenisch Burrough 1978:51; Hoyt 1926:116; Pohl et al. 1997). Likewise, marketplaces were often linked with specific cultural events or sites, the most common of which were religious pilgrimages. Pilgrimage and trade were inseparable in the past and around the world. Goods were often taken on pilgrimage to sell at the destination or bought for the return home to cover the cost of the trip. The city of Mecca and its marketplace were linked to the Quraysh tribe, which would sell incense and other goods only to individuals who came to Mecca on pilgrimage (Simon 1989:60–62).

The annual *hajj* to Mecca had other effects. It helped to establish the port of Mocha as one of the largest export markets for coffee. Coffee was grown in Yemen, and it was on the *hajj* that many pilgrims acquired their taste for coffee, which they took back with them to their home communities (Pendergrast 2010). More generally, Muslims involved in the *hajj* from the Malaccas brought goods with them through India for sale in Mocha and Mecca. The result was that the *hajj* acted as a huge conveyer belt moving goods through the Indian Ocean into Europe (Das Gupta 2001a, 2001b:35, 40, 63). The connection between pilgrimage and marketplaces was important throughout the history of India. Marketplaces were important places of social display and incorporated a processional avenue into their design that included locations reserved for display, worship, prestation, beneficence, and consumption. All pilgrimage sites had market fairs where temple offerings and prayers often involved buying specialized goods at the nearby marketplace. In the indigenous mythology, marketplaces in India were conceived of as spots where the gods and persons of high social rank resided (Sen 1998:26–37).

THE RETAIL MARKETPLACE

Retail markets are those where vendors sell directly to consumers. They are the marketplaces that service households and provide provisioning options for the domestic economy. They benefit households by bringing consumables together in a central location for exchange and sale. They create a repository of resources mobilized from the fields, workshops, and storage facilities in the society that are offered for sale. By so doing, marketplaces *minimize* the costs of resource procurement for households by offering one-stop shopping in a centralized location. Retail markets are, and always have been, the purveyors of consumerism within society, however they were structured.[17] There were many retail marketplaces in the ancient world; for the three described here, there is good information available on their structure and operation. They are the Aztec marketplace of Tlatelolco, the Athenian Agora, and the marketplaces of ancient Rome.

The Aztec Marketplace of Tlatelolco

The second epigraph at the start of this chapter is a first-hand description by Hernan Cortés of the Tlatelolco marketplace[18] in the Aztec capital city of Tenochtitlan (modern Mexico City) in AD 1520. The Aztec marketplaces were centralized and integrated retail markets (Calnek 1978). An integrated market is one where all types of goods are sold, and wholesale and retail activities were carried out alongside one another. Consumers in the Tlatelolco market bought and sold using commodity currencies and barter. This gave the Aztec markets a different character than markets in the Old World that often were specialized by products and were organized as an emporium of shops (see below).

The Aztecs had a strong commercial economy, and the marketplace was at its center. This is interesting for comparative study because the area of Mesoamerica where Aztec society flourished had one of the worse transportation systems in the ancient world. Most goods were transported locally and interregionally on the backs of human porters. The Tlatelolco market was exceptionally large because it was located in the Basin of Mexico's central lake system where food, craft goods, and bulk products could be transported to and from the marketplace in canoes. Market places first appeared in Mesoamerica around 500 BC, fully 2,000 years before the arrival of the Spanish. Market size and the diversity of items sold were the two features that most impressed the Spanish about Aztec marketplaces. Both features are evident in one eyewitness account: "When we arrived at the great market place, called Tlatelolco, we were astounded at the number of people and the quantity of merchandise that it contained, and at the good order and control that was maintained, for we had never seen such a thing before" (Díaz del Castillo 1956:215).

The estimate of 60,000 people attending the marketplaces provided by Cortés (1962:87) in this chapter's second epigraph is generally considered to be accurate for the city's primary market day. While that is a lot of people, the reason it impressed the Spanish was because it was far larger than anything that he and other conquistadors had seen or heard about in their travels through Europe and North Africa. In fact, the Tlatelolco marketplace was larger than most European towns of the era. The population estimates for the Tlatelolco marketplace made it larger than any contemporary Spanish cities except possibly Granada (Chandler 1987).

The reason why Aztec marketplaces were so large is that they were integrated, centralized, and heterogenous in nature. All goods offered for sale could be found in the central marketplace with similar commodities grouped together in different sectors to facilitate comparative shopping and to make supervision easier. Cortés makes this clear when he said, "There is nothing to be found in all the land which is not sold in these markets.... Each kind of merchandise is sold in its own particular street and no other kind may be sold there: this rule is very well enforced" (Cortés 1962:89).

While carefully organized, most marketplaces lacked installations such as shops or market stalls because most markets were not permanent. They were single-day affairs convened on a rotating schedule within the central plazas of the towns where they were held. Except for the largest cities, markets were held on a rotational basis,[19] and town plazas had to be cleaned afterward so other activities could be carried out on nonmarket days. Figure 9.2 is a 16th-century AD rendering in pre-Columbian style that illustrates some of the

9.2 The array of utilitarian items and wealth goods sold in the Tlatelolco marketplace in Tenochtitlan, Mexico. (from Hirth 2016:Figure 3.2)

goods sold in the marketplace that ranged from food and cooking vessels to high-value textiles and jade beads. A review of the contact period sources has identified 705 categorically distinct types of merchandise sold in the marketplace (Hirth 2016:table 3.1), which probably was only a small fraction of the variety of merchandise offered for sale.

The organization of the marketplace by commodity meant that there was no separation of wholesale or retail activities within the marketplace; both

9.3 An Aztec woman selling maize by dry volume. (From Hirth 2016:Figure 5.2)

activities went on side by side with one another. The sources identify four classes of vendors that illustrate the integrative nature of Aztec marketplaces: producer-sellers (*tlachiuhqui*), retailers (*tlanecuilo*), importers of specific goods operating as either retailers or wholesalers, and long-distance merchants (*oztomeca*, *pochteca*) who sold high-value goods and slaves. Most vendors in the marketplace were producer-sellers, individuals who sold what they made, grew, prepared, hunted, or collected in the wild. These often were not full-time vendors. Many artisans who produced goods for sale apparently did so as a major but part-time activity as part of a diversified domestic production strategy to reduce crafting risk, as discussed in the preceding chapter. Also present in the marketplace was an array of other commercial specialists, including money changers (*tlapatlac*), attorneys (*tepantlato*), commercial agents (*tlacuiutiani*, *tlaciuiti*), and peddlers (*tlacôcoalnamacac*). All specialties and professions could be found in their respective locations, and women were as active as men in selling goods within the marketplace (Hirth 2016).

Rulers took pride in their town marketplaces both for providing goods for the people and for what they reflected about the prosperity of their domain. Leading merchants known for their honesty and integrity were given the responsibility of supervising best practices within them. Leading warriors served as constables patrolling the marketplace to guard against theft, and merchant supervisors checked the honesty and reliability of the measures used to sell goods. Unlike the Old World where goods were sold by weight, Aztec goods were sold by volume, count, length, or size.[20] Figure 9.3 illustrates a woman in indigenous dress selling maize by dry volume. To ensure fairness, a council of judges was located in the marketplace to provide immediate rulings on wrongdoers, against those caught using false measures, and to demonstrate publicly what happens to those who broke the law.

The Agora of Athens

Athens was one of the great cities of the ancient world. The Parthenon, dedicated to Athena, the patron deity of Athens, may have been the city's most important religious building, but the Agora marketplace was its cultural center. It was here that political and religious activities blended with commercial, legal, and theatrical displays. The excerpt by the comic Euboulos in the first epigraph at the beginning of this chapter infers that everything was "for sale" in the Agora from food to every dimension of legal and political life, including policemen and the witnesses used to adjudicate law cases. The main buildings housing the Athenian senate (Boule), the city administrators, the central archives, the law courts, and many commemorative altars and religious shrines were located there. Archaeological explorations have recovered more than 7,500 inscriptions from the Agora (Camp 1986:17), which include laws, treaties, decrees, dedications, temple inventories, and the Agora's boundary markers (Figure 9.4).

9.4 A boundary marker from the southwest corner of the Agora of Athens. (Photograph by Mark Munn, used with permission)

Despite its other functions, the Agora was the marketplace of Athens, and it is this commercial aspect that is the focus of discussion here. A great deal of what is known about the organization of the marketplace comes from orators and other literary sources. Xenophon identifies its commercial function in this statement from *Oeconomicus*: "Whatever servant you order to buy something for you from the Agora, and bring it, not one of them will have any difficulty; everyone will plainly know where he must go to get each class of goods. The reason for this, I said, is simply that they are kept in their appointed places" (Thompson 1971:1).

At the center of the Agora (Figure 9.5) was a large, open plaza that became smaller as it filled up with buildings of different functions over time. Small booths constructed of flimsy material known as *skenai* occupied the east side of the plaza. Merchants sold their goods on tables set up within the plaza, and wine sellers are described as having brought their vintages into the Agora on small wagons. The marketplace was regulated, and five inspectors (*metronomoi*) chosen by lots were responsible for checking the honesty of weights and measures within the city (Camp 1986:125). The saying "a place for everything, and everything in its place" ascribed to Xenophon describes the internal organization of the marketplace. Related goods were sold in specific areas referred to as circles. Where these areas were located is unclear, but we know from the speeches of orators that some of the specialized areas included clusters of related merchants selling fish, meat, clothing, perfume, vegetables, fruit, nuts, flour, wine, olive oil, slaves, and horses, to name a few. In general, the circles became the reference to different areas of the city (Wycherley

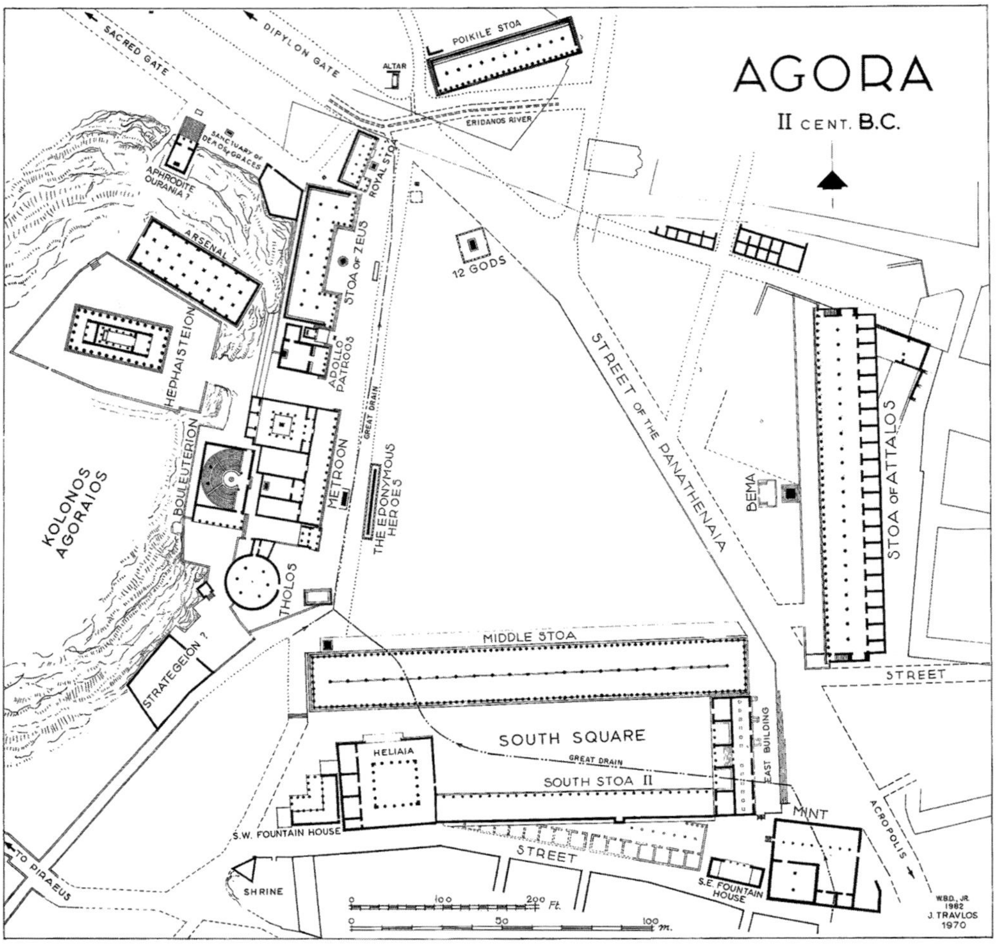

9.5 Map of the Agora at Athens. (Image courtesy of the American School of Classical Studies at Athens: Agora Excavations.)

1978:93–95, 99). The 2nd-century AD grammarian Julius Pollux characterizes this practice by saying, "The Attic writers named places after the things sold there; for instance they might say, 'I went to the wine, the olive oil, the pots'; or again in the words of Euopolis, 'I went to the garlic and the onions and the incense, and straight on to the perfume'" (Wycherley 1978:93).

These areas or circles were not confined to the central core of the Agora but were spread throughout the city along its different streets. Athens was famous for its red and black pottery, and the potters' quarter was located on the northwest corner of the Agora near the Royal Stoa (Figure 9.5) and extending west up the Panathenaic Way.[21] Evidence for ceramic manufacture includes a kiln found at the southwest corner of the Agora near the Tholos[22] and further west along the Panathenaic Way near the Dipylon gate. Many craftsmen, including sculptors, lived in a commercial district on the slopes of the Areopagus hill bordering the south side of the Agora. The house of two marble sculptors named Mikion and Menon was identified on the southwestern corner of the Agora.[23] Wine shops were found in all areas of the city, as were smaller businesses selling goods from the doorways of their houses (Camp 1986:138–143; Thompson 1971:2). The spread of commercial establishments across the city is reflected in the words of Lysias, the late 4th-century BC orator who said, "For each of you is in the habit of frequenting some place, a perfumer's shop, a barber's, a cobbler's and so forth; and the greatest number visit those who have their establishments nearest the Agora, and the smallest those who are furthest from it" (Camp 1986:135).

A significant architectural innovation within the Agora was the construction of long, rectangular buildings referred to as *stoae*. These buildings had one or more rows of columns supporting a roofed colonnade that were used as commercial and administrative areas, and to surround religious sanctuaries. Several *stoae* are believed to have had specific commercial functions. The South and Middle Stoae that flanked the South Square of the Agora very likely were important commercial areas based on both their architecture and the recovery of 240 bronze coins in the South Stoa (Camp 1986:123, 177; Wycherley 1978:102). The Stoa of Attalos, built by King Attalos of Pergamon between 159 and 138 BC, also appears to have had a commercial function. It was built with 2 stories and had 42 shop rooms that could be locked at night and probably contained valuable goods (Thompson 1971:3). Likewise, during the Roman period a great peristyle court with shops behind the colonnade was built with gifts from Julius and Augustus Caesar (Wycherley 1978:102).

Finally, any discussion of the commercial activities within the Agora would not be complete without reference to the first use of formal currencies in Greece and the presence of the Athenian mint for striking silver coins. According to Herodotus, the first coins were minted in the kingdom of Lydia of electrum, a natural mixture of gold and silver in the 7th century BC (Weatherford 1997:30–31). The mint in Athens struck both silver and bronze coins and dates to the beginning of the 4th century BC, although an earlier mint existed somewhere in the city since the 6th century BC. The 4th-century building identified as the mint contained a bronze working furnace along with dozens of unstruck bronze coin blanks recovered from archaeological excavations.[24] Money was also available on loan; a moneylender named Lucian is said to have operated on the north side of the Agora behind the Stoa Poikile, while a second one was located at the Diomeian Gate at the southeastern side of the city (Wycherly 1978:96).

An enthusiast would be tempted to say that the whole of Athens was a marketplace based on the way commercial establishments were spread out through the city. A more realistic characterization, however, is that the central Agora was the original marketplace, with commercial activities spreading out from the core over the length of the city.

The Retail Shops of Rome

With a population of as many as 1 million people, Rome was a commercial megalopolis. It consumed grain and other products from across the empire. The number of books on Rome and the Roman economy is extensive and could consume all the discussion about retail marketplaces (Aldrete and Mattingly 1999; Andreau 1999; Bowman and Wilson 2009; Duncan-Jones 1990; Greene 1990; Holleran 2012; Jones 1974; Morley 1996; Rickman 1980a; Scheidel 2012a; Storey and Storey 2017; Wilson and Flohr 2016). But Rome was atypical of most ancient urban communities in terms of its size and the demands that it placed on its marketplaces. For that reason, the discussion focuses on only one aspect of the urban economy of ancient Rome: the nature of its many retail shops and what they imply about how its commercial economy may have operated.

Rome has been called the city of retail shops, which are known in Latin as *tabernae* (MacMahon 2003:659–661). The *taberna* was a small, single-room shop used for retail and manufacturing activities within Roman cities.[25] They were both associated with residential buildings and part of commercial complexes in primary market areas. As discussed above, the practice of grouping retail shops in business complexes can be linked to the earlier commercial *stoae* of the Athenian Agora. What is different in Roman cities is that *tabernae* also were associated with multistory apartment structures (*insulae*) and individual houses that had one or more *tabernae* facing the street with living quarters behind them on the interior of the building (Figure 8.3). What makes *tabernae* architecturally distinct was their wide entrances, a grooved threshold for vertical wooden shutters allowing the building to be closed at night, and often the lack of a direct connection between shops and the residence to which they were attached.[26] Together these features suggest that they were rented spaces rather than commercial areas used by the residents of specific households (Holleran 2012:99–100; MacMahon 2006).

The point of emphasis is that shops and clusters of shops, whether lining streets or as part of business complexes, were the foci of important commercial activities within cities (J. Anderson 1997:331). The Roman marketplace was an emporium of shops, and it is from this arrangement that the Arabic word *souk* is derived, which means street of shops (Braudel 1986:60). The emergence of a strong shop economy did more than just change the architecture of the marketplace. It also provided a setting for changing the way that retail business was transacted in small but important ways.

While it is always risky to use analogy to infer past behavior, there were two features about the emergence of shops that were important for premodern distribution systems. First, they reflect both diversification and specialization of retail distribution mechanisms within Roman cities. While shops were clustered by craft or retail specialty as a natural practice to attract buyers and increase shopping efficiency, there also were new forms of selling within Rome that included what Holleran (2012:50) calls temporary pop-up shops that varied in terms of the goods sold based on what was available. The proliferation of shops throughout cities reflects not only an increase in the efficiency of distribution but also the increased per capita demand for goods on the part of their residents.

Second, and more important, shops provide a more personalized selling environment that encouraged buyer regularity. The appearance of shops permits the development of personal credit relationships between sellers and their regular customers. This practice has been documented as a regular feature of shop–customer relationships across the premodern and ancient worlds (Benedict 1964:342; Clarence-Smith 2011:138; Cox 2000:146; Davis 1966:151–155; Dyer 2012; Goitein 1967:151, 240; Kicza 1983:59; Khuri 1968; Plattner 1975b:59; Vance 1970:76). Braudel (1986:73) proposes that it was the ability of shops to extend credit for household purchases that enabled them to develop in the first place, with shopkeepers operating between their debts to suppliers and the debts of their customers. While there has been considerable discussion about debt, credit, and the emergence of banking institutions in antiquity (e.g., Andreau 1999; Goetzmann 2017; Graeber 2011; Millett 2002), the development of informal credit arrangements based on personal relationships has gone largely unnoticed because of the lack of records and documentation. Informal credit relationships are also common outside shop economies and are known by a variety of names around the world, including *tanda* (Hodder 1996:226), *dashi* (Nadel 1942:372), *pratik* (Mintz 1964:262), *kameti* (Arderner 1964:203), *hui*, *ko*, or *ho* (Firth 1964; Geertz 1962:250–253).

The establishment of personalized credit between shop owners and customers has been documented in all parts of the world where retail shop economy has been carefully studied. It is what enabled shop owners to weather the fluctuations in sales dependent on ready cash alone, and it provided a way for households to navigate short-term fluctuations in their own purchasing power. The successful reduction and manipulation of debt by shopkeepers kept them in business. Shopkeepers in rural areas might receive in-kind payments at harvest time to reduce debt without clearing it completely to retain an attachment to their customers (Bailey 1964:122; Benedict 1964:342–343). Given the commonality of these practices, there is no reason to suspect that it was not also part of the Roman shop economy. An oration by Seneca mentions a Pythagorean who bought shoes on credit from a cobbler, and when he returned a few days later to pay for them, he found that the cobbler was dead (Holleran 2012:52–53). In her discussion of Roman economy, Holleran states that becoming a regular customer of shops had its advantages: "[It] enabled customers to build up relationships with sellers, and perhaps also to enter into informal credit agreements if necessary. Indeed, credit may have been routinely offered to trusted customers, although given that much of this was probably organized through largely informal agreements, few traces of this practice survive" (Holleran 2012:52).

ENTREPOTS, SPECIALTY MARKETS, AND THE WHOLESALE TRADE

An "entrepot" as defined by *Merriam-Webster* is an intermediary center of trade and transshipment. A specialty market or fair is a marketplace known for the sale of a particular commodity. When the two are combined, the result is a wholesale marketplace where specific commodities are purchased for purposes of resale. In antiquity, wholesale marketplaces were the creation of merchants and their agents who mobilized goods for shipment, distribution, and resale to the individuals, shop owners, and institutions that wanted them. Vance (1970:38) has argued that the development of wholesale trade over the course of history was based on two variables: the geography of distance and the profit of *arbitrage*, namely the difference in value of a commodity at its source, where it is abundant, and at its destination, where it is scarce. The result was that wholesale markets differed from local retail markets that mobilized products for regional consumers in three important ways. First, access to good transportation was important because of the distances over which products needed to move; the result was that wholesale markets were associated with ports, cities, and in locations where goods could be assembled for sale or transshipment. Second, they always contained greater numbers of foreign merchants than regional marketplaces did,[27] and this could result in the wholesale marketplace and its agents being physically separated from the local community. Third and finally, the need to collect, prepare, and hold large quantities of goods for transshipment[28] often led to the development of special infrastructure for the assembly, storage, and marketing of goods in transit as well as activities involving financing, insuring, and transporting goods (Miller 1969:173–176; Vance 1970:130–133).

Specialty markets are one type of wholesale market. These are locations where merchants gravitated to obtain specific commodities for export. Slaves and textile markets are two such examples of this type of wholesale market discussed below. It would be incorrect, however, to think of wholesale markets as dedicated solely to export. They were locations where goods were imported as well as exported,[29] and small retail markets could be held alongside or as part of export markets. Unless merchants brought silver with them, they had to sell the commodities that they brought before they could buy the goods that they wanted. The complexities of commodity exchange were sizable, as Polanyi makes clear in his discussion of the west African slave trade. Here merchants had difficulty calculating their profit because of the different exchange rates they encountered in every port along the west coast of Africa (Polanyi 1966). While the volume of goods transported varied with the type of goods sold, the effect of imported goods on local economies could be immense. Pliny the Elder stated that the amount of money spent on Indian luxury goods such as incense and spice during the mid-1st century AD averaged anywhere from 50 million to 100 million sesterces each year[30] (Young 2001:25).

There were a number of wholesale markets within the Mediterranean world that are well known from literary sources and archaeological excavations. These included Rhodes, Delos, Piraeus, and the Roman ports of Ostia, Portus, and Puteoli. Ports were vibrant, international, commercial centers in their time. Delos was a major grain and slave market, with harborside warehouses used to store goods for resale to other merchants (Hudson 1999a:142–144). Ostia and Portus were major harbors through which grain and many other wholesale goods were unloaded en route to the shops of Rome.[31] The port and wholesale market of Piraeus was the commercial entrepot and naval base of Athens. It was located 7 kilometers south of Athens, and the road between them was walled to protect the connection between port and city from external attack. Commercial dealings in Piraeus were different from those of the Agora in Athens, and illustrate how the external, wholesale trade was separated both commercially and socially from the normal retail trade in the ancient Greek marketplace.

Piraeus had several harbors, and port regulations stipulated where commercial ships could dock and unload based on their cargo tonnage. The *emporion* was the commercial district located along the east and north sides of the Great Harbor and was set off from the port by boundary markers (Figure 9.6). It was walled off from the rest of the city, had a large docking facility, and contained five *stoae* that provided warehouse and commercial functions for foreign merchants and shippers. All goods entering or leaving Piraeus[32] paid a 2% duty known as the *pentêkostê*, which was collected by port inspectors who supervised interactions and regulated the weights and measures of foreign merchants. Goods entering the port were sold at auction after they were set out for display to potential buyers in an area referred to as the *deigma*. The Laws of Solon prohibited foreigners from selling goods in the Agora in Athens, and foreign merchants (*emporos*) were not allowed to go beyond the boundaries of the harbor (Von Reden 1995:33). Piraeus also had a local agora known as the Hippodamian (Figure 9.6), but the goods sold arrived there by land (Wycherley 1978:263). The *emporion* dealt exclusively with the wholesale trade and goods transported to Piraeus from elsewhere in the Mediterranean (Garland 1987:68–97).

Athens, like Rome, depended on substantial imports of grain to feed its population, and Athenian law stated that two-thirds of all the grain entering

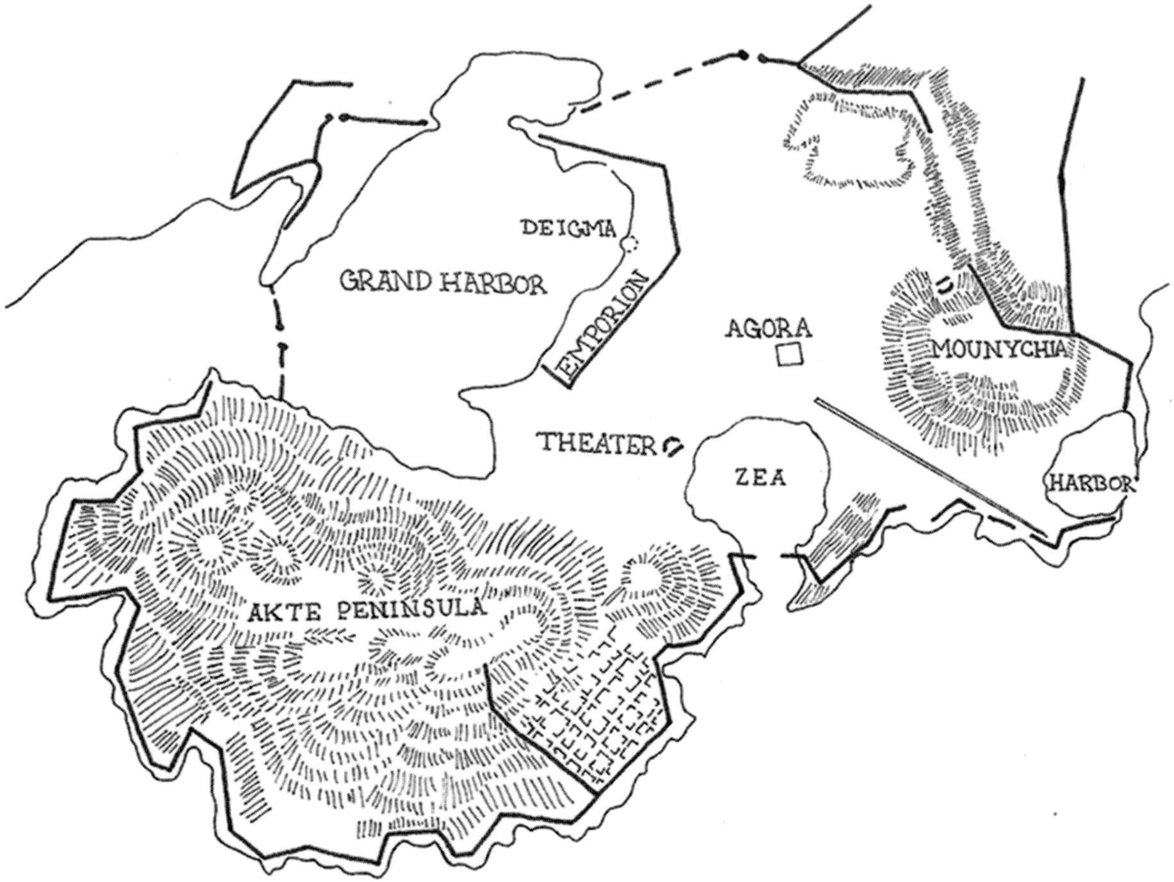

9.6 The port of Piraeus, Greece. (Redrawn from Garland 1987:Fig. 1 by Shea Rider and author)

the port of Piraeus had to be sold there.[33] Moreover, it was considered a capital offense for any resident of Athens to ship grain to any port other than Piraeus, thereby avoiding the controls that the state set on the price of grain (Garland 1987:89). Dependence on Piraeus was high, and it was through its doors that Pericles could make the boast that "[t]he products of the whole earth flow to us on account of the greatness of our polis and we enjoy them just as naturally as we do our own" (Garland 1987:27).

But Piraeus posed a dilemma for the Athenian *polis* because the foreigners and commercial trade they engaged in carried a social stigma. Piraeus was a heterogenous community, and in many ways more democratic in its practices and attitudes toward foreigners than Athens. This heterogeneity is evident in the composition of its resident and visiting population. Funerary plaques from the 4th century BC list individuals from sixty different Mediterranean states (Garland 1987:table 1). Likewise, dedications to seventeen deities have been recovered there, illustrating its ethnic and cultural diversity. Despite the income from the *pentêkostê* tariff and the importance of the navy as its main military defense,[34] Athens kept Piraeus, its merchants, and commercial middlemen at arm's length. They were a world apart (Von Reden 1995) and, like wholesale marketplaces in many other portions of the ancient world, operated in a vacuum within the societies where they were found.

The slave markets of west Africa are another example of wholesale markets operating in a vacuum within the societies where they were found. These specialty markets were responsible for assembling and exporting more than 12 million men and women to the Americas during the 16th through the 19th centuries AD (Eltis and Richardson 2010; Williams 1994). It was the study of the slave trade, the kingdom of Dahomey, and the slave marketplace at Whydah that led Karl Polanyi (1957, 1966) to formulate his port-of-trade model. The model was a good fit for this situation. Dahomey was an inland kingdom that wanted access to a coastal port to sell slaves and conquered the coastal city of Whydah in AD 1727 for that reason. According to an account written by an Englishman named William Snelgrave in 1734, Whydah was a free port that sold about 20,000 slaves each year to the English, Dutch, French, and Portuguese (Comegna 2016). The king of Dahomey required that foreign merchants reside in Whydah and not leave the town without the king's permission and a royal escort. The king dominated the trade since all slaves were owned by him. Slaves were auctioned off to foreign merchants in one specific field for a variety of merchandise that included guns, gunpowder, iron, coral, textiles, and other manufactured goods (Arnold 1957a). Alongside its slave market was the large local market of Zobeme that covered 14 acres, had shops, and sold a range of food and craft goods for local use (Arnold 1957b). While they occurred in the same town, the slave trade was the sole domain of the king[35] and was completely separate from local market activities.

Another well-known set of wholesale marketplaces were the Champagne fairs of medieval France described by Abu-Lughod (1989:51–77) for the 12th and 13th centuries AD. These markets were different from those discussed above in that they were not isolated or semi-isolated commercial areas in the societies where they were found. Instead, they were an integral feature of commercial economies in medieval Europe that were focal points for the production, mobilization, and export of textiles produced both within the Champagne region and beyond.[36] Six fairs were held throughout the course of the year, which rotated between four towns within the region.[37] The sale of wool and linen textiles was the center of the market and went on for 10 days. Merchants attended the fairs and brought textiles from all over France, which were purchased and exported for further processing or sale. The Italian cities of Venice and Genoa were important in purchasing goods for export, as was Florence, which bought textiles in the Champagne fairs to take back and process into luxurious Kalimali cloth (Reynolds 1931). Textiles from Provins and other Champagne fairs are reported being sold in cities as far away as the Levant and Constantinople (Pegolotti 1936). Two fairs were held annually in the city of Provins, which also intensified local production of high-quality textiles to meet the demand for sales within the fairs.

Retail and wholesale marketplaces were dynamic places. While specific marketplaces have been discussed, it is important to realize that they did not exist as isolated places. In developed commercial landscapes, marketplaces were incorporated into broader market systems that mobilized products and resources at the regional level. It is the nature of market systems that is examined next.

MARKET SYSTEMS

Human geographers have written about the ideal and actual structure of market systems under the rubric of central place theory (e.g., Christaller 1966; Lloyd and Dicken 1977; Lösch 1938; W. Skinner 1964, 1965; C. Smith 1976a, 1976b; Vance 1970). That literature is voluminous, and while worthy of discussion, it would move us away from a specific examination of ancient marketplaces. Nevertheless, identifying the relationship of one market to another is important because it provides insight into the development of the commercial landscape. The term "market system" implies a degree of coordination and scheduling between marketplaces. The location and scheduling of marketplaces impacts how goods, people, and information moved across the landscape. The shape of the market network can impact how much physical or social control can be exerted over the movement of products within it. For example, when Rome decided to make the free port of Rhodes more compliant to its wishes in the 2nd century BC, it simply designated the neighboring island of Delos as a free port to change the flow of goods between markets in the eastern Mediterranean. It worked. In a short span of time, Rhodes reported an 85% reduction in its harbor fee income (Finley 1985:130–131). All ports charged harbor fees, and for the wholesale merchant, the costs of operation exerted a strong effect on where they decided to conduct their business.

Reconstructing the structure of a market system is a complex undertaking. The nature of market integration has to do with the frequency and scheduling of adjacent marketplaces. How that scheduling is interpreted, in turn, depends on whether one takes a top-down or bottom-up view of commercial activity. The role of market systems can be examined from two alternative perspectives: as service networks for the retail consumers that they served and as a network through which merchants moved to supply and mobilize resources for both sellers and buyers.

The retail marketplace as an economic institution is designed to meet the needs of the consumer end users. As discussed above, marketplaces provide an efficient, low-cost way for households to provision themselves with goods that they did not produce. The way marketplaces are spaced and scheduled is a means to solve the provisioning problem. In areas where population density is low, and households are largely self-sufficient, marketplaces can take the form of periodic fairs such as those found in medieval Europe. The annual rendezvous of native North America groups are examples of long-cycle, periodic fairs. Conversely, daily markets are more common in urban centers where population densities are high. The issue becomes more complex in moderately dense rural areas where all marketplaces are periodic but are scheduled on shorter cycles in terms of days or weeks.

If market systems are conceptualized as service networks, then three aspects are important to consider for the households that used them: the distance or travel time to markets, the types of goods offered to meet provisioning needs, and the frequency with which markets are held and goods can be accessed. Of these three factors, distance to marketplaces provides a measure of accessibility that can be reconstructed from archaeological data. Goods sold and market frequency are also important but require specific historic information that is more difficult to obtain.

William Skinner's pioneering study of 20th-century AD market systems in rural China identified all three of these variables as features of market development. Skinner found that the development of complex market systems should be associated with increases in the density of markets per unit of area that reduced travel time for market shoppers, the types of goods offered for sale at all market levels, and the frequency with which they were convened (Skinner 1964, 1965). He found that the average service area for rural markets was 50 square kilometers. The average spacing between markets was 8 kilometers, which meant that the maximum walking distance to a nearby market was only

4.5 kilometers for each household. Market scheduling was complex and operated on several traditional calendar cycles, with most markets held every 3–5 days (Skinner 1964:11). This was a well-developed market landscape that provided ready access for goods to all consumers on a regular basis. It provides a baseline for comparison with other ancient and premodern market systems.

The data on market systems are limited for many ancient societies. The pre-Columbian Aztec society had a similarly well-developed market system, at least within their central heartland. Here consumers were located 4–8 kilometers from their closest marketplace (Hirth 2016:290), which, unlike markets in China, were all-day affairs.[38] Records from English manorial courts place the average distance that people traveled to markets at about 10 kilometers (Swanson 1999:32), although Landers (2003:100) notes that travel to specialized (wholesale) animal markets in western Brittany could take 2–3 days.

Luuk de Ligt (1993) provides a comprehensive discussion of periodic markets and fairs across the Roman empire. He does not provide an average distance between markets beyond saying that no rural market was located within 10 kilometers of a market town (de Ligt 1993:129). More specific information, however, is provided by Morley (1996:map 3), who plots the location of rural marketplaces (*nundinae*) in the region of Campania around Pompeii. All these markets were located on roads with an average distance of 21.3 kilometers between marketplaces. This spacing meant that the average distance a householder would have to travel to the nearest marketplace would be on the order of 10–11 kilometers. This makes the Roman system about one-half as efficient as the premodern Chinese rural market system and two-thirds as efficient as the Aztec network in terms of market spacing, depending on the form of travel used to reach marketplaces. Nevertheless, from the point of consumers, the rural Roman markets would have provided fairly good service to rural households that were located within a single day's round-trip travel to market centers.[39]

Market systems were also used by merchants to carry goods for sale to consumers who wanted them, as well as to buy specific goods for resale elsewhere. Periodic markets persist because they permit a denser concentration of marketplaces than daily markets (Skinner 1964:10) while providing cost-efficient means for merchants to supply them. Periodic markets within a region usually occurred on alternate days, which enabled merchants and householders to travel between them with a minimum loss of time. This allowed the merchants to establish a regular market circuit within a region, as well as moving from one market circuit to another when a marketplace was located at the interface between them (Figure 9.7). Traversing market systems allowed merchants to move across ecological regions collecting different resources that could be sold in other marketplaces along the way (Bromley et al. 1975; Gezann 1978:188; Gormsen 1978; Symanski and Webber 1974). Periodic

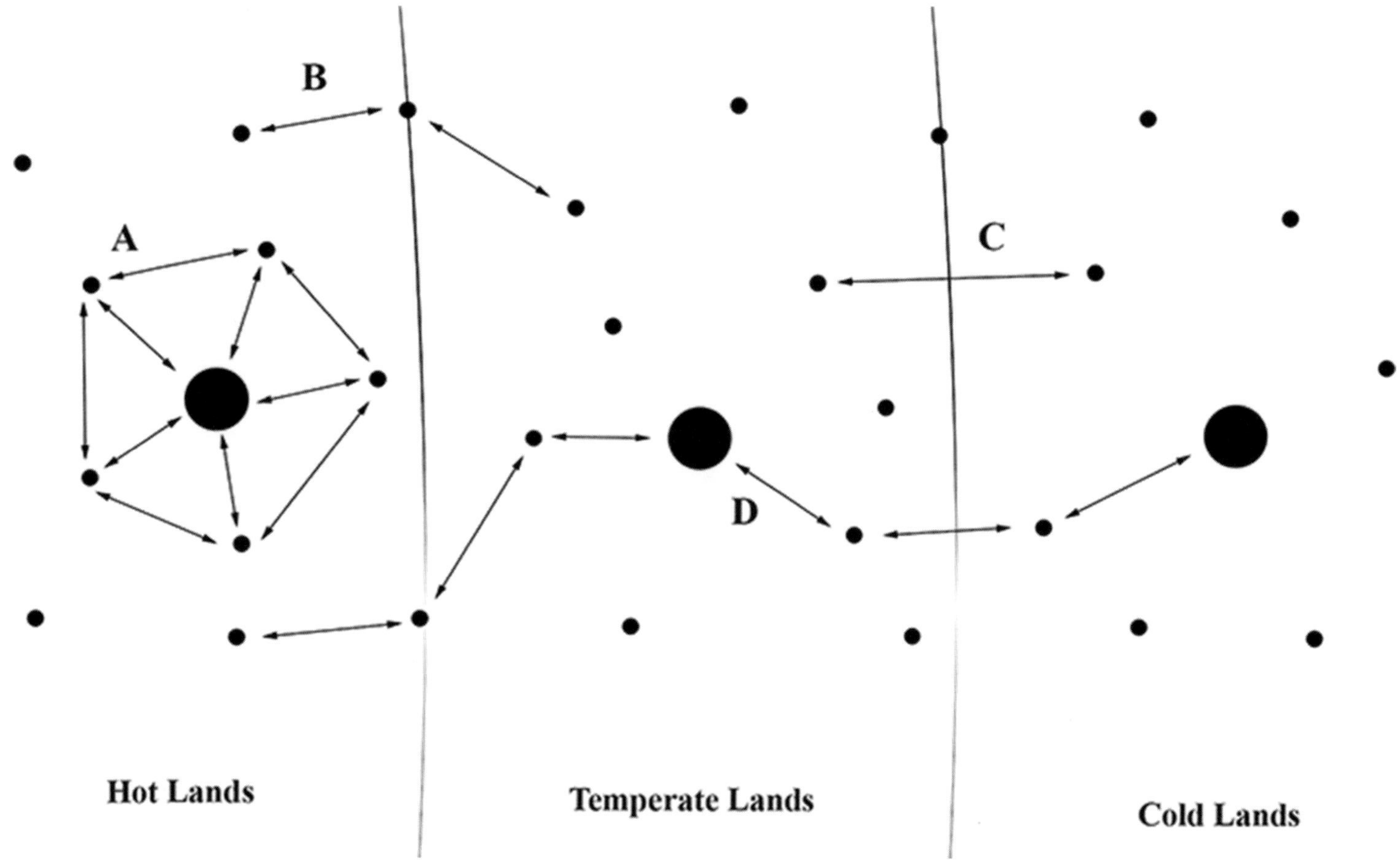

9.7 Merchant circuits between large and small markets across three different environmental zones. (Illustration by Dylan Davis and the author 2019)

marketplaces represent bulking places for goods that householders can sell for other goods they need. They have been an important mechanism for mobilizing rural goods for use in urban areas throughout the premodern world (de Ligt 1993:86; Gormsen 1978; Hodder 1971; Parthasarathi 2011:21; Symanski and Webber 1974).

We know that merchants traveled from marketplace to marketplace supplying goods to consumers who frequented them. But were past rural marketplaces also used as points of supply to mobilize goods into larger commercial networks or for urban consumption? We know they were used as such among the Aztecs. Long-distance *pochteca* merchants traveled as far as 1,000 kilometers buying wealth goods at moderate prices where they occurred and transporting them back to the Aztec capital for sale in the marketplace. The same was true for staple goods at shorter scales of interaction. De Ligt (1993:129, 135) proposed that rural Roman farmers sold produce and craft goods in local marketplaces. If they did so, then these goods could have moved out of the region and into regional urban centers. Morley (1996:166–174) believes that market calendars known as *indices mundinarii* confirm that merchants circulated throughout the Roman hinterland buying and mobilizing products from rural markets for consumption in cities. These calendars provided information on when rural markets convened and would have been useful for merchants interested in buying and selling goods at them. How much of a role rural marketplaces had in provisioning larger urban communities remains unclear, but they did produce goods moving through the Roman commercial system.

ON THE ORIGIN OF MARKETPLACES

The marketplace was a fundamental feature of economic life in the past just as it is today. The examples provided illustrate that marketplaces varied in size and organization at different times and places throughout the past. Whether they were organized as fairs, bazaars, periodic markets, rendezvous, shop economies, or unscheduled spontaneous interactions, marketplaces were an important provisioning mechanism at all levels of society. The ubiquity of marketplaces across the ancient and premodern worlds is clear. What is not clear is how and when marketplaces first originated. The fact that marketplaces occurred under different conditions in both state and nonstate societies suggests that they were present and operating long before written history began to document them. Table 9.2 summarizes some of the models that have been proposed for market origins. Unfortunately, our present understanding of market origins is more theoretical than empirical, but it is a useful place to begin discussing the variables believed to have been important in their development.

TABLE 9.2 *Theories for the development of marketplaces*

Theories of marketplace development	Major advocates
Natural marketplace development	Smith (1827)
Anti-market position	Finley (1985), Polanyi (1944)
External trade origins	Polanyi (1944), Vance (1970)
Urban marketplaces	Appleby (1976)
Labor efficiency	Blanton (1983)
Sponsored market exchange	Polanyi (1944, 1963)

The Natural Market Model

This is the traditional view of market development proposed by Adam Smith nearly 250 years ago. This school of thought sees marketplaces developing from the natural propensity of individuals to truck and barter. Variations in climate, elevation, and environmental diversity create differential distributions of natural resources that fostered symbiotic interactions between groups in different areas (e.g., Sanders 1962). The establishment of interhousehold exchange and interaction networks would have mobilized and moved resources over space. Marketplaces were seen as the natural outgrowth of earlier trading relationships that developed as populations grew in size and complexity. From this perspective, marketplaces were a bottom-up development following the general tenets of central place theory (Christaller 1966; Lösch 1938; W. Skinner 1965; C. Smith 1974). The examples given above for spontaneous trade at pilgrimage sites and religious festivals support the natural tendency of individuals to truck and barter.

The Anti-market Model

This is the view of Karl Polanyi and Moses Finley, and it is diametrically opposed to the natural market model. This school of thought considers market exchange to be an unnatural human activity. Polanyi's anti-market perspective has been the basis for the substantivist approach in economic anthropology and the primitivist school in classical archaeology. Both have been extensively critiqued and debated, and those arguments will not be restated here (but see Cook 1966; Dalton 1968; Hann and Hart 2009; Love 1991; Silver 1985, 1995). But it is important to be terminologically clear. When Polanyi denied the existence of markets in antiquity, he was talking about *market economies* as they are defined earlier in this chapter. For Polanyi the price-setting mechanism was the governing principle of a market economy,[40] and he did not see evidence that it applied equally to all items ranging from food, goods, land, and labor to credit, storage, transportation, and insurance. His conclusion was that the "market" did not exist in antiquity. Barter was seen as too disruptive a force for negotiating price within society. What Polanyi ignored is that mutual trust is often established even in the initial stages of barter (Khuri 1968). Instead, he felt that prices had to be set administratively or through tradition. Polanyi did not deny that exchange took place, but when it occurred between individuals within society, price was established as a precondition for interaction.

Despite what others have said about Polanyi, he accepted the notion that marketplaces existed in the ancient past. He also accepted that barter and forms of market exchange were components of archaic economic systems. But it is better to let Polanyi speak for himself. With regard to Aristotle's analysis of the economy, Polanyi said that Aristotle

> failed to see how impracticable it was to ignore the existence of markets at a time when Greek economy had made itself dependent upon wholesale trading and loaned capital. For this was the century when Delos and Rhodes were developing into emporia of freight insurance, sea-loans, and giro-banking, compared with which the Western Europe of a thousand years later was the very picture of primitivity.
>
> (Polanyi 1944:53)

Regarding local markets, Polanyi states:

> The typical local market at which housewives procure some of their daily needs, and growers of grain or vegetables as well as local craftsmen offer their wares for sale, shows an amazing indifference to time and place. Gatherings of this kind are not only fairly general in primitive societies, but remain almost unchanged right up to the middle of the eighteenth century in the most advanced countries of Western Europe.
>
> (Polanyi 1944:61)

And regarding barter:

> acts of barter are ... usually embedded in long-range relations implying trust and confidence ... As a rule, he who barters merely enters into a ready-made type of transaction in which both the objects and their equivalent amounts are given.
>
> (Polanyi 1944:60)

Karl Polanyi never denied the existence of the marketplace or balanced market exchange (barter) in antiquity. He only asserted that they were *minor*, rather than *dominant*, aspects of the economy that did not lead to the development of internal price-setting markets for goods and services. So, if Karl Polanyi acknowledged the existence of marketplaces in the premodern past, to what does he trace their origin? His views are best characterized as the external trade theory of marketplace origins.

The External Trade Theory

This theory argues that marketplaces were a result of contact with merchants who traded in foreign goods. Marketplaces from this perspective developed as nonlocal goods entered the region from the outside rather than from the exchange of food and other staple goods that readily moved through other forms of exchange. Because the domestic economy was oriented to self-sufficiency, it was assumed the market for external trade goods resided with the wealthy elites. Furthermore, because the demand for nonlocal goods was relatively small, marketplaces were seen as originating as peripheral and periodic places in the economy (Bromley et al. 1975:533).

Support for this theory can be found in ethnographic accounts of African societies where marketplaces often developed because of the outside stimulus for interregional trade (Bromley et al. 1975:533; Schwimmer 1976). A modified version of this theory can be found in the work of Henri Pirenne (1974), who linked the development of markets and cities in medieval Europe to the revival of interregional trade from the 11th century AD onward. In a more general vein, Vance (1970:49–52) argued that external trade was the basis for the general development of retailing. Karl Polanyi, however, has presented the most comprehensive view of the external trade theory. For Polanyi, the marketplace was a foreign element, carried out by foreigners, and operating outside the normal bounds of society.[41] He traced the earliest marketplaces to what was described above as wholesale and specialty markets, such as those of Delos, Rhodes, and Piraeus. In his words,

> The presence or absence of markets or money does not necessarily affect the economic system of a primitive society.... The reasons are simple. *Markets are not institutions functioning mainly within an economy, but without.* They are meeting places of long-distance trade. Local markets proper are of little consequence. (Polanyi 1944:57; emphasis added)

The Urban Marketplace

This model argues that the food needs of large cities will result in the coincident development of marketplaces. Archaeologists beginning with Gordon Childe have reasoned that the appearance of nonfood producers in urban centers resulted in the need to import and distribute food and other resources in large cities (e.g., Silver 1995:153). Both Athens and Rome depended on the importation of grain from the surrounding countryside and beyond (White 1970:393). The same was true for the growth of large medieval cities (Braudel 1986:38; Hodges 1982:24–25). Geographers and historians alike have been concerned with the question of whether large cities were generative and producer communities within their regional economies (Jacobs 1969, 1985) or parasitic and consumer cities draining resources from their surrounding hinterlands to support their resident populations (Harriss and Harriss 2017; Hoselitz 1955; Morley 1996).

The structure of the urban economy in ancient times would have varied with the size of cities and the relationship that urban residents had to their suburban farmlands. Patricia Fall has identified an increase in the rural production of secondary food products coincident with the development of urban centers in the Levant during the Bronze Age, which suggests outlying farms were involved in supplying urban centers with food (Fall et al. 2002). Marketplaces were the most likely way that this food was distributed. Jongman (1988:158, 192), in his analysis of Pompeii's urban economy, proposes that the city was largely a consumer city where resident elites were supported by the rents drawn from land in the rural countryside (see also Kehoe 2007). Ethnographic study of market development in highland Peru reinforces the urban market model since food demand was a primary factor in the development of regional production to supply urban needs (Appleby 1976).

The Labor Efficiency Model

This model links the development of regional marketplaces to the intensification of agricultural production in state-level societies. The marketplace in these societies is a solution to increased labor demands placed on households involved in intensive agricultural production, particularly year-round irrigation. The result to households under these conditions was less time for alternative provisioning activities and the need to rely on craft specialists and the marketplace for provisioning needs of nonfood items that they could no longer meet themselves (Blanton 1983; Blanton et al. 1999:97–98). The development of canal irrigation in the Valley of Oaxaca, Mexico, perhaps as early as 500 BC where this model was proposed, is also linked to the emergence of large regional populations, enhanced state resource demands, and the growth of urban centers. While year-round agriculture can directly affect the work budgets of individual households, this is not a universal theory for market development since large-scale hydraulic societies can develop without marketplaces, which was the case for coastal Peru (Billman 2002; Moseley 1992:162–184; Netherly 1984).

Sponsored Market Exchange

This model accounts for a good deal of the cross-cultural variation found in marketplaces and market behavior. It begins by recognizing that balanced market exchange occurred both spontaneously and through structured social relationships in societies at all levels of complexity and organization. So, in this regard Adam Smith was correct: people do truck and barter to meet their resource needs. But they do more than that. They developed interhousehold exchange networks, gift relationships, and trade partners to access the resources they wanted and needed. Marshal Sahlins (1972) has illustrated that balance and reciprocity in exchange relationships is directly proportional to social distance. The closer the relationship, the less exact balance is expected, and the more credit is employed in the exchange of goods. With greater social distance, exchanges are more closely balanced and immediate. Market exchange as defined at the beginning of this chapter was one component of household provisioning, and it produced the spontaneous trade at small impromptu marketplaces that could spring up at pilgrimage sites, religious festivals, and other social events.

But Polanyi and his substantivist colleagues were correct in one regard. The active negotiation of value through market exchange can be disruptive and contentious. Nowhere is this greater than when individuals of different social rank and from different communities, ethnic groups, or societies come together in a formally convened marketplace. It is for that reason that the "place" where large-scale market exchanges occurred must be different: it must be a place apart, a liminal place where normal rules or modes of social interaction do not apply. That is what formal marketplaces are. They are special, liminal places set aside by sacred and/or social proscriptions so that individuals with no or minimal social connectedness can negotiate value and accept or reject offers of exchange without immediate or later social consequences. In short, the market was established as a liminal place so that what happened in the marketplace stayed in the marketplace. It was why marketplaces were often bounded places, like the Greek *agorae*, and recognized as sacred locales in many societies (Hudson 1999a:142; Rauh 1993:147; Sen 1998:26–37; Silver 1995:18).

Sponsorship appears to have been a key ingredient in the development of early marketplaces. This could take the form of sponsorship by a community leader or prominent individual as was the case of New Guinea marketplaces (Harding 1967:4, 166; Pospisil 1963) as well as in association with recognized religious events, celebrations, and festivals (Abbott 2010; Abbott et al. 2007).[42] Sponsorship provides assurances of safe conduct for attendees traveling to and from the market, and protection within the marketplace should disputes arise. Sponsorship helped to structure the rules of operation and interaction that included setting the value (price) for some goods using traditional means to minimize disagreements.[43] Oversight in some form was, and still is, a standard feature of marketplaces to reinforce the principle of liminality, guard against theft, check the honesty of weights and measures, safeguard against false dealings, adjudicate disputes when they happen, and ensure the safety of all attending participants. Sponsorship of marketplaces continued in complex societies well after the rules of market liminality were well understood by market participants because of the prestige they bestowed to leaders and the fact that not all people play by the rules.

The marketplace was an institution constructed as a safe place for carrying out market exchange on a large scale, with more individuals and involving more goods than could occur through impromptu encounters or intercommunity social interactions (Malinowski 1967a; Mayer 2002). The liminality of the place was often linked to social and supernatural means, while sponsors underwrote and monitored safe interactions within the marketplace. Local and nonlocal goods were exchanged together or separately depending on cultural values of the individuals and societies involved. While the marketplace served the people who made exchanges, it also provided an opportunity for taxation by the sponsors.[44]

So, what can be said about market origins given the diverse and contrasting theoretical perspectives? It is here that a more eclectic theoretical approach pays dividends as there are important developmental insights in several of these theoretical models. We know, for example, that resources are differentially distributed over the landscape and that human societies regularly engaged in trade to procure them at least as early as the fourth millennium BC. So credit needs to go to Adam Smith because, as discussed both here and in Chapter 7, all human societies engaged in some form of gift and reciprocal exchange as a regular feature of the domestic economy. Karl Polanyi recognized this by acknowledging the antiquity and importance of barter for normal domestic provisioning. The practice of trading and the appearance of spontaneous marketplaces (e.g., *gimwali*) reveal that marketplaces can occur anywhere when people come together and there is a demand for goods. The demand for goods drove the operation of rendezvous trade fairs in native North America just as they did at collective feasts and ritual celebrations in Papua New Guinea (e.g., *juwo* feasts) and throughout the American Southwest (Abbott 2010). The appearance of urban centers centralized demand and fixed it on the landscape so that individuals with staple or high-value resources to trade could be reasonably sure of finding a market for them. The danger of the marketplace is that the larger it was, the greater the potential conflict between individuals from different social groups. In these situations, marketplaces operated better when there was some level of supervisory oversight.

There are elements of value in most of these theoretical perspectives. But the differential distribution of resources and the natural propensity of individuals to obtain them through exchange represent the first principles for marketplace development. Group congregations for ritual or informal social activities were opportunities for exchange and for marketplaces to appear. Within these contexts, the need for supervisory oversight provided an opportunity for elite involvement to enhance the safety and regularity of marketplace reunions.

THE MARKETPLACE AS AN INTERSECTING INSTITUTION

However they originated, once they were formed, marketplaces often grew to become one of the primary economic institutions within society. Households may produce food and other goods for auto-consumption, but it is the marketplace that allows them to convert the items they produced into alternative goods as their needs require. As mentioned at the beginning of this chapter, the marketplace was also the place of considerable ad hoc social interaction between members of society. It is where old friends met, new friendships were made, individuals gossiped, and people shared the news of the day. Although the focus here is on the economic functions that marketplaces provided, they were more than just places where goods were bought and sold. Along with periodic ritual celebrations, they provided a significant degree of day-to-day social interaction within the societies where they were found.

Most marketplaces were retail markets whose primary function was to help provision individual households. Provisioning was made possible through the markets' resource mobilization function. They brought together large quantities of food, craft goods, and other resources that were made available to the individuals and institutions that wanted them. As such, they were centers of resource distribution that, unlike forms of administrative redistribution (e.g., Polanyi 1957), occurred with little institutional organization beyond supervisory oversight. Marketplaces provided households with an important conversion function beyond selling their excess production for goods that they could not produce. Depending on the society, they may be the only place that households could convert the food and products they produced into the currency required to pay their rents or taxes. For households involved in specialized craft production, the marketplace often was the lifeline through which they supported themselves. Even where craft production was a part-time activity, the sale of a few textiles or a small quantity of manufactured goods through the marketplace could be an important addition to the total household subsistence budget.

The structure of marketplaces varied to the degree that wholesale and retail activities were integrated or segregated in different places. However it was organized, the market centralized a range of different crafting, retail, and wholesale functions. It was where merchants, shippers, producer-sellers, bankers, and importers interfaced with one another. It is where commercial contracts such as the commenda were struck and financing was obtained when necessary for business enterprises. While loans could be obtained for different purposes, it often was the first step in losing both freedom and property (Hudson 1999c:489). When families fell into distress, the last thing they sold was their land. They sold children first, then livestock, then their labor as bondsmen, and then, when all else failed, they sold their land (Hudson

1999b:461). Where shops were the foundation of retail market activity, households could obtain credit for sales and purchases based on their social relationship to shop owners.

The marketplace also was the location of the money changer when formal currencies became the means through which large and small purchases were made. The use of some form of currency facilitated purchases in the marketplace, and money changers were the agents that transformed a range of products into negotiable currencies whatever they might be. Money could be minted into divisible currencies as occurred in the Old World, or it could take the form of the varied forms of commodity money found in societies around the world. Cacao beans, copper axes, standardized white cotton textiles (*quachtli*), and quills of gold dust were the forms of commodity money that Aztec money changers (*tlapatlac*) regularly worked with. Elsewhere commodity money included items such as cowrie shells, boars' tusks, copper ringlets, brass rods, textiles, and a wide range of beads, bracelets, and necklaces. In premarket economies many of these items were prestige goods and wealth items used in a range of social transactions that included bridewealth, gifts, death payments, ritual exchanges, and debt repayments. As items of value, many of these wealth goods were transformed into units of account to facilitate commercial exchange.

But it was within the context of the marketplace that formal minted and divisible currencies came into existence. The first coins in the Old World were minted in Lydia sometime during the 7th century BC. These coins were made of electrum, an alloy of silver and gold. Both of these precious metals already were used as forms of payment and units of account much earlier in time, and the minting of coins served to standardize and simplify calculating exchange rates and trade. By the 6th century BC, coins were minted in silver across Greece, and the use of coinage quickly became an administrative racket. Cities across the Mediterranean could require that business transactions be conducted in "coin of the realm," and money changers[45] appeared in the marketplace to help make that happen. In Greece and Rome, professional bankers were known as *trapezites*, which comes from the word for table (*trapeza*) on which the banker or money lender converted currencies, made loans, collected debts, and otherwise conducted business (Andreau 1999:30; Goetzmann 2017:82). Money changers in the Greco-Roman world commonly charged 5% for changing coins; some cities required that all changing be done with a specific company from which the city got a commission (i.e., kickback) as a form of conversion tax. This commercial dimension helps explain why cities actively minted their own coins (Andreau 1999:37).

The marketplace was also the place for contacting specific types of services. The New Testament parable of the vineyard workers (Matthew 20:1–16) stipulates that wage laborers could be hired by the day in eastern

Mediterranean marketplaces. The same was probably true for contracting building and short-term hauling services. In wholesale markets commercial agents and factors were in ready supply. A commercial agent is a person who solicits or conducts business for an individual usually for a percentage of the value of the goods. A factor is a commercial intermediary who takes possession of goods and sells them in their name. These individuals were common in interregional wholesale trade, serving as intermediaries and facilitating interaction between individuals of different cultures (Cohen 1965; Das Gupta 2001b:69; Greif 1989). They provided a range of services that reduced the costs and risks of business for traveling merchants, including arranging sales, running hostels, and providing food and safety for transport animals in caravanserai.

The marketplace served as the intersection for all the commercial interests operating within society. It was also where formal institutions such as temples or palaces could convert their wealth and resources into alternative goods that they might require for supporting personnel, hosting events, and sponsoring feasts or celebrations of different kinds. It is not surprising that it is hard to find a state-level society across the ancient world where the marketplace was not an integral feature of its commercial economy. The Inka of the pre-Columbian Andes are perhaps the only exception to this rule.

SUMMARY

Marketplaces were important economic institutions that were extremely difficult to supplant once households came to rely on them for their provisioning needs. Daniel Defoe, in his book *A Tour through the Whole Island of Great Britain*, encapsulates the durability of periodic fairs in the rural English countryside with his description of the annual Stourbridge fair in AD 1724. The fair was held in a large cornfield near Stourbridge; if the crop was not harvested by a specific date in August, it would get trampled by fair merchants coming in to set up their tents and booths. According to Defoe, the fair was diverse and consisted of a wide variety of retailers that included everyone from goldsmiths, toy sellers, braziers, turners, and milliners to hatters, haberdashers, mercers, and drapers. Perhaps in revenge for the lack of respect shown to the owners of the field, Defoe says that plowmen would enter the field on a specific day in September, rousting merchants "with plough and cart and overthrow all into the dirt" (Defoe and Coulson 1991; Vance 1970:66). The market ruled ruthlessly supreme at Stourbridge, at least within its assigned dates of operation.

Market exchange and marketplaces occurred both spontaneously and through structured trade partnerships and organized events in societies at all levels of complexity. The foregoing discussion has attempted to survey the range of different forms of marketplaces and the conditions under which they occurred. Marketplaces could be big or small, spontaneous or scheduled, retail or wholesale, or geared toward selling a broad range of staple goods or a narrow specialty. But the essence of the marketplace was that it was a place with unique rules of economic engagement. It was a place where individuals could negotiate value and refuse or accept offers for exchanges without the fear of social reprisal. How marketplaces became linked in a broader market system of coordinated places is a separate issue, but this occurred after marketplaces were established as a regular feature of the economic landscape. The available evidence suggests that the emergence of interconnected networks of marketplaces (i.e., market systems) was linked to the development of state institutions,[46] urban communities, and the need to mobilize resources to support them (Smith 1976c:50–51).

Finally, the question of how and why early marketplaces developed is an issue that requires specific, additional problem-oriented research. Identifying ancient marketplaces and the effect that they had on provisioning patterns remains a challenging problem that needs to be addressed. Archaeologists are in a good position to do so because they have the tools to directly examine the effects that market interaction has on the consumer populations that use markets (e.g., Hirth 1998). For this to happen, however, more researchers will have to recognize the marketplace as a separate institution worthy of study rather than treating it as an embedded or secondary feature of the societies where marketplaces occur.

TEN

ON FIRST PRINCIPLES OF THE ANCIENT ECONOMY

A Concluding Discussion

He who would do good to another must do it in Minute Particulars; General Good is the plea of the scoundrel, hypocrite and flatterer: For Art and Science cannot exist but in minutely organized Particulars.

(William Blake)

Why should we be concerned about the specifics of the ancient economy? Why not just focus on the broad sweep of cultural development and look for correlates between the economy and aspects of political development, population growth, land reforms, social stratification, wars and trade disruptions, and the appearance of new technologies that could impact forms of production as occurred with the industrial revolution? All of these are important and interrelated historic processes that impacted the development of complex society and shaped the conditions of their economic growth and organization.

The reason simply is that structure is important. That is the point that William Blake is making in the epigraph at the start of this concluding chapter. He is not advocating particularism for its own sake. Good social science requires a thorough understanding of the particulars of how things operate. As in most forms of organization, the devil is in the details. Humans adapt to their environments, not as individuals but in groups of different sizes that anthropologists have identified as families, bands, associations, communities, tribes, and states. Within these groups, the survival of the individual is worked out. When internal or external pressures threaten the livelihoods and survivability of groups, they adapt, reorganize, and do the best they can under changing conditions. Organizational structures, therefore, are important adaptive units involved in cultural evolution and change. Groups may increase or decrease in scale, complexity, or integration depending on the forces or conditions of change that they face. But the greatest improvements in output and production efficiency in the ancient past were the result of small changes or minor adjustments in how work groups were organized. Human groups are flexible, and their flexibility is why they have been so successful.

From this perspective, the economy can be viewed as groups and individuals doing different types of work in different places. How that work was organized in different contexts is important and is the essence of what defines the ancient economy. Did work take place primarily in household contexts or in special places apart from domestic living? What was the range of informal institutions found in society, and how important were they in assisting households in their livelihood pursuits? How did formal institutions that integrated society obtain the resources they used and needed? Did they produce resources to meet their needs, mobilize them from their constituents through forms of taxation, or both? These are all essential questions that need to be answered if the goal is to obtain a comprehensive understanding of how ancient and premodern economies were organized and operated.

The focus of this volume was twofold. The first was to explore the range of variation in economic structures so that researchers have a template for appreciating the diversity in how human societies were organized to produce and distribute resources and get work done. Its goal was to highlight the tremendous diversity of ways that the ancient economy could operate, and which need to be considered when discussing the modes of economic organization in any particular time and place. The second objective was to present a framework for identifying different forms of economic organization that can be used for broader comparative analysis. The framework proposed has three components: the domestic economy and the institutional economy, with its formal and informal sectors. Forms of organization were selected and examined without concern for their historical relationships to one another. They were selected to evaluate whether the analytical framework proposed had cross-cultural relevance for describing a wide range of economic activity.

Karl Polanyi and his substantivist colleagues (Polanyi et al. 1957) argued that the economy was embedded in all aspects of social interaction and therefore could not be examined as a separate domain of study apart from the broader culture. They were correct that it was embedded, but they never attempted to explain why this was the case beyond a general distaste for the principles of maximization and formal economic theory. The result at least within archaeology is that the ancient economy is rarely studied for its own merit and often is subsumed in discussions of political evolution and broad cultural change.

The reality of the situation is that the economy permeated every aspect of ancient society. The exchange of material goods reinforced every important and socially meaningful life event, as well as building, maintaining, and solidifying social interaction and alliances between societies (Dalton 1977). Just as economic exchange creates value (Appadurai 1986a:3; 1986b), so too the exchange of things creates meaning and reinforces memory. This was the essence of why native American societies exchanged wampum to commemorate events and why they wore the clothes and medals given to them by the US government when treaties were broken and renegotiated. It was to reinforce and reactivate the material memory of things established and agreed on.

But the economy was embedded in the society for another reason. Culture often provided a better long-term memory for solving economic problems involving risk than did individual decision makers. People are notorious short-term problem solvers with imperfect knowledge about all the conditions they face and the long-term consequences that economic decisions may have. Halstead and O'Shea (1989) have argued that households only have the capacity to remember and adapt to short-term environmental fluctuations, with longer-term fluctuations left unaccounted for or dealt with by institutions above the level of individual domestic units. From this perspective, tradition provides a framework for guiding the overall survivability of the group. This is why Polanyi (1957) argued that the economy was an instituted process. It was not because it was a secondary aspect of society, but because it was too important to be left solely in the hands of the immediate decision makers with a bounded understanding of their situation. While Polanyi advocated direct institutional involvement, the view favored here is that the cultural norms of society provided guidelines for the economy to run smoothly and with minimal short- and long-term risk to its members.

FIRST PRINCIPLES: DIVERSITY AND THE DOMESTIC ECONOMY

To understand the ancient economy requires that we look first to where it all began. The domestic economy was the foundation of human society and needs to be recognized and incorporated into every discussion of the ancient economy. Households in the past, as they are today, were in business for themselves and their structure varied across time and space as they adapted to new conditions and situations. Households contained the majority of labor and produced and consumed most of the resources within society. Self-sufficiency was their goal and that included an active involvement in exchange networks to obtain resources that they could not produce. Households intensified production where they could and did not always require an administrative agency to construct terraces or irrigation systems for them. The domestic economy could self-organize to get those tasks done. The production capacity of households was illustrated in Chapter 2 by the role they played in the development of the trans-Indian Ocean trade in Indian cotton textiles.

Because households were in business for themselves, it is not surprising that they employed both entrepreneurial and conservative economic strategies in pursuit of their livelihoods. They were entrepreneurial in that they sought new ways of meeting their social and biological needs. But they were conservative by being risk averse. In charactering risk, William Faulkner said that you cannot swim for new horizons until you have courage to lose sight of the shore. Unfortunately, households that took risks and lost sight of fundamental subsistence needs could drown in bad decision making. From an evolutionary perspective, the households that survived tended to be ones that worked hard, avoided risk, and developed informal support networks that could provide social and economic assistance when needed. Intensification of production was not the only or even the best avenue to reduce subsistence risk. Many households mediated risk by diversifying their subsistence pursuits and adopting mixed economic strategies that combined foraging, hunting, agriculture, and/or craft production to produce a balanced and dependable subsistence base. From an evolutionary perspective, successful households were those that produced surpluses that buffered risk, provided the means to mobilize labor, and supplied goods that could be used in both commercial and noncommercial forms of exchange. The diversity of household economic practices is a testimony to their ability to adapt to changing cultural and environmental circumstances.

The second conclusion is that the household was more than just a place where people lived. It was also an organizational body that served as a template for formal institutions in society. The temple was the house of the deity in the same way that the early administrative palace was the house of the ruler. Social and political status was expressed in terms of household, familial, and kinship relationships across Mesopotamia during the Bronze Age. The household was the model for early formal institutions and had amplified versions of the same rights and privileges of normal households. Institutional households mobilized corvée labor for their own support in the same way that domestic households mobilized labor through festive and reciprocal work parties. Feasts and celebrations were important both within and between households, and institutional households followed similar practices mobilizing resources from constituent members for specific purposes. Finally, the house also was the model for many early merchant firms. Just as households accessed community property and diversified their internal economic activities to support themselves, institutional households did the same but on a larger scale.

The question of property rights, resource ownership, and how they originated is an important and challenging topic (Earle 1991, 2000). In Chapter 2 it was argued that claims to resource rights and ownership were based on the labor invested in them, whether they were agricultural fields, herds of domesticated animals, or stands of wild resources. The same principle was used at the community and regional level in terms of landesque capital. The labor invested in agricultural infrastructure (e.g., terraces, irrigation canals), mortuary monuments, and other ceremonial structures demonstrated long-term use and claims to land. Formal institutions can individualize or privatize resources and property claims in the same way by mobilizing labor and intensifying production on a regular basis. Religious institutions have the additional advantage of basing property rights on ideological principles. This could be expressed in terms of "all land belongs to god," the strength of which increased as these principles become universalized. However the concept of private property developed, it is clear that individual property assignments and land purchases were a regular feature of Bronze Age societies in the Old World (Chapter 5). But like hereditary claims to land by individual families, ownership of resources was ultimately based on the labor invested in them.[1]

A major flaw of past research was to classify ancient economies in monolithic terms, as redistributive, market, industrial, or gift economies. This tendency goes back to the Marxist tradition of characterizing societies in terms of a dominant mode of production (Germanic, Asiatic, feudal, capitalistic, etc.). Likewise, researchers often talk about "political economy" without understanding how the economy was structured as a whole. This type of essentialism is easy to understand because it allows researchers to make broad generalizations about the economy in relation to levels of cultural complexity. But it creates the *mutual exclusivity fallacy*: the idea that different forms of production and exchange did not coexist and operate in the same or different sectors of the economy at the same time (Plog 1993:288). If recent research illustrates anything, it is that multiple modes of production and distribution coexisted and continued to do so over very long periods of time (Sinopoli 1988). As a recent discussion points out, "the main problem hindering research is assuming 'mutual exclusivity' of theoretical perspectives, that reciprocity cannot coexist with redistribution, and that neither can coexist with market economies" (Oka and Kusimba 2008:366).

THE REALM OF INSTITUTIONS

Several chapters were dedicated to the discussion of formal and informal economic institutions. Informal economic institutions are voluntary and ad hoc mechanisms, principles, and customs that households employ to mobilize labor, access resources, and obtain the forms of interhousehold support that they require. Informal institutions have been identified (Erasmus 1956; Stone et al. 1990), but their importance in the development of ancient and premodern economies is rarely emphasized (but see Dietler and Hayden 2001). These ad hoc structures did not capture the interest of early ethnographers and are almost impossible to identify in the archaeological record. This is unfortunate because informal economic institutions were key features in the successful adaptation of households in two important ways.

First, households as the primary units of production in society were proactive in solving the resource acquisition problems that they faced. When multiple households faced the same problems, they formed voluntary groups to solve them collectively. One of the main obstacles for household development was limited labor (Chayanov 1966; Durrenberger 1984). Reciprocal and festive work groups were solutions to this problem (Chapter 3) and provided households with the ability to collectively mobilize labor to get work done. Robert Netting (1989, 1993) demonstrated that households can intensify agricultural production in ways that included the construction of terraces and irrigation systems (e.g., Araral 2013:861; Lansing 1987; Ostrom 1992). Interhousehold work groups were a way to mobilize labor when the scale of work required more than one household could manage. Interhousehold assistance networks were structured along the lines of family and friendship and were the first recourse in situations when help or advice was needed. More generally, informal economic institutions were first-order mechanisms used to overcome the limitations in labor, time, and scheduling that households faced in producing the resources that they needed.

Second, informal interhousehold assistance networks were highly flexible and adaptive solutions to the array of problems that households faced. Examples of how these informal collaborations solved household problems were illustrated in Chapter 3. In addition to mobilizing labor, interhousehold networks were indispensable for building social solidarity (interhousehold feasting on the American Northwest Coast), finding spouses (Jacob's bride service), providing group and individual protection (constructing the wall of Jerusalem, fosterage in medieval Iceland), accessing resources through trade (the calumet ceremony), moving to take advantage of better economic opportunities (!Kung *hxaro*), and as emergency support networks in the face of famine or household failure (widows in ancient Israel). Informal institutions and voluntary collaborations were the first step in solving the problems that households faced. When the problems were greater than households could solve on their own, formal institutions emerged at the level of community and society. But for the most part the problems of mobilizing labor for household activities, finding spouses, and providing emergency support for starving families remained issues that households had to solve on their own through the informal institutions available to them.

Formal institutions are special-purpose organizations that operated at the level of community and society. Several chapters discussed formal institutions and the ways they produced the resources and/or obtained the surpluses needed to fund themselves and their society-wide activities. Palace and temple institutions in Mesopotamia organized large-scale textile production and long-distance trade as institutional activities (Breniquet and Michel 2014; Larsen 2015; Michel 2014; Potts 1997). Understanding what those institutions were and how they obtained the resources needed to support their operation is important for reconstructing their origin and organization.

The available information suggests that early Mesopotamian temple and palace institutions were organized as large, heterogenous households. Kinship terms were used to model subordinate and superordinate social relationships both within and between societies. The household as a framework for institutional organization was discussed in detail in Chapter 4 as a form of house society (e.g., Lévi-Strauss 1982; Schloen 2001; Weber 1978). However they were organized, one thing is clear. Once established, formal institutions operated just like households in the domestic economy in the sense that they were in business for themselves. Where they differed from households in the domestic sector was their access to an enormous pool of labor and resources; they needed only to modify the ideological rationales to mobilize them.

Several dimensions of early institutional economies are particularly noteworthy. First, while institutions might be conceived and rationalized as a household (the house of god, the house of the leader), not all its members resided there. Second, the scale of institutional production and distribution activities was immense in comparison to what the domestic economy engaged in. From this perspective, the specialized textile workshops of Mesopotamian temples represent some of the earliest large-scale production facilities found in that society. From an organizational perspective, they were the early predecessors to manufactories and industrial firms that operated for private and commercial purposes later in time. Third and finally, their broad economic strategy was one of self-sufficiency. They produced or traded for what they needed in terms of their own internal consumption needs.

A distinction was drawn between how institutions obtained the resources and mobilized the surpluses needed to finance their activities. One strategy was through direct production, where the institution organized and controlled the production of the resources that it needed. The examples used to illustrate institutional production included the Chinese commodity monopolies, the peripatetic courts of Persia and medieval Europe, and the use of corvée labor for Sumerian, Aztec, and Inka estate production (Chapter 5). The origin of direct production may also be traced to forms of patron–client production used by elites as a means of producing wealth goods for their individual use (Brumfiel and Earle 1987a). The second approach of institutional finance involved the mobilization of resources from the constituents that institutions served either through voluntary donations or mandatory taxation (Chapter 6).

Examples of voluntary donations included the euergetism represented by elite sponsorship of the liturgies in Greco-Roman society. Multiple examples of taxation can be found in the diverse array of tolls, tariffs, leases, and taxes levied on the land and commerce of both natural and conquered subjects.

Systems of institutional finance have been characterized in terms of whether staple or wealth goods were the primary resources used to fund institutional activities (D'Altroy and Earle 1985; Earle 1994; Earle and D'Altroy 1982). While this perspective has provided important information, a different approach was used here. The institutional economy was described in terms of two alternative modes of organization: direct production or resource mobilization. The division between these two modes of organization was more illustrative than real, since most institutional economies were not organized strictly as one form or the other. Instead, both strategies were used together and in different mixes depending on the needs and circumstances of the society in question. The advantage of internal production was that it allowed institutions to determine and fulfill their own needs with minimal intrusion into the activities of the domestic economy.

In agricultural settings, direct production involved using labor drawn from the domestic sector to cultivate land dedicated to institutional use. Scholars who examine the development of institutions from the perspective of surplus production view this labor as alienated from domestic units even when it is voluntarily contributed (Earle 2015; Morehart and De Lucia 2015a, 2015b). Elizabeth Brumfiel, in discussing the development of complex political economies, points out that "[b]ecause the vast majority of production in agrarian societies is household-based, political change almost always involves restructuring of household labor" (Brumfiel 1992:555). The rationale for institutional land assignment followed that used by all households with corvée labor mobilized from the domestic sector in much the same way that commoner households used informal institutions to mobilize labor for communal work groups. The practice of resource mobilization rather than production paralleled that used to fund communal feasting with households contributing food and other resources to collective activities. Furthermore, the use of tolls and tariffs to raise resources was selective; it affected merchants who often were foreigners but did not intrude directly on the domestic economy. The greatest increases in direct taxation of households seem to have been levied on populations acquired through conquest.

Perhaps the most important question that archaeologists and historians seek to answer is how formal institutions and their corresponding economic structures developed over time. It would be naive to assume that they followed a single developmental path. Nevertheless, there are some characteristics of these different resource production strategies that provide some intriguing possibilities. Foremost among these is what can be called the *law of unobtrusive expropriation.* As a working principle, this perspective assumes that people would be more supportive of emerging institutions that made fewer demands on their time and resources than those that made more demands. If this was true, then it is likely that many early institutions were relatively unobtrusive in the demands they placed on the households that supported them. After all, institutional demands for time and resources would directly affect the household's ability to support itself.

In this regard, institutions that employed systems of direct production would have made fewer demands on households than forms of resource taxation would have made. In direct production, the staple resources needed were produced on land set aside for institutional support. The labor used to produce institutional resources was mobilized from supporting households using corvée work groups. The cost to households of removing labor from their domestic work budgets could be minimized by mobilizing labor on a short-term rotational basis as was practiced among the Aztec and Inka. An alternative approach in Mesopotamia incorporated labor as permanent clients into institutional households. The benefit of direct production for commoner households was that it was relatively unobtrusive and did not extract resources produced within the domestic economy. Households kept all the resources produced on their land or through their own activities for their own support. The only cost to households was the labor time donated to or employed for institutional support.

Forms of institutional taxation were different and were more intrusive in the way they affected the domestic economy. As discussed in Chapter 6, classifying corvée labor as a form of labor tax with other forms of taxation confuses the clear distinction between inputs and outputs in a production system. In agricultural settings, labor was an *input* to production in the same way as land, seed, and technology. Taxation on household agricultural production, on the other hand, is a net tax on *output* after all the variable costs and risks of production have been made. By its very nature it is inherently more intrusive on the domestic economy than simple donations of household labor. Furthermore, when corvée labor is mobilized for production in institutional contexts, it is a fixed cost to households calculated against other possible production activities. If crop returns are low on institutional lands, there is no negative effect to the household. However, if the crop returns on household plots are low, and the household still must pay a fixed tax, then the negative effects to the household can be tremendous. Under systems of resource taxation, the institution reaches its hand directly into the pockets and storage bins of households, removing resources needed for their survival. Even if the percentage removed was relatively small, as it seems to have been in some early states (Chapter 6), it still would have been intrusive if it was a mandatory rather than a voluntary donation.

For this reason, it is likely that forms of direct production may have been the initial way that many institutional economies were structured and supported. It is instructive that direct production was the dominant pattern for institutional support in the New World state societies in both Mesoamerica and the Andes. It also was an important component of early Mesopotamian societies and Old Kingdom Egypt before household taxation took hold. Labor was not a free good to institutions in these four societies. Instead, the households providing corvée labor were compensated as if they were in festive work parties with reciprocal rations of food and/or beverage for the work carried out. As a result, it is my preferred candidate for the most common form of early institutional support. Nevertheless, household taxation appears to have been present in Sumer by at least the second millennium BC,[2] since the accumulation of debt to pay taxes was a reason why many households lost their land (Chapter 6). Hudson (1999b:461) has argued that when bad harvests forced households to take out loans to pay tax, it was the first step to losing their family, their land, and their freedom. Rulers recognized this problem and often granted debt amnesty to agricultural households caught in this bind (Graeber 2011).

Of course, the least intrusive form of institutional finance from the perspective of the domestic economy was when elites supplied all or the majority of the resources for institutional needs. The euergetism and liturgies undertaken by elites in the Greco-Roman world to fund festivals, construction projects, and military obligations are examples of this type of system. Its origins probably lie in the practice of elites serving as the sponsors of community celebrations and other civic projects. The role of leader as patron, sponsor, and organizer can be seen in New Guinea big man societies (Nairn and Strathern 2003; Strathern 2007). Of course, this begs the question of how elites were able to produce the large quantity of resources needed to fund the substantial civic and religious undertakings in both Greece and Rome. The answer is that they did so by appropriating land for their own use and producing resources on their large familial agricultural estates. These were not prebendal holdings assigned to specific civic usages like those found among the Aztecs. Instead, they were private estates. In other words, the responsibility for institutional production was moved to the private sector and the land held as private property by elite households.

MERCHANTS, CRAFTSPERSONS, AND THE MARKETPLACE

The commercial sector of the economy, the activities of merchants and craftspersons, and the role the marketplace played in society were important developments in many ancient societies (Chapters 7–9). Merchants were antiquity's aggressive entrepreneurs. They took financial risks, traveled to distant lands, transported goods over dangerous routes, and suffered privations away from their homes and families. Whether they worked independently or conducted business for institutions, the goal of merchant endeavors was profit. This is clear in ancient Mesopotamia where many documents reveal a clear pursuit of profitable gain (Goddeeris 2002:313). The status of merchants varied from society to society and depended to a large degree on the size and orientation of the kingdoms to which they belonged. In large agrarian societies, merchants often were held in low regard because honorable wealth was derived from farming. This was the case in China, Japan, and ancient Greece. Trade was more important in small kingdoms where land was scarce, and merchants often were members of the ruling families. Examples of these instances are numerous and include the Phoenicians and the kingdoms of Ugarit, Assur, Venice, Genoa, Indonesia, and other principalities throughout the Arab world. But merchants ranged from rich to poor and they dealt in a wide array of products from staples to wealth goods according to their knowledge, ability, and the level of capital investment.

Wealthy merchants were the wholesalers or middleman distributors of high-value commodities obtained through long-distance trade. Trade was a high-risk venture because of the danger of theft and possibility of shipwrecks. As a response, merchants diversified their endeavors. Instead of investing in 100% of a single cargo, they preferred to work in consortiums of collaborating individuals. A preference for collaboration was not because they lacked the capital for individual ventures, but because diversification was an effective strategy to minimize business risk. Their preference for investing in 20% of five cargos instead of a single cargo appears to have followed the age-old maxim of not putting all your eggs in one basket. Long-distance trade emerged as a separate enterprise, making those merchants involved in it wholesalers for the goods they trafficked in. Time was the enemy of profit for merchants who had to rely on slow and dangerous forms of transportation. As a result, it was more profitable for merchants to sell goods in bulk or to employ intermediary agents to sell their goods and get back on the road than it was to try to sell all the goods directly to consumers. The basis for all commercial relationships was one of merchant trust and their reputation for integrity. For all the disparagement of merchants, honesty was the best policy and their fundamental calling card, which they pledged both before the gods when contracts were struck and before fellow merchants when transactions were negotiated.

Merchants with limited working capital or who engaged in trade on a part-time basis often sold less expensive goods to consumers within limited geographic areas. Itinerant peddlers sold miscellaneous goods directly to households or in small towns and are examples of this type of merchant. An alternative solution for poor but aspiring merchants was to enter into commenda agreements with a wealthy individual who could supply the working capital for a joint venture. Commenda contracts (Chapter 7), found first among the ancient Greeks, were innovative solutions to conducting business in the ancient world. The number of individuals in a commenda agreement varied, but they usually were individuals who provided three main functions: capital investment, merchant knowledge, and transportation capacity.[3] The commenda is important both as an example of an early business venture and because it illustrates an important operational principle whereby merchants worked on shares based on their respective inputs (labor, capital, mode of transportation).

All merchants faced the *merchant's dilemma* (Chapter 7). The expectation of traditional societies was that all members would contribute to its economic base in proportion to their means and abilities (Gudeman 2001). Leaders led, workers worked, and wealthy individuals contributed their capital. This was a problem for merchants if they stayed in their home communities. Prosperous members of the community were among the first to be called on to sponsor community events, and herein lay the dilemma. If merchants invested in community events, they expended the working capital on which their livelihoods depended. Merchants resolved this dilemma in different ways. One of the most common solutions was to leave the community during the commercially active portion of their lives. If the opportunity was available, merchants could join a diaspora trade community (A. Cohen 1971; R. Curtin 1984) and spend years away from home until they retired from trade. The Assyrian merchants of the Middle Bronze Age (2000–1600 BC) comprise one of the earliest and best-documented commercial diaspora networks in the ancient world (Larsen 2008b; Stratford 2017; Veenhof 1972, 2003b). It was in the coordinated operation and integration of diaspora communities that some of the great merchant houses were formed (e.g., Parks 2005).

Craft production, like trade, was an activity that could be profitably incorporated into the domestic economy as a part-time activity during periods of low labor demand. The addition of small-scale crafting to the domestic economy was compatible with other diversified economic strategies intended to reduce subsistence risk. It is not surprising, therefore, to see small-scale craft production in many different settings across the ancient world. The reason for this was the high cost of transportation, which made it more feasible economically to produce most craft items locally than it was to try to centralize production and take advantage of economies of scale.

The transition from intermittent to full-time craft production was not an easy one outside institutional settings. All independent artisans who worked for themselves faced the *craftsperson's dilemma* (Chapter 8). All artisans had to deal with the problem of variable demand for the goods they produced throughout the year. In broad terms this can be thought of as craft risk. In agricultural societies, the demand cycle for utilitarian goods coincided with harvests, when crops were sold and purchases could be made for a range of items. Major festivals were another time for purchases made from savings. The cyclical demand for goods made full-time crafting a risky business since there were periods throughout the year when no sales might be made, and artisans might not eat.

One solution to this problem was for specialized artisans to relocate to urban centers where the aggregate demand for goods was larger. An alternative was to diversify production activities through multicrafting, which involved producing products that had different demand cycles throughout the year. A more common solution was to combine craft production with farming or herding, which provided a reliable subsistence base for crafting households. This strategy was not confined to small societies with low population densities. It was the predominant way that craft production was organized in the highly commercial societies of Mesoamerica, such as the ancient Aztecs (Feinman 1999; Hirth 2006a, 2009c; Widmer 1991).

On the whole, the scale of full-time crafting units was relatively small, often organized as extensions of family firms, and rarely growing beyond 10–20 persons in size. Larger industries usually developed in collaboration with merchants, who took charge of developing, transporting, and distributing finished goods to markets where they could be sold. Examples of these larger industries were discussed for *terra sigillata* and Chinese porcelain ceramics. The organization of artisans into guilds in medieval Europe regulated the quality of goods produced for export markets at the same time that they operated as protectionist groups restricting the proliferation of craftspersons who might threaten the livelihoods of established artisans. Merchant intermediaries were important for the intensification of craft production across the ancient world. In India, merchants organized and intensified the manufacture of cotton textiles in domestic settings that were the basis for the greater trans–Indian Ocean textile trade (Chapter 2). Merchants across Europe did the same using the putting-out system, which took advantage of the periodic availability of labor in rural areas to intensify production in a variety of different crafts (Chapter 8).

The marketplace was the most important formal economic institution in ancient and premodern societies. Some form of marketplace was associated with most large state-level societies,[4] either to service the local population or as a means for importing or exporting goods (Chapter 9). One of the marketplace's most important economic functions for the society was its role in assembling and provisioning households with the resources that they did not produce for themselves. Marketplaces concentrated demand and provided a locale where craftspersons could offer goods to a large number of potential buyers. Considerable variability is evident cross-culturally in the form, function, and periodicity of marketplaces. However marketplaces were structured, they were where all commercial interests intersected in society. It was where consumers, merchants, and craftspersons met to engage in wholesale or retail trade.

Marketplaces facilitated the peaceful expansion of commercial exchanges that took place between members of the same or different societies. That is what marketplaces did, and there is plenty of evidence that they functioned that way in the ancient past. But the recent work by David Graeber (2011) has rekindled the fires of the substantivists by arguing, like Polanyi, that barter only occurred between strangers in societies because of its tendency to create discord as value was negotiated. This is an important criticism because if it is correct, it affects how the marketplace is viewed, since market exchange, like barter, is about negotiating value and the terms of the exchange. For Graeber, barter and the idea of negotiating value and price was disruptive and could occur only between strangers. Nevertheless, Graeber makes a concession when he states that "barter does sometimes occur between people who do not consider each other strangers, but they're usually people who might as well be strangers – that is, who feel no sense of mutual responsibility or trust, or the desire to develop ongoing relations" (Graeber 2011:33).

Graeber's true interest in barter is its relation to the invention of coined money and the use of credit in economic transactions.[5] In the process, however, he creates a type of marketplace that never existed. His characterization of the Mesopotamian marketplace emerges as a place where prices fluctuated with supply and demand, transactions were made only between strangers, value was calculated in silver, and all exchanges were made on credit instead of through the immediate transfer of goods (Graeber 2011:39). Graeber has not considered how market exchanges and marketplaces actually functioned. Negotiation always went hand-in-hand with judging value and price, and if this occurred only between individuals without ongoing social relations, as Graeber proposes, then you cannot have credit. Both credit and market exchanges operated *within* established and ongoing social relationships even under conditions of immediate barter (Khuri 1968). This is evident in the forms of *pratik* found in the marketplace (Mintz 1964), through the credit extended via one-on-one relationships with retail shop owners (Bailey 1964; Benedict 1964:342; Braudel 1986:73; Cox 2000; Dobbin 1996:166), and within the context of visiting trade institutions in many pre-state societies (Heider 1969).

It is true that negotiating value can be disruptive and that is why goods circulated through gifts and prestations between family, friends, and neighbors without negotiation. But marketplaces can also be the location where commercial interaction provided opportunities for the formation of new and extended interregional social networks. This is what occurred in 18th-century AD Jamaica where Sunday marketplaces organized and run by African slaves became the social spaces where the enslaved passed information, forged their own social networks distinct from plantation society, and created the regional solidarity and social context for organizing the various slave rebellions of the 17th, 18th, and 19th centuries (Hauser 2008:196). The marketplace is not always a place of contention and discord. It can be a place where new friendships, relationships, and social identities are forged and fostered.

Nevertheless, as societies grew in size, they often reached a point where informal exchanges and the noncommercial economy could no longer regulate the distribution of resources. That was when the marketplace emerged as a vital and important economic institution. As discussed in Chapter 9, the marketplace was a liminal place where the normal rules of society did not apply and negotiations took place without broader social repercussions. It is also why marketplaces were usually supervised and in their earliest beginnings were probably held under the sponsorship of individuals or in conjunction with institutional activities or ritual celebrations. Barter and negotiation did happen! Even Karl Polanyi acknowledged this when he said, "Obscure as the beginnings of local markets are, this much can be asserted: that from the start this institution was surrounded by a number of safeguards designed to protect the prevailing economic organization of society from interference on the part of market practices" (Polanyi 1944:60–61).

The ancient economy was complex. Indeed, in many regards commercial dealings were more complex than they are today, where there is little negotiation of price and commercial interactions have become increasingly depersonalized because of the rise of commercial retailing and Internet shopping. In the past, credit, loans, and even access to some goods depended on interpersonal relationships that had to be built and cultivated over time. In the words of Siassi Island merchants who bought and sold goods along the coast of New Guinea, trade was "mainly an activity of the household ... [and] ... therefore a part of private rather than public affairs" (Harding 1967:182).

ON ECONOMIC PLASTICITY

A point emphasized throughout this volume is that ancient and premodern economies were *economically plastic*. The concept of economic plasticity is a simple one. It refers to the practice of adding new forms of economic organization to societies without removing older, preexisting ones (Hirth and Pillsbury 2013). It is growth in economic complexity by addition rather than by replacement. The addition of new forms of organization can relate to production, distribution, finance, the organization of labor, credit relations, contracts, or any other dimension of the economic environment in which households and institutions operate. New, more efficient forms of production can appear without replacing less efficient ones. Older, less efficient forms of organization can continue and even be preferred if they fit the needs of specific sectors of society. Economic plasticity is the reason why many small Internet start-up businesses work out of their homes, and why the putting-out system is still employed in different ways around the world as it is in the dynamic knitwear fashion industry in Italy, the home hammock and embroidery industry in Mexico, and the manufacture of Harris Tweed woolens in Scotland (Chapter 8).

Despite its simplicity, the concept of economic plasticity is often overlooked. One reason is the tendency to view the economy in monolithic terms (i.e., the mutual exclusivity fallacy). The other is our addiction to efficiency models for framing levels of economic development. Efficiency models are well suited to the analysis of industrial societies where costs of production determine price, and price determines sales. They are not so well suited to antiquity where transportation costs were high enough that markets were cellular, and less efficient forms of production could continue to operate if the practitioners could make a living. The protectionism found in the medieval craft guilds is an example of how less efficient forms of production continued to remain viable within small-scale regional markets (Chapter 8).

In a world where people rush to get the latest smartphone, it is hard to imagine a society that resisted technological innovation and organizational change. But this was a feature of premodern rural economies everywhere. It explains why horse-drawn wooden sledges (*dhoukani*), armed with sharp-edged chert blades instead of iron teeth, continued to be used well into the 20th century AD to thresh grain in Cyprus, Greece, and Turkey (Figure 1.1). The reasons relate to the conservative nature of the domestic economy. Farmers continued to use the chert-edged sledges, not because they were more durable than iron, but because they worked and required no additional capital investment. They could obtain the chert replacement blades within the existing rural networks, which freed farmers from dependence on urban suppliers (Kardulias and Yerkes 1996).

Unlike today where large manufacturing industries produce large quantities of goods for sale, ancient economies were composed of many small and diversified production entities that distributed goods within local markets without incurring high distribution costs. Their small scale meant that many production units were distributed across the landscape, producing a diverse array of goods. The result was that ancient societies had a high degree of *economic heterogeneity*. Older forms of production continued in perpetuity as long as they were economically viable for the households or production units involved. Established forms of craft production were durable because the fixed costs of production (i.e., knowledge, facilities, establishing resource procurement, technology) were already covered and access to labor was compatible with existing work cycles.

Economic heterogeneity is evident in many ethnographic cases where multiple forms of economic organization operated alongside one another. Socially based forms of interaction such as gift exchanges, trade partner relationships, and forms of redistribution continued to distribute goods well after marketplaces were an established fixture of ancient societies. These forms of distribution continued to fulfill household needs and maintain informal social networks well after commercial relationships came to dominate the economic landscape. In the same vein, antiquated forms of in-kind barter were still in use in open-air markets alongside the use of formal currencies in areas of Mexico well into the 20th century AD (Chapter 9).

Economic heterogeneity also is reflected by the forms of economic symbiosis found between different ethnic groups (Barth 1956; Varady 1979) or that allows differentiation of work along caste or religious divisions within societies (Appadurai 1974; Lewis and Barnouw 1956). The plasticity of economic arrangements creates heterogeneity. It is what allows reciprocal labor exchanges to remain a viable means of mobilizing farmworkers alongside wage labor to complete agricultural tasks. Most importantly, economic plasticity allows economic systems to develop differentially, permitting changes in one sector without disrupting the status quo in others. It permitted the development of parallel forms of land tenure and the exclusive control of certain fields by temple institutions or elite administrators, eventually leading to the appearance of private property. It is the ability to add new rationales and forms of organization without disrupting the preexisting ones that permitted the emergence of economic inequality and the differential control of resources in society.

Multiple examples were presented in this volume to illustrate the principle of economic heterogeneity in the ancient and premodern worlds. The practice of leaving the corners of agricultural fields uncut (*pe'ah*) for the poor to glean was discussed in Chapter 3, and this practice is still followed by some orthodox Jewish farmers even though gleaning is not. The *locatio–conductio* agreement was discussed for ancient Rome as a basic business principle that was applied to a wide range of economic arrangements, from leasing farmland and renting houses and shops (*tabernae*) to hiring labor and producing craft goods such as *terra sigillata* ceramics (Chapter 8). Perhaps the best example of economic heterogeneity was the multiple ways that Roman estate owners used to market their produce to urban consumers (Morley 1996:160–166). These included (1) taking produce to their own urban *tabernae* and selling it directly to consumers, (2) transporting it to urban centers and selling it to regional wholesalers, (3) auctioning produce at harvest time to merchants at the gate of the estate, and (4) auctioning produce to merchants while it was still on the tree, in the field, or on the vine, in an ancient type of futures market (Chapter 7). Estate owners could select between these different options depending on their individual circumstances.

Where modern economies differ sharply from ancient and premodern ones is in their use of fossil fuels as primary energy converters and the way that high-speed transportation and communication technologies have created a truly global economy. But in terms of the organization of work, that distinction blurs. Assembly-line production, often thought of as a modern development associated with the industrial revolution, was practiced in several areas of the ancient world including Polemarchus' shield factory of ancient Greece and the large-scale ceramic manufactories at Ching-te-chen, China (Chapter 8). But where craft work is still done by hand or where small start-up companies operate out of homes or garages, the distinction lessens except in the use of Internet technology that connects small businesses to the global marketplace.

The organizational structures of ancient economies were varied and complex. Monolithic approaches that attempt to describe an economic system based on a single form of production or distribution are essentially worthless for establishing a comprehensive understanding of the economy. They may serve other purposes, but they shroud the economy in a cloak of reductionism. The way to avoid this problem is to conscientiously apply William Blake's concern for "minute particulars" quoted at the start of this chapter to the study of how ancient economies operated. Even though this can be difficult for archaeological investigations, researchers need to be aware of the multifaceted nature of past economic systems and incorporate that understanding into their interpretations. Only then can investigators begin to develop a comparative framework for discussing the scale, complexity, and integration of production and distribution systems in the societies that they study.

A FINAL WORD

Peter Temin (2006) was quoted at the beginning of this book about the lack of communication between economists and economic historians interested in studying the ancient past. In his words, "Ancient economic history is still in its infancy, both because few economists have learned much about the ancient world and because ancient historians have typically not incorporated economics into their analysis" (Temin 2006:133). It is true that economists and historians do not collectively examine the organization and operation of ancient economic systems. Unfortunately, the problem is much larger than that. The systematic study of ancient economy requires a multidisciplinary approach and the collaboration of historians, economists, archaeologists, economic anthropologists, and where possible, art historians. The economic systems of past are gone, but the residues of what was produced, distributed, and consumed remain. Archaeologists can help with that. Most transactional relationships went unrecorded, but those behaviors can be modeled using ethnographic and ethnohistoric information from different parts of the premodern world and tested using archaeological and historic information about what was consumed and how far trade items moved. The goal of this work was to make a small step in that direction by illustrating some of the variation in how ancient and premodern economies were organized, while presenting a framework for how that variability can be viewed, compared, and analyzed.

NOTES

CHAPTER 1

1 Anthropologists and archaeologist who follow the substantivist position in economic anthropology would argue that investigators cannot and should not attempt to study the economy separately because it is intricately embedded in all other social and political dimensions of society. The entire premise of this volume is that the economy can and should be examined as a specific domain of investigation since failure to do so does not advance the study of the field.

2 Examples of these detailed analytical frameworks can be found in basic anthropology textbooks as well as the Human Relations Area Files where different aspects of culture are broken down into scalable categories (Murdock 1967) for comparative analysis (e.g., Blanton 1994; Pryor 1977, 1985, 2005).

3 The comparative method has long been the foundation for anthropological inquiry. The comparative method explores the similarities and differences found in societies at similar levels of organization. The approach seeks to understand what variables correlate with similar organizational forms in the attempt to explain how they functioned and developed over time (Durrenberger and Erem 2016:4).

4 The position taken here is that there is no truth in a definition, only utility. It provides a starting point for analysis and evaluation. When it no longer fits the situation, a bad definition should be discarded for a better one.

5 LETS are calculated as mutual credit or time dollars based on the inputs that individuals make to the system.

6 It is likely that by the time this book goes to print Uber, Airbnb, and many other similar examples will have been bought up, gone out of business, or been transformed into other business entities. I am confident that the Internet will continue to create new, decentralized forms of commerce that individual households can take advantage of.

7 An example of aligning economic practices and ideological norms can be found in medieval England where market day was often held on Sunday. Clerics knew that people would come to the market, so convening it on Sundays also made individuals available for church services.

8 The field of economics is generally divided into the subfields of microeconomics and macroeconomics. Microeconomics attempts to study the market behavior of individuals and firms in an attempt to understand their decision-making processes. Macroeconomics in contrast is concerned with how the total aggregate economy behaves by examining trends in the gross national product, inflation, prices, unemployment, and money supply.

9 The problems of text preservation are always a problem for historians. An example of economic records that cannot be translated are the Inka knotted *khipus* (Salomon et al. 2001; Urton 2012). An example of where writing was developed for reasons other than recording economic transactions include the Chinese Shang scripts (1600–1050 BC) (Boltz 1986).

10 Institutions can be defined in many ways. The institution of marriage can be thought of as a spiritual union or as a socioeconomic arrangement between two individuals. Marriage as a spiritual union in the Christian tradition would be represented by the view that in marriage two individuals become one flesh (Matthew 10:7–9). Marriage from the socioeconomic perspective would reflect the formation of a household to raise a family and provide for its support. The use of prenuptial

agreements in modern marriages reflects an economic view of marriages operating along the lines of a limited partnership.

11 Examples of the norms and values that can be attached to specific socioeconomic institutions would include the idea that priests in the Catholic Church must be males.

12 This definition of institutions differs from that employed by the New Institutional Economics, which defines institutions in terms of the rules of the game separating them from the groups of players (the organizations) that carry them out (North 2008:22). While this perspective is conceptually useful when studying contemporary societies (North 1995), it can be difficult to apply to the ancient past.

CHAPTER 2

1 Households can maintain stable work regimes for long periods of time but then change very quickly when new opportunities or necessities arise. The speed of these changes makes them difficult even for ethnographers to chronicle and is the basis for restudying ethnographic communities at different points in time (e.g., Foster 1952; Wilk 2001).

2 Early ethnographers believed that households were a transitional group whose form depended on patterns of descent, marriage, and the functioning residence rules of society (Netting et al. 1984:xi). In this sense households were seen as a residual category of other processes rather than a dynamic form of organization worthy of separate study.

3 Sahlins (1972) made the point more than 40 years ago that hunting and gathering groups do not face the resource shortfalls as often as agricultural groups do because of their knowledge of where seasonally available resources occur and the mobility to pursue and obtain them. A recent study has clarified and confirmed much of Sahlin's original position (Bird-David 1992).

4 Most examples of dry field terracing were constructed by the households and groups that used them (Donkin 1979; Van Andel et al. 1986). Examples of household-directed and household-constructed hydraulic agricultural systems include small-scale wet field cultivation among the ancient Maya (Scarborough 2003) and the wet rice cultivation of the Ifugao tribal societies in the Philippines (Conklin 1967: Dove 1983).

5 Other household diversification strategies beyond the production of food and resources for auto-consumption include production of cash crops for sale, involvement in craft production, wage labor, or periodic service in exchange for support. All of these alternative activities are found in ancient, past, and premodern societies.

6 John O'Shea (1989) has identified four fundamental strategies that premodern households used to offset resource risk: mobility, diversification, storage, and exchange. Mobility refers to the practice found in foraging, hunting, and pastoral societies of moving to areas where resources occur. This is effective for dealing with seasonal and regional variation in resource availability. Diversification involved buffering risk by exploiting multiple resources instead of specializing in a narrow range of the most productive ones. Storage is an important foundation in societies where there are seasonal fluctuations in resource availability. It is especially important in agricultural economies where households are heavily reliant on the crops they produce. The fourth strategy is exchange: how households obtained resources that they did not produce themselves. What this strategy entails is using some of the goods they do produce to obtain those that they do not.

7 An example of food diversification is the incorporation of both domestic and wild foods in the normal household diet. Wild foods are available in good years as well as bad years when agricultural crops fail. Having them in the diet provides a fallback for households to draw on. Diversified subsistence strategies are often referred to as mixed economies in the anthropological literature. The incorporation of insects into the diet from the western perspective is an extreme example of dietary diversification (Menzel and D'Aluisio 1998). Another example of diversification would be to spread agricultural plots over space instead of farming one large field to avoid the risk of disease, insect damage, or rainfall fluctuations (O'Shea 1989).

8 The earliest evidence for the specialized production of human and animal figurines and fired clay anomalies using pyrotechnology

come from the site of Dolni Vestoniche (Vandiver et al. 1989). Production took place in small structures removed from the larger camp, and it is assumed that production was by a specialist who produced these items intermittently for ritual purposes.

9 Evidence for the specialized production of chert blades during the Early Neolithic period (7200–5000 cal BC) comes from several areas of the Old World. Long-lever pressure blades produced by specialists have been recovered in the Near East (Altınbilek-Algül et al. 2012:173; Chabot and Pelegrin 2012), in western Europe with the production blades in the *livre-de-beurre* tradition (Linton 2008; Pelegrin 2003:figure 4.14), and in the Linear Pottery Culture (Linearbandkeramik, LBK) from 5400 to 4900 BC. Particularly good evidence for specialized blade production associated with the LBK culture has been identified at the Verlaine site near Liège, Belgium (Allard 2005). Blades of Hesbaye light gray flint reflect production for exchange, and the raw material to manufacture blade cores moved over distances of 50–200 kilometers from the source to production contexts (Allard 2005:figure 6; 2012).

10 The distinction made here is between craft production as a specialized activity for exchange and use outside the household as opposed to the ad hoc production of tools and utilitarian goods for use within the households or as occasional gifts.

11 Seasonal farming regimes are widespread throughout the world in both tropical and temperate environments. In many areas seasonal farming involves a period of intense agricultural activity followed by months of labor inactivity. This seasonality provides an opportunity for additional types of work to be carried out during the nonagriculture period that includes craft production.

12 Examples of micromanagement of household labor include shifting from agriculture to craft work during the heat of the day or during storms when work in the fields is difficult, as well as working at night.

13 The need to obtain spouses is another example of why households could not survive as completely self-sufficient units. Complete self-sufficiency would have denied households the social networks needed to obtain spouses for social and biological reproduction.

14 Most land was held by the state in custody for the people. The best improved land was occupied and in continuous use. Marginal lands could be assigned to migrants by the lords and rulers of each city-state, as they were available. Land tenure relations varied throughout Central Mexico and included both free commoners and renters. Some elite estates were held as large contiguous holdings, while other parcels for elite support were dispersed as very small plots alongside household fields (Harvey 1984, 1991).

15 Households residing in the Aztec capital of Tenochtitlan faced the most severe shortages of farm land since the capital was located on an island in the center of Lake Texcoco. Households made both house lots and agricultural plots (*chinampas*) within the lake bed by building them up with mud dredged from the lake bottom. Pressure was relieved somewhat in the 15th century AD when the Aztecs began conquering cities around the lake margins and expropriated farm land from them for households residing in Tenochtitlan (Durán 1994).

16 Slaves were not used in agriculture in Central Mexico. Some slaves were used in other areas of Mesoamerica, including the Gulf Coast and the Maya area, where they could be employed in the cultivation of cash crops such as cacao (Attolini Lecón 2010:59). There is one reference to the ruler of the Aztec capital of Tenochtitlan granting slaves to the highest quality craftspersons so the latter could work as full-time artisans in the state craft workshop known as the *totocalli*. The slaves were awarded so the artisans did not have to cultivate the farm plots that members of the household normally cultivated.

17 The best agricultural lands near the Aztec capital of Tenochtitlan were lake bed *chinampa* plots, most of which were in the southern Valley of Mexico. *Chinampa* plots in the wetlands and the margins of lakes were cultivated year-round by regulating the water levels, creating perfect conditions for raising two to three crops per year. While labor intensive, these plots are the most likely candidates for supplying fresh vegetables to the city throughout the year (Parsons 1976, 1991).

18 Huexotzinco was an independent kingdom in the Puebla–Tlaxcala basin that was forced to pay tribute during the early colonial period

even though it assisted the Spanish in the Aztec conquest. The *Matricula* was prepared as an appeal to Spanish authorities against the high level of taxation that the native residents of Huexotzinco were required to pay in the face of declining population. The household census documents the exact number of tribute payers in the province of Huexotzinco.

19 The community where nonfarming activities were not recorded is Santa Cruz Atenco.

20 Some of the new activities that households engaged in during the colonial era included the wage labor activities of cart drivers and plow workers, fiscal administrators, and the church-related activities of bell ringers, catechists, and preachers.

21 Early textile impressions during the Upper Paleolithic period are found on fired loess fragments recovered at the site of Pavlov that date around 26,000 BC (Adovasio et al. 1996). Additional evidence includes the use of cordage for bead necklaces, and possibly as netted garments on Venus figurines (Soffer et al. 2000; White 2003:135).

22 Examples of early woven textiles from the Neolithic period include those recovered from the site of Çatal Hüyük in southeastern Anatolia (Helbaek 1963; Ryder 1965), the Early Jomon textiles at the Torihama site of Japan (Aikens and Higuchi 1982), and fabrics from Nahal Hemar Cave in the Levant (Bar-Yosef and Schick 1989). Elsewhere in the world cotton and other plant fibers were spun into thread and used for textiles in the Indus Valley as early as 4,500 years ago (Gulati and Turner 1929; Wright et al. 2012) as well as for nets and fishing line on coastal Peru 5,000 years ago (Moseley 1974). Cotton was also grown, spun, and woven into cloth in Mexico and Guatemala by at least 3,000 years ago.

23 Ethnographic studies have shown that Navajo and Hopi men in the American Southwest were involved in both spinning and weaving. More variation is found within households in terms of weaving. Men dominated weaving in premodern India and southeastern Africa (Beckert 2014:16).

24 Perhaps one of the most extreme examples of foragers integrated into a commercial network was the collection of wild birds' nests by foragers in Borneo and Thailand, which were then exported by merchants for sale in China to make bird's nest soup (Lin et al. 2009). These nests were made from the salivary glue of the Aerodramus swiftlets (*Aerodramus fuciphagus*) and were a delicacy in Chinese cuisine. Their importation into China may have started as early as the Tang Dynasty (AD 618–907).

25 Cotton textiles were produced on an ad hoc basis in both commoner and wealthy households because they were needed by women for their respective dowries (Zurndorfer 2011:56).

26 Li (2011:393) estimates that by the late 19th century the income of women involved in spinning and weaving was about 70% of what a man could make in farming, although on average women worked 265 days in textile manufacture compared with 180 days in farming. The average female worker in 1820 could earn enough in textile production to support 3.7 people, or 82% of household needs at a time when the average family size was 4.5 persons.

27 The merchants operating in the Indian Ocean were a combination of Hindu, Muslim, and Jewish merchants and ship owners. They were referred to in generic terms of *nakhudas* and *nauvittakas* (Chakravarti 2000:34). *Nakhudas* were ship captains or, literally, lords (*knuda*) of the ship (*nau*) (Chakravarti 2000:37). *Nauvittakas* referred to ship owners.

28 Trade in Indian textiles is often characterized as being in the hands of maritime merchants. It was, but merchants also moved textiles overland depending on routes of trade and conditions of travel. During the 17th century AD it is reported that 25,000–30,000 camel loads of textiles reached Persia from India each year (Riello 2013:23).

29 Bayly (1986:299) estimates that the Delhi court alone consumed as many as one million pieces of Bengal muslin each year. How many million were produced for export and to satisfy demand across the length of the Indian trade network remains unknown.

30 According to data collected by Vijaya Ramaswamy (2006:143), there were an average number of 1.3 looms per household, or a household-to-loom ratio of 3:4.

31 Both Hindi and Muslim merchants, sometimes referred to as Moors in medieval documents (Ramaswamy 2006), were involved in the textile trade at various levels. The Chettis,

a group of Tamil merchants who originated along the southeast coast of India, were particularly prominent in the textile trade. Along with general trade in high-value goods the Chettis also were retained by the king of Vijayanagara to conduct his personal trade both inside and outside India (Ramaswamy 2006:85).

32 For a critique of the study of early kinship systems, see Schneider (1984).

33 Lauriston Sharp's (1952) classic study of stone-axe use among Australian aborigines made this important point by showing that elder men "owned" the axes that individuals would borrow when they were needed to engage in specific cutting or chopping tasks. This reinforced the social position of the elders, which was undermined when steel axes were obtained as gifts from Christian missionaries. Likewise, John Dowling (1968:505) observed that among the !Kung bushmen ownership of hunted game was ascribed to the maker of the arrow that brought the animal down, whether it was shot from his bow or from that of another hunter.

34 Individual control over wild resources was found among the Ojibway people of northern Minnesota in the way they apportioned access to wild rice. Families would enter the wild rice fields and isolate sections for exclusive household use by marking stands of rice with distinctive forms of knots and bindings (Vennum 1988:82). Jonathan Carver (1951) reports that an entire rice field in 1767 was marked in this way so that individual families could harvest mature grain as their individual property.

35 Hunt and Gilman (1998:viii) recognize four types of property relationships that affect individuals and households throughout antiquity: (1) open access land often referred to as *res nullius* that can be accessed by all; (2) common pool property held by a corporate group such as a village or kinship group (access to this land is limited to group members and is referred to as *res comunes*); (3) private property held by individuals through specific jural relationships defined by society, with access usually limited to the owner; and (4) state property where access is controlled by a social, political, or religious institution.

36 Usufruct refers to the real or acknowledged right to use open-access and common-pool resources. The term comes from two Latin terms: *usus* (user), which is the right to make use of, and *fructus*, which refers to the fruit and the right to derive profit, return, or enjoyment (Handford 1961).

CHAPTER 3

1 Consanguineal kinship refers to a relationship established as blood kinship according to the kinship system employed in society. Affinal kinship refers to relatedness established through marriage when some form of exogamy is practiced. Fictive kinship refers to relatedness that is assumed because of membership in the same clan or from the same mythical ancestor or totem.

2 The weakness of interhousehold support networks is that they are limited in scope and all participating members suffer to the same degree. In these circumstances, individuals may have to emigrate, resort to begging, or take some alternative action. Prior to the Spanish conquest, a prolonged famine in Central Mexico from AD 1452 to 1455 forced parents to sell their children into slavery to neighboring groups so that they would not starve (Bierhorst 1992; Chimalpahin Cuauhtlehuanitzin 1965:200–201; Durán 1994:239–240).

3 Division of labor by age and sex most often matches tasks to individuals with the physical strength required to carry them out. Men usually engage in more risky tasks or those that require more strength to carry out, while women often engage in work that can be combined with child rearing.

4 Collective labor requires reciprocating in kind. That means if four men come together for a day to help a fifth, the man they help is required to give one day of labor to each of the other four. There are no economies of scale if a single man can do the same amount of work that the group completes in 5 days, the day he works with the group and the other four he needs to provide for the others.

5 Festive labor goes by a wide variety of different names around the world. It is known as *mar muos* (farming for beer) in west Africa (Stone et al. 1990), *convite* or *minga* in Ecuador and Colombia, *ayni* in Peru, and *mingaco* in Chile, to name a few (Erasmus 1956:445).

6 The book of Nehemiah is written in the first person, and scholars credit its authorship to Nehemiah himself. It is not a continuous account, however. Some portions appear to have been added by later writers. Nevertheless, Williamson (1985:15) considers that chapters 1, 2, and 4–6 were written by Nehemiah. Chapter 3 may be a later insertion by the groups involved in rebuilding the wall.

7 The accounts in the Hebrew Bible (Nehemiah 1:3) and the historian Josephus written in AD 93–94 both confirm that Nehemiah learned of the problems in Jerusalem from Hebrews who had come to Susa (Maier 1994:192).

8 A long face was not allowed in the Persian court as it suggested disgruntlement or subversive behavior, and cast suspicion on those who displayed it. Nehemiah's request probably occurred in the month of Nisan (Nehemiah 2:1), most likely during a special *tukta* banquet where Persian kings regularly granted special requests (Blenkinsopp 1988:213). Nehemiah, however, was cautious in how he made his request.

9 While Lebanon was famous for its cedar, it is possible that local resources were used since timber in the form of olive and sycamore wood was also available in the hill country of the Shephelah west of Jerusalem (1 Chronicles 27:28).

10 Community construction projects in the third world often were organized as segmented and unsupervised forms of collective labor. In 1972 I witnessed the construction of a village water line in Mexico that was 3 kilometers long and took 4 months to complete. The community took the distance of the length of the water line to be laid and divided it by the available male labor in the community. Each household dug its prescribed length of line to the requisite depth at their own pace and when it fit into their normal household time budget. The only requirement was that they finish on a prescribed date. This traditional form of collective labor is referred to by the Nahuatl word *tequio*.

11 One has to realize that the wall was not constructed from scratch. Military tactics sought to breach city walls in key spots and then swarm the city. It is likely, therefore, that while the wall was damaged in many spots, there were large segments where it was mostly intact and only needed more modest repair. These sections would have been taken into consideration when the segments of construction were assigned to different groups.

12 While most Bible scholars accept the mid-5th-century BC as the date for the rebuilding of the wall (Stevens 2006:48; Williamson 1985:55), recent archaeological investigations have not been able to confirm this date. Finkelstein (2008) dates the reconstruction to the Hasmonean period (140–116 BC). Because the archaeological evidence is not precise, the 5th-century date is used here as the most likely time frame for Nehemiah's work.

13 Forms of dowry and bridewealth can still be found in India (Anderson 2003; Stone and James 1995), Africa (Dekker and Hoogeveen 2002; Rudwick and Posel 2014), and other countries in the non-western world (Yan 2005). They are no longer common in European or American marriages. Nevertheless, one only needs to tally the type and quantity of gifts given at weddings and bridal showers to see that resources still move from family and friends toward the establishment of new households.

14 Bridewealth is the dominant form of marriage transaction in Africa where it is found in 82% of societies; it is much less frequent in North and South America at 18% and 8%, respectively (Anderson 2007:152).

15 The Babylonian term for brideprice is *terhatu*, which Stol (2016:112) equates with the Sumerian term *nimusa*, which literally translates to "that which belongs to the son-in-law (*musa*)." In contrast the Neo-Assyrian word for dowry is *nundunû*.

16 Other examples of the production of a social surplus (Harris 1959) unrelated to marriage include contributing to community feasts, coming-of-age celebrations within the households, meeting ritual contributions, and paying annual tax or service obligations.

17 The picture of the early household economy comes from Genesis 26 where it says, "Isaac sowed in the land and reaped in the same year a hundredfold" (verse 12), and "He had possessions of flocks and herds and a great household" (verse 14). That hunting was included in the subsistence strategy is indicated by the statement in Genesis 25 where it says, "Esau was a skillful hunter, a man of the field" (verse 27). Esau was Jacob's older brother and in verse 3 Isaac his father tells him to "take your

weapons, your quiver and your bow, and go out to the field, and hunt game for me." It is likely that both sons were familiar with hunting.

18 Whether the story can be taken at face value or not, Jewish weddings went on for several days and involved a lot of drinking. Under those circumstances anything is possible. What is clear, however, is that Laban colluded with his older daughter Leah to make the switch on the evening the marriage was to be consummated by having Leah change into the wedding garments Rachel was wearing.

19 Exodus 22:13 clarifies that if an animal under the care of a shepherd was killed by a wild animal, then "let him bring it as evidence; he shall not make restitution for what has been torn." If an animal was lost due to negligence or stolen, then he had to make restitution.

20 Mongongo nuts (*Schinziophyton rautanenii*) can be collected by hand from trees ranging up to 15 meters tall or collected from the dung of elephants where intact nuts pass through them undigested. These nuts are both a nutritious and highly reliable food source (Lee 1968:33).

21 The formal definition of an egalitarian society according to Fried (1967:33) "is one in which there are as many positions of prestige in any given age–sex grade as there are persons capable of filling them." It is a society where all individuals have equal opportunities, there is no interest in limiting leadership opportunities, social status is based on personal abilities and initiative, and there is no means of fixing or limiting the number of persons able to exert power or to fill a particular social status.

22 The range in the number of *hxaro* partnerships among these 73 adults was quite wide and varied from as few as 2 to as many as 42 (Wiessner 2002:421).

23 European goods also circulated in *hxaro* exchange and were extremely popular for both their uniqueness and their functional quality.

24 According to Tim Parkin (2013:43), Shakespeare's proverb "old age is a second childhood" captures the idea of high infant mortality. It did not refer to a happy retirement, but to the return to that early stage in life of the high risk of mortality.

25 This quote is found in *Meditations*, book 11, paragraph XXX (Casaubon 1906:102).

26 There were always exceptions. Foster children in medieval Iceland normally received equal shares of inheritance with biological children from their foster fathers.

27 There were three recognized social classes in medieval Iceland: the chieftains called *goði* (pl. *godar*), commoners called *þingmenn* or *bondi* (pl. *boendr*) who were clients of a particular *goði*, and slaves (Byock 2001; Miller 1990:17).

28 There were three forms of fictive brotherhood described in the sagas. They are foster brothers (*fóstbródir*), sworn brothers (*svarabródir*), and oath brothers (*eidbródir*), all of which imply support in a dispute or conflict. The term *fóstbródir* is sometimes used to designate a blood brother as well as a foster brother (Miller 1990:173).

29 Medieval Icelanders recognized a bilateral kinship system that allowed claiming descent through both the biological father and mother. This meant that a child of a married couple could have kinship connections to four different families. Households could be large with the addition of foster children, cousins, slaves, and orphaned children from other families. The result was that a single household could have multiple kinship affiliations where household members could line up on different sides of a dispute between two individuals.

30 Arbitration of disputes leading to monetary judgments or outlawry were made at the yearly Alþing, or general assembly of regional chieftains and their supporters. Arbitrators were knowledgeable in the law, good negotiators, and had the ability to win an argument through persuasion and reason. They were influential men most like our concept of lawyers. The injured party needed to have a good arbitrator on his side to win a judgment at the Alþing. As Byock (1993:41–42) puts it, "The prudent man created such obligations ahead of time so that he would have a powerful broker to turn to in time of need. Obligations could be kept alive by giving gifts and feasts."

31 Anna Hansen (2008) draws a distinction found in the law codes between fosterage and guardianship. Children under guardianship came from poor families and did not have financial support as foster children did. Under the law codes close relatives were required to absorb the cost of supporting poor kinsmen such as orphans (Miller 1990:147–154). Nevertheless, some reimbursement of costs for raising a child was possible. A guardian could retroactively

obtain support for having raised a child from a poor home (i.e., the *fóstrlaun*) directly from the child if the latter acquired wealth during their adulthood.

32 There is another instance in the Sturlu saga where Jón Loftsson assists Páll Solvason in a property dispute against Sturlu himself. Jón wins the claim and in a conciliatory effort to Sturlu, in what can be seen as a way to forestall resentment and a possible future clash, Sturlu agrees to bring his son Snorri Sturluson into his household as his foster son (McGrew and Thomas 1970).

33 Rituals are actions wrapped in symbolism. They represent activities that are recognized as being functionally and symbolically different from everyday activities in terms of purpose or action (Dietler 2001:67).

34 Diego Durán was born in Seville, Spain, around AD 1537. He relocated to Texcoco in the Valley of Mexico around 1550 where as a boy he learned the native language of Nahuatl. He entered the Dominican order and became a novice at the Monastery of Santo Domingo in Mexico City on May 8, 1556. He became a missionary, traveled widely across New Spain, and sought to learn local customs as foundation for native conversion and instruction in the Christian faith. He died in Mexico City in 1588. His works remained unknown and unpublished for nearly 300 years (Durán 1967–1980; Horcasitas and Heyden 1971).

35 When a feast was part of a burial ceremony, wedding, or a formal political potlatch, all food preparation was more formal. Slaves were not allowed to serve food or to be present when it was consumed. Furthermore, since a potlatch involved invitations to the whole clan, individuals outside the immediate household would be called on to contribute food to the celebration (Oberg 1973:97).

36 According to Drucker and Heizer (1967:8), the term "potlatch" comes from the Chinook language and simply means to give. This reflects both the feasting and the large-scale gift giving that accompanied the potlatch. The potlatch was a formal procedure for social integration within and between clans. It publicly validated an individual's membership in a group and their status within it (Barnett 1938).

37 After European contact the items exchanged for furs increased to include liquor, guns, knives, blankets, iron cooking pots, and a range of other western manufactured goods (Chittenden 1986; Wood 1980).

38 Our colloquial expression "to smoke the peace pipe" is derived from the Native American calumet ceremony.

39 The best-known prehistoric quarries of argillite used by native North Americans to manufacture calumet pipe bowls are in southwest Minnesota, southeast South Dakota, and north central Wisconsin, although other sources occur in Kansas and the American Southwest (Gundersen et al. 2002).

40 Several examples of the benevolent institutionalized support of the poor in antiquity include the *Lex Sempronia Frumentaria* of ancient Rome, which provided regular food support for its urban poor (Rickman 1980a). An example of onetime support of the poor in the Americas is the great famine of 1 Rabbit in the Aztec calendar (AD 1454) when rulers opened the state granaries in an attempt to save all the people from starving (Bierhorst 1992; Durán 1994:239).

41 Examples of helping the poor and destitute include Deuteronomy 15:4–5; Ezekiel 18:5–9; Isaiah 58:10–11; Job 22:5–9, 29:12–13, 31:16–21; Proverbs 22:9, 31:20; and Psalms 41:1, 82:3–4. There is also the exhortation to provide loans to the poor who needed them in Deuteronomy 24:10–13 and Proverbs 28:8.

42 The sabbatical year was held every seventh year. The Jubilee year was celebrated at the close of seven sabbatical cycles.

43 Leviticus 19:27 says, "You shall not round off the hair of your temples or mar the edges of your beard." Adherence to this command is why males in the Orthodox Jewish community have sidelocks known as *pe'ot*. They are the uncut hair of the temples.

44 Berenbaum and Skolnik (2007:632) have stated that gleaning was allowed at three times of the day, "because some of the poor were nursing mothers who must eat at the beginning of the day, and some were minors who do not wake up early and cannot reach the field until midday, and some were aged who cannot reach the field until the afternoon." So Jewish law also took into consideration not only whether one was poor, but also how the structure of their household might obstruct gleaning the resources needed for their survival.

45 An *ephah* of barley was approximately 3 pecks, or three-fourths of a bushel (Pfeiffer and Harrison 1990:270).

46 The term *hesed* is often translated from the Hebrew as loving-kindness. It is an act of benevolence that an individual does out of kindness rather than any expectation of reciprocation (Eskenazi and Frymer-Kensky 2011: xlviii).

47 The idea in Jewish theology is that Yahweh owned all the land and that no Israelite could lose his property permanently (Leggett 1974:85). The practice of *go'el* worked in concert with this belief, so that if a property was put up for sale the first option to purchase it would fall to a kinsman.

48 While the book of Ruth does not specify what the relationship of Boaz was to Elimelech, the rabbinical sources provide some guidance. They suggest that the unnamed redeemer who does not step forward was the brother of Elimelech, whereas Boaz was the son of a brother, or Elimelech's nephew (Eskenazi and Frymer-Kensky 2011:63).

CHAPTER 4

1 The definition of institutions used here differs notably from Douglas North (1995), who considers institutions to be the rules of operation distinct from the organizations that employ them. I consider them together because in the broad diachronic perspective, organizations shape the rules of operation just as rules of operation shape the form of organizations (sensu Douglas 1986).

2 Scale, complexity, and integration are three important dimensions of social groups that can be measured historically and archaeologically. Scale refers to overall size and geographical extent of a group, community, or society. Complexity refers to the functional differentiation between social units that can be both vertical and horizontal. Vertical differentiation refers to hierarchical organization of units and their centralized decision making and power. Horizontal differentiation refers to the subdivision of groups into different roles or subgroups. Integration refers to the ways and means by which social units and groups are interconnected. For a more complete discussion of these variables, see Blanton et al. 1993 and Feinman 2013b:36.

3 The resources to support formal institutions are most often met in one of two ways. Either they are produced under the supervision of institutional personnel who need and use them or they are mobilized from the households that the institutions serve. The more institutions use the first approach, the less they will intrude on the household economy to fulfill their needs (Hirth 2016:35).

4 Aristotle's discussion of the structural elements of social and political life are found in *Politics* books 1–4 (Jowett 1943). For a discussion of Aristotle's view on political structure, see Weissleder (1978).

5 Recognition that larger size confers advantages to members of society can be traced back to at least as far as Rousseau (1984). In his often-quoted example of the stag hunt, he argues that large hunting parties working together can hunt larger game as opposed to working individually when they might focus on smaller game. His example is accurate for some but not all types of group hunting techniques (Bates 2001; Steward 1938)

6 In Murdock's sample of 565 societies, 564 had some form of unilineal or bilateral kinship system. The single society that did not was one for which no information was available (Coult and Habenstein 1965:491).

7 Anthropologists use the terms "emic" and "etic" refer to the different perspective of events that observers have compared with participants. Emic refers to the insider's view of cultural events. From an ethnographic perspective this is the view that individuals raised in a society have of the activities that they participate in. Etic refers to the outsider's view, which is the view of both the biased and unbiased observer who was not raised in the society under examination.

8 It is not assumed that collective participation in formal institutions is always voluntary. Noncontributors and free riders are a problem in all organizations, and an array of negative sanctions and punishments may be employed to force compliance with institutional activities.

9 For the purposes of discussion, both territoriality (an ecological concept) and land tenure (an economic concept) deal with the same process of restricting access to resources

distributed across the landscape (Cashdan 1989:40). Dyson-Hudson and Smith (1978:22) define a territory as a spatial area "occupied more or less exclusively by an individual or group by means of repulsion through overt defense or some form of communication." Land tenure systems in agricultural groups function in much the same way.

10 Local communities and claims on *ahupua'a* land were stable because of endogamous marriage patterns and low levels of movement between communities (Earle 1977:218).

11 When warriors or soldiers are drawn from the citizenry as opposed to being full-time professionals, war will tend to occur in low points in the agricultural cycle when the greater part of the male population is not involved in farming or other subsistence pursuits. This was the militaristic tradition for the Inka, the Aztecs, and the Maya (Hassig 1988). This tradition was dramatically played out in the Maya caste war in Yucatan when the Mayan army was composed of native farmers. The siege of Merida occurred in the spring of AD 1848 just before planting. When it began to rain during the siege, most of the native army left the battle to begin the spring planting (Reed 1964; Rugeley 2010).

12 Lycurgus, the legendary lawgiver of Sparta, said essentially the same thing when he said, "A city is well-fortified which has a wall of men instead of brick."

13 Jacobsen (1943) called this form of government "primitive democracy" in the spirit of the time in which he was writing. In modern anthropological terms the reference to an assembly reflects a kin-based form of governance common in both tribal and chiefdom societies.

14 An alternative way of creating action groups that cross-cut groups organized by kinship is with age-set cohorts. Age-sets provide a structure that organizes society horizontally by age (P. Spencer 1993). Individuals in this system were initiated into a cohort and moved through different life-cycle stages as a group. They were important in African pastoral societies and often were divided into different cycle categories such as youth, warrior, elder warrior, and elder depending on the society in question (Foner and Kertzer 1978). The age-set cohorts ranged anywhere from 8 to 15 years in length, and each set had its own internal leaders who provided instruction and direction for new initiates. Those in the warrior categories were expected to provide defense and protection within society (Baxter 1979; Gulliver 1953; Hodgson 2001; Larick 1991). Nevertheless, Evans-Pritchard (1940:254) asserts that among the Nuer, the warrior age-set was not a formally organized military association but was grouped into larger fighting units under the direction of tribal elders.

15 Other warrior groups within this setting included the Sioux, Crow, Comanche, Blackfoot, Pawnee, and Kiowa, to name a few (see DeMallie and Sturtevant 2001).

16 The names of the six warrior associations were: Elk, Fox, Shield, Dog, Bowstrings, and Wolf. The Wolf association was formed in AD 1837 by a Cheyenne chief named Owl Man after the Bowstrings were annihilated by the Pawnee (Hoebel 1960:33).

17 The Cheyenne had three kinds of raids or war parties: private, fraternity, and tribal. Private war parties were at the discretion of the participants and were the most common. Fraternity war parties were those of the warrior associations, while tribal parties involved all of the ten Cheyenne bands (Hoebal 1960:70).

18 Hoebel (1967:24) presents the testimony of one Cheyenne warrior named Wolf Lies Down who brought a claim for a horse borrowed without permission by a member of another Cheyenne band. In the process the Elk warrior association resolved the dispute and instigated a new policy for punishing individuals who borrowed goods in illicit ways.

19 Llewellyn and Hoebel (1941:6–9) record an instance of a peace chief by the name of High Backed Wolf intervening on behalf of a rebellious Cheyenne youth of the Fox warrior association named Pawnee who had stolen two Appaloosa horses from their owner. In the words of Pawnee, "One day I took them and headed west. Three days passed and I found myself still safe.... On the fourth day, as I looked back, I saw some people coming up. 'It is nothing,' I thought, 'just some people traveling.' When they overtook me, I saw they were Bowstring Soldiers out after me. 'You have stolen those horses,' they cried as they pulled me from my horse. 'Now we have trailed you down.' They threw me on the ground and beat me until I could

not stand; they broke up my weapons . . . they cut my blankets, moccasins, and kit to shreds. When they had finished they took all my food and went off with the horses, leaving me alone on the prairie, sore and destitute, too weak and hurt to move. The next day I started back, traveling as best I could all day long.... I traveled all day. The next day I thought I would die.... My feet were bleeding and I could not walk farther. I crawled slowly on my hands and knees to the brow of a high hill to find a place to die. As I gazed steadfastly into the south, a hunter came up the hill from behind me.... This man dismounted and hugged me. He wept, he felt so bad at seeing my plight. It was High Backed Wolf, a young man, but a chief. He put his blanket about me and took me home.... Then High Backed Wolf sent for the chiefs who were in the camp. Four or five came, one of whom was a soldier chief. High Backed Wolf spoke to the soldier chief first. 'This is the first time since I have become a big [tribal] chief that I have happened upon such a poor man; now I am going to outfit him.... This is my first good act as a chief. Help this man to tell the truth.'... I told them the whole story. I told them whose horses they were, and told them it was the Bowstrings who had punished me.... High Backed Wolf knew I was a rascal, so he lectured to me.... 'You are old enough to know what is right.... Now leave all of this foolishness.... Now I am going to help you out. That is what I am here for, because I am a chief of the people. Here are your clothes. Outside are three horses. You may take your choice!'"

20 The Aztecs believed that they lived in the fifth and final world, the four previous worlds having been destroyed by cataclysmic events. The fifth world was brought into being by the gods having drawn their own blood to revive human beings. This left the gods in a weakened condition, and it was human sacrifice and the offering of blood and hearts that kept the gods strong and the universe as they knew it in continual operation. They believed that failure to perform sacrificial rituals would lead to the final destruction of the fifth world. The relationship between warfare and human sacrifice is known as the god nourishment complex (Hirth 1989).

21 The dimensions of the Purron dam at this time were 400 meters wide, 100 meters thick at its maximum width, and about 5 meters in height (Woodbury and Neely 1972:86:figure 8). Charles Spencer (1993:52) estimates the volume of construction at 123,000 cubic meters, although it more likely was closer to 200,000 cubic meters based on mathematical estimates. The construction of a secondary coffer dam with a volume of 40,000 cubic meters was also constructed. Together the total volume of the Purron dam constructed at 600 BC was 163,000–240,000 cubic meters.

22 An example of this type of relationship is well illustrated with intergroup feasting associated with the potlatch in native America (Barnett 1938; Boas 1897; Drucker and Heizer 1967) and with Kula and moka celebrations in New Guinea and Melanesia (Dalton 1977; Malinowski 1922, 1967a; Strathern 2007).

23 Feasting that marks the termination of hostilities does not necessarily have to include the aggrieved parties. Among the Tsembaga in north-central New Guinea, the feasting associated with planting the rumbin tree and terminating hostilities with neighboring groups involved only the Tsembaga (Rappaport 1967).

24 Archaeologists often think of population growth at the regional level as a powerful source for social change. While true, I feel that the appearance of large communities was more important as they created an environment where internal disputes could occur and had to be mediated between both kinsmen and nonkinsmen.

25 Anthropologists have referred to network leaders by a variety of terms, including aggrandizers and big men (Godelier 1986; Hayden 2001b; Sahlins 1963).

26 There are more examples of ancient palaces for antiquity than can be cited. The reason is that for more than a century, archaeologists have sought to locate and excavate palaces of the rich and famous. Examples can be found across the world, including China (Ko and Hu 1984), Japan (Ponsonby-Fane 1956), Thailand (Dumarcay and Smithies 1991), Persia (Porter and Thévenart 2003), India (Michell 1999), and in the New World in Mexico, Guatemala, and Peru (Evans and Pillsbury 2008; Inomata 2008).

27 Examples of palaces in chiefdom societies include those in Africa (Evans-Pritchard 1971:166–234; Ojo 1966; Wilks 1989), Central America (Healy 1980:26–28; Oviedo

y Valdés 1959), Mesoamerica (Cyphers 1997), and Polynesia (Kirch 2010:166–176).

28 At the powerful Aztec city of Texcoco, the marketplace was located in what was said to be the first plaza of the king's palace. The reason was the king oversaw the care and operation of the marketplace and its venders for the good of the people (Hirth 2016:32; Ixtlilxóchitl 1891: 233–234). The term "Aztec" is used here in the generic sense since Texcoco was one of the three primary cities of the Aztec triple alliance.

29 Upper and Lower Egypt met near the modern city of Cairo.

30 The first three rulers depicted on the Palermo Stone to wear the double crown (*shmty*) are those with the names of Ka, Narmer, and Aha (Trigger 1983:appendix).

31 Six kingly dynasties define the Early Dynastic (3100–2686 BC) and Old Kingdom (2686–2181 BC) periods from the initial unification of Upper and Lower Egypt to its initial disintegration during the First Intermediate period. The First and Second Dynasties comprise the Early Dynastic, while the Third through Sixth Dynasties define the Old Kingdom.

32 Heqanakht was a moderately well-off official who lived during the Middle Kingdom. His household is listed as containing eighteen people, which included his mother, sister, second wife, a son, two daughters, an older aunt, a younger brother, his estate foreman and dependants, three farmers, and three female servants (Allen 2002:116–117; Moreno Garcia 2012:3).

33 The two most important officials within the religious hierarchy were the high priests of the important temples of Re and Ptah. The pharaoh was the head of both the secular and religious hierarchies (Warburton 2001).

34 For a comprehensive critique of the patrimonial household model as well as other models used in the interpretation of Ugaritic society, see McGeough (2007).

35 The Hebrew word for brideprice is *mēhar*, which appears to have been a common custom throughout Canaanite society.

36 The *mispaha* was an endogamous protective association of extended families and as such it defined the network of related households required to provide *go'el* (kinsmen-redeemer) service for one another. This included the obligation of avenging the murder of a clansman, marrying the widow of a deceased clansman, and redeeming the land of an impoverished or indebted clansman (Gottwald 1999:257–267) (see Chapter 3).

37 The Neolithic period (9000–6000 BC) was an era of independent towns and villages without evidence for a unified political structure that could provide a holistic claim of land proprietorship by any single ruler.

38 An example of flattery and subservience found in royal correspondence is illustrated in the Amarna letters in a dispatch from Aziru, the Canaanite ruler of the kingdom of Amurru in northwest Syria and northern Lebanon, to an Egyptian official named Tutu. The correspondence reads: "To Tutu, my master, my father: Message of Aziru, your son, your servant . . . Moreover, as you in that place are my father, whatever may be the request of Tutu, my father, just write and I will grant it. As you are my father and my master, and I am your son, the land of Amurru is your land, and my house is your house" (Schloen 2001:257).

39 Some of the ancillary palace personnel involved in cooking and entertainment include fowlers, tailors, acrobats, jesters, cooks, singers, a cymbalist, and a barber (Heltzer 1999:435–436).

40 Schloen (2001:270) argues that the 2,000 measures of land in this text represent *GáNA.KI* measures that are equivalent of the Sumerian *iku* of about 0.36 hectare. See Schloen (2001) for discussion.

41 The names of the three sons are Gir-Damu, Ir-Damu, and Napha-Il. The son named as Ingar and to whom the king grants land is probably Ir-Damu (Schloen 2001:276–277).

42 Schloen (2001:54) feels that the patrilineal house model describes the basic political structure of both Bronze and Iron Age societies throughout the Near East, including later Muslim societies. Regarding the latter, he notes that Islamic cities are often organized in quarters where clusters of households are linked by a combination of kinship, factional alliances, and patron–client relationships (Schloen 2001:110).

CHAPTER 5

1 An example of the multifaceted ways institutions raise support for their activities can be

found in how religious denominations in America raise support. While most religious congregations rely on voluntary tithes and offerings to support themselves, they also raise funds through other direct and indirect ways including bake sales, craft projects, voluntary work groups, auctions, collective garage sales, or running auxiliary for-profit businesses like day care programs, religious schools, after-school programs, and sport camps.

2 There is a 1st-century parable from Roman Palestine that summarizes the desire to lay up large stocks of staple goods such as food both as a hedge against future subsistence needs and to reinforce social position. "The ground of a certain rich man produced a good crop. He thought to himself, 'What shall I do? I have no place to store my crops.' Then he said, 'This is what I'll do. I will tear down my barns and build bigger ones, and there I will store all my grain and my goods. And I'll say to myself, You have plenty of good things laid up for many years. Take life easy; eat, drink and be merry'" (Luke 12:16–19). The man in the parable was rich and his social position was reinforced by the wealth he controlled. The size of his barns was a measure of his wealth and social importance within the community.

3 Issuing rations for work was a practice common throughout the ancient Old and New Worlds. Chinese sources identify artisans permanently attached to workshops of the royal Mongol court workshops who also received food rations for their service (Allsen 1997:32).

4 Egypt was one of the largest ancient states to operate with a staple finance system. The reason it could was that the Nile provided a natural transportation corridor to move resources in bulk throughout the kingdom. The current of the Nile carried goods from south to north from upper to lower Egypt, and the prevailing winds blowing from north to south allowed boats to sail against the current from the coast to upper Egypt.

5 Control over the production of wealth goods can be achieved in multiple ways and is often referred to as attached production (Clark and Parry 1990; Costin 1991).

6 While decentralized storage may lower the costs of transportation, it may incur higher costs of storage, monitoring, and protection. In this regard storage and movement costs may be inversely related to one another for institutions that rely on systems of staple finance.

7 The way a temple household was referred to was the same in both Sumerian and Akkadian. The word for house in Sumerian (*é*) and Akkadian (*bītu*, *bītum*) was followed by the name of the god or goddess to signify temple household or house of the named god (Robertson 1995:444).

8 Temple administrative personnel included priests, temple stewards, scribes, archivists, grain storage supervisors, and treasurers (Gelb 1979).

9 Skilled craftsmen who received temple rations included carpenters, woodworkers, leatherworkers, architects and builders, smiths, silversmiths, stoneworkers, merchants, and traders (Falkenstein 1974; Wright 2013).

10 Service personnel included fishermen, bakers, cooks, butchers, brewers, millers, messengers, and boatmen (Falkenstein 1974).

11 Some of the temple personnel involved in agricultural activities included field surveyors, crew chief supervisors, scribes of plow animals, overseers of plow animals, plow team leaders, plowmen, ox-drivers, and gardeners (Falkenstein 1974; Gelb 1979).

12 The activities involved in textile production of woolens included plucking the sheep (equivalent to shearing), cleaning the fiber, spinning thread, dyeing the thread, weaving cloth, and trimming and fulling finished goods (Wright 2013:403–406).

13 According to Wright (2013:398), during Ur III times (2112–2004 BC) herds of sheep reached their largest size. Dan Potts (1997:93) estimates that wool may have been plucked from as many as 203,310 sheep over a 3-month period in the city of Girsu in Lagash province.

14 This estimate was based on a sample of 452 fields from the cadastral texts of Lagash. Measurements in the Lagash texts were in *iku* where 1 hectare equals 2.77 *iku*. Similarly, for this calculation, one hectare equals 2.47 acres.

15 Textual evidence from Uruk levels at Warka record annual tallies of sheep that appear to belong to temple establishments during the fourth millennium. Zooarchaeological evidence of herd management strategies for wool production date to the same time frame from highland western Iran (Green 1980; McCorriston 1997:521).

16 Archaic texts from Uruk record a flock of 1,400 sheep belonging to the city that

probably produced wool used in the early textile industry (Breniquet 2014:64).

17 A proto-Elamite text records an entry for 20,098 bows and arrows (Englund 2001:110, fn 19). A separate Uruk period text records a smaller registry of 740 bows and arrows (Rubio 2006).

18 One such case was the shipment of grain to Oman via the Persian Gulf in exchange for copper and possibly other resources (Ouyang 2013). Other staple goods that were exchanged between regions include fish, lard, wool, and scented oil.

19 In the 21st century we would be tempted to draw a direct analogy between prebends and a salary. This would be partially correct as the prebend was an indirect way to cover subsistence needs like rations did, drawing the resources from direct production within the institution to which individuals were attached. In medieval society the term "prebend" referred to the idea of taking a "man into one's household, to feed and clothe him" (Bloch 1961:68).

20 Interior drainage within the Valley of Mexico created a series of shallow lakes in the center of the basin. The water table could be regulated using a series of dikes and drainage canals to produce an ideal growing environment. These fields when properly managed could produce two to three harvests per year and were resistant to crop failure from drought or frost (Palerm 1955; Parsons 1991). While the system was labor intensive, it produced some of the highest agricultural yields registered in pre-Hispanic Mesoamerica (Sanders 1976: table 9).

21 To complement the protein-deficient diet, animals, including deer and waterfowl, were hunted; insects were collected from wetlands; and fish of all sizes were captured in nets (Parsons 1996).

22 Aztec conquests within the Valley of Mexico allowed the Aztecs to reengineer *chinampa* agriculture within the southern lakes region, greatly expanding both agricultural productivity and the number of individuals that could be supported in the capital of Tenochtitlan. It is estimated that the productivity of newly created drained fields in this region produced enough surplus to support a nonagricultural population of 100,000 people in the capital city (Parsons 1976; Sanders 1976).

23 One of the reasons there were few changes in the way that staple finance systems were organized is that the Aztec state and the growth of its military empire occurred over a very short period of time. From the moment of Aztec independence from the neighboring city-state of Azcapotzalco to the arrival of the Spanish conquistadors was a period of only 91 years. While Aztec elites increased their hereditary control over agricultural land, private property or individual land ownership was not dominant in the Valley of Mexico at the time of the conquest.

24 Kinship was reckoned bilaterally along the Aztec and other Nahua groups in Central Mexico so that an individual could possibly affiliate themself to the *calpultin* of either their father or their mother if they came from different groups. This provided new households with considerable flexibility to access enough agricultural land for their support.

25 The *tecpan* contained a *calpulli* temple, administrative building, and a school for male youth. Male youth typically resided at the *tecpan* school, known as either the *telpochcalli* or the *calmecac* for several years. The food to feed the young men during this period came from land that the youth worked for their own support.

26 Alternative arrangements are known throughout antiquity, including working the land by those who have the prebend, renting it out, sharecropping, employing slaves, or working it with corvée labor.

27 The only exception to rotating corvée labor is when small land assignments were made to individual households located adjacent to their subsistence fields. In these cases, a single household would be responsible for a single small plot. In the Tepeaca region prebendal fields worked by commoner households were only 0.167 hectare in size (Martínez 1984:85).

28 Hirth (2016:41) has estimated that the total time commitment of commoner households to elite agricultural service was 11–17% of the total amount of time spent on agriculture during the rainy season. In the Tepeaca region males had to spend 5–9 days per year in additional labor service. Women were obligated to provide domestic service of 4–6 days per year in addition to 20 days of spinning thread or weaving textiles (Hirth 2016:41).

29 The capital city of Tenochtitlan was built on an island in the center of the Basin of Mexico

lake system. Because all rainfall across the basin drained into these lakes, years with high summer rainfall raised lake levels and typically created floods throughout residential areas of the city.

30 The pickling process is achieved through the lactic acids produced as sugars breakdown during the decomposition process of vegetables. Salt in the proportion of 0.8–1.5% of the weight of vegetables slows the process of decomposition and the formation of yeast that would lead to fermentation and the production of alcohol instead of pickled vegetables (Kurlansky 2002:21).

31 The formal definition of taxation according to international taxation guidelines is a compulsory levy made by public authorities for which nothing tangible is directly received in return (James 1998).

32 The number of salt prefectures changed over time with reorganizational efforts. During the Qing dynasty the empire was divided into eleven salt districts (Ho 1954:130).

33 Salt from each directory was stamped by place of origin, and toll stations were set up along the roads to enforce proper distribution and to attempt to control smuggling.

34 The problem in spoilage was a result of salt absorbing moisture under conditions of improper storage or when cargos were not protected during transportation. Spoilage during transportation decreased when private merchants were incorporated into the distribution system.

35 Salt stolen during transit was replaced with anything that concealed the bulk lost, including dirt, sand, and even feces. In AD 1163 the high-ranking administrator Huang Zhen proposed that the weights and measures of salt be standardized across the directories at both salterns and storage warehouses to minimize the theft that occurred in route. These reforms were apparently ineffective and contamination so pervasive that even the royal court could not escape it (Chien 2004:51, 229).

36 According to Chien (2004:57) an adult male of a master household in the Giangxi directory was required to purchase nearly 12 kilograms of salt, which was well beyond the 1-kilogram annual salt needs of an adult male.

37 The organization and conquest of the Inka state have been discussed in considerable detail by a number of scholars (Bauer 1996; Cieza de León 1998; Prescott 1921; Sancho 1917).

38 Small-scale settings include those of short temporal duration, small spatial extent, or those restricted to specific social settings or groups of individuals.

39 The universal partnership and ownership established within the Zoar community treated men and women equally as share owners in the profits of their efforts.

40 The industries established to provide self-sufficiency for the community as well as profit by selling goods to the outside world included a flour mill, woolen mill, saw mill, planing mill, two blast furnaces for smelting iron, a cooper, cobbler, blacksmith, saddlery, a tin shop, wagon shop, cabinet shop, a warehouse for exports, and a ceramic kiln for making roof tiles and other household wares. Furniture was made in the cabinet shop and the community also made cast iron stoves for cooking used both locally and across the region. All the iron tools and plows were made in the community foundry. A hotel was built within the community to make money from tourists who came to enjoy the community's music and gardens, as well as to house passengers and crew of canal boats operating along the Ohio Canal (Ohio State Historical Society 1952:27–31).

41 The Peruvian coastal desert is the result of the cold Humboldt current flowing north from the Antarctic, which produces the rich marine life found in the offshore waters. Periodic El Niño Southern Oscillation events bring warm waters along the coast that override the cold southern current and lead to catastrophic environmental events, including dying-off of marine fauna and torrential rains.

42 The satellite colonies in the archipelago model could be as small as three to four households or 100 or more. Because they are outside the core, satellite colonies are often situated in areas of other ethnic groups, creating multiethnic communities (Murra 1972).

43 Murra (1980:30) suggests that a family of two adults probably received an area of about 2.5 acres to cultivate, while larger families with more children received additional land.

44 Local land assignments were made to the *curaca*, or ruler, to support political activities, *huaca* lands to support the religious cults and deities, and *ayllu* lands cultivated by commoner households. The validity of this

division is supported after conquest by the Catholic Church's claiming *huaca* lands and those of the Temple of the Sun for monasterial support (Burns 1999).

45 Significant changes in land allocation occurred when local *ayllu* were forcibly moved from their home region and relocated to new areas of the empire as part of *mitmaq* resettlement.

46 The most common textiles were woven from alpaca wool. Fine *kumpi* textiles were also woven from the wool of the vicuña, and were said to be restricted for use by the elite. The unauthorized wearing of vicuña cloth was a capital offense (Murra 1962:720).

47 Little is known about the use of maguey for cloth across the Andes. Garcilasco de la Vega (2014) indicates that maguey was spun into thread and woven into cloth in areas where populations did not have access to cotton or camelid wool. Murra (1962:710–711) identifies the Callejon de Huyalas as one area where maguey cloth was manufactured.

48 The *aqllakuna* were sequestered in special conclaves called *aqllawasi* where they were supervised and taught weaving, cooking, beer brewing, and religion. These *aqllawasi* were located in different provinces throughout the empire, the largest of which are said to have contained up to 200 women of different ages. After 4 years of service they could serve as religious priestesses or be married to young elites (D'Altroy 2002:188–189).

49 Elsewhere, peripatetic consumption was called *veizla* in ancient Scandinavian; *poludye*, *poludovanie*, or *goszczenie* in ancient Slavic; and *makahiki* in Hawaiian (Kobishchanow 1987:108).

50 Peripatetic consumption of the ruler's court in 19th-century AD Georgian kingdoms could, according to A. I. Budberg, consume in a day the entire yearly production from a peasant village (Kobishchanow 1987:109). Whether this is an accurate description of the level of surplus consumed is unclear, but it emphasized that the arrival of the ruler's court drew heavily on the resource stocks of dependent towns and villages.

51 The bishopric of Ely was roughly 70 miles from north to south and 60 miles east to west (Stone 2005:map 2.1). The area if calculated conservatively at 4,200 square miles converts to 10,878 square kilometers.

52 His peripatetic lifestyle is evident in the number of horses he maintained on his different manors. Although it is impossible to calculate an exact total, we know that he had 20–40 horses at two of his main palace residences and another 60–70 at his townhouse in London (Stone 2005:22). How many horses were stabled at his other manors and palace residences is unknown, although it is likely that he would have changed mounts as he moved throughout the bishopric.

53 The Achaemenid empire is often referred to as the first Persian empire. It extends from the conquests of Cyrus (ca. 559–530 BC) and Cambyses (530–522 BC) to the fall of the kingdom with its conquest by Alexander the Great in 331 BC.

54 The procession was much larger, of course, when the king moved with his army. The sources suggest that there was a fixed order of the procession. According to Quintus Curtius, the procession included, along with other individuals, 365 young men clad in purple robes, one for each day of the year (Briant 2002:188).

CHAPTER 6

1 The quote is from the Adam Smith's classic work, *An Inquiry into the Nature and Causes of the Wealth of Nations* (1827:364).

2 In Israel the tithe was known as the *ma'aser*, while across greater Mesopotamia during the Old Babylonian period (mid-second millennium BC) it was called the *esru* (Stevens 2006:93).

3 Bonney and Ormrod (1999) discuss the organization of institutional economy in terms of tribute states that got their support from conquered provinces, domain states that supported institutions from the ruler's personal properties, tax states that derived income from the property of their constituents, and fiscal states that derived resources through economic growth.

4 An example of an early tax is that recorded for linen and oil paid to the Scorpion king of predynastic Egypt sometime during the late fourth millennium BC. This is possibly a tithe or a tribute levy exacted as a result of his early conquests of adjacent nomes at the end of the Predynastic period.

5 Solon is credited with taking a census of property ownership to establish a general estimate

of annual income as the basis for these social orders. The *pentacosiomedimni* were the first and highest class defined by an annual income of "500 measures or more of wet and dry produce" (Scott-Kilvert 1960:59). The second class were the *hippada teluntes*, or knight class, which had an annual income of 300 measures or more of wet and dry produce and paid a horse tax. The third class were the *zeugitai*, who had a yearly income of 200 measures or more of wet and dry produce. All three of these groups could hold public office. The remainder of the population comprised the fourth group known as the *thetes* (Scott-Kilvert 1960:60). Foreigners (*metics*) were not citizens and were not included in Solon's classification, irrespective of their wealth.

6 According to Samson (2002), this tax was calculated initially on land and evolved more broadly to personal property such as ships, carriages, horses, clothing, money, and other possessions. The census established the basis for the tribute, a direct tax levied as a percentage of net worth. It was not seen as necessarily onerous since a higher property evaluation placed individuals in a higher position in the military and political hierarchy and made them eligible to seek high military and civil offices (Levi 1989:79).

7 During the Roman republic, an important source of income was derived from the sale of slaves taken from conquered provinces. The sale of slaves within Italy transformed the Roman economy from one of independent peasant farming to commercial estates owned by the elite and operated using slave labor (Bradley 1987:14).

8 The British perfected an efficient means of taxing a wide array of transactions with the enactment of the Stamp Act on March 22, 1765. This tax was imposed on the American colonies and it required them to purchase a stamp for every piece of printed paper used in legal transactions. The uses covered everything from legal documents to paper for printing books and newspapers, and eventually, to the documentation of the purchase of imports such as tea.

9 In a very practical way Aristotle defined generosity with respect to spending money as the midpoint between excessive wastefulness and stinginess. This made generosity a relative variable in relation to the wealth that an individual possessed (Irwin 1999:49–50).

10 A Greek talent is generally accepted to represent 26 kilograms. There were 6,000 drachmas in a talent where each silver drachma was 4.33 grams in weight (Bresson 2016:440) . In February 2016, the price of a troy ounce of silver was $15, or 50 cents per gram. At this rate a silver talent would be worth about $12,990 at February 2016 prices; 10 talents would be worth $129,900. While it is always risky to evaluate relative worth, given modern swings in the value of precious metals, it is safe to say this was a lot of money.

11 The word *trierarchos* is the title the liturgist held while fulfilling a trierarchy. It is a compound of the name for a warship (*trieres*) and *archos*, the word for commander.

12 The young litigant says that he equipped warships for a period of 7 years at a cost of 6 talents, or 36,000 drachmas (Lamb 1930:477–479). The yearly average of 5,142 drachmas is produced by dividing 36,000 by 7 years.

13 Gabrielsen (1994:126–129) estimates that the size of the Athenian navy was relatively stable throughout the 4th century BC, fluctuating between 300 and 350 seaworthy ships available for service over that period.

14 The 5-year immunity for army veterans was originally established by emperor Marcus Aurelius between AD 161 and 180. The immunity for army veterans was made permanent under emperor Septimius Severus (Duncan-Jones 1990:161).

15 The modern term of euergetism was originally coined by French historian André Boulanger (1923) and subsequently used in the work of Paul Veyne (1976).

16 While especially prominent in the Greco-Roman world, euergetism can also be found in other societies. Isin and Lefebvre (2005) cite the pious foundation of the waqf within the Ottoman empire as another type of euergetistic practice within the Muslim world.

17 Zuerderhoek (2009) argues that a civic ideal of citizenship was especially strong throughout the Greco-Roman world. He feels that members of the urban elite saw themselves first as citizens of their communities, whatever the level of their wealth, instead of members of an upper class as it might exist across communities.

18 Votive offerings were not the same as sacrifices intended to feed or maintain the gods. Instead, they celebrated life events such the birth of a

child, healing from a disease, or a victory in competitive games or in battle. They were given within the context of expected reciprocity, either for things received or for things hoped for in the future.

19 Plutarch says that at the completion of the project, Pericles put the matter to rest by asking for the ostracism of his primary rival. He was successful, and his unnamed rival was banished from Athens and the opposition party was dissolved (Scott-Kilvert 1960:182).

20 *Demes* were local political and landholding units within Attica. Cimon belonged to the deme of Lacia. Attica is believed to have had 139 demes that were grouped into larger tribes.

21 A great deal of public construction was carried out by convicted criminals who were condemned to carry out *ad opus publicum*. This work included the construction of public architecture, building roads, cleaning sewers, and servicing public baths. When the supply of criminals fell short, as it often did, regular citizens were conscripted in a form of corvée labor (Duncan-Jones 1990:174).

22 Zuiderhoec (2009:39) defines small donations as being 1,000 denarii or less, which is the equivalent to provide an annual subsistence cost of 33 denarii per individual.

23 Evidence for one of the earliest pan-Mediterranean food drives for the poor is documented for the 1st century AD in the Christian New Testament where the Apostle Paul raises money from the Christian–Jewish churches in Greece and Asia Minor to support widows and the poor in Jerusalem. Appeals to contributing churches can be found in the books of Acts (6:1–4, 11:29, 24:17), Romans (15:25–28), 1 Corinthians (16:1–4), 2 Corinthians (8:1–4), and Galatians (2:10).

24 In some cases scholars refer to tolls and tariffs simply as a trade tax (Monson and Scheidel 2015). In other cases, it is unclear from the sources as to whether the charges levied refer to import tariffs on goods or market taxes on sellers.

25 The pre-European florescence of the Wanga in Africa was due to their position along a long-distance caravan route (Stevenson 1968:142).

26 The important salt production centers of Taghaza and Taoudeni were brought directly under the control of the Songhai empire during the early 15th century AD as part of their overall strategy to control the trans-Saharan salt and gold trade.

27 It is very possible that tolls existed much earlier in time in the absence of specific treaty relationships between polities. Even where treaty relationships existed, these may only have extended to state-sponsored merchants, with private merchants responsible for paying tolls and customs duties where they were required.

28 Duncan-Jones (1990:194) identifies the level of *portoria* in Spain at 2%, while it was 2.5% in Asia and Gaul, and 5% in Sicily.

29 The other two important taxes during the Republic were the *tributum* tax assessed against property in the time of war and the rents collected from state lands (Tan 2015).

30 Zuiderhoec (2009:49–50) estimates that the 2–4% tax on grain and other market goods entering the city of Myra in Roman province of Lycia was sufficient to cover anywhere from 30% to 60% of the city's total annual expenditures. While this may not have been the case for other Roman cities, it indicates the important of the *portoria* for local civic maintenance.

31 High-value goods listed in the *portoria palmyrenorum* include slaves and camel unguent imported in alabaster vessels. Interestingly, it also identifies a range of charges for local services, including a charge on sex workers (Matthews 1984).

32 The author of the *Periplus Maris Erythraei* is believed to be an Egyptian Greek mariner and merchant. The document is a handbook and guide to merchants engaged in trade with India and down the east coast of Africa. The document is believed to have been written sometime between AD 40 and 70 (Casson 1989:6–10).

33 The route of Pegolotti extends east to the city of Azov in southern Russia and then on to Hang-chou the capital of the Song. Pegolotti calculates the cost of a caravan transporting 25,000 gold florins' worth of merchandise at 1,300–1,900 florins for a caravan of 40–60 pack animals, 1,000 florins for duty on select goods at Azov, and 400–600 florins for tolls and protection along the way. If duty and tolls cost 1,600 florins, this is only 6.4% of the total value of the merchandise transported (Rossabi 1993:356–357).

34 The Mongolian horse pastoralists would be an example of a nonagricultural state-level society (Allsen 1997; Weatherford 2004).

35 The volume of an artaba during the Greco-Roman period was 27.13 liters, while 1 aroura was equivalent to 2,754.8 square meters, or 0.27548 hectare.

36 Tax rates on agriculture greater than one-sixth of the crop are found only on irrigated land where the yields were understandably higher. Prasad (1987) indicates that the state taxed anywhere from one-fifth to one-quarter of the produce on irrigated land. It is possible that the rationale for a higher tax base on irrigated land resided both in the higher yields that they provided as well as in the higher investment that the state made in maintaining them. Conversely, tax on livestock could be quite low. The tax on cattle was one-fiftieth of the herd, or 2% annually.

37 A determination of the complete tax obligation must be determined against the entire constellation of taxes that may be imposed on a given taxpayer. In addition to land or production taxes, farmers often paid poll taxes along with absorbing the ad valorem taxes charged on any trade goods that they might purchase.

38 Using a tax calculation in wheat against annual consumption needs, Hopkins (1980:116–120) estimates that the annual tax levy was equivalent to 10–12% of annual subsistence requirement for a family. Households would have adjusted their production levels to produce at 10–12% above their subsistence needs.

39 One way that debt could be incurred by rural population was to avoid the military draft by making money payments (*ilku*) used to hire mercenaries. This enabled families to keep their workforce on the farm, but it could incur debt beyond that needed to pay their tax share.

40 Herodotus (3.89) writes of the Persian empire, "During reigns of Cyrus and Cambyses there was no fixed tribute at all, the revenue coming from gifts (*dēra*) only; and because of his imposition of regular taxes, and other similar measures, the Persians have a saying that Darius was a tradesman, Cambyses a tyrant, and Cyrus a father" (De Selincourt 1966).

41 Wealth goods such as silver bullion are mentioned occasionally in bala texts, but they are very rare (Sharlach 2004:29).

42 Labor service for men included canal work, towing boats, agricultural tasks, or other service activities. A total of 7,750 workdays are listed in the bala for female workers from Lagash, but their services are not identified.

43 The fifty-five provinces and client states comprising the Aztec empire extended across the modern state of Mexico from the Atlantic to Pacific coasts and from 150 kilometers north of Mexico City to as far south as the border of Guatemala.

44 Chia is the common name for *Salvia hispanica* L.

45 Most craft production in the Aztec world was carried out by independent craft specialists within the context of their homes. Nevertheless, the palace workshop known as the *totocalli* manufactured specialized items with the insignia of the king such as the feather garments mentioned in the epigraph at the start of Chapter 5. The raw materials used to manufacture these goods came from tribute levies. When these did not suffice, additional raw materials would have been purchased in the central marketplace.

46 The main marketplace in the Aztec capital was located in Tlatelolco. It was the richest market in the empire and was well stocked with staple foods, utilitarian goods, and the complete array of wealth goods. Conservative estimates place the population visiting the marketplace at about 60,000 people (Hirth 2016:64).

47 The reason that cotton textiles were a frequently mentioned in the tribute lists was because cotton could not be grown in the Basin of Mexico and had to be imported. It is for this same reason that raw cotton is listed among the tribute listed in Table 6.1.

48 The province of Tlapa was one of the most important within the Aztec empire to produce gold, turned in as gourds of gold dust and gold bars. Since gold was considered a form of money within the Aztec economy (Díaz del Castillo 1956:217; Hirth 2016:72), it may have facilitated its conversion into alternative goods.

49 The Tlapa provincial documents are particularly rich and report the quarterly payments made to the Aztec tribute administrator between AD 1486 and 1522. Gerardo Gutiérrez's (2013) analysis of the regional tribute turned in to the Aztec tribute supervisor in Tlapa has revealed two interesting aspects about the administration of the provincial

tribute system. The first is that the level of tribute increased over time, which is not surprising in and of itself, since the central state often raises taxes. In the case of Tlapa, the increases might also reflect a recognition of the region's growing population able to produce tribute over the 36-year period chronicled in the tribute registry. Second, the value of tribute turned in to the Aztec tribute supervisor as computed from the *Información de 1554* (Scholes and Adams 1957) was 13–14% higher than what was turned in. Gutiérrez (2013) believes that this might reflect a local processing fee by the state.

50 Both the Sumerian and Aztec economies had forms of commodity money with which to calculate exchange equivalencies. Although silver and perhaps copper had equivalency value for calculating relative worth, they did not circulate as fractional currencies. The Aztec were better off in this regard with the use of cacao beans and *quachtli* textiles. Cacao beans served as the small fractional currency used to purchase individual fruit and other items in the marketplace. *Quachtli* were valued in terms of their size in the number of cacao beans. The three sizes of *quachtli* were valued at 65, 80, and 100 cacao beans. Other forms of commodity money included copper axes and gold dust circulating in semi-transparent plumes.

51 Tax farming was widely practiced across the Mediterranean world in Greece, Rome, Ptolemaic Egypt, and Byzantium. It was also practiced throughout the Arab world and within the Ottoman empire (Çizakça 1989, 1993; Fleet 2006:134–141; Gibbs 2013; Kiser and Kane 2007).

52 The period of the contract could be annual or longer. In the Ottoman empire, contracts to tax farmers often were for 3 years (Fleet 2003:215).

53 Horses were fundamental to military power across Asia and were one of the most important imports into India during the 15th and 16th centuries AD. India also exported horses to China where they served the same function. The pivotal role of Muhammed Sayyid Ardestani in providing horses for the mobile cavalry of Indian governments made him an important figure in geopolitical relationships within the Indian subcontinent.

54 See Duncan-Jones (1990:121–142) for a good discussion of types of land and land wealth in ancient Rome.

55 According to Tacoma (2013), the Ptolemaic estates were referred to as *ousia* and passed as personal property from emperor to emperor. With the Flavian emperors (AD 69–96), these imperial estates shifted from being the personal property of the emperor to an imperial patrimony tied directly to the office of the emperor and the resources needed for its operation.

56 According to Renger (1979:250), the term used for a rental field in the documents is a *sukusu* field.

57 This process of granting individuals direct access to palace and temple lands for their personal use and support created prebendholders that over time evolved into some of history's first documented renters (Hudson and Levine 1996:14). Moreover, Postgate (2004:185) observes that when land was leased it was generally rented for 2–3 years at a time.

58 We can assume that the entrepreneurs did not make this arrangement in the hope of breaking even. Instead, they surely were speculating on making a profit from what they would sell over and above the 4.5 million liters of barley and 1.8 million liters of dates to be harvested from domain lands. Dates, of course, would have been harvested from date groves lining irrigation canals and located in other areas.

59 The first systematic coinage to be used across Mesopotamia was introduced by the Persians in the mid-6th century BC. One of the first coins introduced was the gold daric, which Darius I introduced based on the Lydian gold stater.

60 The kingdom of Gyaman, located in what is today the Côte d'Ivoire (Ivory Coast), was an important kingdom of the Akan people in west Africa from the middle of the 15th century to the end of the 19th century AD.

61 While gold prospecting was open to everyone, the chiefs controlled the greatest flow of gold in addition to nuggets because they could mobilize slave labor to work deep mines following veins of ore that normal households could not exploit. The nature of the differences between deep and shallow mining is described by Terray (1974:327–328).

62 Silver was also mined in ancient Greece in the provinces of Thrace and Macedonia.

63 Davis (2014:268) estimates that if Athens had a population of 30,000 male citizens, then the total revenue available for distribution was 300,000 drachmas, or 50 talents of silver. Ober (2015:512), working from the perspective of the mint, estimates coin production at 700–6,000 talents per year in the 5th century BC. A 3–5% minting fee would produce a regular annual income of 21–300 talents of silver.

CHAPTER 7

1 The individuality of decision making was greater in the ancient past than it is today given the ease of communication made possible with cell phones and the Internet. In the past, merchants had to estimate information on price, supply, and demand based on their experience and good judgment. Communication was slow and often inaccurate, which meant that merchants had to make their commercial decisions based on imperfect information and hard-won experience.

2 Stephen Gudeman (2001:98) feels that there is no consistent theory for what profit is within neoclassical economics. As a result, this makes it a fluid term that can be defined in different ways, depending on how individual preferences can vary in different cultural settings. Gudeman feels the term "profit" best fits market settings where gains in value can be measured in monetary terms at the level of individual households.

3 The *Periplus Maris Erythraei* describes the resources to be found in ports for maritime merchants trading between Egypt, the east African coast, the Arabian Peninsula, and the west coast of India (Casson 1989). The document was written in Greek, and while the author is not stated, the account is clearly a firsthand description written by a merchant and navigator who had traveled the route and observed the goods available for sale.

4 The *La Practica della Mercatura* most likely was written by Pegolotti sometime between AD 1310 and 1340. He estimated the travel time from Azov, Russia, and Hang-chou, China, at 270 travel days. He emphasized the security of the route and calculated the costs of hiring individuals for the trip, paying tools, and transporting goods home as a per-animal expense (Rossabi 1993:355–357; Yule and Cordier 1916:143–171). What is remarkable about this account is the detail of costs specified that can be used in planning a trade expedition.

5 Examples of produce that had to be processed before it could be resold include processing pigs into hams and cucumbers into pickles (Vance 1970:76).

6 Hopkins (1978:51) feels that the Geniza merchants of medieval Egypt are a model of how merchants operated. He cites one merchant who traded in flax, silk, olive oil, soap, wax, pepper, cinnamon, cloves, metals, textiles, dyes and tanning materials, aromatics, jewels, coral, shells, chemicals, hides, and pitch, among other commodities.

7 Economic geographers developed central place theory to model human economic interaction in an environment free of natural resource irregularities and restrictions on movement (Christaller 1966; Haggett 1965; Losch 1938). While unrepresentative of the real world, this approach has proven useful for understanding a good deal about the spatial organization of human interaction (C. Smith 1976b, 1976c).

8 The gravity model was one of the earliest attempts to address why transportation networks show strong linkages and commodity flows between some centers and weak linkages between others. In general, the model predicts that the linkages and flows between communities should be directly proportional to their population size, and inversely proportional to the distance between them (Taafe and Gauthier 1973:73).

9 Halstead and O'Shea (1989) have discussed how groups deal with fluctuations in resource availability in terms of the concept of subsistence risk. Groups employ several strategies to mediate resource fluctuations that can endanger their existence. These strategies are diversification (exploiting a wide array of resources to minimize the possibility of shortfall), mobility (traveling to where resources can be found), storage (laying up stores to guard against shortfall), and trade (O'Shea 1989). Trade provides access to resources that are not locally available.

10 The discussion of the Vitiaz Strait tribal merchants is based on the excellent work of Thomas Harding (1967, 1994), who described this trade network as it still operated in the

mid-1960s. The six merchant groups involved in this trade were the Bilbili, Tami, and the four Siassi Island groups of the Aramot, Mandok, Malai, and Tuam. The population of these six groups ranged from 120 to 300 people between AD 1885 and 1926 (Harding 1967:14). It is likely that the trade network was even larger during the 19th and early 20th centuries AD.

11 In the words of Thomas Harding (1967:182), "Trade . . . is mainly an activity of the household. It is therefore a part of private rather than public affairs." Trade partnerships were structured along kinship lines, but while it was good to have kinsmen in faraway places through which goods could flow and exchanges could be made, in the view of Vitiaz merchants it was best to have good trade-friends whoever they might be.

12 Although trade could occur within mini-markets held in coastal villages, this did not expand merchant behavior since the scope of their sales was determined by the limit of their trade contacts and the extended kindreds and trade relationships of their trade-friends.

13 Raising pigs in Melanesia is dependent on growing yams, and since these island merchants lacked agricultural land, they could not breed them and had to obtain them through trade.

14 The transport and sale of goods by merchants over more than 300 kilometers up and down the New Guinea coast stimulated and increased the level of craft production within the communities that manufactured specialized goods for sale. Harding (1967:246) estimated that trade doubled or tripled the demand for craft goods produced by the specialized villages that manufactured them.

15 A modern example of how an innovation in transportation technology transformed the commercial world can be found in the introduction of container shipping into maritime trade. Malcom McLean, a former trucker, recognized that considerable delays were spent in loading and unloading cargo on maritime docks. In 1956 he outfitted the ship known as the *Ideal X* and launched the world into container shipping. This twentieth-century innovation changed where and how products were produced, led the way to transport deregulation, and integrated East Asia into the world economy (Levinson 2016).

16 Geospatial modeling has made it possible to examine the relative costs and time of transportation using different forms of transportation via the website of ORBIS: The Stanford Geospatial Network Model of the Roman World (https://classics.stanford.edu/projects/orbis-stanford-geospatial-network-model-roman-world). This modeling takes into effect time of year, wind patterns, sea currents, and road networks as they can be reconstructed in the ancient Roman world.

17 Trade circuits for obsidian sources in the central Mediterranean were larger than those exploiting Melos obsidian in the Aegean. Here obsidian from Sardinia and Lipardi moved inland and across Italy and France. Obsidian from the island source of Lipardi even reached coastal sites in the northern Adriatic Sea.

18 The British found the Banjaras difficult to control and a potentially disruptive force. They adopted a pass system in AD 1872 to keep them from moving freely across the landscape: groups with more than four males had to have a pass to move together. The pass was obtained from the police, and groups would have to stop to get new passes as they crossed into new districts (Satya 1997). The Banjaras continued to transport goods throughout the colonial era even though a train could move in 1 week what a *tanda* of 20,000 pack oxen could carry in an entire season (Raychaudhuri 1982:339). The introduction of the long platform truck in 1950 led to the quick demise of the Banjaras as long-distance caravan haulers (Varady 1979).

19 When used as pack animals, each ox could carried 265–280 pounds on average (Habib 1993:376). When they pulled carts, they could transport heavier loads.

20 Other goods that the Banjaras bought, transported, and sold included the supari nut, wheat, spices, dry coconuts, plantains, sugarcane, opium, mangoes, custard apple, lac, gum, hemp, and tobacco (Satya 1997:316).

21 The social status of merchants fluctuated within Chinese society. Merchant status increased after the 10th century AD with the development of a meritocratic philosophy that encouraged entrepreneurship and the view that wealth could play a positive role within society (Gungwu 1993:401). Under the

Mongols, the status of merchants was elevated and they were seen as being superior to priests (Weatherford 2004:225).

22 Christian attitudes held that the practice of usury and charging loans with interest was an unnatural way of making a money. To this could be added the New Testament example of Jesus driving merchants out of the Temple (Mark 11:15–17). The general attitude toward merchants is summarized in the Apocrypha in the book of Sirach where it says, "A merchant can hardly keep from wrongdoing, nor is a tradesman innocent of sin. Many have committed sin for gain, and those who seek to get rich will avert their eyes. As a stake is driven firmly into a fissure between stones, so sin is wedged in between selling and buying" (Sirach 26:29–27:2).

23 Gregory, bishop of Tours, summarizes this view in a story about buying wine in the 6th century AD. For Gregory, all traders were suspect outsiders, Jews or eastern Christians. A source of Gregory's hostility was that they would buy cheap food and sell dear, raising the price and leading to hardships of the peasants (Knight 1999:148).

24 Pearson (1991) cites England, Portugal, and the Netherlands as examples of small states that focused on trade as a basis for revenue compared with China and India. Port cities and city-states such as Venice and Phoenicia are other examples but on a smaller scale.

25 Granovetter (1985:492) cites a modern instance of large-scale transactions that take place between individuals based on trust alone. Modern diamond merchants make deals and extend unsecured credit between one another based on a handshake. Of course, diamond merchants are a closely knit group and monitor each other for improper dealings. One act of cheating or malfeasance on the part of a merchant would ruin him and eliminate him from the community.

26 Indigenous cargo systems in Latin America were a way to share the financial obligations of sponsoring important religious events within the normal calendar of the Catholic Church. Cargo means "obligation," and the socially responsible, wealthy members of the community undertook the expense of sponsoring these activities on a rotating basis. Some of these obligations were onerous and required years of saving or incurring debt to cover the cost. What was incurred in terms of cost was rewarded at the community level with increased social stature and prestige. Wealthy individuals who shirked the expectations of the community and conserved their economic capital lost respect and social influence within the community (Cancian 1965; Monaghan 1995).

27 Moses Finley (1985) championed the small view, or primitivist perspective of the ancient Mediterranean economy. For Finley (1985) and Jones (1974), the ancient economy was composed of largely self-sufficient agricultural communities that were integrated through political and religious institutions of the larger towns. The high cost of transportation limited the distribution of staple goods to relatively small regions and stymied the development of centers of craft production and the economies of scale that specialized craft production could achieve. Control of land, not trade, was the source of wealth. Large communities were consumer cities rather than centers of independent production and commerce. The food mobilized to support large communities like Rome took place through the administrative system and its associated forms of taxation rather than relying on the market for resource provisioning. The foundation of wealth was land and labor, and political power was in the hands of those who controlled it.

28 The calculations of worth for the cargo were made using Ugarit (silver) shekels, which weigh 9.4 grams. Fifty Ugarit shekels made up 1 mina (approximately 470 grams), and 60 minas made up the Ugarit talent of approximately 28.2 kilograms. The value of the cargo at 12,000 shekels was equivalent to 4 minas, totaling 112.8 kilograms. The price of 1 kilogram of silver at $15.72 per ounce is $505.41.

29 The ship's cargo included copper and tin ingots, terebinth resin, glass ingots, eighty pieces of Cypriot ceramic fineware, gold and silver scrap jewelry and/or bullion, bronze weapons (swords, daggers, spearheads), bronze and copper vessels, Egyptian ebony logs, ivory blanks, hippopotamus teeth, ostrich eggshells, *Murex* shells for purple dye, and finished ivories. Perishable organic materials in the cargo included almonds, pine nuts, figs, olives, grapes or raisins or wine, safflower, black cumin, sumac, coriander, whole pomegranates, wheat,

and barley. It is likely that woolen textiles were also an important component of the cargo, although none has been preserved (Monroe 2009:11; 2010:21, 26; Pulak 2008:294).

30 Copper onboard the Uluburun occurred as oxhide, bun, oval, and pillow ingots. The tin bullion on board was cast in the form of oxhide, bun, and anchor-shaped ingots (Monroe 2010:table 1).

31 Voyages in the Mediterranean normally did not occur throughout the entire year because of weather conditions and the increased risk of ship loss in bad weather. The 22.5–30.0% interest rate for a 4- to 5-month period represents a per annum rate of 67.5–90.0%. Interest rates were high because risks were high (Casson 1991:102).

32 I use the term "partnership" simply to express that individuals who collaborated in a business venture benefit from their mutual collaboration. I do not use the term in a technical way to distinguish different types of partnerships, percentages of return obtained in each, or whether all participants invested capital or not (e.g., Weber 2003b). For examples of how arrangements could be structured in different areas, see Amselle (1971:264), Dale (1994:118–120), Goitein (1967:170–171), Greif (2000:266–269), and Weber (2003b).

33 It is noteworthy that there is no known transactional agreement from the pre-Columbian New World. The closest known arrangement occurred in the Aztec world with merchants functioning as agents on trade ventures for wealthy individuals.

34 Braudel (1986:122) notes that commenda contracts had high interest rates, with Armenian investors getting 75% of the profits. Merchants could invest their own capital, and for this reason Hovhannes recorded it as such in his account book. Braudel speculates that Hovhannes may also have been counting and using his return of 25% on the total profits from the venture in his dealings once return on investment could be calculated.

35 Areas of the ancient and premodern world where merchant associations have been reported include Africa (Dike and Ekejiuba 1990:69; Skinner 1964:88), China (Cheong 1997:37; Golas 1977:559; Shiba 1977:417), Europe (Braudel 1986:314–315; Epstein 1991:130–135; Weber 2003b:230–235), and Russia (Dale 1994:85).

36 Finley (1985:138) argues strongly that there were no guilds in antiquity and that the Roman *collegia* did not serve as regulatory or protective agencies. While his reference is specifically to trade guilds, he is also correct to the extent that merchant relationships were more often handled through commenda agreements and often with foreign merchants.

37 Mauro (1993) makes the point that Venice lacked guilds because commerce was the concern of the entire city and was too important to be left in the hands of merchants. Instead, the state took it over and negotiated treaties and trade deals directly with the countries where its merchants operated.

38 *Verlagssystem* is the term used to refer to the development of the putting-out system in Germany. Mazzaoui (2011) argues that it appears as early as AD 1350 in southern Germany where it is associated with the manufacture of textiles from imported cotton.

39 Clifford Geertz (1963:63–64) reports a modern application of the putting-out system in rural Indonesia. Here textile traders called engrossers bought manufactured cloth, cut it to design, and farm it out to tailors who made finished garments that were collected and sold in local marketplaces.

40 Cohen and Van Hear (2008) have provided an overview of different types of diaspora in the modern world. Dike and Ekejiuba (1990:196–201, 226) talk about the factors leading to the establishment of diaspora settlement and colonies among the Aro chieftains of Africa.

41 The network-based economy is contrasted by Wai-keung (2005) with the firm-based economy of the modern world. In a network-based economy, family firms are embedded in the diaspora network instead of the other way around. In a firm-based economy, individual firms or enterprises will compete with one another for commercial gain. In China, linkages are based on *guanxi*, the personal relationships that build trust, reputation, and make quick business decisions possible. In a network-based operation, individual merchants are seen as part of the larger group (the *bang*, or trade coalition) rather than as individuals.

42 The Portuguese never gained control of the vital trade of pepper and spice for this reason (Tracy 1993). In Sri Lanka, the Portuguese

relied on the contract system using local ethnic intermediaries to collect pepper, ginger, cardamom, and cinnamon from dispersed foraging and farming people (Morrison 2002). Because of this, the Portuguese did not seek a trade empire as much as they established a protection racket that coerced local merchants to sell spices at below market rates and forced Indian merchants to buy a *cartaz* that entitled their ships to travel safely in the Indian Ocean controlled by Portuguese seamen (Bernstein 2008:174, 194; Serjeant 1974).

43 Jewish merchants taking goods for sale in India during the 9th to 14th centuries AD would often work through a well-known and respected local Jewish or Muslim merchant representative known as the *wakīl al-tujjār* or *peqīd ha-soharīm*. The *wakīl* had a warehouse (*dar wakīl*) and would take charge of goods left with him for sale after the merchant would leave. It was common for a range of buying and selling to be conducted in the (*dar wakīl*) warehouse. The *wakīl al-tujjār* often was a knowledgeable and respected religious judge (*qadis*). He was not the head of a merchant guild, but, rather, "was a self-made, independent agent in a society of independent merchants" (Goitein 1963:201–202).

44 On a smaller scale, the family firm shared these same advantages over independent merchant interactions (Dobbins 1996:126).

45 Trade diasporas in the ancient world include, but are not limited to: the Near East (Dercksen 1996; Kuhrt 1998; Stein 1999b, 2001), China (Gungwu 1993; Liu 1988:140), the Greek and Roman worlds (Rauh 1993: xv), and one case in highland Mesoamerica (Spence 2005; White et al. 2004). In another sense the intentional relocation of community segments in different ecological zones for purposes of producing and redistributing resources within the community can also be thought of as a type of managed interpolity diaspora (Murra 1980).

46 A few of the trade diasporas in the premodern world included Jewish (Grief 1989; Israel 2005), Armenian (Baghdiantz McCabe 2005; Chaudhury 2005), Chinese (Cohen and Van Hear 2008:83–102; Dobbins 1989), Japanese (Wray 2005), Tamil (Abu-Lughod 1989:301), African (Cohen 1971; Dike and Ekejiuba 1990; Sundström 1974:45–47), Muslim (Curtin 1984), and Hindu (Dale 1994; Levi 2002) groups.

47 In Africa the solution to long separations by Hausa merchants was to take prostitutes with them during their travels (Cohen 1971:272).

48 The city of Assur was located in a flat plain that extends east from the Tigris river. The region is poor in resources and did not produce enough food to support its urban population. For that reason, Assur had to rely on trade to get grain to support the city (Aubet 2013:271–272; Moore and Lewis 1999:64).

49 It is believed that Akkadian merchants were already present and trading in Anatolia during the second half of the third millennium BC coincident with the expeditions of Sargon of Akkad. The Warrior King legend suggests that the expansion of Akkad into Anatolia was at the behest of merchants and not the state. The implication is that the Assyrian merchants were following established patterns of trade in expanding their network of trade enclaves across Anatolia (Aubet 2013:309–312; Larsen 1976:216).

50 Three political institutions dominated Assur: the ruler, the city assembly of wealth merchants, and the economic office referred to as the *bit alim*. The official in charge of the *bit alim* was known as the *līmum*, who oversaw procuring and supplying traders with goods to trade. The city assembly (*ruba'rum*) was both a court of law and an influential body made up of city elders and principal merchants who regularly monitored *kārum* enclaves such as Kanesh (Veenhof 2003b:73–75).

51 All of the tablets were correspondence sent in duplicate (Veenhof 2003a:90). One copy was sent ahead of time to alert merchants as to what was coming and/or needed to be sent, and the other with the carrier who was transporting the goods, which served as a bill of lading. Comparison of the letters by the individuals receiving goods allowed them to see if any goods had been removed from cargos before or during shipment.

52 The tax or toll paid along the road was called the *nishatum*. It consisted of 5% of the value of the textiles and 2 minas of silver on each container of tin (Aubet 2013:302; Dercksen 1996:176)

53 A problem with in-laws in Assur appears to have arisen from the fact that Anatolian women were accustomed to greater liberty

in their lives than women in Assur, which chafed against cultural mores in the capital (Larsen 2008b:72).

54 *Kutānu*-cloth, according to Kuhrt (1998), was probably a common textile that may have been used as a kind of sheet. Similarly, *abarnê*-cloth refers to a particular style or weave named after the place (Abarne) where it was made.

55 For a lengthy discussion of the role of gods in commercial dealings across the ancient world, see Silver (1985:7–31; 1995:3–38).

56 The practice of taking an oath before god to testify honestly is evident in a Middle Bronze Age text from Babylon where a merchant has bought the unpaid rent of a farmer owed to the palace. To ensure honesty on the part of the merchant, it was required that the "merchant shall declare an oath before the god 'I did not receive anything referred to in this sealed receipt from the tenant,' and after he has made this declaration he shall bring the tenant's sealed receipt, they shall meet together, and make their mutual deductions" (Postgate 2004:197).

57 In India contracts could be sealed by swearing on the life of a cow or a chicken. Because pious individuals did not kill animals in this society, this was viewed as a most solemn pledge (Levi 2002:134).

58 In medieval India craftsmen such as potters, weavers, and metal smiths were induced to settle near temples because they produced goods needed in temple rituals and by its followers (Sinopoli 2003:272). In a related fashion, frankincense was a sacred crop across the Arabian Peninsula because of its use as incense in religious rituals. For that reason, the resins tapped from wild trees in the region about Shabwa in Yemen had to be brought to the temple to pay a temple tax before they could be sold or exported (Groom 2005:107).

59 Temple endowments often carried guaranteed returns for specific purposes, and temple administrators had to stipulate the value of the annual income in the name of the donor. When food was donated to the temple, up to 25% could be designated for the support of specific individuals. It was the responsibility of temple administrators to oversee these disbursements (Stein 1960:175–176).

60 Most known merchant groups resided in large communities. Much less is known about professional merchants who resided in small communities outside of large urban centers. The one rural merchant community that we know of is the town of Santa Maria Acxotla, Puebla, where merchants and merchant craftsmen make up fully 85% of its residents. In a real sense Santa Maria Acxotla was a separate merchant community (Hirth et al. 2017).

61 The goods that the *pochteca* took for common people included obsidian and copper ear plugs, obsidian razors with leather handles, pointed obsidian blades, rabbit fur, needles for sewing, and shells. Cochineal used to dye textiles was also taken, along with alum, birthwort and sulfur cosmos. High-value items taken specifically for the elite included gold miters, forehead rosettes, necklaces, pendants, and finger rings, as well as ear plugs made of gold and rock crystal (Sahagún 1959:8, 18).

62 These raw materials were important for craftsmen who worked in luxury goods. Featherwork was an especially important luxury craft and was used for capes, shirts, and headdresses as well as covering ornately worked warrior shields and other goods (Berdan et al. 2009). Exotic pelts were used in warrior costumes and garments of office. Shells, jade, and greenstone were used in jewelry and other costuming regalia.

63 The province of Anauac Xicalanco was located on the Gulf Coast of Mexico between the Coatzacoalcos River and the Laguna de Términos (Scholes and Roys 1968:31). The broader province of Xicalanco was made up of several independent kingdoms whose elites were involved directly in long-distance trade. Aztec merchants were prohibited from entering these kingdoms, either because the elites were hostile to the imperialistic expansion of the Aztec empire or because they wanted to maintain a direct monopoly over the goods that they produced (e.g., tropical feathers, pelts, cacao, cotton textiles) for their own commercial purposes.

64 The complete list of the goods that were given to the merchants for Ahuitzotl is the following: large round greenstones, cylindrical greenstones, greenstones cut on a bias, the finest emerald-green jade, fine bottle-green jadeite, turquoise mosaic shields, green pyrites, large red sea shells, red coral shells,

flower-colored shells, yellow and ocelot-colored tortoise shell cups, red spoonbill feathers, toupial feathers, blue honeycreeper feathers, yellow parrot feathers, and jaguar skins (Sahagún 1959:18–19).

65 This practice of depositing cargos with trusted individuals in the merchant community, before returning home where they could be unpacked in private, is described by Sahagún: "And as to goods . . . Not at one's [own] home did one arrive, [but] perhaps at the house of his uncle or his aunt . . . or it was only someone else's house into which he went – one who was of good heart, who told no lies. Nor was he a thief; he was prudent. And this owner of the goods did not acknowledge them; he did not take the goods himself, he did not claim them as his own. And there . . . into as many cities as he bore their goods.. . . He did not claim the goods, the property, as his own. He only told them [those who guarded the goods] . . . 'They are not my goods which I have carried; they are the goods of our mothers, our fathers, the merchants, the vanguard merchants'" (Sahagún 1959:31).

66 Disguised merchants also served as spies, and because of their service they received a special title as *naualoztomaca* due to the dangers they faced when circulating and trading in marketplaces where they were forbidden to enter. One such area where Aztec merchants were forbidden to enter on pain of death was in Zinacantan in southern Mexico (Cardos de Mendez 1959:59). According to Ximénez (1920:360), commerce was in the hands of the elite leaders of the community who wanted to forbid outsiders from gaining access to the valuable tropical bird feathers, skins, and amber that could be obtained here (Hirth 2016:210).

67 *Pochteca* merchants raised their social position both within their merchant community and across Aztec society by becoming a sponsor in the *tealtiliztli*, or Bathing of Slaves ceremony. This ceremony involved dedicating four slaves for sacrifice to the Aztec god Huitzilopochtli. This ceremony involved sponsoring four expensive feasts and giving expensive presents to members of the Aztec elite. Poor performance by individuals who undertook the sponsorship of this ceremony brought disgrace on both themselves and the merchant community as a whole (Hirth 2016:230–235).

CHAPTER 8

1 As a rule, scholars interested in social evolutionary theory are more interested in the conditions and productive processes of change that transformed society than they are in the forms of production and the specifics of how they were organized (Patterson 2005).

2 Examples of institutional craft production included the manufacture of textiles in Mesopotamia and the controlled production and distribution of salt in ancient China.

3 Aleksander Langlands (2017) points out how difficult it is for us to understand ancient economies where so much of everyday life for all households involved making the tools and applying them in a knowledgeable way to day-to-day subsistence tasks. He points out that tradesmen who work with their hands are often looked down on and relegated to the lower class. Moreover, our system of education emphasizes learning principles instead of "learning by doing" (Langlands 2017:22). Any archaeologist who studies past economic processes can tell you the increased insight achieved by replicating the productive processes (e.g., flint knapping, pottery manufacture, basket making) that they are attempting to study.

4 !Kung bushmen make and distribute gifts with friends and individuals in distant groups to reduce subsistence risk by increasing their ability to move to groups in areas with sufficient resources to support them when food becomes scarce in their foraging territories (Wiessner 1977, 1982). While serving as a safety net, the result of *hxaro* gift exchange is primarily social, with the economic option involving movement between groups being activated infrequently.

5 During the Neolithic period, sheep were bred for wool, which was spun and woven into textiles by women for the members of their household. The temple workshops brought people together and reorganized production so that textiles could be manufactured on a larger scale (Gelb 1972).

6 The prestige goods economy and how it operated is a huge topic with an immense literature for readers to consult (e.g., Arnold 2010; Bascom 1948; Brumfiel and Earle 1987a; Clark and Blake 1994; Earle 1987b; Frankenstein and Rowlands 1978; Hayden

1998, 2001b; Junker 1993; Peregrine 1991; Saitta 1999; Trubitt 2003).

7 The choice to engage in crafting (or not) resides with individuals of the household. This brings us back to the entrepreneurship found in individual households to ensure their successful biological and social reproduction. Their incentive to truck and barter, as Adam Smith (1827) described it, or their desire to lower their subsistence risk (Halstead and O'Shea 1989), or expand the size of family households (Chayanov 1966; Durrenberger 1984), would, of course, vary from household to household (Sahlins 1972).

8 Alexander Langlands illustrates how both crafters and noncrafters intentionally modified the landscape around them to propagate the raw materials that they used. Examples of this included pollarding and coppicing trees to produce shafts and shoots to weave baskets or managing stands of trees, as was done on Bermuda for ship building (Jarvis 2010:276; Langlands 2017). Similarly, the domesticated crops such as wheat or barley would be harvested in ways that their stalks could be productively used in a variety of utilitarian and craft activities ranging from thatching roofs to making coiled beehives (*sceppe*) for apiculture (Langlands 2017:93–108).

9 Marciana Lane notes how peasant households in Mexican community of Santa Maria Nativitas near Texcoco incorporated the production and sale of high-risk goods in the form of hothouse flowers into their domestic cycle alongside the less risky but low-return activities such as gathering firewood and the production and sale of flatbread (*cocoles*), hot foods (*sopes*, *tlayocos*), and maguey wine (*pulque*). The combination of a suite of high- and low-return activities with different levels of risk allowed households to accumulate capital in ways that they would have otherwise been unable to do (Lane 1997:129–135).

10 In Indonesia the traditional household crafting system known as *tukang* includes a range of part-time activities such as brick making, cigarette rolling, bean curd manufacture, basket weaving, and charcoal making. According to Glifford Geertz, these industries are "usually treated as an adjunct to farming: when things are slow in the fields, activity picks up in brickmaking, coconut oil manufacturing, or basket-weaving; and vice versa. Such household industries are viewed as additional cash crops, ones whose 'growing seasons' can be inserted in between those of the ordinary crops to give a better balance to the yearly round. The result is an approach to manufacturing which is interested less in steadily increasing efficiency or in continually rising wages and profits, than it is in a reliable, riskless source of supplemental income, in return for the irregular application of otherwise idle unskilled labor" (Geertz 1963:70).

11 There are some craft activities like ceramic production and salt production that are best carried out during the driest portion of the year when rainfall agriculture cannot be undertaken. Pottery production is best carried out during the dry season when it is easier to thoroughly dry vessels prior to firing, which reduces firing errors. The same is true for salt production using both solar and brine boiling techniques.

12 A law during the Late Han period (206 BC–AD 220) made it illegal for an individual to practice two occupations (Liu 1988:48). The purpose of the law was to increase agricultural productivity at the expense of craft and commerce.

13 These subsidiary occupations include crafting (*sana'a*), trade (*kasuwanci*), brokerage or trading on commission (*dillanci*), and wage labor (Smith 1955:155, 162).

14 Among the Nupe, the need to combine agriculture with crafting as a means of diversifying subsistence risk was characterized by blacksmiths who farmed plots near their houses "for the mouth" (Nadel 1942: 264).

15 Carneiro (1974) made the important observation that cultural complexity in the New World was not technology dependent. He noted that the basic technology associated with agricultural production in the New World was basically unchanged from early settled villages up through the emergence of complex states. The digging stick and simple irrigation systems found in early societies continued to be employed with few other changes in agricultural technology up through the Spanish conquest.

16 We often think of craft specialists as sedentary artisans because of the need of large quantities of resources or special tools or production facilities. Peripatetic craftsmen are found in a variety of situations where demand for

products was low or there were high costs involved in transportation, making it more efficient to move the artisan than the final product. Examples would include the manufacture of bricks or large storage vessels that break easily or are costly to move. Peacock (1982:35–38, 127) points out that mobile brick makers were likely present during Roman times, as the same brick stamp can be found in widely separated locales.

17 Karl Marx (1967) was one of the first investigators to identify the differences in organization between nucleated workshop industries and manufactories as examples of what he called the twofold nature of manufacture involving qualitatively different levels of labor segmentation. The examples that Marx used for cooperative production were Dutch papermaking and both German and English needle making (Marx 1967a:338). Marx used the assembly line manufacture of carriages as his example of a manufactory.

18 Other examples of itinerant craftspersons in the ancient and premodern world include steatite vessel makers in Susa and Mesopotamia (Ratnagar 2004:170), traveling artisans in Afghanistan (Olesen 1994), tinkers and gypsies in Europe (Brazzabeni et al. 2015), and ceramicists in pre-Columbian North America (Eerkens et al. 2002). Chester Starr (Starr 1977:88) also believes there were itinerant artisans in ancient Greece.

19 Types of production that might require separate or isolated areas include the production of lithic tools, where sharp debris could cause injury, or where pyrotechnology was used, as in metallurgy or ceramic firing, which created hazards or noxious fumes for household members.

20 Where workshop labor resided and whether these individuals were considered to be members of the master's household is a separate matter entirely, although in many instances the household model of specialized domestic production continued to operate even if the members were not directly related through kinship.

21 An example of a designated work area used on a periodic basis instead of continually would be a workshop reserved to produce military weaponry or for metallurgical production by itinerant artisans or intermittent craftspersons. For example, Moore and Lewis (1999:97) observe that metal-working shops in the Phoenician city of Tyre were connected to or located close to temples that may have been used periodically by the artisans engaged in this craft.

22 Artisans apparently did not offer a warranty for their work or employ the phrase "satisfaction guaranteed" to attract their customers. Curse tablets were a way for an unhappy customer to get revenge on a job done poorly by the artisan. These tablets would be buried in a grave or dropped down a well to get to the spirits of the underworld involved in causing harm to the artisan. A curse tablet of one unhappy consumer that was hidden in a specific house reads, "I condemn Aristaichmos the bronzeworker to those of the underworld and Pyrrias the bronzeworker and his work and their souls, and Sosias the Lamian and his work and soul, and Ages(ion) the Boeotian" (Camp 1986:141–142).

23 The service activities associated with Roman *tabernae* include those of barbers, fullers, physicians, bakers, and bar owners (Holleran 2012:125–149).

24 The *locatio–conductio* contracts from Roman Egypt are from the Middle Egyptian town of Oxyrhynchus and span the period AD 243–269. Two of the potters mentioned in the papyri are the same individual named Claudianus, who was a slave (Cockle 1981; Poblome and Brulet 2005:30–31).

25 Horizontal specialization was where different artisans produced different products and where one worker performed all the steps in the production process (Bayly 1983:400; Ruffing 2016:117). Horizontal specialization did not necessarily mean small production since Adam Smith (1827:12) made the point in his discussion of labor productivity in his illustration of a nail factory, where the specialized nail smith could produce ten times the output in a single day than a smith unaccustomed to the production process.

26 According to Stephen Bushell, local tradition states that large-scale, specialized ceramic production first began in Ching-te-chen during the Han dynasty. The earliest record of production dates to AD 583 and consists of an order for porcelain vessels for use in the royal palace. An official was appointed to the city between AD 1004 and 1007 to monitor production and tax during the Song dynasty (Bushell 1983:175–177).

27 The specialists involved in making a cup included two individuals to clean and beat the clay, four artisans to shape the cup, three to four painters depending on the design, one person to polish the cup, one to two glaziers depending on the type of glaze used, one person to prepare saggers and another to stack the kiln, and finally the specialists who fired the kiln and watched how the firing proceeded over the 8 days that were required. Other specialists are also mentioned who prepared the pigments used to paint the vessels as well as those who moved and stored finished goods before they were taken for sale.

28 Epstein (1991:40–41) identifies a guild or association existing in London in the early 10th century AD that was designed to keep the peace and protect its members. Professional guilds, however, began to be mentioned in regularity in different places during the 12th century. In Germany, the Bishop of Worms granted twenty-three fishermen the right to control the wholesale market of fish, effectively organizing them into a guild in AD 1106. Likewise, weavers were one of the first guilds to appear in Cologne in AD 1149. Guilds also were starting to form in France, and in AD 1152 there is reference to millers forming a collective organization whereby they received one-sixteenth of what they milled as individual income. Moreover, guilds are found in numerous cities in England from AD 1130 onward (Blair and Ramsey 1991:xx–xxi; Epstein 1991: 52–60).

29 The complaint revolved around the fact that "Dyers were driven from dyeing, Carpenters from carpentry, and so on" (Rappaport 2002:111) because these same activities were being practiced by members of other guilds that were not licensed to engage in these activities.

30 The term "grocer" that we use today actually refers to a wholesaler who was a shopkeeper who sold "in gross," that is, selling essentials to the lower strata of society (Cox 2000:204).

31 Other terms used to describe the putting-out system include cottage industries, the domestic system, the rural workshop system, homework, and the domestic system (e.g., https://en.wikipedia.org/wiki/Putting-out_system). All these terms are ambiguous and should be avoided because they can easily be confused with specialized domestic craft production described in this chapter. See Prentice (1983) for an example of using the term "cottage industries" in this general sense.

32 Information collected by Lazerson (1993b:409) in 1998 revealed that one-half (49.9%) of the artisans producing knitwear for the Italian fashion industry in the province of Modena worked as solitary workers manufacturing goods in their individual households.

33 Harmony Methodist is not the actual name of the congregation, which is not reproduced here for reasons of confidentiality. I have borrowed the name Harmony for the congregation from Philip Gulley's (2002) marvelously entertaining and humorous writings about congregational life of the Friends Meeting Fellowship in the mythical town of Harmony, USA.

34 Members make an array of home decorations and craft presents sold at an annual Christmas bazaar, make hamburgers and other food sold at local football events, and have made chocolate Easter eggs sold at a church social. Most of the individuals who engage in these events are mature women, although men also participate. They engage in these events not just to raise money. Although they could perform many of these activities in their individual homes, they prefer to work together because it is both more fun and they like each other. When asked how many pies they each made in a day, they could not tell me. They enjoyed the work and were not counting.

35 Voluntary fellowship and work groups organized for different charity endeavors are an old tradition in many Christian churches. They most often operated as women's guilds or informal associations for service within the church as well as the broader community. Examples include sewing and knitting groups, visitation for shut-ins, meals-on-wheels for the aged, mission activities, evangelism, and single-mother support groups. The list is extensive and can include any help or ministry-related activity that church members identify as a priority for social service.

36 Some people were involved in more than one part of the production process, but the general framework for production breaks down as follows: 1 man bought the apples; 1 woman made the cinnamon–sugar mixture; 8 women mixed the dough, rolled it out, and shaped the piecrust; 8 men peeled 55 bushels of apples;

12 persons trimmed, cored, and sliced the apples; 2 persons made aluminum-foil collars for the pie pans; 8 women made the crumb topping; 9–10 women assembled the pies; and 4 persons filled orders, collected the sales receipts, and carried the pies to the cars of customers in the church parking lot. Piecrusts, crumb topping, and the cinnamon–sugar mixture were prepared the day before so they would be ready for assembly.

37 The use of hand implements such as rolling pins, hand-cranked apple peelers, knives, and a hand apple corer were the major implements used. The only industrial inputs employed were a food processor to mix the dough, wax paper to cover the pies, and aluminum pie pans and foil. The number of pies purchased per customer varied from 1 to 85. Four to five pies per person was common, with larger purchases (e.g., 25, 43, 85 pies) being made collectively for extended families and for unrelated individuals who worked together in businesses within the community.

38 The information on fruit pie consumption in the United States is notably imprecise. It is estimated that 187,000,000 pies are sold commercially each year in supermarkets across the country (www.piecouncil.org/pdf/Pie_Fun_Facts.pdf). The number of households in the United States was estimated at 126,220,000 in 2017 (www.statista.com/statistics/243789/number-of-tv-households-in-the-us/). This makes 1.48 pies per year the average consumption of purchased fruit pies in the United States. It would be slightly higher depending on the number of homemade pies made and consumed.

39 Organic solidarity refers to the division of production tasks on the basis of natural differences in where the resources occur and the economic interaction and trade that results from accessing them. Mechanical solidarity refers to the interaction that occurs between groups that decide to specialize in the production of different products over others.

CHAPTER 9

1 Andean civilization and the institutional economy of their ancient states traditionally have been argued to have operated through top-down administrative control without markets (La Lone 1982; Murra 1972, 1975, 1980, 1985a). Nevertheless, that view has recently been challenged with the possibility that earlier marketplaces throughout the Andes were intentionally suppressed by the Inka as part of the expansion and organization of their empire (Hirth and Pillsbury 2013; Mayer 2013; Stanish and Cohen 2013). Enrique Mayer (2002) documents that marketplaces were present in indigenous communities early in the colonial period that were not a product of Spanish contact.

2 Sidney Mintz (1964:261) makes the observation that young girls in Haiti teach themselves how to sell in the marketplace by beginning their selling career with as little as 5 cents of working capital.

3 The quote from Euboulos is cited in Thompson (1971:1).

4 In ancient Egypt the word *dmi* means port or quay. It was also the location of the marketplace and where news was disseminated and decrees were proclaimed. It was within the *dmi* that local councils met to discuss legal, social, and political issues (Goelet 1999:81)

5 Money changing is a separate concept with considerable antiquity in comparison to the purchase of land on credit through mortgage borrowing, which is a modern concept.

6 Active negotiation over price and value has been documented for both hunting and gathering groups (Steward 1938) as well as in tribal and chiefdom societies (Bohannan and Dalton 1962b; Harding 1967; Heider 1969; Malinowski 1922; Strathern 2007). Market exchange is not restricted to state-level societies.

7 In Papua, New Guinea, the *juwo* pig feast was an important ceremonial event within the traditional Kapauku culture. It also was the context for both marketplaces and market exchange. Pigs were slaughtered to initiate the feast, and the next order of business was market selling for all types of goods to acquire shell money used later to buy more pigs (Pospisil 1963:327–330).

8 Kenneth White (1970) provides an excellent overview of the orientation of Roman agriculture for the urban market. Cato's treatise *De agricultura*, written in the middle of the 2nd century BC, provides farming recommendations on how to achieve an 8% profit on crops (Thielscher 1963). In addition to the profitable

practice of viticulture, estate owners engaged in the production of specialty products for elite tastes, which, according to Varro, included artificially fattened mice, flowers, snails, peacocks, and other avian and aquatic delicacies (White 1970:22–24, 66).

9 The simplest form of trade that could accommodate the exchange of high-value commodities is that of house trade. This form of exchange operates through an agent where interacting parties come to a domestic residence to conduct their transactions (Hill 1966, 1969, 1971). It is found in both rural and urban areas and may be a pre-market form of exchange that facilitated cross-cultural interaction through an intermediary before the establishment of marketplaces. Among the Hausa, the *mai gida* house trade was adapted to the cloistered trade of women, but elsewhere it was a dynamic form of trade facilitating sales, providing credit, and promoting interaction across ethnic boundaries (Cohen 1965).

10 Another form of barter relationships that Malinowski (1922, 1967b:219–220) refers to is called *vava* and involves the direct and immediate barter of fish for vegetables. Where a ceremonial relationship existed between villages, the exchange of fish for vegetables was made through a *wasi* relationship. Within a *wasi* relationship repayment was deferred rather than immediate (Malinowski 1967b:216).

11 Weather was a key factor in the success or failure of merchant expeditions to Iceland and Greenland. In AD 1118 several sagas record that thirty-five ships came to Iceland from Norway but only eight returned after Michaelmas (September 29). The twenty-seven shiploads of individuals who remained in Iceland over the winter had to be fed, which resulted in a famine throughout the island (Miller 1990:16).

12 These debts included payment by the family of a slain man to the warrior who avenged his death. Other payments could be for fostering an adopted son, for brideprice, or for loans in different business ventures (Pospisil 1963:331).

13 A description of a rendezvous on the Green River on June 10 of AD 1837 describes the integration of European trappers with the native Americans: "Here presented what might be termed a mixed multitude, the whites were chiefly Americans and Canadian French with some Dutch, Scotch, Irish, English, halfbreed, and full blood Indians, of nearly every tribe in the Rocky Mountains" (Wishart 1992:193).

14 Springer (1981) feels that prominent leaders of different groups often engineered collective exchanges of large quantities of goods for their respective groups in association with the organization of the calumet dance.

15 Pastoral and agricultural interactions are very durable. Xinru Liu discusses the border markets that existed between Kushan (Hsiung-nu) and the Chinese as far back as the Han dynasty (206 BC–AD 220). The Hsiung-nu were pastoralists who exchanged horses, furs, and other products with the Han for agricultural products, luxury goods, and iron weapons (Liu 1988:14).

16 Francisco Benet (1957:189–191) argued that border markets located in politically neutral areas operated on their own without direct political control because this was necessary to reinforce the overall neutrality on which they were based.

17 Daniel Defoe wrote one of the first serious works describing how one could establish oneself in retail trade in AD 1738. He felt that a flourishing internal market encouraged consumption and contributed to the wealth of the nation.

18 The citation on the Tlatelolco market is from Cortés (1962:87).

19 Pre-Hispanic marketplaces throughout the Mexican highlands were convened on a rotating schedule of 5, 9, 13, or 20 days based on community size (Hassig 1985:79). Only the largest cities had daily markets, and even then, the largest activity in the marketplace occurred every 5 days when there was no direct competition with neighboring city markets.

20 Scales were used to sell goods by weight in Old World, and the Spanish were struck by their absence in Aztec marketplaces. Cortés emphasizes this point: "All is sold by number and measure, but up till now no weighting by balance has been observed" (Cortés 1962:89). Maize and beans, the important food crops in Mesoamerica, were sold by volume (Farreras 1972). The *tlatamachihualoni* was one such measure (Molina 1977) that was adopted because it was like the Arab *almud* of about 7.6 liters.

21 The potter's quarter was referred to specifically as Kerameikos.

22 In addition to the ceramic kiln, other evidence found in the south and southwestern sectors of the Agora include little ceramic figures known as coroplasts (Camp 1986:138).

23 The house occupied by Mikion and Menon at different times dates to between 475 and 275 BC. The workshop of a second marble sculptor was found in the western *stoa* of the library of Pantainos dating to the 1st century AD. Other evidence for craft and commerce in the Agora include the house of bronze workers on the southwest side of the Agora dating to the 4th century AD and a bronze casting pit associated with a small temple on the west side of the Agora dating to around 500 BC (Camp 1986:139–142).

24 The commercial function of the mint is also suggested by its location close to the South Stoa and the South Square, which is believed to have been an important marketplace area within the Agora. While the bronze coin blanks and furnace found in the mint date to the 3rd and 2nd centuries BC, the foundation of the building used as the mint dates to around 400 BC. Likewise, Camp (1986:128) says there are references to the use of silver-coated bronze coins in Athens by 407/6 BC.

25 The Roman writer Varro specifically links *tabernae* to retail activities and associates them with the sale of such things as wine, ceramics, perfume, meat, leather products, and shoes (Gesner 1781; Holleran 2012:118).

26 There certainly is variation in how *tabernae* were laid out and organized. Meiggs (1973:273) has proposed that *tabernae* with single rooms were used as retail shops, while those with an attached back room were possibly used for some form of production. Some *tabernae* had a frontal arcade that provided a protected space for shoppers, while others did not. On the basis of architecture, it is not possible to distinguish shops involved in retail sales from those engaged in wholesale trade; the same *taberna* could be involved in both (Holleran 2012:115–121).

27 I am not suggesting that retail markets and regional marketplaces did not have foreign or nonlocal merchants in them, because they did. George Simmel (1967) identified the stranger within societies as an individual who remained unattached to the society in which he resides. Foreign merchants involved in local and regional trade would fit this category.

28 The importance of maritime shipping in ancient and premodern times created its own problems when weather and the shift in trade winds could require that merchants lay over for periods of time before beginning a return journey. Because of wind patterns, a trip from ports on the Red Sea or the Arabian Gulf to east coast of India or Indonesia could take 2 years. These layovers required special facilities for the merchants, their ships, and the goods that they sought to ship while they waited for safe conditions to travel.

29 Rice (2016:102–103) describes three types of shipping activities that a merchant would be involved in at a wholesale maritime port: (1) the assembly and shipping of export cargoes or local goods either to their ports of destination or to a larger entrepot for sale and transshipment, (2) shipments already in transit but that needed to be broken down for shipment to more than one final destination, and (3) shiploads of imported or return cargo to buy goods to make the round trip profitable.

30 A sesterce was one-quarter of a silver denarius, which contained one-tenth of a troy ounce of silver. In 2018 equivalencies, the value of a sesterce would be 39 cents. That placed the current value of the imported luxury goods at \$19 million to \$39 million. Pliny was concerned with the vice of *luxuria* (luxuries) and the amount spend each year on these imports. He identified the markup on the luxuries from the Indian, China, and the Arabian trade at 100-fold (Young 2001:202–206).

31 Geoffrey Rickman (1971, 1980a) provides careful description and documentation of the different types of warehouses in Ostia and how they were constructed for storing both grain and other merchant goods.

32 Since most shipping involved mixed cargos, goods that were intended for another port remained shipboard and did not pay the *pentêkostê* (Garland 1987:92). Ships were charged only the small harbor fee probably based on their overall size.

33 To take the concern for and control over grain even further, there was a special official named the *sitophulakes* who was specifically in charge of supervising both the wholesale and retail price of grain and made sure that two-thirds

of the grain entering Piraeus was sold in the port (Garland 1987:78).

34 The navy was indispensable for the defense of Athens, and Piraeus had one of the largest military naval shipyards in the ancient world (Lovén 2011). For more information on how the navy was funded, see the discussion in Chapter 6.

35 Palm oil was another controlled export commodity in Dahomey. The king of Dahomey had palm oil plantations that were tended by slaves, the oil from which was also exported at Whydah (Polanyi 1966:53). Other elites in the Dahomey state also had palm oil plantations and were allowed to export their oil as wholesalers (*gletanu*) (Herskovits 1967:55).

36 The development of these fairs was fostered by the support given to them by the independent counts. This included protection of merchants traveling to the fairs and the enforced local justice during the fairs. The counts benefited financially from the fairs by collecting tolls on the roads from merchants traveling to them as well as through fees charged for different activities and for validating financial contracts (Abu-Lughod 1989:58–59).

37 The four towns that held fairs sequentially throughout the year were: (1) Lagney, (2) Bar-sur-Aube, (3) Provins (first fair), (4) Troyes (first fair), (5) Provins (second fair), (6) Troyes (second fair). Then the cycle repeated (Abu-Lughod 1989:60–61).

38 Skinner (1964) reports that traditional Chinese markets operated for only 2–3 hours in the mornings of market days. This allowed consumers to comfortably walk to and return from the market on the same day, as well as allowing the itinerant peddlers that attended them to walk to the next market that convened on the following day.

39 The distance of 25–30 kilometers is used as a normal day's travel. This figure is based on the distance for a long but normal day of foot travel among the Aztec of Mesoamerica (Hirth 2016:18). Distance would have to be adjusted depending on the loads carried by individuals.

40 From a practical point of view, Polanyi felt that communication systems were too poor to allow a price-setting mechanism to operate since a change in price in one market would be too slow for merchants and manufacturers to respond to (Garraty 2010:13). It is true that communication was slow, but when there was a change in price, merchants were quick to act in making purchases or selling their goods. In fact, their livelihoods were based on a keen understanding of price differentials in the areas in which they traded.

41 It was within the framework of foreignness that Polanyi's model of administered trade operated (Polanyi 1957).

42 Whether sponsored or unsponsored, small informal marketplaces or trader stalls were common as piggyback events at religious events, political gatherings, and pilgrimage places in many different societies (Abbott 2010; Blanton 2013:30; Burger 2013).

43 Even where price or value equivalencies are fixed (e.g., two apples for one orange), negotiation can enter into exchange since individuals can disagree on the relative size, condition, or ripeness of the fruit being exchanged.

44 The issue of market tax as an important instrument of administrative operation is a separate and complex subject. As presented in the discussion of the wholesale port of Piraeus, the 2% tax charge was more along the lines of an import duty on foreign goods. When a market tax is charged on local food markets, it must be small or it will stifle normal commerce (see Hirth 2016:75–79 for a discussion of the market tax among the Aztecs). In medieval Europe, monarchs devised an ingenious plan to indirectly tax the marketplace. Marketplaces were established by royal grants and charters as independent entities (Smith 1999:139). In England, local lords set up more than 2,000 weekly markets in villages and almost as many annual fairs in hope that towns would grow and the demand for goods would increase. The rationale behind this was not "altruism" for the sake of consumers, but rather so that peasants could sell their produce to pay their taxes and so the lords could gain revenue from the tolls charged to merchants headed to markets and fairs (Dyer 2005:20).

45 The task of the money changer was far from easy and allowed considerable leeway for fraud. The use of different quantities of silver, gold, and brass in coins minted in different cities made the task of calculating relative worth in silver in different currencies a challenging task. Add to this the practice of snipping of pieces of coins and the use of hack

silver, and this required the use of precise weights and assaying techniques. In the medieval period, Italian bankers would make assessments of silver content, seal coins of different currencies together in a leather pouch, and stamp their value on the pouch's exterior along with their names. Pouches often remained unopened and circulated as currency without their interior being rechecked.

46 In a comparative study, Blanton and Fargher (2010) identified a tendency for market development to be more prevalent in societies with collective political organization.

CHAPTER 10

1 The underlying notion that ownership is linked to the labor invested in property is expressed in our own society in the simple principles of squatter's rights and the axiom that possession is nine-tenths of the law.

2 The inference that taxation was present in the second millennium BC comes in the form of the clean-slate proclamations of debt relief made by rulers to the commoner population who are believed to have borrowed money to pay their taxes. Examples of debt relief proclamations include the edict of Ammisaduqa in 1646 BC and the law code of Hammurabi in 1662 BC. The earliest debt relief proclamation was the reform of Urukagina in the 24th century BC (Hudson 1999b:467; 2000:15; Liverani 2013:113–114; Van de Mieroop 1999:206).

3 In commenda agreements, the number of persons involved could vary. For example, the merchant and the shipper could be one and the same individual, just as there could be multiple investors in the venture.

4 The only area of state-level development where researchers have argued that markets were absent is Andean South America (Earle and Smith 2011; Murra 1980). While they appear to be absent among the Inka, researchers have questioned whether they might have been present earlier and were suppressed by the Inka after areas were conquered and groups were incorporated into the empire (e.g., Burger 2013; Mayer 2013; Stanish 2013).

5 What Graeber is referring to is what he calls the myth of barter, used in reference to the origin of coined money. The traditional narrative is that barter came first, and then coinage was invented to facilitate negotiations, which was followed in turn by the extension of credit. He argues for the reverse order. He feels that credit came first in conjunction with established units of value, followed by minted currencies, and barter after coinage was already circulating (Graeber 2011:40).

GLOSSARY

Arbitrage: The practice of making a profit by using the difference in value of a commodity at its source, where it is abundant and inexpensive, and at its destination, where it is scarce and can be sold for a higher price.

Cabotage: The practice of sailing from port to port to pick up cargo.

Carrying trade: The practice of incorporating trade into the mobile lifeways of pastoral and foraging groups as a secondary but important aspect of their subsistence economy.

Chiefdom societies: A society where individuals are ranked with respect to one another based on their position within their descent group, and the position of their descent group in relation to other descent groups. The number of positions of power and prestige is limited, and the highest-ranking leaders of descent groups are often referred to as chiefs.

Commenda: A business agreement between multiple individuals who shared the profit of the venture based on their involvement as investor, merchant, or shipper.

Contingent crafting: The production of tools or secondary goods in crafting contexts that are needed in the manufacture of a primary good.

Craftsperson's dilemma: The subsistence risk that artisans face because of the uncertainty created by a variable or fluctuating demand for the goods they produce.

Direct production: A form of resource production by formal institutions whereby they estimate and collectively produce the resources required for institutional consumption. Production is on institutional lands or facilities apart from production in the domestic economy.

Domestic economy: The diversity of ways that households and families are organized to access or produce the resources needed to meet their biological and social needs. It was the foundation of all human societies both past and present.

Economic heterogeneity: The diversity of organizational structures created over time as new forms of economic organization are added to economic systems (i.e., plasticity) without discarding existing forms.

Economic plasticity: The practice of adding new forms of economic organization (e.g., production, distribution, finance) to societies without removing older, preexisting ones. The result is that different forms of organization can comfortably coexist in different sectors of the economy.

Economy: A socially mediated form of material provisioning and economic interaction involving the production and allocation of resources among alternative ends.

Egalitarian society: A society where there are as many positions of prestige in any given age–sex grade as there are persons capable of filling them.

Euergetism: The practice of patronage by wealth elite to fund social and institutional activities using their individual wealth. It was particularly important across the Greco-Roman world to fund aspects of the institutional economy. The term is derived from the Greek word *euergetēē*, which means doing good deeds.

Exchange value: The value that an item has on the open market in exchange for currency or other goods. Exchange value is usually applied to goods that are manufactured specifically for the purpose of exchange.

Formal institutions: The special-purpose organizational structures that operate at the level of the whole society for both economic and noneconomic purposes.

Holonic business enterprise: A network of self-regulated production and service units that arrange themselves in a collaborative system to meet a specific production, service, or distribution objective.

Informal institutions: The ad hoc and voluntary structures, mechanisms, principles, and customs that households employ to mobilize labor, access resources, and obtain forms of interhousehold support.

Institutional economy: The production and mobilization of resources needed to support the integrative activities carried out above the level of individual households.

Law of unobtrusive expropriation: The idea that people would be more supportive of emerging institutions that made fewer demands on their time and resources as opposed to those that made more demands.

Liturgies: Patronage duties and responsibilities undertaken by wealthy families in the Greco-Roman world at their own expense to fund institutional activities. Liturgies included both voluntary and compulsory sponsorships that could coincide with the responsibilities of an officeholder or the beneficence expected of a wealthy elite member of society.

Marginal advantage of crafting: The idea that the incorporation of craft activities into the normal work regimes of households when labor is available supplies an additional revenue stream that increases their economic well-being and provides a subsistence advantage over those that do not.

Market economy: An economic system where the production and distribution of products is strongly determined by the connectivity between supply, demand, competition, and price.

Market exchange: A balanced transaction involving the exchange of goods or services between two or more interacting parties during which the forces of supply and demand are active and visible.

Market systems: Networks of coordinated marketplaces that are convened on regular schedules, facilitating the movement of merchants and goods between them and providing efficient access to products by consumers.

Marketplaces: Centralized locales where a large number of market exchanges take place on a periodic or regular basis.

Merchant: An individual who participates and assists in resource provisioning within society as an aspect of his or her livelihood. May be full- or part-time depending on circumstances.

Merchant's dilemma: The problem that merchants faced in maintaining capital sufficient for conducting commercial activities because of the expectation that wealthy individuals in the community would contribute generously and finance the economic base of the community.

Multicrafting: The practice of artisans engaging in multiple crafts in the same household or workshop instead of specializing in a single craft activity.

Mutual exclusivity fallacy: The incorrect idea that very different forms of production and distribution did not coexist and operate in the same or different sectors of the economy at the same time.

Peripatetic consumption: The movement of institutional consumers to where resources were produced for on-the-spot consumption.

Prebend: A resource allocation that serves as an assigned income derived from an institution in return for services that an individual provides.

Premodern societies: Traditional societies where households largely produce for their own consumption; most of the food consumed is produced locally; transportation and communication is slow and costly; and formal financial institutions are lacking. In these societies, the organization of labor is more important in determining output and structuring forms of production than technology or capital investment. They are preindustrial in the sense that they do not make extensive use of energy from fossil fuels.

Putting-out system: A decentralized form of production carried out in rural areas whereby a manager provides the materials to manufacture a product and workers are paid for their labor based on output.

Staple finance: The collection, storage, and use of staple goods and food to support the activities of institutions and the administrators who oversaw them.

State societies: Large, internally complex societies where the central political authority or ruling institutions maintain the right to coerce compliance with social, economic, and political norms. The internal organization of states can bring together diverse ethnic groups and social classes under a common rule.

Tax farming: A means for governments to collect taxes using private contractors who win the contract to collect taxes from regions and make a profit on the margin between the bid price paid for the tax contract and the actual amount collected.

Taxation: An economic transfer that removes food, finished goods, or other resources directly from households after they have been produced. It does not include the mobilization of corvée labor from households as labor tax.

Trade diaspora: A network of merchant communities composed of individuals who share ethnic, religious, and/or kinship relationships that are distributed over space and who reside in foreign areas for the purposes of engaging and long-distance trade.

Use value: The value that a product has related to its function or intended usage. Usually associated with goods produced for use by their maker.

Wealth finance: The use of high-value commodities or prestige goods to fund formal institutions and elite-sponsored activities.

BIBLIOGRAPHY

Abbott, David 2010 The rise and demise of marketplace exchange among the prehistoric Hohokam of Arizona, in *Archaeological approaches to market exchange in pre-capitalistic societies*, C. Garraty and B. Stark eds., pp. 61–83. University Press of Colorado, Boulder.

Abbott, David, Alexa Smith, and Emiliano Gallaga 2007 Ballcourts and ceramics: The case for Hohokam marketplaces in the Arizona desert. *American Antiquity* 72:461–484.

Abé, Takeshi, and Osamu Saito 1988 From putting-out to the factory: A cotton-weaving district in late-Meiji Japan. *Textile History* 19:143–157.

Abu-Lughod, Janet 1989 *Before European hegemony: The world system A.D. 1250–1350*. Oxford University Press, Oxford.

Acheson, James 1989 Management of common-property resources, in *Economic anthropology*, S. Plattner ed., pp. 351–378. Stanford University Press, Stanford.

Acheson, James 1994 Welcome to Nobel country: A review of institutional economics, in *Anthropology and institutional economics*, J. Acheson ed., pp. 3–42. University Press of America, Lanham.

Acosta Saignes, Miguel, Miguel León-Portilla, Ann Chapman, and Amalia Cardos de Méndez 1975 *El comercio en el México prehispánico*. Instituto Mexicano de Comercio Exterior, Mexico City.

Adams, Colin 2012 Transportation, in *The Cambridge companion to the Roman economy*, W. Scheidel ed., pp. 218–240. Cambridge University Press, Cambridge.

Adams, Robert McC. 1965 *Land behind Baghdad: A history of settlement on the Diyala plains*. University of Chicago Press, Chicago.

Adams, Robert McC. 1981 *Heartland of cities: Surveys of ancient settlement and land use on the central floodplain of the Euphrates*. University of Chicago Press, Chicago.

Adams, Robert McC., and Hans Nissen 1972 *The Uruk countryside*. University of Chicago, Chicago.

Adovasio, James, Olga Soffer, and Bohuslav Klima 1996 Upper Palaeolithic fibre technology: Interlaced woven finds from Pavlov I, Czech Republic, "c." 26,000 years ago. *Antiquity* 70:526–534.

Aikens, Melvin, and Takayasu Higuchi 1982 *Prehistory of Japan*. Academic Press, San Diego.

Airlie, Stuart 2000 The palace of memory: The Carolingian court as political centre, in *Courts and regions in medieval Europe*, S. Jones, R. Marks, and A. Minnis eds., pp. 1–20. York Medieval Press, York.

Alba, Carlos 1949 *Estudio comparativo entre el derecho Azteca y el derecho positivo Mexicano*. Ediciones Especiales del Instituto Indigenista Interamericano 3, Mexico City.

Aldrete, Greg, and David Mattingly 1999 Feeding the city: The organization, operation, and scale of the supply system for Rome, in *Life, death, and entertainment in the Roman empire*, D. Potter ed., pp. 171–204. University of Michigan Press, Ann Arbor.

Algaze, Guillermo 1993 *The Uruk world system: The dynamics of expansion of early Mesopotamian civilization*. University of Chicago Press, Chicago.

Algaze, Guillermo 2007 The Sumerian takeoff, in *Settlement and society: Essays dedicated to Robert McCormick Adams*, E. Stone ed., pp. 343–368. Cotsen Institute of Archaeology, University of California, Los Angeles.

Algaze, Guillermo 2008 *Ancient Mesopotamia at the dawn of civilization: The evolution of an urban landscape*. University of Chicago Press, Chicago.

Ali, Abbas, and Abdullah Al-Owaihan 2008 Islamic work ethic: A critical review. *Cross Cultural Management: An International Journal* 15:5–19.

Allan, William 1965 *The African husbandman*. Oliver and Boyd, Edinburgh.

Allard, Pierre 2005 Surplus production of flint blades in the Early Neolithic of western Europe: New evidence from Belgium. *European Journal of Archaeology* 8:205–223.

Allard, Pierre 2012 Détection de spécialistes de la taille de la pierre au Rubané. *Bulletin de la Société Préhistorique Française* 109:267–278.

Allen, James 2002 *The Heqanakht papyri*. Metropolitan Museum of Art, New York.

Allsen, Thomas 1989 Mongolian princes and their merchant partners, 1200–1260. *Asia Major* 2:83–125.

Allsen, Thomas 1997 *Commodity and exchange in the Mongol empire*. Cambridge University Press, Cambridge.

Altınbilek-Algül, Ciler, Laurence Astruc, Didier Binder, and Jacques Pelegrin 2012 Pressure blade production with a lever in the Early and Late Neolithic of the Near East, in *The emergence of pressure blade making*, P. Desroisiers ed., pp. 157–179. Springer, New York.

Amselle, Jean-Loup 1971 Parenté et commerce chez les Kooroko, in *The development of indigenous trade and markets in west Africa*, C. Meillassoux ed., pp. 253–265. Oxford University Press, London.

Anderson, Heath, and Kenneth Hirth 2009 Obsidian blade production for craft consumption at Kaminaljuyu. *Ancient Mesoamerica* 20:163–172.

Anderson, James 1997 *Roman architecture and society*. Johns Hopkins University Press, Baltimore.

Anderson, Patricia, Jacques Chabot, and Annelou Van Gijn 2004 The functional riddle of "glossy" Canaanean blades and the Near Eastern threshing sledge. *Journal of Mediterranean Archaeology* 17:87–130.

Anderson, Siwan 2003 Why dowry payments declined with modernization in Europe but are rising in India. *Journal of Political Economy* 111:269–310.

Anderson, Siwan 2007 The economics of dowry and brideprice. *The Journal of Economic Perspectives* 21:151–174.

Andreau, Jean 1999 *Banking and business in the Roman world*. Cambridge University Press, Cambridge.

Andrews, Anthony 1983 *Maya salt production and trade*. University of Arizona Press, Tucson.

Annis, Sheldon 1987 *God and production in a Guatemalan town*. University of Texas Press, Austin.

Appadurai, Arjun 1974 Right and left hand castes in South India. *Indian Economic and Social History Review* 11:216–259.

Appadurai, Arjun 1986a Introduction: Commodities and the politics of value, in *The social life of things: Commodities in cultural perspective*, A. Appadurai ed., pp. 3–63. Cambridge University Press, Cambridge.

Appadurai, Arjun ed. 1986b *The social life of things: Commodities in cultural perspective*. Cambridge University Press, Cambridge.

Appleby, Gordon 1976 The role of urban food needs in regional development, Puno, Peru, in *Regional analysis, vol. 1: Economic systems*, C. Smith ed., pp. 147–178. Academic Press, New York.

Araral, Eduardo 2013 What makes socio-ecological systems robust? An institutional analysis of the 2,000-year-old Ifugao society. *Human Ecology* 41:859–870.

Arcury, Thomas 1984 Household composition and economic change in a rural community, 1900–1980: Testing two models. *American Ethnologist* 11:677–698.

Ardener, Shirley 1964 The comparative study of rotating credit associations. *The Journal of the Royal Anthropological Institute of Great Britain and Ireland* 94:201–229.

Arnold, Darrell 2008 Georg Simmel: The stranger as a social category. PhD dissertation, Colorado State University.

Arnold, David 1988 *Famine: Social crisis and historical change*. Basil Blackwell, Oxford.

Arnold, Dean 1985 *Ceramic theory and cultural process*. Cambridge University Press, Cambridge.

Arnold, Jeanne 1995 Social inequality, marginalization, and economic process, in *Foundations of social inequality*, T. Price and G. Feinman eds., pp. 87–103. Plenum, New York.

Arnold, Jeanne 2010 The role of politically charged property in the appearance of institutionalized leadership, in *The evolution of leadership: Transitions in decision making from small-scale to middle-range societies*, K. Vaughn, J. Eerkens, and J. Kantner eds., pp. 121–146. School for Advanced Research Press, Santa Fe.

Arnold, Rosemary 1957a A port of trade: Whydah on the Guinea coast, in *Trade and market in the early empires*, K. Polanyi, C. Arensberg, and H. Pearson eds., pp. 154–176. Free Press, Glencoe.

Arnold, Rosemary 1957b Separation of trade and market: Great market of Whydah, in *Trade and market in the early empires*, K. Polanyi, C. Arensberg, H. Pearson eds., pp. 177–187. Free Press, Glencoe

Arthur, John 2003 Brewing beer: Status, wealth and ceramic use alteration among the Gamo of south-western Ethiopia. *World Archaeology* 34:516–528.

Attolini Lecón, Amalia 2010 Intercambio y caminos en el mundo Maya prehispánico, in *Caminos y mercados de México*, J. Long Towell and A. Attolini Lecón eds., pp. 51–77. Universidad Nacional Autónoma de México and Instituto Nacional de Antropología e Historia, Mexico City.

Aubet, Maria 2013 *Commerce and colonization in the ancient Near East*. Cambridge University Press, Cambridge.

Axelrod, Robert 2006 *The evolution of cooperation*. Basic Books, New York.

Ayyagaria, Meghana, Asli Demirgüç-Kunt, and Vojislav Maksimovic 2011 Formal versus informal finance: Evidence from China. *The Society for Financial Studies* 23:3048–3097.

Baghdiantz McCabe, Ina 2005 Global trading ambitions in diaspora: The Armenians and their Eurasian silk trade, 1530–1750, in *Diaspora entrepreneurial networks: Four centuries of history*, I. Baghdiantz McCabe, G. Harlaftis, and I. Pepelasis Minoglou eds., pp. 27–49. Berg, Oxford.

Baghdiantz McCabe, Ina, Gelina Harlaftis, and Ioanna Pepelasis Minoglou eds. 2005 *Diaspora entrepreneurial networks: Four centuries of history*. Berg, Oxford.

Bailey, Frederick 1964 Capital saving and credit in highland Orissa (India), in *Capital, saving, and credit in peasant societies*, R. Firth and B. Yamey eds., pp. 104–132. Aldine, Chicago.

Baines, John, and Jaromir Malek 2000 *Cultural atlas of ancient Egypt*. Checkmark Books, New York.

Banning, Edward 2011 So fair a house: Göbekli Tepe and the identification of temples in the Pre-Pottery Neolithic of the Near East. *Current Anthropology* 52:619–660.

Bar-Yosef, Ofer, and Richard Meadow 1995 The origins of agriculture in the Near East, in *Last hunters, first farmers: New perspectives on the prehistoric transition to agriculture*, D. Price and A. Gebaur eds., pp. 39–94. School for Advanced Research, Santa Fe.

Bar-Yosef, Ofer, and Tamar Schick 1989 Early Neolithic organic remains from Nahal Hemar Cave. *National Geographic Research* 5:176–190.

Barber, Elizabeth 1994 *Women's work: The first 20,000 years: Women, cloth, and society in early times*. Princeton University Press, Princeton.

Barjamovic, Gojko 2011 *A historical geography of Anatolia in the Old Assyrian colony period*. Carsten Niebuhr Institute Publications 38, Copenhagen.

Barker, Graeme, and David Gilbertson 2003 *The archaeology of drylands: Living at the margin*. Routledge, London.

Barnard, Bailey 2011 Euergetism and gift-giving at Eleusis: A case study of ancient patronage structures. Master's thesis, University of Nebraska, Lincoln.

Barnett, Homer 1938 The nature of the potlatch. *American Anthropologist* 40:349–358.

Barth, Fredrik 1956 Ecologic relationships of ethnic groups in Swat, North Pakistan. *American Anthropologist* 58:1079–1089.

Barton, Roy 1969 *Ifugao law*. University of California Press, Berkeley.

Bascom, William 1948 Ponapean prestige economy. *Southwestern Journal of Anthropology* 4:211–221.

Bass, George 1986 A Bronze Age shipwreck at Ulu Burun (Kaş): 1984 campaign. *American Journal of Archaeology* 90:269–296.

Bates, Daniel 2001 *Human adaptive strategies.* Allyn and Bacon, Boston.

Bauer, Brian 1996 *The development of the Inca state.* University of Texas Press, Austin.

Baugh, Timothy, and Jonathon Ericson eds. 1994 *Prehistoric exchange systems in North America.* Plenum, New York.

Baxter, Paul 1979 Boran age-sets and warfare, in *Warfare among East African herders,* F. Katsuyoshi and D. Turton eds., pp. 69–93. Senri Ethnological Studies. Osaka.

Bayly, Christopher 1983 *Rulers, townsmen and bazaars: North Indian society in the age of British expansion, 1770–1870.* Cambridge University Press, Cambridge.

Bayly, Christopher 1986 The origins of swadeshi (home industry): Cloth and Indian society, 1700–1930, in *The social life of things,* A. Appadurai ed., pp. 285–321. Cambridge University Press, Cambridge.

Beale, Thomas 1978 Bevelled rim bowls and their implications for change and economic organization in the later fourth millennium BC. *Journal of Near Eastern Studies* 37:289–313.

Beals, Ralph 1975 *The peasant marketing system of Oaxaca, Mexico.* University of California Press, Berkeley.

Beck, Hans ed. 2013 *A companion to ancient Greek government.* John Wiley and Sons, Chichester.

Beckert, Sven 2014 *The empire of cotton: A global history.* Vintage Books, New York.

Berry, Mary 1982 *Hideyoshi.* Harvard University Press, Cambridge, MA.

Bender, Donald 1967 A refinement of the concept of household: Families, co-residence, and domestic functions. *American Anthropologist* 69:493–504.

Benedict, Burton 1964 Capital, saving, and credit among Mauritian Indians, in *Capital, saving, and credit in peasant societies,* R. Firth and B. Yamey eds., pp. 330–346. Aldine, Chicago.

Benedict, Burton 1968 Family firms and economic development. *Southwestern Journal of Anthropology* 24:1–19.

Benet, Francisco 1957 Explosive markets: The Berber highlands, in *Trade and market in the early empires,* K. Polanyi, C. Arensberg, and H. Pearson eds., pp. 188–217. Free Press, Glencoe.

Berdan, Frances 1975 Trade, tribute and market in the Aztec empire. PhD dissertation, University of Texas, Austin.

Berdan, Frances 1982 *The Aztecs of Central Mexico: An imperial society.* Holt, Rinehart and Winston, New York.

Berdan, Frances 1987 Cotton in Aztec Mexico: Production, distribution and use. *Mexican Studies/Estudios Mexicanos* 3:235–262.

Berdan, Frances 1989 Trade and markets in precapitalist states, in *Economic anthropology,* S. Plattner ed., pp. 78–107. Stanford University Press, Stanford.

Berdan, Frances 1992a Appendix B: Annual tribute in the Codex Mendoza part 2, in *The Codex Mendoza,* F. Berdan and P. Anawalt eds., 1:54–156. University of California Press, Berkeley.

Berdan, Frances 1992b The imperial tribute role of the Codex Mendoza, in *The Codex Mendoza,* F. Berdan and P. Anawalt eds., 1:55–79. University of California Press, Berkeley.

Berdan, Frances 2006 Circulation of feathers in Mesoamerica. *Nuevo Mundo, Mundos Nuevos* (http://nuevomundo.revues.org/1387).

Berdan, Frances 2014 *Aztec archaeology and ethnohistory.* Cambridge University Press, Cambridge.

Berdan, Frances n.d. Guilds in distress in 16th century England. Unpublished manuscript.

Berdan, Frances, and Patricia Anawalt eds. 1992 *The Codex Mendoza.* University of California Press, Berkeley.

Berdan, Frances, Edward Stark, and Jeffrey Sahagún 2009 Production and use of orchid adhesives in Aztec Mexico: The domestic context, in *Housework: Craft production and domestic economy in ancient Mesoamerica,* K. Hirth ed., pp. 148–156. Wiley, Hoboken.

Berdan, Frances, Richard Blanton, Elizabeth Boone, Mary Hodge, Michael Smith, and

Emily Umberger eds. 1996 *Aztec imperial strategies*. Dumbarton Oaks Research Library and Collection, Washington, DC.

Berenbaum, Michael, and Fred Skolnik 2007 Leket, shikhhah, and pe'ah, in *Encyclopaedia Judaica*, M. Berenbaum and F. Skolnik eds., 12:631–632. Macmillan Reference, Detroit.

Bernbeck, Reinhard 1995 Lasting alliances and emerging competition: Economic developments in early Mesopotamia. *Journal of Anthropological Archaeology* 14:1–25.

Bernhardt, John 2002 *Itinerant kingship and royal monasteries in early medieval Germany, c. 936–1075*. Cambridge University Press, Cambridge.

Bernstein, William 2008 *A splendid exchange: How trade shaped the world*. Atlantic Monthly Press, New York.

Betzig, Laura 1988 Adoption by rank on Ifaluk. *American Anthropologist* 90:111–119.

Bianquis, Thierry 1996 The family in Arab Islam, in *A history of the family*, A. Burguiere, C. Klapisch-Zuber, M. Segalen, and F. Zonabend eds., 1:601–647. Polity Press, Cambridge.

Bible, The 1952–1971. *The Bible containing the Old and New Testaments*. Revised Standard Version. American Bible Society, New York.

Bierhorst, John 1992 *History and mythology of the Aztecs: The Codex Chimalpopoca*. University of Arizona Press, Tucson.

Billman, Brian 2002 Irrigation and the origins of the southern Moche state on the north coast of Peru. *Latin American Antiquity* 13:371–400.

Binford, Lewis 1981 Behavioral archaeology and the "Pompeii premise." *Journal of Anthropological Research* 1:195–208.

Binford, Lewis 1982 The archaeology of place. *Journal of Anthropological Archaeology* 1:5–31.

Bird, James 1958 Billingsgate: A central metropolis market. *The Geographical Journal* 124:464–475.

Bird-David, Nurit 1992 Beyond "the original affluent society": A culturalist reformulation. *Current Anthropology* 33:25–47.

Bishop, Charles 1998 The politics of property among northern Algonquians, in *Property in economic context*, R. Hunt and A. Gilman eds., pp. 247–267. University Press of America, Lanham, MD.

Blackmann, David 1982a Ancient harbours in the Mediterranean. Part 1. *International Journal of Nautical Archaeology* 11:79–104.

Blackmann, David 1982b Ancient harbours in the Mediterranean. Part 2. *International Journal of Nautical Archaeology* 11:185–211.

Blair, John, and Nigel Ramsey eds. 1991 *English medieval industries*. Hambledon, London.

Blakeslee, Donald 1975 The Plains interband system. PhD dissertation, University of Wisconsin, Milwaukee.

Blakeslee, Donald 1977 The calumet ceremony and the origin of fur trade rituals. *Western Canadian Journal of Anthropology* 7:81–88.

Blakeslee, Donald 1981 The origin and spread of the calumet ceremony. *American Antiquity* 46:759–768.

Blanton, Richard 1983 Factors underlying the origin and evolution of market systems, in *Economic anthropology: Topics and theories*, S. Ortiz ed., pp. 51–66. University Press of America, Lanham, MD.

Blanton, Richard 1994 *Houses and households: A comparative study*. Plenum, New York.

Blanton, Richard 2013 Cooperation and the moral ecomomy of the marketplace, in *Merchants, markets, and exchange in the pre-Columbian world*, K. Hirth and J. Pillsbury eds., pp. 23–48. Dumbarton Oaks Research Library and Collections, Washington, DC.

Blanton, Richard, and Lane Fargher 2008 *Collective action in the formation of pre-modern states*. Springer, New York.

Blanton, Richard, and Lane Fargher 2010 Evaluating causal factors in market development in premodern states: A comparative study with critical comments on the history of ideas about markets, in *Archaeological approaches to market exchange in ancient societies*, C. Garraty and B. Stark eds., pp. 207–226. University of Arizona Press, Tucson.

Blanton, Richard, and Gary Feinman 1984 The Mesoamerican world system. *American Antiquity* 86:673–682.

Blanton, Richard, Stephen Kowalewski, Gary Feinman, and Laura Finsten 1993 *Ancient*

Mesoamerica: A comparison of change in three regions. Cambridge University Press, Cambridge.

Blanton, Richard, Gary Feinman, Stephen Kowalewski, and Peter Peregrine 1996 A dual-processual theory for the evolution of Mesoamerican civilization. *Current Anthropology* 37:1–14.

Blanton, Richard, Gary Feinman, Stephen Kowalewski, and Linda Nicholas 1999 *Ancient Oaxaca: The Monte Albán state*. Cambridge University Press, Cambridge.

Blau, Peter 1970 A formal theory of differentiation in organizations. *American Sociological Review* 35:201–218.

Bleiberg, Edward 2001 Storage, in *The Oxford encyclopedia of ancient Egypt*, D. Redford ed., 3:327–329. Oxford University Press, Oxford.

Blenkinsopp, Joseph 1988 *Ezra-Nehemiah*. Westminster Press, Philadelphia.

Bliege Bird, Rebecca, and Eric Smith 2005 Signaling theory, strategic interaction, and symbolic capital. *Current Anthropology* 46:221–248.

Bliege Bird, Rebecca, Douglas Bird, Eric Smith, Geoffrey Kushnick 2002 Risk and reciprocity in Meriam food sharing. *Evolution and human behavior* 23:297–321.

Bloch, Marc 1961 *Feudal society*. Routledge and Kegan Paul, London.

Boas, Franz 1897 *The social organization and the secret societies of the Kwakiutl Indians*. Report of the U.S. National Museum for 1895, Washington, DC.

Boenisch Burrough, Joy 1978 The *tamus* of Sabah, in *Market-place trade: Periodic markets, hawkers, and traders in Africa, Asia, and Latin America*, R. Smith ed., pp. 48–63. Centre for Transportation Studies, University of British Columbia, Vancouver.

Bohannan, Paul 1955 Some principles of exchange and investment among the Tiv. *American Anthropologist* 57:60–70.

Bohannan, Paul, and George Dalton 1962a Introduction, in *Markets in Africa*, P. Bohannan and G. Dalton eds., pp. 1–26. Northwestern University Press, Evanston.

Bohannan, Paul, and George Dalton eds. 1962b *Markets in Africa*. Northwestern University Press, Evanston.

Boltz, William 1986 Early Chinese writing. *World Archaeology* 17:420–436.

Bonacich, Edna 1973 A theory of middleman minorities. *American Sociological Review* 5:583–594.

Bongenaar, Arminius 1997 *The Neo-Babylonian Ebabbar temple at Sippar: Its administration and its prosopography*. Nederlands Instituut voor het Nabije Oosten, Leiden.

Bonney, Richard, and Mark Ormrod 1999 Introduction: Crises, revolutions and self-sustained growth – towards a conceptual model of change in fiscal history, in *Crises, revolutions and self-sustained growth: Essays in European fiscal history, 1130–1830*, M. Ormrod, M. Bonney, and R. Bonney eds., pp. 1–21. Shaun Tyas, Stamford, UK.

Bossen, Laurel 1981 The household as economic agent. *Urban Anthropology* 10:287–303.

Bossen, Laurel 1988 Toward a theory of marriage: The economic anthropology of marriage transactions. *Ethnology* 27:127–144.

Boulanger, André 1923 *Aelius Aristide et la sophistique dans la province d'Asie au iie siècle de notre ère*. De Boccard, Paris.

Bourdieu, Pierre 1977 *Outline of a theory of practice*. Cambridge University Press, Cambridge.

Bovill, Edward 1970 *The golden trade of the Moors*. Oxford University Press, Oxford.

Bowman, Alan, and Andrew Wilson eds. 2009 *Quantifying the Roman economy: Methods and problems*. Oxford University Press, Oxford.

Boyd, Robert, and Peter Richerson 2009 Culture and the evolution of human cooperation. *Philosophical Transactions of the Royal Society of London B: Biological Sciences* 364:3281–3288.

Boyd, Robert, Herbert Gintis, Samuel Bowles, and Peter Richerson 2003 The evolution of altruistic punishment. *Proceedings of the National Academy of Sciences* 100:3531–3535.

Bradburn, Daniel 1981 Size and success: Komachi adaptation to a changing Iran, in *Modern Iran: The dialectics of continuity and change*, M. Bonine and N. Keddi eds., pp. 123–137. State University of New York Press, Albany.

Bradley, Keith 1987 *Slaves and masters in the Roman Empire: A study in social control.* Oxford University Press, Oxford.

Bradley, Richard 1984 *The social foundations of prehistoric Britain.* Harlow, London.

Bradley, Richard 1991 The patterns of change in British prehistory, in *Chiefdoms: Power, economy and ideology*, T. Earle ed., pp. 44–70. Cambridge University Press, Cambridge.

Brady, Ivan ed. 1976 *Transactions in kinship: Adoption and fosterage in Oceania.* University Press of Hawaii, Honolulu.

Braudel, Fernand 1973 *Capitalism and material life, 1400–1800.* Harper and Row, New York.

Braudel, Fernand 1986 *Civilization and capitalism 15th–18th century: The wheels of commerce.* Harper and Row, New York.

Braudel, Fernand 1995 *The Mediterranean and the Mediterranean world in the age of Philipp II.* University of California Press, Berkeley.

Bray, Francesca 1984 *Agriculture, science and civilization in China.* Cambridge University Press, Cambridge.

Brazzabeni, Micol, Manuela Cunha, and Martin Fotta eds. 2015 *Gypsy economy: Romani livelihoods and notions of worth in the 21st century.* Berghahn Books, New York.

Bremmer, Jan 1976 Avunculate and fosterage. *Journal of Indo-European Studies* 4:65–78.

Breniquet, Catherine 2014 The archaeology of wool in early Mesopotamia: Sources, methods, perspectives, in *Wool economy in the ancient Near East*, C. Breniquet and C. Michel eds., pp. 52–78. Oxbow Books, Oxford.

Breniquet, Catherine, and Cécile Michel eds. 2014 *Wool economy in the ancient Near East.* Oxbow Books, Oxford.

Bresson, Alain 2016 *The making of the ancient Greek economy: Institutions, markets, and growth of city-states.* Princeton University Press, Princeton.

Bretschneider, Joachim 2007 The "reception palace" of Uruk and its architectural origin, in *Power and architecture: Monumental public architecture in the Bronze Age Near East and Aegean*, J. Bretschneider, J. Driessen, and K. Van Lerberghe eds., pp. 11–22. Peeters, Leuven.

Brewer, John 1988 *The sinews of power: War, money, and the English state, 1688–1783.* Harvard University Press, Cambridge, MA.

Briant, Pierre 2002 *From Cyrus to Alexander: A history of the Persian empire.* Eisenbrauns, Winona Lake.

Brito Guaddarrama, Brito 2011 Huexotzingo en el siglo XVI. Transformaciones de un altépetl mesoamericano. PhD dissertation, Universidad Nacional Autónoma de México.

Broda, Johanna 1978 Relaciones políticas ritualizadas: El ritual como expresión de una ideología, in *Economía política e ideología en el México prehispánico*, P. Carrasco and J. Broda eds., pp. 221–255. Editorial Nueva Imagen, México City.

Bromley, Ray, Richard Symanski, and Charles Good 1975 The rationale of periodic markets. *Annals of the Association of American Geographers* 65:530–537.

Brookfield, Harold 1984 Intensification revisited. *Pacific Viewpoint* 25:15–44.

Brown, Ian 1989 The calumet ceremony in the southeast and its archaeological manifestations. *American Antiquity* 54:311–331.

Brown, Nancy 2015 *Ivory Vikings: The mystery of the most famous chessmen in the world and the woman who made them.* St. Martin's Press, New York.

Brown, Peter 2002 *Poverty and leadership in the later Roman empire.* Brandeis University Press, Waltham.

Bruijn, Jaap 1993 Productivity, profitability, and costs of private and corporate Dutch ship owning in the seventeenth and eighteenth centuries, in *The rise of merchant empires: Long-distance trade in the modern world, 1350–1750*, J. Tracy ed., pp. 174–194. Cambridge University Press, Cambridge.

Brumfiel, Elizabeth 1987 Elite and utilitarian crafts in the Aztec state, in *Specialization, exchange, and complex societies*, E. Brumfiel and T. Earle eds., pp. 102–118. Cambridge University Press, Cambridge.

Brumfiel, Elizabeth 1992 Distinguished lecture in archeology: Breaking and entering the ecosystem – Gender, class, and faction steal the show. *American Anthropologist* 94:551–567.

Brumfiel, Elizabeth, and Deborah Nichols 2009 Bitumen, blades, and beads: Prehispanic craft production and the domestic economy, in *Housework: Craft production and domestic economy in ancient Mesoamerica*, K. Hirth ed., pp. 239–251. Wiley, Hoboken.

Brumfiel, Elizabeth, and Timothy Earle eds. 1987a *Specialization, exchange, and complex societies*. Cambridge University Press, Cambridge.

Brumfiel, Elizabeth, and Timothy Earle 1987b Specialization, exchange, and complex societies: An introduction, in *Specialization, exchange, and complex societies*, E. Brumfiel and T. Earle eds., pp. 1–9. Cambridge University Press, Cambridge.

Brun, Jean-Pierre 2016 The archaeology of Roman urban workshops: A French approach, in *Urban craftsmen and traders in the Roman World*, A. Wilson and M. Flohr eds., pp. 77–94. Oxford University Press, Oxford.

Bruner, Edward 1961 Differential change in the culture of the Mandan from 1250–1953, in *Perspectives in American Indian culture change*, E. Spicer ed., pp. 187–277. University of Chicago Press, Chicago.

Burford, Allison 1972 *Craftsmen in Greek and Roman society*. Cornell University Press, Ithaca.

Burger, Richard 2013 In the realm of the Incas: An archaeological reconsideration of household exchange, long-distance trade, and marketplaces in the pre-Hispanic central Andes, in *Merchants, markets, and exchange in the pre-Columbian world*, K. Hirth and J. Pillsbury eds., pp. 319–334. Dumbarton Oaks Research Library and Collections, Washington, DC.

Burns, Kathryn 1999 *Colonial habits: Convents and the spiritual economy of Cuzco, Peru*. Duke University Press, Durham.

Bushell, Stephen 1983 A description of Ching-te-chen, in *Ching-te-chen: Views of a porcelain city*, R. Tichane ed., pp. 175–185. New York State Institute for Glaze Research, Painted Post.

Butzer, Karl 1976 *Early hydraulic civilization in Egypt: A study in cultural ecology*. University of Chicago Press, Chicago.

Byock, Jesse 1993 *Feud in the Icelandic saga*. University of California Press, Berkeley.

Byock, Jesse 2001 *Viking age Iceland*. Penguin Books, London.

Calnek, Edward 1976 The internal structure of Tenochtitlan, in *The Valley of Mexico: Studies of pre-Hispanic ecology and society*, E. Wolf ed., pp. 287–302. University of New Mexico Press, Albuquerque.

Calnek, Edward 1978 El sistema de mercado de Tenochtitlan, in *Economía política e ideología en el México prehispánico*, P. Carrasco and J. Broda eds., pp. 95–114. Editorial Nueva Imagen, Mexico City.

Camp, John 1986 *The Athenian Agora: Excavations in the heart of Classical Athens*. Thames and Hudson, London.

Cancian, Frank 1965 *Economics and prestige in a Maya community: The religious cargo system in Zinacantan*. Stanford University Press, Stanford.

Caner, Daniel 2002 *Wandering, begging monks: Spiritual authority and the promotion of monasticism in Late Antiquity*. University of California Press, Los Angeles.

Carballo, David ed. 2013a *Cooperation and collective action: Archaeological perspectives*. University Press of Colorado, Boulder.

Carballo, David 2013b Cultural and evolutionary dynamics of cooperation in archaeological perspective, in *Cooperation and collective action: Archaeological perspectives*, D. Carballo ed., pp. 3–33. University Press of Colorado, Boulder.

Carballo, David 2013c Labor collectives and group cooperation in pre-Hispanic Central Mexico, in *Cooperation and collective action: Archaeological perspectives*, D. Carballo ed., pp. 243–274. University Press of Colorado, Boulder.

Cardos de Méndez, Amalia 1959 El comercio de los Mayas antiguos. *Acta Anthropologica epoca* 2.

Carile, Maria Cristina. 2012 *The vision of the palace of the Byzantine emperors as a heavenly Jerusalem*. Fondazione Centro italiano di studi sull'alto Medioevo, Spoleto.

Carneiro, Robert 1967 On the relationship between size of population and complexity of social organization. *Southwestern Journal of Anthropology* 23:234–243.

Carneiro, Robert 1970 A theory of the origin of the state. *Science* 169:733–738.

Carneiro, Robert 1974 A reappraisal of the role of technology and organization in the origin of civilization. *American Antiquity* 39:179–186.

Carneiro, Robert 1978 Political expansion as an expression of the principle of competitive exclusion, in *Origins of the state: The anthropology of political evolution*, R. Cohen and E. Service eds., pp. 205–223. Institute for the Study of Human Issues, Philadelphia.

Carneiro, Robert 1992 Point counterpoint: Ecology and ideology in the development of New World civilizations, in *Ideology and pre-Columbian civilizations*, A. Demarest and G. Conrad eds., pp. 175–204. School of American Research, Sante Fe.

Carrasco, Pedro 1971 Social organization of ancient Mexico, in *Handbook of Middle American Indians*, G. Ekholm and I. Bernal eds., 10:349–375. University of Texas Press, Austin.

Carrasco, Pedro 1978 La economía del México prehispánico, in *Economía política e ideología en el México prehispánico*, P. Carrasco and Johanna Broda eds., pp. 13–74. Editorial Nueva Imagen, México City.

Carrasco, Pedro 1980 Markets and merchants in the Aztec economy. *Journal of the Steward Anthropological Society* 11:249–269.

Carsten, Janet, and Stephen Hugh-Jones eds. 1995a *About the house: Lévi-Strauss and beyond.* Cambridge University Press, Cambridge.

Carsten, Janet, and Stephen Hugh-Jones 1995b Introduction: About the house: Lévi-Strauss and beyond, in *About the house: Lévi-Strauss and beyond*, J. Carsten and S. Hugh-Jones eds., pp. 1–46. Cambridge University Press, Cambridge.

Carter, Tristan 2016 Obsidian consumption in the Late Pleistocene–Early Holocene Aegean: Contextualising new data from Mesolithic Crete. *Annual of the British School at Athens* 111:13–34.

Carver, Jonathan 1951 *Travels through the interior parts of North America, in the years 1766, 1767, and 1768.* Ross & Haines, Minneapolis (originally published in 1781).

Casaubon, Meric 1906 *The meditations of Marcus Aurelius Antonius*, M. Casaubon trans. J. M. Dent, London.

Cashdan, Elizabeth 1989 Hunters and gatherers: Economic behavior in bands, in *Economic anthropology*, S. Plattner ed., pp. 21–48. Stanford University Press, Stanford.

Cashdan, Elizabeth 1990 *Risk and uncertainty in tribal and peasant economies.* Westview Press, Boulder.

Casson, Lionel 1989 *The Periplus Maris Erythraei: Text with introduction, translation, and commentary.* Princeton University Press, Princeton.

Casson, Lionel 1991 *The ancient mariners.* Princeton University Press, Princeton.

Castanzo, Ronald 2009 Ceramics on the side: Pottery making as an augmentation of household economy in the Valley of Puebla during the Formative period, in *Housework: Craft production and domestic economy in ancient Mesoamerica*, K. Hirth ed., pp. 133–147. Wiley, Hoboken.

Chabot, Jacques, and Jacques Pelegrin 2012 Two examples of pressure blade production with a lever: Recent research from the southern Caucasus (Armenia) and Northern Mesopotamia (Syria, Iraq), in *The emergence of pressure blade making*, P. Desroisiers ed., pp. 181–198. Springer, New York.

Chabot-Hanowell, Benjamin, and Lisa Lucero 2013 Water control and the emergence of polities in the southern Maya lowlands, in *Cooperation and collective action: Archaeological perspectives*, D. Carballo ed., pp. 223–242. University Press of Colorado, Boulder.

Chacón, Edgar, Isabel Besembel, Dulce Rivero, and Juan Cardillo 2008 The holonic production unit: An approach for an architecture of embedded production process, in *Advances in robotics, automation and control*, J. Arámburo and A. Ramírez Treviño eds., pp. 301–314. Intech, Vienna.

Chakravarti, Ranabir 2000 Nakhudas and nauvittakas: Ship-owning merchants in the West Coast of India (c. AD 1000–1500). *Journal of the Economic and Social History of the Orient* 43:34–64.

Chakravarti, Ranabir ed. 2005 *Trade in early India.* Oxford University Press, Oxford.

Chandler, Tertius 1987 *Four thousand years of urban growth: An historical census.* Edwin Mellen, Lewiston.

Chapman, Ann 1957 Port of trade enclaves in Aztec and Maya civilizations, in *Trade and market in the early empires*, K. Polanyi, C. Arensberg, and H. Pearson eds., pp. 114–153. Free Press, Glencoe.

Chapman, Stanley 2006 *The rise of merchant banking.* Routledge, New York.

Charvát, Petr 1982 Early Ur-war chiefs and kings of Early Dynastic III. *Altorientalische Forschungen* 9:43–60.

Charvát, Petr 2014 Lambs of the gods. The beginnings of the wool economy in proto-cuneiform texts, in *Wool economy in the ancient Near East*, C. Breniquet and C. Michel eds., pp. 79–93. Oxbow Books, Oxford.

Chaudhuri, Kirti 1985 *Trade and civilization in the Indian Ocean: An economic history from the rise of Islam to 1750.* Cambridge University Press, Cambridge.

Chaudhuri, Kirti 1991 Reflections on the organizing principle of premodern trade, in *The political economy of merchant empires*, J. Tracy ed., pp. 421–442. Cambridge University Press, Cambridge.

Chaudhury, Sushi 2005 Trading networks in a traditional diaspora: Armenians in India, c. 1600–1800, in *Diaspora entrepreneurial networks: Four centuries of history*, I. Baghdiantz McCabe, G. Harlaftis, and I. Pepelasis Minoglou eds., pp. 51–72. Berg, Oxford.

Chayanov, Alexander 1966 *The theory of peasant economy*, D. Thorner, B. Kerblay, and R. E. F. Smith, eds. and trans. American Economic Association, Homewood.

Cheong, Weng Eang 1997 *The Hong merchants of Canton: Chinese merchants in Sino-Western trade.* Nordic Institute of Asian Studies Monograph 70. Curzon Press, Richmond.

Chesson, Meredith 2003 Households, houses, neighborhoods and corporate villages: Modeling the Early Bronze Age as a house society. *Journal of Mediterranean Archaeology* 16:79–102.

Chiang, Tao-Chang 1983 The salt trade in Ming China. *Geographical Review* 65:93–106.

Chibnik, Michael 1994 *Risky rivers: The economics and politics of floodplain farming in Amazonia.* University of Arizona Press, Albuquerque.

Chibnik, Michael 2011 *Anthropology, economics, and choice.* University Texas Press, Austin.

Chien, Cecilia Lee-fang 2004 *Salt and the state: An annotated translation of the Songshi salt monopoly treatise.* University of Michigan Press, Ann Arbor.

Childe, Gordon 1936 *Man makes himself.* Watts, London.

Childe, Gordon 1950 The urban revolution. *Town Planning Review* 21:3–17.

Childe, Gordon 1958 *The prehistory of European society.* Penguin Books, Harmondsworth.

Chimalpahin Cuauhtlehuanitzin, Francisco de San Antón Muñón 1965 *Relaciones originales de Chalco Amaquemecan.* Fondo de Cultura Económica, Mexico City.

Chittenden, Hiram 1986 *The American fur trade of the far west.* University of Nebraska Press, Lincoln.

Christ, Matthew 1990 Liturgy avoidance and antidosis in classical Athens. *Transactions of the American Philological Association* 120:147–169.

Christakis, Kostis 1999 Pithoi and food storage in neopalatial Crete: A domestic perspective. *World Archaeology* 31:1–20.

Christakis, Kostis 2011 Redistribution and political economies in Bronze Age Crete. *American Journal of Archaeology* 115:197–205.

Christaller, Walter 1966 *Central places in southern Germany.* Prentice-Hall, Englewood Cliffs.

Cieza de León, Pedro 1998 *The discovery and conquest of Peru.* Duke University Press, Chapel Hill.

Çizakça, Murat 1989 Tax-farming and resource allocation in past Islamic societies. *Islamic Economics* 1:1–22.

Çizakça, Murat 1993 Tax-farming and financial decentralization in the Ottoman economy, 1520–1697. *Journal of European Economic History* 22:219–250.

Clarence-Smith, William Gervase 2011 The production of cotton textiles in early modern South-East Asia, in *The spinning world: A global history of cotton textiles 1200–1850*, G. Riello and P. Parthasarathi eds., pp. 127–142. Oxford University Press, Oxford.

Clark, Gracia 1989 Separation between trading and home for Asante women in Kumasi central market, Ghana, in *The household economy: Reconsidering the domestic mode of production*, R. Wilk ed., pp. 91–118. Westview Press, Boulder.

Clark, John 1987 Politics, prismatic blades, and Mesoamerican civilization, in *The organization of core technology*, J. Johnson and C. Morrow eds., pp. 259–285. Westview Press, Boulder.

Clark, John 1995 Craft specialization as an archaeological category, in *Research in economic anthropology*, B. Isaac ed., 16:267–294. JAI Press, Greenwich.

Clark, John, and Michael Blake 1994 The power of prestige: Competitive generosity and the emergence of rank societies in lower Mesoamerica, in *Factional competition and political development in the New World*, E. Brumfiel and J. Fox eds., pp. 17–30. Cambridge University Press, Cambridge.

Clark, John, and William Parry 1990 Craft specialization and cultural complexity, in *Research in economic anthropology*, B. Isaac ed., 12:289–346. JAI Press, Greenwich.

Clarke, Michael 2001 Akha feasting. An ethnoarchaeological perspective, in *Feasts: Archaeological and ethnographic pespectives on food, politics, and power*, M. Dietler and B. Hayden eds., pp. 144–167. Smithsonian Institution Press, Washington, DC.

Clarkson, Leslie 1971 *The pre-industrial economy in England 1500–1750*. B. T. Batsford, London.

Coase, Ronald 1937 The nature of the firm. *Economica* 4:386–405.

Coase, Ronald 2008 The institutional structure of production, in *Handbook of new institutional economics*, C. Ménard and M. Shirley eds., pp. 31–39. Springer, Dordrecht.

Cobo, Father Bernabé 1979 *History of the Inca empire: An account of the Indians' customs and their origin, together with a treatise on Inca legends, history, and social institutions*. University of Texas Press, Austin.

Cobo, Father Bernabé 1990 *Inca religion and customs*. University of Texas Press, Austin.

Cockle, Helen 1981 Pottery manufacture in Roman Egypt: A new papyrus. *The Journal of Roman Studies* 71:87–97.

Codere, Helen 1966 *Fighting with property: A study of Kwakiutl potlatching and warfare, 1792–1930*. University of Washington Press, Seattle.

Cohen, Abner 1965 The social organization of credit in a West African cattle market. *Africa: Journal of the International African Institute* 35:8–20.

Cohen, Abner 1966 Politics of the kola trade: Some processes of tribal community formation among migrants in West African towns. *Africa: Journal of the International African Institute* 36:18–36.

Cohen, Abner 1971 Cultural strategies in the organization of trading diasporas, in *The development of indigenous trade and markets in west Africa*, C. Meillassoux ed., pp. 266–281. Oxford University Press, London.

Cohen, Robin, and Nicholas Van Hear 2008 *Global diasporas: An introduction*. Routledge, London.

Cohen, Ronald 1978 Introduction, in *Origins of the state: The anthropology of political evolution*, R. Cohen and E. Service eds., pp. 1–20. Institute for the Study of Human Issues, Philadelphia.

Coleman, James 1998 Social capital in the creation of human capital. *American Journal of Sociology* 94:S95–S120.

Coleman, Kathleen 2003 Euergetism in its place, in *Bread and circuses: Euergetism and municipal patronage in Roman Italy*, K. Lomas and T. Cornell eds., pp. 61–88. Routledge, London.

Collier, Jane 1993 *Marriage and inequality in classless societies*. Stanford University Press, Stanford.

Colpaert, Sabien 2014 Euergetism and the gift, in *Gift giving and the "embedded" economy in the ancient world*, F. Carlà and M. Gori eds., pp. 181–201. Universitätsverlag Winter, Heidelberg.

Comegna, Anthony 2016 Slavery and empire: The destruction of Whydah (www.libertarianism.org/columns/slavery-empire-destruction-whydah).

Conkey, Margaret 1980 The identification of prehistoric hunter-gatherer aggregation sites: The case of Altamira. *Current Anthropology* 21:609–630.

Conklin, Harold 1957 *Hanunóo agriculture: A report on an integral system of shifting cultivation in the Philippines*. Food and Agriculture, Organization of the United Nations, Rome.

Conklin, Harold 1967 Division of Anthropology: Some aspects of ethnographic research in Ifugao. *Transactions of the New York Academy of Sciences* 30:99–121.

Conklin, Harold 1969 An ethnoecological approach to shifting agriculture, in *Environment and cultural behavior*, A. Vayda ed., pp. 221–233. University of Texas Press, Austin.

Cook, Scott 1966 The obsolete "anti market" mentality: A critique of the substantive approach to economic anthropology. *American Anthropologist* 68:323–345.

Cook, Sherburne, and Lesley Byrd Simpson 1948 *The population of Central Mexico in the sixteenth century*. Ibero Americana 31. University of California Press, Berkeley.

Cortés, Hernando 1962 *5 letters of Cortés to the emperor*. W. W. Norton, New York.

Coşgel, Metin 2015 The Ottoman empire, in *Fiscal regimes and the political economy of premodern states*, A. Monson and W. Scheidel eds., pp. 404–428. Cambridge University Press, Cambridge.

Coşgel, Metin, and Thomas Miceli 2009 Tax collection in history. *Public Finance Review* 37:399–420.

Costin, Cathy 1991 Craft specialization: Issues in defining, documenting, and explaining the organization of production, in *Archaeological method and theory*, M. Schiffer ed., pp. 1–56. University of Arizona Press, Tucson.

Costin, Cathy 1993 Textiles, women, and political economy in late prehispanic Peru, in *Research in economic anthropology*, B. Isaac ed., 14:3–28. JAI Press, Greenwich.

Costin, Cathy 1998 Housewives, chosen women, skilled men: Cloth production and social identity in the late prehispanic Andes, in *Craft and social identify*, C. Costin ed., pp. 123–141. Wiley, Hoboken.

Costin, Cathy 2001a Craft production systems, in *Archaeology at the millennium: A sourcebook*, G. Feinman and D. Price eds., pp. 273–327. Plenum, New York.

Costin, Cathy 2001b Production and exchange of ceramics, in *Empire and domestic economy*, T. D'Altroy and C. Hastorf eds., pp. 203–242. Kluwer Academic, New York.

Costin, Cathy 2011 Textiles and Chimú identity under Inka hegemony on the North Coast of Peru, in *Textile economies: Power and value from the local to the transnational*, W. Little and P. McAnany eds., pp. 101–124. Alta Mira, Lanham.

Costin, Cathy 2013 Gender and textile production in prehistory, in *Companion to gender prehistory*, D. Bolger ed., pp. 180–202. Wiley-Blackwell, New York.

Costin, Cathy 2016 Introduction, in *Making value, making meaning: Techné in the pre-Columbian world*, C. Costin ed., pp. 1–30. Dumbarton Oaks Research Library and Collection, Washington, DC.

Costin, Cathy, and Melissa Hagstrum 1995 Standardization, labor investment, skill, and the organization of ceramic production in late prehispanic highland Peru. *American Antiquity* 60:619–639.

Costin, Cathy, and Rita Wright eds. 1998 *Craft and social identity*. Wiley, Hoboken.

Coult, Allan, and Robert Habenstein 1965 *Cross tabulations of Murdock's world ethnographic sample*. University of Missouri Press, Columbia.

Cox, Nancy 2000 *The complete tradesman: A study of retailing, 1550–1820*. Ashgate, Hants.

Crawford, Harriet 1973 Mesopotamia's invisible exports in the third millennium BC. *World Archaeology* 5:232–241.

Crumley, Carol 1995 Heterarchy and the analysis of complex societies, in *Heterarchy and the analysis of complex societies*, R. Ehrenreich, C. Crumley, and J. Levy eds., pp. 1–6. Wiley, Hoboken.

Cuddy, Thomas 2008 *Revolutionary economies: What archaeology reveals about the birth of American capitalism*. Altamira Press, Lanham.

Curtin, Philip 1984 *Cross-cultural trade in world history*. Cambridge University Press, Cambridge.

Cyphers, Ann 1997 La arquitectura Olmeca en San Lorenzo Tenochtitlán, in *Población, subsistencia y medio ambiente en San Lorenzo Tenochtitlán*, A. Cyphers ed., pp. 91–117. Universidad Nacional Autónoma de México, Mexico City.

Dahrendorf, Ralf 1959 *Class and class conflict in industrial society*. Stanford University Press, Stanford.

Dale, Stephen 1994 *Indian merchants and Eurasian trade, 1600–1750*. Cambridge University Press, Cambridge.

Dalton, George 1961 Economic theory and primitive society. *American Anthropologist* 63:1–25.

Dalton, George 1965 Primitive money. *American Anthropologist* 67:44–65.

Dalton, George 1966 "Bridewealth" vs "bride-price." *American Anthropologist* 68:732–737.

Dalton, George ed. 1968 *Primitive, archaic and modern economies: Essays of Karl Polanyi*. Beacon Press, Boston.

Dalton, George 1977 Aboriginal economies in stateless societies, in *Exchange systems in prehistory*, T. Earle and J. Ericson eds., pp. 191–212. Academic Press, New York.

Dalton, George 1981 Anthropological models in archaeological perspective, in *Pattern of the past: Studies in the honour of David Clarke*, I. Hodder, G. Isaac, and N. Hammond eds., pp. 17–48. Cambridge University Press, Cambridge.

Dalton, George 1984 The Kula: New perspectives on Massim exchange. *American Anthropologist* 86:943–953.

D'Altroy, Terrence 2001 The cultural setting, in *Empire and domestic economy*, T. D'Altroy and C. Hastorf eds., pp. 27–53. Kluwer Academic, New York.

D'Altroy, Terrence 2002 *The Incas*. Blackwell, Malden.

D'Altroy, Terence, and Christine Hastorf eds. 2001 *Empire and domestic economy*. Kluwer Academic, New York.

D'Altroy, Terrence, and Timothy Earle 1985 Staple finance, wealth finance, and storage in the Inca political economy. *Current Anthropology* 26:187–206.

D'Altroy, Terence, Ana María Lorandi, Verónica Williams, Milena Calderari, Christine Hastorf, Elizabeth DeMarrais, and Melissa Hagstrum 2000 Inka rule in the northern Calchaquí valley, Argentina. *Journal of Field Archaeology* 27:1–26.

Dandamayev, Muhammed 1999 Land use in the Sippar region during the Neo-Babylonian and Achaemenid periods, in *Urbanization and land ownership in the ancient Near East*, M. Hudson and B. Levine eds., pp. 363–389. Peabody Museum Bulletin 7, Harvard University, Cambridge, MA.

Das Gupta, Ashin 2001a A note on the out-station factories at Mocha, in *The world of the Indian Ocean merchant 1500–1800*, A. Das Gupta ed., pp. 457–461. Oxford University Press, Oxford.

Das Gupta, Ashin 2001b India and the Indian Ocean, c. 1500–1800: The story, in *The world of the Indian Ocean merchant 1500–1800*, A. Das Gupta ed., pp. 34–58. Oxford University Press, Oxford.

Das Gupta, Ashin 2001c The maritime merchant of India, c. 1500–1800, in *The world of the Indian Ocean merchant 1500–1800*, A. Das Gupta ed., pp. 88–101. Oxford University Press, Oxford.

Das Gupta, Ashin ed. 2001d *The world of the Indian Ocean merchant 1500–1800*. Oxford University Press, Oxford.

Davies, Eryl 1981 Inheritance rights and the Hebrew levirate marriage: Part 2. *Vetus Testamentum* 31:257–268.

Davies, John 1967 Demosthenes on liturgies: A note. *The Journal of Hellenic Studies* 87:33–40.

Davies, Susanna 1996 *Adaptable livelihoods*. St. Martin's Press, New York.

Davis, Dorothy 1966 *Fairs, shops, and supermarkets: A history of English shopping*. University of Toronto Press, Toronto.

Davis, Gil 2014 Mining money in late archaic Athens. *Historia* 63:257–277.

De Graauw, Arthur 2013 *Ancient ports and harbours. The catalogue*. (www.ancientportsantiques.com).

de la Vaissiere, Etienne 2005 *Sogdian traders: A history*. Brill, Leiden.

De la Vega, Garcilaso 2014 *Royal commentaries of the Incas and general history of Peru, part two*. University of Texas Press, Austin.

De León, Jason 2009 Rethinking the organization of Aztec salt production: A domestic perspective, in *Housework: Craft production and domestic economy in ancient Mesoamerica*, K. Hirth ed., pp. 45–57. Wiley, Hoboken.

de Ligt, Luuk 1993 *Fairs and markets in the Roman empire*. J. C. Gieben, Amsterdam.

De Selincourt, Aubrey 1966 *Herodotus: The Histories*, A. De Selincourt trans. Penguin Classic, Baltimore.

Defoe, Daniel 1841 *The complete English tradesman*. D. A. Talboys, London.

Defoe, Daniel, and Anthony Coulson 1991 *A tour through the whole island of Great Britain*. Yale University Press, New Haven.

Deimel, Anton 1931 *Šumerische tempelwirtschaft: Zur zeit Urukaginas und seiner vorgänger*. Pontificio istituto biblico, Rome.

Dekker, Marleen, and Hans Hoogeveen 2002 Bride wealth and household security in rural Zimbabwe. *Journal of African Economies* 11:114–145.

DeMallie, Raymond, and William Sturtevant eds. 2001 *Handbook of North American Indians, vol. 13: Plains*. Smithsonian Institution, Washington, DC.

Demarest, Arthur 1992 Archaeology, ideology, and pre-Columbian cultural evolution. The search for an approach, in *Ideology and pre-Columbian civilizations*, A. Demarest and G. Conrad eds., pp. 1–13. School of American Research Press, Santa Fe.

DeMarrais, Elizabeth, Luis Castillo, and Timothy Earle 1996 Ideology, materialism, and power strategies. *Current Anthropology* 37:15–31.

Demsky, Aaron 2012 Jacob's herds in light of ancient Near Eastern sources, in *Looking at the ancient Near East and the Bible through the same eyes*, K. Abraham and J. Fleishman eds., pp. 211–220. CDI Press, Bethesda.

Denevan, William 2001 *Cultivated landscapes of native Amazonia and the Andes*. Oxford University Press, Oxford.

Dennis, Andrew, Peter Foote, and Richard Perkins 2006 *Laws of early Iceland. Grágás I. The Codex Regius of grágás with material from other manuscripts*. University of Manitoba Press, Winnipeg.

d'Entrecolles, Pere 1906 The letters of Pere D'entrecolles, in *Porcelain, a sketch of its nature, art and manufacture*, W. Burton ed. and trans., pp. 84–112. Cowell, London.

Dercksen, Jan Garrit 1996 *The Old Assyrian copper trade in Anatolia*. Nederlands Historisch-Archaeologisch Instituut, Istanbul.

Diakonoff, Igor 1975 The rural community in the ancient Near East. *Journal of the Economic and Social History of the Orient/Journal de l'histoire economique et sociale de l'Orient* 18:121–133.

Diakonoff, Igor 1982 The structure of Near Eastern society before the middle of the 2nd millennium BC. *Oikumene* 3:7–100.

Diakonoff, Igor 1991 General outline of the first period of the history of the ancient world and the problem of the ways of development, in *Early antiquity*, I. Diakonoff and P. Kohl eds., pp. 27–66. University of Chicago Press, Chicago.

Díaz del Castillo, Bernal 1956 *The discovery and conquest of Mexico 1517–1521*. Farrar, Straus and Cudahy, New York.

Dietler, Michael 2001 Theorizing the feast: Rituals of consumption, commensal politics, and power in African contexts, in *Feasts: Archaeological and ethnographic perspectives on food, politics, and power*, M. Dietler and B. Hayden eds., pp. 65–114. Smithsonian Institution Press, Washington, DC.

Dietler, Michael, and Brian Hayden eds. 2001 *Feasts: Archaeological and ethnographic pespectives on food, politics, and power*. Smithsonian Institution Press, Washington, DC.

Dike, Kenneth Onwuka, and Felicia Ekejiuba 1990 *The Aro of South-eastern Nigeria, 1650–1980*. University Press, Ibadan.

Dillehay, Tom 1990 Mapuche ceremonial landscape, social recruitment and resource rights. *World Archaeology* 22:223–241.

Dillehay, Tom, and Lautaro Núñez 1988 Camelids, caravans, and complex societies in the south-central Andes, in *Recent studies in pre-Columbian archaeology*, N. Saunders and O. de Montmollin eds., pp. 603–633. British Archaeological Reports 421, Oxford.

Dixon, John, Johnson Cann, and Colin Renfrew 1968 Obsidian and the origins of trade. *Scientific American* 218:38–46.

Dobbins, Christine 1989 From middleman minorities to industrial entrepreneurs: The Chinese in Java and the Parsis in western India 1619–1939. *Itinerario* 13:109–132.

Dobbins, Christine 1996 *Asian entrepreneurial minorities: Conjoint communities in the making of a world-economy 1570–1940*. Curzon Press, Surrey.

Dodgshon, Robert 1998 *From chiefs to landlords: Social and economic change in the western highlands and islands, c. 1493–1820*. Edinburgh University Press, Edinburgh.

Dong, Fengxia, Jing Lu, and Allen Featherstone 2012 Effects of credit constraints on household productivity in rural China *Agricultural Finance Review* 72:402–415.

Donkin, Robin 1979 *Agricultural terracing in the aboriginal New World*. University of Arizona Press, Tucson.

Donner, William 1999 Sharing and compassion: Fosterage in a Polynesian society. *Journal of Comparative Family Studies* 30:703–722.

Dorsey, George 1904 *The Cheyenne*. Publications of the Field Columbian Museum. Anthropological Series 9.1-2. Chicago.

Douglas, Mary 1986 *How institutions think*. Syracuse University Press, Syracuse.

Douglas, Mary, and Baron Ischerwood 1979 *The world of goods*. W. W. Norton, London.

Douglass, John 2002 *Hinterland households: Rural agrarian household diversity in northwest Honduras*. University Press of Colorado, Boulder.

Dove, Michael 1983 Ethnographic atlas of Ifugao: Implications for theories of agricultural evolution in Southeast Asia. *Current Anthropology* 24:516–519.

Dowling, John 1968 Individual ownership and the sharing of game in hunting societies. *American Anthropologist* 70:502–507.

Drennan, Robert 1984 Long-distance transport costs in pre-Hispanic Mesoamerica. *American Anthropologist* 86:105–112.

Drennan, Robert 1991 Pre-Hispanic chiefdom trajectories in Mesoamerica, Central America, and northern South America, in *Chiefdoms: Power, economy, and ideology*, T. Earle ed., pp. 263–287. Cambridge University Press, Cambridge.

Driver, Harold, and William Massey. 1957 Comparative studies of North American Indians. *Transactions of the American Philosophical Society* 47:165–456.

Drucker, Phillip 1939 Rank, wealth, and kinship in Northwest Coast society. *American Anthropologist* 41:55–65.

Drucker, Phillip 1965 *Cultures of the north Pacific coast*. Chandler, San Francisco.

Drucker, Philip, and Robert Heizer 1967 *To make my name good: A reexamination of the southern Kwakiutl potlatch*. University of California Press, Berkeley.

Dumarcay, Jacques, and Michael Smithies 1991 *The palaces of South-East Asia: Architecture and customs*. Oxford University Press, Oxford.

Duncan-Jones, Richard 1990 *Structure and scale in the Roman economy*. Cambridge University Press, Cambridge.

Durán, Diego 1867–1880 *Historia de las indias de Nueva España y islas de tierra firme*. J. M. Andrade and F. Escalante, Mexico City.

Durán, Diego 1971 *Book of the gods and rites and the ancient calendar*. University of Oklahoma Press, Norman.

Durán, Diego 1994 *The history of the Indies of New Spain*. University of Oklahoma Press, Norman.

Durand-Forest, Jacqueline 1971 Cambios económicos y moneda entre los Aztecas. *Estudios de la Cultural Nahuatl* 9:105–124.

Durkheim, Emile 1984 *The division of labor in society*. Macmillan, New York (originally published 1893).

Durrenberger, Paul 1984 *Chayanov, peasants and economic anthropology*. Academic Press, New York.

Durrenberger, Paul, and Gísli Pálsson 1999 The importance of friendship in the absence of states, according to the Icelandic Sagas, in *The anthropology of friendship: Beyond the community of kinship*, S. Bell and S. Coleman eds., pp. 59–77. Berg, Oxford.

Durrenberger, Paul, and Suzan Erem 2016 *Anthropology unbound: A field guide to the 21st century*. Oxford University Press, Oxford.

Dycherhoff, Ursula, and Hanns Prem 1976 La estratificación social en Huexotzinco, in

Estratificación social en la Mesoamérica prehispánica, P. Carrasco ed., pp. 157–177. Instituto Nacional de Antropología e Historia, Mexico City.

Dyer, Christopher 2002 *Making a living in the middle ages: The people of Britain 850–1520*. Yale University Press, New Haven.

Dyer, Christopher 2005 *The age of transition? Economy and society in England in the later Middle Ages*. Oxford University Press, Oxford

Dyer, Christopher 2012 *A country merchant, 1495–1520: Trading and farming at the end of the Middle Ages*. Oxford University Press, Oxford.

Dyson-Hudson, Rada, and Eric Smith 1978 Human territoriality: An ecological reassessment. *American Anthropologist* 80:21–41.

Earle, Timothy 1977 A reappraisal of redistribution: Complex Hawaiian chiefdoms, in *Exchange systems in prehistory*, T. Earle and J. Ericson eds., pp. 213–229. Academic Press, New York.

Earle, Timothy 1978 *Economic and social organization of a complex chiefdom: The Halelea district, Kaua'i, Hawaii*. Anthropological Papers 63, Museum of Michigan, Ann Arbor.

Earle, Timothy 1980 Prehistoric irrigation in the Hawaiian Islands: An evaluation of evolutionary significance. *Archaeology and Physical Anthropology in Oceania* 15:1–28.

Earle, Timothy 1987a Chiefdoms in archaeological and ethnohistorical perspective. *Annual Review of Anthropology* 16:279–308.

Earle, Timothy 1987b Specialization and the production of wealth: Hawaiian chiefdoms and the Inka empire, in *Specialization, exchange, and complex societies*, E. Brumfiel and T. Earle eds., pp. 64–75. Cambridge University Press, Cambridge.

Earle, Timothy 1991 Property rights and the evolution of chiefdoms, in *Chiefdoms: Power, economy, and ideology*, T. Earle ed., pp. 71–99. Cambridge University Press, Cambridge.

Earle, Timothy 1994 Wealth finance in the Inca empire: Evidence for the Calchaqui Valley, Argentina. *American Antiquity* 59:443–460.

Earle, Timothy 1997 *How chiefs come to power: The political economy in prehistory*. Stanford University Press, Stanford.

Earle, Timothy 2000 Archaeology, property, and prehistory. *Annual Review of Anthropology* 29:39–60.

Earle, Timothy 2001 Exchange and social stratification in the Andes. The Xauxa case, in *Empire and domestic economy*, T. Altroy and C. Hastorf eds., pp. 297–314. Kluwer Academic, New York.

Earle, Timothy ed. 2002a *Bronze age economics: The beginnings of political economies*. Westview, Cambridge.

Earle, Timothy 2002b Hawaiian chiefdoms, in *Bronze age economics: The beginnings of political economies*, T. Earle ed., pp. 71–80. Westview, Cambridge.

Earle, Timothy 2002c The bronze age economy of Thy, in *Bronze age economics: The beginnings of political economies*, T. Earle ed., pp. 293–324. Westview, Cambridge.

Earle, Timothy 2011 Redistribution in Aegean palatial societies. Redistribution and the political economy: The evolution of an idea. *American Journal of Archaeology* 115:237–244.

Earle, Timothy 2015 Conclusions. Surplus and the political economy in prehistory, in *Surplus: The politics of production and the strategies of everyday life*. C. Morehart and K. De Lucia eds., pp. 307–325. University Press of Colorado, Boulder.

Earle, Timothy, and Michael Smith 2011 Household economies under the Aztec and Inka empires, in *The comparative archaeology of complex societies*, M. Smith ed., pp. 238–284. Cambridge University Press, Cambridge.

Earle, Timothy, and Terence D'Altroy 1982 Storage facilities and state finance in the upper Mantaro Valley, Peru, in *Contexts for prehistoric exchange*, J. Ericson and T. Earle eds., pp. 83–101. Academic Press, New York.

Eerkens, Jelmer, Kevin Vaughn, and John Kantner 2010 Introduction: The evolution of leadership, in *The evolution of leadership: Transitions in decision making from small-scale to middle-range societies*, K. Vaughn, J. Eerkens, and J. Kantner eds., pp. 3–17. School for Advanced Research Press, Santa Fe.

Eerkens, Jelmer, Hector Neff, and Michael Glascock 2002 Ceramic production among small-scale and mobile hunters and gatherers: A case study from the southwestern Great Basin. *Journal of Anthropological Archaeology* 21:200–229.

Ehrenreich, Robert, Carole Crumley, and Janet Levy eds. 1995 *Heterarchy and the analysis of complex societies*. Wiley, Hoboken.

Eisenhardt, Kathleen 1989 Agency theory: An assessment and review. *Academy of Management Review* 14:57–74.

Eltis, David, and David Richardson 2010 *Atlas of the transatlantic slave trade*. Yale University Press, New Haven.

Ember, Melvin 1963 The relationship between economic and political development in non-industrialized societies. *Ethnology* 2:228–248.

Engels, Friedrich 1973 Karl Marx, a contribution to the critique of political economy, in *Karl Marx and Frederick Engels: Selected works in three volumes* 1:507–516. Progress, Moscow.

Engels, Friedrich 1978 *The origin of the family, private property, and the state*. Foreign Languages Press, Peking (originally published 1884).

Englund, Robert 2001 The state of decipherment of Proto-Elamite. *Max Plank Institute für Wissenschaftsgeschichte Preprint* 183 (http://pubman.mpdl.mpg.de/pubman/item/escidoc:2273899/component/escidoc:2273897/P183.PDF).

Epstein, Steven 1991 *Wage labor and guilds in medieval Europe*. University of North Carolina Press, Chapel Hill.

Erasmus, Charles 1956 Culture structure and process: The occurrence and disappearance of reciprocal farm labor. *Southwestern Journal of Anthropology* 12:444–469.

Errigton, Shelly 1989 *Meaning and power in a Southeast Asia realm*. Princeton University Press, Princeton.

Eskenazi, Tamara Cohn, and Tikva Frymer-Kensky 2011 *The JPS Bible commentary: Ruth*. Jewish Publication Society, Philadelphia.

Evans, Susan Toby, and Joanne Pillsbury eds. 2008 *Palaces of the ancient New World*. Dumbarton Oaks Library and Research Collection, Washington, DC.

Evans-Pritchard, Edward 1940 *The Nuer*. Clarendon Press, Oxford.

Evans-Pritchard, Edward 1971 *The Azande: History and political institutions*. Oxford University Press, Oxford.

Evers, Hans-Dieter 1994a The emergence of trade in a peasant society, in *The moral economy of trade: Ethnicity and developing markets*, H. Evers and H. Schrader eds., pp. 76–87. Routledge, London.

Evers, Hans-Dieter 1994b The trader's dilemma. A theory of the social transformation of markets and society, in *The moral economy of trade: Ethnicity and developing markets*, H. Evers, and H. Schrader, eds., pp. 7–14. Routledge, London.

Evers, Hans-Dieter, and Heiko Schrader 1994 Introduction, in *The moral economy of trade: Ethnicity and developing markets*, H. Evers and H. Schrader, eds., pp. 3–6. Routledge, London.

Ewers, John 1968 *Indian life of the Upper Missouri*. University of Oklahoma Press, Norman.

Falkenstein, Adam 1974 *The Sumerian temple city*. Undena Publications, Malibu.

Fall, Patricia, Steven Falconer, and Lee Lines 2002 Agricultural intensification and the secondary products revolution along the Jordan rift. *Human Ecology* 30:445–482.

Farreras, Victor 1972 Unidades nahuas de medida. *Estudios de Cultura Náhuatl* 10:197–223.

Faulkner, William 1951 *Requiem for a nun*. Random House, New York.

Feinman, Gary 1995 The emergence of inequality, in *Foundations of social inequality*, D. Price and G. Feinman eds., pp. 255–279. Plenum, New York.

Feinman, Gary 1998 Scale and social organization: Perspectives on the archaic state, in *Archaic states*, G. Feinman and J. Marcus eds., pp. 95–133. School of American Research Press, Santa Fe.

Feinman, Gary 1999 Rethinking our assumptions: Economic specialization at the household scale in ancient Ejutla, Oaxaca, Mexico, in *Pottery and people*, J. Skibo and G. Feinman eds., pp. 81–98. University of Utah Press, Salt Lake City.

Feinman, Gary 2001 Mesoamerican political complexity: The corporate-network dimensions, in

From leaders to rulers, J. Haas ed., pp. 151–176. Plenum, New York.

Feinman, Gary 2013a Crafts, specialists, and markets in Mycenaen Greece: Reenvisioning ancient economies beyond typological constucts. *American Journal of Archaeology* 117:453–459.

Feinman, Gary 2013b The emergence of social complexity, in *Cooperation and collective action: Archaeological perspectives*, D. Carballo ed., pp. 35–56. University Press of Colorado, Boulder.

Feinman, Gary, and Jill Neitzel 1984 Too many types: An overview of sedentary prestate societies in the Americas. *Advances in Archaeological Method and Theory* 7:39–102.

Feinman, Gary, and Linda Nicholas 2007 Craft production in Classic period Oaxaca: Implications for Monte Albán's political economy, in *Craft production in complex societies: Multicraft and producer perspectives*, I. Shimada ed., pp. 97–119. University of Utah Press, Salt Lake City.

Fernandez, Kathleen 2003 *A singular people: Images of Zoar*. Kent State University Press, Kent.

Finer, Samuel 1975 State- and nation-building in Europe: The role of the military, in *The formation of national states in Western Europe*, C. Tilly ed., pp. 84–163. Princeton University Press, Princeton.

Finkelstein, Israel 2008 Jerusalem in the Persian (and early Hellenistic) period and the wall of Nehemiah. *Journal for the Study of the Old Testament* 32:501–520.

Finkelstein, Moses 1935 Emporos, Naukleros, and Kapelos: A prolegomena to the study of Athenian trade. *Classical Philology* 30:320–336.

Finley, Moses 1985 *The ancient economy*. University of California Press, Berkeley.

Firth, Raymond 1939 *We, the Tikopia: Kinship in primitive Polynesia*. Beacon Press, Boston.

Firth, Raymond 1964 Capital, saving, and credit in peasant societies: A viewpoint from economic anthropology, in *Capital, saving, and credit in peasant societies*, R. Firth and B. Yamey eds., pp. 15–34. Aldine, Chicago.

Fishel, Richard, Sarah Wisseman, Randall Hughes, and Thomas Emerson 2014 Sourcing red pipestone artifacts from Oneota villages in the Little Sioux Valley of northwest Iowa. *Midcontinental Journal of Archaeology* 35:167–198.

Fisher, Glenn 1996 *The worst tax? A history of the property tax in the United States*. University Press of Kansas, Lawrence.

Flad, Rowan 2011 *Salt production and social hierarchy in ancient China: An archaeological investigation of specialization in China's Three Gorges*. Cambridge University Press, Cambridge.

Flad, Rowan, and Pochan Chen 2013 *Ancient central China: Centers and peripheries along the Yangzi river*. Cambridge University Press, Cambridge.

Fleming, Daniel 2002 Schloen's patrimonial pyramid: Explaining bronze age society. *Bulletin of the American Schools of Oriental Research* 328:73–80.

Fleming, Daniel 2004 *Democracy's ancient ancestors: Mari and early collective governance*. Cambridge University Press, Cambridge.

Flannery, Kent 1972 The cultural evolution of civilizations. *Annual Review of Ecology and Systematics* 3:399–426.

Flannery, Kent 1973 The origins of agriculture. *Annual Review of Anthropology* 2:271–310.

Flannery, Kent 1999 Process and agency in early state formation. *Cambridge Archaeological Journal* 9:3–21.

Flannery, Kent, and Joyce Marcus 2012 *The creation of inequality*. Harvard University Press, Cambridge, MA.

Fleet, Kate 2003 Tax-farming in the early Ottoman state. *The Medieval History Journal* 6:249–258.

Fleet, Kate 2006 *European and Islamic trade in the early Ottoman state: The merchants of Genoa and Turkey*. Cambridge University Press, Cambridge.

Fleisher, Jeffrey 2010 Housing the market: Swahili merchants and regional marketing on the east African coast, seventh to sixteenth centuries, in *Archaeological approaches to market exchange in ancient societies*, C. Garraty and B. Stark eds., pp. 141–159. University of Arizona Press, Tucson.

Fletcher, Alice, and James Murie 1904 *The Hako: A Pawnee ceremony*. Bureau of American

Ethnology 22nd Annual Report, Washington, DC.

Fletcher, Max 1958 The Suez canal and world shipping, 1869–1914. *The Journal of Economic History* 18:556–573.

Flohr, Miko, and Andrew Wilson 2016 Introduction, in *Urban craftsmen and traders in the Roman World*, A. Wilson and M. Flohr eds., pp. 1–19. Oxford University Press, Oxford.

Foner, Anne, and David Kertzer 1978 Transitions over the life course: Lessons from age-set societies. *American Journal of Sociology* 83:1081–1104.

Fonseca Martel, César 1974 Modalidades de la minka, in *Reciprocidad e intercambio en los Andes Peruanos*, G. Alberti and E. Mayer eds., pp. 86–109. Instituto de Estudios Peruanos, Lima.

Forde, Daryll 1956 *Efik traders of old Calabar*. Oxford University Press, London.

Fortes, Meyer 1949 *The web of kinship among the Tallensi*. Oxford University Press, London.

Fortes, Meyer 1958 Introduction, in *The developmental cycle in domestic groups*, J. Goody ed., pp. 1–14. Cambridge University Press, Cambridge.

Foster, Benjamin 1981 A new look at the Sumerian temple state. *Journal of the Economic and Social History of the Orient/Journal de l'histoire economique et sociale de l'Orient* 24:225–241.

Foster, Benjamin 2014 Wool in the economy of Sargonic Mesopotamia, in *Wool economy in the ancient Near East*, C. Breniquet and C. Michel eds., pp. 115–123. Oxbow Books, Oxford.

Foster, George 1952 Life in a Mexican village: Tepoztlán restudied. *American Anthropologist* 54:239–240.

Fox, James 1987 The house as a type of social organization on the island of Roti, in *De la hutte au palais: Sociétés "à maison" en Asie du Sud-Est insulaire*, C. Macdonald ed., pp. 171–191. Centre National de la Recherche Scientifique, Paris.

Fox, Richard 1977 *Urban anthropology: Cities in their cultural settings*. Prentice Hall, New York.

Frank, Harry 1983 A journey from Kuling to Ching-te-chen, in *Ching-te-chen: Views of a porcelain city*, R. Tichane ed., pp. 339–392. New York State Institute for Glaze Research, Painted Post.

Frankenstein, Susan, and Michael Rowlands 1978 The internal structure and regional context of early iron age society in south-western Germany. *Bulletin of the Institute of Archaeology London* 15:73–112.

Freu, Christel 2016 "Disciplina, patrocinium, nomen": The benefits of apprenticeship in the Roman world, in *Urban craftsmen and traders in the Roman world*, A. Wilson and M. Flohr eds., pp. 183–199. Oxford University Press, Oxford.

Fried, Morton 1967 *The evolution of political society*. Random House, New York.

Friedman, Jonathan 1982 Catastrophe and continuity in social evolution, in *Theory and explanation in archaeology*, C. Renfrew, M. Rowlands, and B. Abbott Segraves eds., pp. 175–196. Academic Press, New York.

Friedman, Jonathan, and Michael Rowlands 1978a Notes towards an epigenetic model of the evolution of "civilization," in *The evolution of social systems*, J. Friedman and M. Rowlands eds., pp. 201–278. University of Pittsburgh Press, Pittsburgh.

Friedman, Jonathan, and Michael Rowlands eds. 1978b *The evolution of social systems*. University of Pittsburgh Press, Pittsburgh.

Friedrichs, Christopher 1978 Capitalism, mobility and class formation in the early modern German city, in *Towns in societies*, P. Abrams and E. Wrigley eds., pp. 187–213. Cambridge University Press, Cambridge.

Fuller, Christopher 1989 Misconceiving the grain heap: A critique of the concept of the Indian Jajmani, in *Money and the morality of exchange*, J. Parry and M. Bloch eds., pp. 33–63. Cambridge University Press, Cambridge.

Gabrielsen, Vincent 1994 *Financing the Athenian fleet: Public taxation and social relations*. Johns Hopkins University Press, Baltimore.

Gallant, Thomas 1991 *Risk and survival in ancient Greece: Reconstructing the rural domestic economy*. Stanford University Press, Stanford.

Gardner, John 1993 *On leadership*. Simon and Schuster, New York.

Gardner, Howard, and Emma Laskin 2011 *Leading minds: An anatomy of leadership*. Basic Books, New York.

Garfinkle, Steven 2004 Shepherds, merchants, and credit: Some observations on lending practices in Ur III Mesopotamia. *Journal of the Economic and Social History of the Orient* 47:1–30.

Garfinkle, Steven 2008 Silver and gold: Merchants and the economy of the Ur III state, in *On Ur III times: Studies in honor of Marcel Sigrist*, P. Michaloswki ed., pp. 63–70. American Schools of Oriental Research, Boston.

Garfinkle, Steven 2010 Merchants and state formation in early Mesopotamia, in *Opening the tablet box: Near Eastern studies in honor of Benjamin R. Foster*, S. Melville, S. Slotsky, and F. Foster eds., pp. 185–202. Brill, Boston.

Garland, Robert 1987 *The Piraeus: From the fifth to the first century BC*. Cornell University Press, Ithaca.

Garland, Robert 2014 *Wandering Greeks: The ancient Greek diaspora from the age of Homer to the death of Alexander the Great*. Princeton University Press, Princeton.

Garraty, Christopher 2010 Investigating market exchange in ancient societies: A theoretical review, in *Archaeological approaches to market exchange in pre-capitalistic societies*, C. Garraty and B. Stark eds., pp. 3–32. University Press of Colorado, Boulder.

Garraty, Christopher, and Barbara Stark eds. 2010 *Archaeological approaches to market exchange in pre-capitalistic societies*. University Press of Colorado, Boulder.

Gasche, Hermann, and Michel Tanret eds. 1998 *Changing watercourses in Babylonia: Towards a reconstruction of the ancient environment in Lower Mesopotamia*. Oriental Institute of the University of Chicago, Chicago.

Gat, Azar 2006 *War in human civilization*. Oxford University Press, Oxford.

Gavin, Kathleen 1987 Forms of finance and forms of production: The evolution of specialized livestock production in the ancient Near East, in *Specialization, exchange, and complex societies*, E. Brumfiel and T. Earle eds., pp. 119–129. Cambridge University Press, Cambridge.

Geary, Patrick 1996 Review of itinerant kingship and royal monasteries in early Medieval Germany, c. 936–1075. *Journal of Religion* 76:110–112.

Geels, Frank 2002 Technological transitions as evolutionary reconfiguration processes: A multi-level perspective and a case-study. *Research Policy* 31:1257–1274.

Geertz, Clifford 1962 The rotating credit association: A "middle rung" in development. *Economic Development and Culture Change* 10:214–263.

Geertz, Clifford 1963 *Peddlers and princes: Social change and economic modernization in two Indonesian towns*. University of Chicago Press, Chicago.

Gelb, Ignace 1965 The ancient Mesopotamian ration system. *Journal of Near Eastern Studies* 24:230–243.

Gelb, Ignace 1969 On the alleged temple and state economies in ancient Mesopotamia. *Studi in onore di Edoardo Volterra* 6:137–154.

Gelb, Ignace 1972 The arua institution. *Revue d'assyriologie et d'archéologie orientale* 66:1–32.

Gelb, Ignace 1979 Household and family in early Mesopotamia, in *State and temple economy in the ancient Near East*, E. Lipinski ed., 1:1–97. Orientaliste, Leuven.

Gelb, Ignace, Piotr Steinkeller, and Robert Whiting 1991 *Earliest land tenure systems in the Near East: Ancient kudurrus*. Oriental Institute of the University of Chicago, Chicago.

Gelsinger, Bruce 1981 *Icelandic enterprise: Commerce and economy in the Middle Ages*. University of South Carolina Press, Columbia

Gesner, Johann 1781 *M. Terentii Varronis de re rustica librii III*. J. Gesner trans. Societas literata, Mannheim.

Gezann, Gary 1978 Itinerant salesmen and the periodic market system of Lushoto district, Tanzania, in *Market-place trade: Periodic markets, hawkers, and traders in Africa, Asia, and Latin America*, R. Smith ed., pp. 186–198. Centre for Transportation Studies, University of British Columbia, Vancouver.

Gibbs, Matt 2013 Tax farming, in *The encyclopedia of ancient history*, R. Bagnall, K. Brodersen, C. Champion, A. Erskine, and S. Huebner eds., pp. 6553–6555. Blackwell, West Sussex.

Gibson, Blair 1996 Death of a salesman: Childe's itinerant craftsman in the light of present knowledge of late prehistoric European craft production, in *Craft specialization and social evolution: In memory of V. Gordon Childe*, B. Wailes ed., pp. 107–119. University of Pennsylvania Museum of Archaeology and Anthropology, Philadelphia.

Gilbert, Erik, and Jonathan Reynolds 2006 *Trading tastes: Commodity and culture exchange to 1750*. Pearson-Prentice Hall, Upper Saddle River, NJ.

Gillespie, Susan 2000a Beyond kinship: An introduction, in *Beyond kinship: Social and material reproduction in house societies*, R. Joyce and S. Gillespie eds., pp. 1–21. University of Pennsylvania Press, Philadelphia.

Gillespie, Susan 2000b Lévi-Strauss: Maison and société à maisons, in *Beyond kinship: Social and material reproduction in house societies*, R. Joyce and S. Gillespie eds., pp. 22–52. University of Pennsylvania Press, Philadelphia.

Gillespie, Susan 2000c Rethinking ancient Maya social organization: Replacing "lineage" with "house." *American Anthropologist* 102:467–484.

Gilman, Antonio 1998 Reconstructing property systems from archaeological evidence, in *Property in economic context*, R. Hunt and A. Gilman eds., pp. 215–233. University Press of America, Lanham.

Gitin, Seymour 1997 The Neo-Assyrian empire and its eastern periphery: The Levant, with a focus on Philistine Ekron, in *Assyria 1995: Proceedings of the 10th anniversary symposium of the Neo-Assyrian text corpus project*, S. Parpola and R. Whiting eds., pp. 77–103. Neo-Assyrian Text Corpus Project, Helsinki.

Glover, Paul 1995 *Hometown money: How to enrich your community with local currency*. Greenplanners, Ithaca.

Goddeeris, Anne 2002 *Economy and society in northern Babylonia in the early old Babylonian period (ca. 2000–1800 BC)*. Peeters, Leuven.

Godelier, Maurice 1978a Economy and religion: An evolutionary optical illusion, in *The evolution of social systems*, J. Friedman and M. Rowlands eds., pp. 3–11. University of Pittsburgh Press, Pittsburgh

Godelier, Maurice 1978b "Salt money" and the circulation of commodities among the Baruya of New Guinea, in *Perspectives in Marxist anthropology*, M. Godelier ed., pp. 127–151. Cambridge University Press, Cambridge.

Godelier, Maurice 1978c The concept of the "Asiatic mode of production" and the Marxist model of social evolution, in *Relations of production: Marxist approaches to economic anthropology*, D. Seddon ed., pp. 209–257. Frank Cass, London.

Godelier, Maurice 1986 *The making of great men: Male domination and power among the New Guinea Baruya*. Cambridge University Press, Cambridge.

Goelet, Ogden 1999 "Town" and "country" in ancient Egypt, in *Urbanization and land ownership in the ancient Near East*, M. Hudson and B. Levine eds., pp. 65–116. Peabody Museum Bulletin 7, Harvard University, Cambridge, MA.

Goetzmann, William 2017 *Money changes everything: How finance made civilization possible*. Princeton University Press, Princeton.

Goitein, Shelomo 1963 Letters and documents on the India trade in Medieval times. *Islamic culture* 37:188–205.

Goitein, Shelomo 1967 *A Mediterranean society: The Jewish communities of the Arab world as portrayed in the documents of the Cairo Geniza, vol. 1: Economic foundations*. University of California Press, Berkeley

Goitein, Shelomo 1973 *Letters of medieval Jewish traders*. Princeton University Press, Princeton.

Golas, Peter 1977 Early Ch'ing guilds, in *The city in late imperial China*, W. Skinner ed., pp. 555–580. Stanford University Press, Stanford.

Goldstein, David, and Izumi Shimada 2007 Middle Sicán multicraft production: Resource management and labor organization, in *Craft production in complex societies: Multicraft and producer perspectives*, I. Shimada ed., pp. 44–67. University of Utah Press, Salt Lake City.

Goldstein, Paul 2013 Embedded Andean economic systems and the expansive Tiwanaku state, in *Merchants, markets, and exchange in the pre-Columbian world*, K. Hirth and J. Pillsbury eds., pp. 361–387. Dumbarton Oaks Research Library and Collection, Washington, DC.

Good, Irene 2001 Archaeological textiles: A review of current research. *Annual Review of Anthropology* 30:209–226.

Goodman, Penelope 2016 Working together: Clusters of artisans in the Roman city, in *Urban craftsmen and traders in the Roman World*, A. Wilson and M. Flohr eds., pp. 301–333. Oxford University Press, Oxford.

Goody, Jack ed. 1958 *The developmental cycle in domestic groups*. Cambridge University Press, Cambridge.

Goody, Jack 1969 Adoption in cross-cultural perspective. *Comparative Studies in Society and History* 11:55–78.

Goody, Jack 1976 *Production and reproduction: A comparative study of the domestic domain*. Cambridge University Press, Cambridge.

Goody, Jack, and Stanley Jeyaraja Tambiah 1973 *Bridewealth and dowry*. Cambridge University Press, Cambridge.

Gormsen, Erdmann 1978 Weekly markets in the Puebla region of Mexico, in *Market-place trade: Periodic markets, hawkers, and traders in Africa, Asia, and Latin America*, R. Smith ed., pp. 240–253. Centre for Transportation Studies, University of British Columbia, Vancouver.

Gottwald, Norman 1999 *Tribes of Yahweh: A sociology of the religion of liberated Israel, 1250–1050 BCE*. Sheffield Academic Press, Sheffield.

Graeber, David 2011 *Debt: The first 5000 years*. Melville House, Brooklyn.

Granovetter, Mark 1985 Economic action and social structure: The problem of embeddedness. *American Journal of Sociology* 91:481–510.

Gray, Robert 1960 Sonjo bride-price and the question of African "wife purchase." *American Anthropologist* 62:34–47.

Grebennikov, Andrei, Vladimir Popov, Michael Glascock, Robert Speakman, Yaroslav Kuzmin, and Andrei Ptashinsky 2010 Obsidian provenance studies on Kamchatka penninsula (far eastern Russia): 2003–9 results, in *Crossing the straits: Prehistoric obsidian exploitation in the north Pacific rim*, Y. Kuzmin and M. Glascock eds., pp. 89–120. Archaeopress, Oxford.

Green, Margaret 1980 Animal husbandry at Uruk in the Archaic period. *Journal of Near Eastern Studies* 39:1–35.

Greene, Kevin 1990 *The archaeology of the Roman economy*. University of California Press, Berkeley.

Gregory, Christopher 1981 A conceptual analysis of a non-capitalist gift economy. *Cambridge Journal of Economics* 5:119–135.

Greif, Avner 1989 Reputation and coalitions in medieval trade: Evidence on the Maghribi traders. *The Journal of Economic History* 49:857–882.

Greif, Avner 2000 The fundamental problem of exchange: A research agenda in historical institutional analysis. *European Review of Economic History* 4:251–284.

Grinnell, George 1972 *The Cheyenne Indians: Their history and ways of life*. Yale University Press, New Haven.

Griswold, Gillette 1970 Aboriginal patterns of trade between the Columbia Basin and the Northern Plains. *Archaeology in Montana* 11:1–96.

Groom, Nigel 2005 Trade, incense, and perfume, in *Caravan kingdoms: Yemen and the ancient incense trade*, A. Gunter ed., pp. 104–113. Smithsonian Institution Press, Washington, DC.

Guaman Poma de Ayala, Felipe 1980 *El primer nueva corónica y buen gobierno*, J. Murra, R. Adorno, and J. Urioste eds. Siglo Veintiuno, Mexico City.

Gudeman, Stephen 2001 *The anthropology of economy*. Blackwell, Oxford.

Gulati, A., and Arthur Turner 1929 A note on the early history of cotton. *Journal of the Textile Institute* 20:1–9.

Gulley, Philip 2002 *Home to Harmony*. Harper Collins, San Francisco.

Gulliver, Philip 1953 The age-set organization of the Jie tribe. *The Journal of the Royal Anthropological Institute of Great Britain and Ireland* 83:147–168.

Gundersen, James 1993 Catlinite and the spread of the calumet ceremony. *American Antiquity* 58:560–562.

Gundersen, James, Gregory Waselkov, and Lillian Pollock 2002 Pipestone argillite artifacts from old mobile and environs. *Historical Archaeology* 36:105–116.

Gungwu, Wang 1993 Merchants without empire: The Hokkien sojourning communities, in *The rise of merchant empires: Long-distance trade in the modern world, 1350–1750*, J. Tracy ed., pp. 400–421. Cambridge University Press, Cambridge.

Gutiérrez, Gerardo 2013 Negotiating Aztec tributary demands in the tribute record of Tlapa, in *Merchants, markets, and exchange in the pre-Columbian world*, K. Hirth and J. Pillsbury eds., pp. 141–167. Dumbarton Oaks Research Library and Collections, Washington, DC.

Guyer, Jane 1986 Indigenous currencies and the history of marriage payments: A case study from Cameroon (Monnaies indigènes et histoire de la dot au Cameroun). *Cahiers d'études Africaines* 26:577–610.

Habib, Irfan 1982 Non-agricultural production and urban economy, in *The Cambridge economic history of India*, R. Raychaudhuri and I. Habib, eds., 1:76–93. Cambridge University Press, Cambridge.

Habib, Irfan 1993 Merchant communities in precolonial India, in *The rise of merchant empires: Long-distance trade in the modern world, 1350–1750*, J. Tracy ed., pp. 371–399. Cambridge University Press, Cambridge.

Habib, Irfan 1999 *The agrarian system of Mughal India 1556–1707*. Oxford University Press, Oxford.

Haerinck, Ernie 1997 Babylonia under Achaemenid rule, in *Mesopotamia and Iran in the Persian period: Conquest and imperialism*, J. Curtis and V. Lukonin eds., pp. 26–34. British Museum Press, London.

Hägg, Robin, and Nanno Marinatos 1987 *The function of the Minoan palaces*. Astrom, Stockholm.

Haggett, Peter 1965 *Locational analysis in human geography*. Arnold, London.

Hagstrum, Melissa 1999 The goals of domestic autonomy among highland Peruvian farmer-potters in peasant craft specialization: Home economics of rural craft specialists, in *Research in Economic Anthropology*, B. Isaac ed., 20:265–298. JAI Press, Greenwich.

Hagstrum, Melissa 2001 Household production in Chaco Canyon. *American Antiquity* 66:47–55.

Hajnal, John 1982 Two kinds of preindustrial household formation system. *Population and Development Review* 8:449–494.

Håkansson, Thomas, and Mats Widgren 2007 Labour and landscapes: The political economy of landesque capital in nineteenth century Tanganyika. *Geografiska Annaler: Series B, Human Geography* 89:233–248.

Håkansson, Thomas, and Mats Widgren eds. 2014 *Landesque capital: The historical ecology of enduring landscape modifications*. Left Coast Press, Walnut Creek.

Halbmayer, Ernst 2004 The one who feeds has the rights, in *Cross-cultural approaches to adoption*, F. Bowie ed., pp. 145–164. Routledge, London.

Haldon, John 2015 Late Rome, Byzantium, early medieval western Europe, in *Fiscal regimes and the political economy of premodern states*, A. Monson and W. Scheidel eds., pp. 345–389. Cambridge University Press, Cambridge.

Halperin, Christina, and Antonia Foias 2010 Pottery politics: Late Classic Maya palace production at Motul de San José, Petén, Guatemala. *Journal of Anthropological Archaeology* 29:392–411.

Halperin, Rhoda 2013 *The livelihood of kin: Making ends meet "the Kentucky way."* University of Texas Press, Austin.

Halstead, Paul 1988 On redistribution and the origin of Minoan-Mycenaean palatial economies, in *Problems in Greek prehistory*, E. French and K. Wardle eds. Bristol Classical Press, Bristol.

Halstead, Paul 1989 The economy has no surplus: Economic stability and social change among early farming communities of Thessaly, Greece, in *Bad year economics*, P. Halstead and J. O'Shea eds., pp. 68–80. Cambridge University Press, Cambridge.

Halstead, Paul, and John O'Shea eds. 1989 *Bad year economics*. Cambridge University Press, Cambridge.

Handford, Stanley 1961 *Langenscheidt's pocket Latin dictionary: Latin-English*. Barnes and Noble, New York.

Hands, Arthur 1968 *Charities and social aid in Greece and Rome*. Cornell University Press, Ithaca.

Hann, Chris, and Keith Hart eds. 2009 *Market and society: The great transformation today*. Cambridge University Press, Cambridge.

Hansen, Anna 2008 Fosterage and dependency in medieval Iceland and its significance in Gísla Saga, in *Youth and age in the medieval north*, S. Lewis-Simpson ed., pp. 73–86. Brill, Leiden.

Hansen, Valerie 2012 *The silk road: A new history*. Oxford University Press, Oxford.

Haran, Menahem 2007 Poor, provision for the, in *Encyclopaedia Judaica*, M. Berenbaum and F. Skolnik eds., 16:371–372. Macmillan Reference, Detroit.

Hardin, Garrett 1968 The tragedy of the commons. *Science* 163:1243–1248.

Harding, Thomas 1967 *Voyagers of the Vitiaz Strait*. University of Washington Press, Seattle.

Harding, Thomas 1994 Precolonial New Guinea trade. *Ethnology* 33:101–125.

Harris, Marvin 1959 The economy has no surplus. *American Anthropologist* 61:385–399.

Harris, Ron 2009 The institutional dynamics of early modern Eurasian trade: The commenda and the corporation. *Journal of Economic Behavior and Organization* 71:606–622.

Harris, William ed. 1993 *The inscribed economy: Production and distribution in the Roman empire in the light of instrumentum domesticum*. University of Michigan Press, Ann Arbor.

Harrison, Peter, and Billie Lee Turner eds. 1978 *Pre-Hispanic Maya agriculture*. University of New Mexico Press, Albuquerque.

Harriss, John, and Barbara Harriss 2017 "Generative" or "parasitic" urbanism? Some observations from the recent history of a South Indian market town, in *Development and the rural–urban divide*, J. Harriss and M. Moore eds., pp. 82–101. Routledge, New York.

Harvey, Herbert 1984 Aspects of land tenure in ancient Mexico, in *Explorations in ethnohistory: Indians of Central Mexico in the sixteenth century*, H. Harvey and H. Prem eds., pp. 83–102. University of New Mexico Press, New Mexico.

Harvey, Herbert 1991 *Land and politics in the Valley of Mexico: A two thousand-year perspective*. University of New Mexico Press, Albuquerque.

Hassig, Ross 1985 *Trade, tribute and transportation: The sixteenth-century political economy of the Valley of Mexico*. University of Oklahoma Press, Norman.

Hassig, Ross 1988 *Aztec warfare: Imperial expansion and political control*. University of Oklahoma Press, Norman.

Hastorf, Christine 2001a Agricultural production and consumption, in *Empire and domestic economy*, T. D'Altroy and C. Hastorf eds., pp. 155–178. Kluwer Academic, New York.

Hastorf, Christine 2001b The Xauxa Andean life, in *Empire and domestic economy*, T. D'Altroy and C. Hastorf eds., pp. 315–324. Kluwer Academic, New York.

Hastorf, Christine, and Terence D'Altroy 2001 The domestic economy, households, and imperial transformation, in *Empire and domestic economy*, T. D'Altroy and C. Hastorf eds., pp. 3–25. Kluwer Academic, New York.

Hauser, Mark 2008 *An archaeology of black markets: Local ceramics and economies in eighteenth-century Jamaica*. University of Florida Press, Gainesville.

Haviland, William 1990 *Cultural anthropology*. Holt, Rinehart and Winston, New York.

Hayden, Brian 1990 Nimrods, piscators, pluckers, and planters: The emergence of food production. *Journal of Anthropological Archaeology* 9:31–69.

Hayden, Brian 1993 *Archaeology: The science of once and future things*. Freeman, New York.

Hayden, Brian 1995 Pathways to power: Principles for creating socioeconomic inequalities, in *Foundations of social inequality*,

D. Price and G. Feinman eds., pp. 15–86. Plenum, New York.

Hayden, Brian 1998 Practical and prestige technologies: The evolution of material systems. *Journal of Archaeological Method and Theory* 5:1–55.

Hayden, Brian 2001a Fabulous feasts. A prolegomenon to the importance of feasting, in *Feasts: Archaeological and ethnographic perspectives on food, politics, and power*, M. Dietler and B. Hayden eds., pp. 23–64. Smithsonian Institution Press, Washington, DC.

Hayden, Brian 2001b Richman, poorman, beggarman, chief: The dynamics of social inequality, in *Archaeology at the millennium: A sourcebook*. G. Feinman and D. Price eds., pp. 231–272. Kluwer Academic, New York.

Hayden, Brian 2014 *The power of feasts from prehistory to the present*. Cambridge University Press, Cambridge.

Hayden, Brian, and Suzanne Villeneuve 2011 A century of feasting studies. *Annual Review of Anthropology* 40:433–449.

Healy, Paul 1980 *Archaeology of the Rivas region, Nicaragua*. Wilfrid Laurier University Press, Waterloo.

Heider, Karl 1969 Visiting trade institutions. *American Anthropologist* 71:462–471.

Heinz, Marlies 2013 Public buildings, palaces and temples, in *The Sumerian world*, H. Crawford ed., pp. 179–200. Routledge, New York.

Helbaek, Hans 1963 Textiles from Çatal Hüyük. *Archaeology* 67:39–46.

Helms, Mary 1988 *Ulysses' sail: An ethnographic odyssey of power, knowledge, and geographical distance*. Princeton University Press, Princeton.

Helms, Mary 1993 *Craft and the kingly ideal*. University of Texas Press, Austin.

Heltzer, Michael 1976 *The rural community in ancient Ugarit*. Ludwig Reichert, Wiesbaden.

Heltzer, Michael 1979 Royal economy in ancient Ugarit, in *State and temple economy in the ancient Near East*, vol. 2, E. Lipinski ed., pp. 459–496. Orientaliste, Leuven.

Heltzer, Michael 1982 *The internal organization of the kingdom of Ugarit*. Ludwig Reichert, Wiesbaden.

Heltzer, Michael 1999 The economy of Ugarit, in *Handbook of Ugaritic studies*, W. Watson and N. Wyatt eds., pp. 423–454. Brill, Leiden.

Hendon, Julia 2006 Textile production as craft in Mesoamerica: Time, labor and knowledge. *Journal of Social Archaeology* 6:354–378.

Hendon, Julia 2007 Production as social process, in *Rethinking craft specialization in complex societes: Archaeological analyses of the social meaning of production*, Z. Hruby and R. Flad eds., pp. 163–168. Wiley, Hoboken.

Henning, Friedrich-Wilhelm 1974 *Das vorindustrielle Deutschland 800 bis 1800*. Schöningh, Paderborn.

Henrich, Joseph 2004 Cultural group selection, coevolutionary processes and large-scale cooperation. *Journal of Economic Behavior and Organization* 53:3–35.

Henrich, Joseph, Jean Ensminger, Richard McElreath, Abigail Barr, Clark Barrett, Alexander Bolyanatz, Juan Camilo Cardenas, Michael Gurven, Edwin Gwako, Natalie Henrich, Carolyn Lesorogol, Frank Marlowe, David Tracer, and John Zikor. 2010 Markets, religion, community size, and the evolution of fairness and punishment. *Science* 327:1480–1484.

Henrich, Joseph, Robert Boyd, Samuel Bowles, Colin Camerer, Ernst Fehr, Herbert Gintis, and Richard McElreath 2001 In search of *Homo economicus*: Behavioral experiments in 15 small-scale societies. *The American Economic Review* 91:73–78.

Herman, Gabriel 1981 *Ritualized friendship and the Greek city*. Cambridge University Press, Cambridge.

Hernandez Xolocotzi, Efraim 1949 Maize granaries in Mexico. *Botanical Museum Leaflets* 13:153–192.

Herskovits, Melville 1965 *Economic anthropology: The economic life of primitive peoples*. Norton, New York.

Herskovits, Melville 1967 *Dahomey: An ancient west African kingdom*. Northwestern University Press, Evanston.

Hicks, Frédéric 1976 Mayeque y calpuleque en el sistema de clases del México antiguo, in *Estratificación social en la Mesoamérica prehispánica*, P. Carrasco ed., pp. 67–77. Instituto Nacional de Antropología e Historia, Mexico City.

Hicks, Frédéric 1984 Rotational labor and urban development in prehispanic Tezcoco, in *Explorations in ethnohistory: Indians of Central Mexico in the sixteenth century*, H. Harvey and H. Prem eds., pp. 145–174. University of New Mexico Press, Albuquerque.

Hicks, Frédéric 1987 First steps toward a market-integrated economy in Aztec Mexico, in *Early state dynamics*, H. Claessen and P. Van de Velde eds., pp. 91–107. E. J. Brill, Leiden.

Hill, Polly 1966 Landlords and brokers: A west African trading system (with a note on Kumasi butchers). *Persée* 6:349–366.

Hill, Polly 1969 Hidden trade in Hausaland. *Man* 4:392–409.

Hill, Polly 1971 Two types of West African house trade, in *The development of indigenous trade and markets in west Africa*, C. Meillassoux ed., pp. 303–318. Oxford University Press, London.

Hiroa, Te Rangi 1932 *Ethnology of Tongareva*. Bernice P. Bishop Museum, Honolulu.

Hirth, Friedrich, and William Rockhill 1911 *Chau Ju-Kua: His work on the Chinese and Arab trade in the twelfth and thirteenth centures, entitled Chu-fan-chi*. Imperial Academy of Sciences, St. Petersburg.

Hirth, Kenneth 1978 Interregional trade and the formation of prehistoric gateway communities. *American Antiquity* 43:35–45.

Hirth, Kenneth 1989 Epiclassic militarism and social organization at Xochicalco Morelos, in *Mesoamerican after the decline of Teotihuacan A.D. 700–900*, J. Berlo and R. Diehl eds., pp. 69–81. Dumbarton Oaks Research Library and Collection, Washington, DC.

Hirth, Kenneth 1993 The household as an analytical unit: Problems in method and theory, in *Prehispanic domestic units in Western Mesoamerica*, R. Santley and K. Hirth eds., pp. 21–36. CRC Press, Boca Raton.

Hirth, Kenneth 1996 Political economy and archaeology: Perspectives on exchange and production. *Journal of Archaeological Research* 4:203–239.

Hirth, Kenneth 1998 The distributional approach: A new way to identify market behavior using archaeological data. *Current Anthropology* 39:451–476.

Hirth, Kenneth 2006a Modeling domestic craft production at Xochicalco, in *Obsidian craft production in ancient Central Mexico*, K. Hirth ed., pp. 275–286. University of Utah Press, Salt Lake City.

Hirth, Kenneth ed. 2006b *Obsidian craft production in ancient Central Mexico*. University of Utah Press, Salt Lake City.

Hirth, Kenneth 2008 The economy of supply: Modeling obsidian procurement and craft provisioning at a Central Mexican urban center. *Latin American Antiquity* 19:435–457.

Hirth, Kenneth 2009a Craft production, household diversification, and domestic economy in prehispanic Mesoamerica, in *Housework: Craft production and domestic economy in ancient Mesoamerica*, K. Hirth ed., pp. 13–32. Wiley, Hoboken.

Hirth, Kenneth ed. 2009b *Housework: Craft production and domestic economy in ancient Mesoamerica*. Wiley, Hoboken.

Hirth, Kenneth 2009c Intermittent crafting and multicrafting at Xochicalco, in *Housework: Craft production and domestic economy in ancient Mesoamerica*, K. Hirth ed., pp. 75–91. Wiley, Hoboken.

Hirth, Kenneth 2009d Intermittent domestic lapidary production during the Late Formative period at Nativitas, Tlaxcala, Mexico, in *Housework: Craft production and domestic economy in ancient Mesoamerica*, K. Hirth ed., pp. 157–173. Wiley, Hoboken.

Hirth, Kenneth 2010 Finding the mark in the marketplace: The organization, development and archaeological identification of market systems, in *Archaeological approaches to market exchange in pre-capitalistic societies*, C. Garraty and B. Stark eds., pp. 227–247. University Press of Colorado, Boulder.

Hirth, Kenneth 2012a La modelización del almacenaje prehistórico: Subsistencia, inequalidad y complejidad política, in *Almenaciemento prehispánico del norte de México al altiplano central*, S. Bortot, D. Michelet, and V. Darras eds., pp. 13–26. Ambassade de France au Mexique and Universidad Autónoma de San Luis Potosi, Paris and San Luis Potosi.

Hirth, Kenneth 2012b Producción azteca de maíz y almancenamiento institucional en la Cuenca de Mexico: Un modelo de descentralización del almacenaje, in *Almenaciemento prehispánico del norte de México al altiplano central*, S. Bortot, D. Michelet, and V. Darras eds., pp. 179–186. Ambassade de France au Mexique and Universidad Autónoma de San Luis Potosi, Paris and San Luis Potosi.

Hirth, Kenneth 2016 *The Aztec economic world: Merchants and markets in ancient Mesoamerica.* Cambridge University Press, Cambridge.

Hirth, Kenneth, and Ann Cyphers 2020 *Olmec lithic economy at San Lorenzo.* University Press of Colorado, Boulder.

Hirth, Kenneth, and Joanne Pillsbury 2013 Redistribution and markets in Andean South America. *Current Anthropology* 54:642–647.

Hirth, Kenneth, Sarah Imfeld, and Colin Hirth 2017 The sixteenth-century merchant community of Santa Maria Acxotla, Puebla, in *Rethinking the Aztec economy*, D. Nichols, F. Berdan, and M. Smith eds., pp. 68–101. University of Arizona Press, Tucson.

Ho, Ping-ti 1954 The salt merchants of Yangchou: A study of commercial capitalism in eighteenth-century China. *Harvard Journal of Asiatic Studies* 17:130–168.

Hobsbawm, Eric, and Chris Wrigley 1999 *Industry and empire: From 1750 to the present day.* New Press, New York.

Hodder, Bramwell 1971 Periodic and daily markets in West Africa, in *The development of indigenous trade and markets in west Africa*, C. Meillassoux ed., pp. 347–358. Oxford University Press, London.

Hodder, Rupert 1996 *Merchant princes of the east.* John Wiley and Sons, Chichester.

Hodge, Mary 1984 *Aztec city-states.* Museum of Anthropology Memoir No. 18, University of Michigan, Ann Arbor.

Hodges, Richard 1982 *Dark age economics: The origins of towns and trade A.D. 600–1000.* Gerald Duckworth, London.

Hodgson, Dorothy 2001 *Once intrepid warriors: Gender, ethnicity, and the cultural politics of Maasai development.* Indiana University Press, Bloomington.

Hoebel, Adamson 1960 *The Cheyennes: Indians of the great plains.* Holt, Rinehart and Winston, New York.

Hoebel, Adamson 1967 *The law of primitive man: A study in comparative legal dynamics.* Harvard University Press, Cambridge, MA.

Hogbin, Ian 2013 *Transformation scene: The changing culture of a New Guinea village.* Routledge, London.

Hollander, David 2013 Roman taxation, in *The encyclopedia of ancient history*, R. Bagnall, K. Brodersen, C. Champion, A. Erskine, and S. Huebner eds., pp. 6551–6553. Blackwell, West Sussex.

Holleran, Claire 2012 *Shopping in ancient Rome: The retail trade in the Late Republic and the Principate.* Oxford University Press, Oxford.

Homans, George 1960 *English villagers of the thirteenth century.* Russell and Russell, New York.

Homans, George 1974 *Social behavior: Its elementary forms.* Harcourt Brace Jovanovich, New York.

Hopkins, Keith 1978 Economic growth and towns in Classical antiquity, in *Towns in societies*, P. Abrams and E. Wrigley eds., pp. 35–77. Cambridge University Press, Cambridge.

Hopkins, Keith 1980 Taxes and trade in the Roman empire (200 BC–AD 400). *The Journal of Roman Studies* 70:101–125.

Hopkins, Keith 1983 Introduction, in *Trade in the ancient economy*, P. Garnsey, K. Hopkins, and C. Whittaker eds., pp. ix–xxv. University of California Press, Berkeley.

Horcasitas, Fernando, and Doris Heyden 1971 Fray Diego Durán: His life and works, in *Book of the gods and rites and the ancient calendar*, F. Horcasitas and D. Heyden eds., pp. 3–47. University of Oklahoma Press, Norman.

Hossain, Hameeda 1988 *The company weavers of Bengal: The East India Company and the organization of textile production in Bengal, 1750–1813.* Oxford University Press, Oxford.

Hoselitz, Bert 1955 Generative and parasitic cities. *Economic Development and Cultural Change* 3:278–294.

Hounshell, David 1984 *From the American system to mass production, 1800–1932: The development of manufacturing technology in the United States*, Johns Hopkins University Press, Baltimore.

Houston, Rab, and Keith Snell 1984 Proto-industrialization? Cottage industry, social change, and industrial revolution. *The Historical Journal* 27:473–492.

Hoyt, Elizabeth 1926 *Primitive trade: Its psychology and economics*. Kegan Paul, Trench, Trubner, London.

Hruby, Zachary, and Rowan Flad eds. 2007 *Rethinking craft specialization in complex societes: Archaeological analyses of the social meaning of production*. Wiley, Hoboken.

Huaycochea Nuñez de la Torre, Flor de Maria 1994 *Qolqas: Bancos de reserva andinos*. Universidad Nacional de San Antonio Abad del Cuzco, Cuzco.

Hudson, Michael 1996 Early privatization and its consequences, in *Privatization in the ancient Near East and the Classical world*, M. Hudson and B. Levine eds., pp. 293–308. Peabody Museum Bulletin 5, Harvard University, Cambridge, MA.

Hudson, Michael 1998 Private landownership, debt, and fiscal crisis in the ancient Near East, in *Property in economic context*, R. Hunt and A. Gilman eds., pp. 139–169. University Press of America, Lanham.

Hudson, Michael 1999a From sacred enclave to temple to city, in *Urbanization and land ownership in the ancient Near East*. M. Hudson and B. Levine, pp. 117–164. Peabody Museum Bulletin 7, Harvard University, Cambridge, MA.

Hudson, Michael 1999b Methodology discussion, in *Urbanization and land ownership in the ancient Near East*, M. Hudson and B. Levine eds., pp. 457–480. Peabody Museum Bulletin 7, Harvard University, Cambridge, MA.

Hudson, Michael 1999c Summary review: From open lands to private ownership, in *Urbanization and land ownership in the ancient Near East*, M. Hudson and B. Levine eds., pp. 481–495. Peabody Museum Bulletin 7, Harvard University, Cambridge, MA.

Hudson, Michael 2000 Mesopotamia and classical antiquity, in *Land-value taxation around the world*, R. Andelson ed., pp. 3–25. Blackwell, Malden.

Hudson, Michael, and Baruch Levine 1996 Privatization: A survey of the unresolved controversies, in *Privatization in the ancient Near East and the classical world*, M. Hudson and B. Levine eds., pp. 1–32. Peabody Museum Bulletin 5, Harvard University, Cambridge, MA.

Huebner, Sabine 2013 Adoption and fosterage in the ancient eastern Mediterranean, in *The Oxford handbook of childhood and education in the Classical world*, J. Grubbs, T. Parkin, and R. Bell eds., pp. 510–531. Oxford University Press, Oxford.

Hughes, Diane 1985 From brideprice to dowry in Mediterranean Europe, in *The marriage bargain: Women and dowries in European history*, M. Kaplan ed., pp. 13–58. Havorth Press, New York.

Hughes, Ian 1973 Stone-age trade in the New Guinea inland: Historical geography without history, in *The Pacific in transition: Geographical perspectives on adaptation and change*, H. Brookfield ed., pp. 97–126. Edward Arnold, London.

Hughes, Ian 1977 *New Guinea stone age trade: The geography and ecology of traffic in the interior*. Terra Australis 3, Australian National University, Canberra.

Hughes, Jason, Nick Jewson, and Lorna Unwin eds. 2013 *Communities of practice: Critical perspectives*. Routledge, Abingdon-on-Thames.

Hugh-Jones, Stephen 1995 Inside-out and back-to-front: The androgynous house in northwest Amazonia, in *About the house: Lévi-Strauss and beyond*, J. Carsten and S. Hugh-Jones eds., pp. 226–252. Cambridge University Press, Cambridge.

Hunt, Robert 1987 The role of bureaucracy in the provisioning of cities: A framework for analysis of the ancient Near East, in *The organization of power: Aspects of bureaucracy in the ancient Near East*, M. Gibson and R. Biggs eds., pp. 161–192. Oriental Institute of the University of Chicago, Chicago.

Hunt, Robert 1988 Size and structure of authority in canal irrigation systems. *Journal of Anthropological Research* 44:335–355.

Hunt, Robert 1997 Property, in *Dictionary of anthropology*, T. Barfield ed., pp. 378–379. Blackwell, Oxford.

Hunt, Robert, and Antonio Gilman eds. 1998 *Property in economic context*. University Press of America, Lanham.

Hutson, Scott 2000 Carnival and contestation in the Aztec marketplace. *Dialectical Anthropology* 25:123–149.

Ingimundarson, Jon Haukur 1995 On sagas and sheep: Toward a historical anthropology of social change and production for market, subsistence and tribute in early Iceland (10th to the 13th century). PhD dissertation, University of Arizona, Tucson.

Inomata, Takeshi 2007 Classic Maya elite competition, collaboration, and performance in multicraft production, in *Craft production in complex societies: Multicraft and producer perspectives*, I. Shimada ed., pp. 120–133. University of Utah Press, Salt Lake City.

Inomata, Takeshi 2008 *Royal courts of the ancient Maya*. Westview Press, Boulder.

Irwin, Terence 1999 *Nicomachean ethics*. Hackett, Indianapolis.

Isin, Engin, and Alexandre Lefebvre 2005 The gift of law: Greek euergetism and Ottoman waqf. *European Journal of Social Theory* 8:5–23.

Israel, Jonathan 2005 Diasporas Jewish and non-Jewish and the world maritime empires, in *Diaspora entrepreneurial networks: Four centuries of history*, I. Baghdiantz McCabe, G. Harlaftis, and I. Pepelasis Minoglou eds., pp. 3–26. Berg, Oxford.

Ixtlilxóchitl, Fernando de Alva. 1891 *Obras históricas de Don Fernando de Alva Ixtlilxochitl*. 2 vols. Oficina de la Secretaria de Fomento, Mexico City.

Izuho, Masami, and Wataru Hirose 2010 A review of archaeological obsidian studies on Hokkaido Island (Japan), in *Crossing the straits: Prehistoric obsidian exploitation in the north Pacific rim*, Y. Kuzmin and M. Glascock eds., pp. 9–25. Archaeopress, Oxford.

Jablow, Joseph 1950 *The Cheyenne in Plains Indian trade relations, 1795–1840*. University of Nebraska Press, Lincoln.

Jackson, Edwin 1991 The trade fair in hunter–gatherer interaction: The role of intersocietal trade in the evolution of Poverty Point culture, in *Between bands and states: Sedentism, subsistence, and interaction in small-scale societies*, S. Gregg ed., pp. 265–286. Center for Archaeological Investigations Paper 9, Southern Illinois University, Carbondale.

Jackson, Thomas, and Jonathon Ericson 1994 Prehistoric exchange systems in California, in *Prehistoric exchange systems in North America*, T. Baugh and J. Ericson eds., pp. 385–415. Plenum, New York.

Jacob, Jeffrey, Merlin Brinkerhoff, Emily Jovic, and Gerald Wheatley 2004 HOUR town: Paul Glover and the genesis and evolution of Ithaca HOURS. *International Journal of Community Currency Research* 8:29–41.

Jacobs, Jane 1969 *The economy of cities*. Random House, New York.

Jacobs, Jane 1985 *Cities and the wealth of nations: Principles of economic life*. Vintage, New York.

Jacobsen, Thorkild 1943 Primitive democracy in ancient Mesopotamia. *Journal of Near Eastern Studies* 2:159–172.

Jacobsen, Thorkild 2008 *Toward the image of Tammuz and other essays on Mesopotamian history and culture*. Wipf and Stock, Eugene.

Jain, V. K. 2005 Trading community and merchant corporations, in *Trade in early India*, R. Chakravarti ed., pp. 344–369. Oxford University Press, Oxford.

James, Simon 1998 *A dictionary of taxation*. Edward Elgar, Cheltenham.

Janssen, Jac 1978 The early state in Egypt, in *The early state*, H. Claessen and P. Skałnik eds., pp. 213–234. Mouton, The Hague.

Jarvis, Michael 2010 *In the eye of all trade: Bermuda, Bermudians, and the maritime Atlantic world 1680–1783*. University of North Carolina Press, Chapel Hill.

Jefferies, Richard 1995 Late Middle Archaic exchange and interaction in the North

American midcontinent, in *Native American interactions: Multiscalar analyses and interpretations in the eastern woodlands*, M. Nassaney and K. Sassaman eds., pp. 73–99. University of Tennessee Press, Knoxville.

Johnson, Allen, and Timothy Earle 1987 *The evolution of human societies*. Stanford University Press, Stanford.

Johnson, Gregory 1982 Organizational structure and scalar stress, in *Theory and explanation in archaeology*, C. Renfrew, M. Rowlands, and B. Abbott Segraves eds., pp. 389–421. Academic Press, New York.

Johnson, Gregory 1983 Decision-making organization and pastoral nomad camp size. *Human Ecology* 11:175–199.

Jones, Arnold 1974 *The Roman economy: Studies in ancient economic and administrative history*. P. A. Brunt, Oxford.

Jones, Richard 2010 Fortifications and sieges in western Europe, c. 800–1450, in *Medieval warfare*, M. Keen ed., pp. 163–185. Oxford University Press, Oxford.

Jongman, Willem 1988 *The economy and society of Pompeii*. J. C. Gieben, Amsterdam.

Jónsson, Guðni 1953 Hungrvaka (Hungerwaker), in *Byskupa sögur*, G. Jónsson ed. and trans., 1:1–31. Islendingasagnaútgáfan, Haukadalsútgafan, Akureyri.

Jowett, Benjamin 1943 *Aristotle's politics*, B. Jowett trans. Modern Library, New York.

Julien, Catherine 1988 How Inca decimal administration worked. *Ethnohistory* 35:257–279.

Junker, Laura 1993 Craft goods specialization and prestige goods exchange in Philippine chiefdoms of the fifteenth and sixteenth centuries. *Asian Perspectives* 32:1–35.

Junker, Laura 2001 The evolution of ritual feasting systems in prehispanic Philippine chiefdoms, in *Feasts: Archaeological and ethnographic perspectives on food, politics, and power*, M. Dietler and B. Hayden eds., pp. 267–310. Smithsonian Institution Press, Washington, DC.

Jursa, Michael, and Juan Carlos Moreno Garcia 2015 The ancient Near East and Egypt, in *Fiscal regimes and the political economy of premodern states*, A. Monson and W. Scheidel eds., pp. 115–165. Cambridge University Press, Cambridge.

Kalinowski, Angela 1996 Patterns of patronage: The politics and ideology of public building in the eastern Roman empire, 31 BCE–600 CE. PhD dissertation, University of Toronto.

Kantner, John 2010 Identifying the pathways to permanent leadership, in *The evolution of leadership: Transitions in decision making from small-scale to middle-range societies*, K. Vaughn, J. Eerkens, and J. Kantner eds., pp. 249–281. School for Advanced Research Press, Santa Fe.

Kaplan, David 1968 The formal–substantive controversy in economic anthropology: Reflections on its wider implications. *Southwestern Journal of Anthropology* 24:228–251.

Kaplan, Marion 1985 *The marriage bargain: Women and dowries in European history*. Harrigan Park Press, New York.

Kardulias, Nick, and Richard Yerkes 1996 Microwear and metric analysis of threshing sledge flints from Greece and Cyprus. *Journal of Archaeological Science* 23:657–666.

Kayoko, Fujita 2011 Japan Indianized: The material culture of imported textiles in Japan, 1550–1850, in *The spinning world: A global history of cotton textiles 1200–1850*, G. Riello and P. Parthasarathi eds., pp. 181–203. Oxford University Press, Oxford.

Keeley, Lawrence 1997 *War before civilization: The myth of the peaceful savage*. Oxford University Press, New York.

Kehoe, Dennis 1997 *Investment, profit, and tenancy*. University of Michigan Press, Ann Arbor.

Kehoe, Dennis 2007 *Law and the rural economy in the Roman Empire*. University of Michigan Press, Ann Arbor.

Kemp, Barry 1972 Temple and town in ancient Egypt, in *Man, settlement, and urbanism*, P. Ucko, R. Tringham, and G. Dimbleby, eds., pp. 657–680. Schenkman, Cambridge.

Kemp, Barry 1983 Old Kingdom, Middle Kingdom and Second Intermediate period c. 2686–1552 BC, in *Ancient Egypt: A social history*, B. Trigger, B. Kemp, D. O'Conner, and A. Lloyd eds., pp. 71–182. Cambridge University Press, Cambridge.

Kemp, Barry 1991 *Ancient Egypt: Anatomy of a civilization*. Routledge, New York.

Kenoyer, Jonathan, and Heather Miller 2007 Multiple crafts and socioeconomic associations in the Indus civilization: New perspectives from Harappa, Pakistan, in *Craft production in complex societies: Multicraft and producer perspectives*, I. Shimada ed., pp. 152–183. University of Utah Press, Salt Lake City.

Kent, Roland 1920 Edict of Diocletian fixing maximum prices. *University of Pennsylvania Law Review* 69:35–47.

Kent, Susan 1987 *Method and theory for activity area research: An ethnoarchaeological approach*. Columbia University Press, New York.

Kern, Paul 1999 *Ancient siege warfare*. Indiana University Press, Bloomington.

Khachikian, Lvon 1967 Le registre d'un marchand arménien en Perse, en Inde et au Tibet (1682–1693). *Annales. Histoire, Sciences Sociales* 22:231–270.

Khuri, Fuad 1968 The etiquette of bargaining in the Middle East. *American Anthropologist* 70:698–706.

Kicza, John 1983 *Colonial entrepreneurs. Families and business in Bourbon Mexico City*. University of New Mexico Press, Albuquerque.

Kieser, Alfred 1994 Why organization theory needs historical analyses – And how this should be performed. *Organization Science* 5:608–620.

Kirch, Patrick 1989 *The evolution of the Polynesian chiefdoms*. Cambridge University Press, Cambridge.

Kirch, Patrick 1997 *Feathered gods and fishhooks: An introduction to Hawaiian archaeology and prehistory*. University of Hawaii Press, Honolulu.

Kirch, Patrick 2000 Temples as "holy houses": The transformation of ritual architecture in traditional Polynesian societies, in *Beyond kinship: Social and material reproduction in house societies*, R. Joyce and S. Gillespie eds., pp. 103–114. University of Pennsylvania Press, Philadelphia.

Kirch, Patrick 2010 *How chiefs became kings: Divine kingship and the rise of archaic states in ancient Hawai'i*. University of California Press, Berkeley.

Kirch, Patrick, and Roger Green 2001 *Hawaiki, ancestral Polynesia: An essay in historical anthropology*. Cambridge University Press, Cambridge.

Kirch, Patrick, and Marshall Sahlins 1994 *Anahulu: The anthropology of history in the kingdom of Hawaii, vol. 1: Historical ethnography*. University of Chicago Press, Chicago.

Kiser, Edgar, and Danielle Kane 2007 The perils of privatization: How the characteristics of principals affected tax farming in the Roman republic and empire. *Social Science History* 31:191–212.

Kiser, Edgar, and Margaret Levi 2015 Interpreting the comparative history of fiscal regimes, in *Fiscal regimes and the political economy of premodern states*, A. Monson and W. Scheidel eds., pp. 557–571. Cambridge University Press, Cambridge.

Klein, Peter 1998 New institutional economics. Available at SSRN 115811, Social Science Research Network (http://ecsocman.hse.ru/data/865/177/1218/0530book.pdf).

Knight, Jeremy 1999 *The end of antiquity: Archaeology, society and religion AD 235–700*. Tempus, Stroud.

Ko, Alfred, and Chui Hu 1984 *Palaces of the forbidden city*. Viking Press, New York.

Kobayashi, Muhehiro 1993a El abastecimiento de alimentos en México-Tenochtitlan: Un análisis del patrón de tributos de Moctezuma, in *Tres estudios sobre el sistema tributario de los mexicas*, pp. 23–49. Centro de Investigaciones y Estudios Superiores en Antropología Social and Kobe City University, Mexico City and Kobe, Japan.

Kobayashi, Muhehiro 1993b *Tres estudios sobre el sistema tributario de los mexicas*. Centro de Investigaciones y Estudios Superiores en Antropología Social and Kobe City University, Mexico City and Kobe, Japan.

Kobishchanow, Yurii 1987 The phenomenon of gafol and its transformation, in *Early state dynamics*, H. Claessen and P. Van de Velde eds., pp. 108–128. Brill, Leiden.

Koestler, Arthur 1967 *The ghost in the machine*. Arkana, Paris.

Kopytoff, Igor 1987 *The African frontier: The reproduction of traditional African societies*. Indiana University Press, Bloomington.

Kosse, Krisztina 1990 Group size and societal complexity: Thresholds in the long-term memory. *Journal of Anthropological Archaeology* 9:275–303.

Kozuh, Michael 2014 *The sacrificial economy: Assessors, contractors, and thieves in the management of sacrificial sheep at the Eanna temple of Uruk (ca. 625–520 BC)*. Eisenbrauns, Winona Lake.

Krech, Shepard 2000 *The ecological Indian: Myth and history*. W. W. Norton, New York.

Kriger, Colleen 2011 "Guinea cloth" production and consumption of cotton textiles in West Africa before and during the Atlantic slave trade, in *The spinning world: A global history of cotton textiles 1200–1850*, G. Riello and P. Parthasarathi eds., pp. 105–126. Oxford University Press, Oxford.

Kroeber, Alfred 1917 *Zuni kin and clan*. Anthropological papers of the American Museum of Natural History vol. 18, American Museum of Natural History, New York.

Kuhrt, Amelie 1998 The Old Assyrian merchants, in *Trade, traders and the ancient city*, H. Parkins and C. Smith eds., pp. 16–30. Routledge, London.

Kumar, Chandra 2009 Credit rationing and the economics of informal lending. PhD dissertation, Cornell University.

Kurlansky, Mark 2002 *Salt: A world history*. Penguin Books, New York.

Kusimba, Chapurukha, and Sibel Kusimba 2010 Leadership in middle-range African societies, in *The evolution of leadership: Transitions in decision making from small-scale to middle-range societies*, K. Vaughn, J. Eerkens, and J. Kantner eds., pp. 223–247. School for Advanced Research Press, Santa Fe.

Kuzmin, Yariskav 2010 Crossing mountains, rivers, and straits: A review of the current evidence for prehistoric obsidian exchange in Northeast Asia, in *Crossing the straits: Prehistoric obsidian exploitation in the north Pacific rim*, Y. Kuzmin and M. Glascock eds., pp. 137–153. Archaeopress, Oxford.

Kwan, Man Bun 2001 *The salt merchants of Tianjin: State-making and civil society in Late Imperial China*. University of Hawaii Press, Honolulu.

La Lone, Darrell 1982 The Inka as a nonmarket economy: Supply on command versus supply and demand, in *Contexts for prehistoric exchange*, J. Ericson and T. Earle eds., pp. 292–316. Academic Press, New York.

La Vérendrye, Pierre 1927 *Journals and letters of Pierre Gaultier de Varennes de la Vérendrye and his sons with correspondence between the governors of Canada and the French court touching the search for the western sea*. Champlain Society, Toronto.

Labib, Subhi 1969 Capitalism in medieval Islam. *The Journal of Economic History* 29:79–96.

Lafferty, Robert 1994 Prehistoric exchange in the lower Mississippi valley, in *Prehistoric exchange systems in North America*, T. Baugh and J. Ericson eds., pp. 177–213. Plenum, New York.

Lamb, Walter 1930 *Lysias*. W. Lamb trans., Loeb Classical Library 244. Harvard University Press, Cambridge, MA.

Lan Pu and Zheng Tinggui 1816 *Jingdezhen taolu*. Chao ji shu zhuang, Shanghai.

Landers, John 2003 *The field and the forge: Population production and power in the pre-industrial west*. University of Oxford Press, Oxford.

Landes, David 1969 *The unbound Prometheus: Technological change and industrial development in western Europe from 1750 to the present*. Cambridge University Press, Cambridge.

Lane, Marcianna 1997 Santa Maria Nativitas. MA thesis, Universidad Iberomericana, Mexico City.

Langlands, Alexander 2017 *Cræft: An inquiry into the origins and true meaning of traditional crafts*. W. W. Norton, New York.

Lansing, Stephen 1987 Balinese "water temples" and the management of irrigation. *American Anthropologist* 89:326–341.

Lansing, Stephen 2009 *Priests and programmers: Technologies of power in the engineered landscape of Bali*. Princeton University Press, Princeton.

Larick, Roy 1991 Warriors and blacksmiths: Mediating ethnicity in East African spears.

Journal of Anthropological Archaeology 10:299–331.

Larsen, Mogens Trolle 1976 *The Old Assyrian city-state and its colonies.* Akademisk Forlag, Copenhagen.

Larsen, Mogens Trolle 1982 Your money or your life! A portrait of an Assyrian businessman, in *Societies and languages of the ancient Near East: Studies in honor of I. M. Diakonoff*, M. Dandamayev, I. Gershevitch, H. Klengel, G. Komoróczy, M. Larsen, and J. Postgate eds., pp. 214–245. Aris and Phillips, Warminster.

Larsen, Mogens Trolle 1987 Commercial networks in the ancient Near East, in *Centre and periphery in the ancient world*, M. Rowlands, M. Larsen, and K. Kristiansen eds., pp. 47–56. Cambridge University Press, Cambridge.

Larsen, Mogens Trolle 2008a The Middle Bronze Age, in *Beyond Babylon: Art, trade, and diplomacy in the second millennium BC*, J. Aruz, K. Benzel, and J. Evans eds., pp. 13–17. Yale University Press, New Haven.

Larsen, Mogens Trolle 2008b The Old Assyrian merchant colonies, in *Beyond Babylon: Art, trade, and diplomacy in the second millennium BC*, J. Aruz, K. Benzel, and J. Evans eds., pp. 70–81. Yale University Press, New Haven.

Larsen, Mogens Trolle 2015 *Ancient Kanesh: A merchant colony in Bronze Age Anatolia.* Cambridge University Press, Cambridge.

Laslett, Peter 1971 *The world we have lost.* Methuen, London.

Lattimore, Owen 1995 *The desert road to Turkestan.* Kodansha America, New York.

Lazerson, Mark 1993a Factory or putting-out? Knitting networks in Modena, in *The embedded firm: On the socioeconomics of industrial networks*, G. Grabherr ed., pp. 203–226. Routledge, London.

Lazerson, Mark 1993b Putting-out production in Modena, in *Explorations in economic sociology*, R. Swedberg ed., pp. 403–428. Russell Sage Foundation, New York.

Le Page du Pratz, Antoine Simon 1758 *Histoire de la Louisiane.* 3 vols. Paris.

Leach, Edmund 1961 *Pul Eliya: A village in Ceylon.* Cambridge University Press, Cambridge.

Lee, Richard 1968 What hunters do for a living, or, How to make out on scarce resources, in *Man the hunter*, R. Lee and I. DeVore eds., pp. 30–48. Aldine, Chicago.

Lee, Richard 1993 *The Dobe Ju/'hoansi.* Harcourt Brace, Fort Worth.

Lee, Richard, and Irving DeVore 1976 *Kalahari hunter-gatherers.* Harvard University Press, Cambridge, MA.

Leggett, Donald 1974 *The levirate and goel institutions in the Old Testament with special attention to the book of Ruth.* Mack, Cherry Hill, NJ.

Lehner, Mark 2000 Fractal house of Pharaoh: Ancient Egypt as a complex adaptive system, a trial, in *Dynamics in human and primate societies: Agent-based modeling of social and spatial processes*, T. Kohler and G. Gummerman eds., pp. 275–353. Oxford University Press, Oxford.

Lekson, Stephen 1985 Largest settlement size and the interpretation of socio-political complexity at Chaco Canyon, New Mexico. *Haliksa'i: UNM Contributions to Anthropology* 4:68–75.

Levi, Margaret 1989 *Of rule and revenue.* University of California Press, Berkeley.

Levi, Scott 1994 The Banjaras: Medieval Indian peddlers and military commissariat. Master's thesis, University of Wisconsin, Madison.

Levi, Scott 2002 *The Indian diaspora in Central Asia and its trade 1550–1900.* Brill, Leiden.

LeVine, Terry 1992 *Inka storage systems.* University of Oklahoma Press, Norman.

Levinson, Marc 2016 *The box: How the shipping container made the world smaller and the world economy bigger.* Princeton University Press, Princeton.

Lévi-Strauss, Claude 1969 *The elementary structures of kinship.* Beacon Press, Boston.

Lévi-Strauss, Claude 1982 *The way of the masks.* University of Washington and UBC Press, Seattle and Vancouver.

Lévi-Strauss, Claude 1987 *Anthropology and myth: Lectures 1951–1982.* Basil Blackwell, Oxford.

Lévi-Strauss, Claude 1991 Maison, in *Dictionnaire de l'ethnologie el de l'anthropologie*, P. Bonte and M. Izard eds., pp. 434–436. Presses Universitaires de France, Paris.

Lewis, M. J. T. 2001 Railways in the Greek and Roman world, in *Early railways: A selection of papers from the First International Early Railways Conference* (www.yieldopedia.com).

Lewis, Mark 2015 Early imperial China, from the Qin and Han through Tang, in *Fiscal regimes and the political economy of premodern states*, A. Monson and W. Scheidel eds., pp. 282–307. Cambridge University Press, Cambridge.

Lewis, Naphtali 1941 Solon's agrarian legislation. *The American Journal of Philology* 62:144–156.

Lewis, Oscar, and Victor Barnouw 1956 Caste and the Jajmani system in a North Indian village. *The Scientific Monthly* 83:66–81.

Li, Bozhong 2011 Involution and Chinese cotton textile production: Songjiang in the late eighteenth and early nineteeth centuries, in *The spinning world: A global history of cotton textiles 1200–1850*, G. Riello and P. Parthasarathi eds., pp. 387–395. Oxford University Press, Oxford.

Li, Yung-Ti 2007 Co-craft and multicraft: Section-mold casting and the organization of craft production at the Shang capital of Anyang, in *Craft production in complex societies: Multicraft and producer perspectives*, I. Shimada ed., pp. 184–223. University of Utah Press, Salt Lake City.

Lieber, David, Moshe Greenberg, Shmuel Safrai, and Aaron Rothkoff 2007 Sabbatical year and jubilee, in *Encyclopaedia Judaica*, M. Berenbaum and F. Skolnik eds., 17:633–630. Macmillan Reference, Detroit.

Lin, Jie-Ru, Hua Zhou, Xiao-Ping Lai, Yan Hou, Xiao-Min Xian, Jian-Nan Chen, Pei-Xun Wang, Lian Zhou, and Yan Dong 2009 Genetic identification of edible birds' nest based on mitochondrial DNA sequences. *Food Research International* 42:1053–1061.

Linton, Jimmy 2008 Consommer, stocker et explorer: Analyse tracéo logique de grandes lames de "livre de beurre" de la région des ateliers du Grand-Pressigny (Indre-et-Loire) au Néolithique final, in *Du matériel au spirituel: Réalités archéologiques et historiques des "dépôts" de la Préhistoire à nos jour*, pp. 16–18. XXIX Rencontres internationales d'archéo logie et d'histoire d'Antibes, Éditions APDCA, Antibes.

Lipinski, Edward ed. 1979 *State and temple economy in the ancient Near East.* Departement Orientalistiek, Leuven.

Littlefield, Alice, and Larry Reynolds 1990 The putting-out system: Transitional form or recurrent feature of capitalist production? *The Social Science Journal* 27:359–372.

Litvak King, Jaime 1971 *Cihuatlán y Tepecoacuilco provincias tributarias de México en el siglo XVI.* Universidad Nacional Autónoma de México, Mexico City.

Liu, Xinru 1988 *Ancient India and ancient China: Trade and religious exchanges AD 1–600.* Oxford University Press, Delhi.

Liverani, Mario 2008a The Amarna Letters, in *Beyond Babylon: Art, trade, and diplomacy in the second millennium BC*, J. Aruz, K. Benzel, and J. Evans eds., pp. 168–169. Yale University Press, New Haven.

Liverani, Mario 2008b The late Bronze Age: Material and mechanism of trade and cultural exchange, in *Beyond Babylon: Art, trade, and diplomacy in the second millennium BC*, J. Aruz, K. Benzel, and J. Evans eds., pp. 161–168. Yale University Press, New Haven.

Liverani, Mario 2013 *The ancient Near East: History, society and economy.* Routledge, London.

Llewellyn, Karl, and Adamson Hoebel 1941 *The Cheyenne way.* University of Oklahoma Press, Norman.

Lloyd, Peter 1953 Craft organization in Yoruba towns. *Africa* 23:30–44.

Lloyd, Peter, and Peter Dicken 1977 *Location in space: A theoretical approach to economic geography.* Harper and Row, New York.

Lobell, Jarrett 2009 Trash talk: Sorting through a mountain of pottery to track the Roman oil trade. *Archaeology* 2:20–25.

López Corral, Aurelio, and Kenneth Hirth 2012 Terrazguero smallholders and the function of agricultural tribute in sixteenth-century Tepeaca, Mexico. *Mexican Studies/Estudios Mexicanos* 28:73–93.

Lösch, August 1938 The nature of economic regions. *Southern Economic Journal* 5:71–78.

Love, John 1991 *Antiquity and capitalism. Max Weber and the sociological foundations of Roman civilization.* Routledge, London.

Lovén, Bjørn 2011 *The ancient harbours of the Piraeus, vol. 1: The Zea shipsheds and slipways-architecture and topography.* Aarhus Universitetsforlag, Aarhus.

Lucero, Lisa 2006 *Water and ritual: The rise and fall of Classic Maya rulers.* University of Texas Press, Austin.

MacDonald, Brian 1986 The diolkos. *The Journal of Hellenic Studies* 106:191–195.

Mack, Raymond 1951 Housing as an index of social class. *Social Forces* 29:391–400.

MacMahon, Ardle 2003 *The taberna structures of Roman Britain.* British Archaeological Reports vol. 356, Oxford.

MacMahon, Ardle 2006 Fixed point retail location in the major towns of Roman Britain. *Oxford Journal of Archaeology* 25:289–309.

Magnusson, Magnus, and Hermann Pálsson 1960 *Najal's saga.* M. Magnusson and H. Pálsson trans. Penguin Books, New York.

Magnusson, Magnus, and Hermann Pálsson 1969 *Laxdœla saga.* M. Magnusson and H. Pálsson trans. Penguin Books, London.

Mahir, Şaul 1983 Work parties, wages, and accumulation in a Voltaic village. *American Ethnologist* 10:77–96.

Maier, Paul 1994 *Josephus: The essential writings.* Kregel, Grand Rapids.

Malinowski, Bronislaw 1922 *Argonauts of the western Pacific.* Routledge and Kegan Paul, London.

Malinowski, Bronislaw 1935 *Coral gardens and their magic: A study of the methods of tilling the soil and of agricultural rites in the Trobriand Islands.* Routledge and Kegan Paul, London.

Malinowski, Bronislaw 1967a Kula: The circulating exchange of valuables in the archipelagoes of eastern New Guinea, in *Tribal and peasant economies,* George Dalton ed., pp. 171–184. American Museum of Natural History, New York.

Malinowski, Bronislaw 1967b Tribal economics in the Trobriands, in *Tribal and peasant economies,* George Dalton ed., pp. 185–223. American Museum of Natural History, New York.

Malul, Meir 1990 Adoption of foundlings in the Bible and Mesopotamian documents: A study of some legal metaphors in Ezekiel 16.1–17. *Journal for the Study of the Old Testament* 46:97–126.

Malville, Nancy 1999 Porters of the eastern hills of Nepal: Body size and load weight. *American Journal of Human Biology* 11:1–11.

Manning, Joseph 2003 *Land and power in Ptolemaic Egypt: The structure of land tenure.* Cambridge University Press, Cambridge.

Marchant, Edgar, and Glen Bowersock 1968 *Xenophon scripta minora. Pseudo-Xenophon: Constitution of the Athenians,* E. Marchant and G. Bowersock trans. Loeb Classical Library. Harvard University Press, Cambridge, MA.

Marcus, Joyce, and Kent Flannery 1996 *Zapotec civilization: How urban society evolved in Mexico's Oaxaca Valley.* Thames and Hudson, London.

Marshall, Lorna 1976 *The !Kung of Nyae Nyae.* Harvard University Press, Cambridge, MA.

Marshall, Lorna 1999 *Nyae Nyae !Kung beliefs and rites.* Peabody Museum Press, Cambridge, MA.

Martin, Janet 1985 Muscovite traveling merchants: The trade with the Muslim east (15th and 16th centuries). *Central Asian Survey* 4:21–38.

Martin, Janet 1986 *Treasure of the land of darkness: The fur trade and its significance for medieval Russia.* Cambridge University Press, Cambridge.

Martínez, Hildeberto 1984 *Tepeaca en el siglo XVI: Tenencia de la tierra y organización de un señorio.* Ediciones de la Casa Chata, Mexico City.

Marx, Karl 1967 *Capital: A critique of political economy, vol. 3: The process of capitalistic production as a whole.* International, New York (originally published 1867).

Marx, Karl 1973 *Grundrisse: Introduction to the critique of political economy.* Vintage Books, New York (originally published 1859).

Marx, Karl 1975 Economic formations, in *Pre-capitalist economic formations,* E. Hobsbawn ed., pp. 67–120. International, New York.

Marzano, Annalisa 2012 Ergasterion, ergastulum, in *The encyclopedia of ancient history,* R. Bagnall, K. Brodersen, C. Champion, A. Erskine, and S. Huebner eds., pp. 2488–2489. Blackwell.

Matrícula de Huexotzinco (http://gallica.bnf.fr/ark:/12148/btv1b7200005f/f1.image).

Matthews, John 1984 The tax law of Palmyra: Evidence for economic history in a city of the Roman East. *Journal of Roman Studies* 74:157–180.

Mattingly, David, and John Salmon eds. 2002 *Economies beyond agriculture in the classical world.* Routledge, Abingdon-on-Thames.

Mauro, Frederic 1993 Merchant communities, 1350–1750, in *The rise of merchant empires: Long-distance trade in the modern world, 1350–1750*, J. Tracy ed., pp. 255–286. Cambridge University Press, Cambridge.

Mauss, Marcel 1990 *The gift.* Routledge, London.

Mayer, Enrique 2002 *The articulated peasant: Household economies in the Andes.* Westview Press, Boulder.

Mayer, Enrique 2013 In the realm of the Incas, in *Merchants, markets, and exchange in the pre-Columbian world*, K. Hirth and J. Pillsbury eds., pp. 309–317. Dumbarton Oaks Research Library and Collection, Washington, DC.

Mazzaoui, Maureen 2011 The first European cotton industry: Italy and Germany, 1100–1800, in *The spinning world: A global history of cotton textiles 1200–1850*, G. Riello and P. Parthasarathi eds., pp. 63–88. Oxford University Press, Oxford.

McAnany, Patricia 2014 *Living with the ancestors: Kinship and kingship in ancient Maya society.* Cambridge University Press, Cambridge.

McCormick, Michael 2001 *The origins of the European economy: Communications and commerce, A.D. 300–900.* Cambridge University Press, Cambridge.

McCorriston, Joy 1997 The fiber revolution: Textile extensification, alienation, and social stratification in ancient Mesopotamia. *Current Anthropology* 38:517–535.

McGeough, Kevin 2007 *Exchange relationships at Ugarit.* Ancient Near Eastern Studies Supplement 26. Peeters, Leuven.

McGrew, Julia, and R. George Thomas 1970 *Sturlunga saga: Shorter sagas of the Icelanders.* Vol. 2. Thorndike Press, Farmington Hills.

McGrew, Julia, and R. George Thomas 1970–1974 *Sturlunga saga.* J. McGrew and G. Thomas trans. Twayne, New York.

McHugh, Patrick, Giorgio Merli, and William Wheeler 1995 *Beyond business process reengineering: Towards the holonic enterprise.* John Wiley and Sons, New York.

McKee, Robin 2006 Family cemeteries: Early settlers buried on homestead, in *Vanished Hamilton II*, M. Houghton ed., pp. 89–90. Canadian Heritage Books, Burlington.

McKendrick, Neil 1982 Josiah Edgwood and the commercialization of the potteries, in *The birth of a consumer society: The commercialization of eighteenth-century England*, N. McKendrick, J. Brewer, and J. Plumb eds., pp. 100–145. Indiana University Press, Bloomington.

McKendrick, Neil, John Brewer, and John Plumb eds. 1982 *The birth of a consumer society: The commercialization of eighteenth-century England.* Indiana University Press, Bloomington.

McKitterick, Rosamond 2011 A king on the move: The place of an itinerant court in Charlemagne's government, in *Royal courts in dynastic states and empires*, J. Duindam, T. Artan, and M. Kunt eds., pp. 145–170. Brill, Leiden.

McNally, Sheila 1975 Diocletian's palace: Split in the Middle Ages. *Archaeology* 28:248–259.

Meiggs, Russell 1973 *Roman Ostia.* Clarendon Press, Oxford.

Meijer, Diederik 2000 State and trade: Toward a case study for northern Syria. *Subartu* 7:219–240.

Meijer, Fik, and Onno van Nijf 1992 *Trade, transport and society in the ancient world: A sourcebook.* Routledge, London.

Menard, Russell 1991 Transport costs and long-range trade, 1300–1800: Was there a European "transportation revolution" in the early modern era?, in *The political economy of merchant empires*, J. Tracy ed., pp. 228–275. Cambridge University Press, Cambridge.

Mendels, Franklin 1972 Proto-industrialization: The first phase of the industrialization process. *The Journal of Economic History* 32:241–261.

Menzel, Peter, and Faith D'Aluisio 1998 *Man eating bugs: The art and science of eating insects.* Ten Speed Press, Berkeley.

Messer, Ellen 1989 Seasonality in food systems: An anthropological perspective on household food security, in *Seasonal variability in third world agriculture*, D. Sahn ed., pp. 151–175. Johns Hopkins University Press, Baltimore.

Meyer, David, and Paul Thistle 1995 Saskatchewan River rendezvous centers and trading posts: Continuity in a Cree social geography. *Ethnohistory* 42:403–444.

Michel, Cécile 2014 The Assyrian textile trade in Anatolia (19th century BCE): From traded goods to prestigious gifts, in *Textile trade and distribution in antiquity*, K. Dross-Krüpe ed., pp. 111–122. Harrassowitz Verlag, Wiesbaden.

Michell, George 1999 *The royal palaces of India*. Thames and Hudson, London.

Miller, Daniel, and Christopher Tilley 1984 *Ideology, power and prehistory*. Cambridge University Press, Cambridge.

Miller, Innes 1969 *The spice trade of the Roman empire*. Clarendon Press, Oxford.

Miller, Walter 1913 *Cicero de officiis*. W. Miller trans. Loeb Classical Library. Harvard University Press, Cambridge, MA.

Miller, Walter 1914 *Xenophon cyropaedia*. W. Miller trans. Loeb Classical Library. Harvard University Press, Cambridge, MA.

Miller, William 1990 *Bloodtaking and peacemaking: Feud, law, and society in saga Iceland*. University of Chicago Press, Chicago.

Miller, William 2014 *Why is your axe bloody? A reading of Njáls saga*. Oxford University Press, Oxford.

Millett, Paul 2002 *Lending and borrowing in ancient Athens*. Cambridge University Press, Cambridge.

Mills, Barbara 1995 Gender and the reorganization of historic Zuni craft production: Implications for archaeological interpretation. *Journal of Anthropological Research* 51:149–172.

Mills, Barbara 2007 Multicrafting, migration, and identity in the American Southwest, in *Craft production in complex societies: Multicraft and producer perspectives*, I. Shimada ed., pp. 25–43. University of Utah Press, Salt Lake City.

Milner, George 1998 *The Cahokia chiefdom*. Smithsonian Institution Press, Washington, DC.

Milner, George 1999 Warfare in prehistoric and early historic eastern North America. *Journal of Archaeological Research* 7:105–151.

Milton, Giles 1999 *Nathaniel's nutmeg*. Farrar, Strauss and Giroux, New York.

Minar, Jill, and Patricia Crown 2001 Learning and craft production: An introduction. *Journal of Anthropological Research* 57:369–380.

Miner, Horace 1953 *The primitive city of Timbuctoo*. Princeton University Press, Princeton.

Mines, Mattison 1984 *The warrior merchants: Textiles, trade and territory in South India*. Cambridge University Press, Cambridge.

Mintz, Sidney 1964 The employment of capital by market women in Haiti, in *Capital, saving, and credit in peasant societies*, R. Firth and B. Yamey eds., pp. 256–286. Aldine, Chicago.

Miyamoyo, Matao 1997 The management systems of Edo period merchant houses. *Japanese Yearbook on Business History* 13:97–142.

Mokyr, Joel 1990 *The lever of riches*. Oxford University Press, Oxford.

Molina, Fray Alonso de 1977 *Vocabulario en lengua castellana y mexicana y mexicana y castellana*. Editorial Porrua, Mexico City.

Monaghan, John 1995 *The covenants with earth and rain*. University of Oklahoma Press, Norman.

Monroe, Christopher 2009 *Scales of fate: Trade, tradition, and transformation in the eastern Mediterranean ca. 1350–1175 BCE*. Ugarit-Verlag, Münster.

Monroe, Christopher 2010 Sunk costs at Late Bronze age Uluburun. *Bulletin of the American Schools of Oriental Research* 357:19–33.

Monson, Andrew, and Walter Scheidel 2015 Studying fiscal regimes, in *Fiscal regimes and the political economy of premodern states*, A. Monson and W. Scheidel eds., pp. 3–28. Cambridge University Press, Cambridge.

Moore, John, Margot Liberty, and Terry Straus 2001 Cheyenne, in *Handbook of North American Indians, Plains*, R. DeMallie and W. Sturtevant eds., 13:863–885. Smithsonian Institution, Washington, DC.

Moore, Karl, and David Lewis 1999 *Birth of the multinational: 2000 years of ancient business history from Ashur to Augustus*. Copenhagen Business School Press, Copenhagan.

Moore, Latetia, and Ana Diez Roux 2006 Associations of neighborhood characteristics with the location and type of food stores. *American Journal of Public Health* 96:325–331.

Moore, Mick 1975 Co-operative labour in peasant agriculture. *The Journal of Peasant Studies* 2:270–291.

Moore, Sally 1958 *Power and property in Inca Peru.* Columbia University Press, New York.

Moorey, Peter 1994 *Ancient Mesopotamian materials and industries: The archaeological evidence.* Clarendon Press, Oxford.

Moran, William 1992 *The Amarna letters.* Johns Hopkins University Press, Baltimore.

Morehart, Christopher, and Kristin De Lucia eds. 2015a *Surplus: The politics of production and the strategies of everyday life.* University Press of Colorado, Boulder.

Morehart, Christopher, and Kristin De Lucia 2015b Surplus: The politics of production and the strategies of everyday life. An introduction, in *Surplus: The politics of production and the strategies of everyday life*, C. Morehart and K. De Lucia eds., pp. 3–43. University Press of Colorado, Boulder.

Moreno, Alfonso 2003 Athenian bread-baskets: The grain-tax law of 374/3 BC re-interpreted. *Zeitschrift für Papyrologie und Epigraphik* 145:97–106.

Moreno Garcia, Juan Carlos 2007 A new Old Kingdom inscription from Giza (CGC 57163), and the problem of *SN-DT* in Pharaonic third millennium society. *The Journal of Egyptian Archaeology* 93:117–136.

Moreno Garcia, Juan Carlos 2012 Households, in *UCLA encyclopedia of Egyptology* 1:1–10. Department of Near Eastern Languages and Cultures, University of California, Los Angeles (https://escholarship.org/uc/item/2bn8c9gz).

Morgan, Lewis 1871 *Systems of consanguinity and affinity of the human family.* Smithsonian Institution, Washington, DC.

Morgan, Lewis 1877 *Ancient society.* World, Cleveland.

Morley, Neville 1996 *Metropolis and hinterland: The city of Rome and the Italian economy, 200 BC–AD 200.* Cambridge University Press, Cambridge.

Morley, Neville 2007 *Trade in classical antiquity.* Cambridge University Press, Cambridge.

Morris, Craig, and Donald Thompson. 1985 *Huánuco Pampa: An Inca city and its hinterland.* Thames and Hudson, London.

Morrison, John, John Coates, and Boris Rankov 2000 *The Athenian trireme: The history and reconstruction of an ancient Greek warship.* Cambridge University Press, Cambridge.

Morrison, Kathleen 2002 Pepper in the hills: Upland-lowland exchange and the intensification of the spice trade, in *Forager-traders in South and Southeast Asia*, K. Morrison and L. Junker eds., pp. 105–128. Cambridge University Press, Cambridge.

Morrison, Kathleen, and Laura Junker eds. 2002 *Forager-traders in South and Southeast Asia.* Cambridge University Press, Cambridge.

Moseley, Michael 1974 *The maritime foundations of Andean civilization.* Benjamin-Cummings, San Francisco.

Moseley, Michael 1992 *The Incas and their ancestors: The archaeology of Peru.* Thames and Hudson, London.

Mujica, Elias 1985 Altiplano-coast relationships in the south-central Andes: From indirect to direct complementarity, in *Andean ecology and civilization*, S. Masuda, I. Shimada, and C. Morris eds., pp. 103–140. University of Tokyo Press, Tokyo.

Murdock, George 1967 Ethnographic atlas: A summary. *Ethnology* 6:109–236.

Murphy, Elizabeth, and Jeroen Poblome 2016 A late antique ceramic workshop complex: Evidence for workshop organisation at Sagalassos (southwest Turkey). *Anatolian Studies* 66:185–199.

Murphy, Robert, and Julian Steward 1956 Tappers and trappers: Parallel process in acculturation. *Economic Development and Culture Change* 4:335–355.

Murra, John 1956 The economic organization of the Inka state. PhD dissertation, University of Chicago.

Murra, John 1962 Cloth and its functions in the Inca state. *American Anthropologist* 64:710–728.

Murra, John 1972 El "control vertical" de un máximo de pisos ecológicos en la economía de las sociedades andinas, in *Visita de la provincia de León de Huamuco en 1562*, vol. 2, J. Mura ed., pp. 427–476. Universidad Nacional Hermilio Valdizán, Huanuco.

Murra, John 1975 Rebaños y pastores en la economía del Tahuantinsuyo, in *Formaciones económicas y políticas del mundo Andino*, J. Murra ed., pp. 117–144. Instituto de Estudios Puruanos, Lima.

Murra, John 1980 *The economic organization of the Inka state*. JAI Press, Greenwich.

Murra, John 1985a "El archipiélago vertical" revisited, in *Andean ecology and civilization*, S. Masuda, I. Shimada, and C. Morris eds., pp. 3–13. University of Tokyo Press, Tokyo.

Murra, John 1985b The limits and limitations of the "vertical archipelago" in the Andes, in *Andean ecology and civilization*, S. Masuda, I. Shimada, and C. Morris eds., pp. 15–20. University of Tokyo Press, Tokyo.

Myerson, Roger 2013 *Game theory: Analysis of conflict*. Harvard University Press, Cambridge, MA.

Nadel, Siegfried Frederick 1942 *A black Byzantium: The kingdom of Nupe in Nigeria*. Oxford University Press, London.

Nairn, Charlie, and Andrew Strathern 2003 *Kawelka: Ongka's big moka*. Shanachie Entertainment Corporation, Newton, NJ.

Nakassis, Dimitri, William Parkinson, and Michael Galaty 2011 Redistributive economies from a theoretical and cross-cultural perspective. *American Journal of Archaeology* 115:177–184.

Netherly, Patricia 1984 The management of late Andean irrigation systems on the north coast of Peru. *American Antiquity* 49:227–254.

Netting, Robert 1972 Sacred power and centralization: Aspects of political adaptation in Africa, in *Population growth: Anthropological implications*, B. Spooner ed., pp. 214–244. MIT Press, Cambridge, MA.

Netting, Robert 1981 *Balancing on an Alp: Ecological change and continuity in a Swiss mountain community*. Cambridge University Press, Cambridge.

Netting, Robert 1982 Some home truths on household size and wealth. *The American Behavioral Scientist* 25:641–662.

Netting, Robert 1989 Smallholders, householders, freeholders: Why the family farm works well worldwide, in *The household economy: Reconsidering the domestic mode of production*, R. Wilk ed., pp. 221–244. Westview Press, Boulder.

Netting, Robert 1990 Population, permanent agriculture and polities: Unpacking the evolutionary portmanteau, in *The evolution of political systems*, S. Upham ed., pp. 21–61. Cambridge University Press, Cambridge.

Netting, Robert 1993 *Smallholders, households, farm families, and the ecology of intensive, sustainable agriculture*. Stanford University Press, Stanford.

Netting, Robert, Richard Wilk, Eric Arnould 1984 Introduction, in *Households: Comparative and historic studies of the domestic group*, R. Netting, R. Wilk, and E. Arnould eds., pp. xiv–xxxviii. University of California Press, Berkeley.

Nichols, Mary 1992 *Citizens and statesmen: A study of Aristotle's Politics*. Rowman and Littlefield, London.

Nider, Reverend Father Frier Johannes 1966 *On the contracts of merchants (De Contractibus Mercatorum)*, C. Reeves trans. University of Oklahoma Press, Norman (originally 1468).

Nielsen, Axel 2001 Ethnoarchaeological perspectives on caravan trade in the south-central Andes, in *Ethnoarchaeology of Andean South America: Contributions to archaeological method and theory*, L. Kuznar ed., pp. 163–201. University of Michigan Press, Ann Arbor.

Nielsen, Axel 2013 Circulating objects and the constitution of south Andean society (500 BC–AD 1550), in *Merchants, markets, and exchange in the pre-Columbian world*, K. Hirth and J. Pillsbury eds., pp. 389–418. Dumbarton Oaks Research Library and Collection, Washington, DC.

Nissen, Hans 1986 The Archaic texts from Uruk. *World Archaeology* 17:317–334.

Nissen, Hans 1995 Ancient western Asia before the age of empires, in *Civilizations of the ancient*

Near East, pp. 791–806. Simon and Schuster, New York.

Nissen, Hans, Peter Damerow, and Robert Englund 1993 *Archaic bookkeeping: Early writing and techniques of economic administration in the ancient Near East*. University of Chicago Press, Chicago.

North, Douglass 1978 Structure and performance: The task of economic history. *Journal of Economic Literature* 16:963–978.

North, Douglass 1981 *Structure and change in economic history*. Norton, New York.

North, Douglass 1985 The growth of government in the United States: An economic historian's perspective. *Journal of Public Economics* 28:383–399.

North, Douglass 1995 *The new institutional economics and third world development*. Routledge, London.

North, Douglass 2008 Institutions and the performance of economies over time, in *Handbook of new institutional economics*, C. Ménard and M. Shirley eds., pp. 19–30. Springer, Dordrecht.

North, Douglass, and Robert Thomas 1973 *The rise of the western world: A new economic history*. Cambridge University Press, Cambridge.

Northrup, David 1978 *Trade without rulers: Pre-colonial economic development in south-eastern Nigeria*. Clarendon Press, Oxford.

Notermans, Catrien 2004 Fosterage and the politics of marriage and kinship in East Cameroon, in *Cross-cultural approaches to adoption*, F. Bowie ed., pp. 48–63. Routledge, London.

Noth, Martin 1965 *Leviticus: A commentary*. SCM Press, London.

Ober, Josiah 2015 Classical Athens, in *Fiscal regimes and the political economy of premodern states*, A. Monson and W. Scheidel eds., pp. 492–522. Cambridge University Press, Cambridge.

Oberg, Kalervo 1973 *The social economy of the Tlingit Indians*. University of Washington Press, Seattle.

Offner, Jerome 1983 *Law and politics in Aztec Texcoco*. Cambridge University Press, Cambridge.

Ohio State Historical Society 1952 *Zoar: An Ohio experiment in commualism*. Ohio State Archaeological and Historical Society, Columbus.

Ojo, Afolabi 1966 *Yoruba palaces: A study of Afins of Yorubaland*. University of London Press, London.

Oka, Rahul, and Chapurukha Kusimba 2008 The archaeology of trading systems, part I: Towards a new trade synthesis. *Journal of Archaeological Research* 16:339–395.

Olasson, P. E. 1932 *The codex regius of grágás*. Levin and Munskgaard, Copenhagen.

Olesen, Asta 1994 *Afghan craftsmen*. Thames and Hudson, London.

Olson, Mancur 1965 *The logic of collective action*. Harvard University Press, Cambridge, MA.

Osamu, Wakita 1975 The kokudaka system: A device for unification. *Journal of Japanese Studies* 1:297–320.

Osborne, Robin 2000 Review: *Tax farming: The Athenian grain-tax law of 374/3 B.C.* by R. S. Stroud. *The Classical Review* 50:172–174.

O'Shea, John 1989 The role of wild resources in small-scale agricultural systems: Tales from the lakes and the plains, in *Bad year economics*, P. Halstead and J. O'Shea eds., pp. 57–67. Cambridge University Press, Cambridge.

Ostrom, Elinor 1992 *Crafting institutions for self-governing irrigations systems*. ICS Press, San Francisco.

Ostrom, Elinor 2007 Collective action theory, in *The Oxford handbook of comparative politics*, C. Boix and S. Stokes eds., pp. 186–208. Oxford University Press, Oxford.

Ostrom, Elinor 2015 *Governing the commons*. Cambridge University Press, Cambridge.

Otero, Clarisa, and Maria Beatriz Cremonte 2014 Local ceramic technology of the Pucara of Tilcara during the Inka period (Quebrada of Humahuaca, Argentina). *Journal of Anthropological Archaeology* 33:108–118.

Ouyang, Xiaoli, 2013 *Monetary role of silver and its administration in Mesopotamia during the Ur III period (c. 2112–2004 BCE): A case study of the Umma province*. Consejo Superior de Investigaciones Cientificas, Madrid.

Oviedo y Valdés, Gonzalo Fernández 1959 *Historia general y natural de las Indias*. Ediciones Atlas, Madrid.

Owen, Bruce 2001 The economy of metal and shell wealth goods, in *Empire and domestic economy*, T. D'Altroy and C. Hastorf eds., pp. 265–293. Kluwer Academic, New York.

Özbal, Hadi, Annemie Adriaens, and Bryan Earl 1999 Hacinebi metal production and exchange. *Paléorient* 25:57–65.

Palerm, Ángel 1955 The agricultural basis of urban civilization in Mesoamerica, in *Irrigation civilizations: A comparative study*, J. Steward ed., pp. 28–42. Pan American Union, Washington, DC.

Pálsson, Hermann 1975 *The confederates and Hen-Thorir: Two Icelandic sagas*. Southside, Edinburgh.

Pálsson, Hermann 2001 Review of *Prolonged echoes: Old Norse myths in medieval northern society*. *Northern Studies* 36:131–140.

Paper, Jordan 1988 *Offering smoke: The sacred pipe and the Native American religion*. University of Idaho Press, Moscow.

Parkes, Peter 2004 Fosterage, kinship, and legend: When milk was thicker than blood? *Comparative Studies in Society and History* 46:587–615.

Parkin, Tim 2013 The demography of infancy and early childhood in the ancient world, in *The Oxford handbook of childhood and education in the classical world*, J. Grubbs, T. Parkin, and R. Bell eds., pp. 40–61. Oxford University Press, Oxford.

Parkinson, William, and Paul Duffy 2007 Fortifications and enclosures in European prehistory: A cross-cultural perspective. *Journal of Archaeological Research* 15:97–141.

Parks, Tim 2005 *Medici money*. Norton, New York.

Parks, Annette, and Larry Caldwell 2004 The burning of Njal as a failure of fosterage. *Edda* 102:150–160.

Parsons, Jeffrey 1976 The role of chinampa agriculture in the food supply of Aztec Tenochtitlan, in *Cultural change and continuity*, C. Cleland ed., pp. 233–258. Academic Press, New York.

Parsons, Jeffrey 1991 Political implications of prehispanic chinampa agriculture in the Valley of Mexico, in *Land and politics in the Valley of Mexico: A two thousand year perspective*, H. Harvey ed., pp. 17–43. University of New Mexico Press, Albuquerque.

Parsons, Jeffrey 1996 Tequesquite and ahuauhtle: Rethinking the prehispanic productivity of Lake Texcoco-Xaltocan-Zumpango, in *Arqueología mesoamericana: Homenaje a William T. Sanders*, A. Mastache, J. Parsons, R. Santley, and M. Serra Puche eds., 1:439–459. Instituto Nacional de Antropología e Historia, Mexico City.

Parthasarathi, Prasannan 2011 Cotton textiles in the Indian subcontinent 1200–1800, in *The spinning world: A global history of cotton textiles 1200–1850*, G. Riello and P. Parthasarathi eds., pp. 17–41. Oxford University Press, Oxford.

Patterson, Thomas 2005 Craft specialization, the reorganization of production relations and state formation. *Journal of Social Archaeology* 5:307–337.

Pauketat, Timothy 1994 *The ascent of chiefs: Cahokia and Mississippian politics in native North America*. University of Alabama Press, Tuscaloosa.

Peacock, David 1982 *Pottery in the Roman world: An ethnoarchaeological approach*. Longman, London.

Pearlman, David 1984 Threshing sledges in the eastern Mediterranean: Ethnoarchaeology with chert knappers and dhoukanes in Cyprus. Master's thesis, University of Minnesota.

Pearson, Michael 1991 Merchants and states, in *The political economy of merchant empires*, J. Tracy ed., pp. 41–116. Cambridge University Press, Cambridge.

Pegolotti, Francesco Balducci 1936 *La pratica della mercatura*. A. Evans ed. Mediaeval Academy of America, Cambridge, MA (originally published 1766).

Pelegrin, Jacques 2003 "Blade making techniques from the Old World: Insights and applications to Mesoamerican obsidian lithic technology." In *Mesoamerican lithic technology: Experimentation and interpretation*, Kenneth Hirth ed., pp. 55–71. University of Utah Press, Salt Lake City.

Pendergrast, Mark 2010 *Uncommon grounds: The history of coffee and how it transformed our world.* Basic Books, New York.

Peregrine, Peter 1991 Some political aspects of craft specialization. *World Archaeology* 23:1–11.

Perodie, James 2001 Feasting for prosperity: A study of southern Northwest Coast feasting, in *Feasts: Archaeological and ethnographic pespectives on food, politics, and power*, M. Dietler and B. Hayden eds., pp. 185–214. Smithsonian Institution Press, Washington, DC.

Peterson, William 1914 *Tacitus: Dialogus, Agricoloa, Germania.* W. Peterson trans. Loeb Classical Library. Harvard University Press, Cambridge, MA.

Pettegrew, David 2011 The diolkos of Corinth. *American Journal of Archaeology* 115:549–574.

Pfeiffer, Charles, and Everett Harrison 1990 *The Wycliffe Bible commentary.* Moody Press, Chicago.

Piddocke, Stuart 1965 The potlatch system of the southern Kwakiutl. *Southwestern Journal of Anthropology* 21:244–264.

Piketty, Thomas 2014 *Capital in the twenty-first century.* Harvard University Press, Cambridge, MA.

Piketty, Thomas, and Gabriel Zucman 2013 Capital is back: Wealth–income ratios in rich countries, 1700–2010. *The Quarterly Journal of Economics* 129:1255–1310.

Pirenne, Henri 1974 *Medieval cities: Their origins and the revival of trade.* Princeton University Press, Princeton.

Pires, Tomé, and Armando Cortesão 1944 *The Suma oriental of Tomé Pires: An account of the east, from the Red Sea to Japan.* Hakluyt Society, London.

Pirngruber, Reinhard 2017 *The economy of Late Achaemenid and Seleucid Babylonia.* Cambridge University Press, Cambridge.

Platt, Tristan 1986 Mirrors and maize: The concept of yanantin among the Macha of Bolivia, in *Anthropological history of Andean polities*, J. Murra, N. Wachtel, and J. Revel eds., pp. 228–259. Cambridge University Press, Cambridge.

Plattner, Stuart 1975a Pedlar: A computer game in economic anthropology, in *Formal methods in economic anthropology*, S. Plattner ed., pp. 197–215. American Anthropological Association Publication 4, Washington, DC.

Plattner, Stuart 1975b The economics of peddling, in *Formal methods in economic anthropology*, S. Plattner ed., pp. 55–76. American Anthropological Association Publication 4, Washington, DC.

Plattner, Stuart 1989a Economic behavior in marketplaces, in *Economic anthropology*, S. Plattner ed., pp. 209–221. Stanford University Press, Stanford.

Plattner, Stuart 1989b Introduction, in *Economic anthropology*, S. Plattner ed., pp. 1–20. Stanford University Press, Stanford.

Plattner, Stuart 1989c Markets and marketplaces, in *Economic anthropology*, S. Plattner ed., pp. 171–208. Stanford University Press, Stanford.

Plog, Stephen 1993 Changing perspectives on north and middle American exchange systems, in *The American Southwest and Mesoamerica: Systems of prehistoric exchange*, J. Ericson and T. Baugh eds., pp. 285–292. Plenum, New York.

Poblome, Jeroen 1999 *Sagalassos red slip ware: Typology and chronology.* Bepols, Turnhout.

Poblome, Jeroen 2004 Comparing ordinary craft production: Textile and pottery production in Roman Asia Minor. *Journal of the Economic and Social History of the Orient* 47:491–506.

Poblome, Jeroen, and Raymond Brulet 2005 Production mechanisms of sigillata manufactories: When East meets West, in *Trade relations in the Eastern Mediterranean from the late Hellenistic period to late Antiquity: The ceramic evidence*, M. Briese and L. Vaag eds., pp. 27–36. University Press of Southern Denmark, Odense.

Pohl, John, John Monaghan, and Laura Stiver 1997 Religion, economy, and factionalism in Mixtec boundary zones, in *Códices y documentos sobre México, segundo simposio*, S. Rueda Smithers, C. Vega Sosa, and R. Martínez Bracs eds., 1:205–232. Instituto Nacional de Antropología e Historia, Mexico City.

Polanyi, Karl 1944 *The great transformation: The political and economic origins of our time.* Beacon Press, Boston.

Polanyi, Karl 1957 The economy as instituted process, in *Trade and market in the early empires*, K. Polanyi, C. Arensberg, and H. Pearson eds., pp. 243–270. Free Press, Glencoe.

Polanyi, Karl 1963 Ports of trade in early societies. *The Journal of Economic History* 23:30–45.

Polanyi, Karl 1966 *Dahomey and the slave trade: An analysis of an archaic economy*. University of Washington Press, Seattle.

Polanyi, Karl 1981 *The livelihood of man*. Academic Press, New York.

Polanyi, Karl, Conran Arensberg, and Harry Pearson eds. 1957 *Trade and market in the early empires*. Free Press, Glencoe.

Pomeranz, Kenneth 2005 Women's work and the economics of respectability, in *Gender in motion: Divisons of labor and cultural change in late imperial and modern China*, B. Goodman and W. Larson eds., pp. 239–263. Rowman and Littlefield, Lanham.

Pomeranz, Kenneth, and Steven Topik 2006 *The world that trade created: Society, culture, and the world economy*. M. E. Sharpe, Armonk, NY.

Ponsonby-Fane, Richard 1956 *Kyoto, the old capital of Japan (794–1869)*. Ponsonby Memorial Society, Kyoto.

Popkin, Samuel 1979 *The rational peasant: The political economy of rural society in Vietnam*. University of California Press, Berkeley.

Porter, Yves, and Arthur Thévenart 2003 *Palaces and gardens of Persia*. Flammarion, Paris.

Pospisil, Leopold 1963 *Kapauku Papuan economy*. Yale University Publications in Anthropology 67. Yale University Press, New Haven.

Postgate, Nicholas 1979 Royal ideology and state administration in Sumer and Akkad, in *Civilizations of the ancient Near East*, J. Sasson ed., 1:395–411. Hendricks, Peabody, MA.

Postgate, Nicholas 2004 *Early Mesopotamia: Society and economy at the dawn of history*. Routledge, London.

Potts, Daniel 1997 *Mesopotamian civilization: The material foundations*. Cornell University Press, Ithaca.

Potts, Daniel 2010 Babylonian sources of exotic raw materials, in *The Babylonian world*, G. Leick ed., pp. 124–140. Routledge, New York.

Potts, Timothy 1993 Patterns of trade in third millennium BC Mesopotamia and Iran. *World Archaeology* 24:379–402.

Pounds, Norman 1994 *An economic history of medieval Europe*. Longman Group, London.

Pozorski, Shelia, and Thomas Pozorski 1991 Storage, access control, and bureaucratic proliferation: Understanding the Initial Period (1800–900 BC) economy at Pampa de las Llamas-Moxeke, Casma Valley, Peru, in *Research in Economic Anthropology*, B. Isaac ed., 13:341–371. JAI Press, Greenwich.

Prasad, Kunwar Deo. 1987 *Taxation in ancient India: From the earliest times up to the Guptas*. Mittal Publications, Dehli.

Prem, Hanns 1974 *Matrícula de Huexotzinco (Ms mex. 387 der Bibliothèque Nationale Paris)*. Akademische Druck -u. Verlagsanstalt, Graz.

Prentice, Guy 1983 Cottage industries: Concepts and implications. *Midcontinental Journal of Archaeology* 8:17–48.

Prescott, William 1921 *History of the conquest of Peru*. J. M. Dent and Sons, New York.

Price, Barbara 1978 Secondary state formation: An explanatory model, in *Origins of the state: The anthropology of political evolution*, R. Cohen and E. Service eds., pp. 161–186. Institute for the Study of Human Issues, Pittsburgh.

Pryor, Frederic 1977 *The origins of the economy*. Academic Press, New York.

Pryor, Frederic 1985 *A guidebook to the comparative study of economic systems*. Prentice Hall, New York.

Pryor, Frederic 2005 *Economic systems of foraging, agricultural, and industrial societies*. Cambridge University Press, Cambridge.

Pryor, John 1977 The origins of the commenda contract. *Speculum* 52:5–37.

Pulak, Cemal 1998 The Uluburun shipwreck: An overview. *The International Journal of Nautical Archaeology* 27:188–224.

Pulak, Cemal 2008 The Uluburun shipwreck and Late Bronze Age trade, in *Beyond Babylon: Art, trade, and diplomacy in the second millennium BC*, J. Aruz, K. Benzel, and J. Evans eds., pp. 289–375. Yale University Press, New Haven.

Putzeys, Toon, and Luke Lavan 2008 Commercial space in Late Antiquity, in

Objects in context, objects in use, L. Lavan ed., pp. 81–110. Brill, Boston.

Quale, Gladys 1988 *A history of marriage systems*. Greenwood Press, Westport.

Quirke, Stephen, Eva Pardey, and Ben Haring 2001 Administration, in *Oxford encyclopedia of Ancient Egypt* (www-oxfordreference-com.ezaccess.libraries.psu.edu/view/10.1093/acref/9780195102345.001.0001/acref-9780195102345).

Radcliffe-Brown, Alfred 1941 The study of kinship systems. *The Journal of the Royal Anthropological Institute of Great Britain and Ireland* 71:1–18.

Ramaswamy, Vijaya 2006 *Textiles and weavers in Medieval South India*. Oxford University Press, Oxford.

Ramírez, Susan 1985 Social frontiers and the territorial base of curacazgos, in *Andean ecology and civilization*, S. Masuda, I. Shimada, and C. Morris eds., pp. 423–442. University of Tokyo Press, Tokyo.

Randall, Emilius Oviatt. 1904 *History of the Zoar Society from its commencement to its conclusion: A sociological study in communism*. Press of Fred J. Heer, Columbus.

Rao, Apama 1987 *The other nomads*. Böhlau Verlag, Cologne.

Rapoport, Yossef 2000 Matrimonial gifts in early Islamic Egypt. *Islamic Law and Society* 7:1–36.

Rappaport, Roy 1967 Ritual regulation of environmental relations among a New Guinea people. *Ethnology* 6:17–30.

Rappaport, Roy 1968 *Pigs for the ancestors: Ritual in the ecology of a New Guinea people*. Yale University Press, New Haven.

Rappaport, Steve 2002 *Worlds within worlds: Structures of life in sixteenth-century London*. Cambridge University Press, Cambridge.

Rathbone, Dominic 1991 *Economic rationalism and rural society in third-century AD Egypt: The Heroninos archive and the Appianus estate*. Cambridge University Press, Cambridge.

Ratnagar, Shereen 2004 *Trading encounters from the Euphrates to the Indus in the Bronze Age*. Oxford University Press, Oxford.

Rauh, Nicholas 1993 *The sacred bonds of commerce: Religion, economy, and trade society at Hellenistic Roman Delos*. J. C. Gieben, Amsterdam.

Ravi, Shamika 2003 *Borrowing behaviour of rural households*. Technical report, Working Paper, Department of Economics, New York University.

Raychaudhuri, Tapan 1982 Inland trade, in *The Cambridge economic history of India*, T. Raychaudri and I. Habib eds., 1:325–359. Cambridge University Press, Cambridge.

Reed, Charles 2003 *Maritime traders in the ancient Greek world*. Cambridge University Press, Cambridge.

Reed, Nelson 1964 *The caste war of Yucatán*. Stanford University Press, Stanford.

Reina, Ruben 1963 The potter and the farmer: The fate of two innovators in a Maya village. *Expedition* 5:18–30.

Renfrew, Colin 1973 Monuments, mobilization, and social organization in Neolithic Wessex, in *The exploration of culture change*, C. Renfrew ed., pp. 539–558. Duckworth, London.

Renfrew, Colin 1986 Introduction: Peer polity interaction and socio-political change, in *Peer polity interaction and socio-political change*, C. Renfrew and J. Cherry eds., pp. 1–18. Cambridge University Press, Cambridge.

Renfrew, Colin, and Arnold Aspinall 1990 Aegean obsidian and Franchthi Cave, in *Excavations at Franchthi Cave, Greece*, T. Jacobsen ed., pp. 257–273. University of Indiana Press, Bloomington.

Renfrew, Colin, and John Cherry eds. 1986 *Peer polity interaction and socio-political change*. Cambridge University Press, Cambridge.

Renfrew, Colin, John Dixon, and Robin Cann 1966 Obsidian and early cultural contact in the Near East. *Proceedings of the Prehistoric Society* 32:30–72.

Renger, Johannes 1979 Interaction of temple, palace, and "private enterprise" in the Old Babylonian economy, in *State and temple economy in the ancient Near East*, E. Lipinski ed., pp. 249–256. Departement Orientalistiek, Leuven.

Renger, Johannes 1999 Comments, in *Urbanization and land ownership in the ancient Near East*, M. Hudson and B. Levine eds., pp. 147–159. Peabody Museum Bulletin 7, Harvard University, Cambridge, MA.

Renger, Johannes 2003 Trade and market in the ancient Near East: Theoretical and factual implications, in *Mercanti e politica nel mondo antico*, C. Zaccagnini ed., pp. 15–39. L'erma di Bretschneider, Rome.

Reyes García, Luís 1997 *Matrícula de tributos o códice Moctezuma*. Akademische Druck- und Verlagsanstalt and Fondo de Cultura Económica, Graz and Mexico City.

Reynolds, Robert 1931 Genoese trade in the late twelfth century, particularly in cloth from the fairs of Champagne. *Journal of Economic and Business History* 3:362–381.

Rice, Candace 2016 Mercantile specialization and trading communities: Economic strategies in Roman maritime trade, in *Urban craftsmen and traders in the Roman world*, A. Wilson and M. Flohr eds., pp. 97–114. Oxford University Press, Oxford.

Richards, Paul 1985 *Indigenous agricultural revolution: Ecology and food production in West Africa*. Hutchinson, London.

Richerson, Peter, Robert Boyd, and Joseph Henrich 2003 Cultural evolution of human cooperation, in *Genetic and cultural evolution of cooperation*, P. Hammerstein ed., pp. 57–88. MIT Press and Preie Universität, Cambridge, MA, and Berlin.

Rickman, Geoffrey 1971 *Roman granaries and store buildings*. Cambridge University Press, Cambridge.

Rickman, Geoffrey 1980a *The corn supply of ancient Rome*. Clarendon Press, Oxford.

Rickman, Geoffrey 1980b The grain trade under the Roman Empire. *Memoirs of the American Academy in Rome* 36:261–275.

Riello, Giorgio 2013 *Cotton: The fabric that made the modern world*. Cambridge University Press, Cambridge.

Riello, Giorgio, and Prasannan Parthasarathi eds. 2011 *The spinning world: A global history of cotton textiles 1200–1850*. Oxford University Press, Oxford.

Rizvi, Janet 2012 *Trans-Himalayan caravans: Merchant princes and peasant traders in Ladakh*. Oxford University Press, Oxford.

Robbins, Lionel 1935 *An essay on the nature and significance of economic science*. Macmillan, London.

Roberts, Richard 1987 *Warriors, merchants, and slaves: The state and the economy in the Middle Niger Valley, 1700–1914*. Stanford University Press, Stanford.

Robertson, John 1995 The social and economic organization of ancient Mesopotamian temples, in *Civilizations of the ancient Near East*, J. Sasson ed., 1:443–454. Hendricks, Peabody, MA.

Robin, Christian 2005 Sabba and the Sabaeans, in *Caravan kingdoms: Yemen and the ancient incense trade*, A. Gunter ed., pp. 8–19. Smithsonian Institution Press, Washington, DC.

Robotham, Don 2012 Political economy, in *A handbook of economic anthropology*, J. Carrier ed., pp. 41–58. Edward Elgar, Cheltenham.

Rodning, Christopher 2014 Cherokee towns and calumet ceremonialism in eastern North America. *American Antiquity* 79:425–443.

Rodrigue, Jean-Paul, Claude Comtois, and Brian Slack 2016 *The geography of transport systems*. Routledge, New York.

Rojas, José Luis de 1995 *México Tenochtitlan: Economía y sociedad en el siglo XVI*. Fondo de Cultura Económica, Mexico City.

Rojas Rabiela, Teresa 1979 La organización del trabajo para las obras públicas: El coatequitl y las cuadrillas de trabajadores, in *El trabajo y los trabajadores en la historia de México/Labor and laborers through Mexican history*, C. Frost, M. Meyer, J. Zoraida Vázquez, and L. Díaz eds., pp. 41–66. El Colegio de México and University of Arizona Press, Mexico City and Tucson.

Roochnik, David 2010 *Of art and wisdom: Plato's understanding of techne*. Penn State Press, University Park.

Roscoe, Paul 1993 Practice and political centralisation: A new approach to political evolution. *Current Anthropology* 34:111–140.

Roscoe, Paul 2013 War, collective action, and the "evolution" of human polities, in *Cooperation and collective action: Archaeological perspectives*, D. Carballo ed., pp. 57–82. University Press of Colorado, Boulder.

Rosen, Steven 2003 Early multi-resource nomadism: Excavations at the Camel site in the central Negev. *Antiquity* 77:750–761.

Rosenwein, Barbara 1999 *Negotiating space: Power, restraint, and privileges of immunity in early Medieval Europe*. Cornell University Press, Ithaca.

Rossabi, Morris 1970 The tea and horse trade with inner Asia during the Ming. *Journal of Asian History* 4:136–168.

Rossabi, Morris 1993 The "decline" of the central Asian caravan trade, in *The rise of merchant empires: Long-distance trade in the modern world, 1350–1750*, J. Tracy ed., pp. 351–370. Cambridge University Press, Cambridge.

Rostworowski de Diez, Maria 1977 Reflexiones sobre la reciprocidad andina. *Histórica* 1:249–285.

Rousseau, Jean-Jacques 1984 *A discourse on inequality*. Penguin Books, New York.

Rovira Morgado, Rossend 2014 Almacenamiento centralizado y comercio multicéntrico en México-Tenochtitlan. *Relaciones (Zamora)* 35:181–208 (www.scielo.org.mx/scielo.php?script=sci_arttext&pid=S0185-392920140002 00007).

Rowe, John 1982 Inca policies and institutions relating to the cultural unification of the empire, in *The Inca and Aztec states 1400–1800: Anthropology and history*, G. Collier, R. Rosaldo, and J. Wirth eds., pp. 93–118. Academic Press, New York.

Rubio, Gonzalo 2006 Review of *Archaische Verwaltungstexte aus Uruk: Die Heidelberger Sammlung*. *Journal of the American Oriental Society* 126:462.

Rubio, Gonzalo 2007 From Sumer to Babylon, in *Current issues in the history of the ancient Near East*, M. Chavalas ed., pp. 1–51. Regina Books, Claremont, CA.

Rudner, David 1987 Religious gifting and inland commerce in seventeenth-century South India. *The Journal of Asian Studies* 46:361–379.

Rudwick, Stephanie, and Dorrit Posel 2014 Contemporary functions of ilobolo (bridewealth) in urban South African Zulu society. *Journal of Contemporary African Studies* 32:118–136.

Ruffing, Kai 2016 Driving forces of specialization: Market, location factors, productivity improvements, in *Urban craftsmen and traders in the Roman world*, A. Wilson and M. Flohr eds., pp. 115–131. Oxford University Press, Oxford.

Rugeley, Terry 2010 *Yucatan's Maya peasantry and the origins of the caste war*. University of Texas Press, Austin.

Ryder, Michael 1965 Report of textiles from Çatal Hüyük. *Anatolian Studies* 15:175–176.

Sahagún, Fray Bernardino de 1959 *Florentine codex, book 9, the merchants*. C. Dibble and A. Anderson eds. and trans. University of Utah Press, Salt Lake City.

Sahagún, Fray Bernardino de 1961 *Florentine codex, book 10, the people*. C. Dibble and A. Anderson eds. and trans. University of Utah Press, Salt Lake City.

Sahlins, Marshall 1961 The segmentary lineage: An organization of predatory expansion. *American Anthropologist* 63:322–345.

Sahlins, Marshall 1963 Poor man, rich man, big-man, chief: Political types in Melanesia and Polynesia. *Comparative Studies in Society and History* 5:285–303.

Sahlins, Marshall 1972 *Stone age economics*. Aldine, Chicago.

Sahlins, Marshall, and Elman Service 1960 *Evolution and culture*. University of Michigan Press, Ann Arbor.

Saitta, Dean 1999 Prestige, agency, and change in middle-range societies, in *Material symbols: Culture and economy in prehistory*, J. Robb ed., pp. 135–149. Southern Illinois University Press, Carbondale.

Saitta, Dean 2007 *The archaeology of collective action*. University Press of Florida, Gainesville.

Sallaberger, Walther 2014 The value of wool in early Bronze Age Mesopotamia. On the control of sheep and the handling of wool in the Presargonic to the Ur III periods (c. 2400–2000 BC), in *Wool economy in the ancient Near East*, C. Breniquet and C. Michel eds., pp. 94–114. Oxbow Books, Oxford.

Salomon, Frank 1977 Pochteca and mindalá: A comparison of long-distance traders in Ecuador and Mesoamerica. *Journal of the Steward Anthropological Society* 9:231–247.

Salomon, Frank 1987 A north Andean status trader complex under Inka rule. *Ethnohistory* 34:63–77.

Salomon, Frank 1988 Un complejo de mercaderes en el norte andino bajo la dominación de los incas. *Revista de Antropología* 4:107–126.

Salomon, Frank, Hilda Araujo, Roy Harris, Walter Mignolo, Gary Urton, and Frank Salomon 2001 How an Andean "writing without words" works. *Current Anthropology* 42:1–27.

Samson, William 2002 History of taxation, in *The international taxation system*, A. Lymer and J. Hasseldine eds., pp. 21–41. Kluwer Academic, Boston.

Samuelson, Paul 1967 *Economics: An introductory analysis*. McGraw-Hill, New York.

Sancho, Pedro 1917 *An account of the conquest of Peru*. Cortes Society, New York.

Sanders, William 1956 The Central Mexican symbiotic region: A study in prehistoric settlement patterns, in *Prehistoric settlement patterns in the New World*, G. Willey ed., pp. 115–127. Viking Fund Publications in Anthropology, New York.

Sanders, William 1962 Cultural ecology of nuclear Mesoamerica. *American Anthropologist* 64:34–44.

Sanders, William 1976 The agricultural history of the Basin of Mexico, in *The Valley of Mexico*, E. Wolf ed., pp. 101–159. University of New Mexico Press, Albuquerque.

Sanders, William, Jeffrey Parsons, and Robert Santley 1979 *The Basin of Mexico: Ecological processes in the evolution of a civilization*. Academic Press, New York.

Sandstrom, Alan 2000 Toponymic groups and house organization: The Nahuas of northern Veracruz, Mexico, in *Beyond kinship: Social and material reproduction in house societies*, R. Joyce and S. Gillespie eds., pp. 53–72. University of Pennsylvania Press, Philadelphia.

Sandstrom, Alan 2008 Ritual economy among the Nahua of northern Veracruz, Mexico, in *Dimensions of ritual economy*, C. Wells and P. McAnany eds., pp. 93–119. Emerald Groups, Bradford.

Santley, Robert, and Rani Alexander 1992 The political economy of core–periphery systems, in *Resources, power, and interregional interaction*, E. Schortman and P. Urban eds., pp. 23–59. Plenum, New York.

Santley, Robert, Philip Arnold, and Christopher Pool 1989 The ceramics production system at Matacapan, Veracruz, Mexico. *Journal of Field Archaeology* 16:107–132.

Satya, Laxman 1997 Colonial sedentarisation and subjugation: The case of the Banjaras of Berar 1850–1900. *The Journal of Peasant Studies* 24:314–336.

Scarborough, Vernon 2003 *The flow of power: Ancient water systems and landscapes*. School for Advanced Research, Sante Fe.

Scelza, Brooke, and Joan Silk 2014 Fosterage as a system of dispersed cooperative breeding. *Human Nature* 25:448–464.

Schaffer, Talia 2011 *Novel craft: Victorian domestic handicraft and nineteenth-century fiction*. Oxford University Press, Oxford.

Schapera, Isaac, and Astley Goodwin 1937 Work and wealth, in *The Bantu-speaking tribes of South Africa: An ethnographical survey*, I. Schapera ed., pp. 131–173. Routledge and Kegan Paul, London.

Scheidel, Walter ed. 2012a *The Cambridge companion to the Roman economy*. Cambridge University Press, Cambridge.

Scheidel, Walter 2012b ORBIS: The Stanford geospatial network model of the Roman world (www.archeonet.be/images/ORBIS_v1paper_20120501.pdf).

Scheidel, Walter 2014 The shape of the Roman world: Modeling imperial connectivity. *Journal of Roman Archaeology* 27:7–32.

Schick, Tamar 1988 Cordage, basketry and fabrics. *Atiqot* 18:31–43.

Schiel, Tilman 1994 The trader's dilemma. The perspective of the longue durée, in *The moral economy of trade: Ethnicity and developing markets*, H. Evers and H. Schrader eds., pp. 15–26. Routledge, London.

Schipper, Jeremy 2016 *Ruth: A new translation with introduction and commentary*. Yale University Press, New Haven.

Schloen, David 2001 *The house of the father as fact and symbol: Patrimonialism in Ugarit and the ancient Near East*. Eisenbrauns, Winona Lake.

Schmidt, Klaus 2001 Göbekli Tepe, southeastern Turkey: A preliminary report on the 1995–1999 excavations. *Paléorient* 26:45–54.

Schmidt, Klaus 2006 Animals and a headless man at Göbekli Tepe. *Neo-Lithics* 2:38–40.

Schmidt, Klaus 2010 Göbekli Tepe – The stone age sanctuaries. New results of ongoing excavations with a special focus on sculptures and high reliefs. *Documenta Praehistorica* 37:239–256.

Schneider, Anna 1920 *Die anfänge der kulturwirtschaft: Die sumerische tempelstadt.* GD Baedeker, Würzburg.

Schneider, David 1984 *A critique of the study of kinship.* University of Michigan Press, Ann Arbor.

Schneider, Harold 1974 *Economic man: The anthropology of economics.* Sheffield, Salem.

Schneider, Jane 1977 Was there a pre-capitalist world system? *Peasant Studies* 6:20–29.

Schoep, Ilse 2010 The Minoan "palace-temple" reconsidered: A critical assessment of the spatial concentration of political, religious and economic power in Bronze Age Crete. *Journal of Mediterranean Archaeology* 23:219–243.

Scholes, Frances, and Eleanor Adams 1957 *Información sobre los tributos que los indios pagaban a Moctezuma. Año 1554.* José Porrúa e Hijos, Mexico City.

Scholes, Frances, and Ralph Roys 1968 *The Maya Chontal Indians of Acalan-Tixchel.* University of Oklahoma Press, Norman.

Schortman, Edward, and Patricia Urban 2004 Modeling the roles of craft production in ancient political economies. *Journal of Archaeological Research* 12:185–226.

Schwimmer, Brian 1976 Periodic markets and urban development in southern Ghana, in *Regional analysis, vol. 1: economic systems,* C. Smith ed., pp. 123–145. Academic Press, New York.

Scott, James 1976 *The moral economy of the peasant.* Yale University Press, New Haven.

Scott, Michael 2003 Ju/'hoansi bushmen of G/am, Namibia, and their pastoralist neighbours: Contact, Hxaro, crisis of identity, and implications for the past. Master's thesis, University of Cape Town.

Scott-Kilvert, Ian 1960 *The rise and fall of Athens: Nine Greek lives by Plutarch,* I. Scott-Kilvert trans. Penguin Books, London.

Segendorf, Björn. 2014 What is bitcoin? *Sveriges Riksbank Economic Review* 2:71–87.

Sen, Amartya 1981 *Poverty and famines: An essay on entitlement and deprivation.* Oxford University Press, Oxford.

Sen, Sudipta 1998 *Empire of free trade: The East India Company and the making of the colonial marketplace.* University of Pennsylvania Press, Philadelphia.

Serjeant, R. B. 1974 *The Portuguese of the south Arabian coast: Hadrami chronicles.* Libraire de Liban, Beirut.

Service, Elman 1962 *Primitive social organization: An evolutionary perspective.* W. W. Norton, New York.

Service, Elman 1975 *The origins of the state and civilization: The process of cultural evolution.* Norton, New York.

Service, Elman 1978 Classification and modern theories of the origins of government, in *Origins of the state: The anthropology of political evolution,* R. Cohen and E. Service eds., pp. 21–34. Institute for the Study of Human Issues, Philadelphia.

Sewell, William 1992 A theory of structure: Duality, agency, and transformation. *American Journal of Sociology* 98:1–29.

Sharlach, Tonia 2004 *Provincial taxation and the Ur III state.* Cuneiform Monographs 26. Brill, Leiden.

Sharp, Lauriston 1952 Steel axes for stone-age Australians. *Human Organization* 11:17–22.

Sheehy, James 1992 Ceramic production in ancient Teotihuacan, Mexico: A case study of Tlajinga 33. PhD dissertation, Pennsylvania State University, University Park.

Sheehy, James 1996 Ethnographic analogy and the royal household in 8th century Copan, in *Arqueología Mesoamericana: Homenaje a William Sanders,* A. Mastache, J. Parsons, R. Santley, and M. Serra Puche eds., 2:253–276. Instituto Nacional de Antropología e Historia, Mexico.

Shiba, Yoshinobu 1977 Ningpo and its hinterland, in *The city in Late Imperial China,* W.

Skinner ed., pp. 391–439. Stanford University Press, Stanford.

Shimada, Izumi, ed. 2007a *Craft production in complex societies: Multicraft and producer perspectives*. University of Utah Press, Salt Lake City.

Shimada, Izumi, 2007b Introduction, in *Craft production in complex societies: Multicraft and producer perspectives*, I. Shimada ed., pp. 1–21. University of Utah Press, Salt Lake City.

Silk, Joan 1980 Adoption and kinship in Oceania. *American Anthropologist* 82:799–820.

Silk, Joan 1987a Adoption among the Inuit. *Ethos* 15:320–330.

Silk, Joan 1987b Adoption and fosterage in human societies: Adaptations or enigmas? *Cultural Anthropology* 2:39–49.

Silk, Joan 1990 Human adoption in evolutionary perspective. *Human Nature* 1:25–52.

Silver, Harry 1981 Calculating risks: The socioeconomic foundations of aesthetic innovation in an Ashanti carving community. *Ethnology* 20:101–114.

Silver, Morris 1985 *Economic structures of the ancient Near East*. Barnes and Noble Books, Totowa, NJ.

Silver, Morris 1995 *Economic structures of antiquity*. Greenwood Press, Westport.

Simmel, Georg 1967 The stranger, in *The sociology of George Simmel*, K. Wolff ed. and trans., pp. 409–425. Free Press, New York.

Simmel, Georg 1996 The stranger (1908) and the web of group affiliations (1908), in *Theories of ethnicity: A classical reader*, W. Sollors ed., pp. 37–51. New York University Press, New York.

Simon, Robert 1989 *Meccan trade and Islam*. Akademiai, Budapest.

Sinopoli, Carla 1988 The organization of craft production at Vijayanagara, South India. *American Anthropologist* 90:580–597.

Sinopoli, Carla 2003 *The political economy of craft production. Crafting empire in South India, c. 1350–1650*. Cambridge University Press, Cambridge.

Skinner, Elliott 1964 West African economic systems, in *Economic transition in Africa*, M. Herskovits and M. Harwitz eds., pp. 77–97. Northwestern University Press, Evanston.

Skinner, William 1964 Marketing and social structure in rural China, part I. *Journal of Asian Studies* 24:3–43.

Skinner, William 1965 Marketing and social structure in rural China, part II. *Journal of Asian Studies* 24:195–228.

Sluyter, Andrew 1993 Long-distance staple transport in western Mesoamerica: Insights through quantitative modeling. *Ancient Mesoamerica* 4:193–199.

Smith, Adam 1827 *An inquiry into the nature and causes of the wealth of nations*. Thomas Nelson and Peter Brown, Edinburgh.

Smith, Alan 1991 *Creating a world economy: Merchant capital, colonialism and world trade 1400–1824*. Westview Press, Boulder.

Smith, Bruce 2001 Low-level food production. *Journal of Archaeological Research* 9:1–43.

Smith, Carol 1974 Economics of marketing systems: Models from economic geography. *Annual Review of Anthropology* 3:167–201.

Smith, Carol ed. 1976a *Regional analysis, vol. 1: Economic systems*. Academic Press, New York.

Smith, Carol ed. 1976b *Regional analysis, vol. 2: Social systems*. Academic Press, New York.

Smith, Carol 1976c Regional economic systems: Linking geographical models and socioeconomic problems, in *Regional analysis, vol. 1: Economic systems*, C. Smith ed., pp. 3–67. Academic Press, New York.

Smith, Carol 1983 Regional analysis in world-system perspective: A critique of three structural theories of uneven development, in *Economic anthropology: Topics and theories*, S. Ortiz ed., pp. 307–359. University Press of America, Lanham.

Smith, Colin 1999 The market place and the market's place in London, c. 1660–1840. PhD dissertation, University College London.

Smith, Joan, Immanuel Wallerstein, and Hans-Dieter Evers 1984 *Households and the world economy*. Sage Press, Beverly Hills.

Smith, Julia 2010 Rulers and relics c. 750–c. 950: Treasure on earth, treasure in heaven. *Past and Present* 206:73–96.

Smith, Michael 1987 Household possessions and wealth in agrarian states: Implications for archaeology. *Journal of Anthropological Archaeology* 6:297–335.

Smith, Michael 1992 Braudel's temporal rhythms and chronology theory in archaeology, in *Archaeology, annals, and ethnohistory*, A. Knapp ed., pp. 23–34. Cambridge University Press, Cambridge.

Smith, Michael 2012 *The Aztecs*. Wiley Blackwell, Cambridge.

Smith, Michael Garfield 1955 *The economy of Hausa communities of Zaria*. Colonial Research Studies 16. Colonial Office Social Science Research Council, England.

Snow, Dean 1996 *The Iroquois*. Wiley-Blackwell, Hoboken.

Soffer, Olga, James Adovasio, and David Hyland 2000 The "Venus" figurines. *Current Anthropology* 41:511–537.

Spawforth, Tony 2008 *Versailles: A biography of a palace*. St. Martin's Press, New York.

Spence, Michael 1981 Obsidian production and the state in Teotihuacan. *American Antiquity* 46:769–788.

Spence, Michael 2005 Zapotec diaspora network in Classic-period Central Mexico, in *The archaeology of colonial encouters*, G. Stein ed., pp. 173–205. School of American Research Press, Santa Fe.

Spencer, Charles 1993 Human agency, biased transmission, and the cultural evolution of chiefly authority. *Journal of Anthropological Archaeology* 12:41–74.

Spencer, Paul 1993 Becoming Maasai, being in time, in *Being Maasai: Ethnicity and identity in East Africa*, T. Spear and R. Waller eds., pp. 140–156. James Currey, London.

Springer, James 1981 An ethnohistoric study of the smoking complex in eastern North America. *Ethnohistory* 28:217–235.

Stanish, Charles 1992 *Ancient Andean political economy*. University of Texas Press, Austin.

Stanish, Charles 2013 The ritualized economy and cooperative labor in intermediate societies, in *Cooperation and collective action: Archaeological perspectives*, D. Carballo ed., pp. 83–92. University Press of Colorado, Boulder.

Stanish, Charles, and Lawrence Coben 2013 Barter markets in the pre-Hispanic Andes, in *Merchants, markets, and exchange in the pre-Columbian world*, K. Hirth and J. Pillsbury eds., pp. 419–434. Dumbarton Oaks Research Library and Collection, Washington, DC.

Stark, Barbara, and Alanna Ossa 2010 Origins and development of Mesoamerican marketplaces: Evidence from south-central Veracruz, Mexico, in *Archaeological approaches to market exchange in pre-capitalistic societies*, C. Garraty and B. Stark eds., pp. 99–126. University Press of Colorado, Boulder.

Starr, Chester 1977 *The economic and social growth of early Greece 800–500 BC*. Oxford University Press, New York.

Stein, Burton 1960 The economic function of a medieval South Indian Temple. *The Journal of Asian Studies* 19:163–176.

Stein, Gil 1994 Economy, ritual, and power in Ubaid Mesopotamia, in *Chiefdoms and early states in the Near East: The organizational dynamics of complexity*, G. Stein and M. Rothman eds., pp. 35–46. Monographs in World Archaeology No. 18. Prehistory Press, Madison.

Stein, Gil 1996 Producers, patrons, and prestige: Craft specialists and emergent elites in Mesopotamia from 5500–3100 B.C., in *Craft specialization and social evolution: In memory of V. Gordon Childe*, B. Wailes ed., pp. 25–38. University of Pennsylvania Museum of Archaeology and Anthropology, Philadelphia.

Stein, Gil 1999a Material culture and social identity: The evidence for a 4th millennium BC Mesopotamian Uruk colony at Hacinebi, Turkey. *Paléorient* 25:11–22.

Stein, Gil 1999b *Rethinking world-systems: Diasporas, colonies, and interaction in Uruk Mesopotamia*. University of Arizona Press, Tucson.

Stein, Gil 2001 Indigenous social complexity at Hacınebi (Turkey) and the organization of Uruk colonial contact, in *Uruk Mesopotamia and its neighbors: Cross-cultural interactions in the era of state formation*, M. Rothman ed., pp. 265–305. School of American Research Press, Santa Fe.

Stein, Gil, and James Blackman 1993 The organizational context of specialized craft production in early Mesopotamian states. *Research in*

Economic Anthropology, B. Isaac ed., 14:29–59. JAI Press, Greenwich.

Steinkeller, Piotr 1987 The administrative and economic organization of the Ur III state: The core and the periphery, in *The organization of power: Aspects of bureaucracy in the ancient Near East*, M. Gibson and R. Biggs eds., pp. 19–41. Studies in Ancient Oriental Civilization No. 46, Oriental Institute of the University of Chicago, Chicago.

Steinkeller, Piotr 2007 City and countryside in third-millennium southern Babylonia, in *Settlement and society: Essays dedicated to Robert McCormick Adams*, E. Stone ed., pp. 185–211. Cotsen Institute of Archaeology, University of California, Los Angeles.

Stevens, Marty 2006 *Temples, tithes, and taxes: The temple and the economic life of ancient Israel.* Hendrickson, Peabody, MA.

Stevenson, Robert 1968 *Population and political systems in tropical Africa.* Columbia University Press, New York.

Steward, Julian 1938 *Basin Plateau aboriginal sociopolitical groups.* Bureau of American Ethnology Bulletin 120, Washington, DC.

Steward, Julian ed. 1955 *Irrigation civilizations: A comparative study. A symposium on method and result in cross cultural regularities.* Pan American Union, Washington, DC.

Steward, Julian 1972 *Theory of culture change: The methodology of multilinear evolution.* University of Illinois Press, Urbana.

Stol, Marten 2012 Payment of the Old Babylonian brideprice, in *Looking at the ancient Near East and the Bible through the same eyes*, K. Abraham and J. Fleishman eds., pp. 131–167. CDI Press, Bethesda, MD.

Stol, Marten 2016 *Women in the ancient Near East.* Walter de Gruyter, Berlin.

Stolmaker, Charlotte 1996 *Cultural, social and economic change in Santa María Atzompa in the late 1960's.* Vanderbilt University Publications in Anthropology No. 49. Vanderbilt University, Nashville.

Stone, David 2005 *Decision-making in medieval agriculture.* Oxford University Press, Oxford.

Stone, Elizabeth 2013 The organization of a Sumerian town: The physical remains of ancient social systems, in *The Sumerian world*, H. Crawford ed., pp. 156–178. Routledge, London.

Stone, Elizabeth, David Owen, and John Mitchell 1991 *Adoption in Old Babylonian Nippur and the archive of Mannum-mešu-liṣṣur.* Eisenbrauns, Winona Lake.

Stone, Glenn 1986 *Settlement ecology: The social and spatial organization of Kofyar agriculture.* University of Arizona Press, Tucson.

Stone, Glenn, Robert Netting, and Priscilla Stone. 1990 Seasonality, labor scheduling, and agricultural intensification in the Nigerian savanna. *American Anthropologist* 92:7–23.

Stone, Linda, and Caroline James 1995 Dowry, bride-burning, and female power in India. *Women's Studies International Forum* 18:125–134.

Storey, Rebecca, and Glenn Storey 2017 *Rome and the Classic Maya: Comparing the slow collapse of civilizations.* Routledge, London.

Stratford, Edward 2017 *A year of vengeance: Time, narrative, and the Old Assyrian trade.* Walter de Gruyter, Berlin.

Strathern, Andrew 2007 *The rope of moka: Big-men and ceremonial exchange in Mount Hagen, New Guinea.* Cambridge University Press, Cambridge.

Strauss, Barry 2012 *Masters of command: Alexander, Hannibal, Caesar, and the genius of leadership.* Simon and Schuster, New York.

Strong, James 1995 *New Strong's concise dictionary of the words in the Hebrew Bible with their renderings in the King James version.* Thomas Nelson, Nashville.

Stroud, Ronald 1998 *The Athenian grain-tax law of 374/3 B.C.* American School of Classical Studies at Athens, Princeton.

Strudwick, Nigel 1985 *Administration of Egypt in the Old Kingdom: The highest titles and their holders.* KPI, London.

Sundström, Lars 1974 *The exchange economy of pre-colonial tropical Africa.* St. Martin's Press, New York.

Swanson, Heather 1999 *Medieval British towns.* St. Martin's Press, New York.

Symanski, Richard, and Michael Webber 1974 Complex periodic market cycles. *Annals of the Association of American Geographers* 64:203–213.

Taaffe, Edward, and Howard Gauthier 1973 *Geography of transportation.* Prentice-Hall, Englewood Cliffs.

Tacoma, Laurens 2013 Imperial estates, Egypt, in *The encyclopedia of ancient history*, R. Bagnall, K. Brodersen, C. Champion, A. Erskine, and S. Huebner eds., pp. 3420–3421. Blackwell, West Sussex.

Tan, James 2015 The Roman republic, in *Fiscal regimes and the political economy of premodern states*, A. Monson and W. Scheidel eds., pp. 208–228. Cambridge University Press, Cambridge.

Tanimoto, Masahuki 2011 Cotton and the peasant economy: A foreign fibre in early modern Japan, in *The spinning world: A global history of cotton textiles 1200–1850*, G. Riello and P. Parthasarathi eds., pp. 367–385. Oxford University Press, Oxford.

Temin, Peter 2006 The economy of the early Roman empire. *Journal of Economic Perspectives* 20:133–151.

Terraciano, Kevin 2001 *The Mixtecs of colonial Oaxaca: Ñudzahui history, sixteenth through eighteenth centuries.* Stanford University Press, Stanford.

Terray, Emmanuel 1972 *Marxism and "primitive" societies.* Monthly Review Press, New York.

Terray, Emmanuel 1974 Long-distance exchange and the formation of the state: The case of the Abron kingdom of Gyaman. *Economy and Society* 3:315–345.

Thaler, Richard 2015 *Misbehaving: The making of behavioral economics.* W. W. Norton, New York.

Thielscher, Paul 1963 *Des Marcus Cato Belehrung über die Landwirtschaft: De Agri-cultura institutum.* P. Thielscher ed. and trans. Duncker and Humblot, Berlin.

Thompson, Dorothy 1971 *An ancient shopping center: The Athenian Agora.* American School of Classical Studies at Athens, Princeton.

Tibbetts, Gerald 1957 Early Muslim traders in south-east Asia. *Journal of the Malayan Branch of the Royal Asiatic Society* 30:1–45.

Topic, John 2013 Exchange on the Ecuadorian frontier, in *Merchants, markets, and exchange in the pre-Columbian world*, K. Hirth and J. Pillsbury eds., pp. 335–360. Dumbarton Oaks Research Library and Collection, Washington, DC.

Torrence, Robin 1986 *Production and exchange of stone tools: Prehistoric obsidian in the Aegean.* Cambridge University Press, Cambridge.

Tracy, James 1993 Introduction, in *The rise of merchant empires: Long-distance trade in the modern world, 1350–1750*, J. Tracy ed., pp. 1–13. Cambridge University Press, Cambridge.

Trigger, Bruce 1983 The rise of Egyptian civilization, in *Ancient Egypt: A social history*, B. Trigger, B. Kemp, D. O'Conner, and A. Lloyd eds., pp. 1–70. Cambridge University Press, Cambridge.

Trigger, Bruce 2003 *Understanding early civilizations: A comparative study.* Cambridge University Press, Cambridge.

Trubitt, Mary 2003 The production and exchange of marine shell prestige goods. *Journal of Archaeological Research* 11:243–277.

Tsutsumi, Takashi 2010 Prehistoric procurement of obsidian from sources on Honshu Island (Japan), in *Crossing the straits: Prehistoric obsidian exploitation in the north Pacific rim*, Y. Kuzmin and M. Glascock eds., pp. 27–55. Archaeopress, Oxford.

Turnbaugh, William 1979 Calumet ceremonialism as a nativistic response. *American Antiquity* 44:685–691.

Turvey, Calum, and Rong Kong 2010 Informal lending amongst friends and relatives. *China Economic Review* 21:544–556.

Ulieru, Mihaela, Robert Brennan, and Scott Walker 2002 The holonic enterprise: A model for internet-enabled global manufacturing supply chain and workflow management. *Integrated Manufacturing Systems* 13:538–550.

Um, Nancy 2011 *The merchant houses of Mocha: Trade and architecture in an Indian Ocean port.* University of Washington Press, Seattle.

Unger, Merrill 1966 *Unger's Bible dictionary.* Moody Press, Chicago.

Unger, Richard 1973 Dutch ship design in the fifteenth and sixteenth centuries. *Viator* 4:387–412.

Urton, Gary 2009 *Signs of the Inka khipu: Binary coding in the Andean knotted-string records.* University of Texas Press, Austin.

Urton, Gary 2012 Mathematics and accounting in the Andes before and after the Spanish Conquest, in *Alternative forms of knowing (in) mathematics*, S. Mukhopadhyay and W. Roth eds., pp. 17–32. Sense, Rotterdam.

Vale, Malcolm 2002 The princely court in Northern Europe, 1270–1380. *History Today* 52:11.

Van Andel, Tjeerd, Curtis Runnels, and Kevin Pope 1986 Five thousand years of land use and abuse in the southern Argolid, Greece. *Hesperia: The Journal of the American School of Classical Studies at Athens* 55:103–128.

Van Buren, Mary 1996 Rethinking the vertical archipelago: Ethnicity, exchange, and history in the south central Andes. *American Anthropologist* 98:338–351.

Van de Mieroop, Marc 1987 *Crafts in the early Isin period: A study of the Isin craft archive from the reigns of Išbi-Erra and Šū-Ilišu*. Departement Oriëntalistiek, Leuven.

Van de Mieroop, Marc 1999 *The ancient Mesopotamian city*. Oxford University Press, Oxford.

Van de Mieroop, Marc 2013 Democracy and the rule of law, the assembly and the first law code, in *The Sumerian world*, H. Crawford ed., pp. 277–283. Routledge, London.

van der Leeuw, Sander 1976 *Studies in the technology of ancient pottery*. Organization for the Advancement of Pure Research, Amsterdam.

van Leur, Jacob 1967 *Indonesian trade and society: Essays in Asian social and economic history*. W. Van Hoeve, The Hague.

Van Zanden, Jan, and Milja Van Tielhof 2009 Roots of growth and productivity change in Dutch shipping industry, 1500–1800. *Explorations in Economic History* 46:389–403.

van Zantwijk, Rudolf 1970 Las organizaciones social-económicas y religiosas de los mercaderes gremiales Aztecas. *Boletin de Estúdios Latino-Americanos* 10:1–20.

van Zantwijk, Rudolf 1985 *The Aztec arrangement*. University of Oklahoma Press, Norman.

Vance, James 1970 *The merchant's world: The geography of wholesaling*. Prentice-Hall, Englewood Cliffs.

Vandiver, Pamela, Olga Soffer, Bohuslav Klima, and Jiri Svoboda 1989 The origins of ceramic technology at Dolni Vestonice, Czechoslovakia. *Science* 246:1002.

Vansina, Jan 1973 *The Tio kingdom of the middle Congo, 1880–1892*. International African Institute and Oxford University Press, London.

Vansina, Jan 1978 *The children of Woot: A history of the Kuba peoples*. University of Wisconsin Press, Madison.

Varady, Robert 1979 North Indian Banjaras: Their evolution as transporters. *South Asia: Journal of South Asian Studies* 2:1–18.

Vaughn, Kevin, Jelmer Eerkens, and John Kantner eds. 2010 *The evolution of leadership: Transitions in decision making from small-scale to middle-range societies*. School for Advanced Research Press, Santa Fe.

Veenhof, Klaas 1972 *Aspects of Old Assyrian trade and its terminology*. Studia et Documenta X. Brill, Leiden.

Veenhof, Klaas 2003a Archival practices at Babylonia in the third millennium, in *Ancient archives and archival traditions*, M. Brosius ed., pp. 78–123. Oxford University Press, Oxford.

Veenhof, Klaas 2003b Trade and politics in ancient Assur: Balancing of public, colonial, and entrepreneurial interests, in *Mercanti e politica nel mondo antico*, Carlo Zaccagnini ed., pp. 69–118. L'erma di Bretschneider, Rome.

Vennum, Thomas 1988 *Wild rice and the Ojibway people*. Minnesota Historical Society Press, St. Paul.

Veyne, Paul 1976 *Le pain et le cirque: Sociologie historique d'un pluralisme politique*. Seuil, Paris.

Veyne, Paul 1990 *Bread and circuses: Historical sociology and political pluralism*. Penguin Books, London.

Vita, Juan Pablo 1999 The society of Ugarit, in *Handbook of Ugaritic studies*, W. Watson and N. Wyatt eds., pp. 455–498. Brill, Leiden.

Vitelli, Giovanna 1980 Grain storage and urban growth in imperial Ostia: A quantitative study. *World Archaeology* 1:54–68.

von Gernet, Alexander 1995 Nicotian dreams: The prehistory and early history of tobacco in eastern North America, in *Consuming habits: Drugs in history and anthropology*, J. Goodman,

P. Lovejoy, and A. Sherratt eds., pp. 67–87. Routledge, London.

Von Reden, Sitta. 1995 The Piraeus – A world apart 1. *Greece & Rome* 42:24–37.

Wachtel, Nathan 1981 Reciprocity and the Inca state: From Karl Polanyi to John V. Murra, in *Research in Economic Anthropology*, B. Isaac ed., 4:38–50. JAI Press, Greenwich.

Waetzoldt, Hartmut 1972 *Untersuchungen zur neusumerischen textilindustri*. Centro per le Antichità e la Storia dell'Arte del Vicino Oriente, Rome.

Wagner, Donald 2001 The administration of the iron industry in eleventh-century China. *Journal of the Economic and Social History of the Orient* 44:175–197.

Wai-keung, Chung 2005 Western corporate forms and the social origins of Chinese diaspora entrepreneurial networks, in *Diaspora entrepreneurial networks: Four centuries of history*, I. Baghdiantz McCabe, G. Harlaftis, and I. Pepelasis Minoglou eds., pp. 287–312. Berg, Oxford.

Wailes, Bernard 1996 V. Gordon Childe and the relations of production, in *Craft specialization and social evolution: In memory of V. Gordon Childe*, B. Wailes ed., pp. 3–14. University of Pennsylvania Museum of Archaeology and Anthropology, Philadelphia.

Walthall, John, Clarence Webb, Stephen Stow, and Sharon Goad. 1982 Galena analysis and Poverty Point trade. *Midcontinental Journal of Archaeology* 7:133–148.

Wang, Yeh-Chien 1971 The fiscal importance of the land tax during the Ch'ing Period. *The Journal of Asian Studies* 30:829–842.

Warburton, David 2001 Officials, in *Oxford encyclopedia of ancient Egypt*. Oxford University Press, Oxford.

Ward, Trawick 1985 Social implications of storage and disposal patterns, in *Structure and process in southeastern archaeology*, R. Dickens and H. Ward eds., pp. 82–101. University of Alabama Press, Tuscaloosa.

Ward-Perkins, Bryan 1984 *From classical antiquity to the Middle Ages: Urban public building in northern and central Italy, AD 300–850*. Oxford University Press, Oxford.

Warden, Leslie 2013 *Pottery and economy in Old Kingdom Egypt*. Brill, Leiden.

Warren, Dave 1971 Some demographic considerations of the Matricula de Huexotzinco. *The Americas* 27:252–270.

Waterbury, Ronald 1989 Embroidery for tourists: A contemporary putting-out system in Oaxaca, Mexico, in *Cloth and human experience*, J. Schneider and A. Weiner eds., pp. 243–271. Smithsonian Institution Press, Washington, DC.

Waterson, Roxana 1995 Houses and hierarchies in island southeast Asia, in *About the house: Lévi-Strauss and beyond*, J. Carsten and S. Hugh-Jones eds., pp. 47–68. Cambridge University Press, Cambridge.

Weatherford, Jack 1997 *The history of money*. Three Rivers Press, New York.

Weatherford, Jack 2004 *Genghis Khan and the making of the modern world*. Random House, New York.

Webb, Malcolm 1975 The flag follows trade: An essay on the necessary interaction of military and commercial factors in state formation, in *Ancient civilization and trade*, C. Lamberg-Karlovsky ed., pp. 155–209. University of New Mexico Press, Albuquerque.

Weber, Max 1978 *Economy and society: An outline of interpretive sociology*. G. Roth and C. Wittich eds. University of California Press, Berkeley.

Weber, Max 2003a *General economic history*. F. Knight trans. Dover Publications, Mineola, NY (originally published 1927).

Weber, Max 2003b *The history of commercial partnerships in the Middle Ages*. L. Kaelbet trans. Rowman and Littlefield, Lanham (originally published 1889).

Webster, David 1975 Warfare and the evolution of the state: A reconsideration. *American Antiquity* 40:464–470.

Webster, David, and Takeshi Inomata 2004 Identifying subroyal elite palaces at Copán and Aguateca, in *Palaces of the ancient New World: A symposium at Dumbarton Oaks*, S. Evans and J. Pillsbury eds., pp. 149–180. Dumbarton Oaks Research Library and Collection, Washington, DC.

Webster's New World dictionary of the American language 1968. Southwestern Company, Nashville.

Weinfeld, Moshe, David Sperling and Aaron Rothkoff 2007 Ruth, book of, in *Encyclopaedia Judaica*, M. Berenbaum and F. Skolnik eds., 17:592–596. Macmillan Reference, Detroit.

Weisberg, Dvora 2009 *Levirate marriage and the family in ancient Judaism*. Brandeis University Press, Waltham.

Weissleder, Wolfgang 1978 Aristotle's concept of political structure and the state, in *Origins of the state: The anthropology of political evolution*, R. Cohen and E. Service eds., pp. 187–203. Institute for the Study of Human Issues, Philadelphia.

Welch, Eric 2015 God, oil, and politics: Hebrew prophetic texts and the dynamics of regional economy in the southern Levant during the 8th–7th centuries B.C.E. PhD dissertation, Pennsylvania State University, University Park.

Wells, Peter 1992 Tradition, identity and change beyond the Roman frontier, in *Resources, power, and interregional interaction*, E. Schortman and P. Urban eds., pp. 175–191. Plenum, New York.

Wendorf, Fred 1968 Site 117: A Nubian Final Paleolithic graveyard near Jebel Sahaba, Sudan, in *The prehistory of Nubia*, F. Wendorf ed., 2:954–995. Southern Methodist University Press, Dallas.

Wenger, Etienne 1998 *Communities of practice: Learning, meaning, and identity*. Cambridge University Press, Cambridge.

Wesson, Cameron 1999 Chiefly power and food storage in southeastern North America. *World Archaeology* 31:145–164.

Wheeler, Sir Mortimer 1968 *The Indus civilization*. Cambridge University Press, Cambridge.

White, Christine, Michael Spence, Fred Longstaffe, and Kimberley Law 2004 Demography and ethnic continuity in the Tlailotlacan enclave of Teotihuacan: The evidence from stable oxygen isotopes. *Journal of Anthropological Archaeology* 23:385–403.

White, Gilbert, David Bradley, and Anne White. 1972 *Drawers of water: Domestic water use in East Africa*. University of Chicago Press, Chicago.

White, Kenneth 1970 *Roman farming*. Cornell University Press, Ithaca.

White, Randall 1993 Technological and social dimensions of 11 Aurignacian-age body ornaments across Europe, in *Before Lascaux: The complex record of the Early Upper Paleolithic*, H. Knecht, A. Pike-Tay, and R. White eds., pp. 279–299. CRC Press, Boca Raton.

White, Randall 2003 *Prehistoric art: The symbolic journey of humankind*. Harry N. Abrams, New York.

White, Randall 2007 Systems of personal ornamentation in the Early Upper Palaeolithic: Methodological challenges and new observations, in *Rethinking the human revolution: New behavioural and biological perspectives on the origin and dispersal of modern humans*, P. Mellars ed., pp. 287–302. MacDonald Institute of Archaeology, Cambridge.

Widell, Magnus 2013 Sumerian agriculture and land management, in *The Sumerian world*, Harriet Crawford ed., pp. 55–67. Routledge, London.

Widgren, Mats 2007 Pre-colonial landesque capital: A global perspective, in *Rethinking environmental history: World-system history and global environmental change*, A. Hornborg, J. McNeill, and J. Martínez Alier eds., pp. 61–77. Altamira Press, Lanham.

Widmer, Randolph 1991 Lapidary craft specialization at Teotihuacan: Implications for community structure at 33:S3W1 and economic organization in the city. *Ancient Mesoamerica* 2:131–147.

Widmer, Randolph 2009 Elite household multicrafting specialization at 9N8, Patio H, Copan, in *Housework: Craft production and domestic economy in ancient Mesoamerica*, K. Hirth ed., pp. 174–204. Wiley, Hoboken.

Wiessner, Polly 1977 *Hxaro: A regional system of reciprocity for reducing risk among the !Kung San*. University Microfilms, Ann Arbor.

Wiessner, Polly 1982 Risk, reciprocity and social influences on !Kung San economics, in *Politics and history in band societies*, E. Leacock and R. Lee eds., pp. 61–84. Cambridge University Press, Cambridge.

Wiessner, Polly 2002 Hunting, healing, and hxaro exchange: A long-term perspective on !Kung (Ju/'hoansi) large-game hunting. *Evolution and Human Behavior* 23:407–436.

Wiessner, Polly 2011 Enga feasts in a historical perspective (Papua New Guinea), in *Feasts: Archaeological and ethnographic perspectives on food, politics, and power*, M. Dietler and B. Hayden eds., pp. 115–143. Smithsonian Institution Press, Washington, DC.

Wilk, Richard 1989a Decision making and resource flows within the household: Beyond the black box, in *The household economy: Reconsidering the domestic mode of production*, R. Wilk ed., pp. 23–52. Westview Press, Boulder.

Wilk, Richard ed. 1989b *The household economy: Reconsidering the domestic mode of production*. Westview Press, Boulder.

Wilk, Richard 1991 *Household ecology: Economic change and domestic life among the Kekchi Maya in Belize*. University of Arizona Press, Tucson.

Wilk, Richard 2001 The impossibility and necessity of re-inquiry: Finding middle ground in social science. *Journal of Consumer Research* 28:308–312.

Wilk, Richard, and Robert Netting 1984 Households: Changing forms and functions, in *Households: Comparative and historic studies of the domestic group*, R. Netting, R. Wilk, and E. Arnould eds., pp. 1–28. University of California Press, Berkeley.

Wilk, Richard, and William Rathje 1982 Household archaeology. *American Behavioral Scientist* 25:617–639.

Wilks, Ivor 1989 *Asante in the nineteenth century: The structure and evolution of a political order*. Cambridge University Press, Cambridge.

Will, Pierre-Etienne, Roy Bin Wong, James Lee, Jean Oi, and Peter Perdue 1991 *Nourish the people: The state civilian granary system in China, 1650–1850*. University of Michigan Press, Ann Arbor.

Williams, Barbara, and Herbert Harvey 1997 *The Códice de Santa María de Asunción*. University of Utah Press, Salt Lake City.

Williams, Barbara, and Frederic Hicks 2011 *El Códice Vergara*. Universidad Nacional Autónoma de México, Mexico City.

Williams, Eric 1994 *Capitalism and slavery*. University of North Carolina Press, Chapel Hill.

Williamson, H. G. M. 1985 *Ezra and Nehemiah*. JSOT Press, Sheffield.

Williamson, Oliver 2000 The new institutional economics: Taking stock, looking ahead. *Journal of Economic Literature* 38:595–613.

Williamson, Oliver 2008 Transactional cost economics, in *Handbook of new institutional economics*, C. Ménard and M. Shirley eds., pp. 41–65. Springer, Dordrecht.

Wilmsen, Edwin 1989 *Land filled with flies: A political economy of the Kalahari*. University of Chicago Press, Chicago.

Wilson, Andrew 2000 Timgad and textile production, in *Economies beyond agriculture in the classical world*, D. Mattingly and J. Salmon eds., pp. 271–296. Routledge, Abingdon-on-Thames.

Wilson, Andrew, and Miko Flohr eds. 2016 *Urban craftsmen and traders in the Roman world*. Oxford University Press, Oxford.

Wilson, Nigel 1997 *Aelian: Historical miscellany (varia historia)*. N. Wilson trans. Loeb Classical Library. Harvard University Press, Cambridge, MA.

Winroth, Anders 2012 *The conversion of Scandinavia: Vikings, merchants, and missionaries in the remaking of northern Europe*. Yale University Press, New Haven.

Winter, Irene 1993 "Seat of kingship"/"A wonder to behold": The palace as construct in the ancient Near East. *Ars orientalis* 23:27–55.

Winterhalder, Bruce 1981 Foraging strategies in the boreal forest: An analysis of Cree hunting and gathering, in *Hunter-gatherer foraging strategies: Ethnographic and archaeological analyses*, B. Winterhalder and E. Smith eds., pp. 66–98. University of Chicago Press, Chicago.

Winterhalder, Bruce, Flora Lu, and Bram Tucker 1999 Risk-sensitive adaptive tactics: Models and evidence for subsistence studies in biology and anthropology. *Journal of Archaeological Research* 7:301–348.

Wishart, David 1992 *The fur trade of the American west, 1807–1840: A geographical synthesis*. University of Nebraska Press, Lincoln.

Wittfogel, Karl 1957 *Oriental despotism: A comparative study of total power.* Yale University Press, New Haven.

Wolf, Eric 1982 *Europe and the people without history.* University of California Press, Berkeley.

Wood, Diana 2002 *Medieval economic thought.* Cambridge University Press, Cambridge.

Wood, James 1998 A theory of preindustrial population dynamics demography, economy, and well-being in Malthusian systems. *Current Anthropology* 39:99–135.

Wood, Raymond 1980 Plains trade in prehistoric and protohistoric intertribal relations, in *Anthropology on the Great Plains*, R. Wood and M. Liberty eds., pp. 98–109. University of Nebraska Press, Lincoln.

Woodbury, Richard, and James Neely 1972 Water control systems of the Tehuacan Valley, in *The prehistory of the Tehuacan valley, vol. 4: Chronology and irrigation*, R. MacNeish, F. Johnson, K. Wittfogel, R. Woodbury, J. Neely, G. Gil Huerta, and E. Hunt eds., pp. 81–153. University of Texas Press, Austin.

Woolf, Greg 1990 Food, poverty and patronage: The significance of the epigraphy of the Roman alimentary schemes in early imperial Italy. *Papers of the British School at Rome* 58:197–228.

Wray, William 2005 The seventeenth-century Japanese diaspora: Questions of boundary and policy, in *Diaspora entrepreneurial networks: Four centuries of history*, I. Baghdiantz McCabe, G. Harlaftis, and I. Pepelasis Minoglou eds., pp. 73–93. Berg, Oxford.

Wright, Ernest, Charles Redman, and Jean Perrot 1974 The tell: Basic unit for reconstructing complex societies of the Near East. *Bulletin of the American Schools of Oriental Research.* Supplementary Studies 20:123–143.

Wright, Rita 2013 Sumerian and Akkadian industries: Crafting textiles, in *The Sumerian world*, H. Crawford ed., pp. 395–418. Routledge, London.

Wright, Rita, David Lentz, Harriet Beaubien, and Christine Kimbrough 2012 New evidence for jute (*Corchorus capsularis* L.) in the Indus civilization. *Archaeological and Anthropological Sciences* 4:137–143.

Wright, Stanley 1980 *Kiangsi native trade and its taxation.* Garland, New York.

Wrigley, Edward 1969 *Population and history.* Weidenfeld and Nicholson, London.

Wrigley, Edward 1978 Parasite or stimulus: The town in a pre-industrial economy, in *Towns in societies*, P. Abrams and E. Wrigley eds., pp. 295–309. Cambridge University Press, Cambridge.

Wycherley, Richard 1978 *The stones of Athens.* Princeton University Press, Princeton.

Ximénez, Francisco 1920 *Historia de la conquista de las provincias de San Vicente de Chiapa y Guatemala.* Tipográfica Nacional, Guatemala City.

Yack, Bernard 2002 Community: An Aristotelian social theory, in *Aristotle and modern politics*, A. Tessitore ed., pp. 19–46. University of Notre Dame Press, Notre Dame.

Yamamura, Kozo 1988 From coins to rice: Hypotheses on the kandaka and kokudaka systems. *Journal of Japanese Studies* 14:341–367.

Yan, Yunxiang 2005 The individual and transformation of bridewealth in rural north China. *Journal of the Royal Anthropological Institute* 11:637–658.

Yanagisako, Sylvia 1979 Family and household: The analysis of domestic groups. *Annual Review of Anthropology* 8:161–206.

Yon, Marguerite 2006 *The city of Ugarit at tell Ras Shamra.* Eisenbrauns, Winona Lake.

Yoshinobu, Shiba 1970 *Commerce and society in Sung China.* Michigan Abstracts of Chinese and Japanese Works on Chinese History No. 2, Ann Arbor.

Young, Gary 2001 *Rome's eastern trade: International commerce and imperial policy, 31 BC–AD 305.* Routledge, London.

Yule, Henry, and Henri Cordier 1916 *Cathay and the way thither.* Munshiram Manoharlal, New Delhi.

Zeder, Melinda 1988 Understanding urban process through the study of specialized subsistence economy in the Near East. *Journal of Anthropological Archaeology* 7:1–55.

Zeder, Melinda 1991 *Feeding cities.* Smithsonian Institution Press, Washington, DC.

Zorita, Alonso de 1994 *Life and labor in ancient Mexico*. University of Oklahoma Press, Norman.

Zuiderhoec, Arjan 2009 *The politics of munificence in the Roman empire: Citizens, elites and benefactors in Asia Minor*. Cambridge University Press, Cambridge.

Zurndorfer, Harriet 2011 The resistant fibre: Cotton textiles in Imperial China, in *The spinning world: A global history of cotton textiles 1200–1850*, G. Riello and P. Parthasarathi eds., pp. 43–62. Oxford University Press, Oxford.

INDEX